To Norma, In appreciation of all of your efforts to help build a better world for everyone

Sincerely,
James Forman
May 16, 1996

"James Forman's **The Making of Black Revolutionaries** is a classic, a personal, no holds barred inside look at the civil rights movement. Written by an insider, it offers an invaluable look at the politics and the personalities that shaped the movement and continue to shape American life."
—Julian Bond

"**The Making of Black Revolutionaries** was the most ambitious politically astute, and emotionally engrossing memoir to emerge from the 1960's. Anyone interested in understanding the present state of Black politics should read this outstanding example of engaged historical analysis."
—Clayborne Carson
Dept. of History, Stanford University

"**The Making of Black Revolutionaries** is an autobiography of one of the most important leaders in the civil rights movement during the 1960s. This book is *must* reading for anyone seriously interested in the Black movement in the United States."
—James H. Cone
Union Theological Seminary

"**The Making of Black Revolutionaries** is, without a shadow of a doubt, the finest analysis of revolutionary action within the United States that I have read. It has all the precision of individual incident and individual character, great mastery of detail, sometimes from day to day, even from hour to hour. I never tire of reading it. And I recommend it to all revolutionaries in every country."
—C.L.R. James

By the same author

Sammy Younge, Junior
(New York: Grove press, 1968)

Liberation Viendra d'une Chose Noir
(Paris: Masperro, 1968)

The Political Thought of James Forman
(Detriot: Black Star Press,1970)

Self-Determination: An Examination of the Question & its Application to the African-American People
(Washington: Open Hand Publishing Inc., 1984)

The Making of Black Revolutionaries

THE MAKING OF BLACK REVOLUTIONARIES

JAMES FORMAN

OPEN HAND
PUBLISHING INC

Seattle, WA

Open Hand Publishing Inc.
P.O. Box 22048
Seattle, WA 98122

distributed by:
The Talman Co., Inc.
131 Spring St., Suite 201E-N
New York, NY 10012
(212) 431-7175

Library of Congress Cataloging in Publication Data

Forman, James 1928–
    The Making of Black Revolutionaries
    Includes Index.
        1. Forman, James, 1928–   . 2. Afro-Americans—Biography.
3. Student Nonviolent Coordinating Committee (U.S.)—Biography.
4. Afro-Americans—Civil Rights
I. Title.
E185.97.F715A3   1985 973'.0496024[B]   85-4828
ISBN 0-940880-10-5

First published in 1972 by
The Macmillan Company, New York, New York

Printed in the United State of America

99 98 97 96 95 94   9 8 7 6 5 4

TO MY SONS

James Robert Lumumba

AND

Chaka Esmond Fanon

AND

ALL THE UNBORN REVOLUTIONARIES

WHO WILL ACCELERATE

AND INTENSIFY THE REVOLUTIONARY PROCESS

BOOK ONE

A CONSTANT STRUGGLE

CONTENTS

BOOK TWO

A BAND OF SISTERS AND BROTHERS, IN A CIRCLE OF TRUST

CONTENTS

Preface

Of all the many issues described in this book and the various international and domestic developments in which I have been involved since its original publication in 1972, the following four topics deserve some attention: (1) the so-called expulsion of white people from the Student Nonviolent Coordinating Committee (SNCC) and my role in that process; (2) the destruction of the SNCC; (3) the issue of the emancipation of women; and (4) the publication of my last book, *Self-Determination: An Examination of the Question and its Application to the African-American People.*

(1) The So-Called Expulsion of Whites from The SNCC

After the failure of the Student Nonviolent Coordinating Committee's initial efforts to utilize white organizers on white southern campuses, some of its principal officers kept raising with white staff members the necessity for them to begin full time work in white southern communities. This advice was usually rejected on the grounds that it was easier for white people to work in Black communities than in white communities. We pointed out that it was also not easy for Black people initially to work in Black communities, but that non-racist beachheads in southern white communities should be established, even though this might take a long time. At that time we had accepted, perhaps incorrectly, the position that it would be too dangerous for Black people to organize in white southern communities.

Following the Mississippi Summer Project of 1964, some of the leadership of the SNCC became even more insistent that the conditions were ripe to begin organizing in white southern communities. The resistance, however, was so great that some of us felt we should pass a rule that SNCC white organizers should work in white communities. We discussed this potential with various white organizers. Thus, at our Kingston Springs, Tennessee meeting in 1966 the SNCC did pass such a resolution. As the maker of that resolution, it was not my intent that white or Black organizers should work in complete isolation or without any consultation with each other.

At the same time efforts were being made to make the SNCC an all Black organization. The reasons surrounding this proposed action are complex. Internationally, some forces in the Pan-African movement were pushing for the expulsion of whites from the SNCC on the grounds that the SNCC would be more viable internationally without white membership. These same forces were stressing Black consciousness rather than race and class consciousness. Many people nationally and internationally, moreover, were beginning to move under the ideology of the late Elijah Muhammed as outlined in his book, *In the Name of Allah: Message to the Black Man.* (Chicago: Muhammed Mosque of Islam No. 2, 5335 S. Greenwood Avenue, 1965). This book supports a third world war in the name of Islam and outright rejection of the Civil Rights movement and Civil Rights workers. Other so-called advance forces used various tactics to render a split of the enormous number of white people who had rallied to the cause of the Student Nonviolent Coordinating Committee and its program for Civil Rights.

The late Ruby Doris Robinson, who is discussed later in this book, and myself took the lead in combatting the tendency that stressed race war or an exclusive racial analysis of the problems facing Black people or any other race of people at home and abroad. We held many meetings with proponents of the race war line, seeking to change their viewpoints. We found that these advocates of race war had a very weak analysis of international economics. We stressed the need for them to study that subject as the first step toward overcoming such beliefs. We also encouraged the study of labor history, as well as the need to promote African and Afro-American history in high schools, colleges, and universities.

In the winter of 1966 at the Peg Leg Bates staff meeting in upstate New York a motion was passed late one night stating that the Student Nonviolent Coordinating Committee should be an all Black organization. Along with others, I voted against this motion, stressing that a viable organization did not expel people from its ranks based on their skin color. The following morning I introduced a motion to dissolve the Student Nonviolent Coordinating Committee and to send any liquidated assets to the People's Republic of Guinea for distribution to African Liberation movements. The motion was seconded; it received a number of votes; but it was defeated.

After the defeat of my motion, a compromise was reached whereby whites could be on the staff of the SNCC, but they could not have a vote. This decision lasted until the June 1967 meeting of the SNCC Central Committee. At that time a white staff member insisted upon the right to have the same voting rights as all other staff members.

Based on an assessment of the potential votes, I earnestly suggested to this staff member that he not press for a vote on his status. I explained in great detail the enormous amount of work that had been done to correct the vote on the status of whites at Peg Leg Bates. I also explained that within a short period of time we would most likely reverse the balance of forces. Many of the people who had accepted the compromise vote or who were at first for the complete expulsion of whites at Peg Leg Bates were no longer with the SNCC. Some had left voluntarily; others had been expelled for various reasons. Unfortunately, this white staff member insisted that a vote be taken upon his request to have immediate full voting rights. We lost the vote.

Many people are quick to leave groups, organizations, parties or countries when they are outvoted or when there is a repugnant turn of events. Unfortunately, their action may leave the formation or country in the hands of very reactionary people. Often without opposition and resistance, such individuals are able to do great harm to many people and to nations of people. My study and experience lead to the conclusion that whenever possible people should join and remain in negative formations and seek to transform them. I stayed, therefore, with the SNCC until 1969 and witnessed many positive changes within the organization and within the world at large. Many of my experiences are described in the pages of this book.

(2) The Destruction of the SNCC

In the original edition of *The Making of Black Revolutionaries* there is hardly any direct mention of the role of governmental forces in the destruction of the Student Nonviolent Coordinating Committee. Lacking sufficient evidence of such role, I, therefore, focused on internal factors within the SNCC that may have contributed to its own destruction. Since that time, however, an enormous amount of documented evidence of governmental interference has been uncovered through the Freedom of Information Act and through the United States Select Committee on Intelligence to Investigate Abuses of the Intelligence Agencies, commonly known as the Frank Church Committee. As a United States Senator from Minnesota, the 1984 Democratic Presidential candidate, Walter F. Mondale, was a member of this committee.

Since the original publication of this book in 1972, I have obtained more than 3,000 pages of personal files from the Federal Bureau of Investigation (FBI) and from the Central Intelligence Committee (CIA). The files of the FBI show that from 1968—1976 I was placed on the Security Index of the United States and labeled an extreme Black nationalist.

Placing a person on the United States Security Index is a method by which the FBI carries out extensive and prolonged investigations of a particular person. The various powers of the FBI under the provisions of the Security Index are not clear at this time, though my family, friends, associates, and I have been subjected to great harassment since 1968.

The Church committee documents may be obtained by writing to the United States Select Committee on Intelligence, Washington, D.C. and asking for a complete set of the Frank Church Committee Hearings. Information on the Student Nonviolent Coordinating Committee may be obtained under the provision of the Freedom of Information Act and from various members of the former SNCC.

Another reference to governmental interference is *The Pied Piper, Allard K. Lowenstein and the Liberal Dream* by Richard Cummings (New York: Grove Press, 1985). Cummings states that the late Allard Lowenstein was an agent of the Central Intelligence Agency. Lowenstein is discussed extensively in the *Making of Black Revolutionaries. The Pied Piper* also has excerpts from *The Making of Black Revolutionaries.*

When I was a graduate student at Cornell University from September 1977 until May 1980 *The Cornell Daily Sun, Umoja Sasa* (a publication of Third World students), and the *Cornell Alumni Review* were all very helpful in publicizing the atrocities of governmental repression in the Civil Rights movement and against myself. I thank them very much for their efforts. The crusading spirit of the Cornell students and faculty in those years has yet to sweep many other campuses and faculties, but that day may not be far off.

McGeorge Bundy

Due to censorship of sections of *The Making of Black Revolutionaries* on the part of a lawyer from Macmillan, publishers of the original edition, I had to suppress a major revelation about the destruction of the SNCC. For many months I agonized over whether to withdraw the book from Macmillan or to agree to delete the following material: After the call for Black Power had become popular in the United States and other countries, McGeorge Bundy, former National Security Advisor under the late President John F. Kennedy, called a meeting at the Ford Foundation in New York City of twenty or more Black leaders. At that time McGeorge Bundy was the President of the Ford Foundation. Bundy announced to the assembled Black leaders that a decision had been made to destroy the Student Nonviolent Coordinating Committee and to save the Congress of Racial Equality (CORE). This decision was based on an assessment that it was possible to wean CORE away from the concept of Black Power through massive infusion of money for its operation. In the case of the SNCC, however, the assessment was that it was too late to save it; it had to be destroyed.

The Executive Committee of the SNCC was in session in Atlanta, Georgia when this meeting was held. We were notified of its decision and advised to be very careful for McGeorge Bundy was extremely serious.

Immediately, I contacted Floyd McKissick, the head of the Congress of

Racial Equality, and asked for a meeting. We met in New York and we discussed the McGeorge Bundy meeting. McKissick said that he would not permit any separation of himself from the concept of Black Power which simply meant political power for powerless Black people. McKissick also said that he had not been aware of that meeting.

(3) Some Thoughts on the Emancipation of Women

During the course of writing the first edition of this book, my friend and personal editor, Elizabeth Sutherland Martinez, raised with me what she felt was a weakness in the book, hardly any material on the theory of women's liberation. I replied I was attempting to deal with this question by portraying the heroic experiences of women in the Civil Rights Movement and highlighting the activities of several women, especially those of Georgia Mae Turner and Lucretia Collins.

After the publication of *The Making of Black Revolutionaries*, another friend, Kathie Sarachild, Editor of Redstockings' *Feminist Revolution*, also stated she felt that the book should have concentrated more on the theory of women's liberation. Kathie said, moreover, that the awareness of a sit-in in the SNCC office in 1963 or 1964 by some women tended to light a prairie fire in the women's movement.

That sit-in grew out of a discussion between some women in the SNCC national office in Atlanta, Georgia and myself about the conditions of women in general and in the SNCC. Many of those who worked in the office stated they felt they could not discuss with some men how they felt about certain matters or grievances they held about various situations.

I suggested at that time that women should begin to become more militant in their demands and that they could start the process by emulating the lunch counter sit-in movement that started on February 1, 1960 in Greensboro, North Carolina. I proposed that they role play, using me as a target. I also suggested they should make a sign or signs and develop a plan of action along with the sit-in in my office.

The Waveland Meeting

Another significant historical event is the paper on women in the SNCC that was written by three female SNCC staff members and presented at the Waveland, Mississippi 1965 meeting. Instead of permitting the body to discuss the paper the three women withdrew it. I urged them not to do this insisting that the body would most likely be criticized for not discussing the paper. Unfortunately, history proved me correct. It is very regretable that the three women who wrote the paper withdrew it instead of letting those in attendance discuss it.

So that there is more clarity about my personal position on the liberation of women, let me state I have always fought for the total equality and emancipation of women, not only in the society but at home as well. When I started working for the Student Nonviolent Coordinating Committee, I already held very firm positive beliefs on the emancipation and equality of women and the necessity to promote the leadership of women as well as that of men. I firmly maintain that all men throughout the world should support the equality and emancipation of women.

Within the struggle for the equality and liberation of women, however, there is a viewpoint that holds that men, because they are men, are the main problem or the principal contradiction in the world. I strongly disagree with this viewpoint which tries to pit women against men because they are men. Men are viewed as enemies regardless of who they are, what they are doing, and what they have done. This viewpoint is similar to the one that says my group, my nation, my race, or my religion and only my group, my nation, my race, or my religion is worthy of support.

(4) Self-Determination: An Examination of the Question and its Application to the African-American People

During the time I was involved with the SNCC and other formations in the deep South, I was unaware of the body of theoretical material on self-determination for the African-American people. I refer the reader, therefore, to my last book, *Self-Determination: An Examination of the Question and its Application to the African-American People*, which attempts to fill this void. I thank Open Hand Publishing Inc. and its president, P. Anna Rodieck, for the publication of the two editions of this book. Written and published as partial requirements for my Master's degree from Cornell University and my Doctoral degree from the Union of Experimental Colleges and Universities in cooperation with the Institute for Policy Studies, the book is a direct outgrowth of many experiences described in *The Making of Black Revolutionaries*.

Conclusion

Unheralded, and perhaps unknown in much of its magnitude, is the consistent, invaluable struggle of many African-American people against bigotry and anti-semitism. Some of us within the SNCC fought manifestations of anti-semitism as well as various forms of Black supremacy, the ideology that the black race should rule over all other races.

As an anti-fascist youth in the United States during World War II, I, along with countless others, strove to stop Hitler, Mussolini, Hirohito, Franco, and others in the Axis Alliance, an alliance that brutally murdered Jews and non-Jews, whites and Blacks, Asians and non-Asians. As a Black anti-fascist youth, I suffered from intense racial discrimination and segregation in the United States and have dedicated my life to the ending of all forms of discrimination, segregation, and inequality.

The Making of Black Revolutionaries is, therefore, an attempt to illustrate the development of myself and of others within the context of a racist, brutal, sexist, and anti-semitic society. At the same time millions of people in this society have been struggling and will continue to struggle to change these conditions and to create a new world for all people. Thanks to Open Hand Publishing Inc. and its president for publishing this current edition.

As this edition goes to the printers, the Civil Rights Act of 1964, with all of its imperfections, still exists. The Voting Rights Act of 1965 is a reality. Its 1982 extension was passed and governs the lives of millions who were once without the vote and without any form of equality. Internationally, overt United States military aggression in Vietnam is over. Though fighting for their survival, the Sandinistas govern a sovereign country, and ending apartheid in South Africa is on the agenda of people of conscience for solution. The Civil Rights movement and the Vietnam anti-war movement have, therefore, been outstanding examples of success. Those models will long be useful as the worldwide struggle against tyranny intensifies.

March 1985
Washington, D.C.

Letter to My Sisters and Brothers

WE ARE NOT born revolutionary. Revolutionaries are forged through constant struggle and the study of revolutionary ideas and experiences. This book describes some of the process that molded not only me into the revolutionary I hope I am, but that shaped many others into revolutionaries. As some of my generation were unaware of much that influenced our development, so there will be future generations unaware of all the forces of resistance that have determined their actions. In the years ahead more and more people will be forced to become revolutionary, for the repression and decay of United States society leaves few options. I hope future generations will profit from these experiences of mine and those with whom I have struggled: study our mistakes, criticize our actions, draw inspiration from our deeds.

As I wrote this book, I constantly thought of some words written by Frantz Fanon, a great black thinker and African revolutionary: "A society that drives its members to desperate solutions is a non-viable society, a society to be replaced."

There are thousands and thousands of people who have affected my life very positively, especially my mother, my wives, my lovers, my friends, my sisters and brothers in the Student Nonviolent Coordinating Committee (SNCC), the Black Economic Development Conference, the League of Revolutionary Black Workers, and the Black Workers Congress. I have drawn inspiration from them and courage to keep my principles. Many have helped me in moments of crisis and all have despised some parts of the despicable system under which we live.

There are many people with whom I have had negative experiences: white racists, southern sheriffs, countless police pigs, FBI agents, government officials. Some black people whom I thought at first to be friends turned sour, leaving deep scars and bad memories. From all these negative forces I learned very much.

The Making of Black Revolutionaries represents the impact of all these positive and negative forces on my life in one way or another. While not minimizing the importance of all the people who were positive forces—some of whom are described in my story—I must single out several people who played a specific role in the production of this book:

LETTER TO MY SISTERS AND BROTHERS

(1) Robert Parris Moses with whom I shared the closest and warmest of friendships from 1961 to 1966. Much of the material in this book relates to heroic struggles in which he was involved. Bob and all the rest of us in the Student Nonviolent Coordinating Committee were victims of some treacherous acts by many we thought were our friends. Wherever Robert Parris Moses is today I hope he will evaluate anew his historic role in light of information I have revealed in this book.

(2) Donald P. Stone and his wife Flora who sat patiently with me in 1968 and 1969 while I unravelled many of the conflicting forces, tendencies, and historical experiences that affected me. We discussed for hours the question of what a political person should reveal in print, of how many secrets a revolutionary should carry to the grave with him. We knew that a great deal of personality conflicts and other pettiness could creep into a book that encompassed experiences such as mine. And we concluded that to remain silent about certain disputes and certain objective facts would retard the revolutionary struggle in the long run. At the same time, we agreed that any book about the revolutionary struggle had to be political and avoid name-calling, criticism of minor personality problems and the many trifling details that are found in the life of any movement, any group of people, any individual person. Out of those discussions came order and focus to this present book.

Donald and Flora Stone, along with Roberta Yancey, are godparents of my sons, James Lumumba and Chaka Fanon.

(3) Ana Livia Cordero, a Puerto Rican militant and doctor who taught me to always affirm the blackness of Puerto Ricans and to understand that they suffer the same general oppression as black people in the United States. In addition Ana Livia found in Puerto Rico a rest and work place for me by the Caribbean Sea, where most of this book was written. While in Puerto Rico, I learned much about its people, and a study of that colonization helped me to better understand what has happened to those of us who live inside the mainland of the United States. My many conversations with Ana Livia, who worked in Africa and attended the first Tri-Continental Conference held in Cuba, have had a tremendous impact upon my life. Today she is busy in the Puerto Rican liberation struggle, indivisible from the struggle on the mainland.

(4) Elizabeth Martinez whom I have known intimately since 1965 and with whom I worked closely when she was involved with SNCC. We have maintained our close and warm friendship throughout the years, and she rendered invaluable assistance on this book. Currently Elizabeth is an editor of *El Grito del Norte*, a Chicano newspaper in the Southwest. In the final stages of editing this book, I traveled to New Mexico, where I met many Chicanos in the movement there who were very instrumental in helping me to understand the dynamics of the Chicano movement, thereby broadening my understanding of the vast and deplorable role of

the United States government in suppressing the rights of all nonwhite people.

My warmest and most tender feelings are for the masses of black people in the United States and poor people the world around. My life has been dedicated to the struggle of all exploited people against their oppressors. It is this objective that sustains me every day in the revolutionary movement.

BOOK ONE
A
CONSTANT
STRUGGLE

CHAPTER 1

Driven Insane

I LEFT Doheny Library at the University of Southern California at about eight o'clock that evening. I had been studying for five hours, getting ready for an examination the next morning. Under my arm was a copy of Karl Menninger's *Love and Hate*.

Standing in front of the library, I looked at the stars that loomed bright and large in the sky. I could even see traces of the Milky Way. I smelled the fresh air and thought of the weather in Chicago. It was cold there, I knew. The streets were surely covered with dirty snow and no green grass grew anywhere except in the hothouses. I thought, how amazing it was that in the same country, on the same day, at the same hour, you could be in a very hot climate wearing only a shirt and looking at the stars, while far away, where you had been born, it was cold and dirty. I just stood there, thinking how good it felt to be out of the Air Force and back in school. Time had destroyed many of my plans and I had changed in many ways, although there was a constant thread running through my life. I had to get an education. I had to use this education. Whatever I did with this education, I had to put it to work for my people; somehow and somewhere, this had to be a reality.

"Hey boy! You there!" A police car pulled up to the curb. Two white cops were in the front seat wearing blue caps and blue uniforms. I heard them insulting me but I went on looking at the stars.

"Hey boy! You there! Come here!" The voice grew louder this time, more insulting.

"Are you talking to me?" I said sharply, looking straight at him in the dark under the street light.

"Who else do you think we're calling?"

"Well, if you're talking to me, I'm not a boy. I'm a man," I said, walking a few steps toward the police car.

"What are you doing here?"

"I'm looking at the stars."

"One of those smart ones, huh!"

"I'm looking at the stars and what are you calling me for? What do you want?" All the years of fighting the police as a child welled up in me. I remembered the cops who stopped us as youngsters in Chicago and searched us for nothing. I remembered the cops in Chicago who stood by silently as I went to them for help once. There could not be any good reason why these cops were calling me. The street was deserted. Something was about to happen.

"There's been a robbery around here," the officer sitting near the window said. I had heard this before too many times in the black community. I thought of Richard Wright's autobiography, *Black Boy*. How many times have the white cops stopped a black person in the white community simply because he is black!

"What does that have to do with me?" I asked.

"There's been this robbery and you look like the one who did it," he said. Oh, I felt the shit flying again.

"Look, how can you say that? I have been in the library for the past five hours studying for an examination. You're just trying to make up something because I'm a Negro."

"You look like the one who committed the robbery," the cop insisted.

"Come on, officer. You can go just inside the library and ask my girl friend who has been on the desk ever since I started studying. There are other students inside who can verify where I've been. Anyway, when did this robbery occur?"

"Not long ago and you look suspicious. What are you doing around here?"

"Look, I told you I go to school here."

"Do you have any identification?"

I felt for my wallet. I had left it at home. I knew that question, like the others, was a trick. The crackers were pulling some shit again, and it didn't matter whether I could produce identification or not. They were destined by their own racism to get me. I looked around, hoping some of my friends would come out of the library. I hoped someone would come by who knew me. The street was quiet and not a soul left the library. The night became hotter and hotter and I became more and more agitated. I thought I knew the cops and the no-holds-barred attitude they often took toward us. But I didn't know the Los Angeles cops.

"I left my wallet at the house. I only live a few blocks from here. Besides, I told you you could check with anyone in the library. I've been studying there for five hours."

"Get in the car. We're taking you to the station," he said matter of factly.

"Taking me to the station for what? I haven't done anything. I've been in the school library studying for the last five hours. What do you mean you're taking me down to the station?"

"Just what we said. We're taking you down to the station. You're suspicious. You look like the one who committed the robbery."

"What robbery? Man, I told you I've been in the library," I said, feeling my face twist and my hands move with impatience.

"Are you going to get in the car or do we have to make you get in?"

It was useless to argue. No one came from the library. No one passed along the streets. Just the cops and I were there. They had the guns. I was a black man at the University of Southern California who was studying political science and all that jazz about democracy. "Do I have any choice? Are you saying that if I don't get in the car then you're going to put me in it?"

"That's right," he answered. I can remember now his smirky face, his half-raised brown eyebrows.

"You mean you won't even go inside and check where I've been? Why don't you just come inside and check? I told you I've been in the library."

"Are you going to get in the car?"

It was hopeless. They had the guns.

He opened the back door of the car. I got inside. Many times since that night, I have wondered what would have happened if I had just stood there on a sidewalk of Los Angeles in front of the Doheny Library at the University of Southern California. Things are bad enough today, but this was 1953, and there I was, a black man standing on the streets of a white community.

Or sometimes I have wondered what would have happened if my manner had been less "belligerent" or more Tomish. But I had taken too much from white cops and I resented them telling me that I looked like someone who had just committed a robbery. They were saying that all Negroes look alike and that I was a smart nigger and we're going to take you down because we have the guns; we have the power. I got even angrier as I thought about the term paper I had just written, on the brutal suppression of the Pullman strike by the police in Illinois. Here was just another manifestation of police violence and power, an everyday occurrence in our lives.

We drove to the station on Thirty-ninth and some corner; I can't recall which one. I was taken inside and put into a cell with another brother. A red-faced cop with bumps all over his face was on duty. As they brought me inside, I asked him to let me make a phone call.

"You can make your call in a few minutes," the bumpy, red-faced white cop said. Then he locked me up.

I was insulted. I was outraged. I was *innocent*.

Five minutes passed.

"When can I make the phone call," I yelled.

"In a minute. I'm busy."

The cell in which the other brother and I were locked stood directly in front of the cop. I could see him sitting behind the desk with the desk light shining on his books. I could not understand the delay in letting me make my phone call. I assumed wrongly at that time that every prisoner arrested had the right to make a phone call and that one could demand that right to call a lawyer or call someone to get a lawyer. No one knew where I was. My friend, Wanda Harris, who worked on the desk at the Doheny Library, did not know where I was. My landlady did not know where I was. I was here in jail and these damn cops were holding me here for nothing.

Twenty minutes passed.

"Say, when are you going to let me make that call? I have a right to make a phone call. You can't just keep me locked up in this jail for nothing."

"If you don't stop making so much noise you'll never make a phone call. Who do you think you are anyway?"

"I'm a citizen," I yelled back at him. "I have a right to make a phone call. And neither you nor anybody else has the right to stop me." I don't think I really believed that; I knew better from years on Chicago's South Side. But I was full of my political science courses just then, reading every day about the right of this and that. Maybe I had begun to believe it, or maybe I still believed. Or maybe, in the panic of knowing that I hadn't committed any crime but was doomed anyway, I was trying to pull hope out of the air.

"All right!" he yelled. "You just keep on yelling and we'll see how many rights you have. You don't have no right to make a phone call. It's up to me to let you make one."

The brother in the cell got up from the bunk and walked over to where I was standing. "You'll never get out this way," he said softly. "Man, there's no need in yelling at those cops. Just be cool, baby."

"I'm sorry. But he ain't got no right not to let me make a phone call. Hell, I haven't done nothing to nobody. And even if I had, I still would have a right to make a phone call."

"O.K. I'm not going to argue with you." The brother sat back down in the cell. He was cool and no doubt knew the ways of the cops. I didn't. I thought I did. I was outraged. I believed in sticking up for my rights. But I didn't fully realize I was behind bars. The cops were out there. They had the guns. They had the guns and that's why I was in here.

I kept shouting at the fucking, white, red-faced, bumpy-skinned cop who was my oppressor. I grew tired. I sat down. I waited for hours, it seemed. I kept talking about my rights. Then the wagon came and took me downtown to the main jail.

The brother in the cell had warned me about this. He had told me to be cool or they were going to come and take me away and when you get down to the main jail they really work you over. "Down there, they don't play with you," he had said.

There I was, behind bars on my way downtown. I was tired, but I was angry and I was insulted and I was outraged and I was innocent and I had a right to make a phone call and I was a student of political science and I knew my rights and I had to make a phone call and I knew these white cops with their red faces had no business keeping me and

I was tired and I was right and I knew you had to fight for your rights and I didn't want no cop or any other white mother fucker messing over me and I became more tired and I felt the wagon shaking as they took me downtown, downtown to the main jail. And the brother had told me they don't play with you and the brother was right. They just don't play. I was finding out why, years later, there would be a rebellion in Watts and then other cities, and why there will be more rebellions and, ultimately, a revolution.

My cell at the city jail had lights at both ends, bright lights that shone constantly in your face. The lights were set in the walls protected by wire screens. There was no bed, just a concrete slab slung along the wall. No blankets. No pillows. No water. No toilet. Only the lights that shone brightly from both ends of the cell.

I was isolated. There were no other prisoners near me. I couldn't hear any voices. In this section of the jail, a big blond white pig was on duty. I wanted to make my phone call. I still assumed I had some rights. I knew I had just a little more fight in me and I called out time and time again to the guard about my right to make a phone call. When I got no response, I began yelling about my right to use the toilet.

"Do you mean I have to stay in this cell and cannot use the toilet?" I cried out. "This is cruelty, inhumane treatment. I am a citizen." I kept up the bullshit about a citizen and my rights. I tried to annoy the jailer by quoting the Constitution, the Declaration of Independence. I knew that those documents did not apply to *us*, even when they were written, but I kept talking about my rights under the Constitution. Finding that this didn't do any good, I took a new tack.

"Look. I have to piss. If you don't hurry up and open this cell, I'm going to piss on the floor . . . I'm going to piss on the floor."

"You better not piss on that floor, you sonofabitch," the blond white pig hollered as he walked around to the cell and began to open it. It had taken that type of demand to wring some concession. He opened the door and said, "Follow me."

I began walking behind him. We reached the corner. He turned and started hitting me hard in the stomach. One-two! One-two! One-two! One-two! I doubled up under the impact of his fast blows to my stomach and fell to the floor. "You still got to piss, nigger?" he yelled, as he pulled back his foot and held it poised to slam against my head.

I rose slowly from the floor. I had no strength to strike back against the cop. My ribs, my stomach, my insides—all were aching from the hard set of blows he had delivered to my stomach.

As I barely got to my feet—One-two! One-two! again. I doubled over once more. This time I did not fall to the floor. I began to stumble toward the cell. He slammed the door on me "Now shut your goddamn mouth and stop all that shit about your rights. You're a nigger."

I fell across the hard cement block. I could not believe what was happening. I could not believe I lay there, the piss literally beaten out of me, unable to think, unable to call anyone for a lawyer, just one more nigger who felt he had some rights in this fucking country. I wanted to sleep, but couldn't.

I turned over on my back. The light hurt my eyes. I rolled over on my stomach. My ribs were hurting. I vowed to fight the cops. I had to get the cops somehow, somewhere, soon. I could not forget that other brothers were in this jail. Maybe they were being beaten like this too, by the Los Angeles cops—the cops whom the brother back in the precinct tried to warn me about, without making too much noise, so that the desk sergeant would not send him down to the main jail. He tried to tell me.

The next two days were pure mental torture.

The minute, it seemed, that I had fallen asleep, plainclothes detectives would come and take me upstairs. Or sometimes they would force me to sit up in my cell. Anything to keep me up and under the lights, those bright shiny lights.

"Look at the light. Look at the light," one or both of them would yell. Then, "Why did you do it?"

"I didn't do anything."

"Tell us, city slicker—why did you do it?"

"I didn't do anything. I haven't committed any robbery."

"You came all the way from Chicago to do this job, didn't you? You're one of those Chicago slicks, aren't you?"

"I told you I was in . . ."

"Don't give us any of that school shit. You've never seen a school. You live by robberies, don't you? Confess to this robbery. Confess! Confess! Confess! Confess! Confess!" That's all I could hear. Under the lights. Upstairs. In my sleep, if I slept. "Confess! Confess! Confess!"

The next morning I was downstairs in the lineup. No one identified me for anything. I thought sure I would leave then. No! They were holding me still. More investigation. Down to the lineup every day. Upstairs under the light. In the closed room. During the day. At night. No food. Could not eat the slop they were handing out. Did not try. Knew I was getting out of there soon. How come my landlady hasn't come for me yet? How come? She must have seen my car outside. I never left my car in the front of the house. Couldn't she tell something was wrong? Upstairs under the lights. More questions.

"Where were you born?"

"How long have you lived on the coast?"

"You've never been in the Army?"

"How come you're not in Korea?"

"Trying to dodge the draft, aren't you?"

"Answer me boy."

"Answer me, smart Chicago nigger."

"Oh, you're tired."

"Well, we're tired of you Chicago niggers coming out here on the coast and robbing and going back to Chicago."

"Oh, so you need sleep."

"Look at the lights."

"Look at the lights."

"Hear me."

"Look at the lights."

"Go back down to your cell."

"We'll be back to get you."

"You're going to talk."

"You're going to talk."

What was there to tell? I had told them the truth. I am black. I am black and the bastards are persecuting me. This is Los Angeles. This is Los Angeles and white cops are white cops and white cops are white cops and I am tired and there is nothing to tell and these white cops are driving me out of my mind. Am I going crazy? These lights are blinding me. Here come some more questions and I want to sleep, just sleep and sleep and go to sleep. There is nothing else I can tell these white cops and I have told them all I could tell them and I was in the library and they have not gone out to check where I was and they know my story is true and why can't I make a phone call and why do they have to ask me all those questions and all . . . those questions . . . and all those questions . . . and I am tired . . . and I can't stand these lights . . . and how long can somebody go without sleep . . . and day and night and how many days have I been here? Can they keep you for more than seventy-two hours? There is no sense in talking about making a phone call—you got no rights here. These white cops, the dirty bastards, one of these days I will get me one or some of these sonofabitches. I can't sleep. Now what can . . . what can I do . . . to get out of this jail. . . . I got to get out of this jail. . . . I am losing my mind . . . something is wrong.

More questions and more questions and how many days have I been here and how can you tell the nights from the days with all those lights on you all the time? If they would only cut those fucking lights off for a few minutes, maybe I could get some sleep and I must get some sleep . . . my nerves are all on edge . . . I feel very jittery and I can't stand up anymore and what is this thing I am in now?

This is a cage. It is a cell that revolves around and around on its axis. They shoot water into it and scream, "You did it, didn't you?" This must be the master torture chamber. Just play crazy. All white folks think niggers are crazy and maybe if you prayed you could get out of here, but I haven't prayed in so many years. Remember what the old folks said, "Son, we got to fool the white man sometimes. We got to do some things and say some things we don't mean. We can't let the white man know all the things we are thinking and doing." You can start reciting your speech about Richard Allen, the founder of the African Methodist Episcopal church. Tell how he fought segregation and how the white people would not let him sit on the main floor and he withdrew in protest and founded his all-black African church.

And I did this, not once but twice, and it seemed the white detectives started getting scared. I heard one of them say, "Get this nigger out of here. He's going crazy."

They let me go. I walked out of the station. I did not have any money. I did not know where I was. I saw a railroad track, it seemed like music to me. Railroad tracks would carry me back to Chicago, away from this city where you had no group of people to fight the cops. It would carry you back to your family and away from all this white army and these white cops.

I walked over to a section of the railroad where two men were working. "Excuse me, sir, but could you tell me how to hop a freight to Chicago?"

"Boy, you better get off of this track before you get in trouble. You can get in some serious trouble talking about hopping freights." They were white and there was no need to tell them what had just happened to me. They wouldn't understand. They would not know why I wanted to hop a freight.

I walked some more. How was I to get home? I didn't know where I was, but I walked into a business section. I hailed a cab. I didn't have any money with me or at home, but I would get the cabdriver to take me home and then give him some cuff links, which had cost more than the fare would be. I had to get home and get some rest. My body was aching. My nerves were on edge. I could hardly sit still.

Day seemed like night as we drove through the black community to where I lived. The lights were on; no, they were out. I asked the driver to wait a minute while I went to get my money.

"Listen, driver, I'm sorry," I said when I came back down. "See, man, I've just come from the police station where I have been beaten and tortured for three days and I don't have any money. But I am going to give you a personal article of mine that will more than pay for your fare. I'm sorry to have to do this to you, but I had no other way to get home."

He looked distressed. "I'm sorry," I explained to him once again. "But these are worth almost ten dollars and they have some sentimental value to me. Not to you, I understand. But their value is still more than the fare." I was being as nice to him as I possibly could, knowing he could call the police if he wanted to. Those were the chances.

He took the cuff links. I won this time.

Inside the house, I did not see my landlady. I did not know where she could be. Upstairs in my room, I picked up the phone.

"Operator, I would like to make a person-to-person call to Chicago . . a collect call from James Forman."

My stepfather answered the phone. My mother was not at home and the operator wanted to know if I wanted to speak to him.

"No operator. Tell the party I'll call back."

I wanted to get some money to come home. I knew my mother would send it, but I doubted if my stepfather would, and besides I just did not want to tell him my problems.

I left the house. The sun was shining. I was going to withdraw from school and leave the city as soon as possible. I would go back to Chicago. Didn't matter if I lost the semester. It had just started a month ago. I didn't need to explain my actions to anyone except a young English teacher. He seemed to be something of a radical; at least, he understood a little about the oppression of blacks in this country. I found him and talked to him, sitting on the grass. I think I told him about my experience with the police.

Memory grows hazy . . . mind goes blank. . . . It happened sometime, not sure when. . . . It happened. . . . Mind is blank. . . . Consciousness is gone. . . . At the edge of the cliff. . . . Time is up. . . . Thin black line. . . . Sanity and insanity. . . . White society. Line grows tight. . . . Thin line tight . . . in the middle. . . . Line begins to break. . . . Line snaps. . . . Vicious circle. . . . Circle grows smaller . . . smaller. . . . Entangles nerves. . . . Nerves are crossed . . . twisted . . . tossed . . . all in a maze. . . . Cops won this round. . . . Racism . . . rooted deep. . . . American culture . . . no exit . . . no way out. Nerves gone. . . . Alone. . . . Sleep. . . . Insane!

No lights . . . no shiny lights. . . . Alone . . . deep sleep . . . sleep. . . . Lights out . . . dark . . . deep . . . sleep . . . cool . . . calm . . . coma.

CHAPTER 2

Childhood and Coca-Cola

PEACEFUL, SURROUNDED by family, friends, and relatives, a large house it seemed then, abounding love, the absence of conflict: These are my recollections of the farm of my grandmother, where I was raised. We lived in a rural section of Mississippi, in Marshall

County, one mile from the Tennessee line. There were no white people and the only white man we saw was the mailman when he stopped at our house or drove past, delivering the mail. At first he came in a car and then later he got a truck. We never knew his name; we just called him the mailman. He came from Moscow, Tennessee, seven miles away, which is where our mail was routed from. Later on, the roads became so bad that the mailman stopped delivering and my folks had to walk a mile to get it.

My grandmother and two cousins had bought a plot of land which they divided into three farms. She had moved onto her farm from Benton County; it was 180 acres, but poor and hilly land, unlike the rich Mississippi Delta. Shortly after arriving there, my grandfather died. Left alone to raise nine children and to pay off the debt from the farm, my grandmother survived by plowing the land and planting cotton, growing corn for the stock, and raising some crops for her own food. She was a subsistence farmer, using the only modern method of farming that she had —the plow and the mule. From the few bales of cotton that she would sell and the food she grew, she barely managed to keep her family alive.

This poverty had driven my mother and the rest of the sons and daughters away from the farm and into the industrial cities. My mother went to Chicago. There she met my father and I was born on October 4, 1928, in Chicago. When I was eleven months old, my mother sent me back to live with my grandmother while she tried to eke out a living in the ghetto.

I grew up in my grandmother's large, four-room house. It had no electricity, and was heated by two fireplaces and the wood stove in the kitchen. The house was L-shaped, with a front porch with a swing on it and a rectangular back porch. My grandmother slept in the front room; next to it was a large hallway, a room by modern standards, which ran from the front of the house to the back porch. Across the hallway was another large room, where I slept with many relatives, often on a pallet. A pallet is a bed made of blankets or quilts and put on the floor; during the wintertime, my grandmother and her daughters and other women would quilt blankets from pieces of cloth and then stuff them with some pieces of cotton. Quilting kept the cotton from dispersing and the patterns were very lovely.

Adjacent to my room stood the dining room, which did not have a fireplace and was unusable in the wintertime. Next to it was the kitchen. On the back porch stood the stand for the water which we carried in from a well; and it was also there that we used to churn. We never had a refrigerator and only later did we buy ice from town; that was to make ice cream for a Saturday treat. Our life on the farm was literally dirt poor; I can remember eating dirt on the side of the road. It was supposed to be good for you; some said it contained vitamins. Whether it did or not, dirt was a staple for us and we were hungry all the time, all the time.

Sometimes we would go down the road visiting, hoping that somebody would give us something to eat. Many times we were lucky enough to get some grease and corn bread. During the wintertime, we had biscuits and molasses in the morning and maybe a little side meat or salt pork with them. There was no regular lunch. Our dinner usually consisted of peas that we had picked during the summer and some onions. Once in a very long time we had meat. But it was rare and the killing of a calf was a communal affair, for nobody raised beef for food on any of the farms there. Whenever a farmer killed a calf, he would give and sell pieces of the veal to his neighbors.

We ourselves raised a few chickens, but they always seemed to be saved for the preacher who came quite often to our house to eat. Mama Jane, as I called my grandmother, would not let us three children sit with the preacher at dinner; we ate afterward when the grown-ups and the preacher had finished. The preacher always ate plenty and the best of the chicken. We got chicken feet, hard, fried chicken feet, whenever the preacher came for dinner.

At the dinner table we played a game about which my Aunt Thelma, who taught school, was dead serious. We had to spell what we wanted to eat. If we wanted meat, then we had to spell M-E-A-T. If we wanted water, bread, salt, or pepper—we had to spell them too. Sometimes we did not get all of our food right away, for if we didn't know how to spell the word, then we had to learn on the spot.

The house had a garden where pears, apples, and peaches grew. Fall was the time for canning. Wood burned constantly in the stove; it was my job and the two other grandsons' to cut the wood and bring it into the house while the daughters and Mama Jane cooked the fragrant fruit. We canned a lot each year so that we would have some food during the winter, but we never canned enough to completely eliminate hunger.

The orchard was also our bathroom. We had no outhouse and would just go outside of the house, winter or summer, usually to the orchard, on the theory that it would help to fertilize the ground. We would wipe ourselves with the leaves from the trees in the summer, with newspaper or corncobs or corn shucks in the winter. We brushed our teeth in the house, using small twigs from the trees for brushes. Occasionally we would put salt on the homemade brushes, but most often we didn't brush our teeth period.

Mama Jane was the center of the farm, the center of the family. She directed the farming and supervised the entire administration of our small place. When I was about five years old, she started courting Daddy Tom. They were both past fifty, he older than she. Mama Jane would always clean the house before his courting visits, and she seemed especially happy. Then they would sit and talk in the living room, which was her bedroom, a room with an old piano in it. The door would be closed and we would hear laughter—great resounding laughter that seemed to shake the house. We wondered why they were laughing, and what type of courting was that, anyway? They soon married and Daddy Tom became my grandfather, the only one I ever knew and I loved him dearly.

Daddy Tom worked hard on the farm to help Mama Jane. One day he caught me and two other grandchildren stealing watermelons from an old man's patch. Daddy Tom put me in front of him on his mule and started talking. The sun had just set and it was not quite dark yet.

"I don't like it that you were stealing. . . . If you steal, I'll have to send you back to Chicago and not let you come visit us anymore. We have watermelons of our own and we do not have to steal."

Daddy Tom was a very easygoing person almost all the time. I didn't want him to send me back to Chicago and I did not want him to tell my mother. I promised that I wouldn't steal any more watermelons and I didn't.

At Christmastime we children would get an apple or an orange and a few nuts. There were never toys, as I remember. I didn't realize these meager Christmases were the result of our poverty. We never questioned our poverty and our people never talked about it. We shared what there was.

Daddy Tom and Mama Jane took me to Moscow with them once, in our wagon pulled by two mules named Jabo and Ol' Henry. The wagon was loaded with loose cotton that had to be ginned and sold. After taking care of that business, Daddy Tom and Mama Jane bought winter supplies for the house and gave me a penny to buy some candy. I bought a red and white peppermint stick.

We were quiet as the mules slowly walked the seven miles back to our house. I had the candy clutched in my hand. Daddy Tom asked, "What are you holding there?" It was dark but he saw that I was just sitting there, thinking of something.

"My candy."

"Why don't you eat it?" he asked.

"I'm saving it till we get home so that I can give Sonny and Bum some." Sonny and Bum were my two first cousins, the children of my Uncle Eddie. My grandmother had raised the three of us and we did everything together.

"That's good," he said quietly.

In the wintertime the family killed hogs. All year the hogs were kept in a large pen where they roamed freely; my job was to slop—to feed—them. When it came time for slaughtering, the hogs were placed in a smaller pen, the fattening pen, where they could not run so much. They got fatter and fatter and fatter each day and then, early one morning, the men would assemble.

It was dramatic to me, the first time I saw the whole process. First, the fact of getting up unusually early—the work had to be done before the sun rose and heated the day. Then I watched as someone took a sledge hammer and knocked a hog on its head. The hog lay there, dead or nearly dead. Then a sharp butcher knife slit its throat horizontally. After the blood had drained, the men took the hog by its hind legs and strung it up on the frame of the water well. Then they sliced the animal open; every part was saved. The ritual of these actions, and perhaps the anticipation of eating some real meat, excited me.

One night after killing a hog some of the family were sitting in the kitchen eating what seemed to me the best piece of meat I had ever tasted. My uncle Ariche came to the kitchen and I told him how delicious it was.

"Do you know what kind of meat you're eating?" he asked with a sly smile.

"It's fresh meat from the hog that was killed today."

"But what kind of hog meat is it?"

"It's hog meat."

"Sport, you're eating hog nuts," he said, laughing aloud. I jumped up from the table and ran outside, trying to puke up the hog nuts. I knew by then what nuts were.

We lived in a crowded situation and I remember often sleeping in bed with my older aunts and uncles. Formal lessons in sex began one day when my Uncle Ariche asked me to water one of the mules. I did it and was riding back to the house when I saw our dog locked with another one. Some kind of rod joined them together. I jumped off the mule in fright, yelled and stomped, and then began beating the other dog who had put this rod in our dog. But both dogs just swirled around.

I ran, pulling the mule behind me. When I got to the house I yelled, "Uncle Ariche, Uncle Willie, help! Come quickly!" They came running through the house. "Hurry, come with me. Our dog is stuck up in the field. Another dog is stuck to him. One is going one way and the other is going the other way. Come on, let's go."

They laughed and laughed. I could not understand what was funny, but then they explained to me how puppies are made and how babies are born.

Sexual play among the children was commonplace and could be rough. One day, coming from the one-room schoolhouse where my Aunt Thelma taught, some of the older boys told me that they would beat me up if I didn't throw my cousin Juanita down on the ground and do it to her. Some of her brothers were in this group of boys.

I didn't want to do it. I loved Juanita and I didn't want to hurt her by playing like we were adults in the open field. But my protests were in vain. I tried to run home, but they caught me and taunted me. In the meantime, some of the boys had caught Juanita and they were holding her. They threw her on the ground and they put me on top of her. "Pull up her dress, pull up her dress! You better," they shouted. We were on the ground in the open field and all around us were these older boys. I pulled up her dress and she had no panties on.

By this time, my cousin Sonny who had been forcing us to play this game had a change of heart and said, "Quit it now. That's enough." I was relieved. Sonny had spoken. His word was law around there.

Juanita and I walked home slowly together, upset and disturbed. Sexual intercourse should be something private, I decided then or not long after. And women—they should not be mauled.

There was one fearful thing during those years: My uncle Ariche died at the age of twenty-three of tuberculosis, in Chicago. His body was shipped back to Mississippi. He had been the youngest son, a favorite among the sisters and brothers, and among us, the grandchildren. I had felt especially close to him and people often told me how much I resembled him.

His was the first funeral I attended and I did not understand it. They told me that Uncle Ariche had died, but I did not understand fully what that meant. The funeral took place at Concord Baptist Church; all the brothers and sisters were there except one. I sat between my mother and Aunt Thelma.

People lined up to view the body for the last time. My aunts were crying profusely and loudly. A strange fear began to envelop me. And then it happened.

Aunt Thelma stopped at the casket, crying and yelling, "Oh, Ariche!. Ariche is dead! Ariche is gone!" She flung herself on the casket. People tried to pull her off but she clung to it. Then she kissed him on the cheek. They pulled her away, but she kept looking back and crying, "Ariche is dead. He's dead!"

A coldness crept into my being. Death was something terrible. Ariche had died at the age of twenty-three and I looked like him. From somewhere, and somehow, that numeral stamped itself on my mind. As I grew up, there loomed a constant fear: Would I live past the age of twenty-three? There was doubt in my mind that I would and it surfaced from time to time, and whenever it did I remembered the image of Aunt Thelma kissing Uncle Ariche's face as he lay high in the casket with its lining of white satin pressing against his dark suit and tie, surrounded by yellow flowers, and, in the background, all my aunts and Mama Jane, people I loved, crying and weeping. I was past the age of twenty-three before I finally expelled this fear from my mind.

But most of those early years on my grandmother's farm were very happy. My Aunt Thelma, a teacher in the one-room Concord schoolhouse, gave me lessons at home. I had gone to that school a few times and then found it too boring, with all those students cooped up in one room. I preferred to stay home with my grandmother and study there.

Aunt Thelma was always surprised when she found me reading at night, almost in the dark. We had only two oil lamps in our house and neither was in my room, but sometimes a little light came in there from the fireplace. I remember one night she asked me, "James, how can you read in the dark?"

"I'm not reading," I told her, "I'm only looking at the Sears Roebuck catalog. I've memorized all the stories in the last book you gave me." From that moment on she began advancing my education as rapidly as possible, and she was a good teacher.

One night when I was reading, a strange thing happened which was never explained. It had been raining all day and now the rain still struck the tin top of our house with a vengeance. My grandmother, some of her children, and the three of us grandchildren were all sitting around the fireplace in the room where I slept. There was a knock on the door.

"Go see who that is," Mama Jane told me.

I went to the hall door and opened it. I was frightened. A man stood there, looking like a ghost. I closed the door and ran into the living room. "Mama, it's a man with a white face," I said in an agitated voice.

"Go see what he wants." She was teaching me not to be afraid.

I went back to the door and he was still standing there, water running down his face, his clothes soaked. It was just a white man, but I had never seen one at such close range before.

"Could you ask your Mama if she could give me some bread or something to eat?" he said.

Mama heard him and told Aunt Hattie to get some leftover corn bread. She brought it into the room to Mama, who took it, walked to the door and gave it to the man.

"Thank you ma'm," he said. "Could I ask another favor of you? If any white men come by here looking for me or asking you about me, please don't tell 'em I was here."

"All right," Mama Jane said. I was standing by her side and didn't know what was wrong, but something was wrong.

The next day Uncle Randolph, the husband of my Aunt Thelma, came down from Slayden. I heard him talking with the other grown-ups. He told them that a white man had been caught not far from our house and lynched. They put a rope around his neck, stood him in a wagon, and drove the wagon out from under him. I knew it had to be the same man. I didn't know much about lynching, but since then I have often wondered what that white man had done to be lynched by other whites, since lynching was usually reserved for us, a fact I began to discover as I grew older.

Sometimes my mother came to visit, and took me up to Chicago for short stays. I think it was from those trips that people began calling me Spote, a country way of saying Sport. When I would go back and forth to Chicago, I was always well dressed and quiet. Supposedly I had an air about me and they named me for it.

Coming back to Mississippi from one of those trips, I stopped in Memphis, Tennessee, to visit my aunt. I remember the day, a summertime day, a very hot day. I left my aunt's apartment located over a garage and started walking down the cinder-filled alley. I walked along Poplar Street into the white section of town, and passed a rich-looking girls' school where young girls in clean, white shorts and blouses were shooting with bows and arrows. Everything was fresh with the smell of neatly mowed and watered lawns. I was five years old, maybe six.

I watched their arrows hit the board, always missing the bull's-eye. I betcha I could shoot better than that, I thought. The yard in which they played seemed full of limitless green grass and many trees. It looked like a "paradise." I compared their surroundings with mine in Chicago and continued my stroll along the broad avenue, whistling here, picking up a twig there, throwing a rock every now and then.

The hot sun felt good on my legs and face. The cars zoomed past on the busy boulevard. I waited for the light to turn green; I was going to cross the street and buy some ice cream.

I walked into an ice cream parlor. The two girls behind the counter were young and gay. They had wide, friendly smiles as I began to question them about the various types of ice cream and the prices of one scoop, two scoops, three scoops. I wanted two scoops, but that cost too much. I asked if they sold Coca-Colas. They told me I could get one next door in the drugstore.

"Well, I'll come back tomorrow and get some ice cream," I said and bounced outside, feeling very good.

I went into the drugstore and hopped on one of the leather-covered stools. There were about six or seven of them and they were all empty. I spun around on the stool several times, waiting for the fountain clerk. I took out my nickel, twirled it around and around on the black marble counter. There was a crack in it and I began moving my nickel along the crack. Finally the fountain clerk appeared. She was an elderly woman, rather fat, without a smile.

"What do you want?"

"I want a Coke and a glass, please." I intended to drink my bottle of Coke there, pouring it bit by bit into the glass, making the most of my day. I could already taste the tangy flavor.

The woman disappeared. I waited and waited and waited some more. Suddenly a man appeared at my side, a tall brown-skinned man wearing a porter's jacket.

"You want a Coke?" he asked.

"Yes."

"Then come with me."

I got off the stool, puzzled, wondering why I had to follow him to get my Coke. He took long strides going toward the back of the drugstore. There stood a big, red box with the words *Coca-Cola* on it in white letters.

He pulled up the top and reached for a bottle.

"That'll be a nickel," he said. "You drink it here."

"But . . . but . . . I don't want a Coke from the bottle. I want to sit up there and drink my Coke from a glass. Why do I have to drink it here?"

The man looked at me. Something was wrong. I didn't know what, but something. A fear swelled up within me, the fear of the unknown.

"Where are you from?" he asked in a sympathetic voice, although there was annoyance in it, too.

"I don't understand."

"You have to drink your Coke back here. You can't sit on those stools."

"But . . . why?" By this time I had the cold Coca-Cola in my hands. It was very wet and very cold, and I felt myself turning cold like the bottle of Coke. Something dreadful was wrong and I could not understand why I was crying, what was the matter, who this man was, what right he had to tell me where I had to drink my Coke, why I couldn't sit on the stool.

"Where are you from?" the man asked again.

"Chicago."

"Well, don't you know?"

"Know what?"

"Boy, you're a nigger," he said in a flat voice.

"A what?" I asked. I heard him and I didn't hear him because I didn't really understand the word.

"A nigger, and Negroes don't sit on the stools here."

I put the Coke down on the box quickly and left the drugstore, sobbing. I walked aimlessly around this block and that block, turning the word over in my mind and looking at this person and that person and concluding that Negroes were those people who did not have white skins. And it meant then there were things we were not supposed to do. There were stools on which we could not sit. We could not buy the type of Cokes we wanted to buy. What else could we not do?

I returned to the cinder alley. I walked toward the garage over which my aunt lived.

Upstairs, I asked, "Aunt Hattie, what are niggers, Negroes?"

"That's what we are. Nigger is a dirty word for us. We are Negroes. Why, James, why do you ask?"

"I just asked. . . . I'm going back outside." She didn't say anything, and I left. I don't think I was asking her to say anything; it was all clear to me. I'm sure I had heard the word before, but I don't think it had any meaning for me. Certainly it didn't have this meaning.

Outdoors again, I thought more about niggers and Negroes. That's what we were and that meant there were certain things we could and could not do, and other people had the "right" to tell us what we could and could not do. My mind was racing in all directions, in a turmoil, and I had no way of knowing that all this was something that happened sometime to every black child.

A taller boy, about fourteen, came down the cinder alley. I was throwing rocks fast and hard at anything and everything. I stopped because I did not want to hit him. He had slowed down as he saw me throwing rocks. He passed me.

"Are you a Negro?" I asked.

"Boy, you must be crazy. Get out of my way," he said and kept on walking.

"Well, you're brown like me and I am a Negro. You must be one too," I yelled at him.

"Fool," he said and walked a little faster.

My experience that day was not unusual—hardly. You could almost call it a cliché of the black experience, so often has it happened to our children in one form or another. But I buried it deep, and "forgot" about that bottle of Coca-Cola for many years. Later, in graduate school, I would write down all the racist confrontations of my life—and only when they were all on paper, and I was racking my memory to make sure none had been forgotten, did this one come to the surface.

It must have been a horrendous day for me, more than I realized at the time. It was, in fact, the first step on the long journey of a black man in a strange land.

CHAPTER 3

Roots of the Black Manifesto

DURING THE summer of 1935, when I was six, my mother and father came in a 1934 Plymouth to take me to live with them in Chicago. I remember the car, for it was new and seemed very clean. We were accustomed to old cars in Mississippi, and used to play "driving" in the Model T Fords that would sometimes be around our house. I felt lonely leaving the country. I knew these were my parents, so there was no question of not going, but inside I felt I was leaving a place where there was love and comfort, hills and open spaces—and entering a great unknown.

My family home in Chicago for twenty-two years was a four-room apartment at 6108 Prairie Avenue, near the corner of Sixty-first Street on the South Side. Once a white neighborhood, it had by the time of our arrival entered the final stage of transition to all-black. Only one white family could still be found on our block, that of the janitor in our building. A big, fat man with graying hair, John lived in the basement and had three sons. Two of them, Elmer and Dickie, used to catch hell all the time; we called them honkies, our term for whites. Elmer and Dickie were sometimes protected by their older brother, who was much larger than we were, and we would never attack them if he were there.

A Kent cleaners, a Kroger supermarket, a drugstore, and a confectionary store owned by a Greek stood on the four corners of Sixty-first and Prairie. Later the Kroger supermarket became a liquor store, owned by another liquor store next to the Kent cleaners. They would deliver whiskey and beer and the delivery "boys," actually men, would ride bicycles. Across the street from us stood a warehouse that later became the Joe Louis milk dairy, and a garage. Down the street, on the other side, stood a Consolidated Edison plant. The Stony Island elevated lines, which we called the El, could be heard and seen from our house. All night the roar of the El rumbled by and you became used to its sound living on Sixty-first and Prairie.

Two blocks east of Sixty-first and Prairie lay South Park; when I first came to live in Chicago, all the area east of South Park was owned and controlled by whites. Any black kid crossing South Park took his life into his hands and had to fight to survive. We often stood on the west side of Sixty-first and South Park and threw rocks at the other side of the street, at the white people. Sometimes we would cross over and steal potatoes from the shops on the other side. We would bring them back to the vacant lot which stood at the end of our block, roast them, and eat them.

Money was hard to come by and we used to steal milk bottles and take them to the store to get a penny for each one. I also used to save paper, old newspapers, and take them to the junkyard to sell them for pennies. We never got more than a quarter for them, but the habit of saving the newspaper is one that we acquired.

I never owned a bicycle or many other toys, but I did own a wagon that was supposedly brought to me by Santa Claus. I never understood why my parents engaged in this myth of Santa Claus when I knew he didn't exist. On the night that he was to bring the wagon, they thought I was asleep, but I could hear them in the next room trying to put it together. I went along with the myth the next morning, although I did ask them how come Santa Claus had not fixed the wagon right. They replied that he couldn't do everything.

In September, just before my seventh birthday, I enrolled in the Catholic school at Sixty-first and Indiana. The choice of the school was mine. One day my mother and I were walking down Sixty-first Street and looking at the various school buildings in that neighborhood. On the corner of Sixty-first and Michigan stood the Greek Orthodox Church and School; opposite it stood St. Anselm's Catholic Church and School. One block farther stood Betsy Ross Grammar School, the public school of my district. As we walked, I noticed the students from St. Anselm's marching out of school for a fire drill. All the girls had on blue dresses with white collars and red bows. The boys wore long pants, knickers, shirts, and ties. They all seemed very orderly and the girls were very attractive. The teachers were white but all the students at this school were black.

"Mother, that's the school I would like to go to."

"Why do you want to go there, James?" she asked. "That's a Catholic school."

"I like the way the girls look." They really did look good in their blue uniforms, marching in unison. I suppose I noticed their cute behinds, too.

My mother may have smiled, I'm not sure. "We'll talk about it. . . . Are you sure you want to go there? They work you very hard, I'm told. And you have to be very good in class. They will whip you if you are not good. You have to be quiet too. I'm not sure if you can be quiet."

I assured her the work wouldn't be hard for me. I considered myself very smart at that age and it did not enter my mind that the work would be difficult. Aunt Thelma had taught me a lot. I could memorize a book very quickly; I knew all my multiplication tables up to twelve and could say them as fast as you snapped your fingers; I could write not only my name, but a whole lot of other things. I was sure I would find whatever work they gave me easy.

My parents agreed to send me to St. Anselm's, and I was put into the second grade—my first experience of being officially in a school. I am not sure why they allowed me to go to a Catholic school. For one thing, they may have thought that it would keep me out of trouble. My mother worried a lot about her son getting into trouble and fighting with the rest of the children. You could say that, as working-class parents, they wanted the "best" for their son. On the other hand, they were strong for the African Methodist Episcopal church and did not like the Catholic church. My mother allowed me to go to this school, I think, mainly because I wanted to do it. She usually took the position that my life was mine and I should make my own decisions.

She was firm, however, on the question of my not becoming a Catholic. Never, not if she had to become a Catholic and take instructions. It is possible that if the school had not required her to take instructions too, she might have allowed me to join the Catholic church. My father, who worked at the stockyards, said nothing against my going to St. Anselm's, although I think he was opposed to it. Later he would always talk to me about doing my homework, and remind me that the Catholic school was not free—it cost a dollar a month plus buying books.

So I went to St. Anselm's and all my classmates were black except one who was white. We used to give him such a hard time. He was the son of a tailor and later the family moved out of the neighborhood.

Most of my public school and Catholic school friends were very conscious of their blackness. We used to fight the Greeks who went to school across the street, as well as among ourselves. In the evenings when we were on the block and wanted to have some fun and get back at white people, we would stand on the corner of Sixty-first and Prairie or in the alley between Prairie and Indiana and wait for a Greek or any other white person to come along—man, woman, child, couple, three or four, the more the merrier. We hurled rocks and cans and some more rocks and then made it through the gangways or up the alley. Sometimes the police would try to catch us, but even they were hesitant to mess with the alley very much. On more than one occasion we threw bricks down from a roof onto the top of a cop car, then made it quickly down the other side and onto Indiana before you could say "boo." We were young "Tarzans."

In school we had the usual courses, plus religion. The sisters would see that we always had plenty of homework. They were all white and I often wondered where the black sisters were, and the black priests. I don't recall ever asking them about this matter, although my schoolmates and I discussed it among ourselves.

At the end of that first year we had final examinations. Father Ecker, a fat, short, red-faced priest, came to our room after-they were scored to give prizes to the smartest boy and the smartest girl in the class.

Gloria Malmore, who sat behind me, was awarded the prize for the smartest girl. Then Father Ecker said, "There's a tie between the two boys who are the smartest: James and Marion."

Both of us were Protestants, the only two in the class. "We have a problem," the Father began to say. "We have to decide which one of the boys will get the prize." It was a tie pin. "Now, since James is a Protestant and since Marion is one, too, we are going to give the prize to the boy who is going to become a Catholic. Marion is taking instructions and we'll give it to him. Maybe next year James will become a Catholic."

I turned to Gloria behind me and said, "I don't think that's fair."

"See there!" the Father exclaimed. "He is talking now. Marion's conduct is better, and that is another reason why he should get the prize."

Didn't matter to me, I said to myself. But it did, because every year thereafter I did not study for final examinations. I may have glanced over some material but I knew it and I believed there was no point in studying hard, staying up late as I had done in the second grade. A non-Catholic would not get the first prize anyway. Besides, even when I didn't

study, I landed in the top five of the class. But each year it became pro-
gressively worse. In the third grade I placed third; in the fourth grade,
fourth; in the fifth grade, fifth. I'll place sixth in the sixth grade, I told
myself.

Not being a Catholic began to cause me more and more anxiety as the
years passed. By the time I reached the sixth grade, my Protestantism
had become a great issue with the priests and the nuns. A nun named
Sister Clevidge, who had pimples all over her flush-red jaws, used to
teach us that the Soviet Union was a bad place because the people were
Communists and did not believe in God. They were atheists. In her class
the distinction between heaven, purgatory, and hell assumed mammoth
proportions. All Protestants were doomed to purgatory; only Catholics
went to heaven. Heaven was like a large city, she told us. There were
slums in the city and streets that were like boulevards. Catholics who did
great works on earth would build themselves fine mansions in heaven,
while those who were good but did not do great work would have to live
in slums. The class distinctions in heaven made me anxious to build a
good place. Sister Clevidge was thus able to con me into staying after
school and sweeping the floors. Boys willing to sweep the floors after
school would build a great place for themselves in heaven, I was told.
They were storing up bricks to build their mansions, while others were
doomed to the shantytowns of that great city where St. Peter had the
keys to the gates.

This con game worked and I spent many hours thinking of how I could
become a Catholic; I wanted to go to heaven. But my parents, who took
me to their AME church while I was attending the Catholic school, said
the sister taught incorrectly. There was no such thing as purgatory. There
was heaven and hell, and Protestants might go to heaven just as Catholics
might go there, but hell was most definitely reserved for those white
people who on this earth mistreated black people. The white man will
get his due in hell, my mother used to say, and my grandmother, too.
All the black people will go to heaven and God will punish those white
people who do us wrong on this earth. God does not like the ugly. He
will repay the evil white man for what he does to black people on this
earth. All we have to do is pray. This was the sermon, and I had my
doubts.

I was caught in a dilemma. We got grades for knowing our religion,
and understanding the class structure of heaven was part of religion.
Understanding, too, that the caste makeup of heaven was the most important factor, for only Catholics would go to heaven. This was a place,
heaven, that was reserved to the special caste group, the Catholics. And
I was no Catholic. I was even used in the classroom at St. Anselm's, as
an example of one who would go to purgatory but not to heaven. This
status in a classroom full of Catholics put me in a great emotional turmoil.

Then there was the conflict with my parents' beliefs. Finally, to give the dilemma a double twist, I was a black person fighting the values of a white society—in addition to struggling with religion. The one problem that St. Anselm's did not manage to give me was sexual repression. The relaxed, open attitude toward sexual activity which I had acquired on the farm stayed with me in the big city. There were birthday parties and games of "Post Office"—with no parental interference—and the usual kinds of experimentation.

Sister Clevidge got on my nerves more and more. I used to play on the streets of Chicago with Kenneth Landry, the brother of Lawrence Landry, who later became active in human rights. One day we were making a snowman and we played a long time after the lunch hour had ended. When we got back to school, Sister Clevidge slapped our hands with a ruler. She was always hitting me for some act that she called bad behavior. The worst time came one day when she was standing next to my desk in the front row, quite near. I looked up and saw the shortly cut hair of her head underneath her black habit. She saw me looking and slapped my face. I thought of Adam being expelled from the Garden of Eden, but this was no Eve and I had only seen some sawed-off hair on the head of a woman.

St. Anselm's had a practice of giving every pupil a punch card to fill out in the fall and in the spring, for selling chances on a box of candy or an Easter egg. These cards, when filled, represented $2.55 in funds raised for the school. Each fall and spring there would be a great descent upon the community in our area. Imagine hundreds of students again and again selling punch card chances to the same merchants and the same neighbors.

Each year I managed to fill my quota, but my motivation sagged as the conflicts over Catholicism and with Sister Clevidge grew. In the spring of the sixth grade, when I was twelve years old, I had reached a low point. I was tired of begging in the community and didn't seem able to get anyone to punch the card. My father said he would pay for it. He couldn't do so on the day that the completed cards were due, but he would give me the money on a Thursday, when he got his check.

On the final day, I entered the classroom and Sister Clevidge asked, "Where is your money for your punch card?"

"My father said he would pay for it Thursday after he gets paid."

"You go home and stay there until you get the money."

I left class and went back home. It was my father's day off and I told him what had happened.

"Octavia," he called to my mother, "you go up to that school and take him out right now. If that school can't wait until I get paid, then I don't want him in the school."

My mother dressed and walked with me to school. I was walking defiantly; I was happy to leave the Catholic school. We went straight to the office of the mother superior and explained to her what had happened.

She was very reluctant to see me transfer. In fact, she assured my mother that things could be worked out. The school could wait until my father got his check. She doubted if I would pass in the public school, since there were only two more months of school that year.

My mother listened attentively to the arguments of the mother superior. Then she turned to me. "James, what do you think? It's you who has to make the decision. Do you want to transfer or do you want to stay here?"

"I want to transfer."

"You understand," the mother superior said, "you might fail this year if you transfer."

"I think I can pass," I said to mother superior and to my own mother.

We walked straight over to the Betsy Ross Grammar School. There I was placed in a 6A class and not only passed, but got a double promotion, skipping the first half of the seventh grade.

Betsy Ross was an overcrowded but pleasant school and I had my first black teacher there, a gym teacher named Mrs. Pearson. I didn't feel challenged by any of my teachers or classes and the scholastic discipline was far less than at St. Anselm's. Mostly I just had a good time. It was a huge relief not to have to take religion, not to be weighed down by the conflict over Catholicism. But religion surrounded my life and it was not to end by merely leaving the Catholic school.

During the summer of 1941 I went south to see my grandmother, as usual. My parents, especially my mother, had the idea that if I spent my summers in the country with my grandparents, I would somehow escape being scarred by the rugged life of Chicago's South Side, a life dominated by gang warfare and petty stealing. She believed that I would somehow not grow up to become a thug or thief or both. This protectiveness in my mother even extended to not letting me wear long pants until I graduated from grammar school. That became a big issue in our house; children younger than I were already wearing them and I fought for my right to look like a young man—but unsuccessfully. At the same time, my mother often insisted that I make my own decisions about my life— such as the one to go to the Catholic school.

There was no hassle about going to the country for the summer, however. I loved the open skies, the farm, the horses, the mules, and, most of all, the endless watermelon patches. Daddy Tom used to tell me that he made three watermelon patches so that there would be plenty when I arrived in the country. In a way I guess I was a favorite grandchild, the only one who lived in the city and came back to the country and imitated radio announcers describing the fights of Joe Louis. That was our way of beating the white man. Joe Louis fought our battles for us in those days.

My grandmother, Mama Jane, belonged to Concord Baptist Church, which was located on the road to Slayden, Mississippi. Across the street from the church stood the graveyard and next to it the one-room school-house. It was a wooden frame church, with the walls and ceiling built from two-inch narrow boards throughout. The church was formerly lighted by small kerosene lights that hung near the front. People would cool themselves with small fans that they brought to church; the men usually stood crowded in the back, wiping off sweat with their greasy handkerchiefs. During my early days, wagons stood outside, but later these became cars and trucks.

Each year there was a revival with a mourner's bench, a place for sinners wishing to save their souls. According to Baptist tradition, when a person became twelve he had reached the age of being responsible for his sins. If your soul was not saved through a process of redemption, you were doomed to hell, with all its fire and brimstone. The devil's men would continually stoke the coals of hell's fire, as well as place wood and logs upon it, and you would burn eternally. The images of this constant torture were enough to make anyone wish to save his soul and stay in grace with the good God above.

All children over twelve were asked to come to the mourner's bench at the yearly revival meetings. Many of my cousins and other relatives who lived near us were going on the mourner's bench to save their souls that Sunday night in 1941 and I went too. I did not know what I was doing or what was supposed to happen to me. The dark church was packed; people were singing and praying and mourning.

I sat there, wishing that I were outdoors talking and playing with the other children. I was going with Celia Mae, the same girl to whom I had been "married" in a Tom Thumb wedding at the age of four. I thought of her and wondered what she was doing, who she was playing with. Inside the church the thump-thump of the feet against the wooden floor became more rhythmic and the voices of people singing and praying more melodious.

We knelt down on the floor and I heard the children mourning and groaning. As I knelt down to ask forgiveness for all my sins at the age of twelve, I asked the girl next to me what I was supposed to do. She replied, "Just say 'Lord have mercy.'" I tried this over and over, and over again: "Lord, have mercy." I told her nothing was happening and that I was getting tired of saying it. She told me to say, "Forgive me for my sins, Lord have mercy on me the sinner." I kept varying these words, saying them over and over again trying to make some pattern out of them, trying to feel sorry for myself. But I could not evoke any tears and I didn't think all of this made sense.

People would come up and pray for all of us, the sinners, who were trying to see the light. They would tell us how one day the hand of God had heard them pray and had come down and lifted them up. God would surely hear us praying, too. Later in life, when I studied African traits in the New World, I was to discover that the rhythmic and ritualistic patterns in this service were comparable to some dances and ceremonies in Africa.

The night passed. No sinners were saved. Late that night we all left the church. We were supposed to keep our minds on God, but I went outside and played with Celia Mae and knew that I was a sinner and not a child of God.

We went through the same routine that Monday afternoon and that Monday night. My knees were beginning to hurt from kneeling so much on the floor. Nothing was happening to me. I didn't feel any different, I didn't feel any sins heavy on my consciousness, but I knew that something was supposed to happen.

We woke up Tuesday morning at our farmhouse and there seemed to be something in the air, a feeling, an expectation, and one of my cousins said that something was going to happen. At the revival that day my cousin Sonny got religion. We were all walking around in a circle and suddenly he started shouting, "Lord, have mercy on my soul!" All the people in the church, and especially the older women who were attending to the mourners that afternoon, began to shout, "He's got religion, Jesus have mercy on him, he's got religion!" I observed all this, trying to figure out how Sonny was different from me. He was one of we three grandchildren who had been raised in the family house. Sonny was older and always received the harshest punishment from my grandmother. He used to pee in the bed and this she couldn't stand. Not realizing that he couldn't help it, or believing in old-fashioned child rearing, or frustrated because she had so much work to do and very few people to help her, Mama Jane would—in my opinion—attack Sonny unnecessarily. I remember how I would crouch down when she told him to go get the bullwhip. Licks with the bullwhip were reserved for very special offenses, but when Mama Jane lashed out at Sonny, she unleashed against his tender skin all the frustrations of living in a racist society and of years of overwork.

Now he was sitting quiet and upright, away from the mourner's bench. Soon he would be able to walk out of the church and to remain forever away from the mourner's bench. The only difference I could discern was that he had publicly cried, thrown his arms back, stomped his feet several times, and shouted, "Lord have mercy on my soul!" If this was all that it took to get religion—to get away from the mourner's bench—then I could do the same thing.

My other friends may well have been thinking just that, too, for no sooner had Sonny got religion, than others started yelling, "Lord, have mercy on me!" The older people shouted that they had got religion too. At the age of twelve, in a Baptist tradition and setting, I did not have the courage to tell my grandmother that I thought all this was nonsense. I simply observed what had been happening around me and knew that I, too, could fabricate some tears in this emotionally charged atmosphere. So I covered my face with my handkerchief and cried, "Lord, have mercy!"

It worked. I was taken off the mourner's bench and the people talked of how many children got saved that day by the grace of the Lord.

When I returned from the country to Chicago my mother told Rev. Joseph Lawrence Roberts that I had gotten religion in a revival and was ready to join the church. He had me stand next to him after a service and the entire congregation passed by, and shook my hands. I felt awful, full of deceit, because I knew I had not experienced any religious conversion and did not believe that anything like that was possible. I knew I had just faked my way through that "conversion" because I wanted to get outside and play with my friends and with Celia Mae. I squirmed under the pressures of those handshakes with people from the South who had got "religion" in their early days and who understood that now I was truly a member of the Christian congregation at the age of twelve because I had confessed my sins—while, in fact, I was sinning all the time.

From the time I was seven years old until I graduated from grammar school, I sold the *Chicago Defender*—the paper that carried on the tradition of the race and told what was happening to black people throughout the land, especially in the South. I started selling the *Defender* every Friday, when it was only a weekly. We bought our papers from Doc, a West Indian who operated a small drugstore on the corner of Sixtieth and Michigan Avenue. We would pay six cents each for the papers and sell them for ten cents, making a profit of four cents per copy. I started out with a list of customers that included some of my mother's friends. At first she would take me around in her car and help me deliver the papers until I learned the route.

I started out with ten customers and never worked myself up to over twenty-five, for I was not an enterprising young salesman and the competition was great. The street would be flooded with boys selling the *Defender*. Some of my friends used to work the open market at the Sixty-first Street elevated stop, hawking their papers each week. I preferred the regular customer type of sale. Only once in the five or six years that I sold the *Defender* did I get robbed of my little change.

More important than the sale of the papers was my reading them and developing a sense of protest, a feeling that we as black people must fight all the way for our rights in this country. Each week the paper would contain the story of a new horror perpetrated against the race. I wanted to do something about these injustices, the lynchings here and beatings there, the discrimination everywhere. I vowed over and over that someday I would help to end this treatment to my people.

I read Booker T. Washington's autobiography, *Up from Slavery*, and also became aware of some of the thought of Dr. W. E. B. Du Bois and his conflicts with Booker T. Washington over the problems of black people in the twentieth century. Washington was an apologist for white philanthropy and United States racism. He felt that black people in the South should not actively challenge the racist political structure of the South. They should not seek political power, but instead should concentrate on acquiring crafts and agricultural skills with which to play what he considered their proper role in the society.

Dr. Du Bois felt we needed all the education we could get, for the demands of a highly industrialized society can only be met by people who are highly trained and can adapt to changing conditions. But, above all, Dr. Du Bois believed that we should seek and get political power and engage in political struggle. He not only believed this was true for black people in the United States but for all African people. He was a pioneer in Pan Africanism. I was greatly influenced by the call of Dr. Du Bois for young black people to get an education, including higher education, for the use of their people.

I went to mass rallies and church meetings called by A. Philip Randolph for the projected march on Washington of 1941. The race issue was on my mind, before my eyes, and in my blood.

I became more and more aware that I was black. I was brown. I was a Negro, and don't you forget it. My friends were red, brown, black, yellow. They, too, were black. They, too, were niggers. And together we were locked in. We were Negroes. And we were not supposed to sit on many stools, nor live on many streets, even in Chicago, especially in Chicago. We had to fight for every block we crossed east of South Park. We fought and we became bitter and we always remembered. We were Negroes and Negroes must fight, 'cause if you don't fight for what you want, ain't no white man gonna give you anything, and don't you forget it.

CHAPTER 4

Ready to Kill

GRADUATING FROM grammar school and entering high school posed a big question in our household: Should I take a general studies course and prepare for college or should I enroll in a shop course and take my chances on getting into college?

Racism and its effects lay beneath this problem. In the Chicago of 1943 few Negroes who graduated from high school went to college. Not that they weren't prepared—but there were very few schools they could attend. Chicago Teachers College had a quota for Negroes: 2 percent of the entering class. The University of Chicago had an unwritten quota of 10 percent. Northwestern University admitted about 5 percent of us. Thus only the upper-middle-class students got a higher education. Then we had the problem of finding jobs when we graduated from high school. Most of us did not have any skills, any vocational training that qualified us for jobs after high school. Without a college education, you couldn't get a good job. And you had little chance of getting a college education. We were in a box.

My parents urged me to take an industrial arts course or a shop course so that when I finished high school I would have something that could help me to get a job. In addition to all the arguments mentioned above, they pointed out that they had no money with which to pay for a college education and there were few schools where you could go free. Also, in my household and among the people who came there, a strong Booker T. Washington feeling prevailed—that all Negroes should have a trade. So my parents even enlisted the aid of their friends to convince me that I should take a vocational course at Englewood High School.

I wanted to take the general studies curriculum, but the whole argument about *us* being Negroes and all the implications of this, and *our* not being able to get jobs and *we* must prepare for the future and *we* have to live and *we* should get some security and four years of shop would give *us* some basis for getting a job if *we* do not go to college and *we* might well not go to college because *we* don't have much money—all those arguments were too much for me. At no point in this debate did anyone consider my personal aptitudes. Some twelve years later, in college, I would take a series of aptitude and personality tests that showed I had capability and interest in many fields of work—with the big exception of mechanics, where I scored at rock bottom. But nobody bothered with black grammar school graduates in Chicago in the forties; everybody knew we were going to the bottom of the job market because we were black, so why bother?

At Englewood High School where all my teachers and half my classmates were white, I enrolled in the shop course in February, 1943. It was a huge mistake. I did badly in all the courses related to shop, mechanical drawing included. I barely passed my first course designed to get me a job—ceramics. Then I enrolled in woodwork for a semester. This was supposed to make us good carpenters if we wanted to build houses. Here I did fine because the teacher made me shop supervisor; I had to keep track of everyone and everything, and did not have to learn anything about woodwork.

After that I went into machine shop, where you were supposed to learn something about grinding tools. This course I cut continuously. It was impossible; I just couldn't understand the complicated process and, therefore, cut and cut and cut. I don't even remember the names of anything in the shop except a lathe. One day the teacher became annoyed about my cutting and my failure in general. "James, if you don't come to class I'm going to kick you out for good," he said.

I turned just as he had his foot raised, I suppose he was gesticulating to make a point. "I wish you would kick me. I'll hit you so hard that you'll never see daylight. You fool."

"Get out! Get out! And don't you ever come back in my course."

I left and never returned. His class was during the first lunch period. Thereafter I had two lunch periods.

My demoralization about the shop classes spread to my other courses, which were not that many since shop took up most of my hours. I became sloppy in my study habits and, in fact, seldom studied. I argued with teachers in an insolent way. All my teachers were white, the student body was roughly half and half, but would soon be all black, and I was taking no shit from anyone, especially some dizzy teacher.

One day, when I was in my second year at Englewood and almost sixteen years old, I arrived late for my first class. The teacher, Mrs. McGovern, asked, "Do you have a late pass?"

I was at my desk by then. "Hell no," I answered. I must have said it loud enough for her to hear, although I did not consciously want her to hear it. I had a rep in the neighborhood and I was just acting it out.

"What did you say? Did you curse at me?"

"Did you hear me curse you?" I said.

"Yes, I did, and I'm not going to have anyone cursing me. You go to the office and tell Mr. Kreowitz I don't want you in my class." That was the assistant principal. I went. She sent a note to him and he looked at me. I had been there many times before and been threatened with suspension. Now the assistant principal told me that if I were sixteen he would expel me and I would never be able to get back into any high school. But since I was fifteen he could only suspend me and send me to continuation school. I could reenter in the spring but I would lose this semester.

I told my parents. They could not understand it. I felt bad, very bad, as I talked to them about what had happened.

"So, get a job," my old man said.

"That's right," my mother added. "No son of mine is going to get kicked out of school and then lay up and sleep. Not in my house." She was serious.

A job. A full-time job. Kicked out of school. The brilliant student who read in the dark. I didn't understand it. I didn't know what it was; but

I knew one thing, I wasn't going to take any shop course when I went back to school. I had sense enough to know that I didn't belong there.

One day a week I had to report to Washburne High, my continuation school. I got a job at the Cuneo Press, a giant printing plant, as a paper roller. We would lift the huge rolls of paper onto dollies and roll them to the presses, where the pressmen inserted them for the books that this plant published in a constant flow. There was an elderly fellow there, an ex-wrestler and boxer, who used to tell me that it was all wrong for me to be out of school and working at a job like this one. He constantly talked to me about this and the work itself, which was boring and dangerous, but the only job I could find.

During the three months that I was out of school and working, I thought a lot about how I had been living up to then. Each payday, I found myself gambling with the older men and losing all my money, so that I was working for zero. I bought a few zoot suits, which were in style then, but the rest of my salary just melted away. I saved nothing. I was going nowhere.

Then there was my involvement with gang activity. My first recollection of Englewood High School was Pee Wee standing on the corner of Sixty-first and Stewart trying to collect protection fees from incoming freshmen. Pee Wee was a short, well-built, young black man who had a reputation for being bad. He was backed up by his older brother, Chili, the leader of our gang. The Sixty-first Raiders, as it was called, centered around the AMO show—a movie house on the other side of Sixty-first and South Park.

In my grammar school days, you couldn't get to the AMO show without fighting the white gangs that resented blacks moving across Sixty-first and South Park and then using the public facilities of that area—including the AMO show. But by the time I entered high school, we held the turf around the AMO. We could claim as our territory the hamburger joint located next to the AMO and we would hang out here during the wintertime. The Sixty-first Raiders were never very organized; we would just ride around our neighborhood, pistols at hand, defending ourselves from the attacks of other gangs and sometimes making intrusions into other neighborhoods. My father had given me the 1934 Plymouth and my role was to drive the guys whenever a rumble started.

But the gang scene had not become a way of life for me, a deep involvement. To a certain extent, I always stood back and looked at it like something foreign and even incomprehensible. Now, in this period of my suspension, it all began to seem completely pointless. Things could have gone the other way; it was a likely time for me to get into marijuana and drugs, as some of my friends were doing then. I didn't, for one thing because I just couldn't learn to inhale. But the main reason was that drugs also struck me as a waste of time and not a way to do the kinds of things I wanted to do. I broke off with the Sixty-first Raiders, with no regrets.

While beginning to think in a new way about my Chicago life up until then, I was also having some new thoughts about going to Mississippi during vacations. When summer came in 1944 and I was asked to pay a visit to my grandmother, I refused.

"I just can't go South this summer," I told my mother. "I'm afraid I'll never come back alive because I ain't gonna take nothing off those white folks. I'm just not going to do it. And I don't want to get Mama Jane and Daddy Tom in trouble. It's best I stay here. I'm sorry."

Mother seemed very upset. My grandmother wanted to see me. I had not been to see her for the last two summers. My cousins had gone into the Army; my grandparents were almost alone.

I loved grandma. I wanted to see her. But this was 1944. The United States was at war. I believed all that bullshit about the four freedoms and that this war would end all wars and that men would live in peace and that black men who died on the battlefield, even though they were segregated, were dying so that black men here in America could be free. Sure, blacks could not vote in the South. Even grandma had never seen a ballot in her life, but she had sons and grandsons on the battle-field in the name of democracy. There are problems, but we are going to correct them. Just you wait until the war is over. Roosevelt, the Great White Savior of the Black Man, was going to make some changes. But damn! They were still lynching my people. They were still beating us. Outside of Chicago, and even within it, there were restaurants off limits to blacks.

My growing awareness of my blackness, my growing inability to com-promise my dignity, and the growing sense of change in the air, all made it difficult for me to go South. This was not a wholly new problem. I had already given my grandparents trouble, because I simply did not know how to behave around the white folks. It was not that I was nasty to them; I was a well-mannered youngster. But I no longer knew how to talk to all those white women who worked as clerks in the stores. In Chicago my parents and Catholic teachers tried to correct our country ways and teach us to talk "properly." In Mississippi my new speech was considered uppity.

There had been an incident on my last visit, when I went to the local store with my uncle to buy some candy. "May I have some of that, please," I asked the white clerk, pointing to one tray. "And may I have some of that, also?" The next week my uncle refused to take me with him. I asked my grandmother why.

"Sport, what did you do the last time you were at the store?" she then asked me.

"I didn't do anything."

"Didn't you sass Miss Jones?"

"Who is she?"

"The woman that works at the corner store."

"No Mama Jane. Who said I did?"

"Uncle Randolph was talking to two white men. They said, 'You had better keep that boy out of town. He might end up in the river.'"

Daddy Tom didn't want to see his favorite grandchild lynched by a white mob, so I was restricted to the farm after that.

Still, I had to pay some kind of visit to my grandmother this summer. "I'll tell you what I'll do," I then told my mother, "I'll go for two weeks and two weeks only."

That was all right. My mother just wanted me to go South, for part of the summer if not all of it.

But I knew my temperament. I was aware of my blackness and my inability to take any shit off of any white man. And I was reading Richard Wright. I did not accept, but I understood fairly well the society's conception of my role and status: I was a nigger, a Negro. At the same time, I would rather die like a man than take insults off crackers. Not me. So in preparation for my trip South I decided not to take many clothes, only a gymnasium bag. In this bag I put a very sharp, very long hunting knife. I would keep the bag close to me at all times and any white man who started some shit would get it. Didn't matter what happened to me. I simply was not going to allow one of them crackers to hit me. Kill me, baby, but one of you will go down with me!

And so I left by train for Memphis, where I would visit my Aunt Hattie and then take the train on to Moscow, Tennessee. From there I would hitch a ride with the mailman and ride out to our farm in Mississippi, just across the state line.

As soon as I got off the front coach of the train from Chicago and took the Memphis city bus for my Aunt Hattie's house, I realized that the time to use that knife might have arrived. A brother in his late thirties had boarded the segregated city bus we were riding, and decided he was tired of going to the back. There were no seats there, anyway. The rest of us had taken them all. The brother decided to sit by a young white man, perhaps in his early twenties. The eyes of those of us in the back followed closely. I was happy to see the challenge and only regretted that I didn't have the nerve to do what he was doing. There he was, a black man sitting in the front of the bus in 1944 in Memphis, Tennessee. He was protesting as Rosa Parks would do ten years later in Montgomery, Alabama.

The young cracker looked at the brother and his face turned red. Then his neck turned red. He began to look up and down at the brother, who kept his black head high, looking straight to the front. I sat in the back, ready in case anything happened, my bag between my feet. Finally the young white cracker stood up and moved farther toward the front of the bus, where he took another seat. Then he got up again and went back toward the brother. His face was still red.

"Did you see my wallet?" he asked, very agitated.

"No, I did not see your wallet," the brother answered as he began to help the young man look for the nonexistent wallet.

"What are you doing, sitting by me anyway?" the cracker yelled when it was obvious that no wallet was lost.

Up straight stood the brother. "I'll sit by you any time I want to. You don't have any right to a special seat."

I placed my bag on my lap. My heart was happy. We were striking back one more time. Here's one cracker who won't have it his way.

"You know you ain't got any business up here in the front. Can't you read those signs?" the young white cracker hollered with his eyes popping open.

The bus driver kept driving. We were in the black community by now.

"I don't care what those signs say. I'll sit where I want to sit on any bus."

"Yeah," said the cracker, "and if you stay on this bus, I'm going to hit you when I get off. I bet you won't get off this bus when I get off."

"Let's get off here," said the brother. "If you want to fight, let's get off right now. Come on, you're so bad, let's get off here." I made up my mind that if the white boy got off, I was getting off too.

The bus driver kept driving. I relaxed the hold on my bag a little. I decided the cracker was shamming. He was not about to hit that black man, not today, not on this bus, and not out there on the street where all our folks were.

"This is my stop," the brother said, as the bus slowed down. "Let's get off here."

But the young white man just sat there. A nigger had sat beside him instead of riding in the back of the bus. Yeah, freedom was in the air. I felt good.

The next morning I woke late and had to rush to the station to catch the train going to Moscow. I dashed up the stairs and saw the train pulling out. I ran, trying to get to the front coach, but I knew I could not make it.

A white conductor was standing in the last coach and he yelled: "Hurry, and grab my hand. You can make it."

I grabbed his hand and caught the train. Now, I knew that I "belonged" in the front of the train and I wasn't planning to challenge the laws of this train. I had become accustomed to some forms of segregation and the train segregation did not upset me. But how could I get up front? Or should I just stay here?

The conductor seemed to know what was on my mind. "I'm the troop train conductor, I'm not the regular conductor. You stay here and I'll tell him you're back here. He'll be back anyway."

"Nice guy," I thought.

In five minutes an old, bony, wrinkled-faced white man came back and yelled at me: "What you doing back here? You know you belong up front."

"The train was pulling out and I . . ."

"Makes not one bit of difference. You got no business back here. When this here train stops, you get off and come up front. Don't come through them coaches either. Get off and come around to the front coach."

"All right," I said.

The train seemed to stop every five minutes, but started again too quickly for me. If I got off, it would probably leave me behind. Having ridden that train so many times in the past, I knew it stopped for fifteen minutes in Covington, Tennessee. There I would get off and go up front and take my place where I "belonged."

Meanwhile, many soldiers started coming back to the end of the train where I was standing. We began talking about the war and the science of military warfare. I was in ROTC at Englewood High School, with no question in my mind about the validity of fighting wars. I was becoming a strategist of modern warfare.

"What kind of rifles are you guys using in basic training?" I asked.

"We use the M-1," one replied.

"I understand it doesn't have the kick of the Springfield. We have to use the Springfield in ROTC at my school."

"Huh," someone grunted. "We have to use the Springfield in basic training, too."

"You what?" I asked, very surprised. "I thought the Springfield went out with the First World War."

"They have some around," he replied.

I was not at ease during this conversation. I kept thinking of the old conductor, who was sure to come back here and start some shit. And I kept thinking about the strangeness of the situation. Here I was, a black man, talking to white soldiers going to war for this nation. They were riding on a segregated troop train. Up front somewhere was the old conductor who wanted me to take my place. I kept hold of my bag because I felt sure there was going to be trouble. I tried to make more and more conversation, since I was afraid of the old conductor and the possibility of his getting a lynch mob together at one of these stops. Although I did not think he would try anything around these soldiers—still—and how could one trust the white soldiers to help in a pinch?

I glimpsed the original conductor who had helped me get on the train. He stood on the other side of the rear platform, listening to our conversation with a nod and a faint smile which indicated approval. He was a friend, you could tell that.

"I thought I told you to come up front when this here train stopped!" the old, bony-faced, white man screamed as he stepped out onto the platform with his hands half-raised. "Goddamn it, you got no business back in this here part of the train. You belong up front!"

"Look," I shouted back, "I'm not Superman, I can't fly up to the front. Every time the train stops, it pulls off right away. I'm not going to get left on the ground trying to get to the front."

"But you got no business back in this here section."

"All right. So when the train gets to Covington, I'll go up front."

"Look," said the first conductor, moving in closer to the old man. "If you want him up front so badly, why don't you take him up front?"

"You know I can't take him up through them there coaches. He can't walk through them."

"Well, if you don't want to take him through the coaches, then you'll have to wait until the train stops long enough for him to get up there. The kid is right. This train has been stopping and pulling off too fast for anyone to get up front," my friend said.

"You really think I could take him through the coaches?" the old conductor asked.

"You're the conductor," the other replied in exasperation.

"O.K. You come on," he said to me, "but I ain't got no business doing this."

"See you guys around," I said, wondering how these soldiers going to fight for democracy felt about the incident. I picked up my bag and started walking.

As soon as we left the rear platform, I worked out the science of killing this white man if he tried to hit me. My long, sharp hunting knife was on top of my clothes in the gymnasium bag. I had unzipped the bag just enough for me to reach the handle. I carried the bag through the two cars at waist height. No doubt the old man would turn to his left if he tried to hit me. I would then swing the bag upward, blocking his right and pulling out the knife at the same time. Within a second I would plunge it into his belly. This I would do, with no regrets. This was the moment when I would no longer accept what "nigger" meant to white people. This was the moment when I would help the brother on the bus. This was the moment I would grow into my manhood. This was the moment I was ready for death. This was the moment I would kill!

We walked through about two coaches and then the old white man turned around. He drew back his fist and said, "I ought to knock your head off for catching that last coach. You got no business back there."

"If you do, you'll never hit anyone else," I said to him quickly, looking straight into his cold, watery blue eyes. In a way, my reaction was strange and ambivalent. On the one hand, I was willing to die if the conductor put his hands on me, yet I was walking willingly toward a segregated coach. Though I may have disliked the idea of sitting in a segregated coach, that emotion was not as strong as my hatred for the man who threatened to strike me. But at the time, I was only aware of one simple feeling: This was the moment when all the white folks in the world would get it for what they had done to me.

As I told him he would not live if he hit me, a loud, deep bass voice behind me boomed, "All right, let's keep moving." I looked quickly over my shoulder and saw a very tall white man standing very close behind me. Close enough to prevent my lunge with the knife if the old cracker tried to hit me. He was a brakeman.

"You tell him to keep moving. He's the one stopping the progress," I said. I could not back down. Things were up-tight at this moment. My mind was clear.

The old cracker looked at me intently for a second, then turned around and kept walking. We reached the front where the brothers and sisters were and I relaxed.

When the train pulled into Moscow, I got off and walked down the red, dusty gravel road leading to Route 2, where I would await the mailman. He had to get the mail off the morning train. Since not many country people did much writing, it took him only about thirty minutes to get his mail together. I sat there on a stump next to the winding stream leading from a river, looking at the green trees and the tall weeds you see near swamps. I was thinking of my life and how I hated white folks and then I thought that I didn't hate all white folks, just some like that cracker who had tried to pull that shit.

I had to tell Grandma that this was going to be my last trip South. I would not come this way anymore. I just couldn't take all the trouble. white people wanted to put on us. I loved her more than anyone else in the world but I couldn't come this way on that train again. Those days were gone forever. She would just have to understand that if she wanted me to live, I could not come South. She would have to come North.

I felt the hot sun burning on my back. I was alone and lonely. Memories of sweet times past were all wrapped up in my grandmother and the farm on which she lived in Mississippi. Here I was, unable to come to see my grandparents because of the cracker system that called me nigger.

I got down off the stump and started throwing rocks. The white mailman pulled up, and I asked if he would take me out to our place. He said, "Yes," as I knew he would.

Then he told me that since I was last South, he had stopped taking the mail all the way down that route. They couldn't drive there when it rained and the state of Mississippi just wouldn't fix up the road. So service stopped at the Tennessee line; I would have to walk about a mile. I didn't mind that, but as I rode on the back of that mail truck, I kept on thinking about myself, my life, what I would do with it. Would I live for the next two weeks? And if I weren't killed by any of these crackers, what then would happen? What could I do to change the situation? Sure, I was going to kill that cracker if he had hit me—but then what? What about people like my Mama Jane and Daddy Tom who just lived on the farm and found ways to get along with these white folks even though they hated them just as much as I did, if not more?

CHAPTER 5

A Family Fight

RACISM, RACISM, hatred, and fear. They dominate the lives of black people and they dominated mine. But of course there were also the universal kinds of conflict between individual human beings.

Throughout my life I had respected the man I called Pop as my father and the idea that he might not be my father never entered my mind. My name was James Rufus. His name was John Rufus; my mother's name was Octavia Rufus. I had a baby brother twelve years younger than I whose name was Bernard Rufus. I didn't have very warm feelings toward my father and thought him to be a cruel person at times. He seemed to feel a great hostility toward me and would often inflict unusual punishment, forcing me to stay inside the house for days on end because of something I had done wrong.

Sometimes my parents would play bridge at home or go out. One night they were having a game at home with friends and my father sent me to the store to buy something. I stayed out a long time, playing with some friends in the street. When I returned, he took me into the other room and started beating me with his fists. So hard was he beating me that some of his bridge partners came in and said, "Leave him alone, Rufus."

When I got older, I began helping my father at the gas station. He had quit his job at the stockyards and leased a Sinclair gas station on the corner of Fifty-ninth and Wabash; it became the center of my parents' lives. Pops, as people called my father, worked long hours. I worked there part-time, pumping gasoline and greasing and washing cars and fixing flat tires. It was wartime and gasoline was rationed, calling for the extra work of dealing with the various types of stamps.

One day when I was fourteen, during the spring of my first semester in high school, I got into an argument with my father at the station. He told me to leave home and I went there to pack. I dressed and put my clothes in a suitcase and took them to the hamburger joint next to the AMO theater. I didn't know where I was going or what I would do. Although I had some money and some United States savings bonds, I felt very loose and just hung around the hamburger joint. My father walked in and asked, "Where is your bag?" I told him that it was behind the counter. He got it and we walked out into the street. He said he was taking me back in the house because my mother was very upset and crying. "That's the only reason I'm taking you back," he told me. Inside me, I said, "Don't do me any favors." But I walked alongside him and I returned.

Then, one day during my suspension, I was searching at home for my father's pistol. He had a .38 Colt and I used to take it out all the time. I thought I had left it in my car but I couldn't find it there. I thought that I might have misplaced it in the house.

As I was rummaging through clothes and papers, I found my birth certificate. On it was written the name James Forman, born October 4, 1928. Continuing to rummage I found the marriage license of my parents: Married 1932. Octavia Allen to John Rufus.

This set in motion a whole series of thoughts and speculations. John Rufus was not my father but I had been going under his name all these years. The incidents of coldness and cruelty I had experienced began to take on a new focus and I wondered if they were related to his being my stepfather. It took me some time to discuss the discovery with my mother. When I did, she said she assumed that I had known all along. But there was no way for me to have known; my grandparents had never mentioned it nor had anyone else.

I did, however, remember a night during one of my summer visits to Mama Jane's house when we were ready for bed and I was saying the prayers I had learned in Catholic school. My grandmother was in bed in her room and the door to the hall was open, so that she could hear me. At the end of the prayer I had said, "bless my mother and father."

"Who is your father, Sport?" Mama Jane had called out from the other room.

"You mean my father in heaven or here on earth?" I replied.

"I'm not talking about God, I'm talking about your father on earth."

"Mr. Rufus," I answered, a little puzzled.

"How do you know that?" she asked.

"I just know it." She had not said anything else, but I thought the conversation strange at the time.

In Chicago, I went on working at my stepfather's gas station, and never mentioned my discovery to him. Saturday at the gas station was a big day, a big money day with plenty of customers. This particular Saturday I pumped a great deal of gas. When we closed up, there was over a hundred dollars in my wallet and many gas rationing stamps.

At about eight o'clock, I went to change my overalls and wash the grease off my hands. My face was dirty and my entire body ached from pumping gas, fixing flats, greasing cars, washing cars, parking cars. I felt dead tired. When it was time for me to check my money in with Pop,

I couldn't find my wallet. There was no possible way I could have lost it, I was sure. But I assumed that one fellow who had been hanging around the station all day had clipped me. His was a new face and we never saw him after that day.

I told Pop about the loss and also about the fellow. "It was my fault, Pop," I ended. "I should have been more careful, but you can take it out of my pay. I'll work free till the hundred dollars is paid off."

"We needed that money. How come you so careless? You ain't got your mind on what you doing," he said angrily, again and again. "You go home and you better find that money by the time I get there," he said with finality.

"I told you I lost the money. I can't find something I ain't got," I retorted quickly.

"You better find it."

I knew he was angry. I knew he would be even angrier when I told him again that I couldn't find the money. But before telling him I didn't have the money, I had thoroughly searched all my clothes and the room where we changed clothes. It wasn't there and it wasn't going to show up.

I left the gas station and went home. I took a hot bath, as I usually did to cut the grease from my body and to ease my tiredness. I didn't mind working at the gas station. I thought it was helping the family. And I earned a decent wage, as decent as I would find anywhere on a part-time basis. Pop used to complain at times about my head being in the books. Sometimes when we were there together on slow days or nights, he had to remind me to catch a customer, to get my head out of a book.

As I soaked in the hot water, I tried to figure what Pop would do when he came home. I didn't have one hundred dollars. I didn't even have my pay for that week. I was willing to forgo it to help make up the hundred dollars, but I could not understand why he wasn't willing to let me make it up. I wondered if he thought I was pulling a hype on him, telling him that I had lost the money and keeping it at the same time. I had never stolen from my parents except one time, the time he put me out of the house when I was fourteen. I had gone to the money box and taken some bills which I never returned. I felt bad about that. But I was angry and had no intention of being put out into the world without a cent to my name. That I didn't return the money disturbed me, but I soon forgot the incident.

The hot water felt good; I almost went to sleep in it. Then I got out, put on pajamas, and pulled out the rollaway bed on which I had always slept. In bed I wondered if Pop would be foolish enough to try to whip me at my age. I hadn't had a whipping in a long time. I used to get them quite often, for most anything my parents felt I had done wrong. My mother used to whip me, but I soon found a way to deal with that. Whenever she wanted to whip me, I would tell her that I had to go to the bathroom first. In there, I would take clothes out of the dirty clothes basket and stuff them into my knickers and into my shirt. When I emerged, I was well padded. By faking loud cries and hopping around, I could soon get my mother to stop. I didn't really mind her whippings because they were a game in a sense.

But my father—I still called him that, in my mind—was something else. He seldom took the strap to me, but when he did he would hold me down with one hand and then bring the belt down very hard with the other. I never tried to fool him, for fear that I would be caught. This would only lead to worse punishment.

I heard the key turn in the lock. "Here it comes," I said to myself. I heard him walk straight to the room where I lay in bed.

"You find that money?"

"Nope. I told you I lost it. I told you I would work and you can take it out of my pay."

My mother was home. My baby brother was asleep. I had not told my mother that I had lost the money, for it was my problem—not hers. In the past, she had never said anything to my stepfather when he scolded or punished me, at least not in front of me. But I had a strong feeling that she often discussed me with him.

"O.K. You lost the money. Now I'm going to whip you for being so careless."

I laughed to myself. He must be kidding. I was simply too old, too big, for a whipping. Besides, there was nothing to justify whipping me.

I didn't answer him when he first said it. But then he proceeded to take off his overcoat and jacket and hang them in the hall closet. He kept telling my mother how careless I was, and that the money wouldn't have been lost if I paid attention to my work. A hundred dollars—that was a lot of money.

I knew Pop was angry, but I was cool. I thought this talk about a whipping must be a joke, but I prepared myself psychologically, just in case. It meant a fight with my father. It meant that I would strike him back for the first time in my life. There was going to be a fight in our house that night if he touched me with a belt or with his hands. That was for sure.

I lay on my rollaway bed, penned between the bureau and the table. He would have to come to the bed if he were really serious. He kept arguing and fussing, talking to himself and to my mother. She was quiet. I waited. "What right does he have to think he can whip me?" I said to myself as I thought of the fact that he was not my real father.

He kept asking me questions about the money, about the man who might have clipped me.

I was becoming irritable.

Angry.

He kept fussing.

I was tired.

He fussed.

I wanted to go to sleep.

He fussed some more.

I didn't have the money.

I should be careful, he went on fussing.

"Damn it, Pop! I told you I lost the money! I'll pay you back, I'll work every day! Now leave me alone!" I said loud and firm.

"Curse me, will you? I'll leave you alone," he said, advancing with his belt outstretched.

"Don't hit me with no belt, Pop. I'm telling you, don't hit me with no belt."

"I'll hit you. Who do you think you are?" he yelled, his eyes flashing as the belt came down.

I caught it before it hit me, rising from the bed.

"Let go that belt. Let go." he yelled.

"I told you not to hit me. I ain't done nothing for no whipping."

"Let go of the belt," he said, pushing me backward onto the bed.

The shit was on.

I let go of the belt as I rose and pushed him backward toward the table. "This kid is fighting me. This kid is fighting me. Octavia, this kid is fighting me!" he cried over and over as we locked arms, pushing, striking, grabbing, and shoving each other. The curtains fell and we were over by the window. A window shade fell. Then another shade. I was holding my own. I didn't want to fight with Pop. I wasn't afraid of him, but I didn't want to fight him. I had no other choice this night.

"All right, goddamn it. I'll kill you. You rotten little bastard," he yelled, rushing toward his room.

I knew he was headed for his gun. I didn't know what to do.

My mother had been yelling to stop it, stop it, all during the fight. She was standing by the door when Pop came charging out with the gun. "No! No! Rufus, no!" she screamed, grabbing his arm. She always called him by his last name.

His right arm went up into the air, gun in hand. "I'll kill him. I'll kill the little bastard. Get out of my way, Octavia. No kid fights me. Get out of my way."

"No, no! You can't do that," she screamed, louder this time, wrestling with him, blocking him from leaving the bedroom.

I decided to go into the bathroom and lock the door. I stooped down behind the toilet, hoping to protect myself from any bullets.

"Come out of there," Pop yelled, banging on the door. "Come out!"

I stayed there. If he shot into the bathroom, he couldn't hit me. I was protected on that flank. If he knocked the door down, which was the only way he could enter, then we would have to fight it out and see what happened.

"Gimme that gun, Rufus. Gimme that gun. Rufus! Rufus!" my mother cried.

"I'll kill him. I'll kill him. Fighting with me!"

"Gimme that gun," my mother screamed for the last time. They were wrestling in front of the bathdoom door. Something heavy hit the floor. One of the two had fallen.

"Mother! Mother!" My baby brother was crying. I was uncertain what to do, but I was not coming out of that bathroom even if it meant spending the night there. As I crouched there, the noise subsided. It was quiet in the house.

My mother had got the gun from my father. She knocked on the door and told me to go to bed.

I got in the rollaway. "I told him not to hit me," I said to myself. "I told him." Then I fell asleep.

The fight was over. The issue was closed, and not mentioned the next day or the next.

I met my real father, Jackson Forman, at the gas station of my step-father. I had made inquiries from my mother as to the type of work that he did and where he lived. She told me she had not seen him for years but that, the last she knew, he was driving a cab for the Party cab company. This was the jitney line that used to run up and down Indiana and one could ride for a dime. Every time I took a jitney, I would look for him. One day, working at the gas station, I saw a man who resembled me very much and who was driving a cab. I asked him if his name was Forman and he replied, "Yes." I told him that I was his son James. He came from Mississippi, too, from Sunflower County.

Since then, I have seen him on many other occasions. He came to my high school graduation; my stepfather did not. But except for the reality that he is my father by birth, few bonds exist between us. From force of habit I still continued to call John Rufus my father.

CHAPTER 6

Dreams and a .38 Colt

ON ONE side of the room were the sophomore students. On the other side sat the juniors. This was "division," a period each day when the two groups would assemble together for twenty minutes. Today we would get our report cards. It was the end of my first month back in school after being suspended and I was in the general studies program, not shop.

The division teacher stood in front of the class and called out the names of the only two persons in the entire division who had made the honor roll.

Jean Perkins.

James Rufus.

James Rufus . . . James Rufus . . . They must be kidding.

All eyes in the division turned toward me. Everyone there knew me as the stud who had a 1934 black Plymouth with red wheels. One of the cats who used to run with a gang that charged protection fees from entering freshmen. One of those Sixty-first Street boys who would come to parties in Woodlawn and disrupt things. They knew I had been kicked out of school last year. I couldn't have made the honor roll. There must be some mistake.

I thought so, too. But there it was on the report card.

A couple of cats insinuated that I had copied off of a girl named Norma. But we didn't even have classes together, fortunately.

While I took their ribbing in a good-natured way, I made up my mind that the capacity I had for education in the Du Bois sense must flourish. When I had come back to school after being suspended, I placed a great importance on being a serious student—not so much on grades in themselves, but on realizing the potential which grade school had told me I possessed. My parents didn't pressure me to do well; they never asked what grades I had got or whether I had made the honor roll. They saw my grades only when they signed my report card. Nor was I afraid of being expelled again. I was just anxious to make up for all the time lost because of Catholicism, my own foolishness, and mistaken choices.

During the next year and a half I continued to make the honor roll every month. Now that I was taking courses which interested me instead of courses to get me a job—maybe in a segregated factory at the lowest possible wages—it was easy to study hard and do well. I felt stimulated all the time, excited about what I read and the talks I had with fellow students.

A key factor was the intense internationalism of this wartime and postwar period. Half the world had united to fight fascism; the United States and the Soviet Union were allies. Our studies at school took place unfettered by the Communist bugaboo that swept in later. No topic was taboo in class. Later the United Nations was born and in my civics class we studied it, as well as the history of the League of Nations, and why the latter had failed. I also remember writing a paper on propaganda and how it manifested itself in *Time* and *Newsweek*. I took the same news story and compared its treatment by *Time* and by *Newsweek*. The latter came out with a relatively higher objectivity (which still holds true).

The level of consciousness was high among students and teachers on the race issue too. Many black soldiers were coming home, only to be frustrated by racism here in the States. Black demands for change intensified. We in high school were affected by the debates, both international and national. Every Friday in division, we discussed some current topic: the UN, capital punishment, the Fair Employment Practices Commission, an antilynching bill. I remember that Lorraine Hansberry, the playwright, who was one grade behind me, and I sometimes found ourselves on the same side and sometimes on opposite sides. I debated Marxism with a fellow student named Frank Wooten; neither of us had read much Marx but we had a general idea of his life and thought. And we did know the theory of surplus value, who got the surplus and who didn't, and why.

For me personally there was another reason why those high school years were a time of real learning and not just something to live through. Englewood High School—like all schools for ghetto children—did not have a curriculum suited to the needs of its students. It offered no courses to give students an awareness of their black experience and culture, to hold their interest. But I was luckier than most; I had been a *Chicago Defender* paper boy since the age of seven. This meant that every week I had read something about *us*, and the way *we* were treated. In high school, now, I could take information and view it in a context that made it mean something to me. The theory of surplus value, for example, wasn't just another piece of abstract economics for me, but a down-to-earth matter of slave owners and racist employers.

Amid all this study, activity, and many friends, I felt alone much of the time. Sometimes I wandered around the park, reciting poetry to myself or to a girl friend. Carl Sandburg's biography of Abraham Lincoln overwhelmed me; not so much for its story of how Lincoln freed the slaves but for the images of Lincoln's poverty, the agony of social change. In the days of reading those volumes, I walked through the cold park, thinking and pondering about the meaning of life. Sandburg's book absorbed me for weeks.

Along with what I was reading and learning, I also found stimulus in the church—not from any doctrines about God or heaven but from its social involvement. I had not been to church for a long time and felt it was for little boys, not a young man of sixteen. But I promised my mother that I would go with her on Easter morning of 1945, and I kept that promise. At the church, the Coppin Chapel of the AME church at Fifty-sixth and Michigan, I noticed a group of young ushers about my age. They comprised the Junior Usher Board and I was eventually talked into joining by Mr. and Mrs. Rogers, senior ushers. The group had meetings and discussion groups in addition to picnics and parties; they discussed current affairs and the role of youth. They were bright young people, another source of learning and challenge.

The junior ushers were also black young people, and that had much to do with my renewed church involvement. Our church was black and all its officers were black. Its entire history was black. Through the church black colleges and universities had been founded. The role of the church at that moment was, among other things, to encourage black children to have hope, to study, to know one's history, to become educated in the Du Bois sense. I read more and more about the history of the church, here in this country and abroad. As I read, seeds of doubt about the validity of God began to grow in my mind. This God was supposed to be just, yet we black people had to pray and pray and hope that justice would come to us one day. This seemed too slow to me. The myth of whites getting their just deserts in hell while we finally got rewarded in heaven was responsible for much of the apathy of black people, I thought. We young people had to make the church a force for change. We, the young black people at Englewood and on the Junior Usher Board, had to forge something from the country in which we lived.

Joining the Junior Usher Board led me into closer contacts with our minister, Rev. Joseph L. Roberts, whom I had known since childhood and who had been one of my customers for the *Chicago Defender*. A graduate of Knox College, Reverend Roberts was more of a lecturer on social issues than a preacher. His sermons, unlike any I had heard before, did not deal with heaven and hell, but with the human condition. He kept raising questions about this world, not describing the next one; he talked about how we must understand our history and what we black people must do to end discrimination.

Reverend Roberts was not dogmatic and worked closely with young people, always encouraging them to aspire. He used to tell us a little story about how life is like a train going up a hill with many heavy coaches. The engine strains and strains and strains and the train sounds like this: "I think I can, I think I can, I think I can, I think I can. . . ." And then, as the train slowly pulls to the top of the hill and goes over, it picks up speed. "I thought I could, I thought I could, I thought I could, I thought I could," the engine says now, racing downhill. For us, children of the ghetto, these inspirational slogans were very important.

In my mind I used to put this story together with a speech given by Charles Wesley, the president of Wilberforce College. It was about dreams. He urged all of us to have our dreams. We as black youth must have dreams. We must believe there is something to be attained on earth different from present reality. We must think as an architect does. He first imagines the building he wants to design, then puts it to paper, and goes on to see the drawings become a reality. This speech was given at DuSable High School and it had a tremendous impact on me. I began to think that all the thoughts I was having about my life and the kind of world I wanted to see were not just idle hopes. You had to have some dreams. You had to act upon those dreams.

I went along in high school, feeling more and more sure of myself, making new friends, dreaming my dreams. I felt good, proud. From time to time, the outside world would come blasting through—once at the end of a Colt .38.

I remember the night, a very cold night in December, 1945. Ice and snow covered the streets and sidewalks of Chicago. I was seventeen. It was the Christmas season, and I wanted to make some extra money. A friend had told me about a job at the Railway Express Company paying one dollar an hour—but you had to work from midnight to eight in the morning. The idea of making a dollar an hour had made me decide at least to try it. Besides, my friend would be there and we could talk about many things. I needed moral support, since both of my parents were agreeable to my working there but very dubious about my ability to stay awake for that long. I didn't have the habit of late nights then.

Aside from almost freezing as I loaded and unloaded the heavy packages, the first night went well. But instead of sleeping the next day, even though I tried, I found myself up and doing various things. Still, I was determined to make that dollar an hour and be able to buy lots of Christmas presents.

When I arrived at work the second night, I knew it was going to be a bad one. My friend didn't come to work. I just didn't know how I was going to make it, but maybe I could steal a little time in the toilet. Maybe I could even catch a nap.

Around three o'clock in the morning, I could hardly keep my eyes open and I decided it was time to take a long shit. I had no one to wake me and must have slept for a long time.

Someone was pounding on the door. "Come out of there, you sonofabitch!"

It was the Man! The White Man! The Boss!

I scrambled to put on my pants. "Don't you call me a sonofabitch," I yelled, half-asleep. "A man don't have any rights around here. Can't even go to the bathroom!"

"Hell, you've been in there too long! Get your ass up and come back to work!"

"All right, but I'm not a machine. I'll come back when I've finished."

"You've got fifteen minutes to be back on the platform."

I was still sleepy, really exhausted. It seemed as if it was impossible for me to rise from the stool. I wanted to get up and make it back to work. I had stolen enough time already. But I just couldn't get up. I fell asleep.

Wham! Wham! Loud knocks on the door again. "Goddamn it! You're fired. Who in the hell do you think you are?"

I was fired, but there was no need to take more from this cracker. "Look, mother fucker, don't you curse me. I'm not your damn slave. My father doesn't curse me and I ain't taking no shit off you," I screamed as I pushed open the door of the toilet. I was furious at this tall white man standing in front of me, dressed in black from top to toe—broad-rimmed black hat, black tie, a long black overcoat, and black pants. He was a very tall, skinny cracker.

"You little bastard. Who do you think you are," he sneered.

The turmoil in me could have made the snow melt outside. "Look, Jack," I said rapidly, "I don't know who you're used to dealing with, but the best thing you can do is to give me my time card and let me out of here."

"Come with me," he said. "I'll give you your time card."

We started walking down the long corridor past many boxes of freight. It seemed like a long walk to the office where the time cards were. As we walked, the cracker had both hands in his coat pocket and then suddenly, and very quietly, he pulled out a gun. "Do you know what this is?" he said.

"Yeah, I know. It's a .38 Colt. My father has one just like it." I had to play up-tight behind the game I had whipped on him in the toilet.

"Well, I'm going to give you your time card," he said, taking long strides toward the office. "But if you cause me any trouble, I'm going to shoot the shit out of you."

We reached the office. "You stand out here and wait," he told me, "I'll watch you from the office."

I felt it would be foolish to leave the building. I sensed that the cracker would shoot me and swear I was running away or that I had stolen something from the place. I decided to ride out events, expecting him to come out and give me my time card and that would be it. But the cracker stayed inside a long time. Finally he came out.

"Here's your time card. Get your money tomorrow. I'll walk you to the door and I don't want to hear any shit."

We walked in silence to the door. He pushed it outward. I stepped in front of him and touched the icy edge of the platform leading to the stairs.

"Stop, nigger, stop!"

I felt the cold barrel of the .38 against my neck.

"I'm from Mississippi, nigger. And I hate niggers. I'm going to blow out your brains. You ain't gonna talk back to no more white folks after tonight!"

I believed him. I knew enough about crackers to believe him. This was it, death. A fear swelled up within me, the fear of being blasted away, of not being able to finish school, of not doing so many things. I would go at the end of a .38. I was trapped. I began to cry, but I didn't want to cry. If I had to go, I wanted to go like a man. Let him blow out my brains but he wouldn't hear me begging for mercy, begging him to let me live. If I could only stop this crying!

I moved forward an inch, a long mile it seemed to me.

"Nigger, didn't I tell you not to move. If you move one more step I'll pull the trigger."

Still crying, still believing this was my last night on earth, I began to wonder if the man was really serious. Why had he said, "if you move one more step, I'll pull the trigger"?

We were on the platform. No other workers or anyone else were around. He could easily pull the trigger. I figured the best course of action was to remain still.

And then, out of the corner of my left eye, I saw someone in a white shirt walk up the platform behind me and whisper something to this cracker.

For what seemed like five minutes I stood there trying to hear their conversation. Finally the cracker said, "Now, nigger, you get off of these premises and don't you ever let me catch you around here. Now you move and get out of here."

What should I do? If I ran he might shoot and there was nothing I could do about that. I would be dead. But I couldn't stand there and argue with him. Then he would shoot me for sure. I had to take a chance that he might shoot as I walked down the stairs. That was the risk.

I walked slowly down the steps and then quickened my pace. At the edge of the building, I turned right. Walking was too slow; I began to run, ducking around boxcars. I headed for the main police station in Chicago, at Twelfth and State.

Two cops were on duty. I was still crying and could hardly talk. Breathing very hard and pointing down the street, I finally got myself together enough to tell the whole story.

Instead of moving fast, these two white cops sat there. "How old are you, kid?" one of them asked me.

"I'm seventeen, but what does that have to do with it? Aren't you going to do something? Aren't you going back there with me?"

They looked at each other. "But you should be in bed," one of them said to me.

"Look! That's not the point," I was getting angry now. "The point is that a man pulled a gun on me and almost killed me and you're just sitting there. Do you mean you're not going to do anything about this? Do you realize I almost died back there, two blocks away from the police station, the main police station?"

"Look, kid," this bastard said to me, "We can't do nothing. The guy is the superintendent. It's his word against yours. We can't leave the station. You want us to call your folks so they can come get you? Ain't nothing else we can do."

"Do you mean to tell me you're going to sit there and let something like this happen and not do anything?" I yelled.

"What can we do? We can't do nothing. You're not hurt or anything."

"See, that's why we hate you cops," I told them. "When you want the cops to do something for you, they can't do it. Naw, you can't go back and arrest that man for holding the gun on me. You can't do that, but you can always come around and stop us from doing what we want to do. You can stop us on the streets and search us for nothing. You can do that, can't you?" I had stopped crying. My hatred for the man at the Railway Express was mild compared to my disgust with these two cops sitting smugly behind a desk telling me they couldn't do anything. All the memories of all the cops in our neighborhood swelled up within me. All our hatred for anything with a gun swinging on his side "in the name of the law" poured forth, especially the hatred for a white cop in a black community.

"All right," I said. "I want you to mark down in your book that I came in here and tried to get you to help me. This isn't the last time you'll hear from me. And if you won't do anything about that man, maybe I'll have to take care of him myself."

"Now look here. You better get on home before you get yourself in trouble."

I began to wolf a little harder then. "Do you think I'm gonna just sit back and take all of this and not do anything? You got another thought coming."

I remember those two cops standing on the marble floor, a bright light shining behind them. All during my visit, no one else had entered the station. I began to see the foolishness of continuing to talk to those cops.

I left the police station and caught the Jackson Park subway train to Sixty-first Street. My parents were sleeping when I entered the house. I had planned to get my father's gun and go back to the Railway Express station. But then I thought that maybe that wasn't such a good idea. Beside, the gun was in my father's room; I would have to wait until tomorrow to get it. The next day I searched for the gun, although my determination to activate my plan was not very high any more. When I could not find it, I dropped the idea. Killing or wounding that cracker wouldn't accomplish much, and it could put me on ice for years.

Then I thought of taking the case to Reverend Roberts, to make it into a social issue and stir up community protest. But that seemed futile, too; it would wind up being the cracker's word against mine. In the end I just chalked the whole incident up as one more experience with the crackers. It was another day in the life of a black man in these United States.

But somehow, somewhere, we had to deal with the police, pigs and hogs that they are.

I had three semesters left of school and went straight through the summer. I did a lot of public speaking, became president of the Orator's Club, and acted in plays. There were many honors; they came unexpectedly out of academic achievement (sports were not my strong point, although I did run track). Then graduation came—in January of 1947.

In Chicago, the *Tribune* sponsored an "honor student award." Every high school graduating class picked from among its members the person considered to be its honor student. This was a process of voting by the members of the class; the teachers had nothing to do with who got elected. I received the most votes in my class, and I have always wondered if the vote was along racial lines. We blacks had pretty solid unity in my class. (Personally I felt that Ernest Gerules, who was white, should have received the award; in fact I voted for him.)

Once named, I went down to the offices of the *Tribune* to be interviewed. The reporter asked what my objectives were in life. What did I want to be? I told her I wanted to be a "humanitarian." She felt this was not clear enough. I tried to explain that this was the general category; under it would, no doubt, fall certain specifics. For instance, at the moment I wanted to be a minister. What type of minister? A minister of the gospel. Oh, you want to be a preacher. But in my mind there were differences between a minister of a church, who worked for humanity, and a preacher. I saw a preacher as one who went around talking about saving your soul and going to heaven and watching out for hell. A good minister of the gospel took the Bible and used it for the advancement of people here on earth. I conceived of the church as a ready-made protest organization. The minister could talk on Sunday about certain issues and then lead the congregation downtown the next day to protest. This seemed to me to be the highest function of the church. When the interview appeared, it quoted me as wanting to be a gospel preacher—and it also put words in my mouth on other subjects.

That was my first experience of how the press twists facts and misquotes people. But more important was the fact that, at the age of eighteen, I had come to such a goal in life—"humanitarian." An ambitious goal. I could as easily have been at loose ends or in permanent trouble or a drug addict or a hustler or just an aspirant to the middle class, as some of my friends became. There were several reasons why not, I think, all of them having to do with my background.

Those early years on the farm in Mississippi imbued me with a sense of security and a certain intellectual curiosity. I had a large, extended family and from it received much love. Even in the turmoil of a Chicago ghetto, stability was maintained. My mother had stopped working after she married my stepfather, and I was strictly supervised at home—too strictly from my viewpoint, but no thought of rebellion against it entered my mind. I had a multitude of friends and relatives in many kinds of circles.

By sending me back South for the summers, my mother not only nurtured this feeling of an extended family, but she also diminished the influence of some destructive community forces. My associations came out of the school scene more than off the street. And, in the school world, popping pills and using drugs were just becoming popular in Chicago but they had not yet swept up large numbers of students.

Both the Mississippi farm world and the climate of my Chicago home generated a pressure to be productive, to make the best possible use of one's time. This was economic in origin, but not just a matter of money. The issue was sheer survival, the survival of black working-class people in a hostile world. I had no patience with activities that seemed to me a waste of time, there was a great impulse in me to do, do, do. Life seemed very short, and so much work had to be carried out for my people.

I saw myself clearly as one of the young blacks destined to take up W. E. B. Du Bois's call to get a deep, true education and use it on behalf of the masses of black folk. My confidence in being able to carry out this mission showed in my choice of the poem I recited at graduation. It was "Invictus," by William Ernest Henley:

> Out of the night that covers me,
> Black as the pit from pole to pole,
> I thank whatever gods may be
> For my unconquerable soul.
> In the fell clutch of circumstance
> I have not winced nor cried aloud.
> Under the bludgeonings of chance
> My head is bloody, but unbow'd.
> Beyond this place of wrath and tears
> Looms but the Horror of the shade,
> And yet the menace of the years
> Finds and shall find me unafraid.
> It matters not how strait the gate,
> How charged with punishments the scroll,
> I am the master of my fate:
> I am the captain of my soul.

At the time, and despite experiences like the one on the Railway Express job, I fully believed in every word of every line. I still had a lot to learn about life and myself.

CHAPTER 7

Corrupt Black Preachers

WHEN I graduated from Englewood no one there even suggested that I might apply for a scholarship to a university on the basis of my strong high school record. No one counseled me or put me in touch with the right people to do this. It was just assumed that a black high school graduate would head for the job market or if he had money a small black college.

My dream was to go to Roosevelt University, but it cost money and I had none. Roosevelt had just opened, in 1945, on the principle of equal education for all people. While this slogan sounds like old hat today, in the city of Chicago in 1945 it was a revolutionary concept. But Roosevelt cost money. Wilson Junior College did not, so I enrolled there with the hope of being able to get a scholarship later.

At Wilson I entered the program in the humanities and took English, French, world history, and other subjects. The school was full of veterans; I always sought their company to discuss events and ideas. They were convinced I could not be serious about God. How could he exist? What type of God was he that would allow all the injustices in the world? World wars? Killings? Prejudices? Define him. Hell was here on earth, man, for black people.

By this time I began to have deep doubts about the existence of God. I had learned that matter cannot be created or destroyed. Therefore, how could God exist? I asked the ministers, the preachers. Youth wants to know the answers to these questions. The important thing about my questions was that a certain intellectual attitude had developed in me. I had to know for myself. I had to be convinced of the correctness of a position before I would accept it. I had to be committed fully to an idea and no one could explain to me the nature of God or what type of person or force he was.

This kind of debate stimulated me enormously and I had a great time during that first semester. I also worked out my long-range educational plans, which led me to a Ph.D. degree by the age of twenty-four.

During the summer of 1947, after that first semester at Wilson, I went to a youth meeting of African Methodist Episcopals from my district.

It took place at a white Methodist camp in Michigan which our church rented. When I left there I had lost still more of my belief in God—and I had completely gotten over the idea of becoming a minister.

I had been assigned to a cabin where most of the ministers were staying. There were no young people in this cabin. One night I woke up and heard some ministers discussing how they planned to curb some of the power of Reverend Roberts, to whom I felt a strong attachment. Roberts was becoming too powerful, they said, and before you knew it he would be talking about running for bishop. This was politics and I did not mind politics, but I didn't think that preachers, ministers, people who were talking about a new world, should be involved in this kind of backbiting and conniving. I began to ask myself if I really wanted to be involved with this type of men. The theory of working from within lay heavy on me at that time, but I now began to think that it was nonsensical for me to dream of reforming the church, of crusading within the church. It would be too difficult, I was sure. And, then, I had some serious doubts about God. These "apostles" of God helped to confirm my doubts.

Then there was the matter of the cook.

It was my job during the meeting to ring the bells for people to go to classes, to worship, to sleep, and so forth. The bell was in front of an administrative cabin. I had to ring a bell at 10:00 for people to go to their cabins and worship, then another bell fifteen minutes later for worship to begin, and a final bell at 10:30 for lights out. One night, during the interval between those first two bells, one of the three white cooks employed by the camp came to talk to me. She was a young redhead named Ethel. I rang the second bell, went to my cabin to worship, and returned. She waited and walked me to my cabin after I rang the final lights-out bell.

The next day, one of the officials of the camp—Reverend Roberts's secretary—told me that I should just ring the two bells for worship and then remain in my cabin. It would be much easier for her to ring the last bell since it was right by her cabin, than for me to return. I thought this was a sensible idea. The next night, I rang the bell at 10:00, talked with Ethel until 10:15, and then she walked me to my cabin.

On the following morning, Reverend Roberts's secretary told me that it would be best for me to ring the bell at 10:00 and then go directly to my cabin and not be late for worship. She would ring the 10:15 bell for worship to begin. Now all this began to sound a little queer to me. Each day the bell-ringing procedure changed.

That afternoon one of the preachers who had been talking about the coup against Roberts came up to me. We were standing in some tall grass and he asked, "How are you enjoying the camp?"

"There are some good things and I have learned some things that I'm thinking about," I said.

"Well, have you seen the picture *Duel in the Sun*?"

"No, I haven't. What makes you ask that?"

"Well, in this picture Lionel Barrymore has two sons on this ranch and there is an Indian girl there played by Jennifer Jones."

He paused, looking very sheepish and then continued, "Well, in the picture Joseph Cotten falls in love with this Indian girl and Lionel Barrymore says to him 'We don't want any half-breeds on this ranch.' "

I looked at him, a preacher, a politician, and I said, "Why are you telling me this?"

"Don't you know?"

"Know what?" I exploded. It was very obvious to me what he was talking about, but I wanted him to say it. I didn't think he had the nerve.

"Well, we don't want any redheaded Negro children coming from this camp."

"Thanks for your advice," I said and walked away. How could he consider himself a preacher, a minister of the gospel, and think that way? You can't even talk to a person and be friendly without someone, a preacher at that, thinking such thoughts and then telling you. I was disgusted. Then I began to wonder if he had some other reason for having changed the ringing of the bell.

It was not until the following week, when I returned to Chicago, that I confirmed my suspicion. I had a conversation with Reverend Roberts's secretary. In the middle of other matters, I suddenly asked, "Why did you keep changing the bells at the camp?"

"Why do you ask?"

She had outfoxed me with this question. Instead of demanding an answer, I told her what that preacher of the gospel had said to me about redheaded Negro children.

"Oh, don't worry about him. You're right, there was a great deal of talk about the possibility of your association with that girl hurting our chances of getting the camp again. To deal with the gossip, I just decided to ring the bells myself. As for that character . . . I wouldn't give it a second thought.

"Listen, he called my house this morning. My husband answered the phone and said Reverend —— wants to speak to you. I was very surprised to get a call from him. And do you know, he began telling me how he had fallen in love with me at the camp and he would leave his wife and four children if I would leave my husband and marry him! I was outraged," she continued. "I didn't know what to say. My husband was in the room so I had to make up something. I'm not sure what I told him, I think I said we could discuss that 'church matter' later. I had to get off the phone.

"The fool did not want to hang up. He kept telling me how much he loved me and he had to marry me. He wanted to leave everything, his family, his children, and all that he had done. He had to marry me! So it doesn't surprise me, what he said to you."

"But how could he do that? How could he, a minister, do that? How can he talk about God and ethics and do something like that?" I asked. I was convinced now that he had wanted to be near Ethel himself. I was convinced that reforming preachers was impossible. I suppose I was look-ing for some kind of consistency in ministers, a superiority to the rest of us.

Then I told her the story of the planned coup against Reverend Roberts and all my feelings about that. We talked for a long time about words and actions, consistency and honesty in your work, and how men should react to women.

God was not quite dead in me, but he was dying fast.

At the end of the summer, when I was eagerly expecting to return to Wilson Junior College for a second semester, an incident occurred which changed my big educational plans and had an undetermined effect on my life.

As in high school, I had been working off and on at my stepfather's gas station. It was a Saturday morning in mid-September and I had gone down there to work for the day, although I wanted to go to the opening football game of Englewood High School. My stepfather hadn't yet arrived and I opened up shop. The first customer was a man who wanted his battery charged. I checked the water, put some in, and then charged it while the customer went off on an errand.

He came back for his car and said it wouldn't start. My stepfather had arrived by then, and went to the car with the battery tester. He said the battery did not charge because there was no water in it .

"I put water in it," I told Pop. "There must be a leak."

Pop continued to insist that no water had been put in the battery. For what must have been the fifteenth time, he scolded, "You got to put water in the battery."

I exploded.

"I told you I put water in. If you say I didn't, you're a shittin' ass liar." Pop froze. "What did you say?"

"Nothing," I answered. I didn't want another hassle with him, we had had enough arguments over the years.

My stepfather called to my younger brother, Bernard, who was also there that day. "What did he say?"

"He said you're a liar," Bernard answered. I was mad at him for tell-ing on me, but glad he hadn't thrown in all the adjectives.

Then Pop said it, though not for the first time. "The house isn't big enough for both of us," he told me. "Get out."

I left and went to the football game. That night and the next I spent at the home of Mr. and Mrs. Rogers from my church. I decided to enlist in the Army. It would interrupt my education and it changed all my plans; but, I told myself, there would probably be a compulsory draft again anyway—and, in fact, it came two years later. Also, I thought the country would be at war again soon (which it was, in Korea). It might be better to get my service out of the way now, in peacetime, and have an uninterrupted education afterward.

There were other factors. I had no money to support myself while in school. The chances of my getting a decent job seemed like a hopelessly long shot. The Army was an assured means of living; I might even learn something from it. Anyway it would only be for two years. Also, I was now eighteen years old and I felt it was time to leave home. Time to get away from my stepfather.

Above all, I had little choice. In feeling that way, I was like a lot of young black brothers then, and still today—just looking for a home and holding little hope of alternatives. I accepted the idea that there might be a draft and I would be drafted. The thought of fighting the draft system did not enter my mind then. I accommodated to the seeming inevitability of the draft and also to the racism which made finding a good job impossible. For all my desire to go on in school right away and to change the society, there was a fatalistic streak in me—as in other young blacks—about our lives. I knew the Army would be segregated; still, I decided without great qualms to go into it, not to fight for so-called freedom and democracy, but to earn money, travel, and fulfill my military obligations to the United States.

That decision reflected the deadening effect that a pervasive system of racism and exploitation has on people. Growing up in a racist society, you become accustomed to a certain way of life. Although I had challenged many forms of racism, I was also inoculated against protest and resistance to a large extent. Perhaps I also had then, deep within me, a hope—a vague wish—that freedom and democracy for all would not always prove to be empty words.

Today I would never volunteer for a segregated army (or the U.S. Armed Forces in general), nor would I take a seat at the back of a bus or in the front of a train. Those battles have been won; the struggle, once so focused on segregation because it was the most blatant form of racism, passed through that stage and now stands on a higher level. And I myself changed.

But this was 1947 and I was eighteen. I had made up my mind to volunteer, and I went back to my parents' apartment just once—to tell my mother of my decision, and say good-bye.

CHAPTER 8

You're in the Army Now

THE ARMY corporal sat behind his desk.

"I want to volunteer for the Army," I said. "I've had two years of ROTC at Englewood High School. I received the Chicago *Tribune* Silver and Gold Medal for efficiency as a noncommissioned officer and I was a lieutenant upon graduation."

"What branch of the Army are you interested in?" the white recruiting officer asked.

"Since my training has been centered around the infantry, I guess I would like that branch," I replied with some mixed feelings.

"When do you want to go in?" he asked.

"Oh, right away. I'm ready to leave next week, tomorrow."

"Well . . . you know . . . there's a problem . . ."

"What do you mean?" I asked, interrupting his slow deliberation. What's going on, I wondered.

"Well, you know, the Army has a quota system."

Here it comes, I said to myself indignantly. *Here it comes!*

"I didn't know there was a quota system," I told him.

"Yes," he replied with more vigor. "There is a quota system in the Army. I personally don't agree with it. And I hate to tell you about it since you are enthusiastic about volunteering. I'm sure you'd make a good soldier with all that experience in ROTC, but . . . I'm afraid we can't accept you this month. Our quota for Negroes is filled. Now, if you want to wait until October, we can take you then. Our October quota for Negroes isn't anywhere near filled . . ."

Maybe I rubbed my eyes. Maybe I shuffled my feet. It's possible I ran my hands through my hair. I could have used some other nervous gesture, but, whatever it was, my plans were crumbling again—because of race. I couldn't even volunteer for the Army. Their quota for *us* was filled for the month of September. While the Army corporal was apologetic about it personally, the fact remained that you couldn't even volunteer for a segregated army because the quota for the segregated army was filled for us, for Negroes, for us, this month. Just wait a month.

"Well," I said, "there are lots of reasons I wouldn't want to wait a month. . . . I think if I have to wait a month, I probably won't go in. It took me a lot of thinking to decide to come here . . ."

That was the truth. It hadn't been easy for me to walk into the recruiting station located downtown on a day my classmates were in college, a place where I wanted to be and thought I should be to carry out my purpose in life. I needed to study my history, my English, my humanities, my French. But I was willing to postpone my education now so that it would not be postponed later, or so I had rationalized my decision at the moment. And now I was faced with a quota system.

"I'm sorry," the Army corporal said. "There's nothing I can do about it. The rules are the rules," he said, almost apologetically it seemed to me.

"But I know something about the Army," I replied. "It's really too bad."

"You know," he said, "you could try the Air Force. I don't think their quota is filled this month. But you have to volunteer for three years if you go into the Air Force. It's not like here, where you volunteer for two years."

"I don't think I could take three years," I told him. Inside I thought, I can see myself doing two, but three years . . . I don't think I can take that.

"It is a long time," he agreed, "but the Air Force does have many technical training schools that the Army doesn't have . . ."

Two years was one thing. Three years in the Armed Services was something else. I had to do some hard thinking about that.

I left the Army Induction Center and went back to the South Side. I talked with several people. "What's the Air Force like?" I asked my cousin, who had spent four years in it during World War II.

"It's not bad. You don't walk as much as you do in the Army. You're not in the direct line of battle. Your chances of staying alive during a war are a little better. You probably would be in the ground personnel. I doubt if they'd let a black man fly."

"I'm not interested in flying a plane, man. But, dig. Do you mean I would have a lot of time to read?"

"Oh, yeah, you can do a lot of reading. You don't really have that much work to do. I don't know how it is now, but when I was in there the guys had a lot of time for reading."

"What about these technical training schools?"

"You can go to these schools now. I never went, but the guys who were reenlisting told me about them."

We talked into the night about the Air Force and his experience. His saying that there was plenty of time to read convinced me, more than anything else, that perhaps I should go down the next morning to see about doing three years in the Air Force.

"Yes, you can join right away," the white sergeant told me.

"Do you have this quota system too?"

"We have it, but we have a larger quota for Negroes than the Army. And our quota isn't filled for this month."

With great reservations, I signed up. On the application, I put down my name as James Forman—the first time since birth that I was officially Forman and not Rufus.

I hadn't been in the Air Force a month before I realized what a disastrous mistake I had made. I could not adjust to the regimentation, the deadly daily routine. Those three years weighed on me like a prison sentence; it was worse than I had ever imagined, a contradiction of my whole existence. My salvation was reading and studying in the library, which brought a lot of anti-intellectualism down on me. That seemed bearable, however. I had a long time ago adopted the attitude that experiences were experiences and that it did not do very much good to bemoan the past. You had to make the best of most situations. But the Air Force also reeked with prejudice, as did all the Armed Forces.

"Airmen," the small white captain said to our flight, Flight 3001, the basic training flight I was assigned to at Lackland Air Force Base in San Antonio, Texas. "Airmen, I have some bad news for this flight. I regret to have to tell you this. It is not something I appreciate doing, but the scores on the Army General Classification Test for this flight were way above the normal standards of the Air Force. Too many of you scored too high for us to permit all of you to attend technical training schools."

What the hell is he talking about, I said to myself.

"Therefore, what we are going to do is arbitrarily raise the standards for people to attend technical training school. Anyone who has a score below 110 will not be allowed to attend a technical training school." To make that score on the Army General Classification Test meant you were in the higher echelon of so-called intellectual ability and could enter almost any technical school. In 1947 a score of only 85 qualified you for more than three-fourths of the schools.

I hit the floor. I was steaming.

"Sir," I boomed. I was known in my flight as the nigger who was always in trouble, but especially the one who was outraged by the segregation in and around Lackland. Most of my flight would go to town when weekend passes were issued, but I didn't want to have a damn thing to do with segregated San Antonio, riding on a segregated bus in an Air Force uniform. My cup was filled.

"Sir, are you saying to us that because everybody in our flight is Negro and that because we as Negroes have scored very high on the Army General Classification Test, there are too many of us who are Negroes in this flight to go to technical training school?"

"That's right, Airman Forman. That is what I am saying."

"Are you saying, sir," I went on, with the most disrespectful slur I could muster, "that you are taking it upon yourself to arbitrarily raise the scores so that you can cut down on the number of Negroes in this flight who can go to technical training school?"

"I'm saying that," he replied.

"Then tell me, sir, how does the Air Force justify all its promises to those of us who enlisted so that we can go to technical training school if we qualify?"

"But you qualify, Airman Forman."

"I'm not talking about myself, sir. I'm talking about the principle. The Air Force makes a great deal of the fact it has all these technical training schools and that it sends people to further educate themselves and that is why the enlistment period is for three years. Now you're telling us that we're too smart in this flight. We have too many people, almost the entire flight, who qualify for technical training schools and now we can't go. I want to know, what is the justification?" I knew what the score was, I had known almost all my life, but acceptance of the score was always something else. Sometimes we reject it outright, sometimes we accept, and quite often we avoid the issue. The choices are always there and we are not consistent at all times in the choices we make. This time I had to reject.

"If it does any good," the captain began, "let me say that I don't agree with what is happening but there is nothing I can do about it. The rules are the rules."

"The rules," I said quietly. "We don't like the rules and we want to know what we can do about it. What is our right to appeal the rules?"

"There isn't any," he said quickly.

"Sir, do you mean to say that you can come into this room and tell us that you are arbitrarily raising the score for entering technical training schools, no matter what is written in the manual, and tell us there is no appeal?" I knew that I was way out there for the Armed Forces. Here I was grilling the captain and, Jack, you just don't do that. But I was out there and I wasn't turning back.

"I mean there is no appeal, gentlemen. That is the decision and that's the way it will have to be. Now . . . the air provost marshal is in charge of the entire base and all the officers at Lackland are under his command. You can talk to him if you like. If there are no more questions, you're dismissed."

We all left the room furious. The men were cursing. "The fucking Air Force . . ." "These goddamn crackers are all the same!" "Man, if I ever catch one of these bastards in combat, I'm going to shoot him in the back!"

"Let's organize. We can't allow this to happen. We got to fight back."

"Let's organize. Let's get together. Let's get a delegation. Let's go to the air provost marshal. Let's draw up demands. Let's tell him man. We got to strike back. We can't take this."

"Yeah, it's our responsibility, those of us who have a chance to go. We got to lead the fight, man. We can't take this. What about all the other Negroes who are going to come into this Air Force, believing the crap some of us believed? Let's go man, let's go!" The seven of us who had made 110 or more went as a delegation to the air provost marshal.

The same old shit. Sorry, the rules. One day they will change. Sorry, there's nothing I can do. We have a quota for Negroes. If you want to, you can appeal to Washington. . . . That seemed like the moon.

Our protest withered away after we left the office of the air provost marshal. He was not there, but the deputy was. He would call the matter to the attention of the provost marshal. Fuck it, man. We're here in this shit and that's that.

And then, when the seven qualified niggers went to the Technical Training Barracks to apply for Technical School, they were told that there were only five schools open to qualified niggers: cooks and bakers, mechanics, clerk-typist, surveyors, welding. You had to be a nigger who qualified for Officer Training School in order to apply for schools that would train you as cooks and bakers, welders, mechanics, clerk-typists, and surveyors.

Now the surveyors' school had a trick to it. If you went there and completed the course, you were assigned to an Engineering Aviation Battalion. This meant a crew that cut hills and made airstrips. Two of the brothers who finished this school had ended up holding strings on hot hills all day. It was clear to me then that nowhere in this country could you believe the words that white people used. You could say "liberty, justice, and equality for all" only as a tool to be used against the man. Garrison was right; the United States Constitution was a contract with the devil. And Du Bois was more than right. We needed to get ourselves together, baby, but fast.

I felt, we felt, double-crossed by the Armed Forces. It was a special kind of anger, caused this time by outrageous hypocrisy and the feeling of having been taken. I had accepted the contradictions of entering a segregated Army Air Force on September 24, 1947, the way I "accepted" other types of segregation—in the sense of deciding not to fight them each time they came up. This "acceptance" was, I think, an answer to the question, how does a person survive psychologically in a society of all-pervasive racism? To fight it every time, all of the time, is to commit a kind of suicide. Even people who are challenging racism as a full-time job find that there are certain things to which they accommodate because those experiences do not raise major issues. Such phenomena vary, according to the consciousness of a person and the stage of the struggle.

But while I worked to find my definitions of the larger struggle, and how to wage it, life in the Air Force continued to press down with its daily insults—above all, its hypocrisy and double-dealing. I began to see the Armed Forces in broader terms, too, as a dehumanizing machine which destroys thought and creativity in order to preserve the economic system and the political myths of the United States. I decided that we should not commit suicide on a mass basis; we should save most of our energy for an organized struggle.

One day in January most of Flight 3001 was shipped out to Fairfield Air Force Base in California. I was wildly happy to leave Lackland Air Force Base and San Antonio, Texas, a city of which I saw only some parts for three hours while waiting for the train to go to California. I took a sight-seeing tour on a nonsegregated bus and that was that. I remember only seeing the Alamo.

At six o'clock in the evening, I got on the train heading west with my Pullman ticket in my hand, looking forward to a night's rest. I was alone; the majority of the brothers from my flight had gone north on furlough. I was waiting for summer to take my leave.

The train rolled. A conductor sent me up front with the rest of the brothers and sisters, saying that he would take care of my accommodations later. Later he said he was still searching for my Pullman accommodations. I had only a ticket and no reservation, he told me.

The train headed west with a vengeance and then another conductor came on and said he didn't know anything about the Pullman accommodations for me. Why hadn't I made a reservation back in San Antonio? We fussed and fussed and I started back toward the Pullman section. I almost had a fight with two MPs who told me to follow the instructions of the conductor.

The train roared ahead into the night. I clutched and waved my Pullman ticket and argued with the conductors and looked at the Air Force uniform I had on and wanted to tear it up. I would rather be' naked. I thought how glad I would be when I got to California and would be out of basic training, so that I wouldn't have to wear this uniform all the time. I was disgraced, humiliated, insulted, outraged; a black man in a military uniform, a volunteer in the Air Force of three months' standing, and these cracker conductors wouldn't even give me the Pullman for which the Air Force had paid. Hell, I knew their game. We were still in Texas and they didn't want to put me, a black man, in the Pullman coach which contained mostly whites and civilians at that.

By now I had convinced myself I didn't want the Pullman anyway, but damn it, there was a principle involved. These conductors were little dictators, shuffling us here and there. I was no longer prepared to take the first coach. I wanted my Pullman. I swore up and down the aisle that I would sue the railroad to high heaven. I wanted retribution for standing half the night talking to the brothers and arguing with anything that looked white about my right to have that Pullman. The more I fussed, the filthier I looked to myself in this monkey suit: a prisoner in a GI uniform. The more I looked at the filthy monkey suit, the angrier I became at myself for being duped into volunteering for this shit. The more I thought about this shit, the sicker I became, because I still had two years and eight months and fifteen days to go.

When I got to Los Angeles I went straight to a lawyer, a civil rights lawyer, and told him I wanted to sue the railroad. I had been injured; he agreed with me, but then said that since the Army had issued the ticket, the Army might be the party I should sue. And they could just say I had failed to make a reservation and give me the difference between the coach fare and the Pullman fare. If I were a civilian, he would love to take the suit because he knew he could get some money out of the railroad.

But "you're in the Army now and you'll never get rich, you sonofabitch, you're in the Army now." And you ain't got no rights as a man in this country and you might as well learn how to live with this mother fucker for the next two years eight months and seven days or else you will be stone crazy. The Army is segregated and there is no use complaining because the whole society you live in is segregated and the Army just reflects that and it don't make no difference about Truman studying how to end segregation in the Army, you're in the Army now and it is too late and so what if Truman does split the Democratic Party and if I were out there I would work for Wallace and the Progressive Party but you're in the Army now and if you think segregation is bad in the Air Force, boy you better be glad you didn't join the infantry.

CHAPTER 9

Okinawa—A Bad Dream

MY ORIGINAL plan had been to save enough in the Air Force so that I could go to school after my discharge. But during those early months, I gambled away my twenty or thirty dollars a month. Most of the soldiers did; life was boring and gambling was one way of passing the time. Since we were always fed, clothed, and lodged by the Army, the loss of a monthly expense allowance did not mean much. For me, it was too little to cover the cost of school even if I saved every cent that I could all three years.

A tremendous amount of money exchanged hands in those poker and crap games. I would look at the winners and wonder what they were going to do with it all. Slowly a new plan began to form in my head.

I decided to begin gambling in a serious way, and use my winnings to finance a higher education. I saw no other way to do it at that time. In November, before leaving for overseas, I went to Chicago on furlough and began asking some of the people I had known when I was growing up there how to become a professional, a scientific gambler. There had to be some techniques to reduce the element of luck and guarantee more winnings. I went to the pool hall where I used to hang out and talked to the owners of several taverns. I talked to my barber who ran a gambling hall in the back of his shop. They gave me tips, and that same month I launched my career as what you might call a professional gambler.

I was timid at first. But while I traveled overseas—to Okinawa—and in the months I spent there, I became more deft in the use of cards, more skilled in the handling of the dice. Soon I always found myself winning. But I was tortured with questions of right and wrong, good and evil. I rationalized my "professional" gambling with a half-baked superman theory based on Nietzsche's writings and on Dostoyevsky's *Crime and Punishment*: My possession of a higher purpose justified my taking money from those who had no special goal in life or use for their money. Unlike most people, I did not have to bow to convention. It was a stupid and dangerous line that I gave myself.

At the same time I rebelled against the conditions that led me into gambling "professionally." I thought of how many young black minds go undeveloped, like precious jewels lying beneath the surface of the earth, because funds are unavailable to meet the competitive cost of education in this country. There had to be some kind of society that would not force people into using any means necessary to acquire money for an education. The society I wanted to create would guarantee from birth the best possible free education to its citizens.

Gambling took up most of my spare time on Okinawa, better known as the Rock, and a desolate-looking place, especially around the 822d Engineering Aviation Battalion. Most of the black airmen served as the road builders, the base builders, the airstrip builders, the truck drivers of the Rock; I was assigned to Headquarter's Squadron of the motor fleet as a personnel classification specialist. There wasn't much to do. You worked eight hours a day and then you had free time. I spent a lot of time observing the Okinawan people and began to realize I had become an occupier. Here lived a brown people, and the white soldiers called them gooks just like they called me nigger. The Okinawans had to take it because the Americans had the guns, just as we had to take it during slavery time. They had captured Okinawa; they had captured us, too. But now I was with them. I was an occupier too.

The saddest thing was that some of the brothers also called the Okinawans gooks. They adopted the superior attitude of the American white man and they, too, thought they were better than the Okinawans. They, too, did some of the things the whites did, especially to the women of Okinawa. Not so much, but enough to open my eyes. Before, I had not seen women as an oppressed group. The girls I knew were students; we had intellectual discussions and they seemed "equal" enough. Okinawa changed my image.

The brothers would come back to the base at night, gloating over their sexual experiences with a local prostitute and speaking of the Okinawan women as if they were things instead of human beings. There came a night when several men in my barracks went out and brought back an elderly woman from a nearby village. They pulled a train on her, passing her from one bunk to another. I saw them and choked on the history of our own black women being raped by white slave owners, of our whole people being taken by force. And I couldn't stop my brothers. What they did was part of being occupiers. But still I choked as I heard her passed from bed to bed and I thought: Brothers, how could you; you who have been exploited and beaten through the ages. How could you put that gun to that woman's head and then rape her like the white soldiers were doing all over the island of Okinawa? When you heard about what the white soldiers were doing, how could you not think of slavery and what the man did to our women? How do you think we got to be all these colors? How could you adopt the white man's ways? How could you go out to kill brown men by day and rape brown women at night? And not dare to kill our real enemies, not dare to love women as women? How could you?

While I was on Okinawa, I often thought a great deal about Mary who later became my first wife. Two weeks before I was to leave for overseas in 1948 I had met Mary through some friends of mine who lived in Vallejo, California. The moment we met, and in the dates we had afterward during those two weeks, I wished that I had met her before I signed up for overseas. I wanted to be with her, to talk to her, to love her. She had been working as a waitress in a club downtown and many of the soldiers at Fairfield had come back to the base talking about how they had tried to hit on her with no success. She was lovely, independent, hard to get, and had no man, they said. What they did not understand was that she was a serious person fighting and working very hard to raise two children. Her husband, the father of her children, had left them one day while he was a soldier in California and she had not seen or heard from him in three years. She was from Birmingham, Alabama, and she had suffered as a black person growing up in the United States. She was active in civic work during her free time and worked hard for the NAACP in the Bay area.

As I had sailed on the U.S.S. *Buckner* for Japan and then Okinawa, I had thought of her often. I wanted very much to see her when I returned;

she was a breath of fresh air that had come into my dull existence as a soldier. I wanted to treat her with all possible care and tenderness.

While on Okinawa I thought of writing her many times, but didn't. Later, when I returned to the States, I would call her. She was lonely; I was lonely. We had been attracted to each other and there was something strong between us. We began to live together as man and wife. I loved her children and often, thinking about how I had been raised, I began to do little things for them, things that I had missed. When I was a child, I had wanted to learn to play the violin. I had seen a man in our church playing one and I was impressed. My parents said we were too poor to buy one and pay for music lessons. I bought Mary's children a piano with some of the money I won gambling so that they could learn music if they wanted to. If they didn't, it would not be because they lacked the opportunity. I also took them to dancing school. As a child in Mississippi, I had often danced to the old piano we had in my grandmother's room. Somehow, when I came to Chicago, I never developed my dancing—probably because my people were churchgoers and viewed dancing not as an evil, perhaps, but not something that should be learned. All the religious indoctrination I got at the Catholic school did not help, either. Mary's children enjoyed the dancing school.

My wife did not have a legal divorce from her first husband when we started living with each other. After it came through, she wanted to marry me officially. I was opposed to this for many reasons. I didn't believe in putting love on paper, because then it falls into that whole world of property relationships and legal contracts which dominates this society. I felt that if we ever stopped loving each other, we could part our ways without the cumbersome problems of getting a divorce from the state. Also, I did not want to be neatly tied up in a marriage package when my life was so unstable. But I agreed to the formal marriage, partly because she had been hurt and I didn't want to hurt her more, and partly because I was sure that if it didn't work out, I would have no hesitation about canceling the formal contract. We both understood that marriages often do not work and that it is best for people to separate if this occurs, no matter how painful.

"Forman, you've been selected to go down to the 625th Aircraft and Warning Company, which is an all-white unit. You are a personnel classification specialist and they need one. You will be the first Negro in that outfit," said the first sergeant of the 822d Engineering Aviation Battalion.

"But, sir, does it have to be me? I don't want to go down there with those crackers. Sir, you understand, we got a hip thing going here. We have a championship football team in the making. We can win the title Battalion. I'm just not up to going down there."

"Orders are orders, my man. I hate to see you go. I know we can win but orders are orders."

"Look, Sarge, you know those crackers are going to start some shit and I'm telling you that if they do I'm coming right back up here and you all can just put me in the stockade for disobeying orders. Now, I ain't kidding Sarge. If those Mother Hubbards start anything, I'm leaving. I don't want to go up for murder. I really don't."

"Take it easy, my man," the first sergeant said, trying to calm me down. He knew I was upset. "You'll do all right down there. They're breaking up this battalion anyway. The football team is going to be shot because they are sending guys all over the island. Just go ahead and keep cool and remember you always have friends up here if you need us. Come back and see us. Get your stuff ready. You have to report for duty tomorrow morning."

That was it. I was the guinea pig. The order had come down; the segregation of military units was scheduled to end in the Armed Forces, and the Air Force was moving to comply. They wanted to see what would happen if I went down there. Old Sarge didn't tell me that, but I knew it. Besides, they wanted to kill our football team. Or if they didn't want to, they were doing it anyway. Damn, going down there fucking with them crackers. Integrate, my ass!

I delayed and delayed going. After packing my belongings, I went out to the football field and talked to Lieutenant Driver, a pilot who got his training at Tuskegee. He had heard the news. He was disappointed to see the one good team he had fielded disintegrate under integration, but orders were orders and things would work out.

I walked around the grounds of the 822d Engineering Aviation Battalion. I didn't like the Quonset huts, but that's what most of us lived in on the Rock. I didn't like the food they served in the morning and I had stopped eating breakfast. It took me a long time to adjust to the Rock, but I had done so in certain respects.

I had lunch with the fellows. They told me what to expect. There would be fights and I would be hit by trays at meals. The crackers were going to really work me over in that all-white outfit. I was going down to the other end of the Rock and coming back in a casket. Going to ship your body home. Killed in action trying to integrate some crackers from Mississippi.

I had planned to transfer that afternoon and get down there in time for dinner, but after all that talk I decided to move in under the cover of darkness, after ten o'clock. If they had planned a reception for me, they would hardly try it late at night. No telling what I might be packing at that hour.

I arrived, way down at the other end of the island, about eleven o'clock. It was dark and the sergeant on duty was helpful. He showed me an empty Quonset hut and said it was mine. There were seven other individual beds in it. It was a small hut, all the Quonsets down there were small and sort of individualized, instead of the dormitory-style ones we had in the 822d.

"Dig, are you saying I will sleep in this hut all by myself tonight?" I asked the sergeant.

"Sure. There are some more people coming in tomorrow, but tonight it's yours."

He's jiving me, I said to myself. He's trying to set me up for the kill tonight. Going to put me in here alone so that I can be picked off easily.

"Dig, are there guards around here?"

"I'm on duty all night tonight. But we don't have any trouble here. Our people work three different shifts. That's why the Quonset huts are small, so that you won't wake up anyone when you get ready to go to work. Your team sleeps together. I understand they're going to make some changes for the office staff."

"I see . . . O.K. If I have any questions, I can come over to the office, right?"

"Right. Just come on over and have a cup of coffee after you get straight."

"Roger."

I made my bed. I kept the lights on. I locked the doors from the inside. I got my shit ready. I got in bed, lights on, clothes on, ready for action. Not a sound, just a voice here or there. Midnight. All's quiet. One o'clock. No action. Two o'clock. I cut out the lights. Three o'clock. It's safe to go to sleep.

It was safe! But I got up early, still full of anxiety. I took my toilet kit and walked out of my Quonset hut into the morning air. It was chilly, the wind was blowing. The island had not warmed up yet. In the Quonset hut serving as washroom I saw two whites. Easy now, I said to myself. They did not speak to me; I did not speak to them. I finished washing my face and teeth and left. They were still taking birdbaths.

I went back to my hut and put down my toilet kit. I walked outside, strolled nervously around the grounds. There were still fifteen minutes before breakfast. I walked beyond the mess hall and looked out into the Pacific, saw some of the Naha Caves, the caves where the Japanese built extensive fortifications to defend the island against the American invasion. To my left I could see parts of the Naha Air Force Base, with its landing strips for the big bombers and fighter planes designed to protect this island and the Far East.

I saw several Okinawan men and women headed for work. They were old, quiet, their backs stooped; they reminded me of slaves going to the master's big house.

I headed for the mess hall. This was the big test. Last night I had prepared for trouble and nothing had happened. Today I really did not want to eat breakfast, but the confrontation had to come sooner or later. I had to face these crackers. I had no idea what they would be like. I did not believe segregation in the Army was correct, but I also knew that I didn't want to be the one to end it in this outfit.

Finally I opened the screen door; here goes. The mess hall was crowded. Men sat to the right. The chow line was directly in front of me; beyond it were Okinawan cooks and two white cooks supervising them. They were walking up and down the line, looking, doing odd jobs.

Fresh eggs. I saw them crack fresh eggs. I did not believe what I saw: fresh eggs. I had been on the Rock some six months and I had never tasted a fresh egg unless I bought it at the restaurant in town. They were cooking fresh eggs, some upside down, some scrambled, any way you wanted them. I saw it, but I didn't understand.

"How do you want yours?" the white cook asked me. I knew it had to be a trick. They wanted to integrate so badly that they were willing to put on a special show for me. They didn't want me to think they were prejudiced. I had heard they were going to make the transition as easy as possible, but damn, did they have to go this far?

"I'd like mine sunny-side up," I replied.

"How many?"

"How many?" I asked in amazement. This was the royal treatment. "Do you mean I can have more than two?" I managed to ask.

"You can have four if you want them. And after you eat them, you can come back and get some more," one of the white cooks said.

That did it. I knew it was a sham. If it had not been for the fact that I could see the eggs when he opened them and put them on the grill, I probably would not have eaten them. It was too much.

"I'll just take two," I finally said. I didn't want them to think *we* were greedy.

"You can have some more if you want them."

"Two's enough," I said. I really couldn't understand this cordiality. It had to be a trick. No one could have made me think otherwise. The fear, the suspicion, the hatred, the ambivalence produced by growing up in a segregated society made me certain that this cook was playing a trick.

Then I got to the end of the line. I saw cartons of fresh milk stacked on top of each other! I hadn't seen fresh milk anywhere except in the restaurants and then only at times. In the 822d Battalion we had had powdered milk—and only occasionally. Here they were serving fresh milk. In the 822d Battalion, an Okinawan poured out the powdered milk because we were not trusted to take just one dipper or two dippers of milk. Here there was no attendant.

"I left my canteen in the barracks," I told one of the white cooks behind the line. "Do you have a cup here so that I can get some milk?"

"Take the whole quart if you want to. You don't need a canteen cup."

I took my quart, not the top container, but a quart underneath. You never know when a trick is being played and I still believed that they had prepared a special feast for me. Then I began to wonder. I looked over at the tables and saw quarts of milk where the other airmen were eating. Suddenly I knew *we* had been tricked and the damn segregated Air Force touched a man not only in his head and his dignity, but even in his stomach. We in the 822d who were black and who did heavy work building airfields and tearing down hills, had to eat powdered eggs and milk in limited quantities while these guys down here were having fresh eggs and milk—all they wanted.

At the table I asked the fellows about the way in which they ate. Some who had been on the Rock for more than six months could not remember a day when they did not have fresh milk. Some days they would not have eggs because there was something else for breakfast, but there were always fresh eggs when there were eggs. No powdered eggs.

I slowly adjusted to my eggs in the morning and my quart of milk a day, fresh milk and eggs. And I cursed the Air Force for its segregation, but I ate my fresh milk and eggs.

There are times in the lives of people that do not seem to have any relationship to anything. They seem meaningless in the context of a person's life, full of disjointed events and actions, without focus. The Air Force was one of those periods for me. My entire service experience was just a long waiting for a bad dream to end. I had made a terrible mistake in enlisting and nothing could change that fact. Okinawa was a place to mark time until the bad dream ended. All my activities there were just attempts to make the dream as plausible as possible.

Football became one of these attempts. Many people were hoping to get positions on the Naha Air Force Base team the day I tried out for center. I was not very big but I was scrappy. A lot of the brothers from good, all-black teams from different parts of the island had been transferred to this integrated base. My buddie, Charles Tribble, from Philadelphia, Pennsylvania, turned up there and we talked about how they had destroyed some good teams. Tribble and I had been friends in California and we shipped overseas together but were assigned to different outfits on the Rock.

"Man, do you think they took some of us from those outfits just so they can get together a championship team down here?" he asked. Tribble was one of the fastest left halfbacks on the island.

"Could be, man," I replied. "Do you think we're going to have any trouble from these crackers?"

"I don't know. I know if one of them fucks with me, he's going to be sorry." I shared Tribble's thoughts.

On the third day of tryouts I was asked to take the center position on the first team. I had learned the basic plays of the T formation we were using. Opposite me was a guard, much older than myself, a lieutenant, although rank was not supposed to matter on the field. I observed his habits, which included a slight delaying motion and then charging at the center. The left guard and I set up a high-low situation on him. The next play I hit low and the guard hit him hard from high. He was really hit clean and pretty. Tribble went through. This was football.

But the lieutenant couldn't take it. On the next play he hesitated and I lost control momentarily, only to feel the full impact of his fingers gouging into my eyes. It hurt and he knew it. I was half-blinded in the left eye for a couple of plays. I said zero to no one and waited for the moment. I had put my elbow into play to ward off any more sudden attacks like that one and to counterattack.

He paused again and then came forward. I lunged hard with my left elbow, striking across the upper part of his nose and into his right eye. I put all of my 175 pounds into that blow to teach the white lieutenant a lesson. His screams could be heard way down the field and the coach came running. "This boy elbowed me! He elbowed me," the lieutenant hollered.

"What do you think you're doing? You're not in a jungle," the coach yelled at me.

"That's what you think. Tell him to stop jugging his fingers in my eyes and I won't have to protect myself." All the brothers came up, for they knew what was happening.

The coach ordered me to the bench, where I sat for the rest of the day. This was not just another incident in a football practice. This was a racial matter to me, to Tribble, and to all the other black brothers on the field. It was an incident that we had all anticipated and it had to be settled with black men letting the whites know we weren't going to take any shit. We were going to play football on this team because we liked football, but we weren't going to take any nonsense.

Throughout the season we played well together, the whites and the blacks, but there was a restrained friendliness on the field. The drive and enthusiasm I felt on my team with the 822d Battalion wasn't there. The camaraderie was missing.

We won the Air Force championship on Okinawa and headed for the Philippines to play Clark Air Force Base. After winning the game at Clark Field, we were flown to Manila for a week of rest before going to Guam for the New Year's Eve Sweat Bowl. I had the name of a black man, Duke, who ran a bar in Manila and the team headed there. The place was full of beautiful Filipino girls serving as barmaids.

I struck up an acquaintance with a young woman nicknamed Colita. She was short, thin, with an engaging smile. We spent a lot of time together every day that I was in Manila. Colita told me stories of how, during the war, the white soldiers had told Filipino women that black men had tails like monkeys. She also told me of an incident that further deepened my hostility toward the Catholic church. During the war she had been living with a black soldier from Chicago. She had a baby by him; after he returned to Chicago, he sent for her and the baby. They were to be married in Chicago. She went to the emigration officials, who ran a check on her to see if she should leave. Her Catholic priest vetoed her going to Chicago to marry the soldier because he was not a Catholic and was not willing to become a Catholic.

But most of all Manila was a liberation of my spirit as a black man.

At the time, I was not very aware of the exploitation of the Philippines by the United States. My friends and I saw mainly a country run by brown-skinned people, a country where we did not experience segregation in public places, a country where it seemed that we were men and not second-class citizens fighting in a recently desegregated Army. We were men who walked the streets and went where we wanted to go. I felt the weight of all the years, the weight of all the forms of racism, begin to lift from my body and disappear into the air. They were gone for the moment and my body felt light. In those seven days, I began to feel what the oppressive load of racism had done to me and other blacks. Here was a culture that had its problems, but racial discrimination did not seem to be one of them.

Later in life, when I read a statement by Richard Wright that there was more freedom in one square mile of Paris than in all the United States, I assumed he was describing his great feeling of relief at the absence of discrimination. Manila was like that for me. It was like a beautiful, intense orgasm. Since the time of Wright's statement, I have been to Paris several times and realized that his statement must be read in a certain context. He said those words soon after leaving behind his experiences of racism in the United States; life in Paris, by contrast, must have seemed a paradise. The racist reality of France as a white colonial nation had not yet touched him.

Still, it is possible for black people to feel complete and totally free as I did for those few days in Manila—and to long for that feeling. Struggle is the essence of life for us, yet the form of struggle makes a difference in the psychology of the individual. I have often wished that our struggle could somehow be less agonized, less emotionally complex for the individual participant, with more promise of clear victory than we have seen after four hundred years of sacrifice and death.

But at that time, on the plane leaving Manila, I could only feel inspired by that taste of wholeness—and eagerly impatient to work toward achieving it in some form.

My last days on Okinawa before returning to the States were painful in one way.

During my time there, the Army had issued some silly regulations to prevent "fraternization" with the Okinawans. One of them stipulated that it was off limits to step more than ten feet from the highway. You could get court-martialed for doing so. Later this was relaxed; soldiers could enter the villages and sit in peoples' houses if they left their shoes outside the door for the MPs to see.

But by that time, I had already taken more than eleven steps off the highway and had become involved with an Okinawan woman, Toshiko, who, by white Western standards, would be called a prostitute. To me she was a woman of dignity, trying to support a family, caught in the trap of occupation and exploitation. I spent much time with her and her relatives, especially her four-year-old daughter. She did not treat me as a trick and I did not treat her as an object existing only for my sexual gratification. We were lovers. Communication was difficult, but Toshiko knew enough English and I knew enough Japanese for the rudiments of conversation.

One day, as we sat in her house, she told me that I would be leaving the island very soon. She told me this before I had had the strength to tell her it was time for me to return to the States. I wondered how she knew. Had she deduced it from the length of time I had spent on Okinawa and what she knew to be the usual length of duty, or had she guessed it from my behavior? Probably both.

Our parting was sad. I was irritable; irritable because I was leaving, irritable because I was a soldier and I hated the way soldiers usually treated women, irritable because I was a part of the United States Army which was occupying Okinawa and degrading the people. Toshiko understood some of this. She cried a lot during our last days together and I tried to comfort her. We knew that each of us was caught in a vicious racist net, trapped by the colonizing nature of the United States Army.

Intense experiences leave their mark in one manner or another. It took me a long time to push memories of Toshiko away from my conscious mind and into the unconscious. She had been the best part of Okinawa for me, a sister who made the long, bad dream bearable.

CHAPTER **10**

Feeling Like a New Car

"I AM the master of my fate. I am the captain of my soul." These words, which I had uttered with so much belief on the night of my graduation from high school, rang in my ears mockingly as I lay in the hospital at Hamilton Air Force Base in California, flat on my stomach.

Three or four weeks before my discharge date, September 23, 1951, I had begun to suffer acute pains at the base of my spine. When I went to the hospital the doctor told me that I had to have an operation to remove a pilonidal cyst and that it would take a long time to heal. There was no way of postponing it until after my discharge unless I wanted to suffer miserably. Since I found it very painful to sit and could hardly move around, I had the operation.

Everything seemed to have gone wrong and I was beginning to feel jinxed. When I had returned to the United States from Okinawa in March, 1950, I was stationed at Hamilton Air Force Base and looking forward to the end of my three-year enlistment period that year. But in August my enlistment period and all others were automatically extended by the government. The United States was at war with Korea.

That extension had floored me psychologically: Another whole year in the Air Force was too much. And how could I be sure of being discharged in 1951? If the government had the power to extend my time for one year, it could do it for ten years. I wanted to leave the Air Force, which I still called the Army—it was all the same to me, the Air Force, the Army, the Army Air Force. It was the Army and I was trapped in it, wasting my time, dulling my mind, supposedly protecting a system of government which I had grown to hate. At least I had escaped being sent to Korea. On Okinawa I had requested a three months' extension so that I could take a trip to Bangkok; the squadron commander turned down my request. Had he permitted it, I would have been frozen on Okinawa. My old outfit, the Aircraft and Warning Squadron, was one of the first to be shipped to Korea to fight for the safety of white America. Now, after that extra year of duty, here I lay in the hospital.

The day before my discharge date, the doctor told me that I could leave the hospital and gave me instructions on how to heal my wound. At that time I did not question his decision. I wanted to leave the Air Force, bloody ass and all. But my wound did not heal. There were days when I couldn't move, although I followed his orders all the way. Eventually, in the summer of 1952, I had another operation which cured the condition, but I spent a miserable year trying to heal the old wound.

In the meantime I was discharged and unsure of what to do. I had been drained by the unwelcome extension, but now I felt milked dry. It was too late for me to enter school in the fall of 1951. I had not applied anywhere; I was too sick to try. I was at sea, all the steam had gone out of me. Then, at the end of 1951, my wife Mary and I agreed to separate; later we were divorced. When we broke up, I moved to Oakland and went back to the streets—broke.

All the money I had saved was gone, as the result of a bad habit I had acquired. Mary had a sport of going to the racetrack every now and then. She seldom bet over two dollars in four or five races, but she loved it. When she took me with her one day, I caught the racehorse bug and found myself losing my hard-earned gambler's money. Although I tried to study the horses by reading many books, I was never able to develop enough sophistication to be a consistent winner. In fact, I became a consistent loser. To my sorrow I found that horses were less predictable than cards and dice.

So I hustled on Oakland's Seventh Street—whenever and whatever, except pimping. I had too much respect for women to try that. Pool halls, card games, crap games—anyplace there was money. I made a little money, but not much because here on Seventh Street everybody had his system and his tricks. I was just one pro among many and the houseman usually got us all. I knew I was wasting my time, as I had known it about the gang activity in Chicago. But I had lost my momentum, and in a way I was content just to hang out in that period. Also, without intending it, I was renewing and sustaining a contact with the street brothers and the field niggers that would be useful later. Seventh Street was a heartland of the urban black experience.

September, 1952, came and I dropped my plan of five years earlier to go to Roosevelt, despite the fact that I could afford it now with my payments from the Veterans Administration, for the cyst problem caused by incorrect treatment. Instead I enrolled at the University of Southern California; it was supposed to be a good school and I had come to like California. The veteran's counselor there told me that there was only one career for which they would rehabilitate me, given my background, and for which I would qualify: something called personnel management number two (I don't know what the number two meant, but I had been a personnel classification specialist in the Air Force so I suppose it made some kind of sense). I therefore enrolled in the field of public administration; fortunately there was a lot of latitude in the choice of courses within that framework.

I dug the course of study and enjoyed being on the debate team, traveling around to different schools and speaking. It was good to be back in school, but I felt very isolated. The university had few black people on campus and it seemed too status-conscious to me. I pushed hard anyway, trying to make up for so much lost time. My grades were very good that first semester.

Then I went to the library that night at the beginning of the second semester. And the Los Angeles cops acted out their racist nature on one more black man. They beat, tortured, persecuted me until my nerves snapped and those bright white lights seared my mind asunder.

My mother came to California after my breakdown and, with a power of attorney that I had given her, acted in my behalf. I will always remember the Los Angeles police, a bunch of filthy white pigs who put me in jail and beat the shit out of me. The Los Angeles police stand indicted in my case. They are guilty of cruel and inhuman treatment, physical and mental torture. I wanted to sue them after I got out of the hospital and talked to several lawyers, but they advised me that it would be difficult to prove anything against the police. I dropped the idea, but did not forget them. If I had my way, I have thought many times in the years since then, I would line these criminals against the wall and coolly, coldly, with calculated aim, shoot all of them through the icy blue of their murderous eyes. If I had my way, I would not order this done, but would personally put my finger on the trigger and with all the love for humanity that surges within me end the lives of those inhuman beings who make monstrous fun and games with the lives of young black people.

If I survived them, and my breakdown, it must have been because of the love I had known while growing up—and again in that period. Although we were separated, my wife Mary acted with great concern and affection. The state hospital in which I had been placed was as bad or maybe worse than most state hospitals. She worked day after day, bringing pressure to bear through friends and veterans' organizations, to get me transferred to a better place, the Veterans' Neuropsychiatric Hospital in Los Angeles. I am not sure to this day of all she did, or how she did it, but it was an act of love I could never forget. Again and again she drove from Vallejo to Los Angeles to visit me and she was there when they discharged me. I went home with her and thought that perhaps I had been too difficult when we were together before. We would make another try. But it didn't work out. I was too restless and did not want the responsibilities of a marriage. In March of 1954 I returned to Chicago. Our relationship was finished.

Back home, I fought hard against feeling shame about my time in the hospital. In this country there are stereotypes about people who have been in mental institutions; they are often looked upon as crazy, nuts, or even worse, no matter what the cause. Quite often the stigma attached to mental disorders prevents people from going to get treatment. Usually the hospitals which treat mental patients are not adequate and poor people do not have twenty-five and fifty dollars to pay some psycho-analyst for an hour that might head off mental illness. The society as a whole has a very sick attitude about its most prevalent disease. I had been lucky enough to get good treatment, and when I had left Brent-wood, I felt that I was whole once again. My body was a car which had needed overhauling so that it could run like new. Now my mind had unloaded a lot of junk that had cluttered it for many years and I was ready for action, a new life.

In Chicago, I stayed with my parents for a few weeks until I found a room. It was good to be home. That summer, I worked at the gas station. My stepfather and I never spoke of the incident which had driven me from home. I held no anger toward him; it was one of those things that happen in life. We could respect each other as men.

Although he was not in fact my physical father, he was in reality my father and I loved him for what he had tried to do: Work and work very hard each day of his life to provide a home for my mother, myself, and later my brother, working first in the steaming stockyards of Chicago as a laborer and then later putting in long, cruel hours as a service station operator for the Sinclair Oil and Refining Company. His work, day and night, Saturday and Sunday, trying to be a small, independent business-man, ultimately killed him. He died that summer of 1954, shortly after I returned home.

That my parents sometimes misunderstood me, as I must not have understood them at all times, wasn't the fault of any of us. There was something on fire in me as a child and young man which, at the time, I could not fully explain. But I think that an intellectual spark had been lighted by my Aunt Thelma in Mississippi, and a sense of justice had been implanted by my grandmother, while I grew up in all their pro-tective arms.

CHAPTER 11

God Is Dead: A Question of Power

THE NEXT six years of my life were a time of ideas. A time when things were germinating and changing in me. A time of deciding what I would do with my life. It was also a time in which I rid myself, once and for all, of the greatest disorder that cluttered my mind—the belief in God or any type of supreme being.

When I finally entered Roosevelt University in the fall of 1954 it must have been one of the most stimulating and brotherly places of study in the country. Its birth in 1945 grew out of a decision by Dr. Edward J. Spaulding, president of the state YMCA college. The board of trustees of the YMCA college wanted Dr. Spaulding to make a head count of the black students there. He knew this meant only one thing: that they were planning to establish a quota because of all the young blacks flooding out of the Armed Forces and into the schools. Spaulding refused to do this and took the issue to the faculty. Its members agreed that, rather than submit to this kind of discrimination, they would found a new university based upon the principle of equal educational opportunities for all people and free from the unwritten quota system for the admission of black people. Spaulding became Roosevelt's first president and the university became a haven for veterans who could not get in anywhere else because of quota systems.

The staff at Roosevelt contained a high percentage of black people, blacks who occupied not just menial jobs but also important administrative positions. This I found very impressive the first day I went there; and I continued to be impressed. It was a very good thing to see that many black people handling administrative posts. It created a feeling of warmth and camaraderie all over the university and a feeling that this school, at least, was serious about its program, serious about its philosophy.

"Do you think that people who want to write are neurotic?" I had asked the doctor during a group therapy session at Brentwood Neuropsychiatric Hospital. "Well, we're all neurotic," he answered, "it's a question of how a person handles his neurosis." I suppose his answer was good enough for me, or that I stopped worrying about what my motivation might be and decided that it was the kind of work I produced that counted. One way or the other, I had left the hospital with a clear desire to be a writer—something I had never thought of before.

At Roosevelt, I wanted to switch my field from public administration to journalism, but this proved impossible. The government was paying for my education and journalism was not a career within its program for veterans; I had to stick with personnel management. But again, the program allowed me to take a wide range of courses—political science, anthropology, economics, philosophy. I made peace with myself about this arrangement by saying that it would provide a good, broad background for journalism; I could always pick up the techniques of my craft at some other point.

Later at Roosevelt I thought for a while of becoming a civil rights lawyer an e en applied to the University of Chicago Law School. They rejected me and I never pursued the idea. As it turned out, the choice of a career to pursue at Roosevelt was less important than my good luck in having a number of exciting teachers and courses.

Walter Weiskopf, a professor of economics, was one of those who impressed me most. He was an Austrian Jew who had to flee Austria because of the Nazis. He had been psychoanalyzed by a student of Freud's, which gave our association additional meaning for me because I was then emerging from my experience at the Brentwood Neuropsychiatric Hospital. I did a tremendous amount of outside reading for his courses: Thorstein Veblen, Karen Horney, and particularly Erich Fromm were some of the writers whom I came to know under Weiskopf's direction.

Lionel Ruby was my professor for Philosophy 102 and important not so much for his personal qualities as for what happened to me because I took his course. Our textbook was *The Way of Philosophy*, by Cartwright, which might be called an atheist's manual; during that course God finally died in my conscious mind. For the final examination, we had to write an essay discussing the most important thing we had learned from the course. This is the essence of what I wrote: The most important things I have learned from this class are a number of intellectual arguments which disprove the myth that there is a God. When I was growing up, I was taught that God was responsible for the creation of the universe and he had the power to judge men, to make them submit to his will.

Then I began to wonder, if he is all-powerful, as we are told, why do we have war and disease and poverty and natural disasters like earthquakes? Why would an all-powerful God create a world where these ills exist? It is said that God leaves these questions to be settled by man. But can he be a just God, knowing that he had the power to change conditions and yet allowing people to suffer on this earth? He cannot be a just God if he has this power and will not use it. And if he is not just, then men should not give him their allegiance, but should seek to destroy him. Which they cannot do, of course, if he is all-powerful.

As I grew older, I began to question the existence of God. If matter could neither be created nor destroyed but simply changed in form— then how was it possible that God, an entity, a being, could create the world. Out of what did he create it?

When I entered this class, I had my doubts about God; I had simply decided that he was the first cause and nothing else. He had no attributes other than being the first cause. I have learned that every cause has its effect and every effect is produced by a cause. This argument goes on ad infinitum. Cause and effect cannot be broken logically. Therefore, if God is the first cause, then what caused the cause?

St. Thomas Aquinas has said that there is a point when one can no longer prove the existence of God by logic. One has to make a leap of faith and accept that there is a God. He is correct, but most often those who believe in God are not willing to say, "I believe in God but cannot prove that he exists." No man can logically disprove the beliefs of someone who insists that his beliefs are correct despite all rational arguments.

It is that leap of faith which I now refuse to make. I reject the existence of God. He is not all-powerful, all-knowing, and everywhere. He is not just or unjust because he does not exist. God is a myth; churches are institutions designed to perpetuate this myth and thereby keep people in subjugation.

When a people who are poor, suffering with disease and sickness, accept the fact that God has ordained for them to be this way—then they will never do anything about their human condition. In other words, the belief in a supreme being or God weakens the will of a people to change conditions themselves. As a Negro who has grown up in the United States, I believe that the belief in God has hurt my people. We have put off doing something about our condition on this earth because we have believed that God was going to take care of business in heaven.

My philosophy course had finally satisfied my need for intellectual as well as emotional certainty that God did not exist. I reached the point of rejecting God out of personal experience and observations; now I had intellectual arguments to satisfy me that my private feelings were correct. It was a great load off my mind to say with conviction, "God is a myth."

The greatest, most direct, and longest-lasting influence on me at Roosevelt was that of St. Clair Drake, who also became a personal friend and collaborator in many ventures after I graduated. St. Clair was the first black teacher that I had throughout my educational experience (except for Mrs. Pearson, my gym teacher in grammar school). He and Lorenzo Turner, with whom I would have a graduate course later, were the only black teachers that I had after grammar school.

My relationship with Drake began when I went to interview him for *The Torch*, the school newspaper, in the fall of 1955. He had just come back from Africa and his excitement about the new political independence of Ghana, about the continuing liberation struggles in countries like Kenya, about the newborn struggles of countries like Algeria, was contagious. He talked in particular about the problems facing black nations with large European populations. In the courses I had with him later, anthropology and sociology, Drake stirred us by the vividness with which he lectured, the energy with which he taught and led discussions, the amount of knowledge he disseminated.

A number of us, both black and white, formed a small cadre or brotherhood, as we called it. Because of teachers like Drake and because Roosevelt had an older student population than most schools, our brotherhood included not only students but also faculty and community people. We read many of the same books, shared similar experiences, had the same basic values. We formed a sort of unity around our common interests—above all, racism U.S.A.

Roy Stell, now a teacher in the Chicago public schools, was my closest associate. He and I used to prick the conscience of many of the black students. Sometimes they didn't even want us to come over to their tables because we would always come talking race. At this time, the NAACP was coming under attack for pushing its many school cases throughout the Deep South and we used to have heated arguments with the black students who didn't want us to talk about the NAACP's struggle. We also argued with white students who felt the NAACP was "pushing too hard."

The Montgomery bus boycott, which began in late 1955, got us even more involved in such debates. There had been a court ruling in the state of Virginia which stated that bus companies could not deny Negroes any seats whatsoever on a bus. The Supreme Court refused to review this decision; this indicated that the court was in agreement with the decision. In Montgomery people continued to boycott the buses while awaiting a decision on their court case. They were testing whether or not the segregation on the Montgomery buses was legal. I was studying constitutional law at the time and believed that, given the Virginia decision and the Supreme Court's attitude, the people in Montgomery should start boarding the buses—and sitting where they wished—instead of waiting for the outcome of their legal case. If they waited, it would set a pattern of people all over the country waiting until their particular desegregation suit was decided. This was one of the weaknesses of the Supreme Court's ruling on school desegregation, that blacks had to apply to desegregate each Southern school district, one by one.

At Roosevelt, I was president of student government then and we decided to try to raise some money for some station wagons to support the Montgomery bus boycott. We made contact—I think Roy Stell spoke to Rev. Ralph Abernathy of the Southern Christian Leadership Conference—to find out what they were going to do. SCLC said that their lawyers felt that there was not enough clarity in the Virginia ruling and that the courts in Alabama would say that it did not apply. We felt that this was a very negative attitude and that King should call for a creative confrontation with the racist bus companies. The boycott had become a passive kind of protest and should be turned into a more positive, aggressive action similar to what Gandhi did at the salt mines. Of course we were sitting in Chicago, judging the situation from a great distance, which is a very dangerous thing to do. Nevertheless, we felt that we had a right to make a comment on the paramount social issue of the day.

The Montgomery bus boycott had a very significant effect on the consciousness of black people throughout the United States. In 1956 our people constantly said, "Well, black folks just can't stick together. We can never act as a unit, we can't unify to protest against this man. We're like a bunch of crabs—the minute one of us crawls through the top, the rest of us drag him back down." This idea had been instilled by the colonizing force of white society, which always played down the importance of the black man. Part of the lack of group identification also rested in the belief that there was no need for it; God was going to take care of the white man when he got him in heaven. Our songs said things like, "I'm gonna tell God how you treat me," and then justice would be done.

Some friends and I had spent hours and hours in the barber shops of Sixty-first Street, trying to talk people out of these self-destructive attitudes, these self-fulfilling prophecies of "we can't get together." When the Montgomery bus boycott came along, you could hear people in the barber shops saying, "Well, at least people in Montgomery are sticking together." The boycott had a particularly important effect on young blacks and helped to generate the student movement of 1960. I remember Ruby Doris Robinson, who became executive secretary of SNCC, saying that when she was about thirteen or fourteen and saw those old people walking down there in Montgomery, just walking, walking, walking, it had a tremendous impact. The boycott woke me to the real—not merely theoretical—possibility of building a nonviolent mass movement of Southern black people to fight segregation. I had already found this notion in Reinhold Niebuhr's book *Moral Man and Immoral Society* and in John Steinbeck's writing. But now, in Montgomery, you could see the real thing.

My philosophy and strategy of struggle were evolving rapidly in the dynamic climate of Roosevelt. I was reading in anthropology and sociology, history and economics, many books outside the required lists, especially with Weiscoff. I had already made up my mind about passive resistance, or pacificism: It was strictly a tactic, not a way of life without limitations. Many students did not agree. Another value in dispute was integration, which had become the subject of keen debate with the 1954 Supreme Court decision ordering that all schools be desegregated. We argued over the merits of integration, which we took to mean total absorption into the mainstream of American life. Day after day, night after night, the discussions went on: "Who wants to integrate into a burning house?" some of us asked. When James Baldwin began writing these things, we had already been saying them for half a dozen years. The difference, of course, is that we just said them while Brother Baldwin put them down on paper.

As the student government president—the second black to hold that office in the school's ten-year history—I invited Autherine Lucy, who had desegregated the University of Alabama, to speak at Roosevelt. I was also working on a local issue, the desegregation of housing in Trumbull Park. Such activities brought my administration of student government under sharp attack from many whites, who felt people in my position should stick to campus affairs.

This was also the position of the National Student Association, which failed to support the Montgomery boycott. I attended the 1956 conference of NSA as head of Roosevelt's delegation and had my eyes opened to how the power structure operates and how whites use blacks to their own ends. This story begins a few weeks before the NSA conference, at the Democratic Convention. My experience there would affect my behavior at the 1964 Democratic Convention.

I went to the National Democratic Party meeting in Chicago in August, 1956, not as a representative of any group but as an individual, a person who lived in Chicago and who was interested in politics—particularly in the platform hearings which preceded nominations. I wanted to see what really went on at these sessions of the Democratic Party. And I began to learn.

One of the delegates to the Platform Committee was a short judge from Alabama, George C. Wallace. Stupid George impressed me at that meeting as an avowed segregationist with a distinctive style. He was constantly jumping up, challenging this statement and that one, arguing that the South and the state of Alabama had no problems of race relations and that people were distorting reality. He jumped up and down so much that I wanted to know what made this jumping jack tick. How could a man who claimed to be a judge jump up and down and make all that noise and know damn well he was not telling the truth? I understood why he was doing it, but I wanted to know more about the man. So one day, during a break, I decided that I would go up and say "hello" to him. I wondered if he was such a segregationist that he would refuse to shake my hand. And if he did, maybe that would embarrass him.

No. Not stupid George. George came over, shook my hand, leaned on a railing, and tried to convince me that he was right. Why, we would be surprised at the progress they were making in getting the right to vote for the nigras in Alabama before that NAACP came along and started pushing too fast. And what the NAACP did with Autherine Lucy was just awful. He went on and on, and I listened. With stupid George I just couldn't get angry. I don't know exactly what made me listen that long, maybe curiosity, but George had a style then, long before he became governor, a style that made me listen to him without getting too angry.

That was not the case with James P. Coleman, a former governor from Mississippi; now he sits on the bench of the United States Fifth Circuit Court of Appeals. To him I reacted with hostility the first time

I heard him open his mouth. I wanted to punch that cracker dead in the nose, right there in the Sheraton-Blackstone Hotel. Maybe it was because he was from Mississippi and that provoked an immediate psychological response in me. I couldn't stand his so-called suave style of condescension: Why, he knew nigras that just loved him to death. Why, even before he left Mississippi, there was Old John whom he had loaned a heap of money to in the past. Old John wanted to borrow five dollars. He asked Old John what did he need it for. Just need it, boss-man. So he loaned Old John the five dollars, knowing full well he would not get it back. He never got it back; that's the way they were. He said he told this story just to show that there was a tradition of goodwill between the races in Mississippi. He just wished all these here Northerners would stop talking about how bad the good white folks of Mississippi treat their nigras.

During the break that day, I saw him entering the hotel and coming up the stairs to the platform hearings. I rushed up and stood by the railing, trying to block his passage, hoping, just hoping he would touch me. He saw me staring at him. He stepped back and went far to the other side of the stairs in order to enter. After he had gone to the other side, I was angry with myself for not stepping over to the other side, too. I guess I made one of those face-saving little vows that a revolutionary often makes, "You just wait."

At the caucuses of the newly formed Leadership Conference on Civil Rights, of which Roy Wilkins was chairman, the feeling was that the Platform Committee would present a very weak platform—with a minority report. The Leadership Conference wanted a floor fight on the minority resolution. If that resolution ever reached the floor of the convention, they were sure that it would be accepted by the convention. The convention just couldn't turn down a strong civil rights plank in the platform of the Democratic Party.

There was some concern that the chairman of the convention would say, "You have heard the report of the Platform Committee. All those in favor say, 'Aye.' Those not in favor, say, 'Nay.' If this happened, according to Walter Reuther, then certainly the chairman would rule on this voice vote that the ayes have it. Platform adopted. Weak."

But the convention certainly had enough labor delegates who were prepared to prevent this steamroller tactic. They would demand a roll-call vote. At that point, there would be a motion to substitute the minority report for the majority. Labor was going to make so much noise before the chairman called for the voice vote that the convention would be in pandemonium. Thus they would stop the steamroller.

I waited. I wanted to see this happen. It was crucial to the civil rights struggle, the destiny of black people. We had to win this one, I thought.

On the night that the Platform Committee was due to give its report,

I sat in the balcony, tense, waiting. The drama was there, the suspense. A feeling of intrigue developed when I saw Carmine De Sapio, smoky glasses and all, walk out of the convention to caucus. What was up?

There was a minority report given and speakers for it. I remember the senator from Illinois, the white-haired Paul Douglas, who spoke in favor of the minority report.

Then came the majority report. The chairman did ask for a voice vote. Where was the noise? I didn't hear anything. I listened. They voted. The ayes had it. The majority report won. I didn't hear one foot hit the floor when the chairman of the convention called for a unanimous decision to support the civil rights plank.

But the trick was greater than I thought. Not only wasn't there a floor fight, but the white people offered up Congressman Bill Dawson, a black man, to speak about the glories of the Democratic Party. I was walking out in disgust as I heard him say he remembered when Negroes were hungry and the Democratic Party came and fed us.

I thought all night about the trick that had been played on the blacks across the country who could not see what I saw or hear what I heard. What a fake the entire platform hearings must be, I thought. They probably had the resolution already written in the National Committee meeting. They had the hearings only as a pretense of democratic procedure, to let people talk.

I learned and I remembered. I didn't know what could be done, except that I could go to the NSA conference held at the University of Chicago. There, as the chairman of the delegation from Roosevelt, I certainly could make a floor fight over civil rights. This time there would be a fight. No compromise. A fight.

The Roosevelt delegation urged that NSA accept the five points which the NAACP and the Leadership Conference on Civil Rights had put forward as a minimum plank for adoption by the Democratic Party:

1. Establishment of a Civil Rights Commission.
2. Creation of a civil rights section in the Justice Department.
3. Calling a national conference on civil rights.
4. Implementation of the 1954 Supreme Court decision.
5. Repeal of Senate Rule 22.

(The last is the rule by which the Senate deals with the filibuster; it requires a vote of two-thirds to end debate. Every time a civil rights measure had come to the Senate, it was killed by extensive filibustering on the part of Southern senators. Those senators wanting to pass civil rights legislation argued that they did not have the necessary two-thirds vote in the Senate to cut off debate. It was this rule that labor, according to Walter Reuther, wanted most to change because it affected labor legislation too.)

To strengthen our position, we lined up the support of the University of Chicago delegation and from there flanked out to get the support of students from Columbia University, the City College of New York, the University of Michigan, some California schools, and others. We were lined up solidly, along with the few black schools from the South, against the Southern whites.

We won. We got the convention to pass resolutions adopting the entire program with relative ease. We were surprised.

And then some tall delegate from a western university moved that we reconsider the vote on the repeal of Senate Rule 22. After all, this was a rule that dealt with how the U.S. Senate governed its business; NSA should not concern itself with such matters.

Our group had successfully argued the importance of civil rights from the point of view of those of us who were black. But in the long run everybody who wanted to make changes through the so-called democratic process suffered from Senate filibustering. Now there was a move to undo all our political and educational work at the convention.

People told us we were fighting an uphill battle because Allard Lowenstein opposed us. Lowenstein, who in 1968 became a congressman from New York, was indeed a powerful fellow, a graduate of the University of North Carolina, a past president of NSA, one who had addressed the convention earlier and received a tremendous response. Lowenstein, we were told, led the fight against us not from the floor but by assisting those Southerners and Westerners who wanted us to leave the business of the Senate to the senators.

It is hard to imagine today the passion and energy with which we fought to keep the NSA convention from rescinding its vote on Senate Rule 22. We were fighting for students to take a positive stand on an important issue of 1956. But the battle was larger than that. We fought to educate people and deal another blow to segregation. In many respects, the NSA convention of 1956 was similar to the halls of Congress. The Southern students lined up with the Western and Midwestern farmers and the Northern conservatives.

Finally Lowenstein pulled out his last and most effective ace. He got the student body president from the City College of New York, a Negro, to stand up and argue against us. The moment this young Uncle Tom rose to speak, I was on the floor and saw with my own eyes how Allard Lowenstein shoved him, literally pushed him, toward the microphone, saying, "Go now. Speak now."

There are some faces and expressions that one does not forget. And to this day I remember the expression on the face of Allard Lowenstein as he pushed the black cat down the aisle. This was the young white who would later build a big liberal image by organizing students to work in the South and by his trips to Africa.

It was a critical moment, for the debate had been wavering and all the blacks at the convention had lined up in favor of keeping the vote on Senate Rule 22. We had decided that this was our fight and that we blacks should speak to this issue. We had decided that if NSA meant anything, it must listen to the black delegates. We had decided that if the Southerners threatened the convention with a walkout, then we would tell the liberals gathered there to kiss them good-bye. We had argued that the question of principle should override any threats from Southern white schools that had not even desegregated themselves. Let them go.

But the black brother from New York stood up and said he was against the convention taking a stand on Senate Rule 22, although he had favored it earlier. He had thought about it and felt this was an unwise position for NSA to take. Not all Negroes were interested in the repeal of Rule 22, he said.

The brother's speech did not affect the black votes but it turned a crucial number of whites around because the argument came from a Negro. So we lost the vote on the repeal of Senate Rule 22, but we saved the rest of the program that had been passed. Afterward I talked to the brother from City College. Not only did I tell him that I felt he had been a Tom for Lowenstein and the Southern opposition, but I asked the brother about what kind of role he would play later in life, given the attitudes he had now. I later learned that this brother lost his position as chairman of his delegation when he returned to City College, primarily because of his stand.

Autherine Lucy, the expelled black student from the University of Alabama, appeared at this conference with Herb Wright, the director of youth activities of the NAACP. Sister Lucy and I had met earlier when she spoke at Roosevelt at the invitation of the student government. Wright announced that, since her case was in court, she would not speak to the body. With Autherine by his side, he proceeded to read a legal document detailing the facts of her expulsion. The white delegation from the University of Alabama and some other crackers got up and walked out, singing "Dixie." Some of us stood, singing the "Star Spangled Banner," of all things.

The last fight we made at that conference dealt with black representation on the policy-making and officer level of NSA. We severely criticized NSA for not having had a Negro as a national officer since its founding. We argued that if NSA were serious about the desegregation of Southern white schools, it should elect a Negro as educational affairs vice-president. We felt that a black would press harder for the desegregation of Southern schools than a white person.

I was then asked to run for this office, in order to make it a real issue. With great reservations I did so, fully aware that having an insurgent as a candidate would reduce us to the level of protesting, making a point. A three-way contest developed. When it was obvious that I would lose, I threw my support to another fellow who was also somewhat opposed to the administration of NSA. Their choice won, nevertheless. Some people argued that my campaigning hurt the liberal candidate. Anyway, the liberal candidate won the position of national affairs vice-president by a unanimous vote.

The 1956 NSA convention was the first and the last one I attended. I knew almost nothing about the organization before this experience. Afterward I felt NSA was irrelevant to the struggle of black people, since it was an extremely conservative organization, dominated by a body of students and former officers who saw themselves moving in governmental circles. But I underestimated the influence of NSA's International Affairs Commission. Since the 1967 disclosures about its involvement with the CIA, its relationship to African students has caused some of us great concern. (Not that we should have tried to reform the organization, but we should have developed alternatives to this government body.) I also wonder to what extent the position I took at that conference affected the way NSA would later play its cards in relation to various groups and individuals in the civil rights movement. Certainly the CIA, FBI, and others must have come to the conclusion in 1956 that I, for one, could never become "witty."

The fight over Senate Rule 22 reinforced my belief that blacks had to take the leadership in waging their struggle. If there were whites who accepted the program and were willing to work under the leadership and direction of blacks, that was another matter. Within that framework, decisions about the participation of whites should be made on the merit of each individual white and how he fitted into the total program and objectives.

The conference revealed to me the distinctions between integration and desegregation which Southerners maintained. As a member of the drafting committee of the Educational Affairs Commission, I could not understand at first some of the quarrels over the words *desegregation* and *integration*. Later I learned that the Southerners believed *integration* meant the total acceptance of the American Negro in the American way of life. *Desegregation* meant the removal of the legal barriers that prevented Negroes from having access to the American way of life.

I became convinced that Southerners deliberately fostered this distinction between integration and desegregation as a rationale for evading the 1954 Supreme Court decision. For instance, the Supreme Court decision of 1954 said that Southern schools should be desegregated. That is a legal question, a legal right which is indisputable. However, when you twist the removal of legal barriers to mean that one must accept (how gracious) us totally into the American way of life, then the justification for hostility increases. The resistance becomes even greater when one takes the word *desegregation* to mean race mixing, as many of the Southern white papers used to call orders to desegregate this or that school, "The court ordered race mixing."

There were a few Southern whites at the NSA meeting who told the truth. One of them was the son of John Patterson, then governor of Alabama, who said "The issue is power. We control the state and we're not going to allow any Negras to run Alabama and take our power from us. That is why we expelled Autherine Lucy. If we allow the Negras to crack our power in any way, that is an invitation to further weaken it.

"Why, in the county where my friend lives, the Negras are nine to one and his father is sheriff of that county. Do you think if the Negras had the right to vote that they would elect his father as sheriff? We got the power and we intend to keep it."

In the contest of power, those with the greatest force, the greatest strength, will win. I was learning.

CHAPTER 12

Keep Your Pride

"MAMA IS DYING, come if you can." The letter from Mississippi arrived a week after the NSA convention, and my mother and I left at once for my grandmother's farm. It was my first trip since 1944, when I had been fifteen and reluctant to face Southern segregation, but able to adjust to it if the crackers didn't push too hard. Now twelve years had passed and I had changed.

We made the trip by car this time, leaving Chicago at four o'clock in the morning and not taking a break until we hit Mount Vernon, Illinois. There we stopped so that I could interview State Senator Broyles for the Roosevelt newspaper, *The Torch*. Actually the interview was an excuse to satisfy my curiosity about Broyles, who had become widely known for his concern about Communist infiltration of the state government. He had introduced a bill calling for all state, county, and city employees to sign a loyalty oath and the bill had just passed. After an hour and a half of lecturing me on the dangers to our great democracy of Communist subversion, Broyles had said good-bye to me with the parting words, "My country right or wrong."

I was disgusted with the senator's fascist mentality and actions and, on an impulse, decided to teach him a small lesson. My mother and I had not yet eaten breakfast, so I drove the car up to a small restaurant in the center of town, knowing it was "for whites" and they probably would not serve us.

Sitting at the counter, I gave our order to the brunette waitress. "We would like two orders of ham and eggs, please."

The brunette wrote the order on her green and white pad with blue lines and walked to the back. Then the manager stepped from the kitchen and asked if he could help us.

"Yes," I answered, giving him a long look, "We gave our orders for two ham and eggs."

"We can serve you but you have to take them out." The man lowered his head as he spoke.

"Why?"

"You just have to."

"Why?"

"We don't serve colored people around here. They all come in and take out their orders."

"We want ours in here, if you don't mind."

"Well, I can't serve them to you.'"

"You will," I said, regretting that I had made it sound like a threat.

We eyed each other. I knew my mother was watching, biting her lips. She had told me earlier to stop on the outskirts of town; she didn't want to come here. In fact she didn't want to stop at all. I wondered if she were thinking about young Emmett Till, a boy from Chicago who had gone to visit relatives in Mississippi and been lynched for not knowing "his place." His body had just been found, and black people all over the country were angry about the vicious killing—but also frightened.

"You can go down to the other end of town. There's a restaurant owned by a Negro. He'll serve you," the white man behind the counter said.

"Look," I said, "I'm a citizen of the state. I was born in this state. I served this country for four years. I know the laws of the state, one of which says you must serve me in a public place."

"Well, I just can't."

"Why not?"

"I've told you, we just don't serve colored people around here. Look, I'm not asking for trouble. Why don't you go to the Negro restaurant like all the other colored people?"

"I'm not here to give you any trouble. All we want is two orders of ham and eggs."

The manager didn't budge; it was obvious that we would not eat there that morning. The time had come to call Senator Broyles and tell him what had happened to us. It would be a small satisfaction to embarrass him with the lack of democracy in his own backyard. On the telephone, Broyles admitted that our experience was a common occurrence. There was nothing he could do about it except invite us to his home for breakfast—which he did. I declined with thanks and did not bother the senator further about what was happening in his hometown—a town not far from where Abraham Lincoln rested in his grave.

When I hung up the phone and turned around, I saw two fat cops standing there in their blue shirts and blue pants and blue caps. My mother murmured softly, "Let's go. Don't start trouble. You see they have called the police."

"Wait Mother. Wait a minute."

I walked up to one of the cops and stuck out my hand. "My name is James Forman."

"I'm the police commissioner for this town. I hear there's a little trouble."

"There is. This man refuses to serve me."

"Well, you know a lot of Negroes come in and try to make trouble. They try to tear up a man's place," the cop said with a grin.

"We're not going to do that. I respect my mother if I don't have much regard for this place." I detested the cop's grin and hoped my sarcasm was obvious. "You're the police commissioner," I continued. "Are you going to see that the law is enforced?"

I turned a little and saw my mother's eyes filling with tears and her hand waving for me to come on and let's go. But I just couldn't walk out now.

"You're right. I am the law. I'm here to see that your rights are protected. I am also here to see that no damage is done to property. He must serve you if you insist. Why don't you just go to the Negro place down the street?"

When my mother had told me earlier not to stop, for she had traveled in the South and knew about the towns in Illinois, I had told her, "Mother, to some extent this is an individual matter. We can't always run, we have to stand up to these situations. We have to force the issue, because if we don't force it now, it will take that much longer." The acquiescence had gone too far and too long.

"Sir," I answered, hoping he would assume I was showing him deference, while in my mind it was annihilation through sarcasm, "I appreciate your reminder that there is a so-called Negro restaurant down the street. It just so happens I didn't know that before I entered this one. Now that I'm here, is it possible for you to enforce the law?"

And the cop answered, "If he serves you, he can make you pay. I'm here to protect his rights as well as yours."

This was the wild deuce. It struck me with tremendous force though it had been laid on the table rather gently. "The price is seventy cents on the menu. He can't make me pay more than what's on the menu."

"He can make you pay," the cop said.

A dying grandmother, a crying mother, these two cops . . . . What shal I do? Make me pay. How much can he get away with? What does the law say? I don't know. I looked at my mother again. Tears fell from her eyes; her face was drawn with tiredness and a little dirty.

"I don't understand what you mean," I finally said to the cop. "Are you telling me that if he charges five dollars for the meal, you will insist I pay the price?"

"I am here to protect private property."

"Does that mean you will insist we pay whatever he charges?"

"He can make you pay," was all the police commissioner would say.

"I see. Thank you, Commissioner. You'll hear from me."

My mother and I walked out and got into the car.

"I told you not to stop," she burst out. "I wouldn't have eaten that food if they had served me. You don't know what they will do to it or put in it back there in the kitchen. You can't take chances like that."

The second wild deuce hit the table. It fell on top of the first one. "You got something there," I mumbled. "I hadn't thought of that. . . . But we could have ordered and left."

It did not end there. I stopped about two blocks from the restaurant and called long distance to Chicago. The lawyer was not in but I talked with his clerk. It would be difficult to prosecute the case, he said. There were no friendly lawyers in the area. He told me to note the name of the place and when I got back to Chicago maybe they could work out something.

I drove on South on U.S. 37 at seventy and eighty miles an hour, thinking over the incident while my mother tried to sleep and the hot sun beamed down on the car. The mockery of it all. America. My country, right or wrong. Me, a man who served four years for the beloved country, who preached its virtues as most of the sixteen million Negroes do. And they tell us to go slow on civil rights, be patient, do not become bitter, wait for time to heal all things.

The 1950 Pontiac rolled on over the hills of southern Illinois and when we reached the Cairo bridge, I got out for a minute to stand there. I formed a ball of saliva in my mouth and spat it down on the turbulent waters flowing under the bridge. "That doesn't help much," I said. "No, there are better ways."

We were not too late. Mama Jane was propped up in the large bed when we entered the room. She smiled and seemed very happy. Mother kissed her. Then I walked over, kissed her on the forehead and on the cheek. She gave me a big hug.

"I'm glad you made it," she said to us.

"You'll be all right," I told her.

"No. My days are over. I've been hanging on, though."

"That's the spirit."

After greeting my aunts and cousins, I took a walk into the dark night. The fresh country air lifted my spirits. I found myself picking up a stick and using it like a cane, as men in the Bible did. I walked for more than an hour up and down the Mississippi road, thinking of death, life, the meaning of life to a black man who has been humiliated.

Everyone was up when I awoke the next morning. They had let me sleep until ten o'clock, an unusually late hour for country people. Aunt Pauline, who lived in Memphis, cooked me some breakfast—bacon and eggs, biscuits and coffee. It was good.

After breakfast I went into my grandmother's room and sat in a chair by her bed. She seemed very gay this morning. She looked better.

"How is school, Sport?" she asked, pronouncing it Spote as always.

"Fine."

"I enjoy reading those copies of the school newspaper you send me."

"You like my articles?"

"Very much. But I want you to be careful. If these white people around here saw those pictures of you and that white girl dancing, they'd have a fit." She smiled.

"I know. It's sickening."

"Just last month, a Negro left Holly Springs because he was afraid. They say he was in the post office and this white girl handed him a note. One of the people in there saw her give it to him. The word went around. The girl asked him in the note to meet her that night by some tree. He got scared. Some of the Negroes in Holly Springs told him he'd better leave for Chicago. He did. He hadn't done anything, they say. They say the girl had been chasing after him. He had been trying to avoid her. I hear you-all got in a little trouble on your way here."

"Not really. Guy just wouldn't serve us anything to eat. It makes me so mad."

"You never could take it, could you? You just be careful. I wouldn't want you to get hurt."

"I know, Mama Jane, but sometimes I boil up inside when things like that happen. It was like the last time I came here. You remember about the train."

"Yes, I remember. I'm old, Sport. I guess I got used to living like I did. 'Course I ain't never had any lost love for these peckerwoods. I just want you to be careful. You got your life ahead of you. No need to get yourself hurt on their account."

"I don't care, Mama. I'd rather die for what I believe is right."

"Hush, boy. Ain't none of 'em worth dying for."

"I wouldn't be dying for them, Mama. I'd be dying for something I believe in. My dignity."

She stretched out her hand and touched me on my shoulder. She looked at me with those bright, brown eyes that seemed years younger than her body. I looked at her brownish-yellow skin, thin, worn from years of toil, ready to return to the earth. I saw her jet black hair.

"The older you get Mama, the blacker your hair gets."

"Isn't it strange?"

"It is."

"Sport, I ain't never been the one to tell you what you should or what you should not do. I always told you to be yourself. If a body can't be themselves, they can't be much. The girls, all of 'em, want me to leave my land. They want me to live in one of them cities. But I can't, the land means too much to me. This is my home. I'm only in this bed now because I can't get up. This is my land. I want to die here. I don't have much longer to live."

"Don't say that, Mama." Her words made me wince.

"It's true. I know it. The Lord's been good to me. It's been a long time since we had a heart-to-heart talk. Not much I can tell you now. But I do want to tell you to keep your pride. It's a good thing, son, a good thing. But try to be careful. You've got a whole life ahead of you."

I rubbed my head several times. Keep your pride and be careful. I thought about what she said. She began to cough.

"Do you want some water?"

"Please."

After I brought her the water, I left the room so that she could rest.

Knowing that someone is dying, waiting for someone to die, what do you do? I sat on the porch of the old frame house that had once been cheerful and decided to tour the countryside, talk to the farmers, visit old hangouts. I spent a lot of time with my Aunt Thelma, who had been mostly responsible for my early intellectual formation. She took me to her schoolhouse where all eight grades were taught in the one room. There were only two teachers for all the grades. The school had only one outhouse, which both the boys and girls used. For books they got the ones discarded by the white children. The white school was not far from Aunt Thelma's one-room shanty; it had large, red brick buildings with neatly clipped lawns. Both institutions were financed by county funds. Blacks comprised 70 percent of the county's population, but another people controlled its government.

I wandered around like that for three days and then it was time for the funeral. Everyone had taken Mama Jane's death very well. There were tears and sobs, of course. I wondered when the hysterics would start. Usually they began at the moment the casket was opened for the last peep at the dead. I detested this practice; the pain of a death seemed accentuated by it—the wailing, the shouting, the crying, the pleas. Don't leave me, come back to me, I can't make it without you—all these cries were heard when the casket was opened.

I was glad that the aunt in charge of the funeral arrangements had told each of the two preachers (who had both insisted on speaking) that they were not to speak more than twenty minutes apiece, if possible. She hoped they would not deliver long sermons about crossing the River Jordan. But, although she had timed the funeral program so that it would last only an hour, it ran an hour and a half. One preacher got carried away into the promised land and tried to carry the church up there with him. When he descended back into Mississippi, they opened the casket and I gripped myself.

I decided I would not walk past the coffin. I wanted to remember Mama Jane as I had thought of her when she was alive, a cheerful person with unfailing hope and courage. She had imbued me with this spirit. I thought of the time she came to Chicago and we had gone to the harness races. As the trotters came around the turn into the home stretch, she said, "Dem some stepping dudes, all right." There was the time I took her to see one of my cousins, who had married a woman not particularly beautiful, though beauty is an individual matter. Anyway, Mama Jane said when we were returning home, "I don't know what that girl got between her legs, but she ain't got much on her face." It was this capacity to laugh at life that I appreciated most in my grandmother.

I sat there, holding up the line. An aunt touched me. "Get up, James, get up. Don't be like that. Get up," she said in a muffled voice.

I got up and walked past the casket. I saw my grandmother lying there, her hair black as it had been in life. She had a smile on her face. I was glad she had died smiling.

After everyone filed past the body, they carried it across the muddy road to the graveyard where some men had just finished digging the grave. There was no sun in the sky, only clouds. I felt a few drops of rain against my face. I stood there, crying within myself, a few tears in my eyes, a handkerchief in my hand.

I looked at the country people around the grave as they watched the casket being lowered into the ground. The farmers liked me and could always tell me some incident in my own life which had touched them. I had forgotten most of the stories until they reminded me. One woman whose daughter was now married liked to tell me about the time I was in the play wedding at the age of five. I had married her daughter. She told me how I became angry after the wedding when my family wouldn't let me go home with my wife. "Sport, you kicked up a storm. You said, 'I married her in the church, why can't I go home with her? She's my wife.' Do you remember that?"

Yes, I remembered. I saw the girl; she had three children now. Her husband had left her. Sometimes he would send money home.

There was another woman who was always reminding me of the first speech I ever made. The country church was the center of social activity and often they would stage week-night socials. On this night, I stepped

out on the platform and said, "I'm going to smoke my daddy's pipe."
I stuck my uncle's pipe in my mouth. "I'm going to wear my daddy's cap."
I put my uncle's cap on my head. "And I'm going to marry me a pretty
little girl just like my daddy's wife." My grandmother and aunts were
there and the church roared with laughter.

The straps were coming up out of the ground now. The casket was
made of pine; this funeral had cost more than the minimum but not too
much more. The daughters felt the eyes of the country upon them. Six
of them were away from the country, living in the cities. They knew
people would never stop talking about how the city daughters could not
give Mama Jane a decent funeral. But the daughter who lived among
the people, my Aunt Thelma, did not give a damn what the people
thought. She couldn't see putting a lot of money in the ground for the
rains to wash away. If the girls from the cities didn't want to stick their
money in the ground, that was their business. Before the funeral I had
talked to one woman who was renting a small piece of land from my
grandmother. She had spent over a thousand dollars on her mother's
funeral. "You ain't got but one mother. When she's dead you might as
well let other people know how much you think of her." And the woman
spent two years trying to pay off the debt.

People watched with interest as the Baptist preacher picked up a clod
of dirt, "Ashes to ashes, dust to dust." One daughter who had been
crying ever since they opened the casket in the church screamed, "Mama,
my mother is gone!"

The dirt went over the casket. The men took turns throwing it rapidly
until you could no longer see the box. Slowly the people began to turn
and walk away.

Almost as if a church service anywhere in America had just ended,
the people began to smile and to embrace each other and say, "I haven't
seen you in such a long time. My, you're looking well. How long are you
staying, child?"

It had stopped raining that Tuesday night when my mother, Aunt
Pauline (who was also returning to Chicago), and I left the South to go
back home. About four o'clock the next morning we pulled into a gas
station. We were in Tennessee, near the Kentucky border.

It was a newly built Standard gas station. "Fill it up and check the oil,"
I said. "Where is your toilet?"

"Straight through that garage door," the young white attendant said.
He looked about twenty-two.

Walking through the garage, I saw the office off to the left, and in it
a door with a sign, "Men." Now I knew the attendant meant that I was
not to turn left and go into this washroom. I was to keep straight until
I found the toilet for Negro men.

I turned left and went into the toilet for men. I closed and locked the door, urinated, washed my hands, used the towel. I unlocked the door, and stepped outside. The young attendant was standing there, his face beet-red.

"I told you to go straight through the big door. You're not supposed to use that toilet."

"It had a sign that said 'Men.' What do I look like to you?"

"That one isn't for you."

"How much is my bill?" I looked out through the window and saw my mother and aunt waving for me to come out of there.

"You're not supposed to use that one," the attendant repeated.

"Look, how much is my bill? We have a long trip ahead of us."

"Four sixty-five."

I gave him a five spot and waited for the change. The redness in the man's face receded some as he handed it to me.

"How's the oil," I said.

"It didn't need any."

"Thank you," I walked out. Even before I got to the car, I could hear my mother say, "Get in here, you fool."

I started the motor. "Hurry up and get out of here." my mother said. "Don't you know he could have shot you and nothing would be said?"

"That's right, James," Aunt Pauline said. "They'll kill you down here. You're not in Chicago, boy."

My mother continued to scold me about the danger in my actions. Finally I said, "That's the trouble with Negroes today, Mother. They're so damn afraid of being killed. They'll take anything just to live."

"This is your last trip South with me," she said. "I'm not going to let you kill me. No sir. And I mean that. You'll never come South with me again."

"You just can't let people stick you in a hole because they think you're not human. Hell, I'm a man, I can't be accepting—always accepting." I was doing seventy; my mother was shouting and I was yelling too.

"Pull over," she said. "Let me drive."

I pulled over. Aunt Pauline said, "Sister, let him drive, there's no need in squabbling. We're out of danger, I think." My mother talked for a while with her sister, who was in the back, and then turned to me.

"You drive, but don't try and kill us."

"I was only doing seventy, Mother."

"O.K. Let's forget it."

We drove in silence, but the incident was whirling through my mind. It was true that I did not mind the idea of dying, if the death was like my grandmother's natural going or if it was for the sake of something bigger than I. Conscious submission to racism seemed to me worse than death. It killed a person's spirit. It took a little from him each time he knew he should not submit—and did.

CHAPTER **13**

Time for Action

LITTLE ROCK! LITTLE ROCK! NIGGERS! NIGGERS! TWO, FOUR, SIX, EIGHT, WE DON'T WANT TO INTEGRATE! NIGGERS! NIGGERS! NINE LITTLE NIGGERS!

I COULD not sleep. I tried to read a book about South Africa but that only made things worse. I went to the kitchen upstairs in the rooming house and tried to calm myself with some hot milk. Downstairs in my small room, I tried to read again. Useless. I tried to write. No luck. I tried walking.

I left my room on Mountfort Street and walked out into the black Boston night. I crossed Commonwealth Avenue walking straight past the chapel of Boston University. Heading for the Charles River, I saw the lights of Harvard and MIT in the distance. I walked and walked and walked some more, up and down the pavement next to the Charles, on the Boston side.

What was I doing here in graduate school at Boston University, studying African affairs and government, when down in Little Rock those young students were facing the man? They were agitating. They were together. I should leave this place. I should quit school now, it just didn't make sense. I should go to Little Rock. There must be some way I can help. My place is in Little Rock, not Boston, not graduate school, not this, strolling along the Charles.

I had graduated from Roosevelt in three years, by going to school straight through two summers. Through his academic contacts, St. Clair Drake had gotten me a grant-in-aid of five hundred dollars for the African Research and Studies Program at Boston University. The department of government gave me a tuition scholarship in exchange for my serving as a teaching assistant. Government was my major. African affairs seemed to me an important field of study; I also had a notion of going to work in some newly independent African country. But I wasn't sure. At the time of my graduation from Roosevelt in January, 1957, I knew that I had to work for black people in some capacity, trying to change the conditions of our lives. This was a certainty, but the precise form of the struggle and the nature of my participation were not clear to me.

My one sure and immediate goal was to write, as a way of dealing with my existence as a black man in the United States. I was keyed up to do a novel; my last semester at Roosevelt and the seven months that followed had been filled with reading and writing and observing and recording my observations. If I could describe the realities of black life, that would be a form of action. I talked with people, always keeping in mind their potential story value. All of us are a book: It is true. Upon the advice of St. Clair Drake, who felt that I needed to break what he called my sociological jargon, I read a lot of novels, American writers like Hemingway and especially Steinbeck, who impressed me very much. I was trying to get a sense of style, trying to loosen up. And this took practice, practice, practice.

In July, I had headed for Boston. A moving company located near the family gas station in Chicago let me hitch a ride with a van going to the East Coast. From Pittsburgh, I hitched another ride to Philadelphia and there looked up Charles Tribble, with whom I had played football in the Air Force. He was the only person I knew in Philadelphia, and we spent time together.

Tribble had a miniature jet set hanging around his house, who spent every evening drinking and going to clubs. They often went to Atlantic City and other beach resorts on the coast, spending the day on the beach and the night in clubs again. I was very alienated from this way of life and kept asking myself, how can young black people get so sucked into the American mainstream of values? They seemed unconcerned about the emerging black consciousness and had few ideas or plans to do something about racism in Philadelphia. In talking to some of them, I began to realize how effective McCarthyism had been. More than one brother talked about how he had joined this or that youth organization and was later visited by the FBI, or could not get clearance for certain jobs. The effects of the McCarthy period on the youth of this country can never be measured, but I would say that they did much to curb protest—until a new generation emerged in the early 1960s.

For a month in Philadelphia I had argued with people about the need for young black people to be involved and doing something, in an organized fashion, about their situation. Each day I would record conversations and impressions; I thought that a play could emerge about the young black jet set. I also did various kinds of day work that summer, to earn money. I left for New York as September drew near and made a short stop there, talking with Lorraine Hansberry who was having success with her new play, *A Raisin in the Sun*. I hadn't seen her since we were in high school. It was a pleasure to talk to her again. She told me that James Baldwin had left the country because he found life oppressive and could not work here. This seemed understandable to me in that period; I felt myself to be living in the worst of societies and could see why a black writer would have to get away, if only to be able to write about it.

In Boston, I arrived with the name of one friend—a woman living in Roxbury who let me stay at her home for a while. Later I would move to a rooming house on Mountfort Street, where I had a room and kitchen privileges for ten dollars a week. The grant-in-aid just did not stretch; I was cooking chicken necks and chicken backs all the time but still could not pay the landlady regularly. It got so bad that I would go up to the university when I wanted a cigarette, collect the butts in the ashtrays, bring them back to my room, and roll the leftover tobacco into a smoke. Worry over my economic state, the lack of food, became almost an obsession.

But there was a bigger problem that fall, and the solution to it could not be bought or sold:

"Little Rock! Little Rock! Niggers! Niggers! Nine little Niggers! Spit on 'em, Burn 'em, Kill 'em!"

Little Rock's Central High School had been desegregated in early September. Only the bayonets of the National Guard, the hundreds of troops sent in by Eisenhower prevented the whites from turning into a giant lynch mob. All through that fall of 1957 and the spring of 1958, I thought about Little Rock. I also read a great deal about South Africa, and the more I learned, the angrier I became. Every time I read about a pass law or some restriction on the rights of blacks in South Africa, the more I thought of home—the South. The South of the United States of America. I even wondered if there were not some historical freakishness in the fact that they were both "South." The more I read about South Africa and the efforts of Africans in general to shake off colonialism, the more I came to doubt whether I should be going to Africa instead of working here.

The African Research and Studies Program was not an action center but purely for research. Little attention was paid to the Algerian War and little research done on French-speaking Africa in general. People, often from the State Department and the diplomatic service, came there to study under the so-called Africanists. Some went on to Africa to do research. But Africa was suffering from white domination and needed to free itself of all colonial influences. Africa didn't need American researchers; it needed its own revolutionaries. If I were going there, it would be to fight with arms.

The department of government at Boston University was worse; it concentrated on a factual, rather than a theoretical, approach to political science. We spent a lot of time learning facts which were bound to change and which we were sure to forget. The classroom lacked the intensity of my undergraduate work at Roosevelt. I argued with my instructors about Africa or other matters in the program; actually I was debating my own life and what to do with it.

I kept asking myself what I was doing full-time to change conditions in this country. My guilt over my own inaction plagued me. The contradiction between my studying in graduate school and those Little Rock high school students facing the mobs haunted me. I wanted to be there with them, to help in whatever manner I could.

Over the months at Boston University, ideas which had begun to take shape at Roosevelt now crystallized. I became convinced that we needed a mass movement of blacks, a popular movement that would awaken our people, show them that "niggers" can get together, and create a desire to go on to the next step. History moves in stages and one cannot leap over certain experiences. People must themselves become convinced that certain moves are the correct ones. That same sense of injustice which I as well as others felt as individuals had to be activated on a mass scale. We needed a mass movement that would aggressively confront racism if we were ever to shake the lethargy of our people and to maintain the momentum that had been sparked by the Montgomery bus boycott and Little Rock. Having lived in many parts of the United States, I knew many brothers and sisters would soon rise up if that momentum could be propelled forward.

That movement would challenge segregation, pointing up the contradictions in the society between ideal and reality and thus heightening conflict. It would begin in the South, where the contradictions were clearest, where the denial of the vote and segregation in public accommodations were most flagrant. There was the white man and then there was *us*; he dehumanized us night and day. Part of my belief that we must start in the South rose from my own intense love for the area, stemming from childhood. I often thought how much I would like to live there, if only racism were absent.

The young, educated blacks would have to forge the consciousness of the movement in the South. I was convinced we were not going to get much help from the preachers and black schoolteachers. They were a very conservative force which had to have fires lighted under it. The students would have to carry the torches. If they were successful in the South, they would light fires under the armchair revolutionaries who sat in the North talking about the man and what has to be done. These were the revolutionaries who never walked on a picket line because that was not the way—although they never worked on what was the way, if there was a way to them. People do need models and what we needed in this country was visible, very visible evidence of blacks staying together, struggling, doing something about our condition.

The movement would utilize the media as a method of disseminating information to change the consciousness of black people. Also, such a movement should try nonviolence as a tactic.

The idea of nonviolence came to me from several sources. One of them was my own disgust with the lack of aggressive action by black people and the need to formulate a program based on anything that would get people into motion protesting the injustices we face. I was, therefore, searching for ideas, for ways that we could move as a people. The Montgomery bus boycott and now Little Rock impressed me; I had to admire the cultural effects of the boycott in changing the mass psychology of black people, showing them that we could do things as a group. Also, I realized that people are motivated to action for many reasons—and one of them is that they get angry when they see their people suffering at the hands of their oppressors. The boycott and Little Rock led me to think that if nonviolent confrontation could heighten consciousness and disrupt the society, then this was a method I should investigate. If the struggles, the beatings, the jailings, would rile up our people to action, then they would be worth it. Therefore, it was always important to make sure that the act, the nonviolent protest, got the widest publicity and had the broadest public appeal.

I further studied the history of Gandhi in South Africa and his concept of *Satyagraha*, "soul force." Looking at Gandhi's work in India, I saw that there, too, passive resistance had been a powerful weapon in dealing with the colonial master—England. On the other hand, however, Gandhi had said something that most apologists for nonviolence seem to forget: "Before I see my people in perpetual slavery I would rather see them fighting with arms." At this stage of my thinking I also made a distinction which has so often been overlooked by advocates of pure nonviolence: Gandhi was forging an independence movement in a country where the colonized formed a majority of the population, with only a small, though powerful, number of European colonists to be defeated. The United States presented a reversal of that situation.

The person who finally convinced me that nonviolent action might be possible in this country was Kwame Nkrumah and his statements that the campaign he led against the English had been based on the principle of direct action, nonviolent if possible, but action nevertheless. Nkrumah was not ruling out violence against the colonial masters and neither did I. He introduced a new term to me, *nonviolent direct action*. In the past people had associated nonviolence with passive resistance or *Satyagraha*, but here was a man—prime minister of the first black country in Africa south of the Sahara to get its independence by using nonviolence—associating nonviolence with action. Without ruling out other forms of struggle, especially the use of violence, I felt Nkrumah's tactic should be tried in this country. I felt this and would continue to feel it despite all those armchair revolutionaries who argued against using nonviolence as a tactical aggressive weapon but were not willing to use any other method either. This was inaction, wasted time.

Of course Nkrumah must be placed in a historical context himself and his limitations understood. Nkrumah had a saying, "Seek ye first the political kingdom and all else shall be added." He and others of the African independence movement failed to deal with the fact that, if the colonial powers yielded only political rule and maintained economic rule, then the people were not much better off and the political leaders themselves were in danger of being overthrown—as many progressives have been in Africa, including Kwame Nkrumah. But I would not understand all this until 1965 or 1966.

The writings of Frantz Fanon were not available in English at that time, a later generation than my own would come to maturity reading his thesis that violence and only violence can totally free a colonized people. It should be clear, however, that nonviolence was always a tactic as far as others and I were concerned, and not the ultimate weapon of liberation. I always said that, if I lived in an African country or some other colony, I would fight with guns and not nonviolence. But nonviolence came to me then because I was convinced that only revolution can solve the problems of black people in this country—and revolutions are not made overnight. They take time and people must be willing to sacrifice all, their lives especially, before revolutions can happen. A mass movement to heighten consciousness would be the first step. Building it called for a hard core, a sacrificial group of people who would be in consistent opposition to the government, but who would help develop the mass consciousness by saying, "we are even ready to lay down our lives by using nonviolence, if this will lead toward revolution."

Such a group always had to view itself in relation to our people as a whole. Individual acts of protest are fine; the collective actions of people are more important. So the elite or vanguard needed to raise consciousness had a responsibility to develop organizational forms that would last way beyond themselves. My theory of leadership was fully developed by the time I arrived at Boston University, but strengthened there as I studied various types of leadership in newly emerging nations and colonized countries. What we needed in the United States, as black people, were committed souls to assist in the development of organizations that would survive the organizer. We did not need charismatic leadership, for this most often led to a disintegration once the charismatic leader was gone. My goal was to build structures that would perpetuate revolutionary ideas and programs, not personalities.

I had a very definite image of the kind of organization needed at that point. It did not yet exist. CORE was dominated by white leadership; the Southern Christian Leadership Conference was dominated by preachers; the NAACP was dominated by a middle-class orientation. The organization we needed would, I thought, be broadly socialistic in its ideology, with the goal of building a revolutionary movement to change the political, economic, and social structure of the country. I viewed its members as a disciplined cadre that would work to develop indigenous leadership and live in the communities—not apart from the people. They must not work for profit or high salaries. They would be principally blacks from the South; the leadership had to be black in order to develop images that would inspire other blacks. Whether whites could actually be in the organization or not, and on what terms, were questions I had not then resolved in my mind. But I did feel that whites should work in white Southern communities; I knew that we would need white revolutionaries too.

My ultimate hope was to organize each rural and urban area into sections, for a mass mobilization. At first, however, I thought that the organization should try positive, nonviolent confrontation.

As I have already indicated, the people in this organization had to be ready to die for their people—if necessary. I had also become convinced that the fear of death was perhaps the biggest single deterrent to mass social action by blacks in this country. We had learned to accommodate ourselves to a few simple pleasures of life and, therefore, did not really want to risk our lives for what we considered our freedom.

Reading the works of Jean-Paul Sartre at Roosevelt and Boston universities, I had been struck with Sartre's ideas on action and the finality of death. By the time I left Boston University, I had formulated my own theory of action based on the finality of death. Much of it, I think, derived from my mother; she had forced me to decide by allowing me to decide. As I grew up, I would often ask her advice and on many occasions she had said, "you must decide. It is your life. When I am dead, you will have to live with your decisions." Several times she had remarked, "Do it now while you have a chance. Because when you're dead you won't have another chance."

To decide to do nothing is to make a decision, I felt. Since we have only one life and there is only one certainty in life, death, then a person must choose what he is going to do with his life. He makes that decision whether he recognizes it or not. We choose by our inaction. Therefore, we as black people had to decide what we were going to do with our black lives. This meant that each black person had to decide what he was going to do and the choice should be made in favor of service to people. We cannot fight racism and exploitation once we are dead. Action is necessary and we must carry it out now, for death always faces us— it is the only certainty in life. When people overcome the fear of death, then and only then are they willing to lay down their lives for humanity. We as black people must develop the love for humanity which will make us act in the name of justice and die for the future of blacks and all humanity, for we are an indivisible part of mankind.

Little Rock! Little Rock! Niggers! Niggers! Young black girls facing mobs of old white men! Tacks in their seats! Taunts in their faces! Old women walking to work in Montgomery. Tired of sitting in the back of the bus. Tired, child, of being treated like dirt. Just downright tired of all this old mess!

Shit, man. You got this scholarship for one year, the second black cat in the African Research and Studies Program at Boston University. Now ain't that a bitch. The second black cat in the program, but what do you expect? Our people have only seen Tarzan on the screen and they have no identification with Africa. The man has played a trick by not putting us in the history books. Even that progressive school you went to, Roosevelt University, used a history book talking about how much better off the slaves were coming to this country and becoming Christians than they were staying in Africa as pagans. True, the teacher didn't like the book and apologized for the section, but the fact that he said it was the best book on other subjects shows you just how much shit is fed into the minds of the brothers and sisters. But this has to change, man!

Ghana is free now and there are going to be a whole lot of other African countries free in the next ten years and the level of awareness of our people will be raised. A whole lot of black people are going to be digging the motherland, some of them late, but nevertheless. . . .

Dig, the man is so up-tight against the East. He's in this East-West ideological struggle and it's our role to play it jam-up. The man is concerned about Africa, not because we are now suddenly such fine people, but because he knows that Africa is important in the East-West struggle and he is going to try to swing Africa to the West. What we got to do is play on the man's politics and the man's fears. Play our game so jam-up that the cat has to give in to our demands because he's hurting in the cold war. How can he go around talking about democracy in this country when it takes bayonets to get into schools in Little Rock?

We got to take the man's education, his contradictions, and throw that shit back into his face hard and furious. Every time we can, hit him with some of his own shit. We got to know his history and we certainly got to know ours. Tell him about his revolution 'cause he was being mistreated. We got a right to ours too. Tell him about his speeches for liberty and death. We can make ours too. Tell him about his documents talking about liberty and equality for all. Hell, we in the *all*, too; so shape up, baby.

Now we got to stop sitting around these here parlors talking about how bad the white man is, 'cause that don't make things no better. We got to hit the streets, and point up those contradictions. Take the vote—

an American tradition. Take public accommodations—an American tradition. Both denied flagrantly in the South. Hit the streets, that's where it's at. It's out there with the people in Little Rock, the people everywhere.

Now what about you? You, James Forman? Here you are, twenty-eight years old, a graduate student, a veteran, an aspiring writer—but, most of all, a black man in a corrupt, dying society. Sure, you, with your technical skills could make it to Africa and help in the construction of a new country there. But what about the masses of black people in this country, all those people who couldn't even raise the fare for a trip to Africa? What's your responsibility to them? What do you owe your family and people like your grandmother and grandfather? They died without ever knowing "how useless it is to vote." At least they should have had the right to find that out.

What right do you have to leave this country and go to Africa, leaving your people here? Some day the struggles will merge, it's all the same, man, but right now agitators are rare in this country. Young blacks who have ideas about social change have a responsibility to stay right here in this fucking country and work for the liberation of themselves and other blacks. Isn't that what Du Bois had in mind when he talked about the talented tenth? Education itself should be for use, right?

If all the young black intellectuals split this country it would be like the South. Young bloods leave the South, get education, go North, start making money and forget all about their poor mamas down south or up north in Miss Ann's kitchen, scrubbing some floors to get that black bastard through school and now he doesn't even want to introduce her to his friends. "Oh, Mama, how many times do I have to tell you to say, 'We are' and not 'We is'?" She-e-e-t.

If all of us cats split the scene and go to Africa as soon as we get some sense into our heads, we're being just another set of individuals. We're just trying to make it for ourselves, baby. We don't want to face the struggle. We want to cop out and say "later" for you-all. That's right, we want to be individuals when we ain't got time for that. There just ain't no time for that.

Frederick Douglass said that no people deserved their rights if they weren't willing to agitate for them. So we got to make people see that they can fight for their rights. "Poor the pen without the gun," yeah, but "poor the gun without the pen." Propaganda! That's it, baby. We need young, black intellectuals to do full-time agitation. Build a propaganda mechanism. We need young writers, storytellers, pamphleteers, our own Tom Paines, some more Richard Wrights. We got to take the forms of the man and put our own substance into them and create new forms of our own. We got to get the word out. Write our own history. Who can write better than us about our frustrations when we read about an

Autherine Lucy expelled? About our joy at the strength of Montgomery? Who can write better than us how it feels to watch the young girls reviled in Little Rock? We got to document these feelings so that the present and future generations can carry forward the movement. We build on Frederick Douglass and Du Bois; let the young build on us.

That means, brothers and sisters, that we must act. The time for talking is way past. Action.

CHAPTER 14

The Great White Rat

THE TRAIN from Memphis could not roll fast enough for me. I stood on the platform with the top part of the door open, looking out at the countryside as the train headed for Little Rock.

Going to Little Rock in September of 1958 was something I had to do for the sake of my existence, it seemed. For months, in Boston, I had felt torn about being in a safe, quiet graduate school while black people in Arkansas risked their lives. Now Little Rock was reactivated and I had another chance to go—a better chance, because I was neither in school nor working full time. It was also a test for me; a test of my reactions to a Southern protest scene, a test of my ability to be mobile and go anywhere necessary on short notice with little or no money. Lee Blackwell, managing editor of the *Chicago Defender*, had given me press credentials and promised to pay for stories filed from Little Rock.

The clickity-clack of the train sounded like music to me. The sun was shining brightly. I waved to the brothers and sisters working in the fields picking cotton, to the old people sitting on their porches smoking corncob pipes or just sitting looking at the blue-colored coaches roll by. I just waved and waved. I was at home, I was with my folks, country folks, the people I loved the best.

When I got to Little Rock, I took a cab to the office of the *Arkansas State Press*, the newspaper owned by the Bateses, L. C. and his wife Daisy Mae, who was the principal black figure in the Little Rock crisis. I did not know her and did not know what type of reception I would receive. When she met me in the office, she began to ask questions. Then she told me, in a polite way, that she did not know me and there was no reason for her to trust me. The White Citizens' Council, an organization of middle-class whites banded together to stop desegregation, had sent black people as paid informers into protest groups to try to discredit them and it was possible that I was an agent of the White Citizens' Council. Her cautious, but forthright position impressed me and I made a mental note of it for future use. I told her that there was no reason why she should trust me; only time would tell if I were trustworthy, and meanwhile I would not push myself on her and her husband or on the movement there. During the next two weeks in Little Rock I became a very close friend of the family and was often invited to their house.

I admired the Bateses very much. Their newspaper had lost all its advertisers except Carnation milk, but even that company was running only a public service ad with no mention of the product. Pressure from the White Citizens' Council had done this. I had been conscious of those councils ever since they began forming after 1954, and could not understand why some influential black organization like the NAACP had not created a public furor and mass protests about them. The Bates's experience was one more example of why this should be done.

When I got to Little Rock, the Supreme Court had just ruled that desegregation of Little Rock schools must proceed. The state then closed down all the public schools in Little Rock. They would stay closed for the entire year; right now the issue was in the courts again. I felt that, for all its greatness, the fight in Little Rock was losing some valuable time. For instance, it seemed to me that the fight should not just be confined to the school issue and, even if it were confined to the school issue, there should be some street confrontation. During my stay in Little Rock, the whites would often take to the streets and demonstrate against "integration." The eyes of the world were upon Little Rock; the United States's image abroad was threatened. There could have been mass rallies in support of the students. Instead, the black community seemed to be passively waiting for court decisions—which was in fact the case. But, although I doubted that the purely legalistic approach was advisable, I did not feel I had the right to make these suggestions to the Bateses since they had decided upon the legal approach and they had to live there, paying the price for their courage. It was an error not to state my feelings.

While in Little Rock I filed several stories with the *Defender*. They were published, but I received no money for them; I would have been stranded in Little Rock if it hadn't been for a lucky night of sociable poker at the Bates's home.

The articles reported on people's reactions for the most part. Several black residents blamed what had happened on Faubus's politicking for a third term by appealing to die-hard segregationists; others brought out an older, deeper racism. In one article, I told how I had gone up to three men and asked them, "What do you think about today's ruling of the Supreme Court?"

"We heard it," the crippled man said. "It had to be. Faubus can't stop the federal government." He was a short dark-skinned man who touched his crutches as he spoke.

"Yes . . . you're right," the brown-skinned man on the grass said. "Old Faubus got a lot of money from those segregationists. He is subject to hide, to run away. You can never tell what that slippery dude will do. . . . What do you think?" he said to me.

After a while, the man on the grass asked me did I see an American flag flying on the State Capitol. "You know every other capitol has a flag they raise in the morning and take down at night. Did you see an American flag up there?"

"No."

"How long you been around here?"

"Not long."

"Well, there hasn't been an American flag up there since they lynched that colored man and drug him down Ninth Street."

"How long ago was that?" I asked.

"Before you were born. It's been a long time."

"It sure has," the crippled man said. "They drug him down this street. They took the benches out of the Methodist church, my church, and they burned the man on Ninth and Broadway."

"When they did that," the man on the grass said, "they took the American flag down and ran up a Confederate flag."

"This is a rough town," the crippled man said. "It's too rough for a capitol. . . . They call it a capitol. But it ain't no capitol. No capitol at all."

"What did he do?" I asked.

"Well," the crippled man said, "they tell me he was trying to catch a runaway buggy that had a white woman in it. I was living around here then. I was on the other side of town but I heard about it. They say he was chasing the buggy and the white men said he was trying to rape the woman."

"And they tell me," the man on my right said (he had been quiet all this time), "that the Negroes left here and went to Hot Springs and Chicago and everywhere. They left the poor man alone. . . . I heard the white woman tried to tell them that the man was trying to help her. . . . But, son, sometimes these white people here don't listen to nobody."

"What was the man's name?"

None of the three men knew.

When I returned to the office of the *Arkansas State Press* I asked the secretary if she knew anything about this murder. She, too, had heard about it. She didn't have any details. However, she called someone and in twenty minutes handed me the following information:

Mr. John Carter of 2000 Monroe Street was mobbed by two hundred white men, shot with 250 bullets, and hung on a telephone pole on Ninth and Broadway, Wednesday, May 4, 1927. The reason for this action was that he was supposed to have raped Mrs. B. E. Steward and her nineteen-year-old daughter, Glennie, on Twelfth Street Pike, the attack occurring at ten o'clock in the morning. He was found and caught just off Hot Springs Pike at the Sipper Inn at six o'clock in the afternoon, by E. V. McElvain. Carter, about twenty-eight years of age, who was believed to be an escaped convict, was identified by the daughter.

On my last night in Little Rock, I interviewed a student who was supposed to enter Central High. She had been writing on a pad before I came into the room and left it on a chair. I glanced at it later and saw that she had written, "Is it dignity to be able to go into a five-and-ten-cent store and buy a coffee pot, but not be able to buy a cup of coffee?" Her words stuck in my mind because they expressed so clearly the struggle against dehumanization that all black people were engaged in. I thought about the incident in Memphis at the lunch counter when I was a child and realized that my purpose in life at this time came down to something very simple: If my life could make it possible for future black children not to have that experience, then it was worth living.

My trip to Little Rock further heightened my consciousness of the need for a mass-based organization that would agitate and organize demonstrations in order to arouse the awareness of black people and embarrass the American image by playing on the contradictions inherent in this society. But the time had not quite come for its birth, nor was I quite ready to commit myself to such an organization. I was still working out my ideas—by writing a novel about my experiences in the South, in Chicago, and at Roosevelt University. The novel was a great wish extension, for, after putting many of my experiences in novelistic form, I had the hero going South to develop a mass movement using nonviolence as a tactic. The novel's characters included a young white Southerner named Robert Atwood who had been a minister and who had to leave his hometown because he favored having a black choir and a white choir singing together at the same church service. The main purpose of my writing his story was to hit white Christian America in the face with a story about a white Christian minister who suffered from the racism of his environment, hit white America where it hurt, in its Christianity and in its whiteness.

The novel contained a detailed definition of the kind of organization needed. But I still felt uncertain about accepting the discipline which this required. I knew that when you join a group, you have to give up something called "personal freedom"; you have to accept rules and policy lines, a whole group discipline that may go against your own grain. This was vital to the functioning of a good organization and necessary to accept, if one was serious about his dedication to the people. But the individualism bred into us by this capitalist society had tremendous power; could I free myself of it? My approach to life had long been a two-step process: first, define what needed to be done collectively and then define my individual role within that plan. But there was one extra little step too: resolving any conflicts between the definition of my political role and my personality—my humanity, including all its weaknesses.

Throughout the winter of 1958 I worked on the novel. I was living at my mother's house and I used to work ten or twelve hours a day, typing and writing, on no particular schedule. If I woke up in the middle of the night and had some ideas I wanted to put on paper I would do so. By the time the summer of 1959 came around the first draft was finished and I had begun to tire of the novel. It was a good year's work.

While writing my novel, I started going out with Mildred Thompson, whom I married in the fall of 1959. We had met each other one Sunday evening when I visited my old church, Coppin Chapel. Our families knew each other and were active together in the affairs of the church. By the fall of 1959 I knew I was definitely going South in the near future to build a revolutionary youth organization and to write about the struggle of black people as I participated in it. I was lonely during that period and agreed to our marriage. Later we were divorced. Today we are the closest of friends. After my divorce from Mildred, I married my present wife, Constancia Romilly, an active revolutionary who is the mother of my two sons.

Since I had to have some method of earning a living and some entrée into the South, I enrolled at Chicago Teacher's College in the fall of 1959 to earn enough hours in education so that I could teach. My plan was to work for one or two years and then go South. I intended to go with my wife. We had no children and did not plan to; it was my feeling that, if a person had cut a pattern of revolutionary life for himself, he could not assume such responsibilities. I loved children, but that did not mean that I had to have them, and certainly not to satisfy an ego desire for "immortality."

I taught school during the spring of 1960, worked as a supervisor on the census team of an area in South Chicago, and took courses at the University of Chicago in French. My interest in Africa had not died, although I had decided that it was first more important to build a movement inside the United States, and the program at Boston University had convinced me that I should learn French. It was spoken in many parts of Africa and I wanted to travel there one day.

That summer I went to the eight-week French Summer School at Middlebury College in Vermont on a scholarship. Events in the world were moving fast. I watched the drama in the Congo from a distance and wished I were there helping Lumumba. In Chicago and Los Angeles, respectively, groups of students had come to the Republican and Democratic conventions and presented their demands. These were youths from the Student Nonviolent Coordinating Committee, just a few months old then and an outgrowth of the sit-ins.

One night during the time when I was writing my novel, I had a nightmare. Awoken by it, I got up and wrote out the dream; later I was able to use it in the novel. Paul, who in the novel had been in the Navy, had the following dream:

He was on a ship taking a test to become a shop supervisor. He had to drop a line into a small hole and reach an object. Through the hole he saw swiftly flowing water. As he dropped the line, it occurred to him that there was no way of really determining whether or not he reached the object. He felt that since he was a Negro all the odds were against him.

His line did not bring up the object. Then a white sailor stepped up to the hole and brought out something that looked like a propeller. One of his shipmates, also a white, came up then and told him to hurry off the ship. Escape or be killed. He ducked through the passageway and ran across the gangplank, stepping onto a narrow path.

He ran downhill and heard a tremendous roar behind him. He looked over his head and saw small pieces of black coal, about the size of ice cubes, rolling rapidly after him. Behind the coals he saw a white mist that covered the path and seemed to be in flight after the coals. The mist became visible. He saw white faces. The coals began to roll past him. As they approached him, they turned into the faces of black people. He stretched out his arms and cried, "Brothers! Stop! Stop this frantic runaway!"

He formed a barricade with his arms and some of the coals could not get past. And they began to listen as they watched the approaching white mist. He shouted, "Resistance! Resistance!" The fight was on. He pushed the coals up the hill, and, while doing this, they gradually pushed him to the forefront. Together they began to push back the white mist in which were discernible white faces.

The struggle of Sisyphus began, but the coals did not seem to give way. Their struggles and advancement were painful, but slowly they pushed the white mist up the hill. They saw light at the top of the mountain. It was like the light that shone into the cave of Plato's *Republic*. They saw the light but their backs were still straining to reach the top.

Then the white mist turned into a huge white rat. Someone gave Paul a stick of dynamite and he crawled along the side of the path, out of the sight of the rat. The rat stood there, hunched on his front legs with a terrifying grin. Its rear end seemed to have been inflated.

The coals were afraid to move. They could not understand this monster which had taken the place of the white mist. They kept their eyes on the rat in order to divert its attention from Paul, who had found a path just below the ridge. He emerged behind the rat. He lit the stick of dynamite. He shoved it hard into the rat's ass. He jumped over into the ravine. As he was falling, unaware of where he would land, he heard a loud pow yow! Down and down he went, his body became lighter and lighter. At last he landed softly in the water.

Paul woke up saying, "If only it were possible!"

On February 1, 1960, the student sit-in movement began to sweep the South. History was enacting what I had advocated in the novel. Now it was useless to talk of publishing my book; once again, fiction had been behind reality. I never regretted doing the novel, for it gave me the chance to clarify many of my ideas and to unburden myself of many conflicts. It was all down there on paper, the suffering, the hope, the plan. It was only left for me to write the ending with my own life in the South.

When I returned to Chicago from Middlebury in the fall of 1960, the mountain was waiting for me. I went to work on behalf of a group of evicted sharecroppers in Fayette County, Tennessee, a few miles from my childhood home, and I thought: It just might be possible.

CHAPTER 15

Georgia Mae Hard Times

GEORGIA MAE Turner sat on the bed, getting ready to go to sleep. She slept in her clothes: a raggedy dress, slip, underclothes, socks, a tattered, lightweight jacket. It was cold and damp outside. In the tent a wood stove gave off heat in its immediate vicinity but did not warm other areas. During the night, when the fire went down, Georgia Mae would become very cold. Chilly air blew in through loose pockets of the tent, mostly around the bottom where the canvas wasn't fastened tightly. It was Christmas night, 1960.

Georgia Mae glanced down at her two-year-old grandson, Little Man, who slept next to her in the bed. Ordinarily she would not be going to sleep at this hour, 10:30 P.M., but she was tired. Two days before she had moved all her belongings—including the large bed—away from the McNamee plantation and onto the tent ground. She was one of seven hundred families of sharecroppers who had been evicted for registering to vote. With some of these other families, she now lived in Tent City, Fayette County, Tennessee.

When she had first come there, she had to tromp-tromp down the large grass. Then she put down some heavy cardboard for a floor, which mixed with the mud of the thawing ground. After the men erected her tent, she worked hard to straighten out her belongings and put them in place. Georgia Mae was used to hard work and her hands looked like a man's from years of heavy labor. Hard work did not bother her, it was the other things—being put out of your home, the home you had for thirty-eight years, the same house you called home for all those many years, and being put out because you registered to vote.

Georgia Mae was a tall woman, not thin and not fat, with a smooth, dark skin. Sitting now in the dim light of a kerosene lamp, Georgia Mae Turner began talking about her life in Fayette County. I had a tape recorder along, and these are her words:

I first was with Mr. Emmett McNamee. That was our boss-man. He rented the McNeil place. He kept us on the McNeil place until I became of age. We worked and we lived on the McNeil place so long till people began to think we belonged to him.

Oh, the good times when he was living! When we didn't make any money, we would go to him, tell him about conditions, and he'd help. He was good to us. He was a widower and he never remarried. He would treat me just as nice as, or better, than our own people. Like he would give us money to get somebody to haul some wood. Well, we wouldn't hire nobody to haul wood. We'd haul the wood ourselves. Ain't never had to hire nobody to help us to get no work done.

Mr. Emmett stick by us with the fever—the typhoid-malaria fever. He would come every day bringing us tomato juice, soup, apples, all kind of fruit, and see after us. Him and the doctor was the only thing that come in and out of the house. That was back around World War I—and I was about nine then. We lost all of our peoples. Lost five brothers, all the brothers I had. The typhoid-malaria killed my brothers, one sister-in-law and my sister's baby. Every three weeks there was a casket going out of my home. I didn't know I was living.

The fever left me, my mother, and three other womenfolk. My father, I didn't see him until I was nineteen. He left my mother when I was young. Stayed away until I was grown, then came home to die at my sister's home. I started working in the fields when I was eight. I been working fifty years. I chopped sorghum, corn, cotton, chopped anything. And I picked. When I first started picking cotton, I couldn't pick but fifty pounds a day, but I kept inching up higher. I started plowing when I was fourteen years old 'cause we didn't have no man. I had to do all that plowing and that rough work to make a living. I have taken an axe and cut wood from about seven o'clock in the morning until it gets dark in the evening. You oughta see the logs that I've hauled.

I could hear the bell ring every morning at five o'clock for you to get up and go feed your mules. I'd be up cooking breakfast when that bell rang. Then they ring it a second time and you go to the fields. You better be there at that hour. Then they'd ring the bell at twelve o'clock for you to come in to dinner and ring the bell at one to go back. You didn't need nobody to ring it for you in the evening.

My mother did all she could. Some days we had something to eat, some days we didn't. I remember on many days we have went to the blackberry bushes and picked berries off the bushes and taken them berries and washed them and mashed them up and get some corn bread and crumble them up in a bowl, eat them for dinner. Then go back to the field. Plow a mule until sundown.

Sometimes I would be sick and if you was sick you had to work just the same. You go to them for a doctor. "Unh–uh, I can't furnish you with no doctor. I can't furnish you with no doctor." You had to be just as low as you could be to get a doctor. Now that's the truth.

I knowed the time when we didn't have light. We had to burn a stump. You know, you clean up new ground and the old stuff done died and it's just settling there. When it gets warm along about April, you go down and light that stump, and that stump would burn there for weeks at a time. That way you have fire —you go there every evening and get you some light. Make fire in the stove, in a lamp. That's all we had to study by, we never did have no other lights in the house.

I knowed the time my mother would take the cotton sacks that we picked cotton in and make me dresses. She would go get bark off the Wonder Tree and take that bark and put it in the pot and boil it and take the sack and put it in there. It would be purple when she took it out. Then I'd have a dress to go to school.

First school I went to was Green Walker, old man Green Walker. It wasn't no rooms, just one long building like this tent. I had about five miles to walk to school. We couldn't go but one month in the winter and one month in the summer each year. In the summertime, we would have to stop to pull fodder and then sell it. In the wintertime, we could hardly get no clothes to wear to school. Come a rain, we didn't have a coat. We would go sometimes two days, maybe three days in a week.

We come home in the evening and wash our dresses at night for the next day. Sometimes I go and wear Mama's dress. Mama weighed two hundred. You know about how I was looking! I used to go to school and they laughed at me. But you would tell them right straight, you going to tell their mama on them if they laugh, and they be whipped.

I made it to the fifth grade. I think I done well to make it that high. I can write a little and read a little. I learned how to count. I can count money— I can count more than I can get! We had a right good teacher. He would whip you and make you learn. When you made it to the eighth grade, you would take an examination and they would get you to teaching school. I always thought couldn't nobody go to teach but the big shots, so I didn't go on in school. If I just had half the education some people got, I'd be something. I got my mother's wit. I remember I was the best speaker. I could say speeches, dialogues. I used to be the speaking girl, they would send me far and near to speak. I never was afraid to get up and say what I knew. And I am that way today.

I felt religion when I was fifteen years old. We used to have a prayer meeting every Wednesday night, have Sunday School every Sunday. I prayed and prayed. I couldn't hardly get my religion, I was hard to believe. I cried mercy until I could hear mercy. When I would go to sleep, I could hear mercy. Crying in the building, "Have mercy, Lord, have mercy."

Somewhere in the cold night, a hound dog sat on his haunches and howled. Georgia Mae pulled Little Man closer to her. The wind blew harder against the large tents bought at an Army surplus store. Eight of them stood like tombstones to freedom in the dark Tennessee night, swaying back and forth in the wind. On the paved road running along the embankment where the tents stood, an occasional car passed by. I wondered how many of the people in those cars knew anything about the life of a Georgia Mae Turner.

Mr. Emmett McNamee, we minded him so good that he decided to buy a place of his own and take us along. He bought the old Chase place and moved us there from the McNeil place. We lived on the old Chase place thirty-eight years. He said to my mother, he said, "Mandy, you have a home here as long as you live." He did for us as long as he lived. If Mr. Emmett would put too much on us, I would tell him. I didn't tell him in no mad way. I'd go there and tell him, "Now, Mr. Emmett, I can't do such and such a thing 'cause you putting more on me than I can stand." Well, then he didn't put that on me.

He knowed me. I remember the time when me and my husband separated. My husband had hit me and blackened my eye. I went up and Mr. Emmett said, "Georgia, did he put that scar on your head?"

I said, "Yes, sir."

He said, "Well, you tell him don't put another track on my place."

I said, "Well, now listen. Now, that's my husband. We just got to fighting, you know. I'm mean, and he's mean too. I know he done wrong, but I want you to have mercy on him."

Mr. Emmett said, "Well, do you want him to come on home?"

"Yes, sir. I want him to come on home."

He said, "Well, I don't have nothing to do with it then."

After Mr. Emmett died, we fell to his brother, Harry McNamee. Mr. Emmett had told him to do by us just like he did. But Mr. Harry said we owed him twenty-two hundred dollars.

We went to work and worked and worked and worked on the debt. That's why we stayed there so long, I reckon, trying to pay that debt. I put one of my girls picking cotton when she was four years old. She picked thirty pounds of cotton. She tells me now I put her in the field so young, I worked her spirits down. She ain't got much spirit now to work.

"Georgia Mae, it's an honest debt and I want to pay it," my mother said.

"But, Mama. I'm tired of working on that debt. . . . You go up there and ask them for some shoes."

She went up there and Mr. Harry said, "Old girl, you got to go back and pick up all that cotton before you get anything." We had to go back in those old raggedy pieces of shoes in the cold and finish picking every bit of that cotton. That's the way it was every year. Then you go up there after it was picked and they would give you so much cloth to make you a dress or a shirt or something like that. Sometimes we get a sack of flour for Christmas. We stayed there and worked there and paid that twenty-two hundred dollar debt. . . .

One day my mother just set down and could never get back up. She couldn't work any more. Fifteen years my mother sat down in my house. She had nothing but me and my little children. And you know, God got a reward somewhere in Glory for me because she weighed two hundred and something, and I had to lift her from place to place. My little self. I got in bad health from lifting my mother.

Then she said one day, "Tomorrow I'm leaving you all at twelve o'clock."

"Mama," I said. "How do you know? You don't know when you are going."

"Yes," she said. "I'm leaving you tomorrow at twelve."

The next day, I caught myself going to make her laugh at what she had said. She was laughing and talking and at fifteen minutes to twelve, I said, "Mama, it's fifteen minutes to twelve."

"Yes," she replied.

Well, she talked on and five minutes after I said that, she was sick as she could be. At twelve o'clock she was dead just like she said. And she talked until she died.

"Georgia," she said, "death is straightening out my limbs. The blood is stopping and it feels like a cold, chilly stream. Take the pillow out from under my head, Georgia. Take care of the children. It won't be long now. My tongue is getting stiff now. Take the pillow out from under my head."

Georgia Mae rose from her bed and went to a box, walking with a slight stoop. She pulled out an old overcoat that had been sent to Tent City by some supporters in the North and put it on. Then she reached under the bed, pulled out a small can, took a dip of snuff, and pulled up a chair by the stove. She put in another piece of wood and sat back in the chair.

Nothing in her kindly face suggested any bitterness about the twenty-two hundred dollar debt, which was not—in fact—an honest debt. It was a typical example of white cheating under the system of share-cropping, a modified form of feudalism.

Every year, the landlord would advance the sharecropper some money to buy seed and to live on from spring to late summer. In the fall accounts would be settled. He would deduct what he had advanced from the sale value of the cotton harvested, together with the cost of any items he had sold to the person. It was not unusual for the sharecropper to end up in debt—according to the boss-man—after working all year. For example, Cora Lee Avant, another resident of Fayette County, picked thirty-one bales of cotton in one year. At approximately $175 a bale, the total sale amounted to $5,425. The landlord took his half, leaving a balance of $2,712 for Cora Lee. But by the time he deducted what she had bought at his store—according to his records—she owed him $221.

In Mandy's case, she owed $100 for a mule—plus interest which piled up over the years, since it was determined by the boss. The boll weevils kept attacking all of Mandy's crops, while the boss-man added other bills to her debt. Thus the $100 became $2,200. Mandy and Georgia Mae had to bear all the losses for the crops they planted in bad years, but if the crops had been good, they would have had to split the profits. For the boss-man, sharecropping meant sharing in the profits but not the losses. For Georgia Mae, it meant permanent indebtedness and perpetual begging. Semislavery is the best word for it.

My baby girl was just a baby when Mama died. I didn't have no shoes. Came a lot of rain.

"Mr. McNamee," I said, "I want to get some shoes."

"Unh-uh," he said. "You can't get them."

"I got to have some shoes," I said. "My baby is young. I can't go to work out there in that field without no shoes."

"I can't let you have none, old girl. Not until you get through picking that cotton. Can't let you have 'em."

Wouldn't let me have no shoes. I went back up the street. I was crying. I went into another man's store, which was Mr. Martin. I sat down. I guess I was pitiful looking. "You around trying to get you something, ain't you?" he said to me.

"Yah, sir. I went down there to try to get me some shoes. He wouldn't even let me have none."

"Wouldn't let you have a bit of shoes?"

"Unh-uh, sir. He didn't."

He got up and didn't say anything to me. He went back there and got a pair of his slippers and gave them to me. And I wore them slippers all the winter long, snow and everything. I didn't have but one pair of slippers. So after we got through picking cotton, the boss-man sent for us to come up to give us some little old thing. I wouldn't even go.

It was bad and it's bad now, but not like it was back in old-time slavery, real slavery. My grandmother said in her lifetime they would take fine children and stand them on blocks and sell them. Why, they would take them to far places and you don't know where some of them was. She said they would work them until twelve o'clock. Those that had babies, they would let them go home at ten o'clock and nurse the babies. If they stayed overtime, they would get a whipping.

My grandmother said they never did sell her. She said they would let them off every Sunday morning. They had about twenty-five or thirty miles to go to see their people. They had to be back by sunset. They would go up there and stay and by sunset they would be walking and running on their way back to the boss.

Grandmother once said there was a talkative slave on the plantation. Said he went down to the field one day and there was an old skull laying down there. Say he took the old skull and took his foot and kicked it. And said, "What are you doing down there?" And it said, "Tongue and teeth brought me here and tongue and teeth going to bring you here." He lit out to the house and told the old boss. You know you couldn't tell the boss no story then. You tell him a story, and he could cut your hand off. He said, "Boss, I found a skull down there and he told me tongue and teeth brought him there and tongue and teeth going to bring me there."

The old boss said, "No, it didn't, John."

"Yes, it did."

"Well, let's go down there," the old boss man said. They went down there and saw the old skull. John walked up and kicked it like he did and it didn't say nothing. Boss said, "Now, John. You see you lied. Now I told you that if you ever lied, I would cut your head off."

He laid John's head down and cut it off and the old skull said, "I told you tongue and teeth were going to bring you here."

My grandmother said once there was a man, he was so lazy. People say, "John is so lazy we going to take him out and bury him alive."

A man said, "Don't go down there and bury him alive. I'll give him a bushel of corn."

John raised up and said, "Shelled?"

Man said, "Naw, it ain't shelled."

"Drive on, boys," John said.

Went to the next house. Man said, "Where you going with that poor man?"

They said, "Going to bury him alive."

Man said, "Don't bury him alive. I'll give you a sack of flour and some molasses."

John said, "Is it here?"

Man said, "Naw, you have to go and get it."

John said, "Drive me on, boys."

Got to another home. They said, "We'll give him some peas."

John said, "Is the peas shelled?"

They said, "Naw, but you can shell them."

John said, "Drive on boys." They carried him on to the graveyard. John was so lazy they buried him alive.

Grandmother used to say their overseer would beat them so bad. When the old boss went home and left the overseer, all of them got him and throwed him in a great big fire. Well, they killed that overseer. Yes, they killed him. They got tired. The slaves on the old McNeil place killed one of the overseers and nothing happened to them. Old man McNeil came around asking about him, but none of the niggers would tell.

My grandmother was singing that song one day, "Thank God Almighty. I'm free at last. I'm free at last. I'm free at last. Thank God Almighty, I'm free at last. I'm free at last." Old Miss said, "Never you mind, you nasty talking heifer. We know you free." My grandmother say that's the first thing she ever knowed about the slaves being freed.

The wind blew harder and harder over Tent City. All the tents were dark now except two. One was Georgia Mae's; the other, which stood next in line, housed one of her daughters and her son-in-law—Early B. Williams. He had lived on another plantation and had to move, too, when he registered. His wife was pregnant again and he didn't know how he was going to find some work. I imagined that he and his wife were probably talking about their problems. Georgia Mae went on with her story.

When Mr. Harry McNamee died, the place fell to his wife—Mrs. Ethel McNamee. She used to call me, want me to come up to the house and work. Regardless of what I was doing, I would lay it aside and go there and work. Sometimes she would give me a dollar or give me some clothes the moths done ate holes in. I would take it and go on. I didn't say a word but take it and go on home. But when I got home I'd say, "She could have kept these old clothes."

She used to tell me so often, "Georgia, I love you. Ya'll is nice and I loves ya'll. Mandy had some good-raised children. We don't have to come there to see if ya'll working or not, because we know ya'll will work."

I would make my boys mind her and stay under her care, just like she was their mother. She would often give us something. She and her sister would give us something every year. It wasn't a year passed they didn't give us all the Christmas greetings they got. You know, people would send them greetings and after Christmas they would give them to us. And we would take them and put them in our house. They gave us all their newspapers. They would give us hangers. They said they did the best they could by us. Well, I guess they did the best they could.

I paid Mrs. McNamee every dime I owed her and got my clear receipt. I worked for my food when I stayed with her. I raised my hogs, raised my chickens, raised my peas, my corn, sweet potatoes, anything that you could call in the eating line. And I had cows—I raised all my meat. She didn't furnish you with nothing during the wintertime. Thirty dollars a month she would give us, from March until August. Then she would stop furnishing it in August, and she didn't pick up until the next March.

This tent is better than my house with Mrs. McNamee. Lord, so many cracks in that house, you could shake hands with me anytime. You didn't have to come to the door to do it, just walk right up to any crack and shake hands with me. When it rained, it would be wet all over the house, the hall, the porch, and the kitchen. It would be just like I done scoured. You couldn't keep a snake or nothing out of that house; cats, dogs, you couldn't keep them out at night.

The chimney go right up through the top of my house. When it was cold, the wind would blow through that house just like it do out of doors. Sometimes I would put all kinds of raggedy clothes on to try to keep warm in that house. Couldn't take a bath in the winter. How can you strip off in the house, and be just as naked as a bluebird, and the wind blowing in there, and you cold and shivering, and can't keep warm with your clothes on? Anyway, you got nowhere to take a bath at. Had to draw water by rope in my house. Didn't have no pump or nothing like that.

I'd go to my boss-lady, "Mrs. McNamee, would you put me up a chimney?"

"Nah," she said, "I'm not able to put a chimney to your house."

"Yes'm," I'd say and go on. I wouldn't say nothing else about it. That was my boss-lady and I always was raised to treat her nice. When you were raised to a thing . . . I just can't help but say, "Yes'm" and "No'm" to every white person I see. I don't think they have no right to have nothing against me 'cause I've tried to treat all of them nice. I just don't believe a colored person would run over a white for nothing. But I'll say this about any person, let him be white or colored. If you up, and you don't want to help me because you're up, you may not be up always 'cause the Lord got a hand in that . . . .

And they wouldn't even build me a barn. I went myself to ask her to build me a barn. She said she couldn't furnish nobody a barn. I went around and asked the other friends to help me build my barn and they come and help me build a barn. She said, "Well, Georgia, I'll furnish you the nails if you can get the barn built." I got that barn built free of charge and she wouldn't even pay a dime to have it built.

You should have seen Mrs. McNamee's house—oh, so pretty! She had gold lamps in her den and in her den she got a great big lion on the floor. He lay curled up in the middle of the floor. Got a rug that deep. Come over your feet, you know. Just soft and pretty. She took me in all her rooms, and let me see all her pretty what-she-haves. Her and her daughter, the only ones that stay there.

I felt like what she had was hers, and what I had was mine. I would just go on back and never think about what she did. Then I'd get home, I'd have some second thoughts. She never put a plank on my house. She said she was going to build a fireplace; she never did do that. I asked her about it in the fall and she said, "Georgia, I can't do nothing." I felt sorry for her when she dropped her head.

Even if we got sick or something, you couldn't get her to help you. Better not ask her to take you to the doctor, even if you had the money to pay her for the trip. No, my boss-lady ain't putting many folks in her car, not colored people. You couldn't get in that car. She would change it every year. And she told me she had the prettiest car on the road. She took me out there and showed it to me, got inside of it, just showing it, making light of me. . . .

I'll tell the truth on my boss-lady. She was good to me until I registered to vote. She would help me with my children through the winter. She would help me every winter, if I didn't make nothing. In August, if I didn't have food, she would let me have it. She wouldn't let the men have it, but I could go and get the food until I registered.

Georgia Mae Turner began to cry. She cried not only because she had lost her home. She cried because she did not understand her boss-lady. Didn't understand how a woman like that could put another woman off the land, take away her home of thirty-eight years—all because she went down to register.

It might seem that Georgia Mae should have been more angry than sorrowful, more indignant than puzzled. But she had lived an isolated life on a farm in the Deep South. Her world had been one of white people in power, white people saying do this and don't do that, a world where the mere fact of whiteness meant power and there could be no question about it. Then there was her religion with its white God and his white son, Jesus. And the white Christian doctrine that in the next world all bad people get their due while the Georgia Maes will inherit the earth. Georgia Mae's religion conditioned her to accept what had been imposed. She was trapped by isolation, by religion, and by the crushing, cheating white world.

The act of registering to vote began to change the world of the Georgia Mae Turners in 1960. The price is high for all acts of rebellion and Georgia Mae had paid dearly for hers.

I heard about the registering long about last May or June. I didn't want to register then, 'cause if I registered then, she would have cut off my check. Mrs. McNamee told my brother-in-law not to go and mess with that mess. So I didn't register until August—got my last check along then. All of them were registering and I wanted to, too. If all the colored people going to be drowned but one, I'd rather drown too. I didn't want to be there amongst the white and there ain't but one colored. I was the first one in my family that broke the ice, the rest followed suit.

I had a hard time after I registered. I went to her and asked for ten dollars one day. "Mrs. McNamee," I said.

"Huh?"

"Will you let me have ten dollars to get some groceries with?"

"Nah, I can't do it."

"You can't let me have no money to get me no groceries? Mrs. McNamee, I have to work out something with you. I got to get me some groceries."

"Ya'll just have to work out something someplace else to get some money to buy some food. We ain't got no money, Georgia, you hear."

I picked all week until Friday with hardly nothing to eat. Then Saturday I went to pick for some money on Mr. Robert's place. I picked 159 pounds of cotton by dinner. And white folks say we lazy.

This last crop, she told me I owed her six hundred dollars. Mind you, I guess I got six checks, thirty dollars each, between March and August and about a hundred dollars above that. I spoke to her about it and I said, "It don't look like to me that I ought to owe you that much."

"You been settling off by my figures. Why can't you settle off by them now?"

"Guess I have to settle off by them, you the one handling them. But it seems to me, Mrs. McNamee, you done run the figures up 'cause I went down and registered."

"That ain't it, Georgia. This is what you owe me."

"Yes'm."

Then later on she sent me word that I would have to move. I didn't take that. Further on, I went down to see her.

"Mrs. McNamee, I came to see you. I got a word. I don't know whether it was right or wrong, but I came to see you . . ."

"What was it, Georgia?"

"I don't know. Ethel was telling me something you said." Ethel is my eldest daughter.

"Yes. I said that you and Ethel would have to move."

"Yes'm . . . Well, Mrs. McNamee, I thank you for what you did for me. You have been good to me up until now. Now you're putting me outdoors."

"Yes, Georgia. You will have to move. You got from now until the first day of January to move . . ."

She made me get out of her house in the snow. I had to get out before winter was even over. That was the first time I knowed her to fool with anything. Somebody told her to do that. Now, I talked to Mr. Leavenworth and he said they all signed a bill that if the colored people registered, they would have to move. I said to him, "If I harmed you all, how did I do it? Would you tell me?"

He said, "Well, Georgia, I'll explain it to you. You didn't, in a way. But we been registering for forty years without you all, and I don't see why you all had to register."

I said, "I ain't got nowhere to move to."

He said, "Naw, you ain't. You ain't got nowhere in Fayette County to go. The next one going to turn you down. You going to have a hard time."

Well, he near about told the truth, you know.

Georgia Mae got up and put some spare wood in the stove. She came back to her bed, bent her knees and prayed. "Lord, I ain't holding nothing in me against her because I'm striving to make heaven my home. I'm bowing down in the morning. Yes, I'm crying in the evening. Lord, I know I got to love everybody. I can't hate nobody. She did me wrong, Lord, but I don't hate her for it. I'm on my way, Lord. And I don't see nothing to turn me back. I'm on my way, pressing forward every day, all the time. Forgive her, Lord, and give me strength to carry on." Then she stopped praying and began to talk again.

It worries me so that I don't have a home. Sometimes I get off and look back at the tents, I can't help but cry. But I thank the Lord to have one for shelter. You know, it's better than nothing. I love the tents sometimes, and I hate them sometimes! I'm just going to get out of here one of these days. If I was to get me a house—just a house—I don't know what I would do.

Sometimes I wish I had a brother. It would be a consolation for me, sometimes to take my troubles there and talk it over with him. I didn't have no brother, no father. Husband—yes, I had one of them. He went off and left us.

Some men are just too jealous-hearted. Can't stand to see you talking to no other man, least that's what they say. I ain't never took up too much time with fellows. I would always have me one, then he wouldn't do right. I would put him down and wouldn't even think about it. Now I'm too old. But I would like to have one to talk with, joke, play, and go on with them.

They say if you register, you going to have a hard time. Well, I had a hard time before I registered. Hard times, you could have named me that—Georgia Mae Hard Times. The reason I registered, because I want to be a citizen. Mr. Ferdie Franklin told me I had as much right to register and vote as anybody else. This here is a free country, that's what he told me. I registered so that my children could get their freedom. I don't figure it would do me no good.

I registered for my children so they won't have to stand around at the back door like I stood in the rain and cold and Mrs. McNamee sat in the front until she got ready to come to the back to see what I wanted. I'd stand there and look up. Sometimes I'd be so cold, I'd be shivering and sometimes she would come there and talk to me through the screen and I would still be in the cold. I come over hard times; I come over hills and mountains. I wouldn't want none of my children, none of my friends, to have to come through it—run, rocking and rolling, over the hills and mountains that I come over.

Georgia Mae leaned over her grandson and stroked his head. "I tell you, child," she whispered. "I done made up my mind. I'm ready to go down right here on this tent ground. Not for my sake. I'm too old. That won't do me no good. But for yours. I'm ready to go down, down right here on this tent ground. For you, Little Man."

It was well after midnight, and I left Georgia Mae to her rest in the cold, silent tent.

Two nights later, at five minutes of twelve, a shot rang out over Tent City and struck the tent of Georgia Mae's son-in-law, Early B. Williams.

That evening there had been a meeting of the Fayette County Civic and Welfare League, a group of black farmers who were fighting desperately against the White Citizens' Council. Because they dared to register and to vote in the United States in 1959-60, seven hundred sharecropping families in Fayette and Haywood counties found themselves evicted from lands where they had lived and farmed for decades. Black farmers found themselves unable to purchase groceries, medical supplies, and gasoline (vital to those who had tractors) or to obtain crop loans to buy seed and fertilizers for anticipated harvests. Local clinics refused to give medical treatment. Anyone on the council's blacklist (let's change that word to *whitelist*) was subjected to a total boycott by the white people who ran the banks and owned most of the stores.

Not only did the merchants organized in the White Citizens' Council want to drive out the Tennessee blacks who registered and to frighten those who had not yet registered, they also intended to preserve Mississippi as a bastion of white supremacy. Fayette and Haywood counties adjoin the Mississippi state line; the crackers knew it was only a matter of time before ferment and change would come to that state too. At stake was political power as well as the maintenance of a feudal economic structure which included sharecropping. The situation presented a crucial test of strength.

The Fayette County Civic and Welfare League was meeting in back of the store of John McFerren, located about two miles from the tents and about fifty miles east of Memphis. McFerren was president of the league. Shepard Towles, who had given the land for Tent City, was also present at the meeting. I had been invited as a member of the Emergency Relief Committee that was sending food, clothing, and medical supplies from Chicago to Tent City.

The league officers had almost finished a strategy discussion when the telephone hanging on the cafteria wall rang. Shepard Towles went to answer it.

"Shot!" he cried out after listening a second. All the farmers who had been sitting around the table rose at the same moment. They guessed immediately that the shooting had been at the tents. "It's Early B. Williams," Towles said.

McFerren grabbed two pump repeater rifles from behind the counter and checked his pistol. In front of the store, men started up their cars. Shotguns and pistols were brought out from behind the seats. Click, clack, click, clack. The men were ready. I joined McFerren in his car.

McFerren led the line of cars rushing through the night at eighty, ninety miles an hour. Taking a sharp curve without slowing down, he said to me, "This baby can go. Faster than this, too. . . . They caught us sleeping tonight. Know we should have put up that defense guard earlier. But the mother fuckers won't be coming back, I betcha."

In less than five minutes, they arrived at the tent site. Black men with guns, guns, and more guns were deployed around the tents, on the side of the road, behind bushes, and in the fields. Others rushed inside Early B. Williams's tent. Georgia Mae Turner was also there.

Early B. had received a flesh wound in the shoulder, fired from a passing car. It was not serious, but he needed hospital treatment immediately —and that meant driving to Memphis, fifty miles away. His wife, who was acting very calmly, wanted to go along but was urged to remain with their young ones. "Don't worry, child," Georgia Mae said. "I'll stay with you to take care of things."

McFerren put Early B. in the back of his car and we started for Memphis with another well-armed car following. With the men on guard back at the tents, McFerren could relax a little. He began talking about his wife Viola and the time six months ago when he had to drive her all the way to Memphis to give birth to their youngest child because his political activity had made it certain that the baby would not be delivered by the nearby white doctor. She had been very frightened when he first got involved, and so he didn't tell her about his work. When the program was fully developed, he was up front and there could be no more hiding. His wife, expecting a third child, tried again and again to dissuade him. She even said that she would divorce him if he kept going. He knew it had been hard for her. A price of two thousand dollars had been placed on his head; there were plans to kill him, threatening telephone calls all night long, people driving by their house. Often he came home very late from meetings. She would tell him how she had gone to bed at nine o'clock, slept until eleven, and then remained awake until three o'clock in the morning. When she tried to talk him out of his work, he hardly answered her or just said, "We'll make it somehow." There was nothing else he could do, and finally she accepted it. She worked with him and helped him now.

The lights of Memphis came up on the horizon and we reached Memphis General Hospital. Our group waited three hours in a segregated waiting room before Early B. Williams was treated. Reporters and police were all over the place. On the drive back to Tent City, dawn broke and it was seven o'clock in the morning when we reached the site. A television crew from NBC was waiting to catch "the story."

A week later, I went to talk to Georgia Mae again and record her account of what had happened at the tents after the shooting. This is what she said:

Right after the shooting, they called the sheriff. The sheriff came thirty minutes later. He and another man were looking at where the bullet came through. The sheriff said to the other man, "Looks like it was shot from the inside."

"Naw," the man said, "It wasn't shot from the inside because if it had been shot from the inside, the cloth would have been pushed out from the inside. This cloth is pushed from the outside."

The sheriff said, "Yeah, yeah, sho' is."

The next morning, lots of different white people come to ask questions. "Were you asleep?" "Were you awake?" "Who do you feel did it?"

I said, "I just feel like it was someone that didn't want us in the tents and was trying to run us off the place. They were shooting to run us out of Fayette County. That's what I feel. I feel like it was some white people."

That was on Wednesday night, the shooting. Thursday night, we sat up all night long. We didn't go to sleep. We was still looking for someone to shoot in. Didn't nobody shoot in Thursday night.

Friday night we sat up too. Long about five minutes after twelve—this time they made it five minutes later—a car came through with a great noise in the west. After a while, twenty or thirty-five minutes, they came back shooting. It was just like a war that night. Laying flat down on the ground and everything. They say our people shot back. I don't know whether they was or not, I couldn't tell which way the shots were going. I just heard shots. After the shooting, we kept quiet for a long time. We didn't hear nobody hollering. After a while, people commenced to move around.

The next morning, old reporters came there. I never saw a reporter before.

You tell them one thing and they go out and say something you never said. You lazy and don't work and all such junk as that.

One man, he wasn't a reporter, said he would give me a home. He had a place down there where they wanted forty hands. That wasn't nowhere else but a penal farm. You know, a man that come way up in the year wanting forty hands—my common sense told me there was something wrong with the place. I told him, "I wish you would leave me alone and not hunt me a home." He was about to worry me to death. I said, "Well, where are you from?"

He said, "I'm from Memphis."

I said, "Well, you ought to stay in Memphis." I was tired of looking at him.

A man said he was from the FBI. There was another man with him, a mean man. He talked so mean. He came on in and he asked us, "Say, Auntie, what is all this shooting going on out here for?"

I said, "I don't know."

He say, "You hear it?"

I said, "Yes, sir. I heard it."

"What you doing woke that time of night?"

I said, "What time was it?"

Then he said, "Who was shooting?"

"I don't know."

"You didn't go to the door and look?"

"Nah, I didn't go to the door. What I look like, going sticking my head out and they shooting at me?"

Then he said, "Well, what you doing woke at that time of night?"

"What do rabbits stay 'wake for? To see who's coming through to shoot 'em and kill 'em. That's the way it was with me. I stayed woke to try to see who was coming through to shoot me so I could dodge like a rabbit."

"Well, what did you say when they was shooting?"

"I stuck my head out from under the edge of the bed and said 'Lord have mercy, save me Jesus.' That's what I said."

"You weren't scared, were you?"

"Yes, I was scared. Wouldn't you have been scared?"

"Naw, them was blanks."

"Well, if a blank going in and kill you, I'm scared of a blank. A blank shot my son-in-law, went through his arm."

He said to me, the mean man, "You reckon somebody up here doing the shooting?"

I said, "I'm going to tell you the truth! I don't know who done it."

"Well, what do you think—do you think white done it or colored?"

"I think the white done it. 'Cause I figured like this—I ain't done nothing to no colored people and ain't done nothing to no white people. They just asked us off their place, and I moved off and then they came shooting in the tents to kill some of us and run the others off. That's the way I feel about it."

He never said nothing when I said that. Then he asked me, "You right sure they were white?"

"Naw, I ain't going to say they were white. Ain't no need of you trying to get me tell no story. I don't know what color they was. But I tell you one thing, if they was blanks—I'm scared of 'em. I ain't got nothing against nobody, and I can't see why they would have nothing against me. I always did mind them. I work harder than they work."

Then I said another thing. I said, "I'm 'pending on the Lord. White people think they got all the power, but they haven't." That mean man, he soon got his hat and went on out the tent, and started asking somebody else questions.

You know, people like that—they can't turn me around. You can drown this old body but you can't harm my soul. I gone too far. I'm too old. I come down too many roads and I dug deep. You know what I got? I got gold. It shines in dark places.

CHAPTER 16

Forgetting the People

WHEN I was asked to work on the Chicago campaign to send food and clothing to Fayette County, it was as though many things fell into place at once. I knew that if the White Citizens' Council was successful in driving people off the land there, it would be most difficult to build any type of movement in Mississippi—the state which interested me the most. Fighting the council appealed to me also because of my general belief that those crackers in business suits should not be allowed to go on trampling people. An organized, mass response was needed, and Fayette could be a focal point for this.

Fayette raised other important issues. Although the immediate struggle concerned the right to vote, economic exploitation—a more basic problem —had also been bared. In addition, Fayette, together with adjacent Haywood County, had what seemed to me exciting political possibilities. The first was 78 percent black (twenty-one thousand Negroes) and the second was 62 percent black. Not a single Negro had registered to vote in the eighty years up to June, 1959. But then twelve men, led by John McFerren, had risked their lives by going to register. After a legal struggle, their right had been confirmed and others followed despite the economic boycott organized by the White Citizens' Council. In the 1960 general election, more than twelve hundred newly registered blacks had voted and turned the county Republican for the first time since Reconstruction. I believed at that time (not now) that one could make changes in this country by aligning with the liberal forces of the North and forcing the Dixiecrats out of the Democrat Party. Fayette offered an opening wedge for this.

For me, personally, the job I was asked to do at the beginning—to publicize the Fayette struggle—was in line with my idea of serving as a pamphleteer and historian of our cause. I would let the people in Fayette tell their own stories and record them; I would write news articles myself when necessary. The inhabitants of Tent City, like the Montgomery bus boycotters and the Little Rock students, had shown that us "niggers" could get together in the face of great pressure. Black people in this country should know about that. The whole world should know how the right to vote and especially the right to make a decent living had been denied.

The Emergency Relief Committee was actually a subcommittee of Chicago CORE. I had known the committee chairman, Sterling Stuckey, for more than two years and accepted his invitation to work on the committee because it functioned autonomously and Stuckey assured me it would continue to do so. I never bothered myself about the politics of its relationship to CORE, which I did not like because it was dominated at the top by whites, and I believed in the necessity of black leadership in the black struggle.

At the beginning, I did the usual publicity work—writing releases, talking to the *Chicago Defender*, seeing people at Johnson Publications. But soon I found myself out in the street, helping to build a support movement. Stuckey and other members of the committee started going to the supermarket at Sixty-third and South Park to ask people for donations of food. I joined them one Saturday morning, in a cold October wind, and noticed that some people would voluntarily drop money in a box standing beside the boxes for food. The elevated stop was close to where we had set ourselves up; I moved over to it with a cardboard box and began asking people for contributions as they came down the stairs. To my surprise, many gave. Then we started asking people catching the bus at Sixty-third and South Park and they contributed too. We began to concentrate more and more on the collection of money, which was important for shipping and other purposes.

A movement developed in Chicago around the plight of people in Fayette County. Our operation grew so that we had to order cans to solicit money; on a good day we would collect three to four hundred dollars. All of us had regular jobs—I was teaching at Kenwood Grammar School—and we solicited contributions during our off hours. We began to organize the churches on the South Side for the collection of food and clothing and within a month we had shipped many truckloads to Fayette County. On a smaller scale, Los Angeles CORE was sending support to adjacent Haywood County, where people had also been evicted.

During Thanksgiving vacation, Stuckey and I made a trip to Fayette County and talked to many people. I had relatives there; one of the founders of the Fayette County Civic and Welfare League was an uncle by marriage, and John McFerren's wife and I discovered that we were third cousins. That first trip to Fayette impressed upon me the importance of getting young people who could help with the technical work, such as writing press releases, collecting affidavits and life stories, writing propaganda, and so forth. The older people had extraordinary spirit but they needed and deserved the technical help of dedicated young people. I hoped that we in the Emergency Relief Committee might broaden our scope and become such a cadre.

We also got our first whiff of internal problems on that trip. For one thing, Scott Franklin—who was president of the league—told us that he was opposed to many of the things that its chairman, John McFerren, was doing. We tried with whatever skills we had to argue for unity, since this was an important fight for all black people. Further trouble began when John McFerren was unwilling, as he told me, to abandon his organization and become a part of the NAACP. I had no love for the NAACP, which I saw as a monolithic, middle-class organization that was not willing to engage in mass struggle and was too closely aligned with the Democratic Party. Aside from that, I just couldn't understand how some NAACP officials could stand in opposition to poor people like the members of the Fayette County Civic and Welfare League. The Nashville NAACP supported the Fayette people warmly but the Memphis chapter did not. When the Nashville NAACP sent a check to a bank in Memphis to be deposited in the account of the Fayette County Civic and Welfare League, an official of that bank, who was an NAACP officer, sent back the check and told them to make it out to the NAACP. They refused to do this.

There was no way for us to fight the NAACP except by working very hard in Chicago to keep food, clothing, and money coming to the people in Fayette County—in other words, to build a base under the NAACP. We could not and did not want to attack it openly.

December was a critical month because all the crops were in and we were sure many more people would be evicted. Many of them had already been told by their neo-slave masters that after the crops were in, they would have to move. Winter lay ahead. We still had not been able to break the news whiteout, though we did get some coverage in the black press about future evictions. Around Christmastime, it was decided that I should make another trip to Fayette County in order to promote some publicity and to be there when a large shipment of food arrived from the United Packinghouse Workers. Through Charles Fischer and Russell Lasley, officials of the Packinghouse Workers, things had begun to move in that union. It was expected that other unions in the CIO would follow suit. The Fischer family included Charles's wife Sylvia, who taught in the same school where I then worked, and their two daughters who attended that school. Together we organized a very successful drive in the Hyde Park–Kenwood community.

While I was in Fayette the shooting occurred in which Early B. Williams was wounded. The media finally woke up. Stuckey and I had made arrangements that if anything happened in Fayette County, I was to call him and he would telephone the news story to the United Press International in Chicago. The bureau there would then send for the news story out of Memphis. (This was a device that activists in the South would employ in the years ahead to get news out. When news was not carried locally, you got a friendly subscriber to the Associated Press or the UPI to request a story.) Stuckey did this now with the shooting. Also, Johnson Publications had a very talented young man, Francis Mitchell, covering the story for them; we became good friends and he was later to work for SNCC.

By early January, 1961, people throughout the United States had been informed about the Fayette situation. In addition, the United States Department of Justice had obtained a temporary order restraining the landlords in Fayette County, to halt eviction of people off their land. This alleviated our plight.

The Emergency Relief Committee had successfully organized mass support in Chicago. The Packinghouse Workers pledged their help on many fronts: they published a pamphlet on the situation, which they got the Industrial Union Department of the CIO to print and distribute in large quantities; they voted to send monthly checks to the Fayette County Civic and Welfare League; they also voted to send a delegation to investigate buying land for the people who were living in the other tents. Then the AFL-CIO Industrial Union Council of Cook County (which included Chicago) voted its support. This was a mammoth breakthrough.

Through these various efforts, the Fayette County Civic and Welfare League was enabled to distribute food and clothing regularly, on Wednesdays and Saturdays, under a system of districts with district officers who submitted lists of those who should receive it. It handled crop loans, paid medical bills, purchased tents. It secured scholarships for children of the county and began a program of adult education in reading, writing, simple bookkeeping. A permanent office to handle league business was set up, with mimeograph machine and other equipment. But certain developments began to undermine all this success.

A factional fight developed which centered around a black lawyer who was dismissed by the league. He played on conflicts which existed inside the league between McFerren and Scott Franklin, and then he began Red-baiting me. Through a series of underhanded tricks, this lawyer got the league incorporated in such a way that McFerren had no legal voice in it and held a press conference announcing McFerren's ouster. This kind of development was typical of what can happen when a group of poor people, having begun with few assets except courage, slowly acquire a certain amount of influence, funds, and national support. Greedy elements materialize to take advantage of their struggle and poor blacks who have been fighting for life against groups like the White Citizens' Council find themselves being knifed by their own people.

I rushed back to Fayette County as soon as I heard about the press conference and tried to help McFerren fight the vicious attempts to undercut him. I returned to Chicago, after promising McFerren to be back very soon, and took with me copies of the Tennessee papers carrying the story on McFerren. The articles quoted some unkind remarks about me and the Emergency Relief Committee. I gave the papers to Stuckey and other members of the committee when I reported to them. The next day, at a meeting, Stuckey and other members of the committee began to object very strenuously to my going back to Fayette County, as I had promised McFerren I would do very soon. They said that I was hurting the image of the Emergency Relief Committee by becoming involved in factional fights and that we had no moral right to take sides in the fight. But, most importantly, they said, I was discrediting the good image of the Emergency Relief Committee.

These charges surprised me very much. The Emergency Relief Committee had been founded to help the Fayette County Civic and Welfare League and we had consistently supported McFerren's leadership. When Stuckey and I first went to Fayette County, he gave a speech urging people to follow the leadership of McFerren (while my speech, ironically, was pitched more to the need for people to organize themselves and build a strong organization). Furthermore, the committee had sent a telegram supporting John McFerren. Our entire history had woven us with the league and we were partisans by our very actions.

But a real and substantive issue lay beneath the charges against me. In the process of promoting the cause of the people in Fayette County, we had acquired a reputation for the Emergency Relief Committee in itself. But this was never our main purpose. Now, I told the meeting, we were getting concerned about the ego of our own organization. We should not do this, especially if it meant sacrificing the Fayette County Civic and Welfare League, for to deny at this late juncture that we had been partisans of the original league and supporters of John McFerren would be to lie so as to save our own image.

The meeting went on very late and the discussion began to teach me how the acquisition of power has its own dynamics. When we had first started standing out in the cold, begging for food, clothing, and money we were just seven to ten people interested in a cause—or so it seemed. We all wanted to do a job. As our work became more successful, the group began to get an identity of its own. That is the nature of groups. But sometimes allegiances get transferred to the group for its own dynamics, and what the group is supposed to be doing fades into the background; this must be fought against.

I also learned about the dynamics of personal power. Working for the Emergency Relief Committee was my first participation in an organized politico-social movement and I made mistakes. Events in later life would make me come to the conclusion that the power and name I had acquired in the Emergency Relief Committee were the underlying problems at that meeting. Stuckey, after all, was its chairman; also, I think he wanted to build the committee as a personal power base in his relationship to CORE —or perhaps as a step toward working independently of CORE.

That meeting was my introduction to the nature of ego and power drives in all of us. There are many books on political theory and history, but few, if any, which discuss egotism and how it affects organizations. As I later came to see, many organizational conflicts revolve around the use and disposition of personal power—although those waging a struggle usually do not come out in the open and say it. To do so would be too honest. In his book, *Psychopathology and Politics*, Harold Lasswell maintains that all politicians have their primary interest and this gets rationalized into the public good. We must assume that the primary interest exists, I came to believe, but the important question is how that interest manifests itself in the public interest. We can never be sure of anybody's motivation, including our own, but we certainly can evaluate the consequences of behavior. My own experience would teach me that among many people, especially young people, the drive for individual power and status is very strong. In 1961 I did not yet fully understand these problems but I had learned enough to be careful in the future about ego drives and I would not again let myself be built up individually, as had happened through unwanted publicity about Fayette.

The meeting that Sunday night put me in a painful position. On the one hand, it was clear that members of the committee did not want me to go back to Fayette County the next morning as scheduled, although the group did not state this. On the other hand, I had given my word that I would return and I felt that I was needed at that point. I went; this decision meant to me that I placed the struggle of the people there above the committee's organizational identity and that I felt that the Emergency Relief Committee's destiny was tied to the league's.

That same week, John McFerren received a call from the Emergency Relief Committee which he asked me to listen in on. Stuckey and others were asking him to send me away from Fayette County. McFerren tried to point out that in Chicago he would never appear anywhere without the committee's permission. The Emergency Relief Committee was "the general" in Chicago. In Fayette County, he was the general and he wanted me there. Not only did he have the right to keep me there, but he needed me, McFerren said; the league did not even have a typist and I was helping them with typing. "We can get you all the typists that you need," was the reply. The committee neither granted McFerren his rights nor his recognized needs. I was not then entirely clear about their motivation and I was very surprised at the amount of hostility exuding toward me. But at that moment I did not care (and this may have been a weakness in my own personality) for I felt they were wrong; they were not taking into consideration the local situation.

This point was another important lesson from the Fayette experience, and when I started working with SNCC I would always try to keep in mind that a central office cannot be aware of all the local, day-to-day problems. It should not dictate all forms of struggle to the local organizer. Local struggle depended upon the level of awareness of the people, their conflicts and aspirations. I felt that the committee shouldn't try to dictate to McFerren what his relationship to me should be. Also, the committee did not understand how well grounded I was in the local scene and how I had moved only with the rhythm of the people who did not view what I was doing as being antagonistic to them, but rather encouraged me in all of my efforts.

I left Fayette County that Sunday; in Chicago, I received a telephone call from the *Daily News* asking me if I had any comment on my "expulsion" from the Emergency Relief Committee. The reporter said that his daughter had been involved in the collection of food and clothing and he could not believe the story; if it were true, he did not want to print it, for he knew all the efforts we had mounted in Chicago would be seriously hurt.

The story was news to me, too, and I called Lee Blackwell of the *Chicago Defender* to ask him if he had heard it. He then read me a long statement which the committee had issued, charging that my recent trip to Fayette County was unauthorized; that I had interfered in a factional struggle within the league, counter to the committee's policy of noninvolvement (as Stuckey called it); that I was undisciplined and, therefore, the committee was no longer responsible for any of my actions or statements. Stuckey denied in the statement that the committee was interfering with the Tennessee project or attempting to dominate McFerren.

In talking with Blackwell, I refused to make any comment on the committee and said only that I had been fighting to prevent the league from being wrecked. But I was extremely concerned about the impact of this news in Fayette County and how it would play into the hands of the White Citizens' Council. Many attempts had been made to break the boycott and to discredit McFerren during the previous year and a half. Now the main supporter of that committee had split publicly within its own ranks, and thus split with McFerren—on top of the split in Fayette County itself. What the White Citizens' Council could not do, some supposed supporters had been able to do.

That was the end of the Emergency Relief Committee. It never again tried to help Fayette County; I never heard any explanation of this failure, directly or indirectly. Efforts that people were mounting in the city just died. Confusion had been sown in the black community of Chicago; people did not know what to think or do. Russell Lasley and Charlie

Fischer met with Stuckey and others of the committee to see if an adjustment could be worked out and to defend what they believed to be my sincere intentions. They told me afterward that nothing could be done; Stuckey would not budge an inch. I had in the meantime learned from an unquestionable source that he was jealous of the publicity I had received and there seemed to be no overcoming that feeling (though I learned from it). All the efforts we had made with the labor unions collapsed.

I had to find some other way to continue my work for the Georgia Mae Turners and their families who had been screwed by forces beyond their control, not the least of which were human greed and egotism.

CHAPTER 17

Diary of Fayette

JULY 7, 1961. You could call my life the Illinois Central. Here I am, riding this railroad once again from Chicago to Memphis. The clickety-clack brings back pleasant memories of the farm, my grandmother, childhood, and some not so pleasant memories. Last night we finished the meeting of the Freedom Council quite early. I think the plan to have everyone write about his actions and evaluate them will be successful and make our group more cohesive. My job in Fayette County will be to do some teaching, try to set up the cooperative, and whatever else the league needs this summer.

I organized the National Freedom Council in March, after the Relief Committee collapsed. McFerren and others have national contacts and are not wholly dependent on the committee, thank god. But I am committed to the Fayette people, and I know there is only a limited amount of work I can do as an individual. The National Freedom Council, mostly composed of teachers and other friends of mine, is dedicated to helping people in Fayette and Haywood as well as other blacks struggling throughout the country, but especially those in the Deep South. Georgia Mae Turner was very helpful in setting it up; she came to Chicago on a speaking tour and many people were moved by her story. She is the poorest of them all.

After the meeting last night, I went over to the house where Paul Brooks and Katherine Burke are staying. They are Freedom Riders and trying very hard to drum up support for more Rides but running into much opposition from the Baptist preachers. The split of the National Baptist Convention into the progressives and the group around Rev. James Jackson makes a lot of preachers support a cause or not depending on whether the people involved in it are lined up with one Baptist faction or the other. I am sick of petty personality things, preachers demanding publicity for the least little contribution to civil rights. I am sick of people confusing morality and religion with civil rights. Justice will not be obtained by appealing to the morality of the oppressor.

Katherine calls the teachers, doctors, and many preachers "stone phonies." The phony Negro is as great an obstacle to racial progress as the most die-hard segregationist.

The stone-phony Negro:
1. Southern teacher and rich farmer who do not register to vote because they are scared.
2. Southern student who fails to participate in a sit-in or stand-in demonstration.
3. Negro who does not believe direct, positive action is of any value but prefers to wait on the courts.
4. Negro who accepts the garbage that the right to vote is going to solve the Negro's problem.
5. Negro who does not want to criticize other Negroes.
6. Negro who contributes a dime, perhaps a dollar, and thinks he has done his share.
7. Negroes with big names who are always ready to talk about civil rights but who seldom, if ever, commit themselves to positive acts to end segregation.
8. Northern Negroes who complain about conditions in the South and whitewash the North.
9. Those who want money, not civil rights.

Later the same day. Our train stopped in Mattoon, Illinois, and I talked to the porter while we were in the station.

"What do you think of the Freedom Riders?" I asked.

"They are doing a good job. What the hell, a hundred years is a long time to wait, don't you think?" he replied.

"Yeah, I agree."

"Man, those young people ain't gonna wait, make compromises like we did. But, you know, what I don't understand is why don't they start at home. Of course, I'm no authority, but something ought to be done in Chicago, Carbondale, and Springfield, Illinois. These places are just as bad as Southern towns."

"Well, I tell you," I said. "It's like this. You strike where you can, when you can, with all your strength. If we can knock out Mississippi, Illinois will be a mopping-up action." (Fool that I was to think that.) "You ain't got no rights in Mississippi."

July 8. Arrived last night around 7 P.M. and immediately noticed several changes. The office of the league has been completed and is in good shape. McFerren is remodeling the store and it looks very attractive too.

Went to a citizenship class and was surprised to find many old people there like Mr. John Lewis, eighty-six. Tomorrow I'll tape an interview with him. The instructor, a former county schoolteacher, is conducting these classes without a blackboard. People were studying the different kinds of sentences, also some history and arithmetic. I spent the night with the McFerrens, with the pistol beside me like last winter.

This morning went to the tents. Not much has changed. There are eleven families in Village Number One and three in the second settlement, near Moscow, Tennessee. John Clive's wife just had a baby—that makes four born here since people moved into the tents. There seems to be a cooperative spirit in the tents, although there is still this petty gossip— he said that he said that you said. . . .

The kinship structure in Tent City fascinates me, and is one reason I think that a cooperative farm would work. Most of the people are related, with Georgia Mae Turner standing as queen mother. The idea would be for the league to set up a Tent City Land Bank, raise funds, purchase land, and turn it over to the people in the tents to work as a co-op. The Beasley farm would be a good farm for this. I went with Early B. Williams, his father, and brother, to Grand Junction this afternoon and we saw the place—it's still for sale. But the price is prohibitive because of that old Civil War hospital on it. We agreed to write President Kennedy a letter asking him to get some land for the tent people—more as an act of protest than anything else.

There is a newly formed Fayette County NAACP here, with Allen Yancey as president. Yancey went to a meeting in Washington in early June to talk about Fayette. One big problem is getting loans from the Farmers' Home Administration. That office is in for a rough time—many people are scheduled to go down Monday and ask for loans.

Something must be done about Wonder Bread, Pepsi Cola, Coca-Cola, and all the other national firms that still will not deliver to McFerren. He is still driving his car fifty miles to Memphis to buy groceries. We should picket these companies and write to Attorney General Kennedy asking that they follow through on their suit against these merchants.

There is also a need for slate to be used as blackboards. There is a need for typewriters. People want to learn to type. We are checking this next week. If we could buy five typewriters from that Army surplus store, I would be willing to conduct a typing class. Dictionaries and teachers are needed! Technical personnel are needed!

July 9. Morning. Birds are singing, chirping away. A mild breeze sways through the trees. Children from the tents are dressed for church; it is their day at the local Baptist church. The heat in the tents is miserable.

Relations between the people in the tents and the league are not the best. Someone at a league meeting called the people in the tents lazy and this remark has hurt the most. There is also the problem with "Freedom Farm." Dr. James Jackson, head of the National Baptist Convention, became interested in Fayette County last spring and organized a day on which all the churches under his jurisdiction were to take up collections for Fayette so that a farm could be bought for the people. This man turned out to be a disappointment too. He got the money, bought the farm, named it "Freedom Farm," and then wanted the people in the tents to be sharecroppers on it—instead of giving them the land as a cooperative farm. The people in the tents had sharecropped all their lives and did not want to go back to it. Only three families have moved in.

Unfortunately the league supported Reverend Jackson's idea, and Shepard Towles became manager of the farm. They did not understand that the people in the tents symbolize the larger fight against sharecropping and tenant farming. The economic system must be attacked along with the denial of the right to vote. But most of the league people are small landowners and in a way feel that a life of sharecropping is not too bad for people who had sharecropped all their lives. The sharecroppers feel they have suffered for everyone in the county. It is a class conflict.

Evening. At a meeting today with the new Fayette chapter of the NAACP, Yancey talked about the desegregation suit he wants to start. Desegregation is not the main need of the people here. Although McFerren trusts Yancey and thinks he can outflank Roy Wilkins by forming an NAACP chapter with Yancey, I am not so sure. The NAACP has a logic of its own and that desegregation suit reflects its politics.

I will sleep tonight in Mrs. Turner's tent. I want to spend more time out here, living with the people, listening to their stories and gossip, eating with them, sleeping in the tents. They are moving forward our history.

It is lovely and quiet now. Outdoors you can see the Milky Way, big and bright. Some children are rolling an automobile tire around in front of the tent where I am visiting. Others are indoors singing religious songs. The older people sit, mostly silent. "Dried eggs make the best food," someone says. "There will be even less work for people now," murmurs a man; the crops are almost laid by.

A mother nurses one baby while the other struggles for the same tit. Early B.'s wife is pregnant again. There is a flurry of activity as the popsicle man arrives and the children crowd around him.

July 10. The surplus food from the U.S. Department of Agriculture arrived today in Somerville. Everyone had been talking about it coming

for days. In the morning, people were getting their children ready to go
—brushing clothes, straightening hair, an air of picnic surrounding everything. They have a right to be happy. It is an important victory.

In Somerville there were more than a thousand people from all over
the county waiting for the food—a fantastic scene. A government official
started assigning numbers at seven o'clock in the morning; by eight
o'clock, he had assigned two hundred. His staff could not process more
than that per day, he said, so the distribution will go on for at least a
week. The food included dried milk, lard, dried beans, rice, dried eggs,
sugar, and other staples. Eligibility was based on Tennessee requirements.
The scale of those eligible began with an income of $60 per month for
a family of one and ran up to an income of $160 for a family of ten.
McFerren said, "There are very few people in this county who will not
qualify."

While the food was being distributed in the National Guard Armory,
white people paraded up and down, glaring at the huge crowd. They
hated what they saw. I asked Georgia Mae what she thought about the
food and she said, "I appreciate it so much. I wish I could go up and
thank President Kennedy myself. The other people done give down and
it was time for some help."

Not all of the people getting food were registered voters. I tried to get
McFerren to hold a mass rally there, to talk about the victory and spur
others to register. Most of the league wanted it but Reverend Dowdy said
people already knew the surplus food was due to their struggle. Some
say he is afraid.

Spent part of the afternoon typing news release. Typed a letter for
Yancey. Later I talked with Viola McFerren and John about the cooperative farm and also my idea of a Fayette County Cooperative Society—
which would be a consumers' co-op at the beginning and eventually
a producers' co-op. They both liked the idea of the cooperative farm, but
John wants to be sure that the people in the tents go along with it. I
agreed, of course, and told him that I would sound them out.

Also talked with Owens from the Justice Department; he and John
Doar have been handling the Fayette case. I pointed out to Owens that
a different economic system was needed so that people could eat and
I told him we needed cooperatives. He said this would defeat the goal
of an integrated society. I disagreed.

At one point Owens made a remark to John about how fine his store
looked—that he must be getting rich. It was a joke, but people from the
tents are saying the same thing—and not as a joke. John feels guilty, I
suspect.

July 11. Distribution of the surplus food is going very slowly since
there are only two interviewers. People are being given numbers and

told to come back in ten days. Some had stood in line for two solid days waiting—not only Negroes but many white families on welfare rolls. A white woman who owns a house in front of the Armory came out with a pistol, telling the niggers to get away. The sheriff made her go back inside. People have commented on the courtesy shown by the interviewers: "The food people sho' are different from white folks around here. But they're learning their lesson." The surplus food has finally broken the boycott.

July 12. I spent the morning at Tent City teaching a citizenship class under the old oak tree. Got L. C. Goodin to write his name. His wife did even better. She wrote:

My name is Louise Goodin. I live in Tent City, Tent number seven. I have many relatives here in the tents. My horses and cows are not in the tents. There are dogs but no rats in the tents. No is no. Not is not. Nothing is nothing.

> I live in the tents
> You live in the tents
> She lives in the tents
> We live in the tents
> You live in the tents
> They live in the tents

Then we worked for a long time on arithmetic, using the fractions of sharecropping. We also discussed Negro history. People did not know we came from Africa. Then people began to complain about the work situation, and discrimination against Negroes in several local plants. But they were not moved to any action. After all the complaints, we got a group together to visit one of the factories—and no one wanted to go into the employment office to see what would happen. There is still fear in their hearts. Much more needs to be done at the tents; a teacher could be busy full time. I can't meet the needs.

This evening, we had a meeting of all the tents and people agreed to the idea of the cooperative farm. They would relocate themselves on eight to ten acres of land each; if someone wanted to sell, he would have to offer it to the group first and then to the league. The people agreed, which was what McFerren had wanted to be sure about.

Later, at a meeting of the league, I reported this—and Yancey moved that the proposal be tabled! He said that the people in the tents were no longer newsworthy enough to raise the money to buy the land. McFerren didn't argue with him. I am not a voting member of the league but I was allowed to speak and disagreed with Yancey. His motion carried, however. The people in the tents saw the plan as a way out for them—and now it's gone.

July 14. People in the tents are having a hard time. Last night, I talked with them; they are reluctant to take leadership. One of the basic problems here is lack of secondary leadership and first-class administration. Later I told John about their need for sugar and coffee. He said the league would have to check its bank account; it had voted out a lot of money. I told him it was rough down in the tents. He said "Yep," and kept on walking. This stunned me. Puckett, another evicted sharecropper, says that John will never get the people in the tents back again.

July 15. I spend the day holding classes under the oak tree. In the evening I talked with James Frazier—the last person who moved into the tents. He said, "This problem is a worldwide problem, as I understand it. You know, this tent is much better than the house where I used to live. I had a tin tub, dish pans, and two buckets hanging over the beds to catch water. Here I haven't had to catch any water at all.

"Work is my best friend. Me and work ain't never fell out. If you want to start working at 6 A.M. and go to 6 P.M., I'll be there with you. I've picked cotton all day and worked at the sorghum mill all night. Get up the next morning and still pick cotton all day. But now . . . the past three weeks, looking for work, has been the hardest in my life."

Later that night, sitting around a small fire on the tent ground, the people talked about something they had never seen happen before. Shots had been fired into the embankment near the tents, two nights ago. People had then begun watching for suspicious cars and noting their license numbers. Mary Williams, the wife of Early B., got one; a 1960 white Chevrolet that seemed to be harassing them, and Shepard Towles reported it to the sheriff. Today the sheriff caught the car and asked Mary Williams to identfy the two youths in it. She did. The sheriff told her they would have no more trouble from that pair. Tonight, somebody asked, "When have you heard of a white sheriff telling a black woman she ain't gonnna have no more trouble out of white folks?"

"I'll tell you," another resident of Tent City said, "This fight we waging must be paying off. That old sheriff knows if he don't do right we gonna put him right out of office."

July 18. Today, just after dark, John McFerren's brother-in-law came to the tents and told me that John wanted me to move all of my things out of his house tonight. I was taken aback but told him I would do it right away. Then I went to ask Shepard Towles if he knew what was the matter; he said this was the first he had heard of it.

I called the McFerrens from Shepard Towles's house. John was not in. I asked Viola, his wife, if she knew what was wrong. In a rapid, high-pitched voice, she began to talk about a report I had sent to the vice-president of the National Freedom Council after the meeting at which the proposal for a cooperative farm had been tabled. She had seen the letter and was angry. She felt that I had said John was making money off the people in the tents when I wrote that "he is trying to make hay while the sun is shining." I tried to explain to her that I had meant he was busy working on the renovation of his store during the summer, in order to finish it before winter. I had gone on to say, in the letter, that, since he didn't have much time to devote to the people in the tents because of that work, I felt someone should do it to maintain communication. McFerren had agreed to this but Viola felt my comments in the letter meant I was taking sides with the tent people against John.

There were other parts of my report which she had misunderstood, but I could not convince her of this. I didn't ask her how she had come to read it; that wasn't relevant at the moment.

Since emotions were running high, I asked Shepard Towles to pick up my things from John's house and bring them to his house. But McFerren had already brought them. When he pulled up in the yard, I said that I would like to talk to him. He told me that he didn't have time.

July 19. Morning. My work is finished here in Fayette County. To stay any longer would be to widen the disunity which already exists. There are enough splits and factions; I won't contribute to the formation of another one—which is what would happen if I stayed.

I can't work where my motivation has been questioned. There is too much work to be done in the South, too much agitation needed, too much organizing for me to remain here where my effectiveness has been impaired. The problem is partly one of language. If I could explain point by point what I meant in the report, I might ease tension. But there is a real problem, a class problem, in the treatment of the tent families and perhaps some people are very touchy about that. McFerren had agreed that my work in the tents might help the overall situation, but I guess one must be very careful of what one writes—especially where there is touchiness. I still do not understand how I misplaced that letter. An organizer has to be more careful about what he writes and where he keeps his material.

I do not know what will happen to the people here in the tents. They will probably move out of the tents one by one, with a bitter taste in their mouths.* Everybody has suffered. But there have been victories here in Fayette. The surplus food would not have come without pressure from all over the country and the embarrassment caused to the United States government by the tents. The White Citizens' Council has been

---

* Since that day, I have been back to Fayette County only once and had a very friendly chat with McFerren when I stopped for gas at his store. He told me that the people in the tents had all moved out. He said Georgia Mae was living on a farm fifty miles from Fayette County.

thoroughly defeated in its attempts to drive Negroes off their land, and the boycott is broken. Many of the landowners are now in court facing Justice Department suits.

July 19. Evening. I talked with McFerren in the driveway between his store and the league office around six o'clock. I explained to him that there had been some serious misinterpretation of the letter and that I had always respected his leadership. But I felt that the only thing for me to do was to leave the county. There was work to do elsewhere and I did not want to contribute to further disunity.

He said that he needed time to think things over. I shook his hand good-bye and went to the tents. I told the people only that I was going to Nashville and would be back someday but I couldn't say exactly when that would be.

I got my bags and that Wednesday night I caught a bus to Nashville, Tennessee, where I knew the Freedom Riders had their headquarters. Young activists of the Student Nonviolent Coordinating Committee, which had been formed in April, 1960, were holding workshops and meetings there. The need to build that organization of young people hummed in my mind with the rhythm of the bus rolling through the soft Southern night.

CHAPTER 18

Lucretia Collins: "The Spirit of Nashville"

IN NASHVILLE, we had been informed that CORE was going to have Freedom Rides that would carry people all over the South, and their purpose was to test the facilities at the bus stations in the major cities. Later, we heard that the bus of the Freedom Riders had been burned on Mother's Day in Anniston, Alabama, and that another bus had been attacked by people in Birmingham. CORE was discontinuing the Freedom Ride, people said. We felt that it had to continue even if we had to do it ourselves. We knew we were subject to being killed. This did not matter to us. There was so much at stake, we could not allow the segregationists to stop us. We had to continue that Freedom Ride even if we were killed in the process.

LUCRETIA COLLINS

The Nashville that I reached just before dawn on July 20, 1961, was an exciting place to be, buzzing with activity and debate in the student community. I went to the office of the Nashville Christian Leadership Conference and found two young men there at six in the morning; the Nashville student movement worked out of that office and at least one person always spent the night. Next door stood the Mecca House, a small restaurant much patronized for its daily, fifty-cent-special dinner. In these two places there were always students gathering to go pick up some "packages" (the code word for Freedom Riders); to talk with Freedom Riders returning from Parchman Penitentiary in Jackson, Mississippi, and other jails; to argue nonviolence or the merits of notables like Martin Luther King. The Freedom Rides had reached their peak in June but were not over, and the ferment stirred up by them had by no means subsided. The students felt they were playing a crucial role in a crucial period of history. It was the Nashville Student Movement that had continued the Freedom Rides when CORE, the original sponsor, had declared them too dangerous and had withdrawn. These students had a right to feel proud and sure of themselves.

In the next few days, I talked to many people in the Nashville movement. I had not arrived there as a stranger. The work I had been doing in Fayette County was known to people involved in the Freedom Rides. Students from Howard University, the Nashville campuses, and other parts of the South had been helpful in sending food and clothing to Fayette County. SNCC, the Student Nonviolent Coordinating Committee, had reported some of the events in Fayette County in its newsletter. Miss Ella Baker, who was most influential in SNCC, had visited the county in January, 1961, and written a news story for the *Southern Patriot*, a newspaper published by the Southern Conference Educational Fund.

Nor were Nashville or the Freedom Rides strange to me. When the Rides had started, I was teaching school on the South Side of Chicago at the Paul Cornell Elementary School. I kept a scrapbook of day-to-day news and had my students collect articles about the Freedom Rides. We put up a map on the wall of our classroom and charted the progress of the Riders. The class and I wrote a letter to James Farmer, the national director of CORE, when he went to jail in Jackson, Mississippi. Later, when I was staying in Tent City, Matthew Walker had come out from the Nashville student movement to recruit Fayette people for the Freedom Rides. The Rides seemed to me the kind of dramatic action needed to raise consciousness and build a national outrage against the injustices perpetrated against black people. Let everyone see and think about this society of "justice and equality for all" that would inflict the type of punishment it did upon students for trying to desegregate interstate bus station facilities.

With my feeling about the Freedom Rides running so high, I had been very glad to meet Paul Brooks when he came to Chicago in late May seeking help from the National Freedom Council with publicity and fund raising. A student at the American Baptist Seminary in Nashville, Paul told me a great deal about his experiences as a Freedom Rider and his political judgments of the people involved. With him was Katherine Burke, also a Freedom Rider; they would later marry. I saw a lot of them both.

Paul was a good-looking, smooth-skinned black man of medium height with a distinctive mole on his chin and a mustache. Katherine, a small and dark-skinned beauty with a lot of hair, had a tremendous sense of humor and smoked a lot. The three of us became tight. It did not matter that we had some differences—especially over the question of religion— which I never pursued. Paul and Katherine had been among those Nashville students who felt the effort must continue after CORE decided to pull out. With money provided by the Nashville Christian Leadership Conference, the group had headed for Birmingham to resume the Ride.

A key person in getting this group together was Diane Nash, a student leader who had dropped out of Fisk to work full time in the movement and then became SNCC's first field secretary. I met her now in Nashville, where she was working as coordinator of student activities for the Nashville Christian Leadership Conference—an extremely impressive person in a quiet way. We spent many hours talking. That she had dropped out of college in the face of much criticism from middle-class blacks endeared her to me at once. While I considered formal education very important, I also felt it took on more meaning if a person had worked. I had not graduated from college myself until I was twenty-seven years old; dropping out of school for a few years had not hurt my education but made it more relevant. Also, a wide work experience seemed to me a necessity for black people in an industrialized society. We needed the resources and skills to be able to survive anywhere—in this country or outside it.

Diane's salaried position placed her square in the middle of a conflict between the adults of the Nashville Christian Leadership Conference and the "Turks"—those from the Nashville student movement who were critical of the adults and nonviolence in general, and certain leaders in particular, Martin Luther King, James Lawson, Kelly Miller Smith (then president of the NCLC). The Turks respected James Farmer, then national director of CORE because he had gone to jail in Jackson and stayed there. But they did not like the so-called big name leaders who seemed to spend so much time in the Statler Hilton.

I recalled Paul Brooks having told me his reaction to King's statement that he was not going to take a Freedom Ride because he was then on probation and his advisors had told him it would be unwise. "I would rather have heard King say, 'I'm scared—that's why I'm not going.' I would have had greater respect for him if he had said that," Paul had told me.

Even Diane Nash, who had strong convictions but tried not to speak evil of anyone, expressed a mixed opinion of Dr. King, "He's a good man but as a symbol of this movement, he leaves a lot to be desired. He has been affected by a lot of middle-class standards. If he wanted to, he could really do something about the South. He could go to Jackson and tell those people why they should participate in and support the Freedom Rides." (Diane was referring to the fact that, while Freedom Riders from all over the country were going to jail in Jackson, students from Mississippi itself were going through the back door to catch the bus or train.) The students expressed praise for Rev. Fred Shuttlesworth of Birmingham, another official of the Southern Christian Leadership Conference, but also some criticism. For the young blacks, concepts of what leadership meant and should mean were very important.

The conflict between students and adults was aggravated by the fact that the students depended on the older people—on NCLC—for money and facilities such as the office. As Diane told me, "Because they control the purse strings, NCLC thinks it can control the movement." In Chicago, Katherine Burke had described to me how students viewed this situation, "Tell the Nashville Christian Leadership Conference what we are going to do and then ask them to give us money with which to do it. They do or they don't. You can't work with the old people—they just don't understand what it's all about." It had become clear to me by then that these black youths were accustomed to making decisions. They were not going to be told what to do; they had been through too much.

The issue of nonviolence ran through all this discussion about old folks versus Turks, leaders versus movements. I did not believe in nonviolence as a way of life and was surprised to see many of the Nashville students still debating nonviolence as a tactic as opposed to nonviolence as a way of life. One student, Bill Hargrove, who had been on the Freedom Rides and been beaten in Montgomery, stated unequivocally that he felt that people should strike back on any demonstration if they were hit. He found many supporters in the Nashville student movement that summer and this growing belief in self-defense among the students was a cause of major concern to some of the leaders. Jim Lawson, who had been involved with the student movement in its earliest days and who wrote SNCC's statement of purpose when it was founded, came to meetings to talk about the spiritual meaning of nonviolence and the need to adopt nonviolence as a total way of life. Many students complained that Lawson had little else to offer.

My first day in Nashville, I went to watch the picketing of H. G. Hill's supermarket for more jobs. The next day and the one after, I joined the line. I had never before participated in a nonviolent demonstration and had grave reservations about my ability to do this. During the spring of 1960, when the student movement was spreading across the South, I had watched a special Huntley-Brinkley program which showed Len Holt, then working for CORE, conducting a nonviolent workshop in Frankfort, Kentucky. As I watched that program, I wondered if it would ever be possible for me to engage in such an action. I couldn't dig anyone hitting me up 'side my head, and I was sure it would be a terrible test of my nerves to submit to this type of group discipline.

This day in Nashville, I decided to make that test. We were demonstrating not in front of H. G. Hill, but another grocery store where students had also been picketing for jobs. There had been fights during the last two days between some of the black students and the white bystanders. At issue was the growing impatience with nonviolence among many of its earlier practitioners.

We lined up in front of this store; I was at one end of the line and Lawson was at the other. He was participating in the midst of the internal debate over violence and nonviolence to demonstrate the need for applied nonviolence. There were not many white bystanders that day and I felt thankful for that, but there was a group of five or six young whites who kept heckling the group. Across the street stood some young blacks who had given up nonviolence—among them, Bill Hargove. They were going to attack any whites who hit us. Each time I walked the line and faced those five or six hecklers, I had to steel myself. I didn't want to break the discipline of the group by striking back. I had agreed to engage in this nonviolent demonstration and I wanted to keep group discipline. It was my belief in collective discipline, more than anything else, that kept me in the nonviolent group at those moments.

We made it through that day of demonstration in Nashville without too many incidents. Coke was sprayed on my face from a bottle and some of the young Turks from across the street began to move forward. But the whites moved back.

My willingness to submit to the discipline of nonviolence arose from my view of it as a means to build a mass movement and to build the self-confidence of our people as a whole. I saw all these demonstrations as having a mass effect which would be negative in some ways but positive in others. I knew that nonviolence would not work, but hopefully the witnessing of terror and police brutality would help create a mass consciousness that would eventually lead to more militancy and action for revolution on the part of the black people. Our protesters that day at the store symbolized this future development. They were forerunners of the Deacons for Defense, whose emergence was an inevitable parallel to the development of nonviolence. Given a nonviolent movement, the deacons had to spring up. Today in major cities where we see black self-defense groups, the rejection of nonviolence emerges from that negative-positive period of history.

As for myself, personally, throughout the many demonstrations in which I later participated, I always reserved the right to hit back. I believed that in a demonstration, you never knew when you would have to hit back and nonviolence did not commit you not to strike back ever. My nonviolence has always been the most tactical of all possible tactical nonviolence.

After four days—good days, especially the long discussions with Diane —I returned to Chicago feeling that I was well acquainted with the Nashville movement. The National Freedom Council was waiting for a report from me and we had to make new plans. I spent a great deal of time with Paul and Katherine, talking about the need to form an organization of young people who would work full time in the movement, and the possibility of building it around a nucleus of Freedom Riders. (At that time I knew of the existence of SNCC but not much more than that; also, it had no staff then and served only as an agency to coordinate student groups.)

One day in June, 1961, at the house where Paul and Katherine were staying, I met another Freedom Rider living there, Lucretia Collins. She made a deep impression on me in many ways. A graduate of Tennessee State and twenty-one years old, her parents both lived in Fairbanks, Alaska, where her father served as a career soldier and her mother as a career nurse. She was beautiful and articulate, with a mild way of expressing great emotion. We developed a bond of friendship, perhaps of love.

Lucretia had gone to school with Katherine and also been with her from Birmingham to Jackson—the Ride continued by the Nashville students after CORE quit. This story had fascinated me when Paul and Katherine told it, but on a superficial level. Lucretia now told me the story in detail, while I asked her many questions and probed deeply for all her reactions. I tape-recorded it, out of concern about the failure of the students in those early days to write down their experiences for future generations—and to write them down while the memory was fresh.

Her account starts with her decision to help carry on the Ride and her leaving school at once although she lacked only nine hours of credit to graduate.

We met that day from 6:00 A.M. off and on until 10:00 P.M. I first went to the dean of women and told her out of respect that I was leaving. It was midnight when I got to the dormitory and packed a few things. We caught a bus that morning at 3:45 A.M.

I kept thinking about what I was doing as I boarded the bus. I observed the traffic outside and the people entering the bus. I felt certain that we were writing history, pages for a history book, some history book, I hope. I kept feeling for the other kids, more so than for myself. Maybe they were thinking the same thing about me, I don't know. But I could see in them the sacrifice they were making. I could see how strongly someone would have to be dedicated because at this point we didn't know what was going to happen. We thought that some of us would be killed. We certainly thought that some, if not all of us, would be severely injured. At any moment I was expecting anything. I was expecting the worst and hoping for the best.

I thought of many things . . . all of my life. I looked back in the past a great deal and I thought a lot about my mother and the little things that she had done, what I had managed to do for myself. I kept thinking about the people in my family who would not understand this and who would perhaps be hurt if anything happened to me. I think at one time even tears came to my eyes, and I began to think how far away I was from my mother. And if anything happened it would be very difficult for her to get to me, which I knew she would like to do. But I had no qualms about going.

I was silent most of the way. We had planned not to identify ourselves with one another because our purpose was to get to Birmingham and not be stopped on the way. Certainly we would have been stopped if we had identified ourselves. This was proven by Paul Brooks, who sat by Jim Zwerg. He should not have done this, for that identified them. Sure enough, they were arrested within the city limits of Birmingham. Black and white just do not ride together in Alabama.

We remained on the bus after they were arrested. A policeman got on at this point, supposedly to escort us to the bus station in downtown Birmingham. I went to get off, but I was blocked. And I was blocked for quite some time.

Since the police were blocking us, we decided to have a stand-in right there in the aisle. I remember saying to other passengers, "Sir, you want to get by, you want to get off?"

And they said, "Yes."

"Come on, let's go together," that sort of thing. But the police managed to pull other passengers through us.

I talked to one policeman who was blocking me for fifteen minutes. I asked him if he was a veteran. "Yes," he replied.

"What did you fight for?"

He didn't answer.

"Are you a Christian? Do you believe in Christianity?"

"Yes."

"Do you believe Jesus Christ died for all people?"

"Yes. But look, this is my job. I'm sorry to have to do this."

He said he didn't want to make trouble for us. He kept saying he was hungry.

"I'm hungry too. Let's go into the station and have some dinner," I said. The man was shaking. All of the policemen seemed very nervous. The one giving them the orders seemed a nervous wreck himself. Finally they let us off the bus and escorted us to the waiting room.

Later, the chief of police came and he told us we were in danger of our lives and that he was placing us in protective custody. At this point, the policemen got very rough with us. It was like a moment of rejoicing to them, as if they had really won something by getting us to go to jail.

We got into the wagon, pleasantly. We went to jail. We sang all the way. It was a rugged ride to that jail; I think they tried to turn us upside down in the patrol wagon because they were turning curves very sharply. And speeding. The patrol wagon caused quite a sensation as we were going through town. People were applauding. This gave us more determination.

They did not fingerprint us in jail. As a matter of fact, we were allowed to carry in most of our belongings, except the suitcases. Money and small articles were taken off us and things we might commit suicide with. They threw us into a cell with all kinds of women who were there for various charges. There were only two whites in the group, Jim Zwerg and Salyn McCollum; they were segregated from us.

In jail, I made as many friends as I could. There was a woman who had a severe speech defect and since that time, I have been reading about that kind of problem. This woman interested me in particular because the others made fun of her and mimicked her. This is very bad to me. I talked with her a long time.

I learned a lot about the people who were there. There were women who had no values at all, really. And they were very rough. Easygoing. I had no fear of them attacking me or anything like this. The only thing that I feared was the fact that there were several homosexuals in the jail. An attack of this sort—I thought very carefully about what I would do. Other than this, most of them were kind. They sympathized to some extent with us.

The following night at 11:30 P.M., Bull Connor came into our cell and said that since we were from Nashville he was taking us in a car back to Nashville. We protested, but that did not do any good. I was pushed out of the cell and Katherine Burke, who refused to go, was carried out. The fellows were pushed and shoved out. During our ride to Ardmore, Tennessee, we made it very clear that we were not afraid of jail and that we were not afraid of being attacked on the road. The driver of our car said that he would kill his daughter before he would allow her to go to an integrated school.

When we got to the Tennessee state line at Ardmore, Bull Connor pointed to a train station and told us to catch a train from there. It was just breaking day. We saw a telephone booth on the corner and we called Diane. She asked what we were going to do and we said we would call her back. This was a gripping moment. We knew that anything could happen to us. We were alone with our luggage and everything in the middle of the street. We did not know if there had been attackers following the so-called police car or if attackers would come at us from somewhere in Tennessee. We were 93 miles from Nashville and 193 miles from Birmingham, Alabama.

Two fellows decided to see if they could find a Negro home. We gave them twenty minutes and they were to return whether they found one or not. We sought refuge behind the little train station. At this point, my mind was just overcome with the idea that the Birmingham police had actually made contact with counterparts in other cities and that we would soon be massacred. I was so sure of it. The two scouts came back in ten minutes and we knew they had found something. So we took our bags and walked down the railroad tracks. The people let us in and we called Nashville again. Leo Lillard, who was coordinator of the Freedom Ride, said he would come right away.

We felt we had to go back to Birmingham because if we went home to Nashville it would be exactly what they wanted us to do. They had put us out in the middle of the night to frighten us. We would lose another fight if we did not return to Birmingham. We knew the dangers we faced, going on the highway with Tennessee license plates.

While we waited for Leo to arrive, we pooled our money and sent for food from the store. Katherine and I cooked. There were eight of us and none of us had eaten for thirty-six hours.

Leo arrived—he drove those ninety-three miles in fifty-five minutes. We planned our trip back to Birmingham so that we would not look so conspicuous. One fellow was on the floor. The other three were slumped down in the back so that it would not look crowded. Katherine and I sat in front with Leo and Bill. I pretended that Bill and I were sweethearts. And I lay on his shoulder. Katherine lay on Leo's shoulder. In this way the car did not look so crowded.

It was very hot but I broke out in cold sweat. We didn't have the windows down for various reasons. I don't know . . . well, there we were. We tried to make jest; it was very difficult. We decided to bypass Anniston, Alabama, since the people there were so treacherous. We heard an announcement over the radio that the students—meaning us—had been taken back to Nashville. This made us happy and quite a bit of tension was relieved, knowing that we had thrown them off, or thinking that.

Within a half hour we heard another radio announcement that the students weren't on their way to Nashville—they were headed back to Birmingham by car. We were on the highway when we heard this and we really became worried. We watched every car behind us with three or four men in it. And parked cars—we watched them. I give Leo credit for being a very good driver. He told us that if a car pulled out after us, he was going to race it.

Katherine was from Birmingham and she helped us find a way to bypass the city and get to Shuttlesworth's house. Several kids from Nashville and two from Atlanta were waiting for us there. Diane, who represented Nashville on the Student Nonviolent Coordinating Committee, "Snick," had called other members and we were happy to see Ruby Doris Smith who had gone to jail in Rock Hill with Diane. There was this great, joyous reunion. We hardly had time to eat because we were so eager to get back to the bus station.

At the station, they wouldn't let us on the bus. Some of the kids slept but I was determined not to go to sleep. I felt as if I had been without sleep for so long that it just didn't matter. I did not want people watching to think that we were so weary, because to me that brings the morale down.

We patronized the little fountain in the bus station. We walked around. Some of the kids played the games that were in the station. We just made ourselves at home in the "white" waiting room. We went to the bathroom at will. Except the fellows; they did not go to the bathroom whenever they felt the need because there were a couple of men in the building who were subject to being very violent. And they would follow them into the bathroom.

During this time, we tried to catch every bus that left Birmingham. The bus drivers said they wouldn't drive if we got on board. They kept refusing us.

It just seemed that all the blood was drained from you or something. And we began to sing. I don't think that song—"We Shall Overcome"—ever had so much meaning as it did that morning. It was really felt that morning, after we had waited so long and been refused so much. Well, we had a little worship right there. A young man prayed. We read scripture. It was unlike any of the other devotional periods we had had. And I saw kids that I knew were not really dedicated before. At this point you could see it come out. I was just filled with mixed emotions.

The next bus, the next bus, we caught. It was a very strange thing—we stood there and we prayed and we sang. And it was so meaningful. And the next bus we caught. It was 7 A.M.

On the ride from Birmingham to Montgomery I was very relaxed. I dozed off. When I awoke in Montgomery, I felt something was wrong.

There was no mob, but I felt apprehensive. Then I looked around and saw no policemen whatsoever. I saw only about eight or ten people standing in the door of the bus station. We were the last people to get off the bus. The other Freedom Riders had walked down a little to the left on the platform. I saw Katherine and John Lewis being televised by NBC. At that point, this very nice man from *Life* was standing in front of these eight people by the door. While Katherine and John were talking to the television man, I saw this *Life* reporter sort of spread his arms out as if to keep those eight people back. I think he must have felt something was wrong and he was really holding up the action that the crowd of eight wanted to take against us.

When we noticed that this crowd was moving toward us, I think John Lewis said, "Let's all stand together." We were standing in a section above an eight-foot drop. A man with a cigar began to beat the NBC cameraman. A crowd started to gather. We were ignored at first and I noticed that there were no cabs or cars to pick us up. The crowd knocked the cameraman down and he dropped his camera. One man took it and smashed it on the ground. He picked it up and threw it down again and it fell into many pieces. I saw the cameraman start moving down the street. The mob was after him. Then some of them noticed us. Two cabs came by. The driver of one said that the best thing was for the girls to leave. There were five Negro girls and two white girls. Four of us jumped into the cab. The cabdriver, a Negro, said, "Well, I can't carry but four." He had a little boy with him. At this point someone pulled the fifth girl down in the cab. The two white girls were still standing outside. "Well, I sure can't carry them," he said. But there was another cab next to us so we told them, "Get in right away." They went in the cab. Some white fellow opened the door and pulled the driver out. I don't think they attacked him in any way, I'm not sure. But anyway, they pulled him out and prohibited him from driving the cab.

At this point, our driver decided to pull off. There were two exits. We went to the exit facing us. There was a crowd coming in this exit. We saw that either we would have to drive over the people or get out of the cab. So we decided it would be best to back up and try the other exit. At the other exit, we were blocked by cars. The driver was really frightened. He told us he was going to get out of his cab and leave us there.

Blocked in by the cars, we looked back. The mob had attacked the fellows. I saw Jim Zwerg being beaten brutally! Some men held him while white women clawed his face with their nails. And they held up their little children—children who couldn't have been more than a couple of years old—to claw his face.

I had to turn my head because I just couldn't watch it.

Finally, our driver, perhaps because we had calmed him down a bit, agreed to stay with the cab. Although we were nervous, frightened and did not know what to expect, we weren't screaming.

We managed to drive out of the parking lot. Then the car began to give us a lot of trouble. We thought the best thing to do would be to find a Negro home. Any Negro home. This little boy in the cab saved the day. He helped us find a Negro home. The car broke down twice. After the second time it broke down, we managed to get to the Negro neighborhood in second gear.

When we got there, Katherine ran into the house. We got out and told the lady what happened. So they welcomed us. They were very warm. Katherine called Reverend Shuttlesworth in Birmingham and she told him what had happened. Then she called some of the people whom he told us to contact in Montgomery. A very nice lady, who I think was a fighter for civil rights, lived around the block. She asked us to her house. We went and listened to the news reports. And of course the report was very biased.

After a while, we just sat there. I don't think anybody stirred. A lady came in, we had a prayer and we sang a song. This was helpful. It was sad, but it was helpful. Because at this time the boys were still down there trapped by the mob.

After this, we went to another woman's house for late breakfast. I think all of us found difficulty in trying to eat. We were still listening to the radio for the outcome of the violence. We heard that the mob had swelled. Other people were being attacked besides the Freedom Riders. Kennedy's assistant, Seganthaler, had been hurt and was suffering a minor brain concussion. We ate. Somehow we managed to eat.

We went to Reverend Seay's house. None of us knew why we were going there, really, or what to expect when we got there. (Rev. Solomon Seay is president of the Montgomery Improvement Association, an affiliate of the Southern Christian Leadership Conference.) We found all the fellows there, except Jim Zwerg and another Freedom Rider who had been taken to a hospital. John Lewis had a patch on his head. The others were beaten badly, but they were all on their feet.

It was a miracle. These boys had taken a beating, a rough beating, and they had taken it bravely and firmly and manfully. And there we were, reunited again. We embraced. It was something.

That same night, we had a meeting at one of the churches. Rev. Wyatt T. Walker was at that meeting and Reverend Abernathy and Metz Rollins from Nashville. We found out there that warrants were out for all of our arrests. We had supposedly violated some injunction. We expected to be arrested at this meeting but we were not. That night we were taken to individual homes where we stayed.

The next day, Sunday, we were to meet at the First Baptist Church. We found out that there were federal marshals in the city and we were being guarded. The city policemen watched us carefully as we moved from one destination to another. A mass meeting in our honor was scheduled for that night, with Martin Luther King as the main speaker. We managed to assemble and spent most of the day in the library of the First Baptist Church, wondering if they would arrest us there.

The time came for the mass meeting. We were introduced as the Freedom Riders. They gave us much applause. The people were very warm. There was an all-out welcome.

We were being televised by most of the networks, NBC, CBS, ABC. There was Associated Press, United Press International, and then the local reporters. Several speakers sat up on the platform: Martin Luther King, Jr., Reverend Shuttlesworth, Jim Farmer of CORE, Reverend Abernathy, Reverend Walker, Diane Nash, and others. Reverend King was going to give the main address of the evening.

Before the address, we received word that a very large mob had assembled outside. There were several federal marshals in town, but they did not have authority to act. All the time, King was in touch with the Attorney General, Robert Kennedy.

Later, we got word that a group of blacks had assembled also. King, with several other ministers, went out and was successful in getting the group to disperse. Then one of the federal marshal's cars was set on fire and the white mob began to stone the marshals.

The Negroes did disperse, I think, but the white mob remained. They began to throw tear gas canisters. The atmosphere in the church filled with this gaseous, suffocating smell. I couldn't help but think how wonderfully Reverend Seay was directing the people. He told them not to panic, not to become hysterical in any way. The gas was choking many people, but they followed him beautifully. We were large in number, very large. The church was over-crowded and the tear gas made it difficult to breathe. People's eyes began to run and they began wiping them.

We sang. We prayed. We were told not to open the windows. Many of these people had been in the Montgomery bus boycott and they knew from experi-ence what it was for people to try to intimidate them. But the desire for free-dom was so strong throughout the group that nothing, nothing the mob could do, would stop us in any way.

We learned that Governor Patterson had ordered out the National Guard. Soon the church was surrounded with National Guardsmen. The mob still had not dispersed completely. Then we were told that we were to remain in the church overnight for our protection, our own protection.

Here we were, a group of peaceable people trying to assemble, to exercise a right which our Constitution guaranteed us.

We decided to make the most of our situation. We sang and the fellowship grew stronger and stronger, person to person to person. All the Freedom Riders had been without food all day. We had sent for sandwiches, but the mob had checked our possibility of getting them. People grew weary, some irritable. Still they managed to discipline themselves. About this time, King gave his main address. It even gave more encouragement.

Eventually, very early in the morning, most of the people were taken home in large Army trucks. The Freedom Riders very carefully mapped out a bit of strategy. We would be getting off at several stops but eventually we were to meet at one point. This was carried out, and we met at Dr. Harris's home. We stayed there approximately three days, having meetings and workshops to decide whether we should continue the Ride. Earlier, we had been advised by some adults that we should return to Nashville and let other people carry on the Ride.

The meetings were very inspirational. All the decisions were made by stu-dents. The adults were there for guidance and advice when we felt it necessary. But we did what we felt was best. We decided among ourselves that we were going on.

The two who offered more inspiration to the group than anyone else were Len Holt, the lawyer, and James Farmer. Holt spoke about our human rights, our constitutional rights, and what we might face if we continued.

Jim Farmer will always stand out in my mind because he decided at the last minute to go with us. Knowing the situation in Mississippi, it was difficult for him to make up his mind. Not that he did not want to go, or that he had any intentions of not going—but there was a great deal of pressure on him from all areas not to go. He finally decided to come along.

From Montgomery we went to Jackson. I was elected a spokeswoman. Most of the kids, wherever they came from, tended to put the students from Nash-ville on a pedestal almost. Perhaps it is because we had been very successful. We made no bones about it. We were so willing to give everything, including our lives.

There was a lot of tension on the ride to Jackson. We didn't know what would happen when we got to the Mississippi line. Whether they were going to implement federal and Alabama state "protection" or turn us over to the Mississippi state police. We didn't know.

This was the most frightening experience. Most of the kids were expecting quite a bit to happen. I wasn't, because I knew that too much had happened already. Due to the political situation and the international situation between the Soviet Union and the United States, I knew the United States would not allow too much to happen. But I did not think they would escort us straight across the state as they did—the federal agents and the state patrol. It was stupid. And the Jackson city police did exactly what they said they would do.

They said they would arrest us. They did. They followed us, literally followed us, through the bus station and into the white waiting room. We were arrested and taken to the Jackson city jail. We went to trial. We were found guilty. Disturbing the peace, trespassing. That's about it.

After my sentencing, I only stayed in jail for thirty hours. I had asked to be bailed out if we were arrested; I wanted to go to my graduation. Not to march down the aisle, but I thought my degree would not be conferred and I wanted to be there to see. I was going to march in the procession. I wanted them to pull me out of the line if they were not going to give me my degree.

I later learned that the school had planned not to confer my degree on me. I also learned that our classmates had planned to walk out if they did not let me graduate. Perhaps because of this, I got the degree.

I want to go back to Jackson because I feel that I have left a job undone. I feel that sometimes one should stay in jail with no bail and sometimes one is more effective if he comes out of jail. I felt I would be more effective by accepting bail. But I feel incomplete. The Freedom Ride—I am willing to do it all over again because I know a new world is opening up. To me, the entire movement is symbolic of the fight for human dignity.

Lucretia Collins later went to New York City to study drama. She was there when the Birmingham church bombing took place in which four little girls were killed, when the Southern cops unleashed their dogs and hoses on hundreds of blacks in different places, when the murders of 1964 took place in Mississippi. Lucretia then went to Ghana for several years and returned to New York after the coup overthrowing Kwame Nkrumah. When I saw her in 1969, for the first time since 1961, I found that somewhere along the line she had ceased to believe in nonviolence as a tactic or anything else. The story she had told me was history now.

CHAPTER 19

Violence or Nonviolence

IN THE debate which raged during 1961 over nonviolence, there was a figure of growing importance, Robert Williams, NAACP chairman in Monroe, North Carolina, an open advocate of armed self-defense. As yet little known, he had begun to symbolize the alternative to both tactical nonviolence and nonviolence as a way of life. When I had returned to Chicago from Nashville, Paul Brooks talked to me about a recent attempt on Williams's life by the Ku Klux Klan following his move to integrate a Monroe swimming pool. The police knew who was responsible, Williams had told Paul by telephone, but they would not issue a warrant for that person's arrest. The man was in danger, isolated, with little support from the nation's black community. He had asked for help and Paul wanted the Freedom Council to sponsor a visit to Williams.

The council members approved Paul's going but thought I should make the trip with him; I had no other important responsibilities at the time and agreed. We called Williams to tell him that we were coming. After our talk—Paul and I both spoke with him—I became very eager to visit Monroe. It seemed to resemble Fayette County in various ways; not physically, but in the sense that both Williams and John McFerren were brave and principled leaders who had stood up against not only white racism but also the national leadership of the NAACP. Both had suffered or were suffering from lack of public attention. Both were indigenous leaders, working in their home communities. I believed strongly in the development of local leadership, of men and women not tied to any power structure, of people willing to fight racism and economic exploitation by whatever means necessary.

Earlier that year, in February, I had read two articles in the *Southern Patriot*, one by Robert F. Williams and the other by Dr. Martin Luther King. The articles were supposed to present two opposed views; in my analysis, they did not seem to be at cross-purposes. I understood from Williams's article that he was arguing for self-defense, basically—not aggressive violence (which would not have bothered me, but it was another matter). Dr. King, as I recall the article, advocated the use of nonviolence as a method of aggressive action against segregation. But I saw both violence or nonviolence as just different forms of struggle.

At various points in a people's struggle they will use one form and then another. So long as one did not advocate nonviolence dogmatically, to be used at all times and all places, I could work with it. I also knew that when a people get ready to use violence against their oppressors they will do so. No so-called leader or leaders can deter them, just as they cannot move a people to it before the people are ready. Therefore, I did not get excited over a debate between nonviolence and the right of self-defense. Self-defense had been a way of life with me and it was the reality of Fayette County.

I did, however, see a difference between "meeting violence with violence," a key phrase of Robert Williams's, and self-defense. Since it was apparent to me, at least judging by his writings, that Williams was only advocating self-defense, I thought he was losing potential support by using the words *meet violence with violence* rather than *self-defense*. The press, whenever it gave the Monroe struggle any attention at all, would harp on that first phrase. I saw no need to bring the inevitable public reaction down on one's head at that point. While I had no qualms about the use of aggressive violence in any liberation movement, I did not believe that in 1961 the masses of black people in this country were psychologically prepared to use aggressive violence. And without that preparation, and the objective conditions necessary, rebellions and revolutions will not occur. One could, on the other hand, build a movement and an organization on the principle of self-defense.

But whatever my small reservations about Williams, I knew that too much noise was being made by his critics and not enough attention paid to the conditions that made self-defense necessary for black people in the United States. I was eager to meet him and write some articles which might help; before leaving Chicago, I made some calls to the black press which would hopefully lead to their publishing such articles.

We left for Monroe on July 21, planning to stop en route in Nashville. There Paul contacted officials of the Nashville Christian Leadership Conference, trying to get an endorsement for his trip to Monroe. He felt he needed some paper to take with him, something that would give him a status other than just Paul Brooks, Freedom Rider. He was promised a letter from the national body of SCLC in Atlanta, saying that he was on an investigative trip to Monroe for Dr. Martin Luther King. (I thought this rather ironic.) The letter could be picked up in Atlanta, on our way.

A workshop of Southern student leaders, sponsored by the National Student Association and under the direction of Tim Jenkins, was then in progress in Nashville and I went to a session. The level of discussion impressed me; people talked of revolution as necessary to end segregation. Without knowing it at the time, I had walked into a meeting of people who were already or would become key full-time activists in the Student Nonviolent Coordinating Committee. They included Charles Mc-

Dew (who became SNCC's first chairman), Charles Jones, Charles Sherrod, Ruby Doris Smith (who became SNCC's executive secretary in 1966), and Stokely Carmichael (elected SNCC chairman, also in that year). Stokely and Ruby had just spent over a month in Parchman Penitentiary in Jackson; they were among the Freedom Riders who had chosen not to be bailed out.

The people in the workshop—especially McDew, Jones, and Sherrod—talked about the need not merely to desegregate bus stations and lunch counters, but also to move on toward political action. We had to deal with the political system, as opposed to just trying to change attitudes, they said. Students must come out of the colleges and work full time on this. To give up a year of study was not too much, they argued; later they themselves would do that, and much more.

Another force was then developing. Bob Moses, a New York schoolteacher, had quit his job and begun to work full time in Mississippi on voter registration. He did not attend the workshop, but his ideas would soon feed into the mainstream of Southern student thinking about what forms of action to take.

Also in Nashville, though not attending the workshop, were other people who would later join SNCC, but whose main interest lay in continuing direct action: Diane Nash and James Bevel (who later married), Bernard LaFayette, Lester McKinney. Bevel and LaFayette had just returned from Jackson, where they were trying with little success to get Mississippi students to test the facilities at the Jackson bus station. Bevel, who was from Itta Bena, Mississippi, felt convinced of the need to build a movement in his home state and wanted to go back there to work. I fully agreed and planned to do the same someday myself.

It was now August 2, and time to get on the road to Monroe. We wanted to spend some days there and then be in Jackson for the trial of the Freedom Riders, a mass trial of all those who, like Lucretia Collins, had been arrested and had posted bond. Diane Nash and James Bevel drove from Nashville to Atlanta, Georgia, with Paul and me in order to attend a meeting of the Freedom Riders Coordinating Committee where the trial would be discussed. This committee consisted of representatives of CORE, SCLC, and SNCC.

In Nashville I had heard the name of "Snick" mentioned often, but at that time no one could tell me exactly what it was like. Diane, who knew the most, explained SNCC as a loosely structured group with students from various autonomous protest groups that met every two months to formulate plans and programs. It had no staff except an administrative secretary, Edward King, a black student from Kentucky State. I decided to visit him and the SNCC office, which was in Atlanta.

SNCC had one room at 197½ Auburn Avenue, directly across the street from the office of SCLC. I walked in and saw the faded clippings on the walls. I examined the map of the United States, with red pins stuck in it to show where student protest had occurred. I smelled the stale, stuffy air resulting from no ventilation and the accumulation of old papers. I observed the one gray file cabinet, the one gray desk and chair. I watched the nervous gestures of Ed King, his neatly pressed clothes and his well-pronounced words. He seemed lonely, dejected.

He was leaving and did not know who would replace him. No decision had been made; it was not his problem, but he was worried. SNCC faced serious problems as an organization, he said. It should have developed more staff and instigated more activity in its own name. It had not developed a fund-raising base and had to rely heavily upon contributions from the Southern Christian Leadership Conference, which was like pulling teeth. In addition, it was identified in many eyes as an arm of SCLC rather than as an independent organization. King seemed to feel frustrated on many levels.

"So this is Snick," I said to myself with disappointment, walking out of that musty, dusty cubbyhole. In my wildest fantasies, I had no idea that in two months I would be sitting in King's chair as the executive secretary. But I would have to live a little more and die a little more before tackling that job.

My desire to build an effective youth organization took new inspiration that evening from a long talk with Ella Baker at her apartment in Atlanta. This was my first meeting with her, although she was known to me for her long history as a freedom fighter. Ella Baker had worked for many years with the national office of the NAACP and knew some of its history intimately. She had served as the first executive director of the Southern Christian Leadership Conference, and was responsible for the initial call for a Student Leadership Conference at Shaw University in Raleigh, North Carolina, in April, 1960. It was out of this conference that SNCC had emerged.

My first impression as we walked into her Atlanta apartment was of a living room cluttered with newspapers, which she was in the process of clipping. I had heard of her speaking ability, and when she talked I could hear the resonance in her voice. She was very quick-witted and precise, and demanded precision in the remarks of others. I had expected her to be embittered by what I knew of her experiences at SCLC but all she would say about that was, "I didn't come there to stay."

We discussed with her our plans to go to Monroe and our intentions to form an organization of young people who would work full time in the South. She thought both ideas good and encouraged us to proceed with their implementation. We left her house more wise about the history of civil rights organizations in this country and with that deepened sense of perspective which was Miss Baker's constant gift to people.

The next morning Paul got his letter from SCLC and we left for Monroe that afternoon by train.

The trip seemed to take forever. Monroe wasn't far, but we seemed to make every possible stop. Dragging along in the hot coach, Paul and I discussed our plan of operation for Monroe.

To avoid being met by a mob, we had not notified Williams of the hour of our arrival. We had his address and his telephone number and were sure that, once there, we could make it to his house or call him from the train station. But, although I didn't feel nervous about the trip, I wanted to go over the whole procedure.

"O.K., suppose we arrive in Monroe and there's a mob?" I asked.

"We'll ignore it and act as if we are just passengers getting off. Besides, no one knows we're arriving and the probability of a mob isn't that big," Paul replied.

"O.K. Suppose we get to Monroe and there's no cab that will take us to Williams's house?"

"Then we'll telephone."

"All right. Suppose there's no telephone at the train station?"

"Not very likely."

"Well, shit, anything is possible."

"We'll just have to wait and see what the situation is when we get there," Paul answered.

I agreed and settled back now, watching the Southern landscape go by, thinking of the vastness and richness of this country and why white people were not about to give it up easily.

"Y'all going to Monroe?" an elderly black porter asked us, leaning toward Paul, who sat on the aisle.

Paul and I looked at each other; we wondered how he knew. It didn't occur to us that he could have gotten this information from our ticket.

"I'm from Monroe," he said, noticing our hesitation. "This is my regular run. I get off at Monroe." He paused, waiting for us to reply.

"Oh, really," I said, following it up, but cool.

"Yep. Y'all know anybody in Monroe?"

"A few people," I answered.

"Monroe's a rough town," he commented. "A rough town."

"Hear Robert Williams been having a little trouble," I said, trying to get to the point.

"Some. Y'all know Robert Williams?"

"We heard of 'im," Paul replied.

"Kinda figured y'all were going to see him. Is that right?"

"Could be. You know him?" I asked, feeling more comfortable and digging the style of this wise old man.

"I know him quite well. Quite well. Be willing to give y'all a lift when we get to Monroe. Got my car at the train station."

"O.K.," we both said. The porter moved on down the aisle.

"Look," I told Paul, "when we get in his car, then we'll tell him where we're going. You never know."

CHAPTER 20

The Klan and a Frame-up

"WELCOME," Robert Williams said as we entered his house. He shook our hands with strength and a warmth exuded from his greeting and from his personality. He was a heavyset man, not fat, his hair cut so that a portion of it came down over his forehead, with a goatee. He looked as though he could be a veteran of the United States Marines, which he was. Thirty-five years old at the time of this meeting, three years older than I, Williams struck me as a determined man.

"Mabel, they're here," he called to his wife, who came out smiling and also greeted us warmly. She was a tall, attractive, brown-skinned woman, thirty-one years old. I knew that she drew the cartoons for the *Crusader*, a paper which she and Williams had started in July, 1959.

The Williams's house was large, with a hallway separating it into two parts. On the left was the living room, dining room, and kitchen. On the right were bedrooms. From the hall a stairway led upstairs. In the living room I could see about forty rifles lying on the floor, stacked on top of each other. I asked Williams if he would object to the public being informed about this little arsenal. He said, "No, not at all. It was John Foster Dulles's policy to carry a big stick to avoid incidents, and that's what we're doing too."

Robert quickly dispensed with the formal names and insisted we call him Robert or Rob, as he was affectionately called by friends. We explained again the purpose of our visit and he promised to make it as easy as possible for us to get together the story of Monroe. He wanted the world to know that law and order had broken down here and that he was going to protect his home and his family by any means necessary.

"But before I talk to you in detail," he said, "I want you to meet Dr. Perry. Ask him any questions you want. He can tell you how all this got started in Monroe. We had to guard his house and he's been through hell ever since." He went to telephone Dr. Perry who immediately came over and took us to his house.

It was a modern brick house, spacious and well furnished, and I could see right away one reason that Dr. Albert Perry had had trouble. He was an uppity nigger to the Klan and the racist whites of Monroe. He was an educated, high-living nigger who was getting too smart for his pants. But not only that, he was an educated nigger who wouldn't Tom, a nigger who wouldn't listen to the white people and do their bidding as so many Negroes did in Union County and throughout the land.

The trouble began in 1957, Dr. Perry told us, when he was elected president of a new human relations group for Union County (Monroe is Union's county seat). The Monroe *Enquirer*, one of the two local papers, carried a front-page story on its formation. Perry handed us the clipping now, so that we could see what a wild, radical outfit the group had been.

Establishment of a Union County Council on Human Relations composed of representatives of all faiths and both races was announced here today. Announcement of the organization came on the eve of Brotherhood Week, which is observed nationally, by proclamation of President Eisenhower, Feb. 17-24. Dr. A. E. Perry is council president, J. Ray Shute, vice president, Mrs. Mabel Williams, secretary, and Miss Frances Cox, treasurer. . . . The Council is the outgrowth of many weeks of quiet effort that began during Christmas. At that time a number of people from various churches curtailed their normal Christmas activity to work at a project which they hoped would help give more lasting reality to the meaning of Christmas. . . . The Constitution and bylaws of the council list the purpose of the council as follows:

1. To promote public awareness and understanding of problems that affect good feelings between the races in Union County.

2. To strengthen the belief that Union County citizens have the courage to face up to problems that must be faced by responsible citizenship in a changing world.

3. To promote equal opportunity for all citizens in employment, education, recreation and all other phases of community life.

4. To encourage a do-it-together movement for development of leadership, exchange of ideas and broader participation in the upbuilding of a good community. . . .

"Let this particular week emphasize an intent for each to live a useful life founded on brotherhood," said Dr. Perry. "Let it strengthen a resolve to build a community in which people are united in mutual love and respect, without regard to race or creed and where everyone lives with benefit of unlimited opportunities. In such a unity people can give each other immeasurable help that benefits all."

Dr. Perry came back in the room with sandwiches and drinks as Paul and I finished setting up our tape recorder. "The vice-president of the council was white, and a Unitarian," he said. "We had a faithful few who attended the meetings and attempted to do something. The organization went on for about a year and finally died out because of lack of nourishment, lack of interest, on the part of most people in the county. In fact, most of the people figured that since the president was a Catholic, which I am, and the vice-president a Unitarian, the Catholics and Unitarians would run the organization. The Protestants said, 'We just won't take any part in it.' It was that form of prejudice that really killed the organization."

In the summer of 1957, a black boy was drowned in a swimming hole. With adequate facilities and supervision, another black youth might have grown into manhood. But the local swimming pool was reserved for whites. The boy's death moved Dr. Perry to action. Perry could not get the new council to do anything about swimming facilities—too touchy a subject—although it had worked on other recreational facilities. He therefore turned to Robert Williams, president of the Union County chapter of the NAACP.

"We were informed that the Park and Recreation Commission was responsible for providing these facilities," Dr. Perry explained. "So a committee from the local NAACP went to the commission, telling them of our aspirations. But we were told that nothing could be done. We'd have to go to the City Council. The City Council held the purse strings for appropriations and so forth.

"We went to the City Council and we talked to them. We could get no relief there. They said that they had swimming facilities for Negroes in the master plan but then they couldn't tell us when this master plan was going to be put into effect. So we asked about the existing pool, which was paid for by tax funds and operated by the city. If we could use that only, say, one day a week.

"They said something to the effect of 'Oh, the water would have to be drained out each time that it was used,' and they couldn't do that. It wound up that we got nowhere, not even a promise, not even some consideration. We met a stone wall there. We had gone to them and they almost threw us out. They laughed at us for the most part.

"After that, Robert Williams took a group of youngsters down to the swimming pool. They were denied admission. And this formed the basis for a suit. The paper carried the news and the surrounding white community figured that they would lose their swimming pool, and so the Klan moved in.

"They started having meetings and aroused the sentiment of the people. In August somebody called my house when I wasn't home and told my wife that the Klan had met that night and they were gonna get me tomorrow night. Well, they didn't get me then or after that. We weren't going to have anybody hurt just because of them youngsters trying to seek their human rights and their legal rights. So a guard was put up. My house was very well guarded. I never was by myself for one moment. Some fifty fellows would stay at the house all night, leave the house and go to their jobs, and another shift would come in the next night. Whenever I would leave my office, somebody would come up and follow me home and so forth. The siege of my home lasted from August to October.

"I kept getting those phone calls during the summer of '57. I would call up the police department and tell them that somebody was worrying me on the telephone and so forth. I might get to talk with the chief. I might not. But whoever I would talk to would not give me any satisfaction about providing protection. The police department would say things like, maybe I shouldn't have lived the way I have lived or I should have been dead when I was a baby or else, 'well, it's your fault that somebody knows your phone number. If you hadn't gone to the City Council meeting, nobody would have called you.'

"We often went to the Klan meetings. We always knew where they were going to be held because they were announced in the local paper. At the meetings, they'd sometimes have curiosity seekers and onlookers; seventy-five hundred people was an estimate that one of the newspapers carried about one meeting. The nucleus of the meeting wouldn't know that we were there, just the people who were around us as we came up into the meeting. We used to wear fatigues and go in two or three cars. We'd have one group of fellows in a car looking out for us and keeping their eyes on us all the time to protect us if anything happened. We would get right up in the group and take a look around. People would see us and then they'd gradually move away. And after a while, we'd find ourselves in a spot all by ourselves.

"They would talk about Sammy Davis, Jr.; they'd talk about Chesterfield cigarettes; they'd talk about the Charlotte *Observer*; they'd talk about anything just to create an emotional feeling in the group. It was interesting to know that people would feel the way that they felt.

"After they'd have the meetings, they'd get in their cars and parade through the colored community, always through the colored community, blowing their horns. They'd have the lights on inside the car. They'd have women in there and they'd have children in there. The men would be clad in robes and caps. I don't remember having seen anybody with hoods on to cover their faces because it was illegal to do that. However, that doesn't necessarily mean that they didn't have any. They'd go through the colored community, disturbing the peace, shooting guns, and insulting colored women. Doing most anything they would feel like doing.

"We tried to get the word out to the national press about all this. But when the reporters called the police chief to check, he would deny that it was true. 'Nothing happened. All's quiet,' he would say."

Dr. Perry paused. "The Klan paraded around my house a couple of times," he continued. "But then we met gunfire with gunfire."

The night of October 5, 1957, was the last time that the Klan came into Newtown, a black section of Monroe, firing their guns and trying to frighten away or maybe kill Dr. Perry. What happened that night has been vividly described by Julian Mayfield, author, actor, and close associate of Robert Williams, in an unpublished manuscript:

It was just another good time Klan night, the high point of which would come when they dragged Dr. Perry over the state line if they did not hang or burn him first.

But near Dr. Perry's home their revelry was suddenly shattered by the sustained fire of scores of men who had been instructed not to kill anyone if it were not necessary. The firing was blistering, disciplined and frightening. The motorcade, of about eighty cars, which had begun in a spirit of good fellowship, disintegrated into chaos, with panicky, robed men fleeing in every direction. Some abandoned their automobiles and had to continue on foot. One carload of men inadvertently turned up a dead-end street. Williams and a detachment of men halted them as they tried to back out.

Anyone familiar with southern customs will appreciate the following dialogue:

Williams: "What are you fellows doing over here?"

Driver: "Oh, Mr. Williams, we just didn't know what we were doing. If you'll just let us out of here, I promise we'll never do it again."

Williams: "Well you fellows want to be more careful the next time. You could get killed."

Driver: "Oh yes, sir, we know."

Williams: "Then get the hell out of here!"

They did.

Self-defense not only stopped the Klan that night but it put an end to the caravans through the black community. "After that, an ordinance was passed by the City Council that said no more parades without permission," Dr. Perry resumed his story. "No more than three cars can be in a group at a time without special permission. So the Klan stopped having these caravans. Incidentally, after we ran the Klan under the ground here, they went on down to Lumberton, about fifty miles from here. There are a lot of Indians there, and they broke the thing up. They had quite a good time chasing the Klan out."

But racists do not give up easily and their power positions make it possible for them to persecute a black man relentlessly if they have decided to get rid of the nigger. Dr. Perry had become a symbol of opposition to the Klan's efforts to castrate the black men of Monroe, especially Rob Williams. So they pulled the oldest trick in the South. They accused Dr. Perry of messing with a white woman . . . of criminally aborting a white woman for twenty-five dollars.

Dr. Perry began the story, "As a Catholic, I have refused to perform legal abortions or sterilizations. It's customary or accepted procedure that in cases where a woman, married or unmarried, has three, four, five children and is having difficulty with delivery and has her husband's consent, that over the signature of three physicians she can be sterilized. Well, I've had those things presented to me quite often, and I have refused to sign them because of religious affiliation. It goes without saying that I wouldn't have done a criminal abortion on this woman. I would have had to be crazy to have done such an act in the face of all the animosity against me.

"There was no evidence at all. She supposedly aborted or lost the baby while she was in the hospital. Yet there was no record of her having had a miscarriage there. There was no record of the examination of the products of conception. Actually, it was just her word against mine. And that was the way it went, all the way through.

"I first had a jury trial in Monroe. This trial, from jury selection to evidence, was all hushed up. I was born dead in a manner of speaking. They were going to get me no matter what. And that they did.

"During that trial, the City Council called a meeting to get its story over to the national press. They invited special Negro citizens to give their views on what was happening and what they thought about the situation. This sprang from the fact that we had been sending all of our news about the Klan straight to the national press agencies and they (the City Council) wanted to get their side over," Dr. Perry added.

"They called the old type of leadership there, but very few of them would go. They figured it was too hot. In instances like this, the white man will say that communication between the races has broken down, but there hasn't been any communication, ever, between the races, except when the white man wanted to fool somebody or fool himself that he was doing right by the Negro. Actually, there is a place for communication and a place for talking and a place for diplomatic maneuvering. But in a situation where you have all for one race and none for another, there's very little room for talk.

"The whites think they can fool us all the time. For instance, Richardson, a trial lawyer, told people I'm not 'umble. He says that he tried to help me during my trial. Well, he volunteered his time to prosecute me. That was helping me a whole lot. But he said that he tried to help me. He told somebody, 'I like Perry, but he's just not 'umble. I tried to fix it so he could plead guilty to a lesser charge.' Actually, one of the Negro lawyers did come to me with that. And I told him to take it and stick it up his ear.

"I appealed the conviction to the State Supreme Court. That court sent it back to the lower court for trial again because the first jury had come from another county, Enson County (where there are more Klansmen than in this one), and this was a technical violation. The second trial was held in an adjoining county. They convicted me too, even though some of the evidence—the records of the woman borrowing money to pay me —turned out to be false.

"I appealed it to the Supreme Court of the United States for a writ of *certiorari*, which was denied. My basis for the application to the U.S. Supreme Court was that I had been denied my constitutional rights of equal protection under the law, that there was discrimination in the Grand Jury which had handed down the first indictment. I had records to show that during the twenty-five years before I was indicted, only one Negro had served on the Grand Jury—one lone Negro in the Grand Jury, and seemingly he was there by mistake. And yet they say there's no discrimination in the selection of the Grand Jury! It's that way all through this Southern hypocrisy. They'll slap you in the face and say, 'No, I didn't slap you. My hand just rested on your face.'

"The U.S. Supreme Court turned me down, and there wasn't much more I could do. It was a two-year struggle and I retained my lawyers myself, Taylor and Mitchell from Raleigh. I paid all the legal fees. I requested legal services from the NAACP, but they turned me down. On one occasion, I went to New York and did get some help from the national office, after seeing a host of people. But almost in its entirety, the bill was footed by me, except where the local people helped me with donations. The North Carolina NAACP was quite disgusting in their absence. Kelly Alexander is the state president and he stayed as far away from it as he could.

"When I found out I would have to go to prison, I talked to the woman who had said I aborted her. She's got quite a history behind her. She was raised down here by Prospect, a little community eight or ten miles from Monroe. And she was so apologetic now! She said, 'Well, Dr. Perry, I'm sorry, I wouldn't have done it if I had known then what I know now. I have gone through hell. I've almost lost my mind. They promised that they'd do a lot of things for me which they haven't done. And I'm just almost crazy. They told me that it would either be you or me, that is, after the thing got started. They told me you were a member of the NAACP and that you and Robert Williams were just trying to ruin the county. So, they had to get rid of you some way and they came up with this idea. And after I got started into it, they wouldn't let me stop.' She said, 'Now, at your next trial, I'm gonna straighten things out.' I told her, 'You're too late. There's no more trial now.'

"She couldn't believe it. She called up the police department to see whether I was telling the truth about going to prison. I talked to her a little later and she said, 'Who issued the warrant on you?' She thought that another warrant had to be issued for me to go to prison. 'The police department doesn't know anything about a warrant for you.' So she was in communication with them.

"But actually, when the Supreme Court denied the writ of *certiorari*, I was automatically scheduled to go into prison. The two years I stayed in court gave me enough chance to get ready to go, because I figured that that's exactly what would happen. Except I didn't expect they would pick me up and take me to prison the way they did. In most instances where a man has been on bond for some time, a judge will sign an order and give the man ten days, at least ten days, to get his personal effects in order. In my case, they just came and got me out of the house. Picked me up one night when I didn't expect them to come. And I was gone off to jail. That's the way it was."

Dr. Perry got up to bring more sandwiches. It was already after midnight and we had become hungry again.

"Prison was one hell of a place," Dr. Perry then continued. "You just have to live till the time you get out. All the guards have an inferiority complex, and they take it out on you. I was sent from one camp to another. I asked one of the guards if I would be able to write my lawyer. 'Just let your lawyer know everywhere you are,' he told me. For having asked that question, I was placed in a little cellblock for eight weeks. I'd go out to eat and then I'd come back to my little cell. They all looked at me as an uppity nigger.

"I was put on parole from July 7, 1960, to July 6 of this year [1961]. I have an office in Charlotte, which is twenty-five miles from here. I stay here at night and practice there during the day. While I was on parole, they wouldn't let me come back to my home county to live or practice. I had to stay away from this county. I had to get a residence in Mecklenberg County. Now I can live here but I can practice only in Mecklenberg County. It would probably embarrass some people in Monroe if I were to practice medicine here on the same level again with some of the doctors who helped to prosecute me.

"I feel that I'll have to be very careful about what I say and what I do until I get back my license on a statewide basis. But that doesn't change me basically. Anything that I have said concerning the rights of man, I believed then and I believe now. I haven't changed as far as my feelings go. I've been a doctor, I've practiced for nine years here in this county. I've been without my license almost two years. I've been a convict in a state penitentiary. I've been an exile from home. And it hasn't changed me.

"The reception that people have given me since I've been back in the county has made me feel very good. I think most people, black and white, realize that it was a frame-up.

"I think most people think of what I did as a sacrifice. Well, I think that we all should sacrifice something. I feel that the lawyers should sacrifice, which they don't. They always go into these cases for the money they can get out of it. I think that the officials of the NAACP should have a firsthand feeling and experience in most of these fights for rights. And surely, I think that I should do my part. I don't think that I'll ever get through doing my part.

"It's that quality in me that most of these people around here don't like. Because they know that if I make up my mind, if I feel that I'm right, I'm going to stick to my guns. They don't like to see that in a professional man, because they figure that a professional man can steer people in a way that they don't want them to go. And that's the reason they hated me most.

"One of the men on the City Council told me, 'Well, doctor, you're better off than I am. You got a good education and you're making money, you got a beautiful home and so forth.' I said, 'Yeah, but I can't do the things that you can do.' The mayor once said to me, 'You know, there are places that I can't go, places down in Florida where I've been that I couldn't go.' Well, I told him the only place that I know that he couldn't go was to the ladies' rest room.

"They just didn't like me because maybe I represented something in this section of the country that is not supposed to be represented. See, a doctor is supposed to practice medicine; he's supposed to be in with the fellas uptown. He can get any favors he wants. But then he's got to help keep the Negro down. Keep 'em in their place, see. Anytime that they don't want to give the Negro something, they'll say, 'Well, doctor so-and-so said that it was his opinion that the Negro wasn't ready for it right now.' The Negro is ready for anything he can get, ever since he's been in slavery."

CHAPTER 21

The Kissing Case

BOYTE STREET was dark when we left Dr. Perry and returned to Robert's house. Not a stir, not a car passing, no one on the street. Williams sat on the porch, his .45 strapped to his waist, a carbine standing on the wall next to his wooden chair. Two or three teen-agers sat in the porch with him. This was Friday night, and Friday and Saturday nights were usually when trouble occurred. There had been threatening telephone calls all week. Last Saturday, some whites had driven down

Boyte Street and shot into several homes down the road from the Williams's house. They had not escaped without a scare. I could see why the Klan had quit coming through here in October, 1957—at least not in parades.

Rob told me that his wife Mabel had gathered together some written materials which might be useful to us. We went inside the house to get them from her. On top was a short account which Julian Mayfield had written, but not published, of the world-famous 1958 "kissing case," the next major chapter of Monroe history after Dr. Perry's frame-up. I sat down on the couch in the living room and read it quickly. These are excerpts from what Mayfield wrote:

On October 28, 1958, two Monroe lads, James Hanover Thompson and David "Fuzzy" Simpson, seven and nine years old respectively, joined a group of white boys playing cowboys. Three white girls in the same age group watched the boys from the sidelines. When the game was over, one of the white girls proposed playing house during which Hanover kissed, or was kissed by, one of the white girls. Later that afternoon, the girl related the tale of her adventure to her mother. Then all hell broke loose.

In describing her reaction several weeks later, the mother told a newspaperwoman: "I was furious. I would have killed Hanover myself if I had had the chance." For an adult woman, of education and presumed intelligence, to express such hostility toward a seven-year-old child may strike many readers as abnormal, even for the South, but consider the reaction of the father who armed himself with a shotgun and went looking for the boys and their parents. Moreover, the girl's white neighbors, in an unparalleled outburst of civic spirit, armed themselves and joined in the hunt. The culprits, Hanover and Fuzzy, were arrested that evening as they pedaled along a roadway on a bicycle.

On November 3rd, at the request of the boys' mothers, Williams hurried to the courthouse, but he was not admitted to the proceedings because he was not an attorney. Juvenile Court Judge, J. Hampton Price, after a brief hearing, found the boys guilty and sentenced them to indefinite terms in reform school. If they behaved well, he said, they might be released before they were twenty-one years old. The boys had no defense counsel.

This last sentence should not be overlooked. Williams had already requested legal help from Kelly Alexander, Chairman of the North Carolina NAACP, and Conrad Pearson, an attorney who frequently represented the NAACP in the state. Mr. Pearson had replied that if Williams would bring the mothers to Durham, 150 miles away, he (Pearson) would talk to them. Meanwhile, Mrs. Thompson's daughter in New York, through an intermediary, brought the matter to the attention of the National Board of the NAACP. Yet, it was not until December 31, after the boys had been confined for several weeks in the reformatory at Hoffman, North Carolina, that Mr. Wilkins announced in a New York meeting with Robert Williams and Conrad Lynn, a well-known militant civil rights attorney, that the NAACP would enter the case on behalf of the boys.

One cannot help wondering about the delay. The case fell clearly within the province of the leading civil rights organization in the country. One would have thought that a sense of outrage would have caused these leaders to immediately channel all available legal resources into the defense of the boys. We must look deeper.

Both James Thompson and Fuzzy Simpson were poor. At the time of the arrest, their mothers each earned $18 a week as domestics and on this income the women each supported several children. As protests over the arrests had mounted, Monroe officials had cast doubt on the legitimacy of the boys' births. Moreover, they had asserted that James and Fuzzy were delinquents who had been in trouble with the police before for stealing hams and a bicycle.

Many of the members of the Negro leadership class cannot help regarding such families as the Thompsons and the Simpsons with misgiving and shame. Propagandists for white supremacy cite such families as examples of the innate inferiority of Afro-Americans. This puts the black leadership establishment on the defensive. After all, they are "educated" and "cultured." These leaders know that the vast majority of black Americans have been denied the opportunity to develop their full human potential. Still, most members of this class cannot help cringing in shame when a fellow black man murders, robs or steals.

During the first several weeks of the boys' internment, Conrad Lynn and Robert Williams were frequently importuned to drop the case. But by that time, thousands of people were wondering why the NAACP had not already entered the case. Ted Posten had been the first to break the story outside of Carolina in the New York *Post* on November 10. And it was a remarkable Englishwoman, Joyce Egginton, who was responsible for focusing the outrage of the world on the little town of Monroe.

White Southerners like to boast of their pure British ancestry, and nothing pleases them more than to lavish their famed hospitality on a visitor from the motherland. If that visitor happens to be a pretty brunette with blue eyes and a shapely figure, no door between Richmond and Atlanta will be closed to her.

To carry out her assignment for the London *News Chronicle*, Joyce Egginton had only to speak in her cultivated British accent. North Carolina officials outdid themselves trying to please her. She received permission to visit the boys at Hoffman, and she took Mrs. Thompson and Mrs. Simpson along. (The mothers had not been allowed to see their children since the "trial.") Cameras were forbidden at Hoffman, but Miss Egginton took hers along at the bottom of a basket of fruit. When Hanover, arms outspread, rushed across the waiting room to greet his mother, Miss Egginton snapped the picture.

On December 16, the readers of the London *News Chronicle* witnessed the moving scene on the front page of their newspaper. The photograph was reprinted throughout Europe and Asia. There were massive demonstrations in Paris, Rome and Vienna. The hugest was in Rotterdam, where the United States Embassy was stoned. An international committee was formed in Europe to defend Hanover and Fuzzy. One M. Sarls circulated a petition in Rotterdam's Franklin D. Roosevelt High School and before he was done he had 15,000 signatures. He forwarded the petition to Mrs. Eleanor Roosevelt who sent it on to President Eisenhower who passed it on to the Governor of North Carolina. We may only surmise what communications passed between these important personages, what strong recommendations citing the intense embarrassment the continued imprisonment of Hanover and Fuzzy was causing. But three known facts may provide a clue:

1. On February 11, 1959, Attorney General Seawell, speaking before B'nai B'rith in Charlotte, N.C., confessed that the Negroes were waging such a "war of propaganda" that the state might be forced to release the boys.

2. On February 11, the mothers of both boys were asked by officials of the state to sign what was in effect a waiver recognizing the legality of their sons' confinement—that is, an admission of guilt—with the assurance that their children would be released. The mothers refused to sign. And,

3. On February 13, the children were released without conditions or explanation.

Yet, just two years later, in a heated reply to an article of mine in the April 1, 1961 issue of *Commentary*, Mr. Kelly Alexander (of the NAACP) wrote about the Kissing Case:

> What an amazing piece of arrogance and falsehood. Whoever heard of any sovereign state bowing under "Pressure of world opinion," and particularly a Southern state? Has this ever happened before?

According to Mr. Alexander, he and journalist Harry Golden, through consultations with Governor Hodges, had effected Hanover and Fuzzy's release. Thus is history often remembered by those, who, however unwillingly, participate in the making of it.

CHAPTER 22

Robert Williams Versus
Roy Wilkins

WHEN I went back outside, I asked Williams to give us rifles. Since he feared trouble, we shouldn't be sitting on the front porch talking to him without some protection. It was important for us to show that we were prepared to help defend his home. Not that he distrusted us; but it was necessary to demonstrate that we were not opposed to self-defense. We didn't want to be labeled pacifists. He got us guns, then sat down to continue the story of his struggle against racism—and against the national NAACP.

Williams had been drafted for the presidency of the Union County branch of the NAACP in 1956, not long after returning to Monroe as a Marine veteran. "Drafted" was the word; the chapter had only six members left in it when Rob came along. Most professional or skilled Negroes had pulled out after the 1954 Supreme Court ruling against segregation because their meal tickets required maintaining the goodwill of whites and the whites were in no mood for advancing colored people. Williams, then working as a yardman and laborer, was not of that class; "the only fool left" for the presidency, as one observer put it. He had, by then, acquired a certain reputation for writing letters to the local papers about the living conditions of black people. His letters had evoked one prophetic response from a white man who wrote to the *Union Mail* saying that just as one rotten apple spoils the barrel, Williams was spoiling all the good colored people. And he should be got rid of, the letter writer advised.

Since a branch was required to have at least fifty members in order to retain an NAACP charter, Williams went out recruiting among the people he knew best; domestic workers, sharecroppers, tenant farmers, and the guys hanging around the poolroom. Not the usual NAACP type. Rob was highly successful; the new recruits thought the NAACP was a militant organization and they had many deep-seated complaints about the racist quality of their lives.

This was enough to make the state NAACP chairman, Kelly Alexander, nervous and perhaps also jealous. According to Mabel Williams, Alexander was the sort of person for whom you have to be pretty big before you can speak to him. "And he considered us nobody. Regardless of how hard we tried to get to him, he was too big to bother with us. He did come down for one meeting and the people seemed to cater more to Rob than they did to him. I think that hurt his ego."

Then came the kissing case and Williams's pressure on the national NAACP to enter the case. Even while that struggle still raged, the seeds of future conflict with the NAACP were being sown.

In January of 1959, a month before the boys finally emerged from the reformatory, a hotel maid of Monroe was kicked down a flight of stairs by a white. She swore out a warrant against him, an unusual action to be taken by black against white in this area.

At about the same time, James Mobley of Monroe was arrested and charged with attempting to rape a white farm wife. Mobley, who suffered from an old head injury, was considered by the black community to be mentally retarded.

But the case which brought tension to a climax involved a white named Louis Medlin. He was accused of having entered the home of a young black woman, eight months pregnant, and attempting to rape her. The charge stated that Medlin had then chased her across an open field and assaulted her while her six-year-old son attempted to come to her defense. The latter part of this incident had been witnessed by a Southern white woman, who was ready to testify in court to what she had seen. Some of Robert Williams's group, according to Julian Mayfield, were all for seizing Medlin and giving him the same treatment that Charles Mack Parker—lynched on April 25, 1959, in Poplarville—had just received. Williams was able to dissuade them, saying that the eyes of the world were on Monroe.

Rape, brutality, lynching—it was enough, enough. Feeling ran high in the black community and highest in Robert Williams. Then the white man meted out his justice On May 4, 1959, the Union County Grand

Jury freed the white man charged with having kicked the hotel maid down the stairs. Within twenty-four hours, a trial jury found Louis Medlin not guilty of assault with intent to rape the black woman. That same afternoon, Mobley received a sentence of two years' imprisonment—which could have been thirty years, if a New York lawyer had not saved him by a technicality.

Robert Williams was at the courthouse when Medlin was acquitted. His people, particularly the women, demanded of him, "How safe are we going to be now?" Rob stood on the courthouse steps and uttered his famous statement:

We cannot take these people who do us injustice to the court and it becomes necessary to punish them ourselves. In the future we are going to have to try and convict them on the spot. We cannot rely on the law. We can get no justice under the present system. If we feel that injustice is done, we must right then and there, on the spot, be prepared to inflict punishment on these people.

Since the federal government will not bring a halt to lynching in the South, and since the so-called courts lynch our people legally, if it's necessary to stop lynching with lynching, then we must be willing to resort to that method. We must meet violence with violence.

Williams's statement, as Julian Mayfield has observed, "was a final chucking off of optimism about a nation that had no place for him at its inception. It was a recognition that all the prayers of colored folks, bolstered by the goodwill of large numbers of whites, could not bring black men their freedom."

At eleven o'clock in the morning on the day after Williams made his statement, Roy Wilkins called him from New York to confirm that he had said those words. Williams replied, "Yes, and I intend to repeat it over several radio and television programs in the next few days." Williams made it clear he was speaking for himself and not for the NAACP. He pointed out, however, that his views represented the thinking of the majority of black people in Monroe. Wilkins argued that it would be impossible for people to distinguish between what Williams said as a person and what he was saying as the president of the Union County chapter of the NAACP.

Williams made a scheduled press appearance and repeated his statement a few hours later. The next day, May 6, he was suspended for six months by telegram from Wilkins.

Propped up by Establishment support and committed as he is to the preservation of the United States government, it is no wonder that Wilkins acted with all deliberate speed in the case against Williams. He heard only those scary words "meet violence with violence" and disregarded the ones which preceded them, "We can get no justice under the present system."

That Williams was arguing for self-defense in 1959 and not for armed, aggressive, revolutionary violence is evidenced by the statement he made in his brief submitted to the Committee on Branches of the NAACP appealing the suspension: "He [Williams] believes the message of armed self-reliance should be spread among Negroes of the South. He is convinced that a somnolent national government will only take action when it is aware that individual Negroes are no longer facing the mobs in isolation, but are acquiring the habit of coming to the aid of their menaced brothers."

The Committee on Branches held a hearing in New York on Rob's suspension. Kelly Alexander was one of those who testified against him. The suspension was upheld. The final appeal would come at the NAACP national convention in July.

Without telling Williams, Wilkins had had a stenographer take down their telephone conversation about his controversial statement; now he distributed copies of the transcript at the convention. There was considerable support for Rob there. But, through a parliamentary device, a vote of 764 to 14 settled the case in favor of Roy Wilkins. That fiftieth anniversary convention of the NAACP was also distinguished by its failure to acknowledge in any way the contribution of W. E. B. Du Bois to our people's struggle on an occasion when many others were honored.

At this point in his story, Rob suddenly fell silent. A car had come down the street and then backed up. "Hit the dust," Williams told us. We immediately got down behind the high hedge which bordered the yard in front of his house and which could provide natural protection for a whole squad of men. There were also two large trees in the yard, one on each side, in which defenders could hide and often did. Paul put a bullet in the chamber of his rifle and we waited. But the car drove on. After it had passed out of sight, Rob said to Paul, "Never put one in the chamber unless you're getting ready to shoot." It was a safety precaution from many nights of readiness.

In 1960 Robert had gone to Cuba to see what that brand new revolution was all about. There he met and talked at length with another visitor, Julian Mayfield, who began to champion Williams's cause. By the spring of 1961, Williams had again been elected president of his chapter and in that capacity he sent a telegram to the Cuban Ambassador to the United Nations at the height of the Bay of Pigs invasion sponsored by the United States. Speaking during a tense debate in which it was Adlai Stevenson's shameful role to lie about what the American government was doing, Ambassador Raul Roa interrupted his speech to read the message: "Please convey to Mr. Adlai E. Stevenson: Now that the United States has proclaimed military support for the people willing to rebel against oppression, oppressed Negroes in South urgently request tanks, artillery, bombs, money, and the use of American airfields and white mercenaries to crush the racist tyrants who have betrayed the American Revolution and Civil War. We also request prayers for this noble undertaking."

According to observers, the crowd in the gallery and the Afro-Asian delegations burst into applause. Stevenson, who was pink with embarrassment, sat in stony silence as Dr. Roa read the sender's name, Robert Williams, President Union County Branch, National Association for the Advancement of Colored People, Monroe, North Carolina.

Rob, Paul, and I sat on the porch until 4 A.M., guns in hand, until Robert told us we should try to get some sleep. He was going to sit by himself for another hour or so until daybreak, and then he would also rest. I thought how important it was for him to guard the house, but I felt that this man ought to be able to live in a country where he didn't have to sit up all night protecting his home. He had been doing this every night since the attacks on his life on June 23 and June 25 of 1961, the attacks which had brought Paul and me to Monroe.

CHAPTER 23

No Room at the Swimming Pool

WE SAT on guard duty the next two nights as well; during the day we talked with different people. These included Mabel Williams and a friend, Mrs. Asa Lee, the wife of the porter who had met us on the train and had taken us to Robert's house. The two women told us about what had happened in June.

The swimming pool was for many years, and in some places still is, the most sacred of segregated public institutions for the average cracker. The whites of Monroe had proven themselves to be no exception to this. By the summer of 1961, black people in Union County still had no swimming facilities. Robert and Mabel Williams decided to renew that struggle on June 16; they took some teen-agers to the "white" pool and began picketing.

Robert had long been a target in Monroe, but now he had gone too far. More than the cold sweat of fear rose on the foreheads of local Klansmen, segregationists, and just plain racists. They were enraged. The bad nigger of Monroe had to be wiped out once and for all. They tried first on June 23. Mrs. Williams and Mrs. Lee told the story:

Mrs. Lee: We were going to the pool, Mrs. Williams and I. Robert, he had just gone ahead of us with a teen-ager in his car. We were carrying some refreshments down to the pool for the boys and girls who were picketing.

As we were traveling along the dual highway, we noticed this car—a very large car—right up behind Robert's car. Mrs. Williams hollered: "Oh look! They're trying to run him off the road!" We speeded up, but another car came in between us to prevent us from getting any closer. The big car rammed Robert in the back, just opposite the highway patrol station."

Mrs. Williams: The big car had two white men in it. The driver was a white merchant. He tried to run Robert's Volkswagen off the road on the right and when that failed, he tried to drive him off on the left. Seeing that he couldn't drive Robert's car off the road, he began to bump it from behind, trying to overturn it.

We were passing the highway patrol station and we yelled to the highway patrolmen who were up there in the station yard, begging them to come on. This is ordinarily a forty-five-mile zone, but they were pushing Robert's car at a rate of about seventy miles an hour, right down the highway past the patrol station. The patrolmen just laughed and looked at the incident while it was happening.

Mrs. Lee: We continued on behind Robert as close as we could. Finally we caught up with him. He had been run off into the ditch. Mrs. Williams was hysterical after seeing her husband about to get murdered there. in front of her eyes. But he told us to continue on. And we continued on.

We found this car; it had been run into a deserted driveway and hid behind some trees. That is when we got the license number. Then we proceeded on to the pool, amid a whole lot of yells and name-calling from the whites.

Mrs. Williams: We went to the police who were down at the pool and asked for an arrest. I talked first to one policeman who turned his back and would not even listen. Then I went to Chief A. A. Mauney. I gave him the license number that we had taken from the car. And later, Robert even gave him the name of the person who was driving the car. But, as to date, no warrant has been issued for the arrest of this man.

After I left the pool, I came back home and called Washington, D.C., to the Justice Department and asked to speak to Robert Kennedy. I was informed that Robert Kennedy was not there. And they wanted to know the nature of my call. So I talked to the secretary in the Justice Department and she informed me that there was nothing that could be done about it and referred me to the civil rights department.

I called the civil rights department and I talked to someone there. I think his name was Barry. I gave him a complete report of what had happened. He also informed me that there was nothing that they could do about it and suggested that I call the local FBI, which is located twenty-five miles from here, in Charlotte. Then I called the Charlotte FBI and reported to them exactly what had happened and they told me there was nothing they could do unless they got orders from Washington.

Despite the attack and the knowledge that he could get no protection, Williams and his followers decided to continue picketing the swimming pool. On Sunday, June 25, a large mob of whites surrounded the pool. Mrs. Lee describes some of the heroism of the Monroe blacks and especially that of Mabel Williams:

Mrs. Lee: Sunday was a beautiful day. We were anticipating a little trouble because, since that other attempt on Robert's life, there had been phone calls and threats made on the lives of people, of Robert and others. The children knew as they left here to go to the pool that perhaps some of them would get hurt, perhaps some of them would get killed. I often think of the look on their faces as they got in the cars to go on with their picket.

As we were going to the pool, we were halted by cars stopped in front of us. We realized, as we moved in farther, that something had happened ahead of us. Mrs. Williams was with me at this time. She got out and got up on the side of my car to see if she could look over the other cars. And she saw Robert's car had been hit. Robert and the others were standing there with their guns in their hands. "Well," Mrs. Williams said, "there's no need of me going down there now. They got things under control. They got the guns." So we sat there until traffic was cleared."

It was Steve Pressen, a member of the Board of Aldermen, who had the highway patrol clear the area. What Mrs. Lee did not mention and may not have seen, was that a mob of some twenty-five hundred whites had gathered at the intersection and that one man—the white who hit Williams's car—was shouting, "Get the nigger. Get the nigger!"

Mrs. Lee: We went down to the pool. Robert was there, and the police. He was showing them how his car had been hit. They were telling him they didn't see nothin' but a little small dent in his car. The left-hand light of his car had been knocked completely out and his tire was scraping the fender, they had hit him so bad. But the police didn't want to take out any warrants or arrest anyone there.

We drove on in and we set there. The children got out and started picketing. In the midst of the picketing of the pool, the crackers was yelling and cursing. And the police were cursing. Robert, he was standing there alone with his wife. *She stood there by him with a gun.* I don't think I'll ever forget that scene that afternoon. To see those people standing there amidst that crowd of whites threatening to kill 'em.

And those pickets, those young pickets, they continued to march. They didn't stop their marching.

Mrs. Williams: I knew that we couldn't depend on the police to protect us. The man who had rammed Robert's car was in the mob. He was pointed out to the police and we told the policemen, "He is the man who hit the car." The policeman just looked at us and laughed.

Well, my feelings then were that if I must die, I'm going to take 'em with me. I heard the chief of police tell my husband, "If you shoot any of these white people, here, I'm gonna kill you." And so I got my gun in my hand and I determined then that if he did anything to Robert, I was going to kill him.

Mrs. Lee: One of the whites went and got a live snake, a black snake, and threw it over there where the pickets was walking. It so happened that this snake turned and went the other way. Then a lot of whites said, "If they can picket, then we can picket, too." So they started in and were going to block the colored people pickets. But those boys just walked right on through 'em. Some of 'em brushed shoulders with 'em. The only ones carrying guns out there were Robert and his wife and myself. I was off a distance.

I often think about that day, how we would have been outnumbered. There was, I guess, two thousand whites there. And they were getting angrier and angrier by the minute. The local police didn't make the whites try to move on or nothin'. They were just lambasting back at Robert, called him all kinds of things.

Then this Howard Troe came in and started agitating that crowd on. Afterwards, the police gave us protection leaving the pool, because the crowd was supposed to have been so bad. I guess they were going to do us in. That is the beginning of a time when I think of America at its lowest ebb. No law and order. If law and order are not upheld in a country, there will be no country.

Mrs. Lee did not mean law and order in the sense that the racists today are trying to use the term *law and order* to apply to rebelling blacks. She meant that in this country, there are laws to guarantee certain rights to all people, but in their application, there have been two sets of laws, one for black and one for white. There has in reality been no law and order for the black man in this country since he was brought here as a slave. Mrs. Lee and Mrs. Williams knew this before, but that Sunday intensified their anger and alienation.

Mrs. Lee: After the affair at the pool and the attempts on Robert Williams's life, we know that these people, white people here in Monroe, they're not content simply with beating him up. That is the reason why we have to protect ourselves with a little more than words. We hope that no violence occurs. But if violence does occur, we are not gonna take it with the other cheek.

I often wonder whether the Negro in every hamlet and village and town will have to go through these procedures. Why hasn't the American government enforced the law to the extent that all of her citizens could be free? Why is it that an Afro-American has to spend most of his life's earnings to obtain his freedom that the Constitution says is his by birth?

It seems that any nation that will allow part of her citizens to be harassed, beaten, for the simple reason of trying to get their freedom, their equal rights, their civil rights, for them to be beaten for that, it seems to me that this country needs a new overhauling or something. Because the white—they have their right and nobody's supposed to interfere with them. They often tell us here that this is a white man's country. But this is God's country. And Negroes fought to win independence for America just as the white man did. In every war that America has had, there's always been the Negro. This is his country; he was born here, his ancestors were brought here against their will, so now this is his country too. And until complete freedom is given all citizens, America will forever be sending money to try to buy friendship of other countries.

Mrs. Williams: All of the people who we thought would help us just turned their heads and let this condition build up to the way it is. The way I feel now, all of the law enforcement officers are my enemies. All of the white people who would deny me my rights are my enemy. And to kill them would be no more to me than killing a snake who was threatening to bite me.

Even after that Sunday, picketing continued at the pool, until the whites did what they have almost always done in such circumstances. A young Monroe activist, Richard Crowder, told the story:

Richard Crowder: We would say to the white man who was running the pool that under federal law we have a right to be here. Every time we would go down there to get in, he'd say, "I'm sorry we have no facilities for colored, for an integrated pool."

The last time we went down there, we told him, well, you better make some facilities. We're going to give you exactly three days. And if there are no preparations made for us to have a pool or to swim here, we're coming in regardless.

He turned purple and green. You could see him turning colors. It was funny. When we went back down, that pool was closed. It's been closed ever since. There's a big sign in front, "Pool Closed."

Just think, we're not losing anything. We didn't have a pool in the beginning. Now they're missing theirs. Save the good white people. Tough shit.

Monroe had come full circle from the day four years earlier when Williams and Dr. Perry had launched the struggle for swimming facilities. Since then, they had endured almost everything from persecution in the courts to attempted murder. But Williams had in some ways become even more isolated. While in the past the press had carried some news on Monroe, there was now a complete whiteout. What was happening in that town remained unknown except what he could publicize in his own newspaper, the *Crusader* and other limited efforts. Many people had forgotten about the racist climate of Monroe; they were concentrating on Williams as an individual and saying repeatedly that violence was not the way. Yet, many of these same critics were practicing self-defense.

Fred Shuttlesworth of SCLC had guards around his home in Birmingham; Martin Luther King had also found a need for this from time to time. But when Williams set forth the concept of self-defense in different language, he found himself deliberately misinterpreted. For Williams was challenging the entire system of the United States and doing so with increasing fervor. This is why the media ostracized him. No longer an NAACP chapter president who made "inflammatory statements," he was becoming a revolutionary—born out of his own experience in trying to get justice for the black man in Monroe, to get the federal government to do its job, to simply save the lives of black people.

It seemed clear to me during that first trip that Monroe was on the brink of an explosion. I wrote down this and other observations in two field reports to Chicago, which read in part:

From: James Forman, Monroe
To: David Ray, Vice-President of the National Freedom Council
  and
  Mrs. Anne Braden, Field Secretary of the Southern Conference
  Educational Fund

I arrived in Monroe last night, Saturday, August 14, accompanied by Paul Brooks, who had a letter indicating he is on an investigating mission for the S.C.L.C. The Rev. Mr. Wyatt T. Walker, Executive Director, had informed Paul he would be calling the Justice Department to notify them of our intention to come to Monroe. Early Saturday morning, Paul called Mr. Walker telling him of the situation here and Walker wanted to know if the FBI had arrived on the scene. They hadn't. He indicated he would try to contact them again. Paul informs me that Walker said Dr. King has been apprised of the situation here and is trying to make contact with either John or Robert Kennedy. (I understand from the papers that John is on vacation in Europe.)

There's a breakdown of law and order here. From the time of our arrival, Saturday, August 5, Robert F. Williams and his supporters were preparing for violent expressions on the part of the white community. Williams has called the White House several times. He called the FBI in Charlotte, N.C., and informs us the agent told him they could not do anything unless something happens. Williams reports that he then asked the agent: "What would it take, my life?" He informed the agent he was not going to sit by and allow someone to kill him without defending himself.

Mr. and Mrs. Williams say they have filed a civil rights suit with the Justice Department through the FBI agent in Charlotte, North Carolina. They are charging that the police chief is failing to guarantee them their constitutional rights under the 14th Amendment. Paul and I have sent a report to John Doar at the Justice Department.

Not only has the federal government been contacted but the state government as well. Williams talked with Hugh Cannon, Assistant to the Governor. He admitted to Williams they have an eye-witness to the incident when Williams' car was pushed into a ditch.

The young people who participated in the picket line at the swimming pool are being picked up by the police without any warrants and investigated. On several occasions they have been fingerprinted, not knowing they have a right to refuse this unless they have been booked. This information has been given to the remainder of the children. One youngster was taken to jail for questioning at eleven o'clock at night. He refused to let them fingerprint him. He indicated the police were trying to say they had protected them at the pool. Youth in great numbers are behind the movement. Children of sixteen and fifteen, even eleven, were on the picket line.

The news blackout continues. This afternoon I talked with Ted Britt, the night editor of the Charlotte AP Bureau, and asked him about it. He indicated they had been receiving Williams' material, but they were unable to get any confirmation from the local police authorities on his reports. He said the police at first denied all charges and now they were very cool toward AP. He said the Sheriff even denied there was any shooting last Saturday night, a week ago.

There are witnesses to this shooting. One witness, Woodrow Wilson, 44, fired two magazines in the air. He said they fired in the air as the two cars carrying white people entered the street. They were not trying to retaliate, they said, because "it is hard to stop killing once you kill a man." However, they wanted to serve notice on the whites that they were prepared to defend themselves. Wilson chased them for more than two miles. Another witness was Augustus Williams, who said the whites fired in front of his house. It is extremely important to note that Negroes here are taking every precaution not to harm the whites who have been harassing them. They have a sense of responsibility and realize the implications of indiscriminate shooting. I assure you the weapons they have and the guard detail would have been sufficient to deter more than two cars.

During the early part of tonight, I personally along with others sitting on the porch heard two loud shots. Williams claims they came from the direction of the railroad. Mrs. Williams called the police, letting me listen in. When they answered, she told them who she was and then asked who was speaking:

"Kenneth Helm," the voice answered.

"I want to report two shootings," she said. He told her to wait and someone else picked up the phone.

"Who is this?" Mrs. Williams asked.

"This is a policeman."

"What is your name? Who is this speaking?"

The voice replied: "This is the Chief."

"Chief A. A. Mauney?"

"Yes, this is Chief Mauney. What do you want?"

"I want to report two shots fired in this vicinity."

"Where? Where?"

"We do not know exactly where."

"Well, we'll send a car right over."

"Sheriff Mauney, I want you to register this complaint." She asked this because of what Britt had told me: that the police denied having any record of the shootings.

"Register this complaint? What do you want me to do that for? I'm sending a car to investigate the situation."

"Well, I want you to register this complaint so that there will be a record of our calling you."

"All right, I'll do that," he said.

In less than six minutes the Highway Patrolman rolled up. In the car was the Sheriff of the County, the Chief of Police, the Highway Patrolman and two other unidentified men. The Chief talked to Williams and asked him from which direction the shots had come. After telling him, Williams referred to the shooting last Saturday night, a week ago. The Chief of Police seemed surprised and Williams said they heard the radio of a patrol car as it passed by. He could not see why the police had not heard all the shooting and screaming that night. They were not going to stand for anything next Saturday night, he said.

Sunday we spent interviewing people to get supporting data. We talked to a woman who had paint spilled on her, to a man who was beaten by some youths. We had a talk with the Police Chief who seemed to indicate everything was fine here and that Williams exaggerated things.

On Monday, Larry Still of *Jet* arrived and we talked with Mr. Ashcraft of the Monroe *Enquirer*. Ashcraft said AP was interested in the shooting but the Sheriff told him there was no incident July 29, 1961. I asked him whether he had contacted Williams and people in the neighborhood. He seemed to think I was getting into his personal business. We tried to talk to the Mayor. He is permitting us to meet with the City Board of Aldermen, Tuesday night, a week from now. (I drew up a petition which is circulating in Monroe. It is hoped the petition will give us better bargaining strength.) We had another talk with the local Police Chief who this time admitted certain things and said he did not hate Williams. He was going to pray for his soul.

Tuesday, Brooks prepared his report for SCLC. I went in the town seeking historical information. I talked with the local extension officer (Negro) who was altogether different from the one in Fayette. He knew all about the FHA loans and Production Credit Association. He said there were many Negroes in both of these agencies and that his relations with the two directors were very good. From his office I went to the Industrial Development Commission and obtained from the clerk some dynamic information. She gave me a list of all the factory employees, which has a breakdown of white and Negro. Williams is going to print this in his paper. I am sure it will create a minor stir. I think the clerk didn't know what she was doing.

I had a long talk with the City Manager, Mr. Hankel, and his secretary, both of whom seemed disturbed about race relations in Monroe. They were extremely courteous and helpful. I obtained much historical information through their office. They really must be getting worried about their image.

Following are certain conclusions:

(1) There is complete disrespect for the local law enforcing agency here; there is hope for the federal government. This last strand of hope must not be lost. Brooks and I are encouraged by the people here to do all we can to help. We are asked to call the news wire services and the Civil Rights Section of the Justice Dept. to keep an eye on Monroe.

The segregationists also ought to be informed that some relationship with the Justice Dept. can be established, for if there is one thing they do not like, it is pressure from the Justice Dept. Requests should be sent to the Justice Dept., the Governor of North Carolina and individual U.S. Senators, demanding an investigation and action to restore law and order here. It's important to realize that in North Carolina it is legal to have arms as long as these arms are visible to the law. It should be stressed at all times that the demands of the people here are for law and order. I have discussed with Williams the difference in connotation between meeting violence with violence and self-defense. It is the latter they are doing, a right guaranteed in the Constitution and practiced by many other civil rights fighters. People and organizations ought to try to understand the historical context of the struggle here and the necessity to formulate courses of actions predicated upon given situations at given times in history. *Monroe is not Nashville nor Montgomery.*

(2) The relationship of Williams to the NAACP is not just Williams vs. Wilkins. Actually, the hostility to this national group goes down to the average member of the Union County Chapter. It exists in Dr. Perry who tried to get the group to help him. All this can be substantiated in the words of the people themselves. It is important to note that a "renegade" chapter like Union County is not apt to get much support from the national. Yet all efforts ought to be made to get some NAACP organizational responsibility into the situation, for there are still legitimate demands of Negro people here and dues paying NAACPers in Monroe.

(3) The role of the southern press in the civil rights fight has to be analyzed, for what we found in Monroe was duplicated in Fayette and I am sure the pattern of the wire services there can be found in other places in the South. (Where there is no bureau, the service depends on local stringers. If they can't get a story or don't want to, the nation never hears it. This is without mentioning the problem of distortion.)

(4) Action should be taken on the national level to get police chiefs indicted on the grounds of denial of equal access to the law.

(5) People from different organizations, depending upon the will of local leaders, ought to make attempts to establish "lines of communications" between the hostile elements. In many instances, it serves to notify the segregationists that the Negroes are not alone in their struggle. This takes some of the heat off of the local leaders.

(6) A Civil Rights Primer has to be written and distributed in millions of copies throughout the South. This Primer ought to include the provisions of the first, thirteenth, fourteenth and fifteenth amendments to the Constitution, spelled out in simple language. It ought to include the telephone numbers of the President of the United States, the Justice Dept., the New York telephone numbers of the Associated Press and the United Press International, along with ANP's [Associated Negro Press] number, *Jet*, the *Afro-American* and a few others, with instructions also to contact local newspapers. Certain historical information about the Negro ought to be included, too.

To return to the Monroe situation: Robert F. Williams has certain values all civil rights leaders ought to have: love for the common and poor man, an awareness that one Negro in an important position does not constitute progress for the race, and a recognition that leaders ought not to ask of others what they are not willing to do themselves. Williams's expression of disgust with segregation has taken many forms. They may not be the iced tea type, but they are still expressions. He will continue to give the segregationists the bourbon type treatment. He is certainly a "masterful propagandist"; he was called this by Mr. Hankel, the City Manager.

There is growing support for Williams throughout the South, for the Negro is becoming impatient and *he is not always going to turn the other cheek.*

On August 8 Paul Brooks and I left Monroe for the trial of the Freedom Riders in Jackson. We would be back.

CHAPTER 24

Eruption in Newtown

WHEN PAUL and I left for Jackson, we had specific instructions from Williams to see if we could get some Freedom Riders to come to Monroe and put an integrated picket line around the courthouse, in support of the struggle led by him. At that time a tremendous amount of national press coverage was given to everything the Freedom Riders did. We thought that getting the Freedom Riders to Monroe might be one way of helping to break the isolation in which Williams and the people of Monroe found themselves. Williams also thought that if an integrated picket line could be thrown up around the courthouse, it might force the city to issue a warrant for the arrest of the man who had tried to kill him on June 23, 1961.

In Jackson the Freedom Riders were all found guilty; those not already put out on bond were then released, and an appeal of the convictions was planned. Many of them wanted to participate in further action that summer, and at a meeting held after the trial various possibilities were proposed. Bob Moses of SNCC called for people to come to McComb, Mississippi, but he wanted only black Freedom Riders. When the chairman of the meeting announced Robert Williams's invitation to come to Monroe, a number expressed interest. Price Chatham, who had fasted for twenty-four days in Jackson's Parchman Penitentiary, and Paul Diderich, another Freedom Rider, talked to us at length about the proposed trip to Monroe. As whites, they did not feel certain that they would be welcome in black Monroe. We assured them that the whole idea of an integrated picket line came from Williams himself (contrary to what some historians would later write about these events), but that they could call Williams directly for confirmation of this. They did so. He not only told them they were welcome, but that he would find places for them to stay and see that they were fed.

Paul Brooks returned to Monroe immediately but I went to Chicago first. There Lee Blackwell of the *Chicago Defender* gave me the call letters of the *Defender* for direct collect Western Union messages. He saw the news value in the Freedom Riders' presence and wanted to be kept informed.

During my absence, the City Council of Monroe met and considered a list of demands which included the desegregation of virtually everything, reinstatement of Dr. Perry as a physician in Monroe, jobs, equal consideration of all people on welfare rolls, and a swimming pool in Newtown itself. The council took no action on any of this. The basic demands had been drawn up by Paul Brooks and myself in consultation with Robert Williams. We strongly suggested that the demands form the basis for a petition by many people in the community to indicate that he had mass support. This suggestion was not taken and Rob, along with two other people, presented the demands to the City Council.

When I arrived in Monroe again on August 22, the Freedom Riders were actively picketing the courthouse. Since there were no reporters from the black press there, I felt that releases should be written and sent out every day. I took this assignment upon myself and for the next three days, Wednesday, Thursday, Friday, sent out a news story along with plenty of other work: meetings, picketing, strategy discussions. Thanks to those releases, a record exists of events during that tense week.

The Freedom Riders were working with a newly formed group of local citizens, the Monroe Nonviolent Action Committee, and used an old, unguarded house for headquarters called "Freedom House." Richard Crowder, a local youth, was chairman of (MNAC). The group was pledged to nonviolence in its actions. As they marched around the courthouse, the Freedom Riders and MNAC members passed out leaflets protesting, "(1) Unfair protection under the law for Afro-Americans and their property; (2) The policy of the taxsupported Industrial Development Commission, which invited industries to Union County and imposed discriminatory labor practices; (3) Arbitrary and cruel administration by the Welfare Department that has deprived destitute Afro-Americans of relief; (4) Separate and unequal recreational facilities."

Shortly after the arrival of the Freedom Riders in Monroe, a new picketing ordinance was passed by the City Council. It restricted picketing to the sidewalk and said that not more than ten people could picket at the same time for the same objective. Picketers must march in single file and fifteen feet apart, it said. Signs may not be larger than two feet in width and length. The chief of police had the authority to allow the "opposition" equal time to picket in the same place. The ordinance also prohibited the carrying of any dangerous weapon while picketing. Finally, the signs carried by the picketers must not carry inflammatory language or words inciting to violence.

Despite the provisions against inflammatory language, the counter-pickets led by local segregationists carried signs reading, "Robert Williams and his half-breed niggers go home"—an obvious attack on the whites who were supporting the picket line. Williams said this was the first time Monroe citizens have seen an integrated picket line in Monroe.

Price Chatham, of Long Island, New York, said an old woman spit in his face. Dave Morton of Minneapolis, Minnesota, was constantly harassed by an old man with a cane who tried to trip him. Failing in his efforts, he started twisting Morton's arm. The Freedom Riders constantly heard, "Your mama is at home in bed with a nigger!"

As the picketing continued, the number of sporadic acts of violence against local blacks increased. On August 23 three white teen-agers attacked a ten-year-old boy, Prentice Robinson. Rev. Lester Dixon, a local Negro minister, saw the attack while making deliveries for the drugstore where he worked. He jumped out of his car and stopped the assault. One of the white youths asked, "Do you want some of it too?"

"Yeah, if you want to give me some of it, here I am," he replied.

As they stood poised for battle, a white man passed by and told the boys they were wrong, that they should not beat up people like that.

"What you got to do with it?" one of them asked. "Are you an FBI or something like that?"

At that point they turned on Reverend Dixon and asked him again if he wanted to do something about it. Dixon reached down and picked up a brick and told them, "Yeah, I want to do something about it. Then he heard someone across the street yell, "Preacher, don't do that. Go call the police."

Reverend Dixon called the police—but the boys fled. The police promised they would make an arrest that evening or the next day, since there was positive identification of the culprits.

When he returned to the drugstore, Reverend Dixon told his employer, Eddie Faulkener, who was a member of the City Board of Aldermen, exactly what had happened. Faulkener told Dixon to tell the chief of police, A. A. Mauney, that he must make an arrest. When Dixon tried to find the police captain at the station, he was told he was at home. When he arrived at the chief's house, he was told the chief was out of town. By the end of the next day the boys were still free.

By Friday, August 25, the whites in Monroe were becoming more and more violent against the picketers at the courthouse. Meanwhile, the city still had not issued a warrant for the arrest of Bynum Griffin. Picketing was therefore extended to other parts of the city. Freedom Rider Ed Bromberg, a former student at Columbia University, was struck by a pellet from a high-powered pump air gun while picketing in front of the dental office of Mayor Fred Wilson. Picketing of the mayor's dental office had started the day before, when Paul Diderich and Richard Crowder attempted to obtain an appointment with the mayor and were refused. A sit-in began which lasted until the mayor closed his office. Picketers reported they saw him peeping out from behind the venetian blinds from time to time. Two Monroe youths were arrested, supposedly because they were less than fifteen feet apart. Both denied this and no measurements were taken.

That Friday night, at a meeting of the Monroe Nonviolent Action Committee, we discussed the mounting violence of the whites. We knew that the next day Saturday, would bring many whites into Monroe from out of town and that violence would reach a new peak. Maximum precautions had to be taken, within the limits of nonviolence. These included insuring group discipline. The need for uniform action is very great in a nonviolent demonstration; decision making must be centralized because of the tensions and dangers which arise. One person who has the respect of the others must be given absolute authority.

On a motion of William Mahoney, a twenty-year-old Freedom Rider from Howard University who later joined SNCC's staff, I was elected "supreme commander" of demonstrations and given the power to make unequivocal decisions in time of emergency. The title and the wording of the resolution embarrassed me but I understood the intent. As later events would show, I wasn't all that supreme.

By this time, both Julian Mayfield and Mae Mallory had arrived on the scene. Rob and Julian had met in Cuba a year earlier; Mae was a key New York supporter of the Williamses' struggle in Monroe. Both had come down from New York City now to help. We would need all the help we could get.

On Saturday, August 26, the sun shone down brightly on Monroe. The sky was clear and blue. The picketers lined up in front of Robert Williams's house, then walked down Boyte Street to Winchester and turned right to the courthouse, we kept our required fifteen feet apart. I was on and off the picket line, taking care of details.

When we reached the courthouse, we found that the number of police had been increased for this day. It seemed that they anticipated special Saturday violence just as we did and, while they could mistreat Robert or other local blacks as individuals, they had to put up at least a pretense of law enforcement because of national projection from the Freedom Riders' presence. The provision of greater numbers of police may also have been a response to some pressure from higher up. In all this, the behavior of the Monroe police was typical of Southern lawmen. In the privacy of their own towns and jails, they would do anything they wished but, if in the national spotlight, they would go through the motions of protection. We were not fooled by this facade.

All day long, whites at the courthouse shouted, "Niggers go home!" "We're going to get Robert Williams!" "Nigger lovers!" "Bet she sleeps with a nigger," referring to Constance Lever, a student from England who had come to Monroe. "Wait until tonight, niggers. You won't live till tomorrow!" They sat in their cars jeering or drove around the block yelling and screaming. Paul Diderich was hit hard on the neck and the right ear by a Monroe man, whom the police arrested. John Lowry, another Freedom Rider, was choked by a white assailant who also broke his watch; police broke up the attack but made no arrest. A third Freedom Rider was struck on the mouth by a white man who fled the scene. Three Monroe youths were arrested for violating the regulation that there must be a fifteen-foot distance between picketers.

At about four in the afternoon, LeRoy Wright and some other blacks were standing in front of the mayor's office when I heard two of the white mob that had gathered say, "Let's go get 'em."

They crossed the street and attacked LeRoy. He began to fight back, striking his opponents with hard blows. The police came and handcuffed him. The two whites followed the officer into the police station. So did I.

"I want to take out a warrant on this colored boy for assault and battery," the police officer told the captain.

"What do you mean, take out a warrant on him?" I demanded, furious. "These two started the fight. LeRoy was defending himself. You can't charge him with assault and battery."

Chief A. A. Mauney, Captain J. D. Elliot, and other officers were standing around inside the police station. I had been there many times that day. "Look, Chief Mauney," I said to him now, pointing to one of the two whites, "this guy here said, and I heard him, 'Let's go get 'em.' Then they proceeded to start a fight with LeRoy."

"That boy is lying, Chief," the man said. "I didn't say nothing to anybody. He's just lying."

"I'm not lying and you stop calling me boy!" I shot back.

"All right, Joe. You go on out of here. You ain't got nothing to do with this," Chief Mauney said to the white man.

"What do you mean, he ain't got nothing to do with it? He was the one who started it. Why are you letting him go? There is no justice in Monroe!" I began a tirade, as a tactic. I didn't want to see LeRoy Wright charged with assault and battery, a felony which these cracker cops would easily impose upon him. The louder I yelled, the greater were the chances of their reducing the charge to mere fighting—if not forgetting the whole matter. "I want to take out a warrant against Joe for starting the fight. I saw him. I was on the street," I continued.

There was no response to this request. I kept pressing the issue. "Book 'em both for fighting," the chief finally told the desk sergeant.

At the end of the day, when we started home from the courthouse, the sky was no longer blue. It had begun to cloud up. We decided that we should all walk home together in a double column. Seeing us prepare to leave, the racists began to line up in their cars. As we marched past the police station singing "We Shall Overcome," they tried to run Julian Mayfield's car off the road. Julian sat there looking at them as they hurled insults. I knew he had his gun. They finally pulled away.

As we walked along Winchester Street headed for Boyte, car after car of whites passed—some loaded with guns, some with occupants throwing stones at us, all hurling insults and threats. A woman from one house screamed, "I told you niggers not to come past my house singing those damn songs." She stood about two feet away, swinging a long knife as if she had the strength of Hercules and had gone completely mad. Keeping formation was a real test at that moment, but to panic and run loose would have invited disaster. The long line of cars bearing racists and Klan members were ready to pick off any individual. We stepped into the streets to avoid her slashes, then had to jump back onto the sidewalk to avoid cars trying to hit us. A man emerged from the same house throwing rocks and bricks. Some white boys were on the top of the house throwing barrages of Coca-Cola bottles. Several of our group were injured, but we kept our formation and went on toward Newtown.

As we approached Boyte Street, local blacks began to return stone for stone and to initiate some rock throwing too. Just then a white man came driving down the street. People—not the picketers—stopped his car and began to stone it. Danny Thomas, a white Freedom Rider, jumped in front of the car to stop our people from retaliating. The driver escaped without great injury, but Danny incurred the resentment of many people. A Freedom Rider who had gone to jail in Jackson, he proved to be an individualistic and undisciplined person whose actions brought down a lot of criticism on the Freedom Riders as a group. There had not, unfortunately, been as much screening as there should have been of each person who came from Jackson.

Williams stood waiting for us on the porch of his house. He told us that he had informed cops in a car patrolling his house that the picketers were being attacked. They just laughed at him.

Newtown was tense that Saturday night and people began to prepare for an invasion by the Klan. About nine o'clock, Danny Thomas ran into Williams's house to report that he and Ed Bromberg, another Freedom Rider, had gone into a café on the highway across the Union County line. They had been attacked and fled but somehow Bromberg lost contact with Danny. People assumed that the worst had happened to him. Paul Brooks called Hugh P. Cannon—assistant to Governor Terry Sanford—to tell him the situation. Cannon said that he didn't give a damn about the missing person; he was getting what he deserved. Bromberg was later found and returned safely. Williams showed his annoyance that the two had gone to a place out on the highway when tension in the area was so high.

At a meeting that night, the nonviolent action group decided to try and attend services at several white churches the next morning and also to picket. I did not attend this meeting, for I was working to locate Bromberg, and I was upset when I heard the decision. I felt that a picket line on Sunday afternoon would be very dangerous. Sunday is like a holiday in Southern towns and I knew the racists would be out in full force. It was also on a Sunday that the swimming pool picketers had faced the greatest danger. There was no reason to expect that this Sunday would be different, especially after a week of sustained picketing during which violence had escalated each day. Moreover, the courthouse would be closed and I didn't see much tactical sense in picketing a closed courthouse.

But Williams was in favor of the plan. "We can't stop now," he said excitedly. "Things are hot but we have to make them hotter." I didn't agree with him, but if he felt that this was necessary, then I was willing to help with the picketing. He has suffered here in Monroe, I told myself, and he should know the local situation. It did not, however, seem necessary for me to go up with those planning to integrate the churches.

Sunday morning went smoothly enough. At some of the churches, blacks were admitted, but at the Episcopal church they were denied entrance. We did get one report—which turned out to be false—that a member of one group had been hit by a car as he headed for a white church. Bill Mahoney, Richard Griswold, and I went up to check on this. At the police station, they had no information but we got into a long discussion with two of the officers and Ashcraft, from the Monroe *Enquirer*, about our objectives in Monroe. They were incapable of understanding the drive of black people for justice.

"What you don't understand," I said, "is that when soldiers fight on the battlefield, the bullet coming toward them is neither white nor black. But, in fact, the Negro soldier is being asked to die in order to protect white people who attack us in the United States."

There was silence. I pressed the point.

"Chief Mauney, you are probably a member of the Rotary Club, the Lions, other civic organizations. You and your associates could spread the word that you don't want any violence in Monroe and no attacks on picketers. You know this would be effective."

They did not answer, but only looked at me. Then Mauney said, "Look, you guys are wasting your time trying to help Robert Williams. He's hated by everybody in town, black and white."

"That's not true," I answered. "Although I'm sure he's hated by the police."

"That's correct," Mauney said and gave me a smug, stupid smile. I wondered why I had wasted this much of my time talking with this joker. I went back to Rob's house to get the picketers together for that afternoon.

CHAPTER 25

Moment of Death

SUNDAY, AUGUST 27, 1961. When we arrived at the closed courthouse at about two o'clock that afternoon, there was hardly a soul in the vicinity except for ourselves and the cops who had followed us there. As if on signal, the square began to fill. Our arrival had been the signal. Many cars with out-of-state license plates drove around and around the square; by 3:00 P.M., at least three thousand people had gathered at the courthouse and the crowd was getting larger. The police were keeping everyone off the sidewalks, around the square except us, the picketers.

A number of young blacks from Newtown came on the scene. They did not picket and did not wish to join us. They stood across the street from the courthouse, and a crowd of whites began to threaten them. It was an annoying problem, for they had no protection—they were not armed and they were not picketers, who, for the moment, had the protection of the police. They were young, black supporters of Rob Williams who wanted to see what was happening—but, if something happened, they were in no position to do anything about it.

I crossed to where they stood, followed by a short man with a club-foot who kept trying to step on my heels. I told them they should leave, but they refused to listen and stayed on the corner. This was at about 4:20 in the afternoon. Richard Griswold, a white photographer who had been taking pictures all week, also came across the street to where they stood. He had been arrested the previous Tuesday for "interfering with an officer." The crackers just didn't want their pictures taken that day and they didn't want them taken now either.

At 4:25 the crowd became unruly. We had arranged, before leaving Robert's house, that a group of cabs would come to get the picketers at exactly 4:30—without fail. I worried about their showing up on time —and now we had additional problems. There would be enough cabs for the picketers, but not enough for the young Monroe blacks who had come to watch. I was furious by this time and there was nothing I could do. The next fifteen minutes were upon me, a nightmare I shall never forget:

4:30. The cabs arrive. They are coming around the corner. There's enough for some, but not for all. I invoke my "supreme powers" and decide that the loose group of Monroe youths have to get in the cabs first. They are in the most danger and certainly cannot be left behind at the mercy of the vicious mob, with all its jeers, its taunts, its threats, its hope of some trouble so that it would have an excuse to move into action. I hastily call some picketers together and inform them of my decision to put the Monroe youths in the cabs. There is some extra room and a few picketers get in the cabs too. We fill the four cabs with as many people as possible, but there are still some twenty of us left on the picket line.

4:31. The four cabs pull off. We are isolated. The cabs are supposed to return, but that will be another twenty-five minutes—if they return. I think of the cab that Lucretia Collins took in Montgomery and wonder if these drivers will be chicken too.

4:32. The crowd begins to close in on all four sides of the square. It will be impossible for the police to contain all these crackers if they decide to charge the remaining Freedom Riders and local citizens. This is their plan without a doubt. Damn. Why did those cats have to come up here to the square today? No discipline. A demonstration is not a sight-seeing tour. If you are not connected, then you are in the way. Damn.

4:35. The crowd is attacking Heath Rush on the south side of the courthouse. Heath is white, from Concord, New Hampshire.

4:35:05. Constance Lever is coming around the corner and a mob is closing in on her. I see Woodrow Wilson's car coming down the street. I wave him down and Constance jumps in. They can get away. Putting her in the car is a gamble. She is surely in for mob violence. I remember those white girls on the Freedom Ride in Montgomery. Constance has taken the most severe jeering this afternoon. I think again of Lucretia.

4:35:10. A cop named Rushing runs to catch Woodrow. He yells to Hegler, who stops the car driven by Woodrow Wilson and asks Captain Elliott if he is going to let that girl ride with these men. He means, let that white girl ride off with those black men.

4:35:30. "Let the car go! Let the car go! Keep the cars moving!" Captain Elliott yells to Rushing.

4:35:45. Woodrow drives off in his car once again.

4:35:46. Rushing is saying that the car driven by Woodrow has a gun in it. He calls to Hegler to stop the car. He is determined to act out his racism, no matter what his superior officer, Captain Elliott, says.

4:36. The car is stopped. Hegler opens the back door; black men with guns are sitting inside. We keep yelling that the mob is attacking Heath Rush and the pigs should go over there.

Rushing says Wilson has broken the law. No pickets are allowed to have guns.

"No one in the car is a picketer!" I yell. "They are not bound by the picket law and it's legal in North Carolina to have a gun as long as it's visible. All their guns are visible."

"He cursed at a police officer," Hegler says. "We don't allow anyone to curse at us."

"Is that his only charge?" I ask.

"Yes."

Woodrow Wilson hears this answer. "Get in the car," he says to Rushing. "You can drive the car. I'm willing to· go to the police station, but I won't be handcuffed. You're not going to kill me."

4:38. The mob is all around the car. Rushing grabs the double-barreled shotgun from the black man in the back. He hands it to a young white man by the side of the car, who looks drunk. Then Don Keziah, an older white, who is supposed to be chief of the Klan, runs up to Wilson and Officer Rushing.

"Get away from me," Woodrow yells. "You get away from me. You're not a police officer."

"He can deputize me and I'll be a police officer," Don Keziah replies.

Rushing tries to handcuff Woodrow. A scuffle ensues between them. Other police officers come to help Rushing. But Woodrow is a strong, muscular black man and he can't be subdued at first. Finally he consents to be handcuffed with his arms in front of him.

The young white to whom Rushing has given the shotgun comes around to the side of the car where I am standing.

"Why did you give him that gun," I yell to Rushing.

"Keep that gun," Rushing says to the white man.

"Take the gun away," I yell.

4:40. "Nigger, stay away from that car," the white man tells me. "If you move one step, I'm going to blow your black brains back to Africa." The shotgun is raised less than eighteen inches from my face. I don't move.

The crowd is yelling, "Kill the nigger! Kill the nigger! Kill him!"

Everything stopped. I thought, this is the moment of death and I must die as a man. I must not cry out. I must not beg this cracker for mercy. I must show strength to those few black people watching. Little Rock.

I have decided.

Circumstances.

Circumstances.

I decided.

There is always a choice, to do or to die.

I decided to come to Monroe. I decided the way to help Robert Williams was to prove that not Williams but racism was the cause of trouble in Monroe. I decided and, when I decided this, I decided that death was of no consequence.

I can see down the barrel of the shotgun, but I must be cool. I must not panic. Look the mother fucker straight in the eye and let him know he has lynched a strong black man.

We all die. It's a question of how and when. Sometimes we cannot decide how we die, but we must defy death. It is the greatest act of defiance, an act of defiance necessary to make a revolutionary.

I hear him, I hear all his curses. I am standing still.

I am hemmed in from the crowd, with Woodrow's car on my left and a car at the curb. Hegler has taken the pistol from LeRoy Wright. He is just sitting in Woodrow's car, a policeman, a defender of the law, a white policeman watching my execution, helping in my lynching.

Police, police, police, all over America, the black man's enemy, their guns swinging, their clubs swinging, dressed up as if from outer space, walkie-talkies, blackjacks, guns, and sticks. No love for the pig. Hatred.

But hatred has turned into love for people, a hatred necessary to defy death, to create a better world where there are no pigs, no fucking cops playing fun and games with young black boys and strong black men. They have the guns, their power.

Force with force.

Violence with violence.

Power with power.

The crowd is yelling, "Kill him! Kill him! Kill the nigger!" Yet I am calm. There is a strange calmness in me. I thought I would be excited if ever faced with this type of death, but no. I cannot explain this quiet within me.

I am cool. I am icy. I have decided to die for my people. I have lived thirty-three years. Strange, Jesus, a revolutionary, died at thirty-three.

There is no hate, no feeling at all.

But, I am not dead yet. I think, he's drunk and I'm cool. I have an edge, I have a percentage. It's a gamble. It might work. Life is a gamble, death is a fact. Be cool. Wait for the moment. Watch his eyes. Watch his hands. Watch his fingers. Watch his whole goddamn body, every move, every gesture, every face contortion. Watch to your right. Look to your left. The crowd is moving in closer from the right. "Kill the nigger! Kill the nigger!"

He has the gun and I must get it. When I make my move, I must move quickly. I must not move until the right moment. I must kick him in the nuts. We will wrestle, maybe, but I must get the gun, get it quickly. Two shots is all I'll have. Two shots at thousands of howling, screaming, red, white, pinky, sun-baked faces of white people yelling, "Kill him! Kill the nigger! Kill the nigger!"

The killer's finger is not on the trigger, I notice. It is loose around the trigger guard. The moment he raises his forefinger to put it on the trigger, then jump!

The car at the curb is moved away. My right flank is exposed. The crowd, the mob, the Klan, is inching forward. They have not started running toward me, but they want blood; a nigger's blood, a black man's blood on a hot Sunday afternoon in Monroe, North Carolina.

I see Paul Brooks driving Julian Mayfield's car. He is stopped cold behind Woodrow's car. There are black men with him, armed. What are they going to do? There is nothing they can do. The crowd is too large. Retribution is the only answer. Revolution the only solution.

Now here comes that clubfoot man again. He has a long, open knife now and he is holding it low. He's coming after my nuts! He's holding the knife in his hand, his hand at his side. He moves with coldness. He is not drunk. He is a killer.

My calmness is gone, my pressure is rising. I cannot be castrated!

There isn't much time. I must move now. Open the front door. Put Constance in the car. Fuck the cop. Fuck the man with the shotgun. The long knife is glistening in the fading sun. It is sharp and the clubfoot man is moving forward. There is no defense against both the shotgun and the clubfoot man swinging the knife. And the crowd is moving in from the right. You will be slaughtered and you will be castrated. "Kill the nigger! Kill him!"

4:45. "Quick Constance! Move now! Get in the car." I open the door and she jumps in. I turn to my left, toward the car. The shotgun comes down on my head.

The hot barrel hits my head, separates my hair, splits my skin, opens my skull, deadens my brain, out comes the blood, gushing like a volcano in eruption, another blow, more red blood down my face, into my ear, past my nose, across my chin, onto my dirty white shirt, blood, blood coming from my head and more blood.

I am inside Woodrow's car, the hot blood running down my face. I roll up the window. Pig Hegler still sits in the back. Another pig drives the car away. Woodrow is sitting in the front seat, handcuffed, his arms in front. We are all jammed in together.

The crowd is yelling. "Niggers! Niggers!"

Julian Mayfield's car, driven by Paul, is stoned furiously. But they also escape.

The hot blood runs through my kinky hair and down onto my gritty, sweaty face.

Let it run.

Run red blood so that the world may see racism. Run red blood down my black, gritty, sweaty face. Run to the words of the poet McKay, if we must die let us die as men fighting with our backs to the wall. Run red blood, run to the rhythm of your ancestors wrung from the land of Africa, run red blood, run, run, run, running in the red sun; tall, dark, proud, black, and beautiful. Let it run! The dirty mother fuckers. Up against the wall. I run no more.

CHAPTER 26

Strong Black Women

WE DROVE to the police station, all of us in one car: Woodrow, Constance, LeRoy Wright, myself, another Monroe black, and pigs Hegler and Rushing. They said we could come inside for our safety; Woodrow was under arrest and they had to book him. "Do you want a doctor, Forman?" Chief Mauney then asked.

"Yes." The police station was buzzing with activity. From outside we heard shots. Boom! Boom! Boom!

A telephone hung on the wall. I called Lee Blackwell of the *Chicago Defender* and gave him the story of what had happened. I tried to call Robert, to tell him we were all right, but his line was constantly busy. I called the United Press International in New York, bypassing the local UPI. They talked to Constance, took her story. I tried to call Rob again but then the telephone went dead for no apparent reason. Just a click, and I couldn't get a line anymore.

A cop came up and asked us to leave the office. "Y'all have to get out of here," he said.

"Are you crazy," a black woman exclaimed, "we're not leaving here till it's safe." We all joined in to protest the request that we leave. We were not going to walk out into a lynch mob.

An agent of the FBI moved morosely around the station taking notes and listening to conversations. He was present when Captain Elliott told Chief A. A. Mauney that if Rushing had allowed the car to pass, all of this trouble would not have developed. At one point, I asked Captain Elliott if he thought it wise for us to take cabs home. He said, "No."

An uproar is not the word to describe what was taking place in the police station. On one telephone a highway patrolman was trying to call someone in Raleigh, telling the operator to break into a busy line—he had an emergency call. Every time the door to the police station opened, we could hear gunfire. Later we would learn that Pig Rushing had been shot in the leg and another cop had had a heart attack. The police were constantly bringing people in for this charge or that charge. Brown Massey had been brought in, moaning from blows he had received from the pigs. He was taken to the back cell, where Woodrow Wilson and others were being kept. Massey's sisters, mother, and a friend came to the station to ask about their brother. At first the officer at the door did not want to let them in. After they protested, he permitted them to enter. Soon afterward, *they* were arrested for inciting a riot.

At one point a cab drove up outside and we urged some of the local people to take it. Eight people got into the car. Ken Shilman of New York, who had picketed with us, got into it too. When he couldn't find us later, Ken came back to the police station seeking information and *he* was placed under arrest.

We were wondering when the police would escort us out of there when a highway patrolman informed us that we were all under arrest—for inciting to riot. Even he had to smile when he said it, the idea seemed so ridiculous. But they were serious about this madness. A cop named Helm told us to go to the back of the station; we were going to be taken to the county jail.

We walked into the Monroe County jail, more than twenty of us, not as defeated persons but as people proud of our arrest. We knew we were being jailed for a just cause and that we were suffering only minutely what black people had been undergoing for years in Monroe. We could hear the women and young girls, who had been taken to the jail first, banging on the doors and yelling at the top of their voices. "No bail," we yelled. "No bail. Everybody on a hunger strike. We must dramatize the issue."

We sang freedom songs and lifted the spirits of our group, of other black prisoners in that jail, who had, no doubt, been put there for other unjust causes. But I began to get weaker and weaker. I knew I had to see a doctor. My wound, which had stopped bleeding for a while, was at it again. I asked for a doctor and one was promised. After thirty minutes, he had not arrived. We started a new protest, "A doctor. A doctor. A doctor. We want a doctor." We chanted these words and we banged on the cell doors. We slammed the doors. Our protest resounded throughout the jail. The jailer then put the girls into individual cells. They began to yell for water.

The strength of the women overwhelmed me. Here they were in jail, but their spirits seemed to rise each minute. They were yelling at the jailer, cursing, singing, ready to fight if someone came to their cell to mistreat them. Images of other strong black women resisting slavery and servitude flooded my mind. I thought of Georgia Mae Turner and Lucretia Collins and the young girls in the cellblock next to me now as the modern-day Harriet Tubmans, Sojourner Truths, and all those proud black women who did not allow slavery to break their spirits. I remembered something Mabel Williams had said to me: "You're not going to get the support of all the people. In most movements throughout history, there hasn't been much popular support at first." As I thought about the women protesting their arrest, I knew that the black liberation movement would escalate, for too many young people were involved. Most of the women in the cells were very young, one of them only fourteen.

The sheriff came over and asked me if I could possibly keep the women quiet. I told him we were all protesting the lack of medical attention and the denial of water to the girls. He said he would see what he could do. He wanted to know if I thought they would then be quiet. I told him that I could not promise him anything. We would cooperate, even in jail, but we would not cooperate if we were denied our "jail rights."

Not long afterward a doctor appeared, accompanied by two cops. Deputy Sheriff McCraven, who was in charge of the jail, unlocked our cell door and took me to the office. My head felt as if it would split open. As the doctor examined the bloody wound, I told him there were other people in jail who wanted to see him.

"Where are you from?" he asked.

"I'm from Chicago, but what does that have to do with my wound?" I asked, knowing that he was getting ready to call me, in his mind at least, an outside agitator.

"I thought so," he replied. I had peeped his hole card.

The individual cell doors of the girls were unlocked for the doctor to go in, and never locked again as long as they were in jail. The doctor gave each a fast look and would not give any of them medical treatment.

Then the doctor said he wanted to take me to his office for treatment. The local police officer told me to go along. I remembered what had happened to Emmett Till, Charles Mack Parker, and all the other blacks who were placed in the hands of white Southerners only to meet their death. I was frightened, more than at any other moment. I absolutely refused to go alone with the doctor. "If I am under arrest," I said, "then I want to leave jail under police protection." Deputy Sheriff McCraven went with the doctor and me. As we stepped out into the night and got into the doctor's car, I still feared the possibility of ambush.

Walking into the doctor's office, I saw a crowd of people on the corner. There were others milling around not far away. "There they are. There they are," someone yelled. I thought, this is it. But nothing happened.

Inside his office, the doctor said he had to put some stitches in my head. We had to go to the county hospital. As we drove there, he said, "I don't understand why some people can't see that bothering y'all is what you want. Giving you attention helps your cause." He may have been right.

At the hospital, the clerk wanted to know how I listed my occupation. "Freedom Rider?" he asked with a sneer. I told him with as much dignity as I could muster, schoolteacher. After treatment, the nurse said I could use the telephone on the desk. She suggested that I not go out into the lobby; a lot of angry people were there and with my bloody shirt, I would be a sure target.

I called Rob's house and talked to his wife, Mabel, telling her that we were all under arrest and asking her to inform my wife in Chicago. She promised she would. It was then about 8:30 in the evening. Helm entered the hospital with a tall state trooper, who immediately put handcuffs on me. I had not been handcuffed when I left the county jail. We left the hospital.

A call came over the radio that all cars should proceed to the bus station. A fight had started. "James, hang on," Helm said, "we really got to roll." We tore into town and came to the courthouse, which was surrounded by whites. Groups of whites roamed the streets looking for niggers to lynch, to beat, to kill. All the corners in downtown Monroe had cops on them surrounded by large numbers of white people. As we approached the county jail, I heard the following announcement on the radio: "Attention all cars. Have any of you heard anything about a hostage being held on Boyte Street? Attention all cars. Have any of you heard anything about a hostage being held on Boyte Street?"

I breathed a sigh of relief when I entered the jail, thinking that it might not be a bad place to be on a night like this. I took off my bloody shirt and lay down to rest. I thought of the radio announcement: a hostage on Boyte Street. I felt sure it was a phony, another pretext to enter Newtown and persecute Robert Williams.

CHAPTER 27

Inside the Monroe Jail

MONDAY MORNING we were worried. We had not heard any news from our friends outside jail. We wondered what had happened in Newtown. Woodrow Wilson had been released from jail before we could organize a list of contacts and messages and now we were not being allowed to make phone calls. I remembered my experience in the Los Angeles jail, and doubted if they would allow us to make a call. But there was a difference: This time, an organized group of people filled the jail.

After a full morning of protest, I was permitted to make a call. As they took me from the cellblock, I explained that the call would be only for myself; the others must have their right to make one also. "Yesterday you acted as if you could talk for everyone, so how come you can't make one phone call?" Pig Hegler said to me. "There'll be only one phone call," the jailer added. "I ain't got time to be bothered with all of y'all."

I called a lawyer in Chicago and asked him to contact Mr. and Mrs. Robert Williams to learn what progress had been made in securing legal representation.

"What is your bail and your trial date?" he asked.

"Just a minute." I turned to the desk sergeant and asked him.

"Bail is a thousand dollars each. Trial date, September 11."

My lawyer promised to take care of the case. As I turned to leave, I saw Captain Elliott and headed toward him. "Forman, have you heard the news?" he asked. I detected a note of sympathy in his voice, but I could have been mistaken.

"What news?"

"Robert's house on Boyte Street is closed down. He's nowhere to be found. There's nobody in the house. He may have left the country by now. He was involved in a kidnapping last night and the police are looking for him all over."

"Thanks. I hadn't heard that." I felt numb for a minute. He might be lying but I felt that he was telling the truth about everything except the "kidnapping." Remembering the announcement over the police radio the night before, I knew they had tricked Robert Williams once and for all. They had set him up for a lynching and now he was gone from Monroe, driven away by the Klan, the police, the pigs, the press, the business establishment, and all the other racists.

We in jail were on our own, in a sense. This did not bother me very much, for I had learned that a person must be able to depend upon only himself at certain times. Our morale was low because we did not have all the facts, low because we feared for the safety of Rob. Also, the cell was crowded and we were constantly bumping into each other, putting our feet on each other. We agreed to take showers. We agreed to rest as much as possible so that we would not become too weak from the hunger strike. And we waited for friends outside the jail to get things together.

We had no paper on which to write but I remembered from reading his autobiography that Kwame Nkrumah used to write messages on toilet paper and sneak them out of jail before independence in Ghana. I started doing this, trying feverishly to reconstruct the events of August 27, 1961, yesterday, which now seemed like a long time ago. Some of this material written on toilet paper was later useful to *Jet* magazine for its September 14 issue on Monroe. I also wrote a letter to my wife:

August 28, 1961

Dear Mildred,

I am writing from the cell of the Monroe City jail. There are twelve beds in our cellblock, a face bowl, a toilet and a shower room. Twenty-eight are in this block. We slept on the floor last night three abreast due to the lack of room. To our right is the girls' cellblock. Most of them were released this morning, although there are four who remain, unjustly arrested and imprisoned. To our left is the cell block holding Bill Mahoney, Paul Dietrich, Ken Shilman and Richard Griswold. Griswold was first in a cellblock with a local white who beat him as he took it nonviolently. I don't think I could have done that. Griswold identified the man as James Elmore, or the one who fought LeRoy Wright of Nashville, Tennessee.

Our cell was very hot last night. My wound did not bother me much.

A trustee promised to mail the letter, and did. The trustees also delivered notes from one cellblock to another. On Monday afternoon Constance Lever wrote me the following:

While in the police station I asked to make a phone call to the British Consul and was told the line was busy. I asked for it again in the prison and repeatedly the next morning. My request was ignored. It was not until a member of the Consulate phoned the prison and asked to speak to me that I was in contact. I asked him to make a protest at my wrongful imprisonment charge—incitement to riot. The date of the trial is set for September 11th (my charter flight returning to England leaves on the 9th of September) and the bail has been put at $1,000, which is a completely unreasonable figure. The Consulate suggested I tell the lawyer to protest the wrongful arrest, highly inconvenient date of trial and unreasonable bail. If this was of no avail, he could ask for a writ of habeus corpus after which the trial must be held within 72 hours.

That night, about twelve o'clock, Constance had a visitor—a British official. We decided to make hay during this visit. We began to sing, "We're on the hunger strike, we're on the hunger strike, we're on the hunger strike oh yes.

"To dramatize the issue, oh yes.

"To dramatize the issue, to dramatize the issue, to dramatize the issue, oh yes."

As we sang, I thought of slavery time and the black music created then. The slaves sang songs with double meanings, understood by friends and overlooked by foes. We thought we were doing the same. We learned that Captain Elliott was with the British Consulate officer. We called for him and he came back to our cellblock.

"Captain Elliott, we don't have enough mattresses in this cellblock. We slept on the floor last night."

"I'll see if I can find any," he said. He went around to the cellblock for whites and brought seven or eight.

"Captain Elliott, we've been trying all day to make phone calls. People want to call their lawyers."

"It's not up to me. I'll ask Chief Mauney tomorrow. I'm sure it can be arranged."

We didn't think that was very likely and the next morning we decided to escalate our protest. We ordered breakfast, although we were fasting. Until then, we had spared the wife of the jailer, Mrs. Reid, the trouble of fixing our meals, but now we switched tactics. It was a small act of protest but important to us. When the trays were brought into the cellblock, we performed a ritual. We placed cigarette butts, match stems, straws from the broom, dirt, and ashes into the grits and gravy. Then we administered the supreme rite of pouring coffee over the bread. No one would ever use any of that food again.

Not long after, Reid the jailer came in and collected the trays. "Give me a break, will you?" he said. "I'm trying to help. I'm sure the phone calls can be arranged. By the way, there's a big shot here to see you."

We all wondered who the big shot was, and then he walked in: a brown-skinned man, muscularly built, wearing a suit and bow tie. It was Len Holt, attorney-at-law.

We knew then that everything would be all right. Although I had never before met Len, he had a reputation and we trusted him. He motioned to me to come to the bars, where we talked in low voices about the case.

He told us to start having classes in jail to pass the time while he worked on getting the bond reduced. Twenty-eight thousand dollars is a lot of money to raise, he reminded us, and we had no organization behind us. We told him we were prepared to stay in jail a long time. I gave him some material I had written. After he left, a cop came and said that we would be able to make calls that afternoon. Later that day, Rev. Wyatt T. Walker, executive director of the Southern Christian Leadership Conference, came to the jail; he was working on the case, too, because Paul Brooks had come to Monroe with a letter of authorization from SCLC. Paul had not been arrested but his involvement remained an embarrassment to that organization.

That Tuesday evening we received toilet articles, cigarettes, and writing paper. We were ready for a long stay. But then we learned that our bail had been reduced from one thousand to twenty-five dollars apiece and that our trial date was set for Friday, September 2, rather than September 11. By one o'clock in the morning, bail had been arranged for everyone. We had mixed emotions about accepting it. In the first place, most of the people from out of town were committed to the principle of jail-no-bail. However, some in our group were weakening from the hunger strike. There was talk of eating the next day and how the hunger strike was difficult. Then, too, our group was physically divided; four of the fellows had been moved downstairs—a change we had accepted after being reassured at length of their physical safety. This arrangement could have been a deliberate trick, as events tended to indicate.

We asked the jailer and Deputy Sheriff McCraven to go downstairs and ask the rest of our group what they wanted to do about bail. The confidence we put in them seems foolish in retrospect. They told those downstairs that we had accepted bail. That group then decided they would accept too. When the cops came back upstairs, they told us that the other group wanted bail. Deputy Sheriff McCraven wanted us out of there so that he could get some rest.

But we were not all out of jail yet. When the last five of us—Mahoney, Griswold, Diderich, Shilman, and myself—went in to sign the warrant for release, we discovered that several other charges, such as carrying concealed weapons, had been added to the "inciting to riot." We were not really worried about them, since the state would have a hard time proving those charges, but we felt we should wait for Len Holt's arrival the next day and not sign the warrant as it stood. So we went back to our cells while McCraven grumbled, "I thought I was going to get some sleep tonight."

Len Holt did not show up that Wednesday morning. We were depending on him and we didn't really trust Wyatt T. Walker; he seemed to be pulling some kind of deal to get us out of town so that SCLC would not continue to be embarrassed by its involvement in a case centered around the name of Robert Williams. But when we read some absurd statement in the papers that Danny Thomas had supposedly made, we decided that I should get out in order to establish some control over the remaining Freedom Riders and to see what was happening on the outside. Griswold was also to get out, so that he could tell the world about his beating.

CHAPTER 28

Justice, Monroe Style

MONROE SEEMED like a ghost town when I emerged from the police station that Wednesday afternoon, and Newtown was like a ghost that had died. Robert's house, where I went to stay until the trial on Friday, had the atmosphere of an ancient monument. By then I had read what the press said happened there after we were arrested up at the courthouse: The Williamses had taken a white couple as hostages and held them at gunpoint. Later Rob released them and he and his wife fled. He was charged with kidnapping.

The story didn't make much sense and I didn't believe what the couple had said. I knew all the law authorities wanted to silence this man, who had been speaking more and more as a true revolutionary and whom the government had begun to consider dangerous. But I decided not to try to find out what had happened. Rob had been indicted for kidnapping, along with Mae Mallory, and both had left. I didn't inquire about the actions of Mae Mallory on this subject but I concluded that this indictment was part of the general witchhunt, because Mae Mallory had been an active supporter of Robert Williams for a long time. If this was the way they had chosen to deal with their situation, then my interference could only jeopardize their chances of escape. An incident which took place shortly after I arrived at Rob's house from jail confirmed this decision. An FBI agent came to question me, asking if I knew this person and that person. He then said that it was a federal crime to withhold information from the FBI. I thought this must be just an intimidating device, but decided in any case that the less I knew and might have to conceal, the better. Too often people pry into delicate situations out of curiosity; this can make them vulnerable personally and of possible danger to others.

I was surprised to find Harold Reape and Richard Crowder still in

Monroe. Not that they had done anything wrong, but I felt they were so closely identified with Rob that it was unwise for them to stay. I told them that they should leave at once. They planned to leave that night at seven o'clock but the police arrested them at four o'clock in the afternoon as accessories to kidnapping. John Lowry of New York, a white youth who had supposedly moved the car of the white couple over to the curb after they were stopped in front of Rob's house, was also arrested that afternoon as an accessory. A nationwide hunt was on for the Williamses and Mae Mallory.

Since then, both Rob and Julian Mayfield have given accounts of the so-called kidnapping. Dozens of black people from Monroe and the surrounding area had poured into Boyte Street, they say, frightened and above all enraged by what was happening up at the square. Rumors and truths were flying everywhere about blacks being beaten, jailed, killed. On Boyte Street shots could be heard coming from the direction of the courthouse. At this high point of tension, a white couple—incredible as it seems—drove down the street and their car was stopped less than two hundred feet from Rob's house. The white man got out or was pulled out of his car while the crowd shouted "Kill him! Kill him!" Williams emerged from his home, tried to reason with the crowd, and finally told the couple to come into his house for their own safety.

Mayfield says that he left the area soon afterward and went to another house. He heard heavy shooting from the area of Rob's house. Williams called him there, said the area was surrounded by state troopers, and advised Mayfield to leave at once so that someone would be free to write the story. He left.

As the world later learned, Rob and his wife escaped to Cuba where they remained as exiles from Uncle Sam's racist justice for several years and then went on to the People's Republic of China. In 1969, Robert Williams returned to the United States. Mae Mallory was arrested and jailed in Cleveland, Ohio, where she fought a three-year struggle against being extradited back to North Carolina. She finally lost that battle and went on trial with Reape, Crowder, and Lowry. The four were cleared in 1965 because the defense successfully contended that there had been racial discrimination in the selection of the Grand Jury which originally indicted them. Today, Mae Mallory is in Cleveland, where she continues the struggle against racism and imperialism.

That Wednesday night in Monroe, we would have had a hard time imagining that anyone involved in this case would ever go free. The cops came cracking down, boom and again boom. At one point, I was calling Len Holt from Richard Crowder's house when a battery of police officers, detectives, and state troopers arrived. When Mrs. Crowder opened the door, they told her that they had a warrant to search the house, I believe. Chief Mauney looked at me with his asinine smile and proceeded upstairs without a word. They brought down many guns. I left the house. There was nothing I could do.

The next afternoon, we were sitting on the porch of Rob's house when a similar battery of police officers walked through the house and into the backyard. They immediately dug up a case of dynamite. From the way they went straight to the dynamite, I thought that someone was singing, giving information that only a person in the know could have had. Or it could have been planted; the house had not been guarded the night before. Assuming that the dynamite had not been planted, it became clear to me what Rob had meant when he said, "If you kill one white man, you might as well go all the way. Otherwise, you won't survive." That belief was why he had been so careful about indiscriminate self-defense, because if he, Robert Williams, had killed somebody in self-defense, the whole state, if not the nation, would have moved to destroy him—all the way. But the most serious implication of the dynamite find was that if it had not been planted, then we had an informer among us.

That incident convinced me that we should not sleep at Rob's house another night. State troopers were everywhere in the town and wherever we went a car followed us. Any car coming into Newtown was followed and usually stopped while the police questioned the driver and examined the vehicle. The police were constantly coming around, snooping, harassing, intimidating. We therefore agreed to disperse and sleep at different homes.

Those were hours of great tension for me, with the trial coming up the next day and the pressure of holding together a group of people who were in some cases bewildered by the turn of events. Mostly I was hoping that Rob and Mabel had reached safety. We had a final pretrial meeting that night, with Rev. Wyatt T. Walker and attorney William Kunstler, whom Walker had brought in. Some of us stated that we wanted Len Holt to represent us in court. He had promised to be there. Walker spoke against representation by Holt; I don't know why, but I did know that there had been conflicts between SCLC and Len in connection with the Freedom Rides. It was finally agreed that Kunstler and Holt would serve as co-counselors for the trial.

On Friday morning we cooked breakfast at Robert's house and those from out of town packed up in the belief that we would be leaving after the trial. We took cabs to the County Courthouse, passing the house of the mad woman with the knife, turning left on the highway where the mob had caused a traffic jam and had attempted to push Williams's car off the highway. We passed the grim-looking police station, which contained so much hate. We saw some of the people who had molested us on the sidewalk in front of the courthouse. They, not us, should have been on trial. Then we walked into the courtroom, took seats on the left and waited.

I knew that Southern courtrooms offered a mockery of justice, but I had never been in one before that day. I knew what a kangaroo court was, but I had never experienced one until that day. Except for Captain Elliott, the police officers lied in describing the events of that Sunday. I sat behind Kunstler and Holt, feeding them questions with which to cross-examine the police. Because of my familiarity with the events, they were able to trip up the prosecution witnesses or elicit favorable testimony; for example, they got Elliott to repeat his belief that if Rushing had permitted Woodrow's car to pass, the trouble could have been avoided. But none of this made any difference. The judge was out to get us and the kangaroos hopped all over the courtroom.

The first one skipped across the courtroom when the defense attorneys Kunstler and Holt pointed out an error in the warrant and moved that the case be dismissed.

"Denied."

The next one bounced in when Holt and Kunstler asked that the witnesses for the state be brought in separately since standing together might influence their testimony.

"Denied. These men have been together for more than a week. They have discussed this case thoroughly. I see no reason to separate them now," the judge pontificated.

A third kangaroo entered when the state said that it rested its case on the fact that the people were picketing and this caused a riot. The defense attorneys objected, pointing out that picketing was legal and that picketing itself did not cause the people to riot.

"Overruled."

Skipping, hopping, and jumping came the daddy kangaroo. The defense attorneys pointed out to the court that the state had not proved that we were armed with weapons, concealed or otherwise, and the other extra charges.

"The fact that the warrant may have said they had firearms and that they did not is only a part of the case," the judge dictated. "Strike that part from the warrant and keep the inciting to riot."

There we were.

Holt did a magnificent job in court. He took every possible opportunity to make the case political, speaking eloquently about race relations in this country and the need for the type of action in which we were engaged. Now he gave his summation, a brilliant one, but this was a kangaroo court and his words were like pearls thrown to swine.

"Guilty! Guilty! Guilty! They are all found guilty," screamed the short, white-faced judge as he banged his gavel. He read out the sentences. We got from six months to two years in the state penitentiary for inciting to riot. But apparently the judge and the rest of the power structure wanted us out of town, for we were offered suspended sentences and a fine of twenty-five dollars if we would agree not to picket or to violate the laws of Union County or the state of North Carolina for a period of two years. The judge gave us thirty minutes to choose between up to two years in jail or suspended sentences and leaving Monroe—for there would be no point in staying if the least activity on our part would land us in jail.

Something weird happened at this point. We all knew that we were not guilty and we wanted to appeal. But Holt said that to appeal would cost money and we had no organization behind us. This left us at the mercy of Bill Kunstler, the lawyer for SCLC. He claimed there was no constitutional issue raised in the case. I thought this absurd; the right to picket, for one, has been guaranteed to all citizens. I could not understand why he didn't see this, and even suspected him of being part of some SCLC deal to get us out of town. Bill has said in later years that he was more of a lawyer at that time than a movement person and he learned a lot from Monroe.

We had only thirty minutes, not enough time to explore alternatives. I was furious as we went back into court and told the judge that we accepted the suspended sentences.

The courtroom emptied out. I stood at the back, thinking about my involvement in Monroe, knowing that I had to leave, aware that even some black people were saying that the problem was Robert Williams instead of racism, feeling distraught, uncertain of the future, frustrated, mad with Kunstler, proud of Holt. Then Captain Elliott walked up to me. "You'd make a good lawyer, Forman," he said, referring to the way I had passed notes to the lawyers to trip up the prosecution. "You know how to handle yourself in the courtroom . . ." He paused. "I'm sorry about the verdict."

I couldn't believe what I was hearing. I couldn't believe this man was serious. We were all alone in the courtroom, just the two of us, a police captain of Monroe and a black man who respected Rob Williams. It is because we are alone, I thought. He wouldn't dare say those things otherwise. Yet I didn't rob him of his sincerity. I believed he meant what he said. He had tried to treat us with some respect as prisoners, and his actions before that had been decent. He knew we were innocent. All the pigs in Monroe knew that, but the one I saw now was a trapped man, trapped by racism in Monroe. I wondered how many other whites in Monroe, in all America, were also trapped as he was, afraid to challenge racism, afraid because they feared for their lives, their jobs, their security. Elliott would not keep his job long, I thought.

"It's one of those things," I replied. "Don't worry about it. We'll make it." He left.

I stood there alone. I was cool. I looked at the judge's seat. I grew cold. Ice-cold. My mind froze. I loved humanity. I hated injustice. Someday we would sit in judgment. We would decide. Monroe. Nashville. Birmingham. Montgomery. Jackson. Fayette County. New York. Chicago. Boston. D.C. Detroit. Newark. Harlem. Watts. Hiroshima. Vietnam. Sharpeville. The Congo. Cuba. Santo Domingo. White America on trial the world around. Racism! Humiliation. Racism! Degradation. Racism! Exploitation. Racism! Napalm. Racism! Guilty. Guilty. Guilty. But. Execute—but. Execute—but. Execute now! Guilty! Guilty! Guilty! Execute now! Case closed. No reprieve. Next.

BOOK TWO
A BAND OF SISTERS AND BROTHERS, IN A CIRCLE OF TRUST

CHAPTER 29

Miss Ella Baker

ELLA JO Baker, one of the key persons in the formation of SNCC, is one of those many strong black women who have devoted their lives to the liberation of their people. Born in 1905, she worked as the director of branches for the National Association for the Advancement of Colored People, as executive director of the Southern Christian Leadership Conference, and without her there would be no story of the Student Nonviolent Coordinating Committee. She has an endless faith in people and their power to change their status in life. She believes strongly in the organized will of the people as opposed to the power of a single leader. She has served black people without fanfare, publicity, or concern for personal credit. Ella Baker's concern for the condition of black people in the twentieth century has led her to think of herself as the one who is willing to work behind the mimeograph machine and to do the work that others are not willing to do, the nitty-gritty, the sweeping of floors, the detailed and tiresome work of administration.

Historians and propagandists have a way of remembering only certain names, but the historical process is pushed forward by such people as Ella Jo Baker and the masses of humanity whose names are rarely recorded. The historical process spirals its way upward, with zigzags, deviations, downward dips, but always inclining upward. It is like the consciousness of a people who are in revolutionary ferment, for no people or group of individuals or single person is born with an intense commitment to the revolutionary process. They are all activated and pushed by forces of history and by individual actors on the life stage.

Throughout the decade of the sixties, many people helped to ignite or were touched by the creative fire of SNCC without appreciating the generating force of Ella Jo Baker. And just as people in SNCC were often unaware of the resistance struggle of their predecessors, so many black people today participate in our liberation without fully understanding the motive power of SNCC. Many black people in the future will carry on that struggle without knowing about the contribution of today's revolutionaries. All this, too, is the historical process.

Ella Jo Baker herself had an acute sense of the historical process and, in the spring of 1960, when the student sit-in movement erupted all across the South, she quickly grasped its significance. She felt there had to be some contact between the various student groups which had sprung up, or they might peter out for lack of the nourishment of ideas and the sustenance of morale that come from such contact. She convinced the Southern Christian Leadership Conference, which she had helped to found two years earlier, that it should call a Southwide Student Leadership Conference where sit-in leaders could gather.

SCLC appropriated eight hundred dollars for the conference and Shaw University in Raleigh, North Carolina, provided facilities; but they were hardly adequate for the number of students who showed up. About a hundred had been expected and over three hundred came, representing fifty-six colleges in the South, fifty-eight Southern communities, and twelve Southern states. Nineteen schools from the North were represented and thirteen observer organizations, to make a total of fifty-seven Northern students and observers.

The Southwide Student Leadership Conference on Nonviolent Resistance to Segregation began on Good Friday and ended on Easter Sunday, 1960. Rev. James Lawson gave the keynote address upon the invitation of Miss Baker, who felt he had the longest commitment to nonviolence and that his struggle in Nashville placed him in a leadership position. Lawson raised some questions about the validity of the legal approach, which earned him strong rebukes from the NAACP. But a much more serious conflict developed at the meeting itself. While Miss Baker had originally thought in terms of a small conference in which the young activists would come together and be able to discuss what needed to be done next, she found herself in the midst of an organizational fight with SCLC over what to do with all these students. The leadership of SCLC —Martin King, Ralph Abernathy, and Wyatt Walker, who was the incoming executive director—wanted the students to form themselves into a youth wing of the Southern Christian Leadership Conference. Images of the NAACP's youth division loomed brightly in the minds of these men. But Miss Baker had by this time become very critical of the leader-centered orientation of the SCLC. She felt that the organization was depending too much on the press and on the promotion of Martin King, and was not developing enough indigenous leadership across the South.

On the second day of the conference King, Walker, and Abernathy called a caucus during which they tried to convince Miss Baker that the students had to become an arm of SCLC. Walker admitted that he was being selfish, but since he was becoming the executive director he desperately wanted the students as an arm of SCLC. This objective could be achieved, these Baptist preachers felt, if someone would just make such a motion. Then they could deliver the votes. King was sure he could deliver the students from Georgia, headed by Lonnie King.

Abernathy felt the Alabama delegation headed by Bernard Lee would automatically follow his lead. And Walker knew he could deliver the Virginia delegation. With these three states in their pockets, they believed the young students assembled in North Carolina would automatically become a part of the SCLC with Dr. Martin Luther King as their spiritual leader.

Miss Baker stated that she felt it was too early for the students to structure their movement, that nothing more should come out of this conference than a continuation committee to explore what kind of structure they might eventually have. She felt the students had a right to determine their own structure—if they wanted one at all at that point; that it was their right to explore all possibilities and make their own decisions, since thus far it was they who had propelled the sit-in movement to national and international importance. She refused to be a party to making a motion that the students become an arm of SCLC and she finally walked out of the private meeting, rejecting the whole caucus procedure.

Realizing the importance of Miss Baker and the influence that she wielded among the young people, the three ministers left Raleigh that night. Their plans had been smashed. The students decided on April 17, 1960, not to become a wing of anything or a permanent organization of any kind, but to set up a temporary Student Nonviolent Coordinating Committee to continue the dialogue established at Raleigh. It would eventually become permanently established as SNCC.

These leaders of the Southern Christian Leadership Conference may never have forgiven Miss Baker for her act of defiance. Throughout the years that followed they consistently made unkind remarks about Miss Baker and her influence in SNCC. What they did not understand, perhaps, is that her position simply reflected the students' attitudes. Many at the Raleigh conference were extremely critical of the adult civil rights organizations existing at that time—including SCLC—and felt a need to form an organization which they could control and direct and which would not be subject to the authority of anyone but themselves. In describing that conference, Miss Baker says that the opposition among the students to becoming an affiliate of SCLC was so hot and intense that at one point during the meeting they had to stop, sing, and pray. Some of the strongest opposition came from Petersburg, Virginia, where Wyatt T. Walker thought he had supreme control.

Aside from this behind-the-scenes problem, the meeting was tremendously inspirational, according to Ella Baker. Writing in the *Southern Patriot* of May, 1960, she described its significance and mood:

RALEIGH, N.C.—The Student Leadership Conference made it crystal clear that current sit-ins and other demonstrations are concerned with something much bigger than a hamburger or even a giant-sized coke.

Whatever may be the differences in approach to their goal, the Negro and white students, North and South, are seeking to rid America of the scourge of racial segregation and discrimination—not only at lunch counters, but in every aspect of life.

In reports, casual conversations, discussion groups, and speeches, the sense and the spirit of the following statement that appeared in the initial newsletter of the students at Barber-Scotia College, Concord, N.C., were re-echoed time and again:

> We want the world to know that we no longer accept the inferior position of second-class citizenship. We are willing to go to jail, be ridiculed, spat upon and even suffer physical violence to obtain First Class Citizenship.

By and large, this feeling that they have a destined date with freedom was not limited to a drive for personal freedom, or even freedom for the Negro in the South. Repeatedly it was emphasized that the movement was concerned with the moral implications of racial discrimination for the whole world and the Human Race.

This universality of approach was linked with a perceptive recognition that "it is important to keep the movement democratic and to avoid struggles for personal leadership."

It was further evident that desire for supportive cooperation from adult leaders and the adult community was also tempered by apprehension that adults might try to "capture" the student movement. The students showed willingness to be met on the basis of equality, but were intolerant of anything that smacked of manipulation or domination.

This inclination toward group-centered leadership, rather than toward a leader-centered group pattern of organization, was refreshing indeed to those of the older group who bear the scars of battle, the frustrations and the disillusionment that come when the prophetic leader turns out to have heavy feet of clay.

However hopeful might be the signs in the direction of group-centeredness, the fact that many schools and communities, especially in the South, have not provided adequate experience for young Negroes to assume initiative and think and act independently accentuated the need for guarding the student movement against well-meaning, but nevertheless unhealthy, over-protectiveness.

Here is an opportunity for adult and youth to work together and provide genuine leadership—the development of the individual to his highest potential for the benefit of the group.

Many adults and youth characterized the Raleigh meeting as the greatest or most significant conference of our period.

Whether it lives up to this high evaluation or not will, in a large measure, be determined by the extent to which there is more effective training in and understanding of non-violent principles and practices, in group dynamics, and in the re-direction into creative channels of the normal frustrations and hostilities that result from second-class citizenship.

After the Raleigh conference, the temporary SNCC met each month between April and September, 1960. Representatives from such other organizations as the YWCA, CORE, SCLC, and NSA were allowed to send observers. In June, 1960, Jane Stembridge, a student at the Union Theological Seminary came to work for SNCC as a secretary, on the recommendation of Fred Shuttlesworth. She joined Miss Baker and others who were trying to disseminate news about this new youth group which did not yet have much of an identity of its own.

At first SNCC had a desk at 208 Auburn Avenue in the back of the SCLC office. Miss Baker spoke to an Atlanta real estate firm, trying to get an empty room in the same building with SCLC. This had been promised, but Martin King decided he wanted the room for the expansion of SCLC. Shopping around again, the real estate agent found a cubbyhole for twenty dollars a month at 197½ Auburn, directly across the street. This housed the national office of SNCC until May, 1962.

One of the functions of Jane Stembridge was to prepare for a conference in October, 1960, in which SNCC would finally be formalized by the election of representatives to a permanent Coordinating Committee. Among the people who helped Jane to prepare for this conference was Robert Parris Moses, who traveled that summer in Mississippi and Alabama and later became a key figure in the development of SNCC.

Someone had approached the AFL-CIO for money to run the October conference. Miss Baker does not know who did this, but the grant from the AFL-CIO presented the organization with one of its first crises. Bayard Rustin had been invited to speak at the conference. At that time he did not enjoy the good opinion of the labor movement as he does today, and the AFL said they would not give the money if he were going to speak. There was a conference with Bayard, who said that he would not stand in the way of SNCC getting the money. He agreed not to speak. But Jane Stembridge felt that this was a violation of principle and the money should have been turned down. She quit after the October conference and Ed King, a young black man from Kentucky State, came to serve as administrative secretary.

There is no way of knowing for sure, but it is my informed guess that the so-called liberal and also conservative forces around the country saw the student sit-in movement as something that could become useful to the foreign policy of the United States. After all, the students were closely allied to the philosophy of Dr. King, who posed no serious threat to the foreign policy of this country. In fact, his emphasis on nonviolence, love, and religion made him a darling of the U.S. State Department. The use of King to show how peaceful change was possible within the American system would reach a peak with the March on Washington when the USIA had a film made of it that was widely—much too widely—circulated all over the world. The government consistently sought to show how dissent was allowed within the United States—unlike the so-called totalitarian countries. Watching the growth of the Southern sit-in movement, the Central Intelligence Agency and other government bodies must have felt a need to control this outburst of "dissent," while simultaneously using it as much as possible. In this same spirit, the AFL-CIO could offer funds to SNCC but with a string attached. And its success in preventing Rustin from speaking must have suggested that it was indeed possible to influence if not control the student movement.

It must be remembered that at this point the cold war was being waged vigorously by the United States. Because the Southern students were somewhat isolated from the effects of McCarthyism, they were not afraid in some ways to take action against segregation and discrimination. But still, the pervasive effect of McCarthyism had certainly influenced the minds of many Southern students. Ruby Doris Smith Robinson, who became the executive secretary of SNCC in 1966 and was active with the Southern sit-in movement from the beginning, told me how some students in Atlanta were suspicious of Bob Moses and felt that he was a communist from New York. Red-baiting became a favorite tactic of the NAACP for discrediting SNCC, an organization that the NAACP leadership despised with a passion. Actually, a struggle for the minds of black people had begun, for the students were critical of adult leadership and felt the legalistic pace of the NAACP was too slow, ineffective. The NAACP, of course, was fully plugged into the American system. Its Red-baiting can be seen as just a variation on the position of the entire liberal Establishment.

When SNCC set out to draw up its constitution that fall, a chorus of liberals and conservatives tried to get the new organization to insert a totalitarian disclaimer. This kind of clause barred from membership anyone advocating a totalitarian form of government. Ostensibly, it applied to everything from fascists to communists but actually it had meaning only for the Left. The League of Industrial Democracy, in which Bayard Rustin was active, had gotten SDS to put such a clause in its early constitution. Rustin tried to get SNCC to do it, too; but SNCC refused all such pressure and this merely intensified the liberal Establishment's determination to control the organization—or to destroy it, if control should prove impossible.

SNCC became a permanent organization at that October meeting and despite the Red-baiting—the fear of SNCC—it was expanding its power. Until September, 1961, it acted primarily as a coordinating agency for the Southern protest groups which met every two months to discuss plans. Significant among the actions that SNCC took in its own name was the petition it presented to the Democratic and Republican party conventions in 1960, and its call to fill the jails at Rock Hill, North Carolina, in February, 1961. During the Freedom Rides, as I have already described, SNCC helped to continue them when CORE abandoned the idea in May of 1961. SNCC had a rotating chairman during the summer of 1960, then Marion Barry became chairman for a number of months and was succeeded by Chuck McDew.

That was the situation, superficially, when I received a telephone call in September, 1961, from Paul Brooks in St. Louis. I had recently come back from Monroe and had just begun teaching elementary school in Chicago.

"You remember that group we have been talking about organizing?" Paul asked. He was referring to our many discussions of the need for a cadre of full-time, absolutely dedicated organizers who could bring to blacks in the South the skills and tools which, I felt, were all they needed to start moving on a mass basis.

"Yes."

"Well, SNCC is going to do it."

"Yes?" I asked.

"They're going to take on a group of people. There's going to be a meeting in McComb in two weeks to talk about it."

"McComb?"

"McComb, Mississippi. Some of the people are going to work on voter registration. Some on direct action. Diane is the coordinator of direct action. She asked me to call you, she wants you to work with us on direct action. Will you do it?"

"Well," I said "Man, just wait a minute now. This requires a slight degree of thought. You don't just say, am I willing to leave my job and so forth—just like that. I need to have more information." I had been through a bad time with one organization, and wasn't ready to leap into another without a full discussion. But more importantly, I knew that joining SNCC would be for me more than just a matter of taking out a year. It was a question of making a long-term commitment.

Paul told me that there was going to be a meeting of the direct action people in Chicago, before the McComb meeting, and I should come to that. He also explained that all the full-time workers would receive forty dollars a week, which didn't sound like much to me, especially since I was married. But I agreed with the idea that a subsistence salary would help prevent the workers from becoming separated from the people. And I agreed to come to the preliminary meeting in Chicago.

We met, and there were more meetings in Chicago. I learned that SNCC was seriously split into two factions—the direct action wing and the voter registration wing. This conflict had developed because some of its members wanted to work for political power for black people through efforts at voter registration—which would also take the student movement into areas of the Deep South that had not been touched as yet—while others like Diane Nash felt that voter registration work would place SNCC too much in the arms of the U.S. Government. It would be necessary to work with the Department of Justice on gathering information about discrimination against would-be black voters and on filing suits. It looked to them as though SNCC would be put in danger of selling out if it concentrated on voter registration. As matters turned out, there really was no conflict, because both the students who favored direct action and those who favored voter registration encountered such repression in the South that any distinction became meaningless. The brutal Southern sheriffs didn't care what kind of "outside agitator" you were; you were black and making trouble and that was enough for them.

There was also a structural problem. The people who were most active on the Coordinating Committee were going to leave school and become full-time organizers—some sixteen of them. This meant that a new structure had to be hammered out for the organization, since the old one would become obsolete when people formed themselves into a full-time cadre. The relationship of this cadre to the student base had to be discussed and ironed out.

These were important problems, but none of them seemed insurmountable and so, with my wife Mildred, I decided to join SNCC. I resigned my teaching job and went on, on a substitute basis, waiting for some money to arrive which had been promised to get me to McComb. While I had some of my own, I felt that if SNCC were serious it should be able to follow through on its commitment or at least to explain why it was not forthcoming. The waiting became unbearable after a while and I made some calls myself. I managed to speak to Charles Jones, in charge of voter registration, at the Burgland supermarket in McComb. He told me that there was no one in the Atlanta headquarters office of SNCC and suggested that I go there to handle the problem.

I caught a plane to Atlanta. Charles Jones had said that the key to the SNCC office, if no one was there, would be at the SCLC office. But no one at SCLC had ever heard of any key. So I wound up jimmying open the door.

There it was—the national offices of the Student Nonviolent Coordinating Committee. The same grubby room that I had seen when I talked with Ed King. Greasy walls. A faint light from a dusty, plastic skylight overhead. The mustiness, the smell, the mail scattered all over the floor. While I stood looking at the mail on the floor, I realized that the telephone was ringing.

McComb had just exploded with the high school students' walkout, which was the reason why the office was empty, and now *Newsweek* was calling for news on McComb. "Sorry I can't give out any information at this time, can I call you back?" I told them. I didn't have any information, but I figured that the national office of a group engaged in what was then the hottest protest going couldn't afford to appear totally ignorant. The telephone again. Another request for news on McComb. "Sorry, I'll take your number and our communications department will be in touch," I bluffed.

Whatever I didn't know about SNCC, I at least realized that the organization was alive. The phone never stopped ringing, but it was always newsmen, no one from SNCC who could give me any information. I asked myself, What time does the next plane leave for Chicago? How in hell could an organization be involved with such a massive protest as the one in McComb and not have anyone in its office all week? The mail all over the floor? Didn't understand it. Papers scattered all over the desks? The room was so small that five people couldn't enter at the same time. There were cases of people coming to work for SNCC and being so discouraged by the first day's experience that they left right away. I can understand and sympathize.

Then I began to realize what was really in store for me. I couldn't leave because if I locked the office I'd have to jimmy it open to get back in. It was clear I'd have to sleep there. I'd have to make arrangements with the people downstairs. But I was in the office. I was in charge. Where was the rest of the group? Was there anyone to answer the phone if I went out? What was my assignment, what was I supposed to be doing? I thought of orienting myself somewhat by looking through the files. What files? There weren't any to speak of. Utter chaos.

Finally, after about two days of this, I saw a SNCC face. It was Charles Sherrod, coming in from McComb. That Saturday everyone came straggling in with tales of violence and fierce civil strife. And murder. The whole story came out in bits and pieces, from oral reports and written ones. For the first time, I knew that I had begun to work for SNCC.

CHAPTER **30**

McComb, Mississippi

BOB MOSES wrote, in a field report from McComb:

On Tuesday, Aug. 29, 1961, we made our third attempt at registration in Amite County. I accompanied two people down to the registrar's office . . . we were to meet Alfred Knox on the courthouse lawn. However, Knox was not there and we had to walk through town looking for him. We found him at the east end of town, by the post office, and were walking back to the registrar's office when we were approached by three young white men.

They came up, stopped, and the fellow who was in the lead asked me what I was trying to do? Before I could answer he began to beat—hit at me. I covered my head and I was kneeling on the ground with my head covered and he was beating me for I don't know how long.

He finally stopped and I got up and walked over to the registrar's office, to the sheriff's office, and asked the sheriff if he couldn't swear out a warrant against him. He said that he couldn't since I wasn't sure whether or not he had an instrument that he was using to do the beating . . . .

The registrar had left. So we came back to Steptoe's where I had the wounds cleaned. (My shirt was very bloody and I figured that if we went back in the courthouse we would probably frighten everybody, so we went to Steptoe's.) Then we went over to McComb where the doctor had to take nine stitches in three different places in the scalp.

Two days later we went back to press charges. The State of Mississippi had to prosecute, and that day they had a very quick six-man Justice of the Peace jury. Dawson and Knox and myself all testified, but the white defendant was found innocent and the case was dismissed.

This report by Moses is a brief one but it suggests all the major elements of SNCC's struggle in Mississippi:

The denial of voting rights, so flagrant that people with master's degrees in political science and even Ph.D.s were turned down in the same automatic way as all other black people.

The violence and terror waiting for anyone who challenged that denial.

The conspiracy of law enforcement and the courts with their "white only" justice.

It was Mississippi, that's all—for some, just to say the name of the state is to tell the whole story.

It was Mississippi: The state which had led the Southern drive to take back from black people the vote and other civil rights won during Reconstruction, the state which had reduced the number of registered black voters from 190,000 in 1890 to 8,600 in 1892, through a combination of new laws, tricks, and murder. It was Mississippi, with a larger proportion of blacks than any other state and the lowest proportion—only 5 percent —of eligible blacks registered to vote. It was Mississippi, birthplace of the White Citizens' Council—a white-collar version of the Ku Klux Klan. It was Mississippi, where years of terror, economic intimidation, and a total, grinding, day-in, day-out white racism had created a black population numb with fear and hopelessness—yet still able from time to time to produce individuals in whom the spirit of rebellion lived.

It was to Mississippi that Bob Moses, then a twenty-six-year-old Harlem schoolteacher with a master's degree from Harvard, had come after working for a period in the New York office of SCLC and in the Atlanta SNCC office. While in Atlanta, Moses had been sent out to get people from Deep South areas to attend a full SNCC meeting in the fall of 1961. On that field trip, he talked with Amzie Moore of Cleveland, Mississippi, one of those individuals who had survived and defied tyranny. Amzie Moore felt that a campaign to register black voters could break the isolation of black Mississippians, replace the brokenness with a fighting spirit, and even possibly win a local political voice which would lead to further change. He convinced Moses of this, and together they laid plans for a voter registration drive to begin that summer.

But, when Moses had returned to Cleveland, he found it impossible to get the project going—no location, no equipment, no funds became available. Meanwhile, however, a man named C. C. Bryant—head of the NAACP chapter in Pike County, where McComb is located—had learned of the proposed registration project and written to Moses, inviting him to come to McComb to start a similar project. Amzie Moore and Moses traveled to McComb and found that it had better facilities. It was decided to make the experiment in that town.

McComb was Mississippi, no doubt about it: A village sitting down there in the southwestern part of the state, Klan country, with a long history of violence and oppression. In Pike County, two hundred of about eight thousand eligible blacks were registered in 1960; in nearby Amite, out of nearly five thousand eligible blacks, there was exactly *one* registered. And in Walthall County, out of three thousand blacks over twenty-one, *none* was registered.

During the first week of August Moses was joined by John Hardy and Reggie Robinson. Hardy was a small, muscular fellow from Nashville who had just finished a jail term resulting from his participation in the Freedom Rides, and Reggie Robinson was from Baltimore, Maryland, where he had been directing a voter registration project. Both students were among the sixteen who had decided to drop out of school for a year to work for SNCC. Together these three started traveling the dirt roads, going into the old, broken-down houses, talking the language and living the life of the oppressed people, and trying to persuade them to face the trials of registration.

On August 6 or 7, 1961, this small group opened SNCC's first voter registration school in Mississippi. The school operated in a two-story, combination cinder block and paintless wood structure which housed a grocery store on the street level and a Masonic meeting hall above it. It was located in Burglundtown, the black section of McComb. There, from 9 A.M. to 9 P.M., people could learn to fill out the intentionally difficult voter registration form. This meant having people read and interpret different sections of the Mississippi Constitution and describe the duties and obligations of a citizen. After doing this every day for two weeks, the workers finally started to get results. People began to go down to Magnolia, Mississippi—the seat of Pike County—to register.

This sudden stir of activity in McComb interested people in Walthall and Amite counties, who then asked the registration workers if they would start schools in their counties. Moses was at first critical of going into such "tough" counties so early in the game; however, he decided to proceed for two reasons: First, because the people had asked for help and were anxious to try to register; second, SNCC couldn't take the position of turning down areas on the basis of difficulty, because the people would then lose confidence in us.

Around the middle of August, John Hardy and two other SNCC workers went into Walthall to start voter registration activities. They also made the first attempt to take people down to the courthouse in Liberty—the seat of Amite County to register. This is Bob Moses's report on that experience:

I [Moses] accompanied three people down to Liberty in a first registration attempt there. One was a very old man and two middle-aged ladies. We left early the morning of August 15th. It was a Tuesday. We arrived at the court-house about 10 A.M. The registrar came out. I waited by the side—waiting for either the farmer or one of the two ladies to say something to the registrar. He asked what they wanted; what were they here for, in a very rough kind of voice. They didn't say anything; they were literally paralyzed with fear. So, after awhile, I spoke up and said that they would like to try and register to vote. So, he asked, "Who are you and what do you have to do with them? Are you here to register?" I told him who I was and that we were conducting a school in McComb, and that these people had attended the school and they wanted an opportunity to register. "Well," he said, "they will have to wait because there is somebody else filling out the form." Well, there was a young white lady with her husband and she was completing the forms. When she finished, our people started to register—one at a time.

In the meantime, a procession of people began moving in and out of the office—the sheriff, a couple of his deputies, people from the Tax Office and Driver's License Office—looking in, staring, moving back out, muttering. A highway patrolman finally came in and sat down in the office and we stayed that way in sort of uneasy tension all morning.

The first person who filled out the form took a long time to do it, and it was noontime before he finished. When we came back after lunch, I was not permitted to stay in the office, but had to leave and sit on the front porch— which I did. We finished the whole process about four-thirty. All of the three people had had a chance to fill out the form. This was a victory because they had been down several times before and had not had a chance even to fill out the forms.

On the way home we were followed by the highway patrolman who had spent the day in the Registrar's Office. He tailed us for about ten miles very closely, twenty or twenty-five feet behind us, all the way back to McComb. At one point we pulled over and he passed us and circled around and came back. We pulled off as he was passing us in the opposite direction and he turned around and followed us again. Finally, he blew us down and I got out and asked what the trouble was. The people in the car, by that time, were very, very frightened. He asked me who I was, what my business was, and told me I was interfering in what he was doing. I said, "I simply wanted to find out what the problem was and what we were being stopped for." He told me to get back into the car, and as I did so, I jotted his name down. He then opened the car door and pushed me and said, "Get in the car, Nigger," and slammed the door after me. He then told us to follow him in the car, and took us over to McComb where I was placed under arrest.

They called up the County Prosecuting Attorney, and he came down. He and the patrolman then sat down and opened the law books to find a charge.

They charged me with interfering with an officer in the process of arresting somebody. When they found out that the only person arrested was myself, they changed the charge to interfering with an officer in the discharge of his duties.

Moses was found guilty and received a ninety-day jail sentence. It was suspended, probably because in jail he had telephoned the Justice Department (collect, and the call was accepted), told an official there that he was being intimidated simply because of trying to help people register, and the powers of McComb realized that they had something a little hot on their hands. Bob left jail—it had been his introduction to Mississippi jails—and returned to the tedious routine of canvassing.

The group was severely handicapped because they had no transportation and the farms in the area are far apart. Finally they got help from E. W. Steptoe, a local NAACP president who lived in the southern part of Pike County and who had already helped the voter registration workers—feeding them when they had no money for food. Steptoe made plans to set up a school near his farm, and Bob Moses, together with a local worker, went to live there for a week. The voter registration project had now spread to encompass the counties of Pike, Amite, and Walthall, with McComb as a sort of headquarters. Other workers came South to help. Hollis Watkins and Curtis Hayes, high school students who were both from McComb originally and who later became full-time SNCC workers, set up the Pike County Nonviolent Movement and served as its president and vice-president respectively.

On August 22, four more blacks went into Liberty to register and this time there was no trouble at all. People felt encouraged and another group planned to go on August 29. This was the day that Bob Moses was viciously beaten.

By this time, McComb had become a hotbed of activity. There was not only a voter registration effort in progress on August 29, but also direct action. Young people in McComb, eager to help in the canvassing, also wanted to engage in something more visible. Marion Barry had come down from Nashville and, with the help of Dion Diamond and Charles Sherrod, conducted workshops in the community on nonviolence and other direct action tactics.

The students decided they wanted to move and they chose as their first target the McComb Library, which did not admit blacks. They first negotiated with the head of the library, who wouldn't budge and then, on August 29, headed down to demonstrate. But the whites had seen them coming and a sign was up on the library saying, "We are closed today." After a quick conference, they headed for the Woolworth's store to demonstrate there against the lunch counter for whites only. The manager refused to yield, they had a sit-in, Hayes and Watkins were quickly arrested and sentenced to six months with a five hundred dollar fine. Both served over thirty days. Hollis Watkins describes their time in jail:

We remained in the city jail for about two days, then we were transferred down to the county jail. When we first got to the county jail they placed us in the drunk tank, the place where they keep the drunkards. There was nothing in there but concrete, to sit or lay on. We remained in the drunk tank for about eight hours. After the eight hours had expired, they carried us upstairs to a better cell, which was not too good. We remained in jail for about thirty-four days, in the county jail that is.

During the time we was in the jail, the food that they would give us was very poor, didn't have any seasoning in it at all and at this time they wouldn't allow anyone to bring us things, such as seasoning, or anything. And when they would bring us breakfast it would be cold, which every morning would be grits and egg, maybe about half an egg, and the grits would be cold.

During the time when we was in McComb the police, as they would question us, would carry us into a room by ourself. And at one particular time they carried me into a room and after entering the room I found about twelve men sitting in the room which seemed to have been just off the street. And as I would answer the questions, yes and no, the officer told me to say yes sir and no sir, but I refused. And by refusing, the men that were in the room, they gathered round me, very close, as if to hit me or beat me if I continued to say yes and no.

So therefore I became very afraid, and at this particular time I decided the best thing for me to do was to make a sentence out of my answer, to keep from saying yes sir and no sir.

And another particular time when the officers carried me into a room to question me, he would look at me and try to frighten me, say bad remarks, call me all different kinds of names, and after all this, he carried me into a room by myself and left me. I didn't know what was going to happen and about five minutes later the police came through and he looked at me for about a minute and then he went into a little room which looked to be like a closet and he got a grass rope out.

After getting this rope he came in front of me and stopped. And he looked at me as I was looking at him, and he said to me, "O.K., nigger, get up, let's go, we're going to have a hanging here tonight and you're going to be first." I became very frightened at that moment, because I didn't know what to expect, but instead of showing my frightenedness, I crossed my legs and reared back in my chair and smiled at him. And he just looked at me for a moment, after which he walked out.

It was that spirit of defiance and determination that kept the local people moving despite the repression, that brought more SNCC workers down as things got tougher, that has sustained black people all over the country. On the night of August 29, after the arrest of Hayes and Watkins, there was a mass meeting attended by two hundred blacks—such a tremendous sight for McComb that the local *Enterprise-Journal* warned that this was no momentary "fussing," that the blacks were serious. At the meeting people decided they would keep on sitting-in and going down to the courthouse.

Two days later there were more sit-ins in McComb and three arrests of high school students including a sixteen-year-old girl named Brenda Travis. In Liberty there was a new registration attempt made in one room of the courthouse while Billy Jack Caston was being "tried" in another room for assaulting Bob Moses. The whites from all over the surrounding area had poured into the courthouse with their shotguns to witness the incredible spectacle of a black challenging the white man's right to hit him whenever he felt like it. The air was heavy with their lust for blood and the sheriff warned the SNCC people to get out of the courtroom while the jury met briefly to find its verdict.

Moses left the courtroom with the two witnesses for his case and went over to the registrar's office to join Travis Britt, a newly arrived SNCC staffer who was down there with the people trying to register. But Britt had been told to get the hell out of the office and went to wait outside the courthouse. As Moses approached him, two shots rang out. Fortunately no one was hurt and the source of the gunfire remained unclear. But the office was closed for the rest of the day and none of the black applicants were registered.

A first attempt at registration was made in Walthall County on August 30, and again two well-qualified applicants, including a senior political science major were found "unsatisfactory." But the surge of activity mounted and continued into September. By this time almost the entire SNCC staff was in McComb. Then, on September 5, Travis Britt was the target of a new white attack when he again went to the registrar's office. He reported:

There was a clerk directly across the hall who came rushing out while we were waiting, and ordered us to leave the hallway. He said he didn't want a bunch of people congregating in the hall. So we left and walked around the building to the courthouse, near the registrar's window. By the time we reached the back of the building, a group of white men had filed into the hall in about the same spot we had been congregating. They were talking belligerently. Finally, one of the white men came to the end of the hall, as if looking for someone. He asked us if we knew Mr. Brown. We said we didn't. He said "You boys must not be from around here." We told him he was correct.

This conversation was interrupted by another white man who approached Bob Moses and started preaching to him—how he should be ashamed coming down here from New York stirring up trouble, causing poor innocent people to lose their jobs and homes, and how Bob was lower than dirt on the ground for doing such a thing. Bob asked why the people should lose their homes just because they wanted to register and vote. The white gentleman did not answer the question, but continued to preach.

At this point, Bob turned away and sat on the stoop of the courthouse porch, and the man talking to him took a squatting position. Nobody was saying anything. I reached in my pocket and took out a cigarette. A tall white man, about middle-age, wearing a khaki shirt and pants, stepped up to me and asked, "Boy, what's your business?" at which point I knew I was in trouble. The clerk from the hallway came to the back door leading to the courthouse with a smile on his face and called to the white man: "Wait a minute!" At this point, the white man hit me in my right eye. Then, I saw this clerk motion his head—as if to call the rest of the whites. They came and all circled around me, and this fellow hit me on my jaw, then on my chin. Then, he slammed me down. Instead of falling, I stumbled onto the courthouse lawn. The crowd followed—making comments. He was holding me so tight around the collar, I put my hand on the collar to ease the choking.

The clerk hollered, "Why don't you hit him back?" This set off a reaction of punches from this man. He was just hitting and shouting, "Yes, why don't you hit me, nigger? Yes, why don't you hit me, nigger?" I was beaten into a semiconscious state; my vision was blurred by the punch in the eye. I heard Bob tell me to cover my head to avoid any further blows to the face. Then, this fellow yelled, "Brothers, should we kill him here?" I was extremely frightened by the sincere way he said it. No one in the crowd answered the question, and the man released me. Moses then took me by the arm and took me to the street—walking cautiously to avoid any further kicks or blows.

The Travis incident was the beginning of a series of blowups.

On September 7, John Hardy accompanied two persons to the registrar's office over in Walthall County. The registrar refused the people the right to register. Said Hardy:

I entered the office to ask, "Why?" The registrar, John Woods, had seen me on one other occasion—the 30th. After telling him my name, he came out—very insultingly and boisterously—questioning my motives and reasons for being in Mississippi, and said I had no right to mess in the "Nigger's" business, and why didn't I go back where I came from. He reached in his drawer and ordered me out at gunpoint. As I turned to leave, he struck me over the head with the pistol.

I staggered out into the street and walked about a block. I decided to go to the Sheriff's office to report the assault and, possibly, make charges. But this was not necessary, because the sheriff found me. He told me to come with him or he would beat me "within an inch of your life." After being put in jail [the charge was resisting arrest and inciting a riot—and later disorderly conduct] about 7:30 that night, after being interrogated at length by a city attorney, and later by the district attorney, I was taken to Magnolia Jail for "your own protection."

The Justice Department entered, immediately, on John Hardy's case. They filed a suit in the Federal District Court in Jackson, asking that a temporary injunction be issued stopping Hardy's trial, which was to take place on September 10. Judge Cox, who was the first appointee of President Eisenhower and a longtime friend of Senator Eastland, refused to give them a favorable hearing. It was probably a victory that he heard it at all. The Justice Department representatives then flew to Montgomery and woke up Judge Reeves in Montgomery, Alabama, at midnight to get a temporary injunction, overruling Judge Cox.

John Hardy was scheduled to be tried in Walthall and Bob Moses went with him. It was announced that the Justice Department had obtained a stay from Judge Reeves in Alabama and that the trial would be held over. As Moses and Hardy tried to leave, the white mob that had gathered grabbed John by the shirt-sleeves and threatened to kill him. They finally got out to their car, at which point a door of the vehicle stuck. A local policeman warned them that he couldn't hold the whites back any longer. The door finally opened and they got away.

Meanwhile, the three high-school students, including sixteen-year-old Brenda Travis, were still in jail with five thousand dollars bail on each for sitting-in. Money had to be raised to get them out. But even under this and all other pressures, the project managed to keep operating; workshops in nonviolent and direct action were being held, while canvassing and citizenship school activities continued in the rural areas.

Behind the scenes, the whites of McComb were moving in a very organized fashion. Bob Moses reported in a confidential memorandum to SNCC:

The Justice Department began a detailed investigation during the week of September 11th. They dug out information about meetings between the whites which were taking place regularly during the last week of August, beginning Aug. 28th, and the first week of September. We believe that as a result of the meetings, the beatings of Aug. 29th and Sept. 5th occurred; a list was circulated with the names of the people who had attended the voting schools; another list was circulated for white people to sign to effect the cutting off of Negroes and whites from the commodities; systematic pressure was put on Negroes connected with the schools to pay their bills.

The next day, September 25, Herbert Lee was killed. Herbert Lee of Liberty, black, age fifty-two, father of ten children, active in the NAACP and then in the voter registration project, was killed with a .38 pistol by Eugene Hurst, white, a state representative.

Hurst was never arrested, booked, or charged. A coroner's inquest ruled that the killing was in self-defense and he walked out free forever.

Three years later, on January 31, 1964, Lewis Allen, one of the key witnesses in the killing of Herbert Lee, was planning to leave Mississippi the next morning and look for work in Wisconsin. That night they found him dead in his front yard. He had been shot with a shotgun three times.

In a society where such things as the killings of Lee and Allen were not the unusual but the expected occurrence, it seems incredible that the spirit of McComb continued to burn as long as it did. It was the high school students who kept on pushing, the students and the SNCC workers. People sometimes said, "You have to be crazy to walk into the face of death like that—on purpose." But they did, and with not much for support except an anger rooted in centuries of oppression and a sense of common cause.

At the Burglund High School, the principal—Commodore Dewey Higgins—indicated that the students who had been jailed for sitting-in would not be able to reenter school for the fall semester. A number of their classmates took the position that, if this happened, they, too, would not attend classes. On October 4 a total of 118 students walked out of school and marched downtown in protest. They marched to City Hall, headed by the three students and the two SNCC workers—Curtis Hayes and Hollis Watkins—who had just been released from jail. Curtis began to pray from the steps of City Hall; a policeman asked him to move along. He refused. And refused again, and again. The police blew their whistles, a mass arrest followed. Bob Zellner, a SNCC worker who had arrived the day before and the only white person on the march, was jerked aside and choked by a white man. Two black SNCC workers threw themselves around him, to protect him with their bodies. The entire group was soon herded up the steps and thrown into jail. They were quickly released, with trial set for October 31.

The students were suspended for three days and then allowed to go back to school—on condition that they signed Commodore Higgins's affidavit acknowledging that they would be expelled if they participated in such a demonstration again. About eighty decided not to sign and many had their parents' strong support. They went to school carrying their unsigned affidavits, expecting expulsion. That afternoon more than a hundred students walked out again. This is the statement they issued:

We, the Negro youth of Pike County, feel that Brenda Travis and Ike Lewis should not be barred from acquiring an education for protesting an injustice. We feel that as members of Burglund High School they have fought this battle for us. To prove that we appreciate their having done this, we will suffer with them any punishment they have to take. In the schools we are taught democracy, but the rights offered by democracy have been denied us by our oppressors; we have not had a balanced school system; we have not had an opportunity to participate in any of the branches of our local, state, and federal government; however, we are children of God, who makes the sun shine on the just and the unjust. So, we petition all our fellowmen to love rather than hate, to build rather than tear down, to bind our nation with love and justice with regard to race, color, or creed.

SNCC workers set up a freedom school, "Nonviolent High," to provide some education to the expelled students. Chuck McDew took charge of history, while Dion Diamond handled physics; Moses took care of math and English, and a little French was also taught. Eventually Campbell College in Jackson said that they would accommodate the students, immediately, and within a short time everyone was back in school.

On October 31, a dozen high school students, along with Moses, Mc-Dew, and Zellner were sentenced to four months in jail each. Robert Talbert, Ike Lewis, and Hollis Watkins, who had organized the walkout, were given six months. Brenda Travis was sent to reform school for a year. The students remained locked up until December 6, when thirteen thousand dollars in appeal bonds was finally raised. It was during this jail term that Moses wrote a moving letter which would become well known in the movement:

November 1, 1961

I am writing this note from the drunk tank of the county jail in Magnolia, Mississippi. Twelve of us are here, sprawled out along the concrete bunker: C. Curtis Hayes, Hollis Watkins, Ike Lewis, and Robert Talbert, four veterans of the bunker, are sitting up talking—mostly about girls: McDew ("Tell the story") is curled into the concrete and the wall; Harold Robinson, Stephen Ashley, James Wells, Lee Chester Vick, Leetus Eubanks, and Ivory Diggs lay cramped on the cold bunker; I'm sitting with smuggled pen and paper, thinking a little, writing a little; Myrtis Bennett and Janie Campbell are across the way, wedded to a different icy cubicle.

Later on Hollis will lead out with a clear tenor into a freedom song. Talbert and Lewis will supply jokes, and McDew will discourse on the history of the black man and the Jew. McDew, a black by birth, a Jew by choice, and a revolutionary by necessity, has taken the deep hates and loves of America, and the world, reserved for those who dare to stand in a strong sun and cast a sharp shadow.

In the words of Judge Brumfield, who sentenced us, we are "cold calculators" who design to disrupt the racial harmony (harmonious since 1619) of McComb into racial strife and rioting; we, he said, are the leaders who are causing young children to be led like sheep to the pen to be slaughtered (in a legal manner). "Robert," he was addressing me, "haven't some of the people from your school been able to go down and register without violence here in Pike County?" I thought to myself that Southerners are exposed the most, when they boast.

It's mealtime now: we have rice and gravy in a flat pan, dry bread and a "big town cake"; we lack eating and drinking utensils. Water comes from a faucet and goes into a hole.

This is Mississippi, the middle of the iceberg. Hollis is leading off with his tenor, "Michael row the boat ashore, Alleluia; Christian brothers don't be slow, Alleluia; Mississippi next to go, Alleluia." This is a tremor in the middle of the iceberg—from a stone that the builders rejected.

Bob Moses

That was the purpose of SNCC—to create tremors in icebergs. And we were succeeding.

CHAPTER 31

The Circle Begins

FOR ME it was a discouraging staff meeting that took place on my first weekend in Atlanta—my first weekend with SNCC. Here were all the people freshly arrived from McComb with many problems to discuss about the future. But in the first stage of the meeting there seemed to be an impasse between the people working on voter registration and those in direct action. Charles Jones, head of the voter registration project, chaired the meeting and his motivation was questioned many times. These arguments revealed the tensions and conflicts which were inevitable in a group of young people who had been active individually and locally (on the sit-ins) and who were now coming together to form a central organization in which each would have to give up some of his or her personal autonomy and sectional interests.

Eventually there emerged a compromise in the organization. There would be a coordinator of direct action and one for voter registration. An executive secretary would remain in the Atlanta office while the others were in the field. Miss Baker was the first choice for this post but she declined. Other names emerged. Some of the people in voter registration wanted James Monsonis to take the job. The people in direct action went on strike in our caucus and said that if I didn't take the job they were not going into the field. They said they were not about to risk their lives if they didn't have someone in the national office they could trust.

I was in a quandary, for I didn't want to work as an administrator. I knew that I had some administrative qualities, more perhaps than any of those assembled, but I felt that my best skills lay in other areas—agitating, field organizing, and writing. It was in these three areas that I wanted to work. But this was a personal wish, and I had enough self-discipline to realize that when you are working with a revolutionary group, which I considered SNCC to be, you don't do what you alone want to, but what the group desires of you. I was prepared to carry out this type of discipline, and agreed to serve as the executive secretary. Still, I had great doubts.

I doubted, first of all, the viability of SNCC with its factional fights over direct action versus voter registration. On the other hand, I felt that this would be overcome if people got out into the field. My experiences in Fayette County made me realize that working on voter registration was indeed a dangerous thing in the South and those working on it would get all the direct action they needed once they ran up against Southern sheriffs. This had happened in McComb, as the voter registration wing pointed out repeatedly at the meeting.

Second, I doubted the discipline of the group. At one point in the debate, everyone agreed that we should go around the table and speak of our motivation and why we wanted to work full time for SNCC Everyone did except Moses, who passed. He also wanted to leave the meeting and get back to McComb where things were still hot and people he had worked with were in trouble. I did not know Moses very well and certainly had not shared his experiences in Mississippi, but I urged him to stay in the meeting until there was some resolution of the impasse which seemed to haunt the organization. I felt that it would be very bad for a new organization, trying to get off the ground, if he were to leave the meeting and return to McComb without some solution. There was another aspect of the problem: SNCC's chairman, Chuck McDew, had stayed in McComb rather than come to the meeting. This already suggested a lack of concern with internal organization and I felt that we needed everyone to evidence a sense of responsibility in that direction. Bob eventually agreed to stay an extra day.

But a more important cause for my doubts about the group's discipline was the manner in which people thought. That is to say, there seemed to be no order to the discussion—no going from this point to the next point on to the next one—but instead a constant introduction of new matters for discussion, forgetting what the other speakers had said. In the process, a great cartharsis took place. This type of thought pattern characterized the group for many years and reflected in part a need to talk out many problems facing the individual in the field—personal problems and problems stemming from the nature of the work, which was indeed dangerous. Through this process the individual no doubt was reinforced by the group and was thus able to sustain himself for a while longer in his hazardous work. But the process was shattering to the mind of someone who wanted order, point-by-point discussion, and resolution.

At the same time, I realized that what was lacking in the group was a sense of direction; all of us were groping and, perhaps the only way to build some cohesion was to allow people to speak about their frustrations, lay them on the table, look at them, and then move on to the work. In reality there was nothing I could do about this situation at my first meeting. I was a stranger to the group of people assembled in Atlanta, although I made many suggestions which they found useful and which were, I am sure, one of the reasons that they wanted me to serve as executive secretary.

I also felt at the meeting the lack of a clearly defined code of staff ethics and methods of work. This related to a generalized disdain for "leadership": All of us sitting in the room were leaders, people said. This was true in many respects, but the group had come together under difficult circumstances and there was distrust—directed primarily toward the intentions of many of the people gathered and aggravated by the failure of some to communicate. This made it difficult to work out common approaches.

I think that the distrust was largely a product of anxiety: The SNCC staff was almost brand new as a group, working in a geographic area brand new to most of us, engaged in activity brand new or at least different in many ways from anything we had done before. Full of self-doubt, people projected that doubt onto their colleagues. This distrust had to be overcome, for the work was too difficult and dangerous, and people could not sustain themselves if they distrusted those with whom they were working. I felt that each member had to have confidence that the other was doing his or her job, regardless of whether one heard from the person.

Although I had agreed to serve as executive secretary, I was still not sure I wanted to cast my lot with those gathered in the room. For all the reasons mentioned here, I had serious doubts as to whether the group could build the mass organization of which I dreamed. And, as I had told Paul Brooks, for me, joining SNCC meant not just deciding to take a year out of school, but making a lifetime commitment. I was older than those in the room, by ten years for the most part. I respected everyone in the room for their youth and realized that at their age I was not involved in the type of service to people that they were, that they represented a small, small minority, only fifteen people, who believed in an idea and believed that they could change the course of history by working full time against racism in its most obvious form and against the value system of this country and by working toward revolution. This determination, this courage, this spirit, endeared everyone of them to me and made me realize that since no one is perfect—least of all myself—and since the dynamics of a group are something other than those of the individuals in the group, one had to look at the overall situation and see if the advantages outweighed the disadvantages.

I was convinced that there existed in SNCC the energy, the talent, the brain power, the determination, and the courage to change certain values in this country. One of the most important values to be changed was that a person should work for money. These students were saying that they were more concerned with human rights than with money. They were not driven by the profit motive which dominates this society. They were against the profit system, which placed them against capitalism. And they were willing to demonstrate this with their lives. They were willing to build a community of brothers and sisters who would take care of each other insofar as possible and by their very actions demonstrate that money—the making of money—should not be the highest value in the United States, in "the American way of life." Or, if it was the highest value, then they rejected this way of life.

I felt that if this idea could grow among young black people, we would usher in revolutionary change. For there was no mass organization which said by the way in which its members lived that it stood against capitalism. The labor movement, which ought to be against it, had become part and parcel of the system in many ways by the kinds of salary that it paid its representatives. In many instances salaries equaled those of government officials or the labor leaders' counterparts in business. This worked against militancy, for when a person becomes high-salaried there is a general tendency for him to become more interested in getting that salary than in the cause for which he is working. The U.S. Government had demonstrated its awareness of how this happens by its very deliberate offers of high salaries to young people for working in various poverty programs— knowing that this is a way to wean them from any revolutionary impulse, to make them develop a vested interest in the status quo, and to plug them into the consumer society.

People at the meeting looked at the other civil rights organizations and saw that they were money-oriented; their staffs wanted to get a "decent wage" out of working for the cause. This meant that on occasion they would sacrifice principles in order to keep the money coming in. This remains a key problem with the Urban League, the NAACP, SCLC, and CORE: They are oriented toward capitalism and this is reflected in their attitude about personal moneys received (or not received) for their work. It was clear to me and others present that we had to keep our militancy by structuring ourselves in a different way from the conventional organizations and by setting a wage scale that would make it impossible for anyone to develop a vested interest in the survival of the organization.

SNCC also recognized that we had to build a people's movement. We had to develop leadership outside our own, to carry forward the struggle whether or not we in SNCC were around—whether or not SNCC was around. For some people this idea meant that we in SNCC were supposed to work ourselves out of business, for, if we were successful in developing a mass consciousness and producing many leaders, then the importance of our own particular role became more and more minimized. While agreeing completely with those ultimate goals, I disagreed strongly with the idea that it meant SNCC would become unimportant. Later this interpretation came to be used as a justification for the fear of power which staff members manifested in 1964, when SNCC's power as an organization rose to an all-time high. It was used to negate that power and thus dissipate it, not because the power was being used wrongly but because of an undirected fear—a fear of power itself, a lack of understanding about how to use power.

At the 1961 staff meeting this problem could not yet be perceived. We were just aware of the need to build a people's movement, and of the fact that preparing people for the next step meant that often one had no control over what would happen—but that the work itself would lead to more and more progressive changes. We had faith in this dynamic, and the dynamic would often work in the years that followed.

But at the same time the government would move to co-opt the work of community organizers. It would pay people to work in its poverty programs—a reformist trap designed to militate against basic changes, for the government is not about to finance programs that are working to destroy the present economic and political system. The government would also emphasize "participation by the people," a borrowing of the early rhetoric of such organizations as SNCC and SDS, and use it to give the people the impression they have power when in reality they do not. This is not to say that we were always right in our rhetoric. The cry for community control is a false one within the present structure of this society. Nevertheless, action geared to achieving community control can help people realize the impossibility of that goal if the proper political education goes along with the action.

It is on this point, political education, that SNCC has always been weakest. But in those early days, and at that meeting, the need for a clearly defined political education program for the cadre was not stressed and, conversely, the results of not having one were not clearly understood by the participants—including myself.

The lack of such a program stemmed from the lack of a clearly enunciated ideology. But again people did not, in 1961, feel that lack. So long as we were working on voter registration and public accommodations, there was a broad consensus under which everyone could move. It seemed important then just to do, to act, as a means of overcoming the lethargy and hopelessness of so many black people. Also, we had no adequate models for what we were doing, for how we should proceed. Rather than set up rigid definitions of goals and tactics, it seemed best then to experiment and learn and experiment some more and draw conclusions from this process.

This lack of an ideology made it possible for us not to get hung up on questions of nonviolence and religion, and especially on SNCC's first statement of purpose which placed so much emphasis on love and godliness.

In its first year of existence a dominant influence in SNCC had been the appeal of changing the conscience of mankind, and especially white America, through redemptive suffering. This line of thought had been advocated by Jim Lawson, Martin Luther King, and the other religionists who had been influential in the drafting of the statement of purpose for the organization in the spring of 1961. With the emerging emphasis upon the nation's political structure as the primary cause of the problems of black people, the original religious thrust of the Student Nonviolent Co-ordinating Committee became a contradiction.

However, the rhetoric of SNCC from those early months did not generate much debate after 1961, for the issue had been firmly decided by October of that year. The organization by then was involved in concrete activities that directly challenged the power structure of this country. The majority of its new recruits firmly believed that the problems of black people were racial and social in character, not religious or spiritual. As the years passed, the religionists became fewer and fewer within the ranks of SNCC, while the revolutionaries increased.

The fact that the statement of purpose had become obsolete did not seem important to SNCC in 1961 or in the years that followed. It did not seem important because of that absence of a clearly defined ideology. Working in the rural South, facing constant death, trying to heighten consciousness, seemed in itself an ideology around which all could rally. There was too much work to be done to spend endless hours hammering out a statement of purpose. By common agreement SNCC had an ideological position: Black people in the United States suffered from racism, from political and economic exploitation, and there was no mass organization fighting to change these conditions, especially in the rural areas of the country. SNCC had to play this role. If you were willing to work to change these conditions, then you subscribed to the broad, general ideology upon which the organization rested.

It would not be until the spring of 1968 that a new statement of purpose was hammered out by the organization. This isn't to say that no ideological discussion took place within the organization. Far from it. There would be very intense discussion as our work to change the political and economic structure of the country continued. But at no time did this discussion center around the use of "love" or the "appeal to conscience" as a method for changing the society. (This in itself proved that the original statement of purpose was dead in the minds of the activists.) From time to time nonviolence would be discussed, but most SNCC workers accepted it as a tactic—only that—and felt no need for philosophical probing.

The lack of an ideology would become a serious problem for SNCC when the problems of voter registration and segregation of public accommodations were largely resolved with passage of the 1964 and 1965 Civil Rights acts. Our long-range goals, the kind of society we wanted to see built, the question of whether the fundamental problem facing black people was strictly racism or a combination of racism and capitalism, the role of whites—all these issues had to be dealt with and failure to do so tore the organization apart. But they were not yet issues in 1961, and at that October staff meeting the dominant question was: What do we do next, and how?

SNCC's future program, as hammered out at that October meeting, included a long-range project called Operation MOM, March on Mississippi. The original plan to send field secretaries to various states was abandoned and all the direct action staff went to Mississippi with the goal of developing a locally based attack on the state power structure. Jackson would be the kickoff point. Action in McComb was to continue, with efforts to get national support. SNCC staffers Charles Sherrod and Cordell Reagan were assigned to start a voter registration project in Albany, Georgia—a new area for SNCC which would become the new hotbed of activity in a short time.

By the end of that month Bob Moses was back in jail. He got out, thanks to the Southern Conference Educational Fund (SCEF), which raised the bail money. This help from the much Red-baited SCEF was used by the NAACP and others to Red-bait SNCC with guilt by association, a problem that would intensify as the organization became more and more active, more and more visible. I myself was Red-baited, by the NAACP and others. I was "the communist sent down from Chicago," just as Moses had been "the communist sent down from New York." But this was hardly my biggest problem in those first months with SNCC. I just had too much nitty-gritty to deal with.

CHAPTER 32

Inside a Cubicle

THERE WAS, first of all, the office, the windowless cubicle at 197½ Auburn Street, with its little plastic dome. The room was allegedly air-conditioned in the summer and definitely heated in the winter; but, without ventilation, it became unbearable that winter and would have been a torment in the summer if we had stayed. We had to clamber up on the desk to unscrew the dome so that some air might come in. We were lucky not to have any of our staff suffocate.

Then there was the tiny size of that office. Norma Collins came down from Baltimore to work with me and she was an excellent typist and calculating machine operator, very efficient. But her coming brought the problem of a second desk. First we had to figure out how to get one, then how to fit it into the office and still have space to move.

Fortunately we had friends in the building. Mr. Mangrum, office manager of the Southeastern Fidelity Insurance Company which was located in the same building as SNCC, became our staunch ally. There were the girls who worked for the insurance company. That office was downstairs but they had a room across from us where they ate their lunches and relaxed. When they saw our crowded situation, they felt sorry for us and relinquished their lunchroom for our use. Then there was Mrs. Turner who ran a physical therapy center. She opened her office to us, and soon one or another of the staff was sleeping on the bed there. Eventually we also began to use her massage room for storage. Little by little we were creeping all over the building, infiltrating everywhere out of desperation.

Mr. Mangrum went around the neighborhood and lined up some services for us. He persuaded a laundry on Hunter Street to take our clothes free. Mr. Beamon, who had a restaurant, let us use it for meetings whenever we wanted. Some weeks, we monopolized the rear of his restaurant for two or three days in a row and he never raised any objection.

People in the community generally were very sympathetic to what we were trying to do and aware of the difficulties. They knew we were borrowing from Peter to pay Paul, and literally matching pennies to skimp along.

Very important to our being able to function at all during this period was Mr. Kasuth Hill, owner of Hill's Office and Church Supply Company. He sold us all our office supplies and gave us a discount as well as long-term credit. By August of 1962 we owed Mr. Hill five hundred dollars for supplies. It seemed as though we would never catch up on this debt —as soon as we could pay him a little, we'd run down and get the two reams of paper and box of carbon that we just had to have, so the debt continued.

We opened the office at 8:30 A.M. and closed anytime after midnight. At first, only Norma and I were working there full time. Occasionally field people would come in and Charles Jones would be there sometimes. Then Dorothy Miller Zellner and Julian Bond started coming in from time to time to help.

In those early days, our critical weakness was in the area of communications. I had some experience in writing news releases, but physically it was a nightmare to get out a mailing. We had to go to another office to use its mimeograph machine; we couldn't spread things out and there was no room to maintain decent files. We tried to get Julian Bond to come and work full time in communications, but he had to take a job with the Atlanta *Inquirer* (a semiliberal paper which he had helped to found) because he and his wife were expecting a baby. That happened just when we had begun to develop an effective communications section, thanks to Julian and others. This experience led us to revise our subsistence pay scale to give married people a little more—as soon as we could afford it.

I remember that when I was first elected to serve as executive secretary

Miss Baker asked me if I thought I could submerge myself and project the chairman. I told her that I could. Thus, one of my jobs as executive secretary was to issue statements in the name of the chairman. At first we tried to contact McDew on all statements issued by SNCC over his name, but this became difficult, since he was constantly traveling around to raise funds, so he gave us blanket approval to put his name on statements. Julian and I would fire off statements from the chairman, but it continued to be very difficult to break the information barrier.

The mass media of the country printed very little news at that time of what was happening to black people. Except for occasional stories in a few black weeklies, there was little information getting out. To compound this the wire services had a habit of always checking out a story with their local stringers. The stringers were usually racists who had good relations with the police chief and the sheriff, and who would seldom verify any story of atrocities that we might send them. One of the ways we got around this was the method I had developed in Fayette County, Tennessee: Get a friendly radio station or some sympathetic reporter in a Northern city to ask for a story on a particular event. This put some pressure on the Southern bureaus of the Associated Press or the United Press International to produce some of the facts.

There was another technique which we developed and put to great use. The wire services would not take our news stories as news stories, but friends at the services told us that some attention would usually have to be given to stories about telegrams sent to the government or affidavits and complaints filed with government agencies. So we would get out the story of an incident of racist repression by issuing a press release saying we had sent a telegram about the incident to Robert Kennedy, then attorney general, and President Kennedy. Or that an affidavit had been made by the victim. There were many stories that we attempted to break that way, but I remember one in particular on which we tried desperately and never succeeded. It was the story of Bessie Turner. Following is the text of our original release, issued in January of 1962:

ATLANTA, GA., January 30—The Student Nonviolent Coordinating Committee today released the full text of an affadavit sworn by Miss Bessie Turner of Clarksdale, Mississippi, who charges that two policemen forced her to remove her clothing and then beat sensitive areas of her naked body with their belts.

SNCC called the policemen's actions "brutal and insane," and asked the Justice Department to intervene in her case.

The full text of Miss Turner's affidavit follows:

"My name is Bessie Turner. I live at 1214 Lyons Avenue, Clarksdale, Mississippi.

"On Friday night, January 19, I went to Tutwiler with Luster P. Turner, Hunt, and Charlie Howard. We went to the Blue Moon Cafe and remained there until early Saturday morning. Upon coming home Saturday morning about 4 A.M. I was in the company of Luster P. Turner. We went by his house and finally we all left. Luster P. lives in the 400 block on Florida. Saturday morning, January 20, I went to the field to pick cotton. When I came in that afternoon, my sister told me that the police had been looking for me. I called down to the police station to find out what they wanted but could not find out because the man I was talking to told me not to say 'no' to him but 'no sir,' and he hung up without talking with me anymore. I had in fact answered him 'no mam' because I thought it was a lady I was talking to and he thought I said 'no.'

"About four o'clock Sunday afternoon, January 21, two policemen came to my house, one short and stocky with either white gold or silver teeth at the bottom and a tall slender policeman. [Here Miss Turner mentioned the names of the two policemen.]

"They told me to get in their car and they carried me to the City Hall, they carried me into a small room and began questioning me about some money they said Luster P. Turner said I had taken from him. I told them I knew nothing about the money. Luster P. Turner is a Negro employee of the City Light and Power Department.

"The short policeman told me to lay down on the concrete floor in the jail and pull up my dress and pull down my panties. He then began to whip me across my back with a wide leather strap, asking me all the time where was Luster P. Turner's money. He told me after I got sore he was going to whip me until I told him where the money was. He hit me several times and I could not tell him where the money was for I did not know.

"He then told me to 'turn over and open up your legs and let me see how you look down there.' At this time the tall policeman left the room. He hit me between my legs with the same leather strap he had whipped me with. He told me if he heard anything I had said about what he had done to me he was going to bring me back down to the jail and really whip me. He told me then to get up and fix my clothes and wipe my face, as I had been crying. He then told me to pull my dress down from my shoulders and pull down my bra and expose my breasts. He said he was looking for the money in my bra. The two policemen then brought me back home. The short policeman came into my house and searched it. He did not show us any papers giving him the authority to search it. My sister, Machie Strong, was home also. We permitted him to search because he was the police and we were afraid not to let him search. When they left the short policeman said, 'Be sure you remember what I told you about not telling anybody what I did to you.' After the police left I was hurting and swollen. I then went to Dr. L. W. McCaskill's office and he treated me."

We sent telegrams not only for publicity reasons, but also because we knew that it was necessary to arouse public opinion in favor of our cause, our work. Requesting help from the President and Attorney General was a tactic to bring attention to the suffering of the people. Also we were hardly partisans of the Democratic or Republican parties, and we felt that the politicians should be put on the spot in a public way. In addition, the telegrams were one way to play on the contradictions between the federal government—what was supposedly official American "democratic" policy—and the state governments of the South with their blatant racism. Finally, we felt that this exposure by way of demanding help from the federal government did provide a small form of protection for our workers. Some years later we would drop this tactic because there was a final whittling away of all belief that any positive action could come from the feds and it had become clear that people had to move to protect themselves.

From the outset we also faced two major public relations problems as an organization. The first was simply to establish in the minds of the public that we existed, who we were, and what we were about. The second was related: To remove from the minds of those few people who knew we existed the idea that SNCC was an arm of SCLC and being financially supported by that group. This notion grew out of the relationship we had initially, when we worked out of the SCLC office, and it was fed by such errors as Louis Lomax writing in the *Negro Revolt* that the student activists got 10 percent of all SCLC income. The result, of course, was that any supporters we had—and there must have been many, because the student movement was the thing at that time—saw no need to send us contributions directly. We had to establish that we were independent, had our own programs, needed support—and we had to do this without getting into a public fight with SCLC. We began putting into our releases the words *SNCC is an independent student organization.*

I remember how concerned Mr. Mangrum was about this problem. He became very upset about conditions in the office—people sleeping on the desks and the floor or in Mrs. Turner's physical therapy office—and he wanted us to put out a fact sheet proclaiming: "Do you know that SNCC has no money for itself? Do you know that SCLC is not supporting SNCC?" I felt that this would be divisive and we didn't do it, but I knew we had to do something.

I recall that in the fall of 1961 we met with Martin Luther King and Reverend Abernathy to discuss our new program for Mississippi, MOM, and asked them to join us in sending a wave of volunteer workers the next spring. Both thought it was very creative planning. We mentioned a budget need of twenty-five thousand dollars, hoping for some help inasmuch as there had been a consensus at the Raleigh conference of 1960 that funds would be provided by SCLC, with Martin Luther King acting as chairman of a fund-raising committee for the students. Now Martin and Abernathy told us that they had received eleven thousand dollars from a union local called District Sixty-five in New York, of which about a third had been earmarked by that union for the Southern student movement. Abernathy said that he would have the books checked and let us know about getting the money to us.

Ella Baker was at that meeting and began, in her principled and very gently direct manner, to raise a series of questions about organizations having allegedly received funds earmarked for the student movement that never reached the students. She also mentioned certain public relations techniques of SCLC which projected the impression that they were more involved in certain action situations than in fact they were. For example, SCLC had the habit of sending out and publicizing telegrams that protested conditions in a certain area where the students—not SCLC —were working. Presenting a united front was a fine thing in principle, but the SCLC telegrams had the effect of creating an impression that the sender of the telegram was also the agent of the protest movement in that area.

SCLC gave SNCC a check for $1,000 from the District Sixty-five funds shortly after that meeting—and that was the end of it. Our desperate financial situation did not improve, and there was a meeting of interested Atlanta citizens at the Phyllis Wheatley YMCA in Atlanta that I shall not easily forget. I was there talking with Jim Woods of SCLC, and someone raised the question of how SCLC got its funds. Woods replied that this was done mainly on King's image. "That image is worth $250,000 to us annually," he commented.

"How does SNCC raise its money?" I was asked.

I replied that we weren't raising any to speak of, but that we wanted to do so on the basis of our program rather than any single image of a leader's personality. Too often have we seen masses of people out in the streets, aroused and willing to stay there in the face of brutality, only to have some big leaders off in a cosy negotiating room making decisions which do not really represent the wishes of the people. Our emphasis on program rather than personality was a position SNCC took then, when it was extremely difficult to do so. That philosophy would stick with SNCC, even in later years when the media foisted personality images on us, and we reaped great strength from them.

Then, at the meeting in the YMCA, I told the group about our need for a car and for a movie projector in Mississippi. About how, in this country with all its wealth and affluence, it seemed impossible for us to get just four hundred dollars to buy a projector. Here was a group of young people willing to renounce comfortable jobs, to devote themselves on a basis of real personal sacrifice to doing the work for which the society had declined responsibility, and it seemed they would not be permitted to survive. I think I was almost crying—actually I was crying inside. But I finally said that it was all right, we were going to make it—it would be only a matter of time.

One reason that I felt so disturbed at that particular meeting was that I had, in a sense, humiliated myself a few days before. I had gone to Dr. King's house to ask him for five hundred dollars for SNCC so that the payroll could go out. I asked not for a gift, but that SCLC should turn over another part of the money earmarked for us by District Sixty-five, of which we had to date received only one thousand dollars. He said that he would have to check with his organization. I then said that if they couldn't turn the money over outright, then at least lend it to us. We would get some money and pay it back. He said he would check and let me know the following Monday. There the matter ended once and for all.

Obviously the money problem had other causes. We were based in the South and few staff people were willing or felt able to leave the field and go North to get money. We had been depending on NSA and SDS to raise funds for us and this didn't work out. We needed to develop our own fund-raising machinery, but there was just too much to do at that time.

Somehow we made it. We borrowed a great deal that year, surviving on the Peter and Paul tactic. Chuck McDew did an excellent job of combing college campuses, picking up a bit here and there to keep us afloat. But by June of 1962 we were thirteen thousand dollars in debt.

What made all this so painful was my awareness that people in the field were not eating for extended periods, sometimes riding a mule for lack of a car, trudging fifteen miles a day along highways to get to the people, sleeping in cars parked in alleys—and all this in the face of extreme danger. They were creating a history of fortitude and courage and there was so little we in Atlanta could do to help. I felt a deep responsibility to the field people, who were not as safe as I was in Atlanta. It was always clear to me that our office in that city was, first and foremost, there to service the field and to provide a link between them and "the outside world." People would often call the national office, talking of the problems they faced in their areas, the need for money, the need for people, the need for advice. It was immensely frustrating to be able to offer so little. At the same time my belief in the strength and viability of SNCC as an agency for constant agitation and eventually for revolutionary change was steadily rising. For me personally it was my awareness of what the field people were doing that got me through.

That winter of 1961, so trying and sometimes so bitter because of the administrative struggle to survive, was also the time of the Albany Movement. Mississippi had been the scene of SNCC's first battle as an organization. The focus now switched to Georgia, where another drama of repression and resistance was being played out and new lessons learned.

CHAPTER **33**

Albany, Georgia

THE NIGHT of the first mass meeting came. The church was packed before eight o'clock. People were everywhere in the aisles, sitting and standing in the choir stands, hanging over the railing of the balcony upstairs, sitting in trees outside near windows. . . . Soon a young doctor of the community took charge of the gathering, leading in the freedom songs which have grown out of the student movement during the last two years. . . . Then arose a tall, silver-haired, outspoken veteran of the struggle. He spoke slowly and determinedly. . . and filled in with vivid detail the developments up to the date of the mass meeting.

Appearing also on the program was the indefatigable [the only local Negro lawyer] C. B. King. He stood flat-footed and thundered with his explosively deep voice, striking at both the inaction of the church and its hypocrisy. He also condemned local leadership for procrastination in other areas. At times he sounded like the prophet of doom but before he had finished, he declared our only hope was unity. This had been the real reason for the mass meeting —to weld the community into one bond of reason and emotion. The force to do this was generated by accounts of the released students who individually described the physical situation and mental state of each, in jail.

When the last speaker among the students, Bertha Gober, had finished, there was nothing left to say. Tears filled the eyes of hard, grown men who had known personally and seen with their own eyes merciless atrocities committed by small men without conscience. As Bertha, with her small frame and baby voice, told of spending Thanksgiving in jail along with other physical inconveniences, there was not a dry eye to be found. And when we rose to sing "We Shall Overcome," nobody knew what kept the top of the church on its four walls. It was as if everyone had been lifted up on high.

I threw my head back and closed my eyes as I sang with my whole body. I remembered walking dusty roads for weeks without food. I remembered staying up all night for two or three nights in succession writing and cutting stencils and mimeographing and wondering—How long? I remembered thinking about home, a thousand miles away and fun, games, dancing, movies, boat rides, tennis, chess, swimming—Life; this was history.

But when I opened my eyes something good happened to me. I saw standing beside me a dentist of the city, a man of the streets singing and smiling with joyful tears in his eyes, and beside him a mailman with whom I had become acquainted along with people from all walks of life. It was then that I felt, deep down within where it really counts a warm feeling, and all I could do was laugh out loud in the swelling of the singing.

The words are Charles Sherrod's, the place was Albany, Georgia, and the time late November of 1961. Within the next two weeks, a mass movement would be consolidated and almost a thousand local people would go to jail. They would go to jail for reasons that today seems like an anachronism—affirming the right of blacks to use the facilities in a bus station, and the right to protest denial of those facilities to blacks. They would go to jail singing the freedom songs that today sound like anachronisms. But a bus station could be a real battleground then. And the songs had not, up to the time of the Albany Movement, been a basic element in our resistance struggle, as they would be for the next four years. It was only at Albany that they burst into their full beauty and power, the unforgettable voice of Bernice Johnson Reagan leading the way, herself led by the awakened spirit of an awakened people.

On the basis of a field trip in the spring of 1961, SNCC had agreed that Charles Sherrod and Cordell Reagan should go into Terrell County, Georgia, to start a voter registration project that winter. "Terrible Terrell," as it was known, sits down in southwest Georgia along with other counties with names like "Dogging Douglas," "Unmitigated Mitchell," "Lamentable Lee," "Unbearable Baker," and "Unworthy Worth"—all of them forming a notorious pocket of exploitation and oppression with a history of violence matched only by such areas as the counties around McComb or Lowndes County, Alabama.

Sherrod and Reagan later decided that they could not plunge right into voter registration work or direct action in Terrell County but would first have to break the grip of fear and lethargy by some means. Sherrod did his homework well, and came to the conclusion that to register voters in southwest Georgia it was first necessary to build a mass movement in Albany—a city of some sixty thousand people located in the middle of these counties. The fear of the police and the hopelessness which existed in the Deep South cannot be overstressed, and indeed the first step toward change is to convince people they should not be afraid. In the Deep South in the sixties, and in some areas still today, the effects of the past had never been erased. Exploited and suppressed through slavery, blacks were then subjected to the system of sharecropping introduced after so-called emancipation. That system maintained the reality and psychology of servitude while the reign of terror that came with it kept many blacks afraid of the white man and his power.

The area around Albany had at one time been plantation country, with Albany its slave trading center. Du Bois describes in the *Souls of Black Folk* how it was then: "For a radius of a hundred miles about Albany stretched a great fertile land, luxuriant with forests of pine, oak, ash, hickory, and poplar, hot with the sun and damp with the rich black swampland; and here the cornerstone of the Cotton Kingdom was laid."

At the turn of the century blacks outnumbered whites by five-to-one in Albany, but in 1961 the black population had been reduced to 40 percent of the total. Albany looked, on the surface, to be a quiet town that had made a few meaningless concessions to black needs, with what the whites liked to call "good relations" between themselves and the blacks. Some care was taken to preserve that liberal image, for the purpose of encouraging outside industry to come in and discouraging outside agitators.

But, even before SNCC went into Albany, a struggle was brewing. Early in 1961 a group of leaders from the black community presented the city commissioners with a request to begin desegregating certain city facilities; the commissioners didn't even bother to answer. The strictly segregationist Albany *Herald*, edited by the chairman of the Georgia Democratic Party, ran an editorial rejecting the blacks' request. Then, in February and March, there was a series of incidents in and around the black Albany State College campus. Drunken whites in cars threw eggs, fired shots, and once tried to run down a student. The college administration was reluctant to defend the students and, before that semester ended, students staged a protest march on the president's office.

In early October of that year field secretaries Sherrod and Reagan arrived and set up an office in a small, run-down building two blocks from the Shiloh Baptist Church. They began registering voters. Some people called them Freedom Riders, which gave the two SNCC workers a certain status with many blacks. But, in general, the black population of Albany was at first "very apprehensive," Sherrod relates.

It was known that we had little money, and there were doubts as to who we really were. . . . But when people began to hear us in churches, social meetings, on the streets, in the pool halls, lunchrooms, nightclubs and other places where people gather, they began to open up a bit. . . . We would tell them of how it feels to be in prison for the cause. . . . We explained to them that we had stopped school because we felt compelled to do so since so many of us were in chains. We explained further that there were worse chains than jail and prison. . . . We mocked the system that teaches men to be good Negroes instead of good men. We gave an account of the many instances of injustice in the courts, in employment, registration, and voting. The people knew that such evils existed but when we pointed out time and time again and emphasized the need for concerted action against them, the people began to think.

Sherrod and Reagan gradually were accepted by a large segment of the black community and stayed in the home of Bo Jackson, the black circulation manager of the Albany *Herald* (who was later fired). But, at superconservative Albany State College, where they went talking to students, they were called in one day by the dean of students. "He assured us of his hopes for the better society of our dreams," Sherrod reported, "but pointed out the relative value of his JOB." Shortly afterward the two SNCC workers were told to leave the campus within fifteen minutes. "But," wrote Sherrod,

It was too late. We had delivered the idea that would disrupt the system, if one person would find the commitment to suffer all consequences. We found more than one; disruption was forthcoming.

But Albany State College was not the only obstacle we had in our way, [Sherrod continued]. From the beginning we had, as SNCC field people, visited the NAACP Youth Chapter, introduced ourselves and outlined our project for Voter Registration. We pointed out the differences between the two organizations and advanced the hope that we could work together.

From this point, we initiated meetings in the churches of the city. We had introduced ourselves to the Baptist Ministerial Alliance and the Interdenominational Alliance. We were given their support as groups and many churches opened their doors to us; others were afraid for one reason or another.

[Sherrod continued, describing a workshop in nonviolence:]

To these churches we drew the young people from the College, Trade and General High Schools, and from the street. Some of these were members of the NAACP Youth Chapter. They kept coming to the workshops we were holding every night at different churches, where we had some shocking responses in role-playing. After the second night of workshops, a beautiful young lady, about twenty-two, and a tall, very dark but not so handsome young man participated in a proposed act in which the male was to be a white brother of unrestrained anger and the young lady was to be a "sit-inner." He was to strike her—HE DID! You could hear the smack resound across the empty air of the high ceilinged church. Everyone felt it as his heavy hand came down across her jaw, and the whole body of people raised themselves together straining in their seats. Hands over faces; fingers in mouths; wide-eyed, one girl shouted aloud. It marked a significant point in our recruitment and education of the people. That started it off and every night we grew larger and larger; the need to unify emotion and direct common anxieties had been met.

By this time it was November 1 and on that date a ruling of the Interstate Commerce Commission (ICC) was scheduled to take effect: No bus facility, bus, or driver could discriminate against blacks. The efforts of the Freedom Riders had won this ruling, but it remained to be seen how the South would react. SNCC worked out a plan for the simultaneous testing of the Trailways terminals in Atlanta and Albany.

In Atlanta, Charles Jones, another person—I forget who it was—and I went at 1:30 in the morning of November 1 to make a test case of a restaurant named Jake's in the terminal, adjacent to the luggage department. Trailways had a policy of leasing space to other concerns for facilities such as this, but we knew the ICC ruling applied to Jake's. We entered, ordered something, were arrested, and eventually released. That same day Sherrod and Reagan left Atlanta for Albany—only four hours' drive away—to test the Trailways terminal down there.

Plans had been made in advance to test the Albany station. But Sherrod and Reagan had to go back to McComb for trials on October 30 and so they missed a meeting of the Youth Council of the NAACP at which it was decided to cancel the test. When they got back to Albany early in the morning of November 1 and learned of this, they quickly moved to line up a new plan. At three o'clock that afternoon, nine students headed down to the bus station. Local blacks, sensing some kind of action, came out to watch from the lunchrooms, poolrooms, other places of business.

"The bus station was full of men in blue [Georgia's state police] but up through the mass of people, past the men with guns and billies ready, into the terminal they marched, quiet and clean," Sherrod wrote. "They were allowed to buy tickets to Florida but after sitting in the waiting room they were asked to leave under threat of arrest. They left as planned and later filed affidavits with the ICC." Salyn McCollum, a young white girl who had been assigned as observer in the station, witnessed the students being ordered out of the white waiting room and took the bus to Atlanta to report that the test had been completed.

As a result of a request by Mayor Asa D. Kelley for a meeting with black leaders, a number of representatives from such local organizations as the NAACP, the Baptist Ministerial Alliance, and the Federated Women's Clubs of Albany met together with SNCC on November 17 to organize a group for the meeting. Nothing ever came out of the meeting with the mayor, but that night the Albany Movement was born, a coalition to support all efforts at desegregating the bus terminal. All the groups except the NAACP agreed to yield their identity as separate organizations and to cooperate under the name "Albany Movement."

An article of mine, which was printed in the *New University of Chicago News*, describes some of the action-filled days that followed. It was written very shortly after the events described and is worth quoting here because of its immediacy:

On November 22, three persons representing the NAACP were arrested in the Trailways terminal. They were released on bond immediately after their arrest. However, Bertha Gober and Blanton Hall, SNCC volunteer workers, were arrested and declined bail.

In an interview with Bertha Gober she told this writer: "On November 22, about 5:20 P.M. I went to the ticket window. I stood directly behind a white man that was purchasing his ticket. I stood there for five seconds when this uniformed officer said: 'You'll never get your ticket there.' I asked why. Still no answer. Then Detective Friend came up and introduced himself and said my appearance there 'was tending to create a disturbance.' He gave me a choice of going to the Negro waiting room or to be arrested. I informed him that I would not leave until I had purchased my ticket. He took me outside where Chief Pritchett was waiting. We then went to the station."

When asked why did she try to purchase her ticket at the so-called white window, Bertha replied: "I felt as a human being not of Albany but of the United States of America that I had a right to use all facilities. I felt it was necessary to show the people that human dignity must be obtained even if through suffering or maltreatment. . . . I'd do it again anytime. . . . After spending those two nights in jail for a worthy cause, I feel I have gained a feeling of decency and self-respect, a feeling of cleanliness that even the dirtiest walls of Albany's jail nor the actions of my institution cannot take away from me."

Not only were there policemen from the city of Albany at the bus station when Bertha and Blanton were arrested but the Dean of Students of Albany State College also appeared, attempting to convince them they should not transgress established conditions.

On Saturday morning Bertha received the following letter:

> I regret that your recent behavior as a student at Albany State College necessitates the following action.
>
> As a student of Albany State College, you are subject to the rules and regulations of the institution and the Board of Regents, the governing body of the University System of which the Albany State College is a unit.
>
> Please be informed that as a result of your being apprehended and arrested, charged with violation of the law on Wednesday November 22, 1961, you are hereby suspended indefinitely as a student at Albany State College.

We need not discuss the violations of the first amendment, but it must be clearly understood that Bertha checked out of Albany State to go home for Thanksgiving. The Supreme Court, moreover, has ruled that State institutions cannot dismiss students without a hearing. Yet Albany State College has not indicated to either Bertha or Blanton that their case will be reconsidered, despite a petition by the student body of Albany State or the requests of Albany citizens for a hearing.

On Monday morning, November 27, more than six hundred (600) people gathered around the City Hall for the trial of the arrested five. The police asked them to disperse. At this point Charles Jones led the group in prayer. Afterwards they marched around the city block while the trial was in process.

Sherrod interrupted courtroom procedures by sitting on the side of the court "reserved" for whites. A policeman tried to eject him bodily, but he was finally allowed to disturb the pattern of segregation.

On Tuesday November 28, 1961 Sherrod was arrested for trespassing on the campus of Albany State. He spent the night in jail. Although warrants had been taken out by the police for Jones and Reagan, they were never arrested. The next day William H. Dennis, Jr., President of Albany State, said the college withdrew the warrants on the advice of the State Board of Regents who preferred that the three SNCC "agitators" be prosecuted by the State Attorney General. All three were told further trespassing would result in such a warrant.

I came to Albany myself on December 10—by way of a Freedom Ride. We had decided to test the allegedly segregated seating policy of the Georgia Central Railroad, four blacks and five whites. When the conductor told the blacks in our group to move to the next coach, we refused and there was no further incident. But arriving in Albany, where about three hundred blacks were at the station to meet us, we went into the white waiting room and the police closed the doors behind us. Chief Laurie Pritchett then moved in and arrested eight of our group, although by that time some of us were no longer in the waiting room but just standing outside the station.

Chief Pritchett told the press, "We will not stand for these trouble-makers coming into our city for the sole purpose of disturbing the peace and quiet of the city of Albany." Pritchett appeared to be following the same policy used by the Jackson, Mississippi, police toward the Freedom Riders of 1961: Arrest quickly, quietly, and imprison. Move before white mobs can form, avoid brutal actions which can mobilize national support. Play it cool. "Peace and quiet," of course, meant maintaining segregation and oppression. There was no disturbance at the terminal, no one gathering, not even a traffic problem. As S. C. Searles, black editor of the *Southwest Georgian* commented, "The students had made the trip to Albany desegregated without incident. Things had gone so smoothly I think it infuriated the chief. There was a good feeling in the group. They wanted to stop this."

But the "good feeling" couldn't be stopped. The Albany Movement was in full swing. The next morning there was to be a prayer pilgrimage at City Hall during the trial of our group. My article tells what happened to the hundreds of people who came then, and of the events on the day following—an almost solid day of demonstrations:

As we went to trial Tuesday morning, the City dealt with the crowd of Negroes praying on the steps of City Hall by permitting them to pray for a few minutes and to walk around the block once. When the marchers appeared before the City Hall the second time, they were told they were under arrest and huddled into the alleyway between City Hall and an adjacent building. It started raining. People were excited. We could hear Sherrod: "We are going to stay in jail. We Shall Overcome!"

Although the trial took all day, the court refused to rule on it and adjourned until Wednesday at 9:00 A.M.

That Tuesday night at the mass meeting, it was decided a group would go to the City Hall and kneel during our trial, protesting it and the jailing of 267 persons that morning.

On Wednesday morning, the city had an attorney at the trial for the first time. He moved to continue the case until Thursday at 1:00 P.M. because of his prior involvement in another court. His request was granted. As we left the courthouse, we saw around 85 people kneeling on cold, wet concrete, singing and praying. Personally I felt it was the most pathetic sight I have ever witnessed, pathetic because it was in mid-century America with a so-called tradition of humanism. . . . Yet, it was moving to know that a community had developed an awareness of social justice to the point that young people, old people, rich people, and poor were able to unite to protest injustice, an awareness that made the community feel what affected one affected all.

Judge Abner Israel, who also tried us, found Slater King in contempt of court for leading the praying and singing Negroes while his court was in session. Sentenced to five days in jail, Slater King refused to appeal his sentence. On Monday, Mrs. Slater King had been arrested and also refused bond. The Kings' three children were at home under the supervision of a housekeeper. The determination of Slater, a prominent businessman in Albany, to join his wife in jail reflects the overcoming-of-the-fear-of-jail and the willingness of the Negro community in Albany to demonstrate to the power structure that no longer could it resist the demands of Negroes.

Around four o'clock Wednesday afternoon the Negro community was informed the Mayor was coming to Shiloh Baptist Church for a meeting. At four-thirty his so-called emissary appeared stating that the Mayor could not meet with them. The Negroes immediately left the church and marched around the courthouse. No one was arrested. However, after returning to the church, it was decided another group should proceed to the City Hall. Led by Bernice Johnson and Bobby Birch, two dynamic young leaders, the group left the church full of enthusiasm. Just as they reached the street on which City Hall is located a loud siren announced: "You are all under arrest." The people started singing "We Shall Overcome" and continued to cross the street, going directly to the alleyway where they were immediately jailed and shipped out of the county. The papers announced: 265 more arrested.

Despite the mass arrests, in a situation where federal law had clearly been violated, the Justice Department wasn't saying "boo." We wanted to force its hand, or at least expose its inaction, and planned a demonstration at the Trailways terminal, together with demonstrations at the library, parks, and train station for Thursday morning. And Chief Pritchett did it again: Ten blacks went into the terminal lunchroom, were served coffee, were arrested, and jailed. They were later released and escorted back to the terminal, but the other demonstrations had to be canceled.

That same day, the city dropped charges against me and seven others (the trial had continued from the day before). But we were rearrested in the courtroom on state charges of conspiring to breach the peace and unlawful assembly, and we went back to jail—this time for a week. By now some 560 people had been arrested and there were at least 300 still in jail. The jails of Albany and of several nearby counties were jammed. National Guardsmen had been called up by Georgia's governor and telegrams were flowing into Attorney General Kennedy's office. At this point, the mayor of Albany contacted the Albany Movement and requested "a biracial meeting."

By noon the next day, Friday, the city had agreed in principle to desegregate bus and train facilities and to release those jailed. We were on the verge of winning our immediate objectives. More importantly, we had helped to create a movement in which—for the first time since the sit-ins—not only students, but also adults were actively participating in large numbers. Adults of all ages and class backgrounds. The older people of Albany had demonstrated their willingness not merely to boycott, collect food, and provide other kinds of material support, but to march in the streets, confront the police, go to jail.

I was extremely proud of this achievement, for it had the potential of spreading to other areas of the Deep South. SNCC's organizers had come into the area and worked so closely with the local people, blended themselves in so well, that no one could charge the Albany Movement with being simply a creation of the Student Nonviolent Coordinating Committee. We had helped to generate a people's movement without dominating it—our goal as a band of organizers. I felt sure in my jail cell in Albany that black people throughout the United States would read and hear about the demonstrations and be deeply affected by this proof that as a people we could come together and forge a unity against our oppressors. I couldn't know it then, but a photograph of the people kneeling in prayer outside the courthouse on Wednesday, December 13, 1961, had already been flashed around the world.

The potential effect of this people's movement on black people—in Albany, but even more so in the rest of the country—was the main reason why I had opposed Dr. Martin Luther King's being invited to Albany. That story developed as follows:

The president of the Albany movement was Dr. W. G. Anderson, a man of conservative persuasion, who had been elected because people felt he could help unite the community through his prestige as a doctor. Others, such as Slater King and Mrs. Irene Wright, were strong leaders, but they lacked his prestige in the minds of some people. It happened that Dr. Anderson had gone to school with Rev. Ralph Abernathy of SCLC and, during the height of the demonstrations, Abernathy called Anderson. He told him that if the Albany Movement would send a telegram inviting Dr. King to join the demonstrations, King would come and his presence would get headlines for the Movement.

This had been discussed at a strategy meeting which took place while I was out of jail. I opposed the move, pointing out that it was most important to keep the Albany Movement a people's movement—to keep the focus on the ordinary people involved in it, especially the unusual number of adults—and that the presence of Dr. King would detract from, rather than intensify, this focus. Also, we had already been getting attention from the media. It was not a situation of desperate struggle taking place in a vacuum of public awareness where a big name might be vitally needed. A strong people's movement was in progress, the people were feeling their own strength grow. I knew how much harm could be done by interjecting the Messiah complex—people would feel that only a particular individual could save them and would not move on their own to fight racism and exploitation.

I had received no support for my position at the meeting, not even from Charles Jones, and was accused by C. B. King (no relation to Martin) of introducing "factionalism." I dropped the argument, for it was obvious that it would not prevail and I was already under personal attack from another quarter. Officers of the NAACP, an organization with which SNCC maintained a queasy relationship in Albany, had interjected the issue of communism into the Albany Movement and had tried to discredit us on the basis of my being a communist.

Once the motion had been passed to send the telegram to Dr. King, I had asked that a resolution be passed inviting other civil rights leaders, too, hoping by this to flank some of the implications of just inviting Dr. King. This was done.

King arrived Friday night, December 15, and spoke at a mass meeting attended by more than 1,000 people. The next day negotiations with the city resumed but were broken off by early Saturday afternoon. That evening, some 250 people, with Dr. King and Dr. Anderson in the lead, marched to the county courthouse and all were arrested for parading without a permit. They were moved into an alley; police cars sealed off the alley, and one by one people were led into the police station. Late that night sound trucks drove through the city calling military personnel back to the nearby Air Force and Marine Corps bases, while bars and liquor stores were closed. The combination of those two developments was a serious blow to the town's saloonkeepers.

I was in jail during all this, but heard about the events. I also learned of a serious rift which had supposedly developed between SNCC and SCLC. I never got full details on this from anyone, but while I was in jail *The New York Times* carried an article by Claude Sitton about conflicts between the two organizations and SNCC's opposition to aspects of King's strategy and style of leadership. Never before had there been criticism of that type in the press, and SCLC was very upset about the impact of this criticism on their fund raising. As its officers often pointed out, King's image was worth plenty of money and they had to see it wasn't damaged.

There were no more demonstrations after Saturday's and the Albany protest began to bog down that weekend. Negotiations with the city resumed Monday morning and, by the end of the day, it was agreed by all local authorities that train and bus facilities would be desegregated; all prisoners except the Freedom Riders would be released on simple property bonds and our group of eight would have their bond reduced. All future demonstrations would be called off and the city would hear the black community's case at the first business meeting of the new City Commission (this last promise was not kept).

By Wednesday everyone was out of jail. They came out from many places—when the city and county jails in Albany and the National Guard armory had run out of space, prisoners had been taken to the county jails at Americus, Dawson, Leesburg, Camilla, and Newton. Conditions had ranged from just bad food and discomfort to sickness and beatings. For me it had been my longest stretch in a Southern jail so far and I had learned a lot. The jails of the United States are not designed to speed up justice or to rehabilitate prisoners. They are reminders of the general decadence of the society.

In the Albany jail where I found myself in December, 1961, I talked to many people who had been sitting there for more than six months without ever having had a hearing. They had been arrested on one charge or another, but did not have the money to pay their bail. The grand jury, which met only twice a year, had to decide on the evidence presented whether or not they should be freed or bound over for trial. This meant that, whether they were found guilty or not when finally brought to trial, they would already have spent at least six to nine months in jail. One man had been in the jail for nine months without a decision by the grand jury on his case. I was filled with horror as I saw these black men rotting away in jail, men going physically soft from waiting to find out if they were going to the chain gang or if they had to spend more time in the Albany jail, men who were becoming homosexuals from their jail time.

I also talked to men who had jumped their bail and crossed the state line into Florida. They told me how the bond companies had their own detectives who would come to their houses at night, handcuff them, beat them, put them in cars, and bring them back. I later found out that this practice, like keeping men in jail for long periods without a trial, was common across the South. The formality of extradition proceedings went out the window when a black person left one Southern state and went to another, hoping to find some justice. He had jeopardized some white man's money and this was another crime in itself. The nigger had to be returned.

As I listened to the prisoners, I took down affidavits from some of them on paper towels, of which the following is the most brutal:

I, Johnnie Frank Morris, 34, born in Larry, Georgia on September 11, 1927, do willingly and of my own free will give the following statement to James Forman who has identified himself to me as Executive Director of the Student Nonviolent Coordinating Committee.

On or about the 18th September 1961, I was at 1711 Tangerine Street, Sanford, Florida. I was alone in the house in the bed. [Two white men]* came to my house around 6 A.M. They yelled: "Open the goddamn door." They then pushed the door open, threw a gun on me. They made me lie down on my face. One stayed there with a gun on me until the other went around to my uncle's house, J. B. Thomas 1702 Roosevelt. They had first gone there and he told them where I was living. He stood out in front of the house while they were there.

Then they chained my feet and my hands to the chains on my feet. We arrived here around 12:30 P.M. in Albany. They carried me into their office. One of them asked asked me where had I been working in Florida. After I told him, he kicked me in the eye and stomped me in the stomach. The other came in and hit me with an iron blackjack.

* Names withheld.

They then took me over to the Sheriff's office while a man in the office said: "That nigger needs twelve months." They wrote me up over there and then brought me over here. They took the chains off of me here in the county jail. . . .

I was charged in September, 1960 for sideswiping five cars. I was fined $5 or my license. Then I was charged with drunken driving. Stokes, a bail bondsman, went my bond $250.00 I sold my '47 Chevrolet and paid him the 10 percent of the bond, $25.00.

I am freely giving this information in front of two witnesses. I understand this may be used in court.

In addition to the small number of people charged with criminal offenses, the Albany jail was full of civil rights fighters, most of them facing jail for the first time in their lives. Their enthusiasm was high but many were wondering when they would get out of jail. In other jails, as we learned later, things were worse. Charles Sherrod had been taken over to another county. Sherrod later reported:

The sheriff came into our cell block, called twenty-one of us out, lined us up against the wall and hollered, "Didn't I say there wasn't going to be no demonstrations in here. . . . This is my jail and I'll run it like I please . . . when you come in here you lose all your rights."

When he had finished his speech . . . I stepped forward and said, "May we ask a question?" He turned in surprise and walked toward me. I went on, "We would like to have two devotional periods a day, as we are religious people."

He retorted sharply, "There'll be no singing and praying . . . you can pray to yourself . . . you lose all your rights and privileges here."

I responded, "Yes, but we're still human beings and Christians."

In the same time that I was finishing the sentence, he was coming down on the side of my face. I was knocked back about two steps and I returned to the same place saying immediately, "but we're still human beings and Christians."

Then he took me out of the group. . . . Back in another room, the Sheriff and his henchmen reiterated their stand and I proposed to make responses. When the Sheriff made a statement that we would have a hard time changing anything down here, I began "Yeah," but another open hand was on my face. My whole face was numb and my jawbone ached for two days. . . . My lip was busted and there was a bruise on my face.

When I had first started that week in jail, Charles Jones, Bernard Lee, and I were placed in a cell with the regular prisoners, in an attempt to isolate us from the civil rights fighters. But we could yell across the hall from time to time and the orderlies were willing to take messages throughout the jail for us. I kept up a regular correspondence with Leonore Taitt and Bertha Gober, writing on toilet paper. We could hear others singing in jail and we sang with them, often starting songs ourselves. The singing kept our morale high. We knew that throughout the counties of southwest Georgia other people were in jail—over four hundred.

It was a ripple on the waters of segregation, disturbing and agitating, one of the many ripples, and I was not sure where they would lead, but they were important ripples. Albany had been the center of the slave trade in southwest Georgia. We in 1961 were facing the white sons and daughters of the plantation owners, telling them we were no longer slaves, no longer willing to pay them any homage or deference. In jail, listening to the other black men who had been brutalized by the white laws of the racist United States, thinking about all the freedom fighters behind bars, all doubts about whether or not I would remain with SNCC ceased to plague me. I knew there was tremendous merit in the type of work we were trying to do in 1961 and that history would judge our actions positively.

Lee and Jones were bailed out on Friday, December 15, but I stayed in because I felt that someone in a leadership position should remain with the other prisoners, who were unable to bail themselves out. Sitting in jail wasn't my cup of tea. I wanted to be on the outside, helping to plan the action and assisting in the negotiations. But group morale seemed more important at that point.

It was a sunny afternoon when I finally got out. Dr. King and his entourage had left town; there was no explanation of why. The black community had won its concessions from the city—small concessions which seemed to me less important than what had happened inside the people. In the article published in the *New University of Chicago News,* I wrote the following evaluation of our work:

In Rock Hill, South Carolina, the Student Nonviolent Coordinating Committee called upon people throughout the south to fill the jails. Many beds were empty. In Jackson, Mississippi, most of the civil rights organizations wanted to see the jails filled. Yet, it took more than three months to get 302 arrested in Jackson. In Albany, Georgia, it took less than a week to mobilize more than 800 people to go to jail.

Jail without bail was becoming a reality not to people living outside of a community but within its very limits. People were exposing themselves to the dirt of their city—its jails. They were placed twenty to thirty in a cell made for four. They saw amongst their numbers, pregnant women, sick men and hungry children suffering for what they considered Freedom.

Within the context of their life experience—and this is the only context in which a valid judgment can be made, I believe—they felt their demonstrations against police brutality and threats of massive jail-ins would produce a new Albany. The gains may appear small to a non-Albanian, but those who went to jail and with whom I have talked said they would go to jail again if ever the need arose. Most of them are agreed the week-long demonstrations have helped to solidify the Negro community for future power struggles, including the current boycott of white stores by the Negroes. Without a doubt, Voter Registration not only in Albany but in other Southwest Georgia counties will intensify.

I might have added to these comments a word about the striking inaction of the federal government throughout the events of December, 1961.

When Salyn McCollum notified us of the ejection of the nine young blacks from the Trailways terminal on November 1, this was reported to the FBI. There was no apparent result. On November 22, when five students were arrested for using terminal facilities, there was no federal action. When Chief Pritchett ordered the Freedom Riders outside the railroad waiting room on December 10, then arrested them in the street, there was no action. Every one of these actions by the police violated an express federal ruling. With the demonstrations and mass arrests that followed, the local police were violating not merely a single ruling, but broader American law—the Bill of Rights and its provisions for freedom of assembly, the right of petition.

Our telegrams to Attorney General Kennedy brought no response, although we were graciously informed through *The New York Times* on December 14 that, "The Justice Department was watching developments closely." That same day, Kennedy talked by telephone with Georgia's Governor Vandiver and Albany's Mayor Kelley. The mayor assured Kennedy that "law and order" could be preserved without federal aid. Also that day the assistant attorney general talked with Dr. Anderson of the Albany Movement. White Albany maintained that it could handle things.

On December 18, when the settlement was announced between the city and the Movement, Mayor Kelley said Kennedy called within an hour to congratulate him for doing a good job. That appears to have been Kennedy's most positive action all through the month of December. The federal government could have stepped in at any time, with clear power to enforce its own orders. But it didn't; the black people of Albany had to see to it that a federal ruling was complied with. They did, with their suffering and sacrifice—not with federal authority.

Our appeals to the federal government, which would be made again and again in the years to come, in uncountable situations, were just a tactic for some of us. But others actually felt the federal government should and could act. At that time there was a general conviction that no justice would be forthcoming from the Southern states; only the federal government, which was supposed to stand in contradiction to the state governments, would or could offer any hope. As the years passed, it became clear to all that the federal government was a partner in the crimes against black people.

Southwest Georgia would continue to be a hot spot and one of SNCC's most important projects through the next two years, with voter registration work intensifying in Albany and the surrounding counties, as did direct action projects and boycotts. A spark had been struck and a fire lit. Nothing had been more important in creating the spirit of Albany than the freedom songs and the voice of Bernice Johnson Reagan. The words and notes of our revolutionary music would change but not the strength of its singers.

To Bernice Johnson Reagan, I say today, almost ten years later: Your voice echoes in my mind and your songs can sing what I felt in Albany better than the few words I put on paper. I remember seeing you lift your beautiful black head, stand squarely on your feet, your lips trembling as the melodious words "Over my head, I see freedom in the air" came forth with an urgency and a pain that brought out a sense of intense renewal and commitment to liberation.

Your eyes were closed, your head back, your nose parallel to the ceiling, and perspiration poured from your lovely black skin as you tried to heal the wounds and inspire to further action the weary black people of Albany who sang, "freedom in the air," responding to your lead as our people in Africa responded to the lead singer. You knew they were weary, they had suffered. You were weary, though you were young. Your pain and sorrow were the anguish of the people, and you comforted all of us. You brought us to your bosom as you sang "there's a balm in Gileam."

And when the call came to protest the jailings, you were up front. You led the line. Your feet hit the dirty pavement with a sureness of direction. You walked proudly onward singing "this little light of mine," and the people echoed, "shine, shine, shine."

Your beauty was too great for Albany alone. The world had to hear you, to appreciate your warmth, your strength, your love, your passion for justice. And you sang across the length and breadth of these United States, in the cold of winter, the heat of summer, in large auditoriums and in small living rooms. Everywhere you sang—committed, disciplined, trying to help your brothers and sisters in the fields and bayous of the Deep South, your brothers and sisters in the Student Nonviolent Coordinating Committee.

Your understanding of the historical process of liberation keeps you singing. You have been able to forge new words to meet changing conditions. You have grown with the demands of the struggle. Your life is forever unfolding as the lives of your people unfold and move down the path of liberation. Your songs today of Africa fit the transition in which we find ourselves. From the dusty roads of Albany, Georgia, through the cities of the United States, from many years ago and for many years to come, the music you make is only a reflection of your total understanding. Through the years your love for humanity and hatred of oppression will keep you singing.

But I know, sweet Bernice, that singing is not an end for you. Your songs reflect the different stages of liberation and liberation is the goal for you. I know, too, that the day is not far off and long overdue when you will do as the women of Algeria have done, as the women of Vietnam are doing, as women have done and shall do in the future, when the songs of the wars are sung before and after the heat of battle, when the high note is reached after the machine gun has cooled, been cleaned, and is ready for the next battle. You will sing with a grenade hidden beneath the blue, brown, green, red, and black colors of your long, flowing buba. Or you will sing with your .45 strapped openly on your multicolored battle fatigues.

I know, for I have heard your music. I have marched to your rhythm, I have struggled alone and with many others as your voice echoed in my mind and drove me beyond what seemed the last ounce of energy, down the path of liberation and toward the new day for humanity.

I know, for you have not given up the fight as many others have. Your ability to change and adapt your music to new forms of struggle proves your long-range commitment and understanding, your willingness not to waiver, and if you have waivered, as we all waiver from time to time, then your faith in our people, your desire for an end to tyranny, your willingness to work and fight, have not abated.

Sing on, dear Bernice. Sing on. Lift those lovely eyes upward, tilt that beautiful head back, and sing on with the spirit of our Zulu ancestors, with the determination of a Chaka, the tenacity of a Harriet Tubman, the sweetness of a Bertha Gober, the spirit of all fighting people.

Sing on! We have heard you. We shall never forget! We fight too! Sing on, Bernice. Sing on.

CHAPTER 34

Attack the Power Center

AS THE year 1962 opened, there was a feeling in SNCC that the decision to go to work full time against segregation and racism had been a correct one. People also felt that despite the danger, the difficulties, and our constant poverty, we had to go on. By now there were too many people depending on us, too many people who had become committed through us. We couldn't leave them hanging in the air. And for me, personally, there was no longer any question of whether or not I would stick with SNCC. All doubts had vanished in that Albany jail.

While our work in southwest Georgia continued and expanded with its own momentum, it was not so easy to find a way to move in Mississippi. On December 6, 1961, Bob Moses and twelve students from McComb, Mississippi, had been released from the Pike County jail on a thousand dollars bond each. The expelled students from Burgland High were enrolled in school in Jackson, and activity in McComb ceased. Diane Nash and others in the direct action cadre had found that the repression in Jackson made it impossible at that time to launch demonstrations against segregated facilities. Instead, they had turned their attention to voter registration, payment of poll taxes, starting a newspaper, and running black candidates for the U.S. Congress (the old debate over voter registration versus direct action had become obsolete, as I had thought it would).

Black candidates had no chance of winning in Mississippi, but it was felt that they needed to run in order to shake loose some of the fear many blacks in Mississippi had at that time. Rev. R. L. T. Smith was at first the only person in Jackson who was willing to run for Congress in the June, 1962, primary. Later he was joined by Rev. Theodore Trammell, running from another congressional district. Trammell died of a heart attack before the election and was replaced by Merrill Lindsay.

Bob Moses became Reverend Smith's unofficial campaign manager. At an executive meeting of SNCC the role of Moses as an undercover campaign manager was thoroughly discussed. Bob felt that too much pressure would be directed against Reverend Smith by the local racists if it were known that Bob was running the campaign. Charges of "outside agitation" and "New York Negro runs campaign" would certainly be launched. So Moses worked unofficially. Reverend Smith lost as expected, and so did Merrill Lindsay, but people felt the campaign had been very significant because it provided a forum for airing issues from a black viewpoint and an opportunity to point up the denial of the vote, the racism in the entire electoral process.

SNCC decided at that same executive meeting to attack another important symbol of political power—the state legislature—and especially its racist practice of seating black visitors in a special section of the balcony. In early 1962 we carried out several demonstrations in the Mississippi and Georgia legislatures. Julian Bond, who would later win a seat in the Georgia legislature after fighting for it all the way up to the Supreme Court, took part in the Atlanta demonstrations.

On February 1, after two days of attempts by integrated groups to take seats in the unreserved (all-black) section, a group of us, including students from the Atlanta University complex, went to the capitol. Howard Zinn, a white professor from Spellman, and a white student joined us in the gallery designated for Negroes. The lieutenant governor, serving as speaker of the house, interrupted the workings of the legislature and asked aloud if the gallery was integrated. When he heard shouts of "Yes!" he ordered Dr. Zinn and the white student to leave. When they hesitated, he ordered them thrown out and arrested. Afterward we left the legislature and began picketing outside with a hundred students.

A week later I went with other SNCC people to try again. This time

I asked a secretary for a pass to the regular gallery. It was refused (while she gave passes to forty cub scouts) and I was told to go ask the house speaker. But his office was locked. At that moment, a white man—later identified as a member of the legislature—ran up to me and spit out, "If you know what's good for you, nigger, you'll pass your black ass out of here fucking quick!" Then he motioned to hit me and ran away.

And on February 13 eleven blacks picketing the capitol to protest the segregated galleries were arrested. The same day, twenty-two persons were arrested in connection with an attempt to desegregate the white clinic at Grady Hospital. This kind of activity in Atlanta lasted only a short time and served only to expose one more nerve in the festering body of the racist United States. There were a thousand others to be exposed. I had long been convinced that this had to be done, that a group of people like SNCC had to work constantly at attacking the symbols of racism and degradation. I churned away at full speed in those days, striking out at this or that symbol, and by now considered myself a full-time, professional agitator. I was extremely proud of the term *professional agitator* and wanted to do nothing more than organize agitation. At the same time I was all too aware of the administrative problems, the lack of funds and staff. So from January to June, despite my orientation to action, I stayed pretty close to the Atlanta office except for some demonstrations in Talladega. I pursued my concept of the administrative function, which was to find people to handle many different kinds of activities, including those of the office. I also believed I had to delegate responsibility and teach others as much as possible.

SNCC was taking shape in those first months of 1962, and so was its commitment for the next year and a half to voter registration work as a tool by which consciousness might be aroused, politicized, and organized. Our particular focus was on the rural South, the Black Belt areas. At that time—this was before the U.S. Supreme Court's "One Man, One Vote" reapportionment decision of 1965—the rural areas of this country had a degree of power in the state capitals that was disproportionate to their populations. Under the old so-called "rotten boroughs" system of apportionment, the rural vote in both the electoral college and the state legislature sometimes approached three times the value of the urban vote. It was thus possible, in principle, to take advantage of this by registering large numbers of rural blacks and thereby win an increase in black political influence. The Deep South contained 137 rural counties with a black majority.

It happened that while SNCC was proceeding with its registration work, policy makers in the Kennedy administration were pondering how the energies of black students could be used to help line up Southern black voters for the Democratic Party. The flagrant denial of the vote to blacks and their low registration were not only an embarrassment to the government but also hurt "liberal" Democrats in the South and left that section of the country open to rank exploitation by the most verbally vicious racists in the country. In the summer of 1961, before I joined SNCC, contact had been made with the organization by representatives of the government and foundations sympathetic to the Kennedy administration. By January, 1962, many meetings had been held and the Voter Education Project was almost ready.

The name "Voter Education Project" was a tax dodge. The Democratic Party and friendly foundations, especially Field and Taconic, were together interested in using tax-exempt money to register Democratic voters. Simple registration would have come under the heading of political activity, but to register voters in order to collect information on registration procedures and problems was deemed by the Internal Revenue Department as "educational activity" and, therefore, tax-exempt funds could be allocated for it.

SNCC's goal was to lay bare the injustices perpetrated upon black people—among them denial of the vote—in the hope that this would lead to greater mass action. In other words, we were interested in trying to register voters so as to expose the dirt of the United States and thus alienate black people from the whole system. And the United States, through the Kennedy administration, was interested in trying to register voters for the sake of the Democratic Party. By cooperating with the Voter Education Project, sponsored by the Southern Regional Council with the federal government's blessing, we saw a way to finance what we wanted to do. We would be walking a thin line of contradiction in the American system, but we felt able to do it.

Had we been content to register voters in the cities of the Deep South, we would have fallen victim to the intent of the federal government. For, in the cities, there was an absence of the kind of repression that existed in rural areas and our activities in the cities would have primarily centered around fighting apathy, an apathy created by years of frustration. But in the rural areas we knew that the fear of the sheriff and the Ku Klux Klan, together with the desire of the whites to hold onto their power by any means, would surface. Struggling against this situation, we could create more exposure and thereby more consciousness.

In this project we also saw the powers of the federal government as an instrument to be used over the state governments of the South—a tactic I have mentioned before. We were particularly interested in the sections of the 1957 and 1960 Voting laws which said the federal government had to provide protection to those engaged in registering voters or helping them to register. This was the clause we felt would help us stay alive longer as we faced the wrath of the Southern racists, providing we dramatized our plight and won political support from Northern areas that would force the U.S. Justice Department to act.

In retrospect it would have been better to organize self-defense units while working on the Voter Education Project. But we were not thinking in terms of organized self-defense units at that time and certainly not in terms of armed struggle. Also, we were still confined to the theory that we could get help from the U.S. Government, and many of our organizers were committed to the practice of nonviolence, a commitment that would erode as the struggle became more intense. In any case, we were right in 1962 to assume that the struggle against repression of political rights would raise the consciousness of black people. The next few years proved this. Eventually, as I have said, the fine line of contradiction would wear thin and we would become open antagonists of the U.S. Government.

In February, 1962, Charles McDew and I sat in a meeting at the offices of the Southern Regional Council, which was sponsoring the Voter Education Project. Assembled were many different leaders from civil rights organizations. Roy Wilkins voiced his opposition to our plan to work in the rural South. He felt that one could not register voters in Mississippi or any other part of the rural South, that we should concentrate on the metropolitan cities of the Deep South. We did not argue with him, for we knew his position and had anticipated it in our proposal.

The proposal which we presented at that meeting, and which was approved, described the specific areas of operation in this way:

We have developed in detail only the plans for Georgia; our intentions in the other states are only sketched. At this time we are prepared to move ahead in Georgia, Alabama, and Mississippi; the program in the other states must be delayed until we have adequate financial resources.

GEORGIA:

In Georgia the Student Nonviolent Coordinating Committee proposes to work in two heavily populated Congressional Districts as the initial thrust of our efforts.

Several counties have been chosen as focal points. In the Third Congressional District, we will work the following:

1) Terrell County—Located in the southern part of the Third District, it touches upon the Second District. This places it in a central location where it serves as the symbol of oppression in southwest Georgia. It was here that the first court action under the Civil Rights Act of 1957 was brought. The county is presently under a court injunction against further discrimination in the registration process. Since Negroes comprise 67.7% of the total population, the county is a point of high focus for all of southwest Georgia.

2) Peach County—The presence of Fort Valley State College increases the potential for student activity in this county. It could serve as a training area for students for other counties. Negroes outnumber the white population by a two to one ratio, but out of the 8,000 Negroes in the county only 679 were registered in 1958. From Peach County, Houston, Macon, and Taylor Counties are easily accessible.

3) Marion County—This is the beachhead to the Northeast. With 62.5%

of the population Negro, only 3.8% of the registered voters are Negro. It could serve as an example of the possibility of progress in the Northeast.

4) Lee County—Lee will be the focal point for the southeast section of the District. We have had strong support already indicated for a summer voter registration program. Since 67.7% of the population is Negro, success here would have strong positive effect upon the neighboring counties.

In the Second Congressional District, four counties have also been chosen:

1) Dougherty County—Here lies the crossroads for people in the rural areas for miles around. It holds tremendous potential, since most of the students at Albany State College live in south Georgia. Negroes comprise 38.1% of the population in the county. A suit has been filed against the county and city officials for enforcing segregation in voting facilities, and has been upheld. The result of this has been that there is a greater awareness of the voter registration process as it relates to the destruction of segregation. It is the home of the only Negro lawyer in south Georgia, and thus has a helpful resource for legal difficulties. And finally, it is in Albany that we have persons willing to study and evaluate our gains in registration through statistical analysis.

The Student Nonviolent Coordinating Committee has been active in Dougherty County for many months, has a good knowledge of the county, and is well known to the inhabitants.

2) Early County—On the northwestern border is Early County, which has a Negro population of 9,300, 54.7% of the total population in 1958. It lies on the Alabama line and has a record of atrocities against Negroes, which may account for the recent Negro population shifts. Whites are also apparently leaving the county: in 1958 the 228 registered Negroes accounted for 4.7% of the registered population, while in 1960 the 214 accounted for 6.5%.

3) Baker County—This is another symbol in Georgia which must be shattered: "no hope for Baker County." People in this area have a strong motivation to register. Baker is one of the forty counties in Georgia where over 50% of the total population is Negro: the percentage in 1958 was 63.3%. At that time no Negro had been allowed to register. At present, there are nine Negroes registered, despite a Federal injunction against the discrimination practiced in the registration process. Baker is said to be worse in police brutality and judicial injustice than the well-known Terrell County. We feel that when Negroes register in Baker County, the effect will be felt across the south of Georgia.

4) Worth County—While Negroes compose 50.8% of the population in the county, they represent only 4.8% of the registered population. We have many contacts in the county and can work here in voter registration.

In Georgia, the methods used to systematically exclude the Negro from citizenship participation through the ballot have had one goal: the obliteration of all motivation toward suffrage. Whatever the apparent procedure, purging or inflating of voter lists, economic warfare, police brutality, etc., all attempts to nullify the right to vote among Negroes have aimed at a psychological enslavement which has increased in effectiveness through the years.

The Student Nonviolent Coordinating Committee will use a similar approach to that of segregationists, but with opposite goals. We also intend to engage in a battle for men's minds. Interest in the pursuit of happiness exists in people under the most atrocious conditions of servitude. If we lift the veil of fear from the eyes of the people and provide in its place the motivation to become responsible citizens, the people will rally among themselves toward the achievement of this goal.

Our operations are based on the premise that we cannot and should not do the work ourselves; it is desirable to involve local citizens and groups as much as possible. They should and must want to do the footwork. The people—ministers, students, the man in the street, businessmen, housewives—must be motivated to feel their responsibility for the entire task. Each is vital to the campaign. . . .

MISSISSIPPI:

A large part of our total effort will be directed towards producing a larger electorate in one of the toughest Southern states. To effectively register voters in Mississippi there must be a system whereby everyone who is working in the state can be brought together to work as one. This system is being promoted through the formation of the Mississippi Federated Voters League, an organization which has representation from all over the state and provides the best contact for the various people working in the field. The role that the Student Nonviolent Coordinating Committee plays in the League is as follows:

We help provide part of the leadership within the state organization and some funds to aid in its operation. We also help by providing part of the manpower needed to get out into the rural areas and teach the people. We have people serving as the liaison between the farms and the central office of the Voters League. We provide the "door knockers" and instructors for the registration schools.

We have people strategically located in each of the five Congressional Districts within the state. We are prepared to place workers in Marshall County of the Second District; Bolivar County of the Third District; Hinds and Pike Counties of the Fourth District; Kemper County of the Fifth District; and Jefferson Davis County of the First District. The field workers will operate out of each of these counties and coordinate the registration activities in the surrounding counties. In this way we hope to establish a well-coordinated statewide organization which will provide the needed unified "community" effort needed to increase the electorate in Mississippi.

ALABAMA:

Since the largest number of Negroes extends through the middle of Alabama we will concentrate on that area. We intend to have people stationed in Marengo and Clarke Counties in the extreme Western section of the state; Dallas and Butler Counties in the central part of Alabama; and Bullock and Lee Counties in eastern Alabama. The idea here will be to establish a base in these counties and move through the rural areas and teach the people on a door-to-door basis.

SOUTH CAROLINA:

This particular state has a situation which will easily adapt to the type of work we will be doing. In most of the areas where we would like to work, there is a sizeable city we can work out of in order to reach the people in the rural areas. We would like to work on a district-by-district basis and cover five of the six Congressional Districts in South Carolina. In the First District we would have people in Allendale and Colleton Counties; in the Second, in Orangeburg and Sumter Counties; in the Third, we would have people stationed at Newberry and Edgefield Counties; in the Fifth District, in Chester and Kershaw Counties; and in the Sixth District, Darlington and Georgetown Counties. In every District except the Fifth we will attempt to work in all of the counties surrounding the area in which we are based. The voter registration program has been carried out quite well in general along the coast, and we do not feel that we can do much in adding to the existing progress. This also holds true in Richland County in the Second District. The ultimate success

in effecting a meaningful change in the political structure of the state will come from breaking the strangle-hold that the rural areas have on the urban centers in the state's political makeup.
CONCLUSION:

In order to increase registration in rural Southern areas there can be only one approach. We are going to have to penetrate the rural areas, live with the people, develop their own leaders, and teach them the process of registration and effective use of the franchise. There will have to be workers travelling from county to county doing just that, making sure that the people are qualified and that registration is being carried on at a steady rate.

Although the traditional methods of increasing voter registration have concentrated upon the large, heavily populated urban centers, our work will be directed primarily toward the rural areas of the South with particular emphasis on areas that have large concentrations of Negro people. We intend to tap the potential power of the people in the black belt.

This original proposal also listed Louisiana as a work area, but SNCC was unable to extend the project into that state. Nor did it send workers into every single one of the Georgia counties listed. However, the Voter Education Project would become an important instrument that helped SNCC develop a number of its bases—particularly in Mississippi—within the next year and a half.

Our relationship with the Voter Education Project would always be strained, for the activities of those receiving subsistence from it were supposed to be confined solely to voter registration work and not direct action. Staff members felt that this regulation was too restricting. In November, 1963, the staff in Mississippi would begin to run candidates in a mock election. This became the excuse for the Voter Education Project to withhold all funds in Mississippi. Walking the fine line of contradiction —our participation in an Establishment-sponsored project—would thus come to an end. Most of us knew in early 1962 that this had to happen, but we were ready and willing to walk the line as long as we could do so and without compromising basic principles or goals.

CHAPTER **35**

Broke, Busted, But Not Disgusted

AS THE summer of 1962 approached, SNCC faced a debt of thirteen thousand dollars and no funds from the Voter Education Project had yet come through. There was no prospect of raising money from any other source. Through the winter we had continued to exist on a deficit basis, borrowing from people on a short-term basis and then borrowing from others to pay off the first debts. No regular subsistence checks were issued and no money for field expenses. Telephone bills were mounting, with the constant threat of service being cut off. Our office supply bill stood at five hundred dollars.

I was the principal administrator, perplexed and disturbed by the financial condition of the organization. But the attitude of the field staff toward fund raising was even more vexing. Many of our people had a notion that we should not get involved in that kind of activity. All we had to do was live with the people and somehow funds would come to us. One staff member disliked fund raising so much that he went on his own to CORE and asked them simply to allocate a certain amount of their budget each year for SNCC. CORE, of course, refused to do this and pointed out that such a proposal would limit the possibilities of SNCC's own growth.

SNCC staff opposed setting up a fund raising mechanism because they said that would mean creating a bureaucracy. It would make SNCC like other civil rights organizations, in which we had indeed seen the corrupting influence of too much concern with money. These organizations often seemed to exist primarily for raising funds—they had no programs in the field. In 1961-62 SNCC had the largest field staff of any civil rights organization although it was the poorest. This situation reflected our values and they were good ones—but we still had to do something about money.

There was also a contradiction in the staff's attitude because Charles McDew was running around the North raising funds and no one objected to that. It seemed that for one person to do the job was acceptable, but creating an administrative apparatus was threatening. The staff's attitude implied an assumption that it is possible to maintain an organization without the means to support it. I think the basic cause of that attitude was a lack of organizational experience.

SNCC staff members opposed fund raising among the local black people in a project area for different reasons. I remember urging Charles Sherrod to do this in Albany, Georgia, at the height of the Albany Movement. Sherrod vetoed such fund raising and Mr. Searles, editor of the *Southwest Guardian*, had asked me to overrule the veto. I explained that I didn't have the power to do that, but I did discuss the question with Sherrod because I felt that, if Albany blacks wanted to support us, we should encourage them to do so. He said that if we did people would think we were in town only to get money. In retrospect I think Sherrod had been made to feel sensitive by all the pressure and attacks on SNCC in Albany —accusations that we were just vagabonds, that we were communists, that we were going to run out on the people when the excitement died down. This sensitivity had, in turn, made him feel reluctant to take money and anxious to protect the work of the organization—its image with the people. If SNCC could say, "We don't want your money, we just want to work and help change things here," our position was strengthened.

Eventually Sherrod and others felt ready to raise money in Albany, but by then SNCC had lost much of its popular support there. The NAACP, however, set its well-greased Freedom Fund Dinner Committee to work and raised over three thousand dollars in one night, capitalizing on the excitement generated by the Albany Movement. I think Sherrod's decision greatly affected the course of our fund-raising activities, that we could and should have moved differently. But hindsight choices are just a different story, they don't reflect the reality of the actual times. Under the circumstances—the personalities and experiences of the SNCC staff, the dynamics of the situation in Albany—I doubt that there was much else he or we could have done.

At the June meeting of SNCC's Executive Committee, I argued for passage of a resolution to open offices in six cities of the North with a large black population: New York, Washington, D.C., Chicago, Detroit, Philadelphia, Cleveland. I saw these offices as forming a fund-raising network, among other functions. There was hardly any opposition to this plan, for by this time everybody was acutely aware of our serious financial situation. But the solution of one problem creates another. Having voted that we should open offices, the problem of staffing them became acute. Paul Brooks went to Chicago and Bernard Lafeyette to Detroit; we could not immediately find staff for the other cities. I was learning that, just as important as making a decision, or perhaps more important, is the process of implementation.

The Northern offices had another function, closely related to fund raising, but also with a political content. One of the problems we faced in the South was our isolation from the news media. We were getting out some information about the repression being suffered by Southern black folk and what SNCC was doing, but not enough. I saw the Northern offices as providing an information network and bases of political support. In those Northern cities with large black populations it should be possible to build an awareness of what was happening in the South together with pressure on the federal government for action. With such a network it would have been possible, for example, to make more people aware of what happened to Bessie Turner, who was so brutally beaten in Clarksdale, Mississippi. This awareness would also sensitize black people around the country to SNCC's activities, thereby generating an impulse in them to do something active and frontal in their own cities.

By this time our grand office staff in Atlanta had expanded from two to three people—Julian Bond had come to work full time in communications. We had also moved, thanks to Mr. Hill—who had helped us so

much with credit on office supplies and who, in May of that year, had
let us move into a huge upstairs loft in a warehouse he was leasing nearby
at 135 Auburn Street. We could have it rent free, he said, but it needed
paint. We leaped at the chance and held a painting party—Bill Hansen,
a white SNCC field secretary who would later head the Arkansas project,
happened to arrive in Atlanta then, just in time to have a paintbrush stuck
in his hand. Our new space was about three times the size of the old
office and we had four desks with four telephones.

We opened the office every day no later than nine o'clock in the morning and closed it at eleven, twelve, or one o'clock at night. We were working much too hard, way beyond the limits of human capacity, but we
worked on and on and still some more, writing press releases, answering
telephone calls, sending out letters for money and material assistance,
listening to the pleas of staff people for assistance when there was no
money. My nights were restless, for I had become totally committed to all
my brothers and sisters who were working for SNCC and I shared deeply
their conflicts with Southern sheriffs and other racist whites who had
vowed to keep white supremacy intact, and with the misguided Uncle
Toms and Negro schoolteachers who opposed what we were doing. Day
after day, night after night, always there was some telephone call about
harassment, some field secretary coming to Atlanta reporting new
repression.

While SNCC faced the viciousness of the Southern way of life, we
were also under constant attack by the white liberal Establishment—
especially in New York and especially by way of Red-baiting. In February, 1962, demonstrations were taking place at Southern University in
Baton Rouge, Louisiana. Dion Diamond, a SNCC field secretary, was
arrested for trespassing, disorderly conduct, and vagrancy when he
stepped out of a taxi onto the campus, and he was held on six thousand
dollars bond. SNCC chairman Charles McDew and Bob Zellner, the white
field secretary who had been choked by a racist in McComb, went to
visit him in jail. They were arrested as they were leaving for "criminal
anarchy"—described as "an attempt to overthrow the government of the
United States or the state of Louisiana"—because they were members of
SNCC, an organization which allegedly opposed the laws of Louisiana by
force and violence. McDew and Zellner were held on seven thousand
dollars bond. Fortunately the Southern Conference Educational Fund
(SCEF) came to our aid once again and bailed them out. Not long after
that I was in New York with McDew and went to see Andrew Norman
and a colleague of his from the Norman Fund. We were told that it would
be impossible to get money from them as long as we accepted help from
SCEF—which was still being intensively Red-baited. McDew asked
what the people were supposed to do—stay in jail indefinitely? The
Norman Fund was later implicated as a CIA conduit in the exposure of
the operations of the CIA and the National Student Association.

In the Baton Rouge case, we tried to bring publicity and pressure to bear on the federal government in the way that I hoped the Northern offices would eventually do. William Mahoney, who headed the Non-violent Action Group (NAG) in Washington, D.C., and who would later come to work for SNCC full time and also publish a book *Black Jacob*, led demonstrations at the home of Senator Ellender of Louisiana and at the Justice Department. The actions of NAG were typical of the kind of support that we in the Atlanta office tried to coordinate during emergencies. We saw our role, as I have said, as coordinators of support action. We were not spokesmen, interpreters, or philosophers. We existed to serve the field.

In the field the situation improved somewhat for our Mississippi staff when five thousand dollars in Voter Education Project funds finally came through in June, 1962. This enabled our work in the Delta to move into full swing. SNCC had also opened a summer front of demonstrations in Cairo, Illinois, and in Charlestown, Missouri—which is just across the state line from Cairo. I visited both places and was especially glad that segregation in that area had come under attack, for since those times in my youth when I traveled from Chicago to Memphis, Tennessee, the racism of southern Illinois had keenly angered me. At last it was being challenged.

The project in southern Illinois stemmed out of service being denied to four SNCC staff members en route to Chicago early in the spring of 1962. Then, on June 22, SNCC field secretary Salyn McCollum was seriously slashed on the thigh when she intervened between a local white racist and a black high school student at a "white" restaurant. The Cairo Nonviolent Freedom Committee tested restaurants, the swimming pool, a local bowling alley, and a roller-skating rink, with at least forty-two students arrested during the summer. The story of what happened at the T-Wood Roller Bowl during several weeks of picketing that August is a classic: A mob of white hoodlums beat demonstrators with chains, blackjacks, and sticks and shot at them, while the local sheriff leaned back against his car seeing nothing and a local white woman told a bloodied picketer, "Oh, you probably fell down."

All public facilities were eventually desegregated but, in September, when people began picketing a market for fair employment, police tear-gased and arrested them. Charles Koen was the sixteen-year-old leader of the Cairo Nonviolent Freedom Committee. In later years he would return to Cairo as an advocate of self-defense and armed struggle and become a national popular hero.

Over in southwest Georgia action was relatively slow in the early months of 1962. Voter registration work began in "Terrible Terrell," Lee, and Dougherty counties; a training school was closed down by a student boycott; a boycott of stores and buses began; Charles Sherrod, Cordell Reagan, and Charles Jones were arrested a number of times—once on that same old battleground, the Trailways terminal. Fifty persons who marched to protest the murder of Walter Harris were arrested and twelve blacks from Albany went to Washington, D.C., to picket the White House. The litany of events became all too familiar after a while, and the pileup of incidents almost numbing. In a SNCC report on the southwest Georgia project, the mere listing in chronological order of outstanding incidents from January, 1962, to December, 1963, takes up eight single-spaced pages.

It is worth quoting just a few excerpts from that report:

July 24. ALBANY: Mrs. Marion King struck, kicked from behind, knocked to the ground while visiting jailed demonstrators in Camilla, Ga. She was five months pregnant at the time and also carrying her three-year old daughter. (Baby was later born dead.)

July 28. ALBANY: Bill Hansen beaten in county jail and placed in hospital with broken jaw and broken ribs.

Attorney C. B. King hit up-side the head by a law enforcement officer, when he went to county jail to inquire about reported beating of Bill Hansen.

18 arrested on prayer vigil.

9 pickets arrested.

July 30. TERRELL: Ralph Allen, Charles Sherrod arrested in front of Dawson Courthouse for "vagrancy."

Charles Jones struck in face while in county jail.

July 31. ALBANY: 21 arrested at library.

Aug. 1: ALBANY: 39 arrested attempting to use public library. Six more arrested at City Hall in prayer vigil.

Aug. 3: WASHINGTON: President Kennedy: ". . . It is wholly inexplicable why the leaders of the Albany government will not sit down with citizens of Albany and try to solve social issues."

In July, Martin Luther King and Dr. Abernathy returned for trial on charges from the march in December, 1962, and went to jail. Efforts were made to mobilize a great number of people to protest King's jailing, but they proved in vain. People had tired of marching; they were being asked to get arrested again, when they did not feel deeply aroused, and they knew what Chief Pritchett would do. Finally there was a small march and thirty-two arrests.

Shortly after King emerged from jail, an important issue came up—the power of federal injunctions. Such injunctions, obtained at the request of local authorities, had been a common way to try to stop protest movements. But the courts of the United States had firmly decided that they were applicable only if specific persons were named and served with the injunctions.

An injunction against marches and demonstrations was issued in Albany on July 20, naming Dr. King and Charles Jones. Dr. King, with whom we discussed the question, indicated that he was in constant touch with Bobby Kennedy, who urged him to obey the injunction—and to get all the people in town also to obey it. Some of us, myself included, felt that an entire movement should not be stopped by the injunction and that we had to teach the people that such an injunction wasn't valid. I felt that, even though Dr. King was named in the injunction and did not want to violate it, he could have used his status and moral authority to stand before the people and tell them the true facts of the injunction procedure. It seemed to me vital to defy the federal government and have a march.

We began working with Reverend Wells, a grass-roots preacher who had been helpful to us in the past. We discussed the injunction question with him; he agreed and began preaching to the people. The result was a night march, led by Reverend Wells after a stirring address. Over one hundred people filed out from the church, moved by the experience of that night. They were arrested and violence broke out. The black youth of Albany began to stone some whites. The police marched in formation through the black community and some of them were stoned.

The next day Dr. King issued a statement on his own. By this time, he had given up any pretense of consulting with local leadership. When I arrived at his house the next morning, the press had already been called. I saw the statement, repudiating the local blacks and asked him not to do this. The whites were responsible for the violence and people were only reacting to a long history of violence and repression. But my arguments had no effect.

The press conference took place in the backyard of Dr. Anderson's home, where King was staying. As I heard the statement, I thought to myself, this is more than a repudiation of the violence of the blacks against whites, this is an attempt to save a fund-raising base. So the statement was issued and Dr. King's reputation for nonviolence was upheld. But it was not the end of our discussions with Dr. King, of our attempts to resolve the essential conflict—namely, the role of leadership in relation to the importance of building a mass movement.

Outside of Albany both SNCC activity and racist repression heightened that summer. In a field report dated September 20, 1962, Charles Sherrod described their work and summarized the "broke, busted, but not disgusted" attitude which prevailed throughout SNCC:

September 20, 1962

ON CRACKERS, CUCUMBERS, AND COLLARDS

The importance of the Albany Movement is only now being realized. The eyes of the world have been on Albany, Ga., since the mass demonstrations in December. Millions were shocked that "white people" would do such things to those "poor Negroes" in the South. Thousands were appalled at the brutality of the city officials here. Twelve hundred were arrested, many beaten. . . and on runs the blood into the streets of Albany where it is seen across the country, but there are only a few who really understand what we are doing, where we are going and what it all means.

Perhaps the people in Lee and Terrell counties are the only ones who grasp the depth, the meaning of the Albany Movement. Lee and Terrell are two counties among many that surround Albany, the only urban area in southwest Georgia. Strange things have been happening in these counties.

Since June 10th, SNCC has had workers in Lee County—Kathy Conwall of Skidmore, Donald Harris of Rutgers, Penny Patch of Swarthmore, Isaac Martin of Rocky Mountain College, and Peggy Desmond of Boston University. Dr. Robert Johnson of New York City College was present during the early part of the summer. There we were, about sixteen miles away from Albany, the mighty fortress, and eighteen other miles away from every other where, way back in the deep woods. We stayed at "Mama Dolly's" house. She is a gray-haired old lady of about seventy who can pick more cotton, "slop more pigs," plow more ground, chop more wood, and do a hundred more things better than the best farmer in the area. We received threats on the telephone, strange automobiles approached under cover of darkness, and a shoe box-sized package was found in the mail box, possibly a bomb. It disappeared before it could be investigated. We were steadily making a "bee line" to the registrar's office and having meetings each Saturday night. Can you imagine what this means—Saturday night in a small county which knows only wine, women and song for recreation—on Saturday night, those people are singing Freedom songs in a little wooden church somewhere in the back country. And the meeting is peopled by the folk of Sumter County, Albany, and Terrell County; all come together on Saturday night in Lee.

At the same time we were also engaged in a similar program in Terrell County, living there as in Lee on the three C's of health, well, at least our health—crackers, cucumbers, and collards. We had a few squash thrown in by well-wishers. But half-starved, holes in the bottoms of our shoes, we were walking long country miles in Lee and Terrell counties, hearing "I'm scared" over and over and over and wanting to yell "hell lady, I'm scared too, so what!"

It was in Terrell, called "Terrible Terrell" or "Tombstone Territory" by the high school students, that opposition first crystallized. It was about 8:30 on the evening of our Voter Registration meeting and we had just begun. In walked about ten white men into our church, smoking, hats on, talking, flashlights, guns, clubs and billies, and looking mean. They took over after asking for a word. They stayed for more than an hour. They took names of people at the meeting and finally left—to remain [outside] in front of the church. This was not the only time they had "taken over," the people were afraid and so were we, but nobody showed it. That night we sang as if they were listening in New York. And they were, for the *Times* carried the story the next day.

They were also listening across the country when, in Lee County, where we used to meet—Shady Grove Baptist Church—the first burning occurred (Aug. 15, 1962). The Sheriff said that it might have been lightning. The burning was undoubtedly a scare tactic. On Saturday night we had a full crowd walking and talking and singing and praying about Freedom. The people of Lee County were angry and showed it. Some came now who had previously had been afraid to.

There followed the two burnings in Sasser in Terrell County (Sept. 9, 1962). The churches had been completely destroyed, leveled to a ground of hot cinders. The only thing standing was the chimney.

Only a week before, our headquarters had been shot up. In Terrell we live with Mrs. Carolyn Daniels, a young divorcee, in a three-room cinder block structured house. She is the "mama" for us there. There is always a "mama." She is usually a militant woman in the community, outspoken, understanding, and willing to catch hell, having already caught her share. This night, "mama" was in Albany. It was about midnight, I had hopped in the sack, being sick, and Prathia Hall of Temple, Ralph Allen and Jack Chatfield of Trinity College, Christopher Allen of Oxford, and Roychester Patterson, Mrs. Daniels' son, were busy running about in the kitchen hunting syrup, mayonnaise, or butter sandwiches. . . .

Out of the night that covered us, pitch black, there were two blasts. Chatfield crouched, gliding into where I was. Suddenly, he snaps around, explaining quite surprisedly but not too excited—"I'm hit." Prathia Hall and Christopher Allen were grazed, one on the finger, the other on the arm. We were all on the floor. We were working together on Voter Registration. We had been shot at. Some were hit. There was blood. We were afraid. Where was the Federal Government? We crawled about on that floor as if we were in Korea on Pork Chop Hill.

There were some shootings in Lee County. In one home there were twenty-four shots. We had about twelve. Four homes were fired into. The meetings continued in Lee and Terrell. Another church was burned—I hope Baptist Church (in Terrell County on Sept. 15). An attempt was made to disconnect this from any effort to register Negroes. They found men who admitted to the burning. They had been drinking. But the head deacon there is a staunch supporter of the drive to register people. Plus the whole family of Braziers go to this church. The 1960 report of the Civil Rights Commission describes the brutal killing of one James Brazier and the injunction proceedings brought against the officials because of it. . . .

This is "the Movement." These are the people on whose backs, in the heat of the day, the South was built. It will be through them again that the South as it exists today will be destroyed. Albany means progress to these people, the possibility that White is not always right and Negroes may stick together sometimes. Last Wednesday we met in a tent on ground which has been cleared off for the rebuilding of the church. We had about fifty people from Albany. Six months ago, maybe four, maybe less or more, you couldn't have paid these people of Albany enough to come to Dawson, Sasser, or anywhere else in Terrell County. But something has happened here in southwest Georgia which has a good chance of becoming the pattern for our grand strategy in the South. And we go about our way, feeling in the darkness. . . . And the world listens and looks on, wondering.

Charles Sherrod.

CHAPTER **36**

Terror in the Delta

THE NIGHT was very dark in Mississippi as Reggie Robinson and I drove into the Delta, an area along the Mississippi River, full of rich, fertile cotton lands, considered a Black Belt area because blacks generally outnumber whites in its counties. This was my first trip to the Delta and all the horrors of its history flooded through my mind—the lynchings, the beatings, the killings, black people dying by the dozen at the hand of the Klan, the White Citizens' Council, the state authorities themselves. As I thought about all this, my admiration for Bob Moses and his band of guerrilla fighters swelled up. They were resisting a tyranny imposed over hundreds of years. They were writing history with their lives.

It was mid-August, 1962, and the Voter Education Project had finally started. My life had become a very mobile one, traveling from one hot spot to another—first Albany, then Cairo and Charleston, and now Mississippi. I drove to all these places, my tension increasing as I passed each Southern town, wondering exactly what it had done to black people in the past and what it would do in the future. Now I was on my way to Cleveland, Mississippi, to see how SNCC's voter registration work was going there and to attend a meeting.

Reggie and I arrived in Cleveland, a small town in the Delta. Moses and his fellow workers were not there that night but I had a long talk with Amzie Moore, at whose house we were to stay, the same man who had helped Moses back in 1960. I had grown up in the United States as a black man; I had been threatened, almost killed, a number of times; but as I listened to Amzie, I wondered how we as a people had ever survived the racism of white America. This is the story of Amzie Moore's life as he told it:

My name is Amzie Moore. I was born September 23, 1912, in Grenada County, Mississippi. I grew up in Grenada and Leflore counties. I attended public school in those two counties. My first knowledge of the freedom movement came in 1942. In that year some ten thousand Negroes assembled at the Delta State Stadium. Our speakers were from Tuskegee, Washington, and various places. The president of Alcorn College, Mr. Bell, brought a vivid picture of the condition of Negroes in the field of education in the state of Mississippi.

Then, on August 8, 1942, I was drafted from Cleveland, Mississippi, to serve in the Armed Forces of the U.S. I really didn't know what segregation was like before I went into the Army. I was sent to a segregated training field in Alabama, where I received my basic training in infantry. From there I went to Tucson, Arizona, as a construction worker in the signal corps. And then, after spending about six or eight months in Tucson, Arizona, we went to Texas. El Paso, Texas, to be exact. We lived in some little black barracks in a desert, away from everything. We were not allowed to go to the main PX, Post Exchange; we were not allowed to go to the recreational facilities provided for soldiers on the place; we had to ride in the back of the buses from the base into El Paso; and it was the first time I really knew how evil segregation really was.

Now here's one strange thing that happened: We were just a short distance from Mexico, as a matter of fact, Juarez is right across the Santa Fe bridge. It was the only place that we could go to get just a little freedom. The Southern officers who were always in charge of Negro troops certainly didn't think much of having Negro troops go to Mexico. They were afraid, I think, that the Negro troops might be seen with the Mexican girls. So, in order to keep Negroes out of Mexico, they would plan trips up into the mountains. The last trip we planned to the mountain, four men were killed, some fourteen seriously injured.

We had investigation after investigation from Washington about the segregation in the area, about having nothing in the post exchange but funny books and loud music, for Negro soldiers. And finally we were shipped from El Paso, Texas, to Lingley Field in Virginia. The condition was no better, and we found ourselves being shipped from one air base to another, allover the country. Everywhere we went, we were faced with this evil thing—segregation. Kept wondering, why were we fighting? Why were we there? If we were fighting for the four freedoms that Roosevelt and Churchill had talked about, then certainly we felt that the American soldier should be free first.

After spending 2½ years in the States, I was shipped from Long Beach, California, thirteen thousand miles to Calcutta, India. Getting to Calcutta, India, we found that the enlisted men's club was segregated, even in Calcutta. We spent a while there, then we were sent over the hump, that's what you call the lower chain of the Himalayas, to Burma, and even in Burma we found segregation. The Japanese, who broadcast day and night about segregation in America and how American soldiers were being treated, simply reminded us daily that there would be no freedom, even after the war was over. They themselves claimed that they were fighting for our economic, political, and social emancipation. We had to counteract this Japanese propaganda by giving lectures to our soldiers. That was my job—to fly from Lashie to Kuming to Mishinaw, Burma, to give these lectures. We were promised that after the war was over, things would be different, that men would have a chance to be free. Somehow or another, some of us didn't believe it, others did.

Then came August, 1945, when the Japanese surrendered and we were ready to come home. We set sail December 13, 1945, coming through the Indian Ocean up to the Red Sea, through Egypt, through the Straits of Gibraltar, and out into the Atlantic. We arrived in New York January 18, 1946. I got home about the twentieth. When I arrived home, Cleveland, Mississippi, in January, 1946, I found that the local white citizens had organized a "home guard." Now as I understand it, the purpose of this "home guard" was to protect the families against Negro soldiers returning home. *Newsweek* had carried a number of pictures showing white German women sitting in Negro men's laps. This had created quite an excitement in the Mississippi Delta. For about six or eight months, at least one Negro each week was killed. I think the purpose of the killing was to frighten other Negroes. It certainly had its psychological effect.

Finally, when we could bear it no longer, we called in special agents of the FBI to investigate some of the killings. This slowed it up for awhile, and then in 1950 a group of Negroes from all over the Delta got together and decided to organize the Regional Council of Negro Leadership. It was organized at the H. M. Nailer Elementary School in Cleveland, Mississippi. Our first mass meeting was held May 7, 1950. At that time we had thirteen thousand people from forty counties in Mississippi assembled at Mt. Bayou, Mississippi. Our first speaker was Mr. [William] Dawson, from the First Congressional District of Illinois. We talked about freedom and we talked about the purpose of this organization, the Regional Council. We decided that the purpose of the Regional Council would be to teach Negroes first-class citizenship, the preservation of property, the paying of taxes, the holding of public office, the changing of the economic standpoint. We were very happy that our first meeting was a success, as far as people were concerned, because they were there.

And then we moved along toward our goal of making first-class citizenship for at least six hundred thousand Negroes located in the eighteen Delta counties. We felt that it could be done, but then we were not sure how long it would take. Our second meeting was in 1952. We brought in Mr. [Thurgood] Marshall, the noted lawyer for the NAACP. He told us that he had argued before the Supreme Court about abolishing segregation in all public schools. Then in 1954, on May 17, we heard that the Supreme Court had handed down its momentous decision.

At first the local whites in my town thought it was a wonderful thing. They said the change was overdue. They felt sure that the schools would be integrated without trouble. They recalled that at one time, when the rural white kids came into the city schools, they were kind of segregated, but finally after about two or three years, everything was all right. But then the politicians didn't think much of this idea of integrated schools. They felt that if the poor whites and Negroes could get together, very soon the politician wouldn't be able to play one against the other.

Then on October 12, 1954, at Indianola, Mississippi, the White Citizens' Councils were born. Now the purpose of the council, as far as I understand it, was to maintain what they called racial integrity. Their problem was to see that at least a half million Negroes over twenty-one years of age could be gotten out of the state of Mississippi in a ten-year period. They felt like they needed the exodus of Negroes from the Delta area, because otherwise they figured that the Negroes might dominate them politically and I think that this is really the beginning of our trouble.

On January 1, 1955, I was elected president of the Cleveland branch of the NAACP. I think at that time we had a membership of about 87. By the middle of the year we had 564 members of that branch. But then we had other things happen in 1955. Rev. George W. Lee, who lived at Belzoni, Mississippi, had complained to the Regional Council in 1952 that the Negroes in Humphrey County did not pay their poll tax. Mr. Lee had gone to the United States Federal Court, Northern District, to ask the Federal Court to enjoin the sheriff of Humphrey County and allow them to pay their poll tax.

On May 7, 1955, about 11:30 at night, Mr. George W. Lee was ambushed and killed. Following Mr. Lee's death in May, 1955, we had Jack Smith, who was killed at Brookhaven, Mississippi, for participating in what they called politics. Then, in September of 1955 we had a terrible thing happen . . . a boy named Emmett Till, thirteen years of age, was visiting his grandfather, Reverend Wright, at Money, Mississippi. He, along with some other boys, had been sitting around on the store porch there in Money. As I understand it, he whistled or somebody felt like he was whistling at a white woman. Finally he went home to his grandfather's house, and then the next night, two white men came to Reverend Wright's house, asked for Emmett, picked him up and disappeared into the darkness. When Emmett was seen again, he was fished out of the Tallahachie River, somewhere in Tallahachie County. He had been mobbed.

Following the Till case in September, 1955, we had Gus Coates, who was then a civil rights worker in Humphrey County where Reverend Lee had been killed. Gus Coates had been warned by local white citizens that he'd better stop his activities, running to registration and voting. And when he refused, he was shot through the window of his store, maybe in October, 1955. Gus

Coates was hospitalized in Mt. Bayou, and after he was discharged from the hospital, he was advised to leave the state. He now lives in Chicago, Illinois.

Quite a number of leaders left the state. T. R. M. Howard, the militant president of the Regional Council of Negro Leadership, had to leave. Dr. Battle, who was located in Sunflower County, a militant leader, had to leave. A doctor from Natchez, Mississippi, had to leave. So we had a great exodus of leaders from the state due to the pressure that was being brought on by white organizations bent and bound on maintaining slavery. As the year came to a close, 1955, we found that there had been seven deaths, many people had been hurt, it was a real rough year for Mississippi.

Came 1956, we decided to start trying to get people to vote. Our first effort was to try in the East Cleveland precinct. Fourteen Negroes went to the East Cleveland precinct with their poll tax receipts in their hands, to try to register in the first Democratic primary. Coleman was running for governor of Mississippi. When they came into the polling place, there were ten burly men sitting over behind a counter. At the box, where they were to drop our ballots, a man stood with a .38 Smith and Wesson on his side. We marked our ballots and came to the box to drop them in. We were informed by the man standing at the ballot box that we could not put the ballots in the box. There was a brown envelope there on the table by the box. He suggested that we put the ballots in the brown envelope. One man, E. B. Hopkin, who is now in Chicago, said he was not going to put his ballot in the brown envelope. He was going to put it in the box. We almost got into trouble. I suggested that we do as we were directed and then we would contact the U.S. Department of Justice to see what could be done against these people who had kept us from voting. I went immediately to a telephone and called the Department of Justice. I don't remember who I talked to, but then they said they would have it investigated. The special agents of the FBI from Memphis came in to investigate. We didn't hear any more from it.

However, in the second primary, in the fall, some of the fellows did vote. In 1957, the state legislature had passed a new law requiring that people give an interpretation of the Constitution to the satisfaction of the circuit clerk. Then we decided we would set up a citizenship school. In the citizenship school we had planned to teach Negroes the Constitution of Mississippi. We felt like it was almost impossible, but we were going to try. Because think of trying to teach a man something about double jeopardy, who probably doesn't even know how to read well.

Then we went about it. First we had hundreds of copies of the Constitution mimeographed. We set up the school at the Gabriel's Mission at Mt. Bayou, Mississippi, under the supervision of Father John Lebouvre. We went to Washington to talk to Mr. Tiffany, who was then in the Eisenhower administration, in the U.S. Department of Justice in charge of civil rights. We talked to people from New York, from Illinois, and from all over. We had breakfast with quite a number of congressmen and senators in Washington to talk about this problem. Then we came back to Mississippi to start working. We taught maybe 150 people that year. We had less than 20 who passed the test.

At the end of 1957, we decided that we would do something different, but by that time, Father John Lebouvre, the devoted priest who worked so hard, had been transferred to Pennsylvania. And I decided that I would have to try to go it alone. Finally the new priest came in, he decided it wasn't in the best interest of the church to allow us to continue our voter registration classes in Mt. Bayou. And that was out.

Then, in 1959, I had quite a number of personal problems at that time and I didn't do too much in the field of civil rights. In 1960, SNCC sent Bob Moses from Atlanta into the Delta. I talked with Bob, and Bob suggested that I go to Atlanta in October of 1960 to the organizational meeting of SNCC. I went into that meeting and it was decided at that meeting that SNCC would work, would have a voter registration project in the Mississippi Delta. Then, the next year, 1961, came the Freedom Riders, from Anniston, Alabama, where the bus was burned, into Jackson. Everybody was excited, peace officers were alerted all over Mississippi, they were racing from the bus stations to the train stations, checking every bus, looking for Freedom Riders, even when there weren't any Freedom Riders in the Delta, all the activity was going on in Jackson. And this went on probably about six or eight months. Then Bob Moses came in, to work in voter registration. We directed Bob to a fellow named Bryant, who lives in McComb, Mississippi, who was the president of the McComb branch of the NAACP. And Bob began his voter registration work in Amite and Pike counties. You know the story. . . .

The voter registration project of which Amzie Moore spoke had finally gotten off the ground that summer and Bob Moses had shifted his base from Jackson to Cleveland. In early August the staff fanned out across the area. Some of them had just returned from the Highlander School in Tennessee, where its director, Myles Horton, had set up workshops in voter registration. But no workshop in the world could prepare anyone fully for what the staff had encountered.

In the Delta town of Greenwood, SNCC field secretary Sam Block—who was from Cleveland, thirty miles away—had started a voter registration project around a police brutality case. On July 28, 1962, a fourteen-year-old local youth named Welton McSwine had been picked up. Somebody had supposedly peeped into a white woman's home, and the police accused McSwine of doing it.

They took him into the back cell and first beat him on the head with a blackjack. Then he was put in a chair and surrounded by five officers questioning him. When he continued to insist, "Please Mr. Policeman, I swear I don't know anything about that. I was in the field [picking cotton]," one of the cops beat him in the face with his fist while another hit him in the stomach with a billy stick.

Next, they made him pull off his clothes and lie on the floor where they beat him with a bullwhip until welts were raised on his thighs and his screams could be heard outside. The beating was interrupted by the buzzer used to signal the arrival of someone in the station and the necessity of stopping screams. It was the boy's father, whose boss had called to tell the police to release the boy into the father's custody.

The police returned to the cell to make the boy stop crying, wash his face, and dress. In the meantime, Sam Block had learned about the incident and, after McSwine was released, had him fill out affidavits. The boy's picture was also taken and the material sent off to the Justice Department and the FBI.

After that, Sam Block—tall, lean, dark-skinned, with a deep voice and a dry sense of humor—began working on voter registration in Greenwood all alone. That may seem like a small thing, but in the Greenwood of those days it took a kind of courage that defies imagination. Sam tells what his early days in the town were like:

I'm Sam Block, a field secretary for SNCC. I've been working in Leflore County, Greenwood, Mississippi. Leflore County is the adjoining county to Tallahachie County where Negro Emmett Till was killed by two white men. . . . They were brought to trial and they were not convicted or sentenced to any time whatsoever.

Greenwood, Mississippi, was a very difficult place to work in when I first went there, and still is. I was accused of going out and spending two hundred and something dollars, buying whiskey, stuff like this. When the people found out what I was there for, they said it was best for no one to have anything to do with me because of what I was doing, and I was only going to stir up trouble and be there for a short length of time, and then leave.

One day I went around and talked to as many people as I possibly could, talked to some of the ministers there and no one was in favor of what I was doing because they felt it would bring too much economic pressure on them and the people that are there. So I didn't get discouraged, I thought that I should continue, regardless, because I had been sent there to do a job and my intention was to do this job that I was sent there to do.

I kind of got myself organized and I got some people to work with me. I canvassed practically every day and every night until I found about seven or eight people to carry up to register, since I had been sent there to work on voter registration instead of direct action. We went up to register and it was the first time visiting the courthouse in Greenwood, Mississippi, and the sheriff came up to me and he asked me, he said, "Nigger, where you from?" I told him, "Well, I'm a native Mississippian." He said "Yeh, yeh, I know that, but where you from? I don't know where you from." I said, "Well, around, some counties." He said, "Well, I know that, I know you ain't from here, cause I know every nigger and his mammy." I said, "Well, you know all the niggers, do you know any colored people?" He got angry. He spat in my face and he walked away. So he came back and turned around and told me, "I don't want to see you in town any more. The best thing you better do is pack your clothes and get out and don't never come back no more." I said, "Well, sheriff, if you don't want to see me here, I think the best thing for you to do is pack your clothes and leave, get out of town, cause I'm here to stay, I came here to do a job and this is my intention, I'm going to do this job."

The sheriff got angry and he left. So I carried the people in and they registered—at least they were given the literacy test that you have to take in Mississippi in order to become a registered voter. We went back home and the next night I received a telephone call and I think it was from the White Citizens' Council and they told me the same thing that the sheriff had told me, to get out of town, nigger. "If you don't, we're going to kill you."

And they meant it. SNCC field secretary Luvaughn Brown, who came with Lawrence Guyot on August 15 to work with Sam Block, tells what followed those threats—on their second day in town:

My name is Luvaughn Brown. I am eighteen years old, and a field secretary for the Student Nonviolent Coordinating Committee. The following is a report of the events that occurred just prior to, and during, my stay in Greenwood, Mississippi.

In the summer of 1962, a workshop was held in Edwards, Mississippi, to plan and learn voter registration strategy. This was in preparation for a mass voter registration drive in Mississippi—specifically in the Delta. People in this workshop were sent to various areas in the Delta. Lawrence Guyot and I were sent to Greenwood, Mississippi, to work with Samuel Block.

We arrived there August 16 and took a taxi to the Greenwood office located on the corner of Avenue I and Broad Street. There we were met by Sam Block, who was standing with a group of three men. We learned that they were newspaper men trying to get information about the plans that we had working in the Greenwood area. Sam was refusing to give them any information. This is easily explained because Sam had given them stories before, and they had ripped them up. We had also learned that it was unsafe because of the closeness of the relationship between the press and the police. After trying without success to learn the reason for the arrival of Guyot and myself, they left.

Sam, Guyot, and I went into the office so that he could tell us of the plans he had, what he had done, and how effective he had been. We then made plans for a small meeting of the volunteer workers from Greenwood that night. The meeting was held in the office—we made plans for canvassing the neighborhood the next day and drew up a plan as to how we would approach people. There was a tremendous amount of fear in the workers that night. We all had the fear that someone would shoot in the window, and the shades were drawn. We learned of and discussed some of the sufferings that some of the workers and their parents had incurred—loss of jobs, threats by phone, etc.

The next morning approximately seven volunteers reported to the office to canvass. We split the city into areas. Then we all met back at the office around twelve to eat and evaluate our canvassing. Approximately one hundred people had been talked to and of these, ten had agreed to go down and attempt to register. Two of the workers had been stopped by the police, and when they told of this incident, the rest refused to go back out that day. Guyot, Sam, and I went back out to canvass near the office. . . .

Out of the ten that had agreed to go down, three reported to the office. We explained the Constitution and the literacy test to them. Then, Guyot and I went to those people near the office who had agreed to go, and see if we could find out what had happened to them. Once again, we encountered a tremendous amount of fear. We tried explaining to them the need to stand up and demand their rights and vote—but to no avail. When I got back to the office, Guyot and one of the taxi drivers from the community left to take the three ladies down.

When they returned to the office, Guyot explained to us that they had been met at the courthouse by the chief of police. The officer had cursed and threatened them and the ladies had become afraid to go into the courthouse. Sam then suggested we meet some of the people in the community who had given him financial and moral support. This was when we learned of the pressure that was being put on the man that we were renting the office space from. The police were threatening to arrest him for bigamy unless he put us out—so far, he had refused to do so.

That night, after having a small meeting in the office with the volunteer workers, Sam, Guyot, and I decided that we needed to have a long talk and discuss the project. We had to find a way to get some of the fear out of people we were working with. We were still at it about one o'clock. Then, Sam decided it was time to make his daily call to Bob Moses in Cleveland. (This was another safety measure.) The phone was situated near the window of the office and we told Sam to pull the shades down so that he wouldn't be seen.

As he started to do so, he noticed a police car parked outside with an officer standing near it. He called our attention to this and then told Bob [over the telephone]. The only thought that came to us was that we might all be arrested. We pulled the shades and put the light out. We then noticed the officer talking to someone on the radio in the car, although we could hear none of what was said. Sam went in back to lock the door. There was another room directly opposite the one where our office was, and Sam and I went into it to watch the side of the building.

About ten minutes later, the police car pulled off in the direction of Broad Street. At the same time, a car approached from Broad Street and stopped in front of the office. We noticed a couple of guns being held by the man. This was when we began to get afraid. Sam, then, tried another call to Bob Moses, but we couldn't get through. After about a minute, Guyot tried to make a collect call to Rev. R. L. T. Smith in Jackson, but Smith refused to accept it saying that he knew nothing of us and that he didn't accept long distance collect calls. Because we couldn't contact anyone, our fears began to mount. We knew now that our lives were in danger. [Sam Block reported that he also called Burke Marshall of the Justice Department, at home, and was told they could do nothing until a crime had been committed.] Then came the decision as to whether we should remain in the office or try to find a way out.

Sam then thought of the FBI agent that lived in Greenwood. We called him and asked him to come over. He said that he would be right over. Then, he asked if we had called the police. We said that we felt they were the cause of the whole thing, since a police car had been there prior to the group in the car. Sam hung up.

We, then, heard footsteps on the stairs and the sound of chains rattling. We went into a room where Sam slept (a part of the office). This was where we decided to make use of a window that led onto the roof of the café next door. We climbed hurriedly out of the window and at the same time heard the beating on the door. We cautiously went to the front of the building on the roof. Then we saw another car loaded with men pull up, and as they were getting out of the car, we went to the back of the roof. We discovered a TV antenna that extended to the ground: Sam went first, followed by Guyot, and then me. Sam led us (running) through a path between the houses. We went to the home of one of the ministers that had befriended Sam. He was frightened, but told us we could come in until we figured out what to do. Sam asked to use the phone so that we might call Bob Moses. The man reluctantly agreed —explaining that he was afraid his phone might be tapped.

Sam, finally, reached Bob and we explained what had happened. After we hung up, the man decided that we should try to make it to his father's house. After he had searched the street from his door, we left. His father accepted a brief explanation and told us where we could sleep. He then gave us a hammer in case someone had followed us, and told us that we would have some defense. We were not bothered the rest of the night.

The next morning, when we arrived at the office, we found Bob Moses and Willie Peacock asleep there on the couch. They told us they had arrived early in the morning, and had found the office door broken open and some cards laying around outside. We then looked at our file cabinet and found that most of the records were missing. . . .

Willie Peacock of Charleston, Mississippi, also a Delta town, described in a field report the arrival of Bob Moses and himself at the Greenwood office:

I spent the night in Cleveland which was August 16, 1962, at least I thought I was going to spend the night in Cleveland, but we got a call from Samuel Block, telling us that he was in trouble over there. That it seems a mob was going to come up in the office any minute. So we began making calls to the JD [Justice Department] after trying to find out why is it that they couldn't do something right away instead of waiting until a crime was committed. Sam called us a second time and told us that they were out of the building and that they were going to try to seek refuge in one of the person's houses that they knew pretty well. So we told them just to hold on and we were going to try to come over as soon as possible.

So we made it there at about 2:00 A.M. We just walked in and Bob Moses went ahead of me into the office. He didn't see anything ruffled up or anything of that nature, so Bob turned the light on in the office, let the couch out and put the covers on, turned the fan on, which makes a lot of noise and went to bed. I was very—I was scared. I just didn't understand what kind of guy this Bob Moses is, that could walk into a place where a lynch mob had just left and make up a bed and prepare to go to sleep, as if the situation was normal. So I guess I was learning, and I said, well, if Bob can go to sleep, I can go to sleep, so I guess about five minutes after I got in the bed I was asleep.

Those guys, Samuel Block, Lawrence Guyot, Luvaughn Brown, woke me up the next morning. I found that I was still in the land of the living, so we had a great discussion that day as to what our policy was going to be in the next two weeks to come. We'd been advised by our executive secretary in Atlanta, Georgia, that we should have more or less a cooling-off period to give the JD time to act, since this thing had been committed. So we broke the session, I guess about ten o'clock, because we were interrupted by the FBI, Everett. This time he came and he talked to Samuel Block, first, which didn't last very long because Sam was very displeased about his delay in coming. That's when the impact really hit me, how unprotected we really were. Here were our great heroes that we depended on in Washington that seemed to have let us down. I had heard that these kinds of things happen, the FBI didn't act when you needed them sometimes, in cases like that, but I just couldn't believe it, but here it had happened. I heard him when he walked in, the FBI, I heard him give this lousy excuse. . . .

So we went down to the café where we eat, which is the same café that they escaped over the roof of that night, and we sat down, Bob Moses, Lawrence Guyot, Samuel Block, and myself, to decide what we would do. We knew that we shouldn't give up the Greenwood project because this is what the Citizens' Council wanted us to do. At the same time we had been told by Mrs. Burns, Mr. Burns's wife, that we would have to move our office, we would have to get out, that—see, her husband had been arrested on the charge of bigamy, later dropped, and the white people who were supposed to go lenient on him and get him off the hook had told her this is the only way he could be gotten out—"get those educated niggers out of the building."

So she told us to get out and we were thinking about where we were going to go. We knew that we should stay and in view of all this violence that was going to be put up on us, it was a hard decision to make. Then finally I got patriotic, since I had waited an hour I guess for somebody to get patriotic, I said, "well, I'll stay" and no one challenged me. Well, so there I was.

For the most part we had to stay in Cleveland until Sam found somewhere else for us to stay, which was with Mrs. Hattie Mae Smith. . . . After returning to Greenwood we began to canvass again, talking to people about going down to register and finally we kind of got immune to what was happening and so we were walking, we didn't have a car, at the time, we had to walk around . . . we had also to protect the person that we were living with, cause we had stayed at other places prior to this and we had been put out every time because of these people sweeping around at night, peeping in windows trying to find out where we lived. . . . So we did all we could to protect her by not letting anyone see us go home or leave. So this kept up for awhile until we got a car. We got a car. . . .

There was an interesting sidelight to the story on Mr. Burns, the workers' first landlord, and his arrest for bigamy. According to Sam Block, a white attorney had gone to Burns's first wife and asked her to sign a paper which, he said, would help them get a final divorce. And she signed it, not knowing that it was in fact an affidavit for his arrest on a charge of bigamy. In jail, Burns was told by the attorney, "You called those fellows into town. You're one of those smart damn niggers and that's why we got you here now."

The search for housing continued to be a desperate problem. Once Sam Block had to sleep in "an old raggedy car on the side of the road in a junkyard." The whites came again one night to a home where they were staying, again they switched out all the lights, but this time there was no way out of the house. "We decided to take watches until morning," Luvaughn reported. "Equipped with two hammers and with the advantage of a small door, we decided we would have to fight it out if they came in." The whites finally left, apparently because the owner of the house had several teachers living there and the mob did not know which room the SNCC workers were in; they didn't want to burst in on the teachers by mistake.

Sam Block would eventually receive a severe beating from three whites, which fractured his ribs and put him in bed for a week. Yet, in some ways the physical danger and violence seemed no worse to the SNCC workers than the loneliness and other psychological strains.

"People would just get afraid of me," Sam reported. "They said, 'He's a Freedom Rider.' Women told their daughters, don't have anything to do with me, that I couldn't carry [take] them out because I was a Freedom Rider. I was there to stir up trouble, that's all. So if I walked down the street, people would say, 'There's the Freedom Rider. Look at him.' They'd say, 'Ain't that the Freedom Rider?' 'Yeah, that's him.' Anything you do there, their eyes are dead on you. So you couldn't afford to do anything wrong . . . you want to hold the respect or gain the respect of the community . . . and make these people feel a part of you and make these people feel a part of the movement . . . which was a very, very hard job to do."

This was the background of SNCC's voter registration work in Mississippi, where I had now arrived myself to learn about that work and to attend a meeting on August 26 of the Council of Federated Organizations. The meeting took place in the basement of a church in Clarksdale, about an hour's drive from Cleveland, with Aaron Henry presiding. COFO was supposed to bring together the civil rights organizations working in the state under one banner, but the unity was more in name than reality, for there was never any surrendering of autonomy by the organizations. Fudamentally it was the desire of the SNCC people to see COFO work that kept it alive.

The initial impulse for the creation of COFO had come in 1961 from the desire of the Voter Education Project to avoid directly giving SNCC a grant of thirty-six thousand dollars for voter registration work in the Delta. SNCC had previously received five thousand dollars directly and more than earned it. (All staff people received twenty-five dollars a week for subsistence; this money was pooled and all those who could eat off the limited total were placed on the staff.) Additional grants were to be made on the basis of the number of unregistered, potential voters—and, in the Delta, this constituted a vast number of people. But, according to Wiley Branton, director of the project, it was politically impossible to award so much money to SNCC because of opposition from other civil rights groups. There had been intense pressure against granting the initial five thousand dollars, but he did it anyway. And so COFO was established.

COFO plans and staffing were now under discussion at the Clarksdale meeting. Wiley Branton insisted that, regardless of attitudes toward SNCC, Bob Moses had to be appointed field director for voter registration —if COFO was to get the grant. This was accepted. The group also reelected Aaron Henry as president of COFO, and the coordinated effort was underway.

The meeting lasted until after midnight and this was past the curfew hour. All the black people in Clarksdale had to be off the streets by twelve o'clock every night and we wondered if there would be trouble. The curfew system in Clarksdale seemed to me the most obnoxious insult to black people I had ever encountered, something out of slavery days. I was becoming inoculated against the horrors we had to suffer in the United States, yet new forms of insult and degradation could still leave me staggering. The curfew made me think of South Africa and I wondered what life must be like for our brothers and sisters there. The realities of our own South Africa in the United States smacked me in the face that night.

The trouble began as we were leaving town and heading for the highway that would take us back to Cleveland. Reggie Robinson and I were in the lead car. We were pulled over by a squad car and a tall sheriff's deputy came over. Reggie and I sat still, expecting trouble, not knowing exactly what to expect.

"Where you going, boy?" he said as he approached the driver's window where I was sitting.

"I'm going to Cleveland, but I'm not a boy." I could not resist trying to save my dignity at 12:45 A.M. in the dark Mississippi night.

"Are you trying to get smart with me, nigger?" he replied taking the strap off his pistol and putting his right hand on the car door handle.

I sat quietly, thinking it unwise to have an argument with a Southern sheriff while parked on the side of a deserted highway.

"Let me see your license."

I handed him my driver's license and he looked at it for several moments. As he gave it back, he said, "You get your ass out of town and don't you ever let me catch you in this town again after midnight."

I started up the car and pulled off as Reggie and I both let out a sigh of relief. We drove slowly down the highway, trying to let the other cars catch up. When we got to Cleveland, Amzie Moore informed us that one carload of people had been arrested for "vagrancy" and the other car had been stopped but was proceeding to Jackson. Someone had called him with the news.

As I talked in later years about the role of SNCC's organizers, I always said that we lived and worked on the fine line between life and death in the back roads of the South. I shall never forget one night in the spring of 1962 when a group of us were coming back from Talledega College in Alabama, where the students were mounting demonstrations against segregation in Talledega. We were stopped in a small town near the Alabama-Georgia border. The police officer seemed weird, slightly deranged, but I am sure he was just acting out his racist instincts.

I had been driving slowly through the town but he sighted us as a bunch of black people driving late at night. This was enough of a pretext to stop our car and order me out of it with his pistol drawn. He wanted to look into the trunk and ordered it opened with his gun still drawn and pointed at me. With his left hand he tried to read some of the literature I had in the back, leaflets about McDew and Zellner, who had been arrested in Baton Rouge on those criminal anarchy charges.

"You work with the AANCP?" he asked, meaning, of course, the NAACP. "I work for the Student Nonviolent Coordinating Committee," I replied, deciding to play it straight. The gun was still in his hand.

He kept reading the first few lines of the leaflet and then looked at other items in the trunk. "Go ahead," he finally said, waving the gun for me to close the trunk and keep moving.

Without knowing it or thinking about it very much at the time, such incidents had begun taking a toll on my nerves. I was learning about the pig power of the Southern police in a hurry. Another confrontation took place on that first visit of mine to the Delta—but this time I was more disgusted than frightened.

Right after the COFO meeting, SNCC opened its beachhead in Sunflower County, the home county of Senator James O. Eastland. One very hot day we canvassed in the town of Indianola—the county seat. We were organizing people to come to a mass meeting at one of the local churches and asking them to sign a petition stating that if they had been able to vote in the primary of June 5, 1962, they would have voted for Merrill W. Lindsay, the black candidate who had taken the place of Reverend Trammell. Moses felt that if enough signatures were obtained showing that people would have voted if they had been allowed, this would exert pressure on the Congress of the United States and perhaps force a challenge in Congress over the right of Jamie Whitten to sit as representative from the Delta.

There were not many people willing to sign the petitions that day, all evidencing fear. At noontime we bought bologna, bread, and mayonnaise, and made sandwiches on the streets of Indianola. By afternoon, the white power structure of the town knew we were there and were planning to have a mass meeting. They moved quickly to stop the preacher from letting us have his church or any church in town. The unavailability of churches always stood as a key barrier to our work, and once again we had to cancel our proposed meeting that day.

As we were getting ready to leave town, the chief of police—a fat, short white man—stopped us and said he wanted to talk to two of the leaders. The group decided that James Bevel and I should be the ones to go with him. Inside his office he began telling us that he didn't want "no outsiders, which are called agitators, coming into Indianola messing with my negras." I sat there almost stupefied at his ignorance and gall, to call the black people of Indianola *his* "negras."

Bevel did most of the talking for I was too angry. I had heard of police chiefs such as this one, but never had I seen or talked to one who seemed the fool he was. *His* negras. "Outsiders who are called agitators."

Before we left the Delta, we attended the first mass meeting in Ruleville, a small town in Sunflower County, where we met Mrs. Fannie Lou Hamer for the first time. At the meeting, she told the story of what had happened to her only a short time before—when she registered to vote—the story that would in the next two years be told from one end of the United States to another and even to the 1964 Democratic Convention:

I lived on the B. D. Marlowe plantation all my life. One day in early August, I heard that some young people had come to town [Ruleville] teaching people how to register to vote. I have always wanted to do something to help myself and my race, but I did not know how to go about it. So, I went to one of the meetings in Ruleville. That night, I was showed how to fill out a form for registration. The next day, August 31, 1962, I went to Indianola, Mississippi, to fill out a form at the registrar's office. I took the test. That night when I returned home [the plantation], I was told by a friend that Mr. Marlowe had been telling everybody in the field what he was going to do to me, if I didn't go back and take my name off the book.

That night, Marlowe came to the house where I was staying, and called Mr. Hamer to the door. I could hear him telling my husband what he was going to do to me if I did not withdraw my registration, so I went to the door. Marlowe asked my husband if he had told me what he had said. Marlowe saw me in the door and asked me why I went to register. I told him that I did it for myself not for him. He told me to get off the plantation and don't be seen near it again. That night I left the plantation and went to stay with Mr. and Mrs. Tucker in Ruleville.

Not long after that, Mrs. Hamer would be hauled off a bus, taken into a jail and brutally beaten by police for her efforts to help others to register. She would be beaten until even her tormentors grew tired, and that beating would combine with the effects of a childhood polio attack to leave her permanently debilitated. Yet this woman, who had picked cotton and fought to survive for so many years, didn't turn back. Instead she went on to become a worldwide symbol of black heroism, or revolutionary black womanhood, a warm and always human symbol of the power of people to struggle against hardship, adversity, terror—the living realities of the Mississippi Delta.

CHAPTER **37**

Ulcers and Carnegie Hall

STRESS OF the kind that our workers experienced in the Delta and other areas of the Deep South surely takes its toll—sooner or later. As I have watched the revolutionary process unfold among people in the United States and especially among my people, I have seen many— including myself—work under intense stress without taking the time to renew their energy with rest periods or removal from the scene of action. The day-to-day demands have been so great that people felt they could not take time out. Burning with anxiety, confused from exhaustion, these revolutionaries still refused to rest. The result has been faulty decision making, unnecessary quarrels, escapism in the form of drugs and liquor.

I have often witnessed people talking about revolution and armed struggle under the influence of alcohol or drugs, or both. They make inconsistent statements and commit erratic actions. The use of drugs and liquor is caused in some by the drive to escape the tensions of the struggle. In others, it has deeper psychological roots. I have seen persons, some of them well known, act out their neuroses on others—rationalizing those neuroses in political terms. Some have had to abandon the struggle because their personal problems and relationships created too much havoc in their minds.

Often workers can benefit from discussion with revolutionary psychiatrists—few in number that they are. There are two basic schools of psychiatry operating in the United States: one that reflects a strictly Freudian approach to human behavior and another with a societal approach. It is the latter school that can be of help to those engaged in the revolutionary process.

The importance of dealing with the problem of stress came home to me with special force in January, 1963. I fell ill then with a bleeding ulcer, resulting from the tensions of the movement, and nearly died.

At that time, SNCC had been active in protests over housing conditions in Atlanta. Mayor Ivan Allen had erected a barricade on Peyton Road, a street in that city which separates the black and white communities. It was a catastrophic blunder on Allen's part. We erected a freedom torch in front of the wall and mounted a publicity campaign that eventually helped to force its removal and to create the possibility for black people to buy homes in that area. Unfortunately, the black real estate operators in Atlanta profited greatly from our actions while refusing to help us financially. But we felt it was a worthwhile protest, for the wall on Peyton Road stood as another affront to the dignity of black people and had to be challenged.

The Atlanta Summit Leadership Conference emerged from this protest as a coalition of Atlanta's black people opposed to the mayor's wall and seeking other changes as well. I was appointed coordinator of its action program. Meanwhile, SNCC had to move from its office at 135 Auburn Avenue to 6 Raymond Street. Our new headquarters was a house with six rooms and a little heat; we had to burn wood at times. But everyone was elated by the space.

I continued to be overworked, worried about the lack of money and the survival of SNCC, and tense from the fieldwork in the Deep South. Everything piled up until one day when I was sitting in a meeting of the Atlanta Summit Leadership Conference and became nauseated, then violently ill.

I went across the street to see a doctor, who gave me some mild medicine and told me to rest. I felt faint in his office and could barely stand up. That night I rested, but the next day there was a meeting of the Action Committee which I headed and I went to it. That was a mistake, and eating some popcorn was an even bigger mistake. I began vomiting and it seemed I couldn't stop, until it was decided to put me in the hospital. My hands were white from internal bleeding.

I had a choice between segregated Grady Hospital or McLendon's— where they had one bed left, fortunately, because I probably would have refused to go to a segregated hospital. But the conditions at McLendon's were atrocious. The doctor ordered blood transfusions for me, but there was only a practical nurse on hand, who banged and banged and banged again at my arm, trying to get the needle into a vein. That Saturday night was a total nightmare.

By Monday my doctor was sure I was suffering from a bleeding ulcer, but McLendon's did not have the proper X-ray equipment to make sure. This meant a trip across town for the X-rays and I was close to death; the doctor wasn't sure I could make it without the loss of too much more blood. He gambled and won. I survived, went on a soft diet, and rested for several weeks.

While I was still in the hospital, SNCC held its first benefit concert at Carnegie Hall on February 1, 1963, as a birthday event. Organized primarily by Ella Baker, Joanne Grant, and William Mahoney, this concert marked the beginning of a support base among many black artists and writers together with liberal and progressive whites. Lorraine Hansberry, Harry and Julie Belafonte, Diahann Carroll, and Sidney Poitier were among those who consistently supported SNCC from 1963 to 1966.

To me fund raising has always been a political act. I believe that, if people give money, they are performing a political service to the movement. I also reject the popular notion that he who pays the piper calls the tune, for my experience has been that you can put radical policies up front and stick to them and still get financial help. This refusal to compromise our politics for the sake of support had been SNCC's position from its earliest days. As mentioned earlier, we resisted attempts to make us put a disclaimer in our constitution. In December, 1962, the issue arose again when SCLC was under attack because the press was publicizing the fact that a member of its staff—Jack O'Dell, one of its most competent fund raisers—allegedly had past connections with the Communist Party. SCLC eventually gave in to the witch-hunt against O'Dell and asked for his resignation. SNCC, on the other hand, adopted from the first a stand in favor of freedom of association and never waivered from it, despite much pressure. It is interesting to note that even Tom Hayden, who is today sometimes considered a spokesman for the New Left, warned us not to associate with Joanne Grant—a writer then working for the *National Guardian.* We refused to change our policy.

The benefit at Carnegie Hall represented an affirmation of our position and a victory for it—but also something broader in scope. By accepting the support of radicals and progressives, we helped to create an atmosphere that made it possible for many people scared by McCarthyism to come out of the woodwork and engage once again in active struggle. SNCC's role in helping to create a climate for radical thought and action was a most important contribution, in my opinion. It was one more way in which SNCC helped to accelerate the course of history.

The Red-baiting by liberals stood as a minor problem, of course, in comparison to the problems we faced in the Deep South. Down in Greenwood the resistance of black people and the repression of the white racist system were rising to a new climax.

CHAPTER 38

Notes from the Greenwood Jail

BULLETS CRACKED the silence of the Mississippi night and sprayed the car driven by SNCC field secretary Jimmy Travis, a native of Jackson. He slumped over, critically wounded, and fell into the lap of Bob Moses. It was February 28, 1963. White racism had struck again in Greenwood—this time with a submachine gun.

This is Jimmy Travis's own story of that night, which begins with Travis, Moses, and Randolph Blackwell (of the Voter Education Project) going from Greenville to Greenwood to attend a staff meeting of the office there:

Durirg the meeting, I noticed a white '62 Buick parked across the street from the office with three white men in it. I felt a little suspicious, so I decided to go out and investigate. I got into my car in front of the office and circled around the block and pulled up behind the white Buick to check the license plate number. Then I discovered that the car didn't have any tags. I quickly parked in front of the office again, went inside, and warned the other people in the office that there was a car floating around outside with no tags on it.

Moses felt we should break the meeting up in case there was any trouble. Block agreed and took the staff home in his car. I then got behind the wheel of my car, Moses in the middle, and Randolph on the outside by the door, and headed towards the highway for the trip back to Greenville. Then, I noticed through my rear view mirror that we were being followed by the white '62 Buick. I pulled into a gas station [Highway 82 Gulf] to fill up and with hopes of getting away from the car that was following us.

The Buick pulled up about a block on the other side of the service station. After filling up, I cut off my lights and backed out of the service station and headed up a dark street—going back towards the highway. I was starting to feel that maybe I had lost them, but as I swung the car onto the highway towards Greenville, I spotted the car again coming towards us. It slowed down, made a U-turn and started following us again.

Something inside of me made me feel as if there was trouble ahead. The marker on the highway said sixty-five miles an hour. I slowed down to thirty-five miles an hour, hoping that maybe that would force him to pass me. I tightened my grip on the wheel and held my speed. The car continued to follow until there were no other cars in sight, and then it pulled up alongside of us as if to pass. At that time, I thought they were going to throw something at us or try to run us off the road. I felt something burn my ear and I knew what they were doing. They had opened fire on us . . . it sounded like a machine gun. I yelled out that I had been shot, as I let go of the wheel. Moses grabbed hold of the wheel and brought the car to a stop on the shoulder of the highway. I was scared. I didn't know what was happening. The Buick had disappeared down the highway. Moses drove on to Itta Bena, Mississippi, to the Mississippi Vocational College, to try and get medical help for me. I had been shot in the head and another bullet had ripped through my shoulder.

There was no doctor on campus, so a doctor was called from Greenville. He came out, took one look, and said that they should take me to the hospital in Greenwood. At the hospital, the doctor cleaned the wounds and wanted to operate, but said I would have to have the bullet removed in Jackson. The bullet remained in the back of my head until the next morning when I was transferred to the University Hospital in Jackson. In Jackson, on March 1, the bullet was removed without anesthesia—my chances of pulling through were fifty-fifty.

Jimmy did not explain the reason for his not being given anesthesia.

Greenwood, Mississippi, became the focal point of SNCC activity after the shooting of Jimmy Travis. There was only one thing we thought we could do at that time, send as many people as possible to Greenwood and heighten activity. Tension mounted as field staff from across the South came to help—to say with their bodies that they were standing behind Jimmy Travis.

The town of Greenwood is located in LeFlore County, where, in 1963, 56.9 percent of the total eligible population was registered to vote—but only 9 percent of the black people. And black people comprised 64 percent of LeFlore's population (30,443 to 16,699 whites). In 1963 whites owned 310,080 acres of land in LeFlore while only 24,116 acres were owned by blacks. The median family income for blacks was $595 per year. Whites in LeFlore County completed a median of 11.9 years in school while blacks completed 4.3 years. Primarily a rural area depending on the single crop economy of cotton, LeFlore's population had been steadily declining over the years. Black people were going first to Chicago and then sometimes on to other cities in the North to earn a living and to escape the racism of the South—which was exactly what the whites wanted, as Amzie Moore had explained in telling the story of his life.

These realities of LeFlore County in general and Greenwood in particular were all on our minds one way or another as we walked the streets trying to get people to go to the courthouse. We were interested in more than registering people. Going to the courthouse was a symbol of defiance.

And the whites had recognized it as such. In October of the preceding year, the Board of Supervisor had cut off shipments of surplus food commodities into LeFlore. This was clearly an intimidation tactic, a reprisal against voter registration, for there were few whites in the county getting surplus food. That winter many blacks had gone hungry. The situation for the poorest families was grim. To combat the whites' inhuman tactic, SNCC organized the collection and shipment of food from all over the United States for distribution in Greenwood. People received food with the understanding that they would go down and register to vote, although adherence to this principle was not absolute. Registration lines at the County Courthouse grew longer every day.

At the same time, the pace of violence was also stepped up. Jimmy Travis had been machine-gunned on February 28; on March 4, the windows of Aaron Henry's drugstore in Clarksdale were smashed. Dr. Henry found the damage when he returned from speaking at a mass meeting in Greenwood.

On March 6, 1963, Samuel Block and Willie Peacock were sitting in a car in front of the SNCC office with two young ladies from Greenwood when a shotgun blast shattered the windows on the driver's side. No one was hurt.

On March 24, 1963, the SNCC office was set afire. All the office equipment was demolished. The telephone was ripped from the wall, but most of the records were saved, except for some that later appeared as news in the local Greenwood paper. Witnesses stated they saw two white men running down the alley after smoke began to pour from the building.

And then, on March 26, 1963, two shotgun blasts shattered the front door to the home of Dewey Greene, Sr., father of George and Freddie Greene, two young high school students who had been working on the voter registration campaign and who would later work full time with SNCC. No one was injured. But Freddie Greene was considered by many local people "the nicest girl in Greenwood," and people were aroused to a pitch of anger by this last incident. They felt now that they had nothing to lose. They were really ready to move.

On March 27, the day after the shooting into the Greene house, I was getting ready to leave Greenwood and return to Atlanta when I saw Bob Moses and a crowd of people standing in the yard of the church where we distributed food and clothing. Moses and I had been discussing the futility of our efforts to register people under the existing Mississippi laws. Most of them simply could not pass the test, assuming it was administered fairly (which it usually wasn't); the questions called for interpretation of complicated clauses in the state Constitution all phrased in legalese. Moses had been pushing the Justice Department to take the position that illiterate blacks had the right to register, especially since thousands of illiterate whites registered with no problem because the registrars were racists.

Standing outside the church now and seeing all those people, I had an instant conviction that they should immediately march from the church to the courthouse in order to dramatize their right to register and to protest all the violence in Greenwood. We talked to the people, urging them to go "tell the mayor" that the violence against people who want to register must stop. The people cried "amen, amen," for they were ready to move. You could feel it. And they began moving, a hundred of them. The whites of Greenwood, watching us march to the courthouse, were stunned by the long, long line of black people. The police went berserk.

SNCC field secretary and poet Charlie Cobb, then over in the town of Greenville, tells how he learned of what happened to the marchers and the events immediately following:

I, Charles Cobb, was in Greenville, amiably walking down the street in tacit peace with the system—but laying plans for the next war. A honk from a car horn, and a yelled-out "Charlie," drew me to a halt. One of the SNCC cars—the green Valiant—pulled up beside me, with SNCC field secretary Emma Bell, and SNCC field secretary George Greene in it.

"They've arrested everybody in Greenwood," Emma said, "just George and I got out the back way—all the roads are blocked. Forman, Bob, Mac, Willie, everybody's in jail. They had dogs. Bob got bit." In gasps, almost as if they'd come from Greenwood on foot, they spit out the story.

As George and Emma ran it down, about a hundred people walked from the church to City Hall; intending from there to go to the County Courthouse to attempt to register. At City Hall, they gathered, demanding to see the mayor. Naturally there was no response, except for an increasing amount of sullen-looking policemen. As the people began to move on to the courthouse, the cops began to move in on them. They [cops] lined up to prevent passage to the courthouse. The sullenness sort of became a snarl, and, appropriately, a dog was loosed on the crowd. Shortly thereafter, ten people were arrested—all on SNCC's staff.

I went back to Greenwood with Emma and George. Everybody was at Westly Chapel when we got there, in the process of preparing for the next day's issuance of food and clothes, and the mass meeting slated for that night. People were drifting in from around the state. . . . The mounting pressure was dramatizing the whole voting issue in the state, and we decided that the best way to keep the pressure (which for the most part was on the city and county) on, was to continue bringing large numbers of people to register.

The city of Greenwood was strengthening its forces also. Law officials from nearby counties were being drawn into Greenwood. Civil defense volunteers were being mobilized. Good white housewives brought food for the policemen, who were on twenty-four-hour shifts. Mayor Sampson thanked "the good colored people of Greenwood" for not listening to those "outside agitators." I'm sure the Citizens' Council met nightly.

The next morning (March 28), we began funneling people to the courthouse from about 9 A.M. on. I got down to the courthouse at about 10:00. By that time, there were approximately fifty people waiting to register. Standing on top of the courthouse steps, I got an overview of the war. At least a hundred cops in multicolored helmets were standing in front of barricades on the street adjacent to the courthouse, talking about "ain't never seen so many niggers wanted to vote" and "black sons of bitches," which of course is familiar music in your ears, probably the white folks' parallel to "We Shall Overcome."

Inside the courthouse were county officials from several counties, and at least one guy that I recognized as a marshal. All they seemed to be doing was looking, and soothing itchy fingers by rubbing them on gun barrels. I wasn't sure that this was cool, because Landy McNair and I were the only staff people down there at this point, and it occurred to me that I had left Greenville with nothing but the clothes I had on, which was a Howard sweat shirt and a pair of dungarees. The sweat shirt focused some of the attention on me as "one of them school niggers"—but I was there, and there was nothing to do but shuffle about and appear unconcerned at the hostility directed at us.

As noon drew near, Landy went out to check the transportation situation, and discovered that there was none, so the next best thing to do was to walk back in a group. News cameras whirring, we lined up in twos, in front of the courthouse, and started down the street. Young, virile, hero-type minister Reverend Tucker was leading, with shuffling, not-optimistic-about-the-whole-scene me alongside of him. We got about two blocks. This cop, with dog-on-leash, came running to the front of the line yelling, "move on, break it up, or I'll turn him loose." Other cops jumped out of a nearby squad car with those long billy sticks that seem so much longer in these situations. Someone yelled, "Get that one, he walks too casual" (me?) as the dog came sniffing around my pants leg. (I saw some picture of me fending off the dog with my clipboard in some magazine.)

The crowd was breaking up in at least four different directions. Another cop yelled, "Get that nigger preacher," while I was calming a lady down who had been evicted from a store she had sought refuge in. Dog jaws chomped down on Reverend Tucker's ankle. Doc Henry was passing by in his car, and Reverend Tucker was put in there and carried to a doctor. By this time, I was at the tail end of the group (now about twenty people) and we headed towards the office, escorted by the police, or whoever those folks were wearing helmets (at least one was an Ole Miss student at home for spring break).

Back at the church, John O'Neal, John Churchville, and Don Harris, all SNCC workers, had come in from southwest Georgia. We nibbled sandwiches, discovered that there had been no arrests, and that Reverend Tucker was all right, except for a couple of holes in his ankle.

With the events of the morning of the twenty-eighth, the issues in Greenwood broadened beyond voter registration and became more basic. The issue now was, Did people have a right to walk the streets which they had paid for, with whomever they please, as long as they are orderly and obey all traffic laws? The city's answer was, Not if you're a nigger! There was a very direct link between this issue and voter registration, because for years attempting to register to vote for Negroes meant preparing alone to suffer physical assault while making the attempt, economic reprisals after the attempt, and sometimes death. To go with friends and neighbors made the attempt less frightening and reduced the chances of physical assault at the courthouse, since cowards don't like to openly attack numbers. It also reduced the chance of economic reprisal, since the firing of one hundred Negro maids would put the good white housewives of Greenwood in a bind ('tis a grim life for Miss Ann without Mary, Sally, or Sam).

The next day, another hundred people lined up and started down to the courthouse and were again stopped by the police. Charlie Cobb reported that he could hear the dogs barking, but off in the distance—they were never used again because of the tremendous amount of unfavorable publicity about their use the previous day. It was the first time in recent history that dogs had been used against black people. I had been lucky enough to get some photographs of the dogs before they arrested me, and we were lucky again when SNCC field secretary Charles McLaurin managed to get my camera away from a cop after a short tussle, and escape with it.

Knowing that those photographs—later to be seen around the world—would get into the right hands was one of the biggest helps to my morale in jail. There were eight of us in there, for "disorderly conduct"; two of those arrested had been released. We eight had decided to go jail-no-bail, since there was absolutely no basis for the arrest. We hoped this would force the Justice Department to file a suit for our release. In Indianola the city had finally agreed to drop the cases against some SNCC workers as the result of JD pressure—but there we had paid bail, which we never got back. This time we would stay in jail.

Facing the possibility of a very long stretch behind bars, I kept a sort of diary—a record I called "Some Random Notes from the LeFlore County Jail":

April 2, 1963: We have been in jail one week today. Our morale is good, although there are serious undertones of a desire to be free among some members of the group. Now and then, the jokes of one or two turn to the outside. John Doar and the Justice Department received some sharp but still humorous comments from some of the fellows. They actually believed the Justice Department would have had them out by last Monday. When we received news that the temporary injunction had been denied, Lafayette Surney and Charles McLaurin, in particular, were somewhat disappointed. Some of us tried to explain that we must prepare ourselves psychologically to spend six months in this jail.

The cell in which we are being held is not so bad so far as American prisons go. (The entire penal system needs reforming.) We are eight in a cell with six bunks. We have two mattresses on the floor. There is an open shower, a sink, a stool. It took us two days to get a broom and five days to get some salt for our food. The inner cell in which we are "contained" is approximately 15′ x 12′. Not much room is there?

You see, we were at first put in a very large cell. Later we discovered that one of the inmates had T.B. We raised a mild storm. The jailer, Boll Weevil Stiles, tried to assure me that the fellow did not have T.B. He had been a victim of the disease at one time, but the case was supposedly arrested. On the other hand, our fellow prisoner maintained that he was taking fifteen pills a day and had not had one in 30 days. You may imagine how we felt. . . . Saturday night, I grasped the chance to explain to the Sheriff about the T.B. case. He was alarmed and immediately put us into our present cell.

People outside send us food. When we were in the city jail, we got food twice a day. Here we received a great deal Sunday, enough to last us till today. We are counting on someone to replenish our supply. However, Dr. Garner—a young black woman doctor—has been to see me about my ulcer three times since I have been in the county jail. Each time she brings some food which I share with the fellows. It is really not for me. . . . I am really not suffering due to my ulcers, but my sickness helps the group—through the visits of the doctor, a contact with the outside.

We are also improving our minds. We have been allowed to keep our books and we have sufficient cigarettes. I even have my pipe and some tobacco. Personally, I have tried to organize our lives. Do you expect anything else of me? We have occasional classes. Moses gave us an excellent math lecture the other day. I gave one lesson in writing and English. Guyot has delivered several in biology. We are always having discussions. Sometimes one of us will read a passage from a book and then we will discuss the meaning of it. We have had several stimulating conversations on Thoreau's essay on Civil Disobedience and Nkrumah's thoughts on Positive Action.

As I write this, it is quiet in the cell. Moses is to my right holding a book in his hand looking out the window. He is squatting on the lower bunk. He has a view that looks upon the parking lot of the county court building. It is very warm outside and a beautiful tree with swaying, green branches sends in waves of fresh air.

Peacock is reading a novel, *Rizpah*. . . .

Surney has been the sleeping bug of the bunch. He snores so loudly that it is a common source of laughter.

Guyot reads consistently and always gives us some well-spoken gem. James Jones is the quiet one in the bunch.

Around eleven o'clock we usually turn out the one large light in the middle of the room. We do not have sheets or blankets. We sleep in our underclothes. I suppose if it got cold, we would put on our clothes.

In the morning when we get up we have grits, biscuits, and a piece of salt pork for breakfast. Then we sweep the cell. For the last two days Bob, Guyot and I have swept the cell and scrubbed it on our hands and knees. During the morning we usually have discussions, showers, play chess, talk and wait for beans or peas and cornbread which arrives around two o'clock. We do not have any more meals from the county until next morning.

My personal opinion as to the significance of our staying in jail follows: I am convinced that all the people connected with SNCC are busily engaged in protesting our unjust imprisonment. This is as it should be. I am also convinced that others sympathetic to the cause of Freedom are also alarmed at this travesty of justice. Only our bodies are confined to this cell. Our minds are free to think what we wish and we know our stay here will also pass away. Our imprisonment serves to dramatize to the nation and to the world that the black man does not even have the right to *try* to be an American citizen in some parts of our so-called democracy. Our jail-without-bail may also serve to remind others in the movement of the need for some of us to stay in jail to dramatize the situation.

On a local and state level it is important that we stay in jail, for people are remembered more by what they do than by what they say. We have been telling Mississippians that we must prepare to die. We have encouraged them to accept our beliefs. Thus it follows that we must lead by example rather than by words.

Moreover, many acts of violence have been committed in Greenwood. The people are not afraid, but perhaps when they see our spirit and determination, they will have more courage. Then, too, the government must assume its responsibility for our release. If the Civil Rights Act of 1960 is ever to mean anything, then those arrested in connection with voter registration activities must be released by the efforts of the U.S. Government. . . .

Perhaps more important than these social and political reasons is the personal significance that our imprisonment has for us. I have not yet asked each person for his personal reaction. As for myself, I am glad to make a witness for a cause in which I believe. I am glad for the chance to meditate, to think of many things, and to see the world continue as I sit here. All of us are determined that once we are out we will walk to the courthouse with some more people.

I am also happy to know that the central office is still functioning. You know, it is my personal belief that my presence there is not really significant anymore. I believe I can make a better contribution traveling from one area to another. . . .

Later: We sing of course. We are singing now. We love "We'll never turn back." We have added a new verse:

> We have served our time in jail,
> With no money to go our bail.

We place this as second stanza. Every night when the lights are out we sing this song. It is beautiful and it symbolizes our state—the entire song.

April 3, 1963: It is rather early, seven sounds by the village clock. All is quiet in our cell except the sound of slow running water in the shower. Moses is taking one. I have just finished one—Guyot is reading. All the rest are sleeping. Outside the cell I can hear cars winding up for the day's work.

We are trying to work out a schedule. Peacock suggested last night that our time might be better spent if we had a schedule. At the same time, Guyot was suggesting that if ever a dispute arose, two people should take one side, two the other and the remaining four should decide. Consequently the question of a schedule was put before the floor. Surney & Smith objected to the schedule. Forman, McLaurin and Guyot favored. All arguments were presented as if we were speaking before a court. James Jones just consented to act as judge. Then he resigned and Peacock accepted the judgeship.

Smith presented some *reductio ad absurdum* arguments which were easily shattered. Finally the judge ruled in favor of the schedule. By this time Lafayette was sleeping. The next incident around which there was disagreement was the light bulb. There is one light bulb in the middle of the room. Each night it seems that someone has objections to it's being turned out. Usually a compromise is worked out.

Interestingly, people are quoting Thoreau—"Government is best which governs least"—and then applying it to the cell. There are many divergent wills operating in this cell; a few people seek to have their own way at all times and seldom, if ever, indicate a willingness to understand others and give a little.

A picture of this cell cannot be obtained unless it is at least indicated that there are many conversations about girls. Some seem to be proud of certain "conquests." Moses and I do not partcipate in these discussions. When I say something, it is usually in an attempt to direct thoughts away from the outside and to the inside. Frankly, I seldom like what is being said, and then I think morale can be lowered by such discussions. . . .

John Doar paid us a visit this morning. . . . Sather and Martin are here collecting evidence for the Justice Department. Sather was at the hearing they held on Thursday. Thursday evening the Department called the city officials and asked them to release us. It told them the Department would sue for our release. Doar said they learned Friday evening that we had been convicted. He arrived here Saturday morning at two and filed the request for a temporary order restraining the city from making arrests like ours.

Judge Clayton did not hear their motion Saturday but did hear it Monday. He made a statement from the bench saying that he deplored violence and felt that all people should have the right to vote on the same basis. On the other hand, he felt that issuing an injunction without a chance to hear from the city would be unfair. . . . Clayton is known to run a strict courtroom. We were also asked to be clean in the courtroom. Therefore we are sending for some more clothes, for we are in bad shape.

12:30: Sather of the Justice Department interviewed me about the events leading to our arrest. While we were talking, I heard some singing on the outside and our fellows yelling. Later we found out that 19 more people had been arrested. We sang and sang.

There are five women in the cell next door. One old woman is now praying as the old folks pray in the South. Her voice has a musical quality as she appeals and prays to God. She is praying for freedom in Greenwood. She is praying for mercy on Greenwood. She is praying for forgiveness in Greenwood. "Please," she cries, "go into the hospital, hold the church of God, you told us to love one another, there does not seem to be any love in this, look this town over, Jesus, and do something about the condition. Whatsoever a man soweth, that also shall he reap!" She prays that we might have our equal rights.

Now there is singing:

> I will let Chief Larry know, before I go,
> I'll have my civil rights—
> Which side are you on, boy?
> Which side are you on, my Lawdie,
> Which side are you on, boy?
> Which side are you on?

Song: "You better leave segregation alone"
Song: "Freedom is coming, and it won't be long"

6:07 P.M. April 3, 1963. We are now in the Washington County Jail. We have been transferred so that we might testify in the injunction hearing tomorrow morning.

We were brought from LeFlore County by Federal marshals. When we came down from our cell, we saw these Federal marshals with handcuffs and chains.

Each person had a chain placed around him and was handcuffed to the chain. Serious protests were made about this treatment. Cynical remarks about the powerful Federal government were uttered. It was somewhat ironic because upstairs we were all depending upon the Federal government.

> Song: "Well, I stayed in jail and thought I'd change
> "Here comes the Marshalls and put me in chains."

9:20 A.M. We have been really singing the last 30 minutes. . . . Mr. Carter brought some milk, donuts, cottage cheese to the cell. Moses asked him to bring some more for the prisoners. He did.

Moses is heading the songs now. He is in rare form, he is standing behind the bars singing alone, talking about freedom, chanting "Do you want your freedom, are you ready to go to jail?" There is a ready-made audience. Most of the prisoners are young people waiting for court. There is a man who came here in January and he has to wait until June.

The prisoners are now requesting that we sing songs. Our plan has worked: we wanted to get them in the freedom mood. One wonders what the preachers are doing today. They are not in the Mississippi struggle, nor do they visit the jails.

April 4, 1963, 8:30 A.M. We have been up for two hours and we are all dressed up in our best clothes, which is not to say very much for most of them are borrowed clothes and hand-me-downs. Clothes in the movement are not very important. We often interchange from necessity. Most of the people working now complain that they have lost a few items in the movement. Peacock says he came into the movement with six pairs of shorts, now he has one. James Jones says that if Jessie Harris came up here now and demanded his clothes back, he would be naked. . . .

Moses looks like he's ready for Commencement at Hamilton.

We sang this morning at the request of the prisoners. Many of them joined us. . . . We had a good breakfast—Rice, butter, jelly, light bread, eggs, gravy, coffee and half an orange. Compared to the diet of the Greenwood jail, it was a sumptuous meal. . . . We never had a cup of coffee during the entire week we spent there. I shall speak to the Sheriff about this. The type of food one gets is indeed a morale booster. . . .

11:45 A.M. We are Free!

We had been released from jail on the basis of what could be called a deal between the Justice Department and Greenwood officials. The JD withdrew its request for a temporary restraining order that would enjoin intimidation of voters together with further detention and prosecution of the jailed group. Greenwood officials, in turn, released us. The JD did not, however, drop its move for a permanent injunction.

When we got back to Greenwood, there seemed to be a state of indecision among people involved in the protest action. Dick Gregory, who had come to Greenwood several days earlier to support us and had been pushed around like us by the police, wanted to march downtown with a group of people. His plan was to get his wife, who was there with him but played an anonymous role, arrested by the police and then let the press know that she was the wife of a famous comedian. Wiley Branton was running around trying to work out some compromise with the power structure. Everyone else seemed to have been waiting for us to make some decision.

It was finally decided to have people go down to the courthouse, but in cars. Gregory told me in the car, heading downtown, that the police commissioner had discussed with him the possibility of our using buses. I realized then that white Greenwood was on the verge of making some concessions.

Later that day, Police Chief Hammond appeared at the courthouse and I suggested that he provide us with a bus to get the people back home again, since he had given us a bus a week ago to go to jail. Lo and behold, a very short time afterward a bus appeared and started moving our way. Newsmen and photographers gathered around as we piled on board and sang all the way home, for we knew that it was our unrelenting pressure —the constant presence of blacks marching through the streets—that had won this small but symbolic victory. We wanted the bus, and by then the police wanted us to have a bus, so that our interests coincided—but only because they knew we weren't going to be turned around.

That night there was a mass meeting at which Dick Gregory spoke. I also talked, about our experiences in jail, about the oppression of black people in the South, about the Citizens' Council, about the meaning of fighting for the vote. At one point, I said:

In Leflore County, the Negro has the majority of the population. There is no reason why we should not have a black man for sheriff. There is no reason why we should not have a black mayor, a black chief of police, and black city commissioners. I'm telling you why they don't want us to register to vote. It's not because they hate us. My God, our mothers have raised most of 'em—how could they hate us? They simply do not want us to control the mechanisms of this government. That's what they don't want.

Let's not kid ourselves, brothers. It's not attitudes, it's that political power. In Africa, they're saying today: seek ye first the political kingdom and all else shall be added unto you. And that's what we have got to do!

The key word in those comments was *power*—but it would be some years before all of SNCC was ready to articulate its goals in those terms.

I left Greenwood and hurried back to Atlanta for a full meeting of the SNCC staff which took place Easter weekend, from April 12 to 14, 1963, at Gammon Theological Seminary. Over 350 students from across the South attended, and the staff of SNCC had grown to 60 people. Dick Gregory was one of the featured guest speakers at the meeting. Bob Moses gave a brilliant summary of the Greenwood situation, comparing and contrasting it with McComb, and indicating some broad outlines of how voter registration activity should continue in Mississippi.

He had arrived late, Bob explained, because the day before about sixty workers and supporters had left Greenwood. There had long been a great fear in the local black people that everybody would jump up and walk out on them at some point—a fear strongly encouraged by the white racists. But the transition had been carried out very smoothly: people were continuing with voter registration and had also started on a project of creating "freedom gardens" with seed distributed to the people by SNCC and local workers. The sixty people who departed had left no visible hole.

Moses continued with his analysis of the Greenwood situation:

We have at least five forces working in Greenwood. You have the civil rights organizations that are working on this voting program and you have the Justice Department. You have the local Negro community, the local white community, and then you have the state-wide set-up of the Citizens' Council and the political machinery. What is going on essentially is that you are fighting psychologically for the minds of the Negro people. They are being bombarded on the one hand by the local white community and the state political machinery, and on the other hand by the civil rights organizations and by the work of the Justice Department and the local F.B.I., such as that is.

At this point, it is not clear which way they are going to go. It's not clear whether the mass of the Negroes are going to make that decision which might jeopardize their jobs and mean considerable amount of discomfort to their families and go down to register. Or rather will we get just a small percentage. Now, we have had over five to six hundred people going down, and for us that's a big number—that's a big breakthrough. But there are thirteen thousand Negroes of voting age in LeFlore County. And what you need is not five hundred but five thousand going down, and whether we will reach that kind of figure depends to a large extent on what takes place in the next few weeks.

A lot of people are asking, "what did you win, and exactly what happened" in Greenwood. . . . The people who have been going down to register to vote have been primarily people who are very black and very poor. The people come off the plantation areas, who have not this year had enough food for their families . . . came to the church when Sam and Willie began distributing food and were encouraged to go down and register. They went down in the face of their fears because they were starving. That's the basic motivation of hunger. And out of this drive came the number of people going down to register. To us it was a breakthrough when you got over a hundred people in one day trying to vote at the courthouse—at any courthouse in Mississippi.

Now most of these people cannot read and write, and it forced us to make another policy decision. Our position, which we outlined to the Justice Department and which we are psychologically trying to sell to the Negro community . . . is that: 1) white people who are illiterate do vote in almost every county in Mississippi; 2) most of these Negroes have not had the opportunity to get a decent education, so they have been denied equal protection under the laws and . . . the strenuous literacy test should not apply to them; 3) the country owes them either the right to vote as a literate or the right to learn how to read and write *now*. It cannot take the position that the illiterate cannot vote and still have these people, who have been denied an education and who express a desire to read and write, left illiterate; 4) we feel that they know the people who govern their daily lives—not only do they know them, in all probability they knew their papas and mamas—so they know the people who are running for office and whether this guy is a good guy or going to beat them over the head.

This means that around the country pressure needs to be put on the Justice Department for them to incorporate these kinds of demands in their current suit in Mississippi. At this point, at least, what they are fighting for is a simple literacy test and the right of people who are well-educated to be able to go down and register to vote. But this would comprise maybe 10% of the Negroes in Mississippi. . . .

What has happened in the meantime is that we have gained a degree of freedom, because every day at the courthouse now we have people stationed there who not only watch the people who come in and out but teach the people how to register. It's not very many places in Mississippi where you can actually stay around the courthouse all day long and . . . I don't know of any where you can actually stay in there and teach people. The city has agreed to supply bus transportation. . . .

Actually, Greenwood serves as the center for around five different counties —LeFlore, Holmes, Carroll, Tallahatchie, Sunflower and part of Humphrey. And what we hope will happen is that we will get a drive in all these counties with Greenwood as a focus. And if you do that, then that will crack the heart of the Delta. People in Holmes County have been going down to register as of this week . . . the first time anybody can remember that people in Holmes County have been down to try to register. . . .

The final thing, I think, that happens is that you get young people to get out and work. The whole question of the possibility of change in Mississippi depends upon finding the agents to produce that change. Every place in which we have worked in Mississippi, we picked up young people and began to build a nucleus of people who were spreading out across the state to work. . . .

You know, there has been little follow-up in McComb and there has been a great deal of criticism about what took place. One thing, surely, we have to go back into McComb. Secondly, three young people from McComb have been working with us full time. In that sense I feel we haven't left McComb because certainly the things they have learned in the meantime will be taken back with them. The other thing about the McComb situation which contrasts with the Greenwood and Delta situation is that McComb was isolated where Greenwood essentially is not. People from Clarksdale, Ruleville, Tallahatchie, Cleveland have been continually moving in and out of Greenwood in leadership capacity. . . . You didn't have that in McComb, there were no other cities around there.

To my mind, it's still not clear that we haven't won any victories and it's still not clear if there will be a victory. It's still not clear to my mind, even on the voting issue, that Negroes will gain the vote rapidly enough. The squeeze is always the automation of the cotton crops, the inability of the Negro with his poor education to adapt to new technology, and the unwillingness of the white people to train them, and the programs of the Citizens' Council to move them out [of the state]. And if these programs are successful, and if they are moved out before gaining the right to vote and you lose the population balance which you have now, then I think we will have lost.

The country is in effect asking all white people in the Delta to do something which they don't ask of any white people any place. . . . And that is to allow Negroes to vote in an area where they are educationally inferior but yet outnumber the white people and hence constitute a serious political threat. Because in every other area in the country, the Negro votes are ghettoized, the Negroes elect their leaders but they don't elect leaders to preside over what we could call a numerically inferior but educationally superior white elite. I don't for one minute think that the country is in a position or is willing to push this down the throats of white people in the Delta, and it will have to be pushed down their throats because they are determined not to have it done.

And really the issue is: not only do you gain the right to vote, but you begin to change all of the other educational values at the same time so that you are able to present a different kind of situation. . . . I think that we are in danger of fighting for some things which some of the black bourgeoisie will reap the benefit of.

We are trying to get workers and train them, and most of them are out of high school or college and they need to go back, or we think they need to go back. In the meantime, it's hard to get other people and train them in time so that they can carry on the work. That is the big dilemma. . . . Perhaps one way out would be to provide for the workers a mass education program while they are working. Because it doesn't seem to me that what's required is a college degree, even though this is the accepted union card of status symbol. What's needed are people who can get up and talk or analyze and verbalize and articulate the problems that the Negro faces and a solution they envision to these problems. Now if that person doesn't have the college degree and still can do this, he will do the job and win the support of the masses of Negroes.

The question of on-the-job education was becoming an important one, with SNCC's staff having grown to sixty people—some of them had college degrees while others had completed as little as the fifth grade. At that staff meeting, however, there were few new programs initiated and most decisions involved the continuation or extension of existing activity. The most important thing about the meeting to my mind was its spirit.

SNCC had struggled merely to exist in the early days of political activity—now its survival was no longer in question. The "Freedom Singers," led by Bernice Johnson Reagan, were singing the tales of the student movement across the country and helping to raise necessary funds. Bill Mahoney was working hard in the New York office, opened at last, to raise funds and create political support. But we had achieved more than a certain sense of organizational security. The meeting was permeated by an intense comradeship, born out of sacrifice and suffering and a commitment to the future, and out of knowledge that we were indeed challenging the political structure of the country, and out of a feeling that our basic strength rested in the energy, love, and warmth of the group. The band of sisters and brothers, in a circle of trust, felt complete at last.

CHAPTER 39

Freedom Walk

THE FIRST day of May is celebrated in many countries around the world as Workers' Day. SNCC celebrated May 1, 1963, together with CORE by beginning a Walk from Chattanooga, Tennessee, to Jackson, Mississippi, to protest the murder of William Moore. A white postal employee who was a native of Mississippi but then working in Baltimore, Moore had gone on a "Freedom Walk" to present a letter to Mississippi governor Ross Barnett urging decent treatment for all citizens. Just before leaving, he had taken a letter to the White House addressed to John F. Kennedy, which explained his purpose:

I am not making this walk to demonstrate either federal rights or state rights but individual rights. I am doing it . . . for the South and hopefully to illustrate that the most basic of freedoms—of peaceful protest—is not altogether extinguished down there.

Moore's life was extinguished by a .22 bullet from an unknown assailant near Gadsen, Alabama. I talked to his widow, who felt that he would have wanted the Walk to continue. SNCC felt that the Walk must be continued, for the best weapon against death is always to show an absence of fear—and to carry on where the slain one has fallen. "When you kill one person, you got to deal with all the rest"—that was the message we wanted to put across. So we had an emergency meeting in Norfolk, Virginia, to iron out details and finally CORE decided that it, too, wanted to participate. A joint march was planned and ten people started walking on May 1.

Through Tennessee and Georgia there was no trouble, but the hecklers became many and more intense as the ten marchers approached the Alabama state line. The night before crossing was spent in Rome, Georgia, in a black church—the usual sleeping place. Tension had mounted the next day, for the state of Alabama had said it would not allow the Freedom Walkers to walk in Alabama. It would deny them the use of the highway.

My function on the Freedom Walk was mainly logistical—I helped transport food, water, and messages in my car. I had no trouble up to that point. As the line of Freedom Walkers approached Alabama, Landy

McNair and I decided to cross the state line ahead of the marchers to see what would happen. Georgia and Alabama state troopers lined the highway, and nearly five thousand yelling and heckling racist whites had turned out to molest the Freedom Walkers.

We drove on, slowly. Over the Alabama state line, we were stopped.

"Are y'all a part of that group?" one burly state trooper asked. The troopers were under the direction of famous Al Lingo.

"What group are you talking about?" I replied.

"Those Freedom Walkers."

"No, we're not a part of the Freedom Walkers," I said, feeling that we might escape arrest this time . . . maybe.

"Well, do you know any of them?" another state trooper came up shouting.

"Yes, we do," Landy replied.

"Don't you be saying 'yes' to me. You say 'yes, sir,' to me!" blared the trooper.

At this moment, a man in plainclothes ran up to the car and said, "Say, this is the car that has been helping them all day, bringing food and water.

"O.K. Get out. You're under arrest."

As we got out of the car and into a state trooper's car, I could only think of Len Holt's dictum, "You got no rights. Don't look for logic. You got no rights. You're black and you ain't got no rights."

I had my camera and I knew that it would be taken from me, so inside the police car I began taking out the film. I could see the Freedom Walkers approaching the state line. They were told they could not enter the state of Alabama. They were asked to disperse. They refused and stood there in a single line, holding their signs in front of them, the crowd yelling "Kill 'em!"

The troopers moved in to arrest them and some went limp, forcing the police to carry them to the highway patrol cars, but not before they were stomped and kicked in the head.

We were all taken to the Fort Paine jail, a modern jail located in Eutaw County. Robert Zellner and another white refused to cooperate with the jailers. They were dragged upstairs and put into cells by the guards. From the time I was arrested, and later while sitting in the interrogation room of the jail, I was busy tearing up pieces of paper I had on my person. I didn't want the pigs to have any extra information. I sat there, certain that they were going to take my camera—I'd never heard of a jail where they allowed you to keep your camera. But as I watched them lead other prisoners upstairs without taking their wallets and other personal items, a strange feeling crept over me that I might be allowed to keep the camera. It was too good to believe and I began to curse myself for not having any more film. Sure enough, I was allowed to take my camera upstairs to the cell and to keep my money, my wallet, everything I had on me, although there was a search for weapons. I could hardly believe it.

Before being led off to a cell, I asked to see a doctor about my ulcer problem—playing it up for the same reason that I had done so in the Greenwood jail. Also, I did think I should watch my stomach closely. I was taken to a doctor in Fort Paine, who gave me a thorough examination and some medicine. When I mentioned a hemorrhoid problem also, he checked that too. "Someone in your condition," he said at the end, "ought to stay in one place, stop agitating and get yourself well."

I didn't heed his advice, nor did I plan to.

The jail had such a relaxed atmosphere that the next day, Saturday, I decided to gamble on how I could get a roll of film from my car, which was parked outside, into the jail. I asked the jailer if I could go to my car and get a change of pants and other clothes from my suitcase. He consented.

When I got out to my car I noticed that a thorough search of it had been made. The back seat was pulled out. Instead of trying to get just one roll of film, I decided to bring my whole attaché case into the jail. And so I was allowed to take an entire bag of film inside. I was rather nervous, for this was hard to believe. A camera inside the jail with complete freedom to take pictures! The idea of being able to make this kind of historical record was tremendously exciting. I must have shot five rolls of film and I even had someone take a picture of me holding the bars of a cell window. (This picture was later published in *The Movement*, a book of photographs with text by Lorraine Hansberry.)

That Saturday evening it was decided by the group that I should get out of jail. I was not a Freedom Walker and I had been arrested on a fluke even by Southern standards of no-justice-at-all. (Later that summer, Landy McNair and I were acquitted—my first and only acquittal in many arrests.) The Freedom Walkers stayed in jail for thirty days and got tied up legally waiting for an injunction. With the momentum of the Walk lost, and the intense heat of summer settling in, it was decided to discontinue it.

As soon as Landy and I got out of jail, we drove to Birmingham where the massive demonstrations which shook the world were under way. We went to help.

CHAPTER **40**

Betrayal in Birmingham

A GROUP of us from SNCC had been to Birmingham earlier that year, in April of 1963, on the way from Greenwood to Atlanta. Dr. Martin Luther King and SCLC had just staked out Birmingham as the city where they would try to mount marches against segregation—a tactic learned from the people of Albany. But things were going slowly at that point and Dr. King was finding it difficult to mobilize people to follow him to jail.

I had spoken at a mass meeting in Birmingham for SCLC, and talked about the struggle in Greenwood and how the dogs had been brought out. At the meeting the call was made for people willing to march downtown and get arrested as Dr. King and Ralph Abernathy had recently been arrested. Some twenty people stood up and began walking downtown from the church—the Sixteenth Street Baptist Church, where six young girls would be bombed to death later that year.

It was a hot Sunday afternoon in Birmingham and many black people were in the park across the street from the church. As the group of twenty walked past the people, who were by now standing and watching them, police dogs appeared on the scene. The Birmingham police had brought out the dogs.

The dogs snapped at people, including those who were just bystanders, and many started to run. I yelled over and over, "Don't run, don't run, back away slowly!" As I saw the first dog in Birmingham actually jump on the first black man, I thought of the high price we were paying in this long struggle. But the man wrestled with the dog. He would fall to the ground and then get up, wrestling with the dog once more. He was winning the fight with the dog and the black people were yelling for him to get the dog, "get him, get him, get him!" Then the black man reached into his pocket and the police put two more dogs upon him. He came out with a knife and started swinging at the dogs. The police themselves moved in, got him to the ground and started kicking him. It was a horrible sight but it was only the beginning of the brutality that would make Bull Connor a household word in the United States. As chief of police in Birmingham, he didn't understand that brutality often brings forth more demonstrations. Repression breeds resistance.

When I returned to the Gadsden Motel, the headquarters for SCLC staff in Birmingham, Dorothy Cotton and Wyatt Walker were jumping up and down, elated. They said over and over again, "We've got a movement. We've got a movement. We had some police brutality. They brought out the dogs. They brought out the dogs. We've got a movement!" It was a disgusting moment to me, for it seemed very cold, cruel, and calculating to be happy about police brutality coming down on innocent people, bystanders, no matter what purpose it served.

The demonstrations did escalate in Birmingham. And the students of Birmingham—as in other cities in '63—also escalated in their militancy. They were the backbone of the demonstrations.

When Landy McNair and I arrived in Birmingham after our release from the Fort Payne jail, we found that William Porter, a SNCC organizer, was heavily involved with the students. The organizing committee of the students wanted to affiliate openly with SNCC. This created a delicate problem, for I knew of the sensitivity of Dr. King and especially of Fred Shuttlesworth, who considered himself the leader in Birmingham at that point. To allow the students to affiliate publicly with SNCC would cause serious arguments with SCLC and I felt we were not ready for that fight. I suggested that we wait and continue to operate as if SCLC was calling the shots in Birmingham. But we agreed that we should try to make the demonstrations as militant as we could. Willie Ricks had come to town from Chattanooga, with the reputation of being an excellent student organizer, and we all went to work together.

On Sunday, May 5, 1963, about three thousand people left from a church to go pray across from a police station where there was a group in jail. Just as the lines began to emerge from under a bridge, the police, with five fire trucks and hoses, stopped the demonstrators. Someone yelled, "Kneel down." William Porter kneeled on a bank and began to pray. While the people kneeled, a local minister walked out into the street to talk to the police officer in charge. The minister explained the purpose of the demonstrators and they were waved on through. The minister told me afterward that the police officer had given orders to the firemen to turn the hoses on the people but the all-white firemen had "frozen," according to the minister—they just couldn't do it.

Many people called it a victory, the ability to go to a public park across from a police station and pray. I had some doubts about that, and my doubts about the whole operation began to increase. The next day Dick Gregory, Ella Baker, and attorney Len Holt arrived in town. Gregory became the first of nine hundred people to get arrested that Monday. Theoretically, people were supposed to march from the church on Sixteenth Street to the downtown section of Birmingham. But the police were arresting them as they walked only one block from the church. I did not see much strategy in people walking from the church and into waiting police vans.

That Monday evening, it started to rain. Len Holt and I went to see some of the arrested students who had been put into a compound. They were standing out in the rain, huddled under what few coats were available. We talked to the police, insisting that they move the students indoors. They said they would, but we had our doubts. Later that night, it was reported that the students were still out in the cold. I became very angry and worried, and went to one of the mass meetings where Reverend Billips was presiding.

I asked for the microphone and described the conditions under which the children were in jail, emphasizing the rain and cold and the need for blankets. Many parents were ready to go home and get blankets and take them to the jail, but Reverend Billips got up and said they should not do that. We should wait to hear from Dr. King and see what he had to say. I was furious, for Dr. King was at a mass meeting where it was warm and the students were out in the cold and rain. I insisted that we go see Dr. King that minute.

Reverend Billips and I found him and we began to talk, sitting to one side of the platform while someone was speaking up front. I explained to Dr. King the conditions in the jail and the need for blankets. In my mind, I was also thinking that if the parents saw their children out in the cold they would become more indignant against the police and thereby more involved. Dr. King said it would be unwise to tell the parents about the conditions in the jail under which their children were suffering. Other parents, he said, would hear about it and wouldn't let their children demonstrate the next day and he felt we needed all we could get.

"What would you do if your daughter or son was in jail?" I asked. The insensitivity to the conditions of the troops on the part of Dr. King deeply disturbed me. I exchanged some hot words with him and finally he said he would go and see the conditions in the jail himself.

Reverend Billips, James Bevel, Dr. King, and I drove to the compound. Students were still standing outside in the cold, wet night. Bevel argued furiously with Bull Connor, who had come to the compound, about the situation. Dr. King said that he was going to call Burke Marshall and talk to him about this situation. In one last effort, I tried to point out to him that constant calls to the Justice Department lessened the militancy of the people. It would be far better to have parents bring blankets. In any case, no matter what Marshall said, there could be no absolute assurance that the students would be placed inside a shelter. But Dr. King called Burke Marshall anyway, and then went back to the mass meeting. King told the people that Marshall had assured him the students would be housed and fed. Both Bevel and Reverend Billips were dissatisfied with this course of action and also felt that parents should take blankets to the students standing out in the cold, wet night.

On Tuesday Dorothy Cotton and I were put in charge of demonstrations. We decided to call our demonstrations "Operation Confusion." I did not see any point in people marching straight into the vans. If the goal of the demonstrations was to get downtown and create some disturbance by sitting-in, then our tactics should maximize our ability to get there. So we split the people up into about fifteen groups and sent them all downtown by different routes. Some headed for the bus station, others to the post office. And we sent a small decoy group straight down the usual street of the marches, to fool the police.

It worked. People got downtown while the police were thrown into confusion. In one incident, a group of students came up to a cop standing on the corner near the Sixteenth Street Baptist Church. "We want to go to jail," they told him. "Jail's that way," the cop answered. The group broke into a run across the park, yelling "We're going to jail!" The mass of black humanity that had been standing around in the park started after them, also running, and within a few minutes a great sea of people was surging downtown. It was a beautiful fluke.

Downtown Willie Ricks and I placed ourselves at the front of a group and began weaving people in and out of stores and around corners. People were singing, picketing, sitting-in. No arrests occurred; the police had been taken completely by surprise. We stayed downtown for over thirty minutes and then started bringing people back to the Sixteenth Street Church. By this time, Bull Connor had brought out a tank and the police were sealing off the streets.

At the church, I tried to convince Andy Young of SCLC and Bevel that this was the time to negotiate. They had been trying to get a meeting with officials of the city. Here they had a power situation in their hands. The church was full of people who had successfully invaded the downtown section of Birmingham.

Reverend Shuttlesworth appeared on the scene. He had already told me that morning that he did not like the idea of my coming to Birmingham and organizing "a SNCC chapter." He would not hear of it. Because of his attitude, I didn't try to convince him of the merit of trying to negotiate at that moment. He then gave a short speech to the people, saying that they should get ready to go back downtown en masse. I tried to point out to him that the police were setting up barricades and fire trucks, that it would be impossible to get people back downtown in a huge mass. And, I asked him, "Who's going to lead them? You can't just send out a mass of people at this stage, just say 'Run on back downtown.'" He said that Martin had sent the word, that Martin said the students had shown how to get downtown—just go. They could do it again.

I knew the reality of what had happened that morning, that the march downtown had been planned in the beginning and then become largely spontaneous. In many ways its success was due to flukes. The police would not be taken by surprise again. Dr. King had not been present that morning and could not understand the dynamics of the events, yet he would determine the next move. I felt my only recourse was to go directly to him, explain that a mass of people could not get through the barricades and that it was wrong to ask students to face those difficulties without any leadership.

When I arrived at the Gadsden Motel and knocked on the door of his room, Dr. King came to open it in his robe—still in pajamas. A freshly cooked steak was on the room-service table. He was busy on the telephone and asked me to wait. I left. It was past one, perhaps after two o'clock, in the afternoon and I felt thoroughly disgusted. I could not understand any leadership that would send down an order for young people to face the barricades while that leadership was busy on the telephone, eating steak, and not yet dressed for the day.

Dr. King did not change his order—the people should go.

The park was barricaded. The fire trucks were out en masse. Bull Connor sat in his bulletproof tank. A few students ran around the barricade and others were able to join them. Ricks and I went too. The police had cordoned off the intersections leading to downtown and started shooting water on people. Bricks and rocks started flying back at the police and the firemen. For over forty-five minutes, there was a chase in and out of alleys and streets. Other black people joined in the fight against the police.

We finally retreated in the direction of the church. As we rushed past the Gadsden Motel, King, Abernathy, Shuttlesworth, and other leaders of SCLC came up and yelled at me, "Jim, try to get the people back into the church!"

Kiss my ass, I said to myself as I hurried down the street with the people. "Get 'em back yourselves," I shouted, and kept on going, angry at the situation that led to the entrapment of the students, but glad about the retaliatory violence.

The "riots" that day in Birmingham received wide public attention—they were a prelude to Harlem '64, Watts '65, Newark and Detroit '67. One of the people seriously hurt by the water hoses was Colia LaFayette who was helping to direct a voting project in Selma, Alabama. Shuttlesworth was hurt and had to be hospitalized. He came out the next day when he heard that Dr. King had agreed to a compromise without discussing it with him. The compromise was merely an agreement to negotiate with the city. But in reality Burke Marshall and Bobby Kennedy had influenced Dr. King to call off the demonstrations because of the violent resistance actions. People had become too militant for the government's liking and Dr. King's image. I felt that the masses of young people who were the backbone of the protest in Birmingham and throughout the South had been cheated once more. The mighty leader had proven to have heavy feet of clay.

In a sense, it did not matter. There would be more white violence in Birmingham—the Gadsden Motel bombing, the murder of the six young girls in church that September, people beaten on the streets. And black resistance would continue to rise across the nation. There were no more demonstrations in Birmingham for the time being, but history would pick up the irreversible thrust of black people in other times and places.

CHAPTER 41

Selma: Diary of a Freedom Fighter

ASK YOURSELF THIS
IMPORTANT QUESTION:
WHAT HAVE I PERSONALLY DONE TO
MAINTAIN Segregation?

If the answer disturbs you, probe deeper and decide what you are willing to do to preserve racial harmony in Selma and Dallas County.

Is it worth four dollars to prevent a "Birmingham" here? That's what it costs to be a member of your Citizens' Council, whose efforts are not thwarted by courts which give sit-in demonstrators legal immunity, prevent school boards from expelling students who participate in mob activities and would place federal referees at the board of voter registrars.

Law enforcement can be called only after these things occur, but your Citizens' Council prevents them from happening.

Why else did only 350 Negroes attend a so-called mass voter registration meeting that outside agitators worked 60 days to organize in Selma?

Gov. Wallace told a state meeting of the council three weeks ago: "You are doing a wonderful job, but you should speak with the united voice of 100,000 persons. Go back home and get more members." Gov. Wallace stands in the University doorway next Tuesday facing possible ten years imprisonment for violating a federal injunction.

Is it worth four dollars to you to prevent sit-ins, mob marches and wholesale Negro voter registration efforts in Selma?

If so, prove your dedication by joining and supporting the work of the Dallas County Citizens' Council today. Six dollars will make both you and your wife members of an organization which has already given Selma nine years of Racial Harmony since "Black Monday."

Send Your Check to:
The Dallas County
Citizens' Council
Selma, Alabama
Your Membership is good for 12 months.
[From the Selma *Times Journal*, Sunday, June 9, 1963.]

Selma, Alabama. A name that would echo around the world in 1965, when black people would be brutally beaten by horseback riding police and Dr. Martin Luther King would lead a series of mass marches culminating in the one from Selma to Montgomery. But Selma, Alabama, in 1963 was a largely unknown little town. Whites kept blacks "in their place," with an iron hand. How did the change come about? The answer to that question lies in the dogged, day-to-day efforts of a handful of SNCC workers.

Many times people in this country and around the world have asked me exactly what it was like to be a SNCC field secretary in the South—what were the obstacles and how did we overcome them, what were our organizing techniques, what was the daily reality of the struggle. As executive secretary, I felt very strongly about the importance of field staff sending in frequent and detailed reports on their activities—so strongly that at one point, we in the Atlanta office took the position of "no field report, no subsistence check." The point was not to burden the already overworked field secretaries with another task but to strengthen our network of communication. At the same time, I felt that we were making history. Nothing that might be written in retrospect could capture the full reality of our work so well as on-the-spot recording.

One of the finest accounts of just what it meant to be a SNCC field worker was written by Rev. Bernard LaFayette in June of 1963 from Selma, Alabama. Bernard and his wife Colia, both twenty-two years old, had gone there in February to start a voter registration project. They went to Selma to make a frontal attack on one of the most vicious and oppressive places in the Deep South.

Dallas County, of which Selma is the seat, is one of several in a Black Belt area where blacks form the majority of the population. In Dallas, the ratio was 57.7 percent "nonwhites" to 42.3 percent (census figures for 1960). Of the blacks, 84 percent existed on less than three thousand dollars a year and 82 percent of those who worked held jobs as maids, janitors, farm and other kinds of laborers, truck drivers, and helpers. Of the blacks over twenty-five years old, 95 percent had less than a high school education, while 62 percent had completed six years or less of school. Among the whites on the other hand, 81 percent had incomes of three thousand dollars a year or more while 73 percent fell into the better-paid and more desirable job categories, and only 11 percent had six or less years of school.

In Dallas County, only 130 black people were registered to vote out of an eligible 15,115 according to a 1961 Civil Rights Commission Report. Adjoining Wilcox County had never had a black voter, although its population was 78 percent black. Lowndes County, which also borders Dallas and also has a huge black majority, had never had a registered black person either. That was the way things had been for almost seventy years and that was the way whites intended them to stay. During the Civil War Selma had been one of the most important military depots in the lower states of the Confederacy. In 1963 it was the birthplace and stronghold of the White Citizens' Council, the authors of that advertisement in the Selma *Times Journal*. Nothing had changed.

Bernard and Colia LaFayette survived their first few months in Selma despite armed attacks by night riders and lesser forms of harassment. By May they felt that the black community was ready for a mass meeting. I was invited to speak and went.

Many people were on edge that day, for reports were coming back that the whites intended to break up the meeting. And they came: Shortly after the meeting had started, a crowd of armed whites gathered not far from the church. We immediately got in touch with our Atlanta office, which began to work with that fine line of contradiction between the federal and state powers. They telephoned around the country, asking people to apply pressure on their elected representatives and on the Justice Department to prevent violence from being inflicted upon the mass of people who had come to the voter registration meeting.

Inside the church we decided to stay until we felt that it was safe to have people leave the meeting. We remained until one o'clock in the morning, singing and talking freedom, until the crowds of whites had disappeared. It was, in retrospect, a mistake not to have been prepared with an armed self-defense group of our own that could fight against those who would attack us. But this type of consciousness would become widespread only later.

I left Selma shortly afterward. Bernard and Colia LaFayette went on with their work—quietly laying the foundations for events that would rock the world in the near future and make the name of Selma a byword like Birmingham. This is Bernard's account of how things went during the month after that first mass meeting:

A REPORT ON SELMA
By Rev. Bernard LaFayette

Introduction: In spite of the deep fears among the Negro community, we have been able to move along with some degree of success. We have been able to get very little cooperation from the Negro ministers and Church leaders, as a whole.

I feel that many people are afraid to identify with the Voter Registration Project, either out of fear or just plain apathy. Many people who would be active have lost hope because of other pressures put on those who failed in the past. The economic pressure put on those who signed a petition to integrate the schools in 1957; the harassment and intimidation of the members of the N.A.A.C.P. and final disbandment of the organization.

The White Citizens' Council is and has been the most powerful pressure group in this state. The Dallas County Branch is an agent of the county government and Dallas is the birthplace of the White Citizens' Council in the State of Alabama. It is also the Stronghold of the Ku Klux Klan.

June 1: June the first was a normal day for us, we passed out leaflets announcing the classes and also the fact that the coming Monday was a day when Negroes could go down and apply to the Board of Registrars for Registration. We emphasized the importance of going down. We talked to several people telling them about the different days that were available to them. We went to some night clubs and some bars and some taverns, telling the people about the meetings. We also went to a dance that was held at the Elk's Club and we also went to a place called the Chicken Shack, passing out leaflets and talking to people about going down to register to vote, and helping them with the program.

June 2: This was a normal day and also was a Sunday. We went to church and that morning we passed out leaflets in all of the churches telling the people about the first Monday in June, which was the next day. We worked that Sunday morning carrying leaflets around to the different churches to make sure that they were passed out. We didn't want them to get stopped in someone's hand that didn't want them passed out. The people who worked with us were young and were from 12 to 15 in number. . . .

June 3: This was a Monday and we went down to Mrs. Boynton's office helping the people fill out Voter Registration forms and we assisted them that day. This day certainly showed a great breakthrough ever since we had our last Mass Meeting. It is difficult to keep an accurate account of the people going down because some of the people go on their own without coming to the classes. In many cases they failed to report to us that they had gone down. We realized that there was a problem amounting and we wanted to do something about it. We came to a suggestion that on the next Monday the Registrar's Office would be open and we would have people go down there to get the names and addresses of people who were applying. . . .

We had a meeting of the Dallas County Voters League, which was called to be held at Brown Chapel A.M.E. Church, and there we discussed our progress. I gave a report of what we had been doing. We talked in terms of bringing younger people into our groups. . . .

June 4: This was the day when Alexander L. Brown came, a student from Birmingham, Alabama. He is sixteen years of age and he came to work as a volunteer.

He is one of the students that Colia, my wife, recruited when she was in Birmingham. He came in and we immediately got to work. We went over in East Selma and we went again canvassing and to see what the possibilities were of setting up a clinic in a little church that we discovered was over there. We're sort of shut-off from the rest of the community. . . . We talked to the people asking them would they like it if we set up a clinic in their neighborhood. We got very good response in that area, that evening.

June 5: We went to Beliot, Alabama and we met with Mr. D. L. Pope who was a man that had been referred to me as very interested in the program and a man who was militant and wanted to help in the movement. I understand that he has given us financial support in the past and he is a Registered Voter. He is also interested in getting others to register. He is a man of dignity . . . he was able to give us a list of 80 people. Mr. Pope agreed to do what he could to influence these people who he had listed.

June 7: This is the day we decided to go down to Wilcox County to attend the meeting that the Wilcox County Civic League was supposed to be having.

I thought that since we had such a hard time getting young people to the meetings, I decided to take the Freedom Trio to sing "Freedom Is 'A Coming and It Won't Be Long." This trio is made up of three attractive young ladies and we thought that it should draw some young people to the meeting. We took them but unfortunately, this night the meeting was postponed because of a regular monthly meeting that was to be held at the church. We decided to go to Mr. Roman Petteway's store, which is the hangout for most of the teen-agers in that community, and we rounded up around thirty students. They helped us to get older people to become Registered Voters. We taught them Freedom Songs and talked about Freedom in general. We left Alexander Brown down in Wilcox County because he met some of his relatives that night and they agreed that he could stay over with them. He was going to work over in that area, for the purpose of setting up a Mass Meeting.

June 8: We were passing out leaflets announcing our Voter Registration Classes and letting the people know about the Board of Registrars being open on the first and third Monday in each month and that they were free to go down and register. We went to Lowndes County, which was the second time I have ever stopped in Lowndes County, although it is between Montgomery and Selma. We went to this Negro store that was out on the Highway, and we left some leaflets there. We know that the Negroes in Lowndes County are afraid, because when we start to talk about Voter Registration the people become fearful even though they were talking to us friendly at first. After we mentioned something about Voter Registration, some of them refused to talk at all.

When I came back home, I made a phone call to Reverend Menifee, who is the pastor of Brown's Chapel, and told him that we were having a problem of a place to have our Mass Meeting and I asked him what were the possibilities of having one at his Church. . . . We realized that if our Mass Meetings died down then, our Voter Registration Program would also die down. He consented that the doors of his church would be open to let us have a Mass Meeting at his church. We discussed June 17 as the date. . . .

June 9: I visited Beliot, Alabama, and it was on a Sunday and I went to Sunday School at Mr. Pope's church. After being introduced in the Sunday School, I got a chance to stress the importance of Voter Registration and tell them something about the work that we have been doing in Dallas County and the need for others to join the program and help others to become registered voters. Most of the people were pleased with the talk that I gave, and I stayed to the service, and Rev. Thomas, who is pastor of this church and lives here in Selma, Alabama, gave me an opportunity to speak again, after the sermon. I made it very brief, telling who I was and what I was doing in the area.

I was asked to come to the 3:00 Program, which was the Pastor's Anniversary, and he consented that I make a speech there. . . . I went home to dinner with Mr. Lawrence Carter and returned and made a speech there. After the main message, I also met Rev. A. C. Burks who was a minister who gave the message for the Anniversary. He seemed to be very interested and enthused about the program. He told me about a committee of three white men who came to his home and told him to give them any information that he would have on these meetings that were taking place and this Voter Registration thing. And he responded (according to him) "I don't have anything to tell you because the meetings are not a secret and everyone knew about them and you will have to find out about them the very best way you can, and I don't have anything else to tell you and you will have to leave my house."

June 10: We passed out leaflets and went to Mr. Pritchett and had some leaflets made about the Mass Meeting that would be on the 17th June and we had secured James Bevel for our main speaker. We had his name printed on the program. In the later part of the day, I learned about a man that had been beaten and arrested at the Quik Check Store. The charge was "Trying to steal a piece of meat." He was beaten by five of the clerks. I tried to trace this rumor down to find out who the man was and check it out to see exactly what happened. I have learned that this man's name is Mr. L. C. Banks and he lives on Philpot Avenue in the 1500 block.

I went by his home but he was not there, and his wife told me that this thing had happened to him and that it was all true. I thought that I would talk with him to get the details and facts of the situation. I understand that he has a serious eye injury, as a result of this beating. Later on I learned that there was a boycott being launched by the beer companies against Mr. Robert Anderson, who is the owner of Bob's Cafe. This boycott was allegedly because he attended the Mass Meeting that was held some time back in May.

June 11: I talked to a man who was fired because he attended the Mass Meeting. I was concerned about this because I thought that this firing and intimidation would make people fearful about going down to register. We also wanted the people to know that we were definitely with them and we would make it public what they were going through and the suffering they were bearing, and we would try to do something about it. I finally traced this down and found out who he was and we had heard a lot of rumors and we went to get the facts of the situation. I found out that the man's name was Mr. Woodrow Foster, and he lives at 86 Small Avenue.

When I first went by his home, he was not at home. Then I went to a meeting at a clinic because this was a Tuesday night. It was held at Mrs. Boynton's office on Franklyn Street. After the meeting was over I went and found Mr. Foster at home. We talked about the situation and he explained that he had been coming to the Mass Meeting and that he had come to the last meeting that we had had. He thought that the man who fired him didn't really want to fire him but he had to fire him because of pressures that were being placed on him. Mr. Foster worked in the Dallas Glass factory.

When I got back home I parked in front of my house and noticed a two-tone '57 Chevrolet with a white top and a rose bottom parked on the other side of the road. A white man was under the hood as if to be fixing something and another was at the steering wheel. . . . I had a lot of books and papers and other things in the car and I had some leaflets in my hand. This man that was under the hood came over to my car and asked me how much would I charge for a push-off. It was about 11:00 that night and ordinarily I would be very leary about this but since the man had come all of the way to my car, and since it was so dark under the trees, I felt that if he wanted to do anything he could have done it then. I told him that I would not charge him anything to give him a push.

I pulled my car up and came behind him to match bumpers. This man who was under the hood let it down and went over to the right hand side of the driver's position and had a brief conversation with him. Then he jumped over the bumpers of the two cars, as if to check to see if they were matching. He looked doubtful about if they were matching. I asked him how did they look, and he said that maybe I should get out and see for myself, what I thought about it.

It was late, and I was getting sleepy, so I got out and took a quick glance at them and saw that they matched. But when I started to lift my head up, this man had circled around me and had struck me on the forehead with a blunt instrument. That caused blood to fountain out of my head onto my shoes. I fell to the pavement and as I started to get up he hit me on my head two other times. I don't know how many times he hit me altogether, but when I began to stagger to the house and call my neighbor Mr. Mack Shannon, I called out "Mack," and at this time the man who hit me jumped into the car and sped away from the scene.

I came and knocked on Mack's door and told him to open quick, he did and they gave me temporary first-aid and washed the blood from my head and my face. They took me down to my apartment and I made a phone call to the police and told them what had happened and they said that they were on their way. I called the FBI of Selma but I couldn't get them so I called Mobile and they said that they had FBIs in Selma, Alabama, and they gave me their home number. Then I called the SNCC office and reported the incident.

Then I got in my car and drove to the Berwell Infirmary where we got in touch with Doctor Dinkin and he placed six stitches in my scalp. Then I got questioned by the police. . . . I got instructions from the nurse that I was to stay there overnight for observation and a friend of mine took some pictures of my wounds. . . . I was still in the hospital on the morning of June 12th and after the doctor came I asked permission to leave because I had so much work to do. . . . This was the day when the FBI came over to my house. . . . They got their fingerprinting equipment and since I had put my car in a safe place they were able to get a few smears but they did get a clear print of the man's palm (from the bumper).

June 13: I was still recuperating somewhat from the incident that happened to me three nights before. Alexander L. Brown came back from Wilcox County after he heard about the incident. We decided not to have the youth meetings at night, as they were usually held, this was because of the brutality that had started in Selma and we didn't want any of the students to get hurt.

June 14-16: I got a call from Ruby Doris [Robinson] that there was a SNCC meeting in Atlanta, Georgia, and they wanted me to attend it. On the 16th when I got in to Selma, Alabama, we went straight to bed. When I got up that morning, I went to Jesse Grimes's house to see if he had delivered the leaflets announcing the Mass Meeting. He mentioned something about the meeting being called off at Brown's Chapel A.M.E. Baptist Church.

I immediately went over to the Pastor's house, but I didn't say anything to him until I showed him the leaflets that I had had made to see what his reactions would be. He told me that he was having some difficulties with his trustees and as far as he was concerned the meeting was still on. The trustees were going to have a meeting after church to discuss it and it would be up to them to decide what they wanted to do.

Since the First Baptist Church was only about a block away, I went to the Pastor and asked him could we have a Mass Meeting at his church. . . . He said that it would be available and that the doors would be open for us to have the Mass Meeting there.

June 17: This was the day of the big Mass Meeting and it was the second one that we would have had. . . . Earlier that day, I was at Mrs. Boynton's office helping people coming by there to fill out forms before they went down to Register to Vote. We had gotten complaints from the people that were going down that they were pouring questions at them and in some instances they were raising their voices at the people and yelling "speak up, I can't hear you," and this sort of thing, and trying to confuse them. I asked Alexander Brown and Bosie Reese to go down and check on the situation. . . . Alexander Brown came back. He was driving the car and he came in very hurriedly and excited and said "Bosie's in jail" and that "the sheriff had grabbed Bosie and with what seemed to him as a blow threw him into the sheriff's office." He also said that "An alarm started to ring all over the courthouse" when he was running away.

At this time I didn't know just what to do but I loaded my camera with film and got some bulbs and called the FBI before I went to the courthouse. They advised me to come by there before going to the courthouse to see what had happened to Bosie. Terry Shaw and I went to the Sheriff's office and asked to see the Sheriff. The receptionist got up and went where the Sheriff was and he came in and asked me what was it that I wanted. I told him "I want to know what happened to Bosie Reese." He asked me my name before answering the questions; I answered, then he asked me other questions and I answered them also. He told me that Bosie Reese was under arrest.

I asked him what the charges were and he said that they were at that time failure to obey an officer and resisting arrest. I asked him what was the bond set at, and he told me that he could give me no more information and that I would have to see Judge Mallory for more information. Then he started to pour questions at Terry Shaw, asking him what was his name and where he lived and at first he acted like he couldn't hear him and he yelled "Speak up" in a very angry manner. We both turned and walked out of the office and reported the situation.

The FBI agent said that he couldn't do anything about it and that he took his orders from Washington and that he had no jurisdiction here in Selma. Mrs. Boynton and I went up to the County Jail and (this was about 5:00) we asked if they had one Bosie Reese there. They did but when we asked to see him the jailer said that he couldn't let us go back there because they were cleaning up and everything and this thing was entirely out of his hands and we would have to see the Sheriff about seeing him and he didn't know what the charge meant or the situation that led to his arrest. He (the Sheriff) seemed to be quite puzzled and confused about the charges that were made, and he said that there had never been a charge made like this before that he knew. We asked him for the bond forms and he filled them in for us and gave them to Mrs. Boynton.

This night was the night of the Mass Meeting and we reported the incident. Rev. Bevel did a very good job at the Mass Meeting. The Mass Meeting was well attended and I estimated approximately 700 people although the local paper reported the next day that we had only 250 people. . . .

June 18: This was a normal day for me and I got out that morning to hear the results of the reactions to the Mass Meeting. You could see the new hope and smiles as they walked along the streets and talked about the Mass Meeting. They felt proud of themselves and Selma and they felt proud of the people who were helping them. I talked to several people that had not attended the Mass Meeting and although they were afraid to attend the Mass Meeting, they were happy to hear that the Mass Meeting was successful and some of them said that they were definitely going to be at the next Mass Meeting. I guess that some of the people had felt that the Mass Meetings had died down and would never be revived again.

I went to a Meeting and we went to a Clinic that was held at Mrs. Boynton's office, we had a late meeting but none of the people showed up for the classes.

Several of the workers and Voters League Members came later on and we discussed the last Mass Meeting and discussed plans for a future Mass Meeting. We also talked about getting some legal defense for Bosie and about another person to sign the bond so he would be able to get out . . . we thought to get Attorney Solomon Seay as another attorney for the defense of Bosie Reese. I called his home and tried to get in touch with him but he was not at home and I left a message for him that the trial would be coming up that Thursday and we needed him to be there.

After we left the meeting, I was driving Terry Shaw home and it was about 10:30 or about a quarter to eleven. As I was driving around the corner, I noticed that a police car was following Mr. Gildersleeve, who had pulled off earlier. (Mr. Gildersleeve is the vice-president of the Dallas County Voters League.) I turned down Washington Street and going North crossed Alabama Avenue toward Selma Avenue and just as I crossed the street, the Sheriff's car pulled up behind me and started flashing a light. I pulled over to the side of the road and the Deputy Sheriff got out of his car and walked over to my car and I got out of my car. The Deputy Sheriff, Chuck Webber, asked to see my driver's license. When I pulled out my wallet to show him my driver's license, he said that he had a warrant for my arrest. I asked him, under what charge? He said, "vagrancy." Mrs. Foster had been following us at the time. She saw the Sheriff pull me over and stopped. Mr. Shannon, who was attending the Voters League Meeting, also stopped. Terry got out of my car into Mrs. Foster's car and the other deputy sheriff drove my car back to the City Hall. My car was impounded and I was imprisoned.

I was booked, and they told me I would be fingerprinted and photographed the next morning; so I stayed in jail overnight. It sort of stirred in the community, and later that night I understood several citizens had gone to Attorney Chestnut's house and waited for him very late (about 12:00 P.M.) in order to do something about my arrest. I had been put into a dark cell by myself. It was a normal case because I had been arrested many times and it was no strange place for me; so I made myself at home and relaxed for the rest of the night.

June 19: When I woke up the next morning the cell doors were opened in order for all the prisoners to go into the day room and the first person that passed by my cell was Bosie Reese. He was so surprised to see me in jail with him that we had a brief conversation. I told him about the things happening on the outside and that we were working on his case. I told him that we had reported this case to the Justice Department.

Mrs. Foster and Mr. Henry Shannon signed the bond (for me) but they couldn't seem to locate the Sheriff. Finally, Attorney Chestnut located the Sheriff and he signed the bond, but I wasn't sure if I should get out of jail at this particular time. I finally made up my mind to sign the bond and get out, to see what I could do about getting Bosie out. Attorney Chestnut informed me that the Justice Department wanted to talk to me about the arrest and Bosie's case. I talked with them and they said they also wanted to talk to Bosie when we got him out of jail. It was almost impossible to get someone that owned that much property ($1,500) to sign the bond for him but we continued to try.

June 20: This was the day for me to be tried for the vagrancy charge. Bosie's trial was to come up also. We went into the courtroom and Mr. Gildersleeve sat on the so-called white side. After conferring with the Judge, Deputy Sheriff Virgil Bates came over and asked him to move to the so-called colored side and he did so. . . . When they got to our cases, Bosie Reese and mine, our lawyers asked for more time because they hadn't had much time to confer with us . . . but the Judge said that he wouldn't give a continuance; so both cases had to be that day. I was tried and the Sheriff testified as a witness for the prosecution of the State. . . . When I was put on the stand, and it was established that I did have visible means of support from the Student Nonviolent Coordinating Committee; that I get regular expenses from the organization, that my rent was paid in advance, and I had a house and food and twenty-seven dollars and seventy-five cents at the time of the arrest, the Judge decided that he would have to find me not guilty. . . .

The Judge saw fit at this time for a continuance of Bosie's case at the request of Attorney Seay and Attorney Chestnut. Attorney Seay offered a great deal of motions and this sort of thing, striking at the violations of Civil Rights in this case. He also complained about the excessive bond of fifteen hundred dollars on Bosie Reese's case and the Judge said that he would make it five hundred dollars on each charge and that would make the total bond one thousand dollars. . . .

We were still unable to get Bosie Reese out on bond because the Judge would not approve any bond until the tax assessor had found the property valued above six thousand dollars. . . . I continued to go around that day and the Rev. McDole drove me around to see if I could find someone to sign the bond. Finally that late afternoon, I was able to get the Rev. C. C. Brown, pastor of the Reformed Presbyterian Church here in Selma and Mr. Charles Moss, who is a contractor and also the owner of a motel and an amusement park here in Selma, to sign the bond. Then it was the problem of finding the Sheriff again to approve the bonds. After Attorney Chestnut finally found the Sheriff, he said that the tax assessor's office was closed. Even though the Sheriff knew that the people who signed the bonds were worth the bonds, he would make us go through the trouble of getting the tax assessment from the tax assessor the next day. We got Bosie Reese out that Friday on a thousand dollar bond and he was able to talk to the Justice Department. . . . I spent the rest of the day bringing myself up to date . . . and I also discovered that some more people had lost their jobs when they came to the Mass Meeting the past Monday.

June 22: It is Saturday and I spent the rest of the day gathering facts for the Justice Department . . . we also got out some leaflets and publicized the Mass Meeting which was to be June 24th . . . we got out letters to all of the ministers announcing the Mass Meeting.

June 23: This is Sunday. We spent most of the day talking to the Justice Department and getting our affidavit prepared, and going over and over again the facts and the case.

June 24: We got our final publicity out and we had our Mass Meeting. Miss Ella Baker spoke and over 500 people attended. It was a very educational meeting and we feel that this Mass Meeting was more enthusiastic than all the others we have had. It seems that every meeting gets better and better, and we are able to bring in new people. Many people who attended this Mass Meeting were people from the rural area, and it was the first time we had that many people from the rural area attending the Mass Meetings.

June 25: I learned that three beer companies had come to Bob on Monday the 24th and asked him if he wanted any beer, because they were able to sell him beer at this point. Bob told them that he would have to check with some of the people in the community to find out if it would be all right if he bought beer. June the 25th he bought beer from three of the companies that had started boycotting him. When he asked them why had they started boy-cotting him they replied "Just let the past be the past."

We had a meeting of many of the Voters League members at the clinic in Mrs. Boynton's office and only one person showed up. We could see from the harassment, no doubt, or something, that the people were afraid to come downtown to the clinic. So we had this committee meeting and started making plans for the coming Mass Meeting which would be on July 1st. We discussed Bosie Reese's trial and the seating arrangement in the courtroom. We hope to have enough people there to fill up the Negro section and to spread over into all of the courtroom. We were discussing the possibilities of what might happen at this trial. I pointed out several possibilities. I thought they would ask all of the Negroes that were sitting in the white section to leave the courtroom or they might let them all sit together, because the Justice Department might be there, and they might change their policy and integrate the courtroom, or they might ask everyone to leave the courtroom and declare it a closed trial because of the seating arrangement. We will only be able to tell Thursday what they will do. . . .

So the days went for Bernard and Colia Lafayette, and a month like that must have seemed like a year. The fruits of his patience and hard work were beginning to show, and would become clearer later that year. For most people, Selma, Alabama, hardly existed before the marches of 1965. But people like the Lafayettes, of whom the world at large knows nothing, were there long before, turning the first stone, breaking the first earth, planting the first seed.

CHAPTER 42

Machine Guns in Danville

BLOOD GUSHED from lacerated scalps, people lay groaning in pain on emergency tables jammed into the corridors of Winslow Hospital, doctors and nurses worked at a frantic pace to keep up with the mounting stream of patients. Relatives of the injured watched anxiously. Everywhere, blood dripped on the floor. It looked like a war scene but it was only that the police of Danville, Virginia, had once again done their "duty" to protect white supremacy.

Leo Branton, Danny Lyon, and I had arrived in Danville just in time to see this mass of bleeding black people trying to get medical attention. It was Danny Lyon's first photographic assignment for SNCC. Leo, the brother of Wiley Branton, director of the Voter Education Project, was an attorney from Los Angeles who wanted to see some of the conditions in the South. We had taken a plane north from Atlanta and were delayed more than an hour trying to rent a car in Durham, North Carolina, to drive in to Danville. Only a fluke, that delay in Durham, had prevented us from being on those hospital tables too.

It was June 10, 1963, "Bloody Monday," as the day came to be known. The fifteen thousand black people of Danville were fed up with the reality they knew. It was not the reality described in a bulletin put out by the local Chamber of Commerce, which said in part, "Danville's civic and social organizations have shown a consistently progressive spirit, adding much to the civic development as well as to the cultural and social life of the city. . . . The city maintains a high moral and spiritual tone." The public relations assistant to the mayor of Danville in 1963 happened also to be the public relations director of Dan River Mills, described as the largest single-unit textile mill in the world. Dan River dominated the town's economy. It employed twelve thousand people in 1963—of whom approximately eleven hundred were black. But the maximum wage paid to a black worker there was eighty dollars a week.

On top of this base of economic oppression rose the social superstructure of segregation: Danville's theaters had a balcony reserved for blacks, restaurants and motels were closed to black people, Winslow Hospital was segregated. It was also understaffed for black patients. The streets in black neighborhoods were unpaved, poorly lighted, and full of uncollected garbage. Whether it was jobs or public services or homes or schools, white was right and black had to get back. The black people of Danville, knowing the realities of their lives, their consciousness lifted by the demonstrations in Albany, Greenwood, Birmingham, and by the impending March on Washington, had decided to move again.

When the sit-in movement started in Greensboro, North Carolina, in 1960 black people of nearby Danville had also been stirred to sit-in. Their main focus then was on desegregating the "public" library. As everywhere in the South, black people were denied the use of the town's main library and assigned (in Danville, but not in all Southern towns) a miserable branch library with a few torn books. The Danville Library fought desegregation to the death, for it was not just another library, but a Confederate Memorial sacred to the white folks, the site of the last full cabinet meeting of the Confederacy before General Lee announced his surrender. Eventually faced with a court order to desegregate, the library chose instead to close from September to November, 1960, and reopen desegregated—but without chairs, and with the cost of a library card raised to $2.50 a year.

The 1963 summer campaign in Danville began on May 31. For a week, Rev. Lawrence Campbell and Rev. A. I. Dunlap, both leaders of the Danville Christian Progressive Association (DCPA) led marches demanding equality in municipal employment. They wanted blacks employed as firemen, policemen, city clerks, meter readers, and typists.

On June 5 the two ministers and other citizens tried desperately to see the mayor, Julian Stinson, but Stinson was in no mood to see demonstrating black people. They decided to stay in City Hall until the mayor would see them. The police pushed Dunlap down a flight of stairs and choked a young black girl, who then swung her pocketbook and hit a cop in the face. She and the two ministers were jailed. A grand jury then indicted Campbell and Dunlap for inciting to riot and "inciting or encouraging a minor to commit a misdemeanor." Their bond was set at fifty-five hundred dollars each.

One of the characteristics of SNCC at that time was that it had a disciplined staff willing to go anywhere in the South to help mount demonstrations against segregation. This mobile character of the field staff did not lessen the intense voter registration work being carried out on a day-to-day basis. So when Reverend Dunlap and Reverend Campbell requested help from the national office of SNCC, field secretaries were immediately dispatched. Ivanhoe Donaldson, Avon Rollins, and Robert Zellner, who had just been released from jail as a Freedom Walker, went to Danville and stayed throughout the summer and into the fall.

On Monday afternoon, June 10, the police arrested thirty-eight persons including Rollins as they marched to City Hall, still pressing for their demands of municipal government jobs for blacks and an end to segregation of the town's public facilities. The Danville police turned fire hoses on them and beat them with clubs. Dorothy Miller, who worked with Julian Bond in the press section of SNCC and later married Bob Zellner, described the scene that evening and its aftermath in a pamphlet which SNCC published carrying the vivid photographs of Danny Lyon:

A group of sixty-five Negroes (and one white woman, a SNCC office worker) walked five abreast from Rev. Campbell's church to the city jail. SNCCer Zellner was along, photographing the march. Mrs. Campbell was at the head of the line. The group, led by Rev. H. G. McGhee, sang hymns and circled the jail once, passing several policemen who stood there watching.

As they began the second trip around, police halted them. Chief of Police E. G. McCain snatched a camera from Zellner's hands, smashed it on the ground, and had him hauled into jail. McCain told Rev. McGhee to stop singing and disperse the group. Instead, Rev. McGhee broke into a loud prayer and asked forgiveness for the police "who know not what they do."

Chief McCain bellowed, "Let 'em have it" and firemen turned hoses on the people, many of them women and teen-agers. Nightstick wielding police and deputized garbage collectors smashed into the group, clubbing Negroes who were bunched for safety against parked cars. Some were washed under the cars; others were clubbed after the water knocked them down. Bodies lay on the street, drenched and bloody. Police and garbage collectors chased those demonstrators who were able to walk for two blocks.

At the Bible Way Church, pastored by Rev. Campbell, bloody men and women came in by twos and threes and were shuttled to the hospital.

Of 65 demonstrators, 40 were hurt.

The next day, the two Danville newspapers, the *Register* and the *Bee*, mentioned casually that "demonstrators were dispersed with the use of hoses and nightsticks."

The next day, Rev. L. W. Chase, pastor of the High Street Baptist Church and President of the DCPA, led a group of 200 Negroes to the city hall to protest the police brutality of the night before and to again assert the need for equal employment. Many of those who paced slowly up and down in front of the city hall wore bandages on their heads and arms, and one young man walked with a crutch. Mayor Stinson was not available to see them.

Three days later, June 13, Rev. Chase again led about 250 Negroes to the city hall to speak to the Mayor. The crowd waited on the steps as Rev. Chase and five others—all victims of the attack June 10—tried vainly to get into the city hall. The doors were locked, and sullen white faces peered at them unblinking as Chase called, "We want to see the Mayor."

Rejected, Chase and his group rejoined the crowd on the steps and everyone decided to stay all night, if necessary, to see the Mayor.

They stayed nine hours.

Women from the High Street Church and other ladies from the community brought several hundred sandwiches and several hundred cokes for the dem_instrators. The young and old people sang Freedom Songs, talked, occasionally danced, heard a lecture on Negro history by James Forman, SNCC Executive Secretary, and waited.

At 11 P.M., when some of the demonstrators had stretched out on the narrow stairs prepared to sleep, if possible, a sudden huddle took place among the police, who had previously blocked off the area for four blocks around.

Then the fire trucks appeared. And police suddenly appeared in back of the demonstrators, on the top steps, after they had come from inside the city hall. They had clubs in hand. An old lady, trembling, cried, "Are they going to hurt us again? Are they going to beat us?"

Dr. Milton Reid, Virginia representative of the Southern Christian Leadership Conference, Chase, and Forman conferred. The demonstrators huddled together, one hand protecting their faces, the other clenched tightly around the railing which ran down the steps of the building.

Some in the back, closest to the police, began to flee but about fifty persons were prepared to brave three high-pressure fire hoses not more than fifteen feet from their faces.

Forman jumped up and said to Chief McCain, "What are you doing?"

Reid and Chase spoke together as Forman confronted the Chief. It was this confrontation, many people believe, which gave the demonstrators time to get out of the way of the hoses. High pressure hoses could have, at that small distance, blown eyes out and broken bones. So the group got up and descended the stairs. Police followed them, brandishing nightsticks, to the Negro neighborhood.

After that night's mass meeting at Rev. Campbell's church, police, armed with submachine guns, set up roadblocks near the church and searched several cars. Standing near the four patrol cars loomed a riot tank with four machine guns mounted on top. . . .

It was this sight that greeted us as we left the church and headed toward the section of town where I was staying. Bob Zellner was driving. We were ordered out of the car, told to put our hands on top of the car, and the frisk began in earnest. But it was more than a frisk, for several pigs surrounded me with their submachine guns pointed at my head.

"So you're Forman," one of them drawled. "Say something now. You been talking all day at the courthouse. Give us a speech now." He brought the barrel of his machine gun closer to my face. "Say something, nigger!"

I didn't say a word. I was just cool, man. I wasn't shaking. I knew that he had it within his power to let me have it. But I also knew that the worst thing in the world was for me to say something. They wanted to get me—I had been one of the principal organizers of the demonstration that day, giving speeches on the courthouse steps about the history of black people and their current political situation in the United States. They wanted to get me, and the slightest excuse would do it.

The long moment passed. The pig lowered his gun and we were finally allowed to leave. The next day, for security reasons, I left my identification with the woman at whose house I was staying. While we were downtown, the police came to her house. She became frightened as they knocked on the door and hid my identification, including my driver's license. She hid them so well that she was unable to find them ever again. On several occasions I tried to get a driver's license from the segregated bureau of licenses in Georgia, but I always managed to fail the test—according to them. I have not driven since 1963 and one reason was certainly my experiences in Danville.

On June 21 the grand jury handed down indictments against fourteen persons charging them with an ancient Virginia statute, "inciting the colored population to acts of violence and war against the white population." This statute was passed in 1830 after the Nat Turner slave uprisings. It was used to hang John Brown after his Harpers Ferry raid. On June 22 the police kicked in a door in the main sanctuary of the High Street Baptist Church and arrested three SNCC workers named in the indictments. Eventually thirteen of the fourteen people charged were arrested and jailed on five thousand dollars bond each.

I was the fourteenth person, but I got away. After a final talk with attorney Len Holt, I left Danville in a clandestine fashion. Len, a brilliant and aggressive lawyer, was handling the Danville cases and charged that it was impossible for black people to get a fair trial in the Danville courts—where Judge A. M. Aitken presided with a pistol strapped to his waist. As a result of Len's work, none of those indicted was ever sent to jail to serve sentence, and the charges were eventually ruled unconstitutional.

The police brutality and the machine guns of Danville stayed on my mind a long time. My commitment to the building of a mass base of consciousness helped me to hold up under the nightmare qualities of Danville and sent me on to further scenes of action where black people struggled in various ways to assert their dignity as men and women, their "peoplehood," their pride, and their determination to rid themselves of their oppression. We were in fact trying to deal with the colonial nature of our existence, although the perception of our existence as that of a colonized people would come later. Meanwhile, accumulating experiences with Southern "law and order" were turning me into a full-fledged revolutionary.

CHAPTER 43

The March on Washington

ORIGINALLY PLANNED as a march for jobs and freedom, with the emphasis on black people and their demands, the March on Washington of 1963 turned into a victory celebration for the Kennedy administration and its supporters. There was only one discordant note and that was struck loudly by the Student Nonviolent Coordinating Committee.

In June, 1963, John Lewis had been elected chairman of SNCC, replacing Charles McDew in that position. McDew had concentrated most of his efforts in the last two years on fund raising in the North. His efforts had been of tremendous importance, but there was a general feeling that SNCC needed a chairman who would concentrate his energies on building local protest movements. John Lewis, people then felt, might be able to do this. A Southern black student for the ministry, Lewis had been a central figure in the Freedom Rides and spearheaded militant demonstrations in Nashville in the spring of 1963. He had been arrested twenty-four times before becoming chairman of SNCC.

One of Lewis's first assignments as chairman was to represent SNCC at the March on Washington Committee. The day-to-day work would be handled by Courtland Cox and Joyce Ladner. There was some discussion in the organization as to who should speak at the March, Lewis or myself, but that was settled easily. John should clearly represent the organization. He was the chairman and spokesman and my role, as in the relationship with McDew, was to support the chairman. We were a team.

Lewis and I were invited to a meeting called by Bayard Rustin and A. Philip Randolph. Present were Cleveland Robinson of District Sixty-five, James Farmer of CORE, a representative from the National Council of Churches, Lewis and myself. Agreement had already been obtained from Dr. King as to the purpose of this meeting, namely to present Roy Wilkins with a fait accompli. Rustin felt that all the action organizations should agree to hold a March on Washington and then ask Wilkins and Whitney Young of the Urban League for their support. He was confident that, if all the action organizations were in agreement, Roy Wilkins would go along too—although he would fuss and steam and pitch a fit at first. With Wilkin's acceptance, Whitney Young would not stand outside in the cold; he wanted to be considered as some big-time militant.

It was all very amusing to me and not of much importance, for I did not believe that a large March on Washington would accomplish much. But I felt that it was absolutely essential for SNCC to participate, as one means of ending the isolation under which we had been working. We had to find more support in our fight against the racist white South. At the meeting, however, we insisted that the March had to include demonstrations against the United States Justice Department. Only recently in Albany, Georgia, the federal government through the Justice Department had brought charges of perjury against leaders of the Albany Movement. There was no serious opposition to this idea but somewhere later in the negotiations the plan was dropped—unquestionably to satisfy the white liberal contingent.

Following that meeting, there was another with Wilkins. Rustin wanted all of us to go in to it but I refused, saying that Lewis alone should represent SNCC. I was sensitive to the protocol of the meeting—which was supposed to be "heads of civil rights organizations"—and did not want any snide remarks from Wilkins about double representation. My decision proved correct, for Bayard Rustin and Cleveland Robinson later came walking out of the room to where I was waiting for John. Wilkins had objected to their presence, adding that Bayard represented "zero." He even objected to the presence of Abernathy, but Ralph had refused to leave and insisted that he had to stay with Dr. King.

Notwithstanding this shaky start, the March on Washington proceeded to develop. Wilkins and Young agreed to go along. And behind our backs, they and the Kennedy administration developed plans of their own as to how the March on Washington could be used to advance their own respective interests. The United States Government as a whole worked diligently to make the March appear as one where black and white could come together in the "democratic" U.S.A. and peacefully protest. Uncle Sam's image was hurting from those Birmingham police dogs and fire hoses, from photographs which traveled around the world of blacks kneeling in prayer for rights which the United States ostensibly denied no one, from the specter of violent rebellion that rose faintly on the horizon.

SNCC, on the other hand, felt that the March on Washington had to be used to launch a blistering criticism of the society in general and to state some of the passion with which we had been working since 1961.

The March on Washington had to be the forum from which we articulated to the nation a militancy not heard before from civil rights organizations. In other words, SNCC's intent was running in direct conflict with the intent of the power structure and most of the March leaders. A blowup was inevitable. But I didn't become fully aware of this until the last moment. Throughout the summer of 1963 I was busy with local protest movements in Atlanta, Rome, and Savannah, Georgia; Selma, Alabama; Greenwood, Mississippi; Danville, Virginia; Cambridge, Maryland. I was not involved with the development of the March on Washington after those first meetings in New York.

Consternation first hit the nation's capital the day before the March, when the speech John Lewis planned to give became known to some of the politicos flanking the Democratic Party. It was a stinger, and it had already been released to the press. I was sick with a cold and decided to go to bed early. At the Statler Hilton, I met Brother Malcolm for the first time—he had come to observe the March (which he would later term "the Farce on Washington"). We talked casually for a few minutes and then I left to get some rest.

On the day of the March, the SNCC people gathered at the Statler Hilton and we went as a group to the Washington Monument and from there to the Lincoln Memorial. We sang freedom songs to amuse ourselves and discussed the hypocrisy of the March. Everywhere there were large groups from labor unions and especially the United Automobile Workers, all with prominent signs. We had asked them for financial help and they had refused. We felt that not only the UAW, but many other so-called liberal forces were shamming and this was just another march. It would not solve the problems of the people we worked with. We talked of the expense involved in getting all these people to Washington and thought of our own desperate financial situation. We saw bus after bus full of people arriving and our hearts grew sick. In Mississippi we had been desperately trying to buy two cars and we needed a few buses to transport people from place to place. Amid the affluence of the March on Washington, we became more bitter at the established civil rights groups and the white liberals who were fronting off black people. We talked about the poverty of the people with whom we worked and wondered when people, including civil rights organizations, were going to stop putting on displays of wealth such as we now saw. We knew that many groups had large signs only for the benefit of the press and the television cameras. They had not done a damn thing for civil rights and they certainly were not helping us in the Deep South.

But we also knew Lewis had a dynamite speech that would puncture the tranquility of the March and the efforts of the Kennedy administration to make this look like a popular uprising in favor of his Civil Rights Bill.

As I approached the top floor inside the Lincoln Memorial, I was met by Chuck Neblett and Matthew Jones of the Freedom Singers.

"Hey, man. Did you hear what they did to John's speech?"

It was 1:00 P.M. The program was due to begin at 1:15.

"What do you mean? What are you talking about?"

"They don't want Lewis to give his speech."

I started toward a group of the March speakers, very excited, my blood pressure starting to rise. I knew that there was hostility to Lewis's speech and felt sure they had pulled some trick.

"Now be calm," Abernathy said to me. "We're going to work it out. Just stay calm, Jim."

In a few minutes, enough of the story emerged to outrage me. The night before, in the hotel, there had been a meeting of Bayard, John Lewis, Courtland Cox, and some other officials of the March. Archbishop Patrick O'Doyle had said that he would not appear on the platform with Lewis if John was going to say, as planned, that SNCC could not support the Civil Rights Bill of John Kennedy. There were some other objections to a section where Lewis planned to say that we will "march through Dixie like Sherman, leaving a scorched earth with our nonviolence." John had agreed to delete the section about Sherman from his speech. Other passages of not too much consequence were also changed.

But new objections were now being voiced, especially by Rev. Eugene Carson Blake of the National Council of Churches. Even the archbishop was not satisfied. A committee was appointed to work out the differences: King, A. Philip Randolph, Abernathy, Bayard Rustin, Courtland Cox, John Lewis, Eugene Carson Blake, a representative from the Catholic Interracial Committee on Justice, and myself. The group closeted in a small anteroom on the top floor of the Lincoln Memorial. We of SNCC began to lecture them on the importance of John's speech and the suffering that speech expressed. I was furious, scornful, and deriding the federal government for all its inaction in places where we had worked.

Meanwhile, outdoors, the speeches had to be delayed. Indoors, A. Philip Randolph began to plead for unity. Bayard started telling us that John's speech would take longer than the five minutes allotted to each speaker, although in the end Dr. King spoke for twenty or more minutes about his derams while the black people lived in nightmares.

Finally we got down to brass tacks. Eugene Carson Blake objected to the fact that the words *masses* and *revolution* were used in the speech. He was afraid that people would label the March as communist. Even A. Philip Randolph had to speak out against that argument, saying that he used the word *masses* and also called for a social *revolution*.

Then came the key point. SNCC had agreed a day or two before to change Lewis's speech from saying "we cannot support" the Kennedy Civil Rights Bill to saying "we cannot wholeheartedly support" it, because there were sections of the bill that members of our organization did support. (This change was omitted from the text released to the press, by an oversight.) Now, however, Eugene Carson Blake began to object to the word *wholeheartedly*. We said that possibly we could change the phrase to read "we support with reservations." It seemed like a small matter to us, then; we thought that Blake and the others siding with him were just masturbating over words.

At that point, the SNCC people decided to caucus separately—John, Courtland, and myself. We discussed the situation and found that we were not in a bad position. The press had copies of the original speech. Any deviation from that text was certainly going to call further attention to it and indicate disagreement. In addition, there were members of the press who already knew that there was conflict over the speech. We did not know at that time that Burke Marshall had leaked to the press a statement that the archbishop would not speak if John's speech went unchanged. This might have made a difference in our approach. But we figured that news coverage of John's original remarks, plus portions of the actual speech and editorial comments on the dispute, would put us in a favorable position.

We then agreed that I should take all the changes they had agreed to the night before and that day, and rework the speech. I felt that there were ways we could make the speech still stronger, reflecting more intensely our anger and frustration, our aspirations and hopes. After we did all that, we were not going to change one comma. If the church people didn't like it, they could go to hell. I started to work, as fast as I could, with the program starting before I had finished. I included the change to "we support with reservations" and there was no further dispute.

It would be years after the March, only after more experiences with the churches—especially at the time of the Black Manifesto—that it became clear to me why Eugene Carson Blake felt that change to be significant. It was not just quibbling over words, but a matter of substance, given the underlying purpose of the March.

Somewhere along the line, the church and labor people had been told that this was a march to support the administration's Civil Rights Bill, which was passed in 1964, after Kennedy's death. Who did this and how it happened, I do not know. But people all over the country thought they were marching for jobs and freedom when in actuality the sellout leadership of the March on Washington was playing patsy with the Kennedy administration as part of the whole liberal-labor politics of Rustin, Wilkins, Randolph, Reuther, King, the Catholic and Protestant hierarchy. If people had known they had come to Washington to aid the Kennedy administration, they would not have come in the numbers they did. Moreover, if I personally had had any idea of the true purpose of the March on Washington, I would have resisted our participation in that March.

In this context, it is clear why Blake and others preferred that "we support with reservations." If it was the intent of the Kennedy administration for the white liberals and sellout Toms to create a base of support, then to have apparent unanimity of support for the civil rights bill was important. It did not matter that one group supported "with reservations"; it supported, nevertheless. If, on the other hand, we had said "we cannot support wholeheartedly" or "we cannot support" period, the whole game would have been shot.

All this we did not, as I said, realize for some time. But we soon saw how the March was used by the U.S. Government and the liberal-labor syndrome to improve the American image abroad. The USIA film on the March, of which hundreds of prints were made, was shown all over the world as proof of how it was possible for peaceful "dissent" to take place in this country—how people exercised their "democratic rights" under this best of all possible systems. At the same time the March served to stifle manifestations of serious dissent and to take the steam out of the black anger then rising in the South, eventually to explode in many parts of the North as well. We were beginning to see the whole process by which fancy productions like the March on Washington tended to "psych off" local protest and make people feel they had accomplished something— changed something, somehow—when, in fact, nothing had been changed. In 1965 the Selma-to-Montgomery March would confirm this feeling once and for all. Such marches could be compared to the antipoverty program and other government-backed efforts with a veneer of popular participation: All are tools to subvert mass discontent and must be guarded against carefully.

The speech John Lewis finally delivered, despite its concession on the phrase about support, was still a strong indictment that could not have made the bosses of the March very happy. This is what he said:

We march today for jobs and freedom, but we have nothing to be proud of. For hundreds and thousands of our brothers are not here. They have no money for their transportation, for they are receiving starvation wages . . . or no wages at all. While we stand here, there are sharecroppers in the Delta of Mississippi who are out in the fields working for less than three dollars a day for twelve hours of work. While we stand here, there are students in jail on trumped-up charges. Our brother, James Farmer, along with many others is also in jail. We come here today with a great sense of misgiving.

It is true that we support the present civil rights bill in the Congress. We support it with great reservations, however. Unless Title Three is put in this bill, there is nothing to protect young children and old women from police dogs and fire hoses, their penalties for engaging in peaceful demonstrations. In its present form this bill will not protect the citizens of Danville, Virginia, who must live in constant fear in a police state. It will not protect the hundreds of people who have been arrested on phony charges. What about the three young men—SNCC field secretaries—in Americus, Georgia who face the death penalty for engaging in peaceful protest?

As it stands now the voting section of this bill will not help thousands of black people who want to vote. It will not help the citizens of Mississippi, of Alabama and Georgia who are qualified to vote but lack a 6th grade education. "One man, one vote," is the African cry. It is ours, too. It must be ours. Let us tell the Congress: One man, one vote.

We must have legislation that will protect the Mississippi sharecropper who is put off his farm because he dares to register to vote. We need a bill that will provide for the homeless and starving people of this nation. We need a bill that will ensure the equality of a maid who earns $5 a week in the home of a family whose income is $100,000 a year. We must have a good FEPC bill.

Let us not forget that we are involved in a serious social revolution. By and large, American politics is dominated by politicians who build their careers on immoral compromises and ally themselves with open forms of political, economic and social exploitation. There are exceptions, of course. We salute those. But what political leader can stand up and say, "My party is the party of principles?" The party of Javits is also the party of Goldwater. Where is *our* party? Where is the political party that will make it unnecessary to have Marches on Washington?

Where is the political party that will protect the citizens of Albany, Georgia? Do you know that in Albany, Georgia, nine of our leaders have been indicted not by Dixiecrats but by the Federal Government for peaceful protest? But what did the Federal Government do when Albany's Deputy Sheriff beat Attorney C. B. King and let him go half dead? What did the Federal Government do when local officials kicked and assaulted the pregnant wife of Slater King, and she lost her baby?

To those who have said, be patient and wait, we must say that we cannot be patient, we do not want to be free gradually. We want our freedom and we want it *now!* We are tired of being beaten by policemen. We do not want to go to jail if that is what we must pay for love, brotherhood and peace.

All of us must get in this great social revolution sweeping our nation. Get in and stay in the streets of every city, every village and every hamlet of this nation, until true Freedom comes, until the unfinished revolution of 1776 is complete. In the Delta of Mississippi, in southwest Georgia, in Alabama, Harlem, Chicago, Detroit, Philadelphia and all over this nation—the black masses are on the march. You must go home from this March and help us to get our Freedom.

We will not stop now. All of the forces of Eastland, Barnett, Wallace and Thurmond will not stop this revolution. If we do not get meaningful legislation out of this Congress, the time will come when we will not confine our marching to Washington. We will march through the South—through the streets of Jackson, Danville, Cambridge, Nashville and Birmingham—with the dignity and spirit we have shown here today. By the force of our demands, our determination, and our numbers, we shall splinter the segregated South into a thousand pieces and put them back together in the image of God and democracy. Wake up, America!

CHAPTER 44

Americus, Georgia

IN THE fall of 1962 I had read Che Guevara's book on guerrilla warfare and drew some lessons from it for our work. I saw SNCC establishing bases throughout the South, bases that would grow into larger units. As we consolidated our power in the rural areas and the smaller cities, the time would come when we would work in larger cities. We would have to attack problems other than the vote, problems we faced as a people in our daily lives: jobs, housing, education, welfare, medical care. There was never any doubt in my mind that we would confirm the right to vote and win unlimited use of public accommodations. The March on Washington had indicated that the administration and the liberal-labor forces were prepared to push hard on those issues out of their own self-interest. We were, in the fall of 1963, approaching a new era in the struggle.

But the first stage was by no means ended. Nothing could have made this clearer than the horrendous bombing of the Birmingham church in which six girls were killed—the bombing which came right on the heels of the March and made a mockery of it. The South was still crying "never," and using every vicious, bloodthirsty, inhuman tactic at its disposal to stop the wheels of history. Although the urge toward retaliatory violence was growing stronger and stronger, as events following that bombing showed, it was still necessary to begin at the beginning—to conquer the fear of many blacks. Although the Southern way of life was no longer a sacred cow for increasing numbers of black people, there were still many pockets of feudalism where the grip of white supremacy had not begun to loosen.

One of these was Americus, Georgia.

SNCC workers had come into Americus in January of 1963, living with the people as usual and helping the local Sumter County Movement to register voters and to organize attempts to use the front door of a local movie theater. In July close to a hundred people had been arrested in connection with the theater demonstrations and spent forty-six days in jail. In this case, the manager was willing to let black people enter, but local police wouldn't allow such a transgression against gracious living in the South. As elsewhere, the demonstrators were almost entirely high school students. And Willie Ricks of SNCC was busy on the scene, working again with young people and charged now with contributing to the delinquency of minors.

Then came August and the longest, hottest month of all in Americus. On the eighth, some 250 black people were attending a mass meeting at the Friendship Baptist Church. Police stood by, but the people—mostly teen-agers—decided to go outside and walked down one block to a "colored" café where they began singing "We Shall Overcome." The police tried to surround the group but, as one participant reported, "we surrounded them."

Police began shooting in the air and told the crowd to disperse, the participant said, "but we just kept on singing. They started shooting, but nobody moved." The police and troopers then moved in with guns and billy clubs, slugging their way through the group to arrest SNCC field secretary Don Harris—whom they considered its leader. He was beaten and dragged to a squad car. SNCC workers Ralph Allen and John Perdew were also beaten and arrested. The three were held initially on bonds totaling forty thousand dollars apiece and several charges. The main one became "attempting to incite insurrection," a crime for which the death penalty can be given in Georgia—and for which they were not allowed to be bonded out. Two local youths were also beaten and arrested that evening, and held on bonds of twenty thousand dollars apiece. (Naturally, the charges against them included "assault and battery.")

The next day 175 black people went to protest the brutality and the arrests. "They left the church," said John L. Barnum, Jr., treasurer of the Sumter County Movement, "and walked four blocks in orderly columns of twos, not blocking the sidewalk. The police officers were armed with guns, two-foot clubs, electric cattle prodders and blackjacks . . . the City Marshal and Police Chief asked them if they had a permit to parade and asked them to disperse. But before any response could be given, the officers started bludgeoning groups of boys and girls with clubs and cattle prodders, which give a severe shock and leave burn marks on the flesh." Most of the persons in the group were arrested. One required twenty stitches in his head, another six, another four, and so on, while others had scars from the burns. You didn't have to be in the demonstration to be hurt—several persons just sitting or walking in the area were beaten and one man had his leg broken.

It went on and on. Another group of twenty-five people was arrested while kneeling in prayer at the police station. A black youth was shot at while out walking, seventeen police officers then beat and arrested him, and his mother was arrested when she went to the police station to ask about his condition. A thirteen-year-old boy who had participated in the demonstrations was kicked and viciously beaten by police, then arrested. On August 17 another thirty-five were arrested while praying at the police station. A CORE worker who was with the group before it reached the police station found himself charged with attempting to incite insurrection. On August 20 a thirty-year-old Korean War veteran named James Brown was shot and killed by a local policeman with a bullet in the back of his neck. His offense, apparently, was walking through a white section of town.

Among the many affidavits collected by SNCC workers during this time were these two:

James Williams, being duly sworn, deposes and says:
On Friday night, Aug. 9, I went from a fish fry in Brooklyn Heights to a barber shop at the corner of Lee and Ashby Streets, in Americus, Ga. The barber shop was closed and Gene Mann and I started across the street to the cafe. A policeman shouted, "Halt!" and we were scared and stopped. Then Gene Mann ran away. I talked with the policeman on Lee Street facing Ashby. Then a panel truck came with two state patrolmen. The policeman made a big knot on my head behind my left ear with his billy club. He didn't say anything to me before he did it. I fell down and the two state patrolmen started hitting me up the side of the head, they hit me with something like a baseball bat. I can't describe the pain. But my whole head felt swollen and the blood was gushing down my face.

I told them I couldn't get up. The state patrolmen had asked me and then the policeman with them said, "Let me have him," and he stomped me on the leg. They kept asking me to get up. Then the state patrolmen pulled out a "hot shot," a long silver-looking stick run by batteries and burned me in the right rib section. I still have a big old blue-looking spot there. After they got through doing that they got Gene Mann back and some other fellow and had them put me in the truck. And then they took me to jail. Then they laid me down by one of the cells and went out. And a lot of the guys already in there crowded around me.

About a half hour later they took me outside on the concrete steps, they said, "Who do you work for, boy?" I told them I worked for the same man they did, the mayor. I cut steel for the nail plant that Mayor Griffin Walker's wife manages. . . . Then they said, "We better carry this son of a bitch to the car and get him to the hospital."

During the week of Aug. 12 I talked with men from the FBI. I was in the hospital at the time. They asked me what happened and I told them. I explained that my leg was broken by the patrolmen and they asked me about my head.

Lena Turner, being duly sworn, deposes and says:
I, Lena Turner, am willing to testify in court that I saw the police of Americus, Ga., bring into the jail the beaten bodies of Milton Wickerson, James Williams and Mr. McClendon, who is 67 years old. I could clearly see that they had been beaten and told the FBI investigators that during the week of Aug. 12.

After they came in, I saw Milton with blood all over his shirt. I said to Milton, "What happened?" And he said, "It was rough, it was rough." He turned his head and I could see blood all running down his face. By this time they brought James Williams in, and he was crying and moaning and the others who had been arrested crowded around him. Someone hollered out, "His leg is broken, call the cops!" The cops had gone out the back into the hall leading to the white cell. Then they stood aside and I could see him lying down on the floor. He was stretched out on the floor and I could see the blood on his pants and his head was rolling from side to side. I could tell he was in pain. I was in my cell. They kept yelling and yelling that James' leg was broken and finally the cops came back with more prisoners. They were told again that his leg was broken. So they said, "Okay, all you guys who are hurt bad enough —let's go." The prisoners said, "We can't carry him, his leg is broken." Everybody crowded around him again and then moved through the back door and someone must have picked him up and carried him out.

When they came back, Milton Wilkerson had his head bandaged. Mr. McClendon had a bandage on the top of his head and others had bandages on their heads and arms. You could see cuts on their arms. They were open wounds, not exactly bleeding, just that somehow the skin had been opened. It was awful. I had never seen anything like it before. The cuts looked like what you see when you go to the movies, see weird tales.

About thirty minutes before the arrests I had seen the policemen come in, go to their lockers, get their equipment. They got their hats, the kind they use to play football, the billy sticks and a box with wires and something on the front of it. One of the officers said, "You want to use that tear gas?" But I don't know whether they ever got it.

The following week of Aug. 12 I was upstairs in the courthouse cleaning the floors. Lorine Sanders and I were singing freedom songs as we mopped the floors and the men who later turned out to be the FBI men went into the courtroom. We went into the courtroom and Lorine asked one of the two men for a match. He introduced himself as an FBI man by showing us his credentials. He asked us why we were there. He asked us if we were among those arrested Friday, Aug. 9. I told him that we weren't among them, but that we surely know about it. He said he already knew about it. That was the reason he was there, he said.

I then volunteered to tell him about the fact that several people had been beaten, that James Williams had his leg broken by the police and about the others, too, although I didn't actually mention their names. I did tell him that many had required stitches and gone to the hospital. I explained to him that there was a man 67 years old, Mr. McClendon, still in the city hall and that he had been beaten.

In a few minutes I saw him talk with McClendon and I saw him talk with three or four cops.

It must have been the cops that the FBI chose to believe. For, despite a mountain of evidence like those affidavits, the Justice Department managed to announce on August 12 that it had uncovered "no evidence of police brutality."

This finding was made all the more disgusting and infuriating by an action which the federal government had taken just three days earlier. It found no police brutality against blacks in Americus, but over in Albany it found reason to indict eight black citizens and a SNCC worker for crimes supposedly committed against the white world. This piece of upside down justice was the result of a complicated case rising out of the fact that a white-owned supermarket in the black neighborhood had been picketed and boycotted in April, 1963, for failing to give blacks anything but menial jobs. The owner happened to have been a member of the all-white federal jury which had ruled in favor of the local sheriff over a black man charging him with brutal violation (including three shots in the neck) of his civil rights. "Intimidation of a federal juror" was the whites' charge against the blacks for their picketing—and a federal grand jury chose to believe them.

It also indicted for perjury Joni Rabinowitz, a white student from New York working with the local movement, who had testified that she had not been present at the picket line. The grand jury indicted her despite the fact that another young lady testified that she was the white girl present, and not Joni Rabinowitz. Five others were similarly indicted for perjury. The group included Slater King, whose wife had lost her baby after being assaulted, and Rev. Samuel Wells, who had also been active in the Albany Movement and who had been dragged to jail by his genitals on July 8. The trials in this infamous case would take place later in 1963 and heavy sentences were handed down which took years to appeal and finally win.

It was all too clear whose side Uncle Sam was on. And it was these cases that we had wanted to protest during the March on Washington— but that had been too heavy for the liberals involved.

With the police on a rampage of uncontrolled violence, and no hope of protection from the federal government, intimidation pervaded the black community of Americus. One black businessman refused to allow any Movement worker to enter his restaurant, pool hall, or liquor store. In mid-August there was no restaurant where workers could eat—they could only order food "to go out," that was all. There was one restaurant owner who seemed fearless in the face of intimidation—a big, strong black woman. Once, when the city marshal tried to get tough with her, he found a gun pointed at him. But even she came to the point of refusing to serve Movement people. Her beer license had been revoked, her son and son-in-law had been arrested several times on phony charges, and it was rumored that she had been threatened with foreclosure on a debt incurred to start her business. In other ways, however, she remained a fighter—she would not sell Coca-Cola at her restaurant because of a nationwide boycott organized by civil rights groups demanding fair employment for blacks.

Meanwhile, more than a hundred young people remained in jail for weeks on end because they could not post a two hundred dollar cash "appearance" bond, and the judge had taken a long, so-called vacation and no hearings took place. In addition, jailed blacks were no longer permitted to call the only bondsman in town friendly to Movement people. Bonds by then totaled two hundred thousand dollars for all those arrested since August—the setting of exorbitant bonds being another white tactic. Conditions in the jail were described as "unbelievable" by one observer, like animal cages. Children under the age of twelve slept on the floor of a filthy building, with no working toilet facilities or showers. Affidavits taken by SNCC from two girls describe the conditions in more detail:

> Lorine Sanders, being duly sworn, deposes and says:
> I was arrested July 19 with 42 others while on the way to city hall to protest the arrest of the seven people that were arrested for trying to purchase tickets at the Martin Theater. The group consisted of eighteen young adults and twenty-four adults. . . .
> While the group was standing and singing, Chief Chambliss said, "All right, you people are under arrest." He had not told us to disperse. All of us sat down except two other people. A girl, Lena Turner, stood reading a Bible and a boy knelt. Sheriff Chappel screamed to the boy "Sit down, nigger, with the rest of the crowd." He then looked at the girl and said, "You sit down, too. You feel like a frog, too—jump, damn it."
> Chief Chambliss called for the paddy wagon that was a feed and seed truck. When the truck arrived he said, "I'm going to ask you orderly to get up and get on the truck." We got on the truck and were carried to jail.
> After we arrived the Chief came to the back of the jail and called Lena Turner. He took her inside. I was placed in a cell with seven others. Four bunks were in the cell. We put the bunks together and I slept between four other people.
> In my cell there were dirty mattresses. We asked for soap but were refused. There was no hot water in the cell. We used a nasty wash basin to wash our face and hands. The ventilation was poor and the place was hot all the time. We were given two meals on Saturday and a sandwich. Sometimes the hamburgers were spoiled and half cooked.
> Once when we were singing, the guards came back and yelled at us, saying "Stop that damn fuss" but we continued to sing.
> The Monday after the arrest we went to trial. (Four of us had already been arrested before, but our sentences had been suspended.) This time we spent forty-nine days working on the street and in the jail. One day we cut the grass on the street. Another day we carried parking meters up three flights of stairs.
> I spent fifty-two days and fifty-three nights in the city jail of Americus.

And Lena Turner would state in her affidavit that police had shoved her into a cell, alone, where "the sink was clogged and filled with dirty water. The commode was clogged with waste. The mattresses were filthy and infested with bedbugs and roaches. The floors were littered with decayed paper. . . . One day I was sick and asked for a doctor. But the guard refused. He said, 'The city doctor ain't got time to be bothered with you.' He started in my cell with a stick. I told him my disease was contagious, in order for him to leave."

The three SNCC field secretaries—Don Harris, Ralph Allen, and John Perdew—remained in jail for three months without bond, facing a possible death sentence. On November 1, 1963, a three-judge federal panel ruled the "incitement to insurrection" charge against them to be unconstitutional. But five days later, Ralph Allen was found guilty by an all-white jury of another charge against him from the same arrest: assault with intent to murder. Sentenced to two years in prison, he appealed his case. It is worth noting that the insurrection charge brought against this group had been used only once before, against Angelo Herndon, a black man from Atlanta and a member of the Communist Party, who organized workers in the 1930s and who was in fact sentenced to death. Only a decision by the U.S. Supreme Court saved his life. Things hadn't changed much in thirty years, it seemed.

But they were changing. Not so much in the external lives of black people, the way they existed from day to day, as in their minds. And the white man knew it, saw it as the greatest of threats, moved to crush it. The change and the attempts to crush change were taking place in other parts of Georgia besides Americus. SNCC's work in the town of Albany and in Terrell County went on. In "Terrible Terrell" thirty blacks were registered in November, 1963, so the house of Mrs. Carolyn Daniels, serving as a voter registration headquarters for SNCC, had to be riddled by bullets and bombed early Sunday morning, December 8. Half the house was blown away; Mrs. Daniels luckily escaped with only a bullet in her foot.

The continuous brutality in Americus and nearby areas occupied much of the attention of the Atlanta office that fall. We issued many news releases, reports, appeals for intervention and help. We brought groups of Americus blacks to Atlanta to talk to the press. But, to my regret, I was unable to visit Americus in person and probably for that reason the national office received some severe criticism by the southwest Georgia staff for giving insufficient attention to its activities and problems. No excuse can be adequate, but the fact is that events all across the South had reached an overwhelming pace. Everywhere there were projects developing and repression mounting. It was impossible to meet all the demands as we should have met them. By September of 1963 we had projects going in Alabama, Mississippi, Georgia, Arkansas, Tennessee, Maryland, and were planning new ones in North and South Carolina and Texas. The Arkansas project was gaining steam—it had started in Pine Bluff that year; students had conducted sit-ins, then been suspended and thus radicalized, and momentum grew from that point.

In the process of establishing and developing our projects, SNCC was constantly seeking new ways to attack white supremacy—imaginative forms and styles that would involve more black people in mass actions. The "Freedom Day" was one of these and its first test came in Selma, Alabama, that October.

CHAPTER 45

Selma Freedom Day

ON SUNDAY, September 22, 1963, a group of prominent whites in Selma, Alabama, ran the following full-page advertisement in the local *Times Journal*:

A DECLARATION OF BASIC RIGHTS AND PRINCIPLES

The white and Negro races have lived together in Selma and Dallas County for many generations in a state of peace and tranquility; and Selma will continue to be the home of both races long after agitators have done their evil work of poisoning the minds of some of our Negro citizens.

We have enjoyed mutual confidence and trust between the races, and this will again prevail regardless of current unrest. . . . Through the efforts of white leadership in the county, great strides have been made in the field of industrial development; and this has created thousands of jobs for Negro workers. Without such leadership there would never have been such opportunities for these Negroes. . . .

To maintain such a society of mutual confidence, trust and respect between the races, there must be mutual recognition of and respect for certain basic rights and principles. These include:

1. The right to sell and rent property according to individual inclination and amenable to the written laws of the country.
2. The right to own and operate private business in such manner as is deemed sound and proper by the operators thereof with unchallenged authority to select such personnel as the owner desires and to use such methods as have demonstrated themselves to be most conducive to sound and profitable management.
3. The right to select one's own associates, whatever the occasion.

These basic rights are to be enjoyed by all people of both races, and the white citizens of Dallas County are firmly united in their determination to preserve them, because of their conviction that freedom as conceived by our Founding Fathers, does not grant any minority, be it white or Negro through threats or otherwise, the right to force its will upon the majority. Neither do we believe that the majority has the right to impose its will upon a minority. We believe that freedom means equal and untrammelled opportunity for all citizens to better themselves through their own efforts—not by legislation and not by demonstrations backed by threats, which inevitably result in both force and reprisals.

We further believe it to be axiomatic that any action taken by any group whether by a minority or majority, if such action is either unlawful, or is lawful with unlawful intent, will bring reprisals which are frequently more detrimental to the innocent than to the guilty. These guilty ones are usually agitators, who having done their evil work, will probably vanish from our community, leaving us to pick up the pieces and repair the damage.

Time is fast running out. . . . Responsible Negro leaders should take immediate steps to put down agitation among their people. In this effort, they can count upon the full cooperation of our white citizens, the governmental bodies of our city and county and all of our law enforcement facilities.

We believe that through mutual understanding and efforts of the responsible citizens of our community, both white and Negro, confidence, trust and respect between the races in Selma can and will be restored and maintained.

The undersigned stand firmly united in their belief in, and adherence to, these basic rights and principles of people of both races.

SELMA RETAIL MERCHANTS ASSN.
Julius M. Lillienthal, President

DALLAS COUNTY FARM BUREAU
Walter C. Givhan, President

SELMA RETAIL CREDIT BUREAU
Frank Wilson, President

DALLAS COUNTY BAR ASSN.
Theodore L. Wade, President

SELMA AND DALLAS COUNTY CLEARING HOUSE ASSN.

THE PEOPLES BANK & TRUST CO.
Rex J. Morthland, President

THE SELMA NATIONAL BANK
Roger C. Jones, President

CITIZENS BANK AND TRUST CO.
J. Bruce Pardue, President

THE CITY NATIONAL BANK OF SELMA
William B. Craig, Pres.

MARION JUNCTION STATE BANK
James M. Gilmer, Ex V.P. & Cashier

SELMA AUTOMOBILE DEALERS ASSN.
W. F. Driggers, Pres.

DALLAS COUNTY DRUGGIST ASSN.
E. O. Ward, Pres.

SELMA BOARD OF REALTORS
William H. Hicks, Pres.

DALLAS COUNTY CATTLE-MEN'S ASSN.
W. R. Martin, Pres.

SELMA & DALLAS COUNTY CHAMBER OF COMMERCE
R. E. Ellzey, Pres.

SELMA RESTAURANT ASSN.
William Speed, V.P.

DALLAS COUNTY DENTAL STUDY CLUB
E. A. Wilkinson, Pres.

ALA. SERVICE STATION ASSN.
Nick Patterson, Pres.

1st FEDERAL SAVINGS & LOAN ASSN.
Charles S. Frazer, Pres.

ACCOUNTANTS OF SELMA & DALLAS COUNTY

SELMA JUNIOR CHAMBER OF COMMERCE
Robert J. Robinson, Pres.

COMMITTEE OF 100 PLUS
Otis G. Adams, President

Some three months had passed since that first full-page advertisement in the same newspaper asking, "What Have You Done to Maintain Segregation?" It was a tribute to the work of Bernard and Colia LaFayette that the tone was now a little more worried, more careful, more defensive. For those who know the South, both advertisements were issued by the same people, despite the fact that the first was signed by the Citizens' Council while this one carried the names of many "respectables."

It is often thought that only so-called "white trash" provoked violence against black people. But in most Southern towns, the truly powerful forces of intimidation and repression rest in the hands of the moneyed classes—who in turn constitute the White Citizens' Council. In Selma, the council was the leader of opposition to SNCC. It controlled the Dallas County power structure. Its president was the president of one of Selma's largest manufacturing companies, and whites who did not support the council found it impossible to get loans at local banks.

The council went about its racist business with a thin veneer of respectability, leaving the dirty work to Sheriff Jim Clark and his three-hundred-man posse. Its members included about a hundred men wearing old army fatigues, helmets, and boots, and the whole posse was empowered to carry weapons and make arrests. Jim Clark himself set the style for their enforcement of the law: Gun on his hip, electric cattle prodder in hand, he would stand watching at every mass meeting held by SNCC, the Dallas County Voters League, or the Dallas County Improvement Association. Big Belly Jim Clark, we called him.

And behind both the sleek, double-talking council and Big Belly Clark stood the awesome power of the U.S. Air Force itself, in the form of Craig Air Force Base, located on the outskirts of Selma, with a payroll of six hundred thousand dollars a month—most of which was spent with Selma businessmen. This meant that federal money was one of the mainstays of Selma's economy, but black servicemen stationed there were subjected to discrimination of every type when they left the base, and they were not even admitted to the local USO.

On June 7, 1963, Secretary of Defense Robert McNamara issued a directive stating that:

Discriminatory practices directed against Armed Forces members . . . are harmful to military effectiveness. Therefore, all members of the Department of Defense should oppose such practices on every occasion while fostering equal opportunity for servicemen and their families *on and off base* [Italics mine]. . . . Every military commander has the responsibility to oppose discriminatory practices affecting his men and their dependents and *to foster equal opportunity for them, not only in areas under his immediate control, but also in nearby communities where they may live or gather in off-duty hours* [italics mine].

In September of that year, SNCC field secretary Worth Long obtained an appointment with the commander of Craig Air Force Base, Col. Richard Ault. He went to see Ault on September 21, together with a Selma student leader and Mrs. Amelia Boynton, a local businesswoman.

The group requested that Selma be placed off limits to base personnel because of the town's racist practices. The request was refused. SNCC chairman John Lewis then wired the Defense Department in Washington repeating the request and it, too, refused to act. The reason: Their request was based on "alleged discrimination against civilians rather than servicemen." Two months later the Air Force announced that it planned to expand operations at the Craig Base considerably. More money for the White Citizens' Council businessmen of Selma, more blacks to be taught "their place."

Worth Long had been placed on SNCC's staff as an assistant to me, with the title of staff coordinator, and Selma was one of his first assignments. Bernard and Colia LaFayette had left in the summer of 1963 to return to school, as originally planned. This kind of turnover in personnel was a constant problem in SNCC; fortunately the LaFayettes had left behind an organized cadre of young people to carry on. There was also a handful of adults like Mrs. Amelia Boynton, a tall, stout, very strong black woman, long active in Selma, always ready to help, who let us open an office in the back of her insurance agency. Then Worth Long came in September and began working not only on the Air Force issue but also on segregation policies in the town.

On September 15 five black high school students were arrested while sitting-in at a number of lunch counters. One of them, Lula Brown, fifteen, was knocked off a lunch counter stool at a Carter-Walgreen drugstore and shocked with an electric cattle prodder by a man believed to be one of Jim Clark's posse. A nineteen-year-old boy was hit from behind by another posse member, and later required seven stitches in his scalp.

Later that day close to a hundred high school students set out to march in protest against the arrests and beatings. They, too, were arrested. Worth Long, who was not even on the march, was also arrested and then beaten in the county jail. The pace of events quickened rapidly in the next few days, with up to a thousand students boycotting classes to protest segregation. Selma had clearly become an important center of resistance.

When I arrived there in the last week of September, my first objective was to turn the demonstrations and the whole climate of protest into a thrust for the right to vote and against Jim Clark. Students agreed that they would begin holding demonstrations and carrying signs that talked about the right to vote. Our strategy as usual was to force the U.S. Government to intervene in case there were arrests—and if they did not intervene, that inaction would once again prove the government was not on our side and thus intensify the development of a mass consciousness among blacks.

Our slogan for this drive was "One Man, One Vote"—a phrase which had been the cry of many African nations during the years when they had been negotiating for independence from their colonial masters. I had learned about it from my studies on Africa, and John Lewis had used the phrase in his March on Washington speech as an appropriate cry for our struggle, too. Who could deny the justice of "One Man (or one woman), One Vote"? Jim Clark, of course.

On September 25, John Lewis was jailed along with twenty-seven students from Selma University for leading a picket at the county courthouse demanding "One Man, One Vote," and all were sentenced to one hundred days. Then Dick Gregory came to town with his wife, Lillian. Instead of Dick's participating openly in the demonstrations and getting arrested yet another time, Lillian carried a sign saying "One Man, One Vote." She was arrested two days after John Lewis and the students. At that point, I shot off a telegram to Attorney General Robert Kennedy asking for an immediate temporary restraining order against Jim Clark and others "who are interfering with peaceful picketing to encourage voter registration." We were building a trap for Jim Clark, and we knew that he knew it—he was getting jittery. The White Citizens' Council, as its advertisement of September 22 clearly showed, didn't like us outside agitators. On the other hand, we were just asking for the right to vote— and the U.S. Department of Justice had already filed a suit in 1961 to enjoin practices which prevented black people from voting in Dallas County.

The climax of our strategy came on October 7, 1963: Freedom Day in Selma, Alabama. "Freedom Now" had become a popular slogan, but making it come alive in Selma was rough going. The event was based on the fact that there were only two days a month when people could register. On those two days, the registrar would take an hour for each person—if the people were black. At that rate, it would take ten years to enroll as many blacks as whites in Dallas County. We wanted to demonstrate that this situation was a perpetual hindrance to black registration. More importantly, we felt that if we could get a large number of our people to stand in line at the courthouse, it would be a show of strength and give heart to other blacks in Selma. Large crowds had been attending the mass meetings, but it is a long way from a mass meeting to standing out in the hot sun in front of a county courthouse trying to register to vote. We needed a psychological victory—for the brave people who had already stuck out their necks, for the skeptical blacks in town, and for ourselves—the organizers.

I woke up early that morning, feeling the tension. It was there, under my eyelids. My whole body ached with the strain of many demonstrations. The summer of 1963 seemed to weigh on me as I put on my blue overalls and white shirt. I put my bottle of Maalox in my pocket—I tried to protect my health by constantly watching my diet and taking my medicine, although my sleeping habits were something else again. Mrs. Amelia Boynton cooked a good breakfast of eggs and toast and grits that morning. We had no idea where or when our next meal would be.

A group of us were in the office by eight o'clock. We did not know just how many people would show up at the courthouse to try to register, but we had done everything possible to get them there: singing and exhorting at mass meetings, initiating a "ten-and-ten" telephone campaign in which we urged everyone at the mass meetings to call at least ten people and ask each of them to call ten more. We wanted the entire black population of Selma to know of this Freedom Day and its significance.

We also wanted black people beyond Alabama to hear about it, and for this reason had invited author James Baldwin to join us that day. The inclusion of personalities from the world of entertainment, from the arts, was a tactic we developed from our analysis that many people in the nation identified with them. Whatever they did, other black people would in a sense feel it. They represented part of the national consciousness, especially of black people. To involve people like Gregory and Baldwin was to involve many thousands more who could not come to Selma or Greenwood or whatever the place might be.

In an article published in the *New Republic* on October 26, 1963, Howard Zinn, a history professor and for several years a SNCC adviser, describes Freedom Day:

By 11:00 A.M. there were 250 Negroes in the line, which extended the full length of the block, around the corner, and halfway down the street. Two hundred of them would never get inside the courthouse door.

Standing over these men and women, were helmeted men with clubs and guns, members of Sheriff Clark's posse. By noon, the line of Negroes reached 300. The sun was hot, and the line did not seem to be moving.

Directly across the street from the county courthouse in Selma is the Federal Building. Here are the federal court, the draft board, the social security office —all the visible manifestations that the Civil War was won by the Union and that the national government is supreme all over the United States. In this building, on the first floor, its windows looking directly at the county courthouse, is the office of the Federal Bureau of Investigation, the police force of the national government, created to enforce the laws of the United States.

Four FBI agents and two Justice Department lawyers spent Freedom Day in this building. The FBI agents were taking pictures, and watching. The Justice Department men were just watching.

Through all that happened on that Monday, while federal law was broken again and again, these law enforcement officials of the federal government stood by and watched. By the time Freedom Day was over in Selma, the Constitution had been violated in a number of its provisions, several statutes of the U.S. Congress had been ignored, the Civil Rights Acts of 1957 and 1960 had been turned face down on the sidewalk. For all the good the federal officials did, George Wallace might have been President of the United States.

What happened in Selma on Freedom Day?

A Negro registrant, before he got to the door of the county courthouse, had to run a gauntlet of armed troopers and a local cameraman whose pictures could cost the Negro his or her job.

The registrants waited from 8:30 A.M. to 4:30 P.M., standing in the sun without food or water, without being able to go to the toilet. State troopers told them they could not leave the line and return. (When I asked a Justice Department lawyer standing by if he would go over to the state troopers and say that these Negroes had a right to get a drink of water, he said: "I think they do have that right. But I won't do it.")

There were two "incidents":

1. At 11:55 A.M. I looked away from the line of registrants, across the street to the Federal Building. On the steps of the building—so still that for a weird second I thought they were statues—stood two young members of the Student Nonviolent Coordinating Committee facing the county courthouse across the street and holding signs. One, in overalls and a fedora, carried a sign saying "Register Now for Freedom Now." The other, in a polo shirt and slacks, carried a sign which read "Register to Vote."

I crossed the street to get a better look. At that moment—it was a few moments before noon—Sheriff Jim Clark and two members of his posse also crossed the street, walked up the steps of the Federal Building, snatched the signs, and pulled the two young fellows down the stairs and into a police car. I have seen a number of examples of the invisibility of federal power in the South, but I didn't believe this. I turned to the Justice Department man and asked, "Is that a Federal Building?" "Yes," he replied.

2. Lunchtime passed, but no lunch for the more than 300 Negroes on the registration line. The sun was hotter now. Jim Forman, in charge of the day's operations, sent some people for sandwiches and water. By now, Al Lingo's blue-helmeted state police—commanded by Major Joe Smelley—had taken over from the posse, but Sheriff Clark and his men were still around. Jim Forman and Mrs. Boynton (a local Negro leader) walked over to talk to Sheriff Clark (it was 1:55 P.M.). Forman said: "Sheriff, we'd like to give these people some food." Clark replied: "They will not be molested in any way." Forman said: "We don't want to molest them. We want to give them food and to talk to them about registration." Clark shouted: "If you do, you'll be arrested. They will not be molested in any way and that includes talking to them."

Forman and Mrs. Boynton went back across the street to the alley alongside the Federal Building, where a shopping cart with a keg of water and sandwiches were set up. Newsmen were called over. Mrs. Boynton said: "We want to see if to Mr. Clark 'molesting' means giving people food." Forman told the newsmen: "We wired the Justice Department last night for marshals; we figured Clark might be violating federal law today. But we've had no reply."

Two SNCC members, Chico Neblett [brother of Chuck Neblett], a tall, good-looking former student at Southern Illinois University, and Avery Williams, dark, quiet, stepped forward and filled their arms with sandwiches and registration material. It was an unreal scene: food was going to be delivered to people standing in line in front of a public building and it was as if paratroopers were preparing to drop into enemy country in wartime.

"Let's go, man," Neblett said. He and Williams crossed the street. We—newsmen, photographers, a few others—followed. The state troopers converged on the two young men as they approached the line. Major Smelley yelled: "Get 'em!" Suddenly the two were on the ground. I saw Chico Neblett stretched out, troopers over him. I saw them jab at him with their clubs and saw him writhe under what looked like shock induced by the electric cattle prods the troopers carried. Four of them picked him up and dragged him away and then I saw them throw him and young Williams into the green arrest truck at the corner. In the meantime state troopers and posse men were pushing and shoving all of us standing nearby, cursing, threatening, ripping one photographer's clothes. We retreated across the street. The Justice Department men hurried in and out of the Federal Building. The FBI watched.

I walked down to the corner a few minutes later, to see if the line that had extended all the way around it and halfway down the block was diminished by the tension. Some 30 more Negroes had joined the line. I went back to the steps of the Federal Building and waited for Freedom Day to be over. At 4:30 P.M. it was, and the several hundred men and women in line drifted away. A young Negro lawyer, visiting from Detroit [this was John Conyers] who had observed the day's events, said with emotion in his voice, pointing to the people walking quietly from the line: "Those people are heroes. They should be given medals."

Then what would be given the President and the Attorney General of the U.S.?

That evening, we had a mass meeting in Selma. James Baldwin spoke, among others, and he talked about the hatred that he had seen in the faces of the whites on that Freedom Day. In the face of that hatred—and the power to implement it—black people had not flinched. Their courage and determination in Selma changed the course of the freedom movement in the state of Alabama and affected its development across the country. Freedom Day was a major step in building a mass consciousness among blacks. When I heard, in 1965, that young people in Watts were throwing rocks and Molotov cocktails, crying "this is for Selma!" or "this is for Birmingham!"—I knew that our long-range strategy had worked. It was a high price, but at the time I didn't know of any other method that might work in the Deep South and also develop a national consciousness about the realities of racism. People had come to see the unwillingness of the federal government to do anything real about the injustices committed against people in the South. And militancy—meaning a readiness to go all the way for what one believed, regardless of personal sacrifice—had increased. For me, personally, the brutality of the blue-shirted Alabama police and the club-swinging posse of Big Belly Jim Clark were putting the finishing touches on my experiment with nonviolence. My patience with it, even as a tactic, was drawing to a close.

As a national organization, SNCC moved immediately to use the events in Selma to build pressure on the federal government, expose its inaction, build up that national consciousness. Within twenty-four hours after Freedom Day, an "action memo" went out from the Atlanta office telling supporters in the North about events in Selma and what they could do. This memo was typical of our working methods in those days. Part of it said:

WE NEED YOU:

1. To organize your friends and associates to continue telegramming the Justice Department, the Attorney General, the President, and the Civil Rights Commission for these three most legitimate demands: federal marshals in Selma, a temporary restraining order against Clark, and arrest of officials interfering with voter registration.

   Telegrams are more effective if they go from individuals rather than groups.

   Night letters (50 words at a reduced rate) could be used.

2. To throw up sympathy picket lines at federal buildings all over the country, protesting the federal government's refusal to act within its *present* jurisdiction to protect persons in the process of voter registration in Selma.

   Pickets may take place at federal post offices, a branch of the Justice Department, or any federal building.

   Leaflets should be prepared in advance to inform the press and passers-by of the background of your effort.

3. To consistently pressure your local newspapers for adequate coverage of news.

4. To continually keep the wire services on their toes by your pressure. Their interest wanes as quickly as the interest of persons in other parts of the country wanes. They are most active when their subscribing newspapers demand coverage.

5. To have letters published in local newspapers interpreting the social, economic and political (voting) background of areas where SNCC is working, especially in crisis situations.

6. To keep your Congressman informed, and especially to urge your Congressman to speak from the floors of their respective bodies denouncing the use of violent repression of persons attempting to register to vote.

What will you do between now and then to insure that Negroes who are trying to win the vote (many for the first time in their lives) will be guaranteed this essential right, without fear of violence?

Now, instead of our demonstrations being aimed at some small café, we were mounting increasingly heavy pressure on the federal government. The FBI was, and is, the enemy of black people. We did not say it that way in 1963, but we did know the FBI was a farce. It wasn't going to arrest any local racists who violated any and all laws on the statute books. Instead, it would play a game of taking notes and pictures. The files in Washington must have been growing thick even then with documents from the civil rights movement and with photographs of us all—doing everything but screwing, and maybe even that.

With Freedom Day SNCC had established a firm beachhead in the heart of Alabama's Black Belt—a beachhead that would later service field work in Lowndes County, birthplace of the Black Panthers, and Greene County, where one day black officials would get elected. Freedom Day in Selma also laid the legal trap for Jim Clark, as planned. During the Selma-to-Montgomery March a federal decision would be finally handed down that obstructed the acting out of his sadistic racism.

There would be other events called Freedom Day in various parts of the South. But there would never be one like that first Freedom Day: the day when a century of Southern fear and terror—of night-riding Klansmen, of the smooth-talking, but equally murderous, White Citizens' Council, of vicious George Wallaces—when all these forces had not been able to stop the forward thrust of a people determined by any means necessary to be free.

CHAPTER 46

The Freedom Vote

THE DAY before Selma's momentous Freedom Day, a "Freedom Vote" campaign was launched in Mississippi by COFO—the umbrella organization which theoretically included SNCC, CORE, the NAACP, and SCLC. With the Freedom Vote, SNCC moved into the stage of consolidating established bases of popular power—a consolidation which we saw as the next logical step in building a movement. The time had come for us to expand our voter registration work in separate communities into active political organizing on a statewide basis. And we felt ready to do so in Mississippi. The Freedom Vote campaign—actually a mock election in which "freedom candidates" ran for local office at the same time that the racists were holding their lily-white "regular" elections —aimed to bring about that consolidation and expansion.

The Freedom Vote had two other purposes. One was to demonstrate that, if black people could vote, they would, and in great numbers. Furthermore, they would not vote for bigots. They would not vote for men like Congressman James Whitten from the Second District in the Delta, and this could indirectly raise serious questions about the legality of Whitten sitting as a legitimate representative of his constituency. The second purpose was to make a further breakthrough in the fear and self-doubts of black people, to provide them with a forum for speaking out their own political ideas.

Aaron Henry of Clarksdale ran for governor and Ed King, a white chaplain at Tougaloo College in Jackson, for lieutenant governor, on a platform calling for desegregation, the right to vote, fair employment, a $1.25 minimum wage, and better schools. Their names, together with those of the official candidates, would appear on a "freedom ballot" which could be cast at special polls by anyone—whether registered to vote or not. Registered voters would be urged not only to cast freedom ballots but also to write in the names of the freedom candidates on the official ballot. November 3, 4, and 5 were the dates set for the Freedom Vote.

Bob Moses became campaign manager, and a central office for the campaign was set up in Jackson, to coordinate activity around the state. A statewide WATS line (Wide Area Telephone Service, permitting unlimited telephone calls between all points for a set monthly fee) was installed. About sixty white students from Yale and Stanford came down for a two-week stint of volunteer work on the campaign, supplementing our lack of personnel. With them we were able to penetrate communities and make valuable contacts where we had never been able to do so before.

Once, three years earlier, Bob Moses had talked with Amzie Moore and together they had envisioned a project that might break the grip of fear on black Mississippians. Now SNCC was on the move across the entire state, reaching thousands of people. It was a dream come true in many ways, but not without the usual nightmares of white racism. During the month of the Freedom Vote, over a hundred incidents involving harassment and arrest of election workers were recorded.

The Yale and Stanford students did not escape jail or physical violence. One of them, Bruce Payne, was beaten by four whites on November 1 and found himself the next day being pursued in a car by some of the same assailants. George Greene of SNCC was driving and the two were just outside Natchez. For half an hour Greene tried to evade or lose the pursuing car by turning around and by outracing it, but the top speed of 105 miles per hour on their car was no match for the newer and more powerful car driven by the pursuers. Finally they were forced off the road against a bridge and one of the men walked up to Greene, pulled out a pistol, and told him to get out.

Greene, whose door was locked and window rolled up, shifted instantly into low, swerved sharply and escaped back onto the highway. As they drove off, the white man shot three times—apparently to disable the vehicle so that the two could be captured. With a slow leak in the left rear tire, Green again tried to lose his pursuers—going through three red lights, crossing double lanes, driving in oncoming traffic lanes. Finally he managed to get three cars ahead of the whites and turned out of sight onto a backwoods road. And there they changed the tire. Greene's fantastic driving—which became a legend in SNCC—was the only thing that saved the lives of those two campaign workers.

Ivanhoe Donaldson, a SNCC field secretary long active in Mississippi, reported an experience he had with three other SNCC workers in Jackson one day during the campaign. The group had already been threatened with arrest on two occasions that day when they were stopped once again, at a gas station. Three of the workers were forced by the police to stand outside with their hands on their car, palms down, for an hour and a quarter while the police interrogated Donaldson inside the car. Ivanhoe continues the story about himself and his co-workers in that laconic manner which came to typify SNCC staffers' reports on the dangers that they faced: "Donaldson was asked if whites were better than Negroes, and when he replied 'No,' the interrogating officer took out his pistol and rapped him on the knuckles with the butt of the gun. On answering another question, he was again rapped. Finally the officer placed the muzzle of the pistol against Donaldson's temple, cocked it, and said 'Nigger, I think I'm going to kill you right now.' At this point, another officer interrupted and said, 'No, you can't kill that nigger now—it's not time.' The four were finally released."

Intimidation throughout the state undoubtedly cut down the number of participants in the Freedom Vote. And yet eighty thousand freedom ballots were cast. Ivanhoe Donaldson summed up the results as follows:

It showed the Negro population that politics is not just "white folks" business, but that Negroes are also capable of holding political offices. It introduced a lot of Negroes, for the first time, to the idea of marking ballots. For the first time, since Reconstruction, Negroes held a rally on the steps of the Courthouse, with their own candidates, expressing their own beliefs and ideas rather than those of the "white folks." There was less fear in the Negro community about taking part in civil rights activities.

Aside from these points, it indicated that SNCC, as an organization, was capable of mobilizing quickly, and concentrating its energy in one particular area. The drawing-in of staff from different protest areas to help supplement the deficiency in manpower, also demonstrated SNCC's flexibility. The presence of both Jim Forman and John Lewis out in the rural areas helping to bring in the vote also demonstrated the basic difference between SNCC and the other major civil rights organizations.

The Freedom Vote paved the way for the historic Mississippi Summer Project of 1964. It also contained an omen, a warning, which we did not fully recognize as such at the time. That omen took the form of Allard Lowenstein's presence in Mississippi during the campaign.

It was Allard Lowenstein who had recruited the white students from Yale and Stanford to work on the Freedom Vote, and he himself turned up in the state. Seven years had passed since I had seen him in action at the NSA conference, slickly manipulating a conservative victory, arrogantly using a black delegate for that purpose, wheeling and dealing all over the place. I was disturbed to see him in Mississippi now and very briefly mentioned to Bob Moses that I had reservations about Lowenstein. I did not press them because Moses was in charge of the operation and I did not want to infringe on his authority and because Lowenstein's presence was a fait accompli. In any case, it soon became clear that Moses was developing his own reservations about Lowenstein.

One night in the Jackson COFO office, the campaign headquarters, a white volunteer from Stanford was about to leave town to go to Yazoo City—a notorious stronghold of white violence, where we had done no groundwork. Bob either told him not to go or that he should wait for George Raymond, a CORE field secretary. Whatever Bob's remark, the volunteer came to me and said that he was working under Lowenstein and that Al wanted the volunteers to converge in Yazoo City, or something to that effect. I told him, in a manner that left no room for doubt, that Moses was the project director in Mississippi—not Lowenstein. If Lowenstein told him to go to heaven and Moses said he should go to hell, then he'd better start packing his summer clothes and make it. Either he and the rest of the volunteers accepted this discipline or they should go home the next day. The volunteer insisted that he was under Lowenstein's direction. In the end, he did not make the trip and left the state a few days later. But it was not this single volunteer who represented the real problem—it was what his attitude suggested about how Lowenstein had projected the setup in Mississippi. A few months later, when plans for the 1964 Mississippi Summer Project went into high gear, our suspicions would be confirmed: Lowenstein was traveling around the college campuses telling students that he had charge of recruitment and people would go to Mississippi under his direction.

It would take us still longer to understand the full implications of Lowenstein's presence in Mississippi in 1963. We would discover that he represented a whole body of influential forces seeking to prevent SNCC from becoming too radical and to bring it under the control of what I have called the liberal-labor syndrome. The syndrome's first step was just to observe—and I am sure that is why Lowenstein showed up in Mississippi that year.

The liberal-labor syndrome played an important role in American politics at that time and incorporated many powerful elements. We do not know exactly what role was played by each of these forces in relation to SNCC. But we had had, or would have, direct experience with certain elements and, from that experience, we can say that the syndrome was typified by its close links with the Kennedy administration and later to liberal Democratic elements in the Johnson administration, by the influence of Walter Reuther of the United Automobile Workers, by its violent Red-baiting, and by its social democrat line—as embodied in Norman Thomas. Individual white members included Joseph Rauh (general counsel for the UAW), author and poverty "expert" Michael Harrington, and various church leaders.

Lowenstein, Rauh, Harrington, and Bayard Rustin had several meetings in 1962 and 1963 to discuss what might be done about the "Stalinists" who had "taken over" SNCC. I was supposedly the key "Stalinist." Paul Jacobs, at that time a notorious Red-baiter in the service of the government, was invited to the meeting to help plan strategy for an attack on the "Stalinists" and the saving of SNCC for the liberal-labor syndrome, specifically for those who followed the line of the social democrats represented by Norman Thomas. He went. Jacobs later repudiated his past position and activities, and it was he who told me about these meetings during a conversation we had in 1967 after the disclosures initiated by *Ramparts* magazine concerning links between the Central Intelligence Agency and the National Student Association.

According to Jacobs, the key decision made at that first meeting which he attended was that Allard Lowenstein should infiltrate SNCC on behalf of the liberal-labor group, to check the power of the supposed Stalinists and keep SNCC out of the orbit of the communists.

The disclosures in *Ramparts,* combined with the history of Lowenstein's activities in the NSA, Spain, and Africa made me suspect that he was close to CIA circles if not actually on its payroll. One of the "high spots" of Lowenstein's serpentine career was when he went to the Dominican Republic with Norman Thomas to observe the 1966 elections which followed the U.S. Marines' occupation of the island. Juan Bosch, a progressive leader, ran against the candidate preferred by Washington —Juan Balaguer. Surprise: Balaguer won. Thomas and Lowenstein reported back that the elections had been "free and open"—to reassure Americans who might have thought there was something a little undemocratic about the whole affair. It is reported that Lowenstein was in constant touch with the U.S. Embassy while in the Dominican Republic. No doubt this helped to make him "a truly impartial observer."

Bayard Rustin played a particularly important role in the liberal-labor syndrome because he was the one person in the group who had the personal trust and respect of some SNCC staff members in these years. In 1960 Rustin had not been in the good graces of the labor movement or the established civil rights organizations, and it will be remembered that the AFL-CIO threatened to withdraw a grant to SNCC if Rustin was allowed to speak at a SNCC conference. But somehow he had won them over—just how remains a mystery to me, but no doubt they came to see from Rustin's actions that he was not the raving radical some people had once thought.

Bayard at one time had great influence in the Young People's Socialist League, which developed a strong chapter at Howard University. A number of SNCC staff members from the Washington, D.C., area, who had been Howard students at one time, came to know Bayard in this way. Some of them became active in the YPSL, the youth arm of Norman Thomas's so-called Socialist Party—so-called for it had become a strictly reformist outfit of social democrats who were more vehemently anticommunist than the loudest rightwingers. It was the young SNCC people in Washington who organized a conference in November, 1963, at which both Norman Thomas and Bayard Rustin spoke, and meetings were held with the Industrial Union Department of the AFL-CIO. The entire conference represented a thrust to pull SNCC closer to the liberal-labor syndrome.

Within a year, all of SNCC would be disenchanted with Bayard Rustin. But at the time we were too young, too idealistic, and too uninformed to see the traps that were being laid. We should have been more suspicious. We should have recognized that as the power of SNCC grew and was consolidated, the opposition would move intensively to control or destroy SNCC. John Lewis's speech at the March on Washington had symbolized the approaching, final divorce between ourselves and the government. All elements of the nation's power structure sensed an inability to control SNCC. We had to be watched closely, infiltrated if possible, and destroyed if necessary. One indication of the Establishment's attitude and tactics was given in a November, 1963, issue of *Life* magazine—not long after the March on Washington. An article by Theodore White accused SNCC of planning a "putsch" against the government. SNCC hotheads, said White, were responsible for the violence initiated by black people after the killing of the six girls in Birmingham, Alabama, and the murder of Medgar Evers in Mississippi that year. White's attack would be followed by the steady bludgeoning of syndicated columnists Evans and Novak, who spread their lies and fantasies about SNCC across the nation's newspapers for several years.

The growing power of SNCC was not a power of numbers or financial resources or friends in high places. It was the power of an idea whose time had come, the power of a reawakening people. SNCC was also becoming more solid and more effective as an organization. The administrative infrastructure of the national office had developed to the point where we had a brilliant communications section headed by Julian Bond, a campus program coordinator, a Northern support coordinator, a research department, and a constantly expanding printshop. We also had a receptionist, bookkeeper, and a WATS line which covered the South and North, and extended as far west as Texas. Since spring of that year, we had had on the staff the extremely talented Ruby Doris Robinson, who acted as my administrative assistant. Altogether this tightly knit, highly disciplined, and hard-working team made it possible for the Atlanta office to service the field projects more adequately than ever before and for me to be away for extended periods. It is hard to describe adequately the importance of the people in SNCC's infrastructure. But there was a deep sense of doing a job that had to be done, of doing it well and with integrity, of sustaining ourselves on love for each other and for our brothers and sisters throughout the movement.

As executive secretary in charge of the Atlanta office, I followed the principle of delegating authority but not responsibility. There were tensions inside the office as well as complaints from the field—a normal situation—and I always felt ultimately responsible for them. I imagine that I was often deemed tyrannical or dictatorial but there was no work that I wouldn't do—sweeping the floor became my specialty—and I asked no one to work as hard as I did. It seemed to me that only through intense work on my part could I inspire the same in others. And nothing was more important in my view than building an effective administrative apparatus. Too often workers in revolutionary movements do not spend enough time on this because it seems dull or burdensome, but not to do so becomes a betrayal of the people.

Most of the Atlanta staff naturally had one constant complaint: They wanted to participate more in action projects. In the winter of 1963 they got their chance. Oginga Odinga came to town and the office workers had a field day.

Oginga Odinga was at that time minister of home affairs in the new Kenya Government headed by Jomo Kenyatta. In 1969 he would be placed under house arrest after a series of events described in his book, *Not Yet Uhuru*. But in the winter of 1963 Kenya had just become a member of the United Nations and Oginga Odinga came to this country to accept his government's seat in that body. A tour under State Department sponsorship was arranged for him. When some of us in SNCC heard that he was coming to Atlanta, the last stop on his tour, we knew that a visit to our office was not on his agenda as prepared by the U.S. Government. So we decided to visit him.

On a Saturday evening in December, a group of us went to the Peachtree Manor where he was staying, brought him gifts, sang freedom songs and chanted "Uhuru"—freedom—with him. Inspired by the visit, we went on to a Toddle House restaurant for coffee. Seventeen SNCC people, including Chairman John Lewis, were arrested. Some went limp and had to be dragged to the paddy wagon, and some were bruised when being dragged. At the jail, most of the group refused to identify themselves and told policemen their names were "Freedom Now."

The campaign against the Toddle House restaurants accelerated. As a tactic SNCC bought token shares of stock in the corporation that owned this chain, in the names of two staff members—Roberta (Bobbi) Yancey and Prathia Hall. A share was also bought for me. (Earlier, in Danville, Virginia, stock in Dan River Mills had been bought for Ivanhoe Donaldson.) At the very least, we could go to board meetings and create a furor. Then the police of Atlanta did just what we wanted. They arrested Bobbi and Prathia along with another stockholder, Lillian Gregory, for what amounted to being on their own property. Everybody spent Christmas in jail. We never had to go to those board meetings because Toddle

House agreed to serve black people (we should, however, have pushed them on the issue of jobs for blacks).

In January there were more demonstrations and arrests at Atlanta hotels and restaurants, with up to five hundred people participating while robed and hooded Klansmen stood by. Close to two hundred people went to jail, including myself. By now we had expanded our repertory of names to give the cops from "Freedom Now" to "Abe Lincoln" and "Super Snick." We had groups out at the airport and in front of the hotel where a United Nations commission on discrimination was meeting, with signs saying "Welcome to Atlanta, a Segregated City." The white powers of Atlanta, anxiously projecting the image of a "liberal," "progressive," Southern city, were squirming.

All these activities, beginning with our visit to Oginga Odinga, must have made some people on a higher level squirm too. Here was a high-ranking foreign dignitary, on an official visit, commenting that the racial situation in the United States was "very pitiful" and that the United States "practices segregation—which is what we are fighting in Africa." The racist image of this country that SNCC's work projected was in sharp conflict with the picture of democracy at work painted by the bureaucratic beavers in Washington, D.C.

The super-Establishment was unhappy with SNCC. The white liberal-labor syndrome, actually part of that Establishment but thinking of itself as a little different, was unhappy with SNCC. And then there were the black flunkies of the liberal-labor syndrome: the super-Toms. The brothers whom we would have liked to call brother, but could not. They are a story in themselves.

CHAPTER 47

The "Big Five" and SNCC

Congress for Racial Equality (CORE)
National Association for the Advancement of Colored People (NAACP)
NAACP Legal Defense and Education Fund
Southern Christian Leadership Conference (SCLC)
Urban League
and, the *Student Nonviolent Coordinating Committee* (SNCC)

RELATIONS BETWEEN SNCC and other civil rights organizations had always been stormy because, from the beginning, SNCC developed as an antithesis to all the other civil rights groups. SNCC strove to be a group-centered or people-oriented organization while others were leader-centered. It constantly stood in opposition to the Republican and Democratic parties while others sought favors from the two-party system. It vigorously attacked the Kennedy administration for its inaction in the field of civil rights while others thought that discussion and conciliation with the executive branch could win concessions. It fought against the American value system of making money and paid its staff only subsistence while others were seeking wages for civil rights works beyond the necessary living requirements. It believed in sending its staff to work with the most wretched of the earth while some of the organizations thought this a waste of time. It believed in the absolute right of freedom of association while other organizations acted as fearful as McCarthy of communism. It argued for a basic revolution in American society (even in the days when it was confused about the method by which this might be achieved) while others always advocated change within the present system.

These basic differences were accentuated as the years unfolded, causing sharp antagonisms and eventually irreconcilable differences, although at times SNCC cooperated with this group or that one and sometimes with all of them.

In November, 1961, a meeting took place between SNCC and the NAACP, ostensibly to discuss the McComb situation. Marion Barry, who, in the summer of 1961, was working on a SNCC direct action project in McComb, had sent Roy Wilkins a letter asking for legal assistance. Wilkins had pointed out that NAACP did not usually give help in situations where it had not been involved in making policy. After several months of discussion, a top-level meeting between SNCC and the NAACP was arranged. Representing the NAACP were Ruby Hurley, director of the southeastern region of the NAACP; John Morsell, assistant to Roy Wilkins; Medgar Evers, field secretary in Mississippi; Vernon Jordan, field secretary in Georgia; and a representative of their youth chapters. From SNCC came Charles Sherrod, James Bevel, Bernard LaFayette, and myself. Jean Fairfax of the American Friends Service Committee (AFSC) was also present.

The McComb cases were discussed and it was agreed that the NAACP would handle them. The meeting then centered around charges by NAACP officials that we were "raiding" their youth chapters. Vernon Jordan and Ruby Hurley were furious with Sherrod for his activities in Albany. Evers was especially adamant that SNCC had come into Jackson, Mississippi, and "stolen" members of their youth chapters. Bevel, who was then working in Mississippi with SNCC, replied it was not a question of "stealing." If our actions and program appealed to members of the youth chapters, that was more of an indictment of the NAACP than of SNCC.

As I sat there listening to this petty talk of "stealing members," I thought of Dr. W. E. B. Du Bois and his efforts to make the NAACP into a relevant organization of black people. The narrow sectarianism of the organization at this point was certainly not what he had hoped for, and only reflected the NAACP's growing ineffectiveness among black people. I was also struck by what I had to call organizational paranoia. My feeling about the defensiveness of some of the NAACP leadership was confirmed by my first direct contact with Roy Wilkins.

In January, 1962, a top-level meeting of the heads of civil rights organizations was called by Alan Chalmers in upstate New York. Chalmers had been involved in some aspect of the Scottsboro case and was currently helping to raise money for the NAACP Legal Defense Fund. He had recently received some money from the Phelps Stokes Fund to hold such a meeting. Present were Dr. King and Wyatt T. Walker of the SCLC, James Farmer of CORE, Whitney Young of the Urban League, Jack Greenberg of the NAACP Legal Defense and Education Fund, Roy Wilkins of the NAACP, Charles McDew and I representing SNCC, and Jean Fairfax of the AFSC.

Chalmers opened the meeting by stating that its purpose was to create a forum for discussion by the heads of civil rights groups in an atmosphere of unrestraint. Each participant should tell of his program or the program of the organization he represented, and speak his mind freely.

Wilkins offered to begin, and remarked that he wanted to talk about "the house of the NAACP." He explained that there was no organic relationship between the NAACP and the NAACP Legal Defense and Education Fund. They were separate organizations with separate boards, fund-raising machinery, and styles of operation. He made a blistering attack on the method by which Jack Greenberg operated. Before the two organizations became separate, he said, the NAACP would take on a case and raise a great deal of money with appeals to help pay legal fees. Now, however, there was a separate Defense Fund which handled cases. Greenberg's method was to work directly with lawyers in the South, not coordinating court cases with the national office of the NAACP or its branches. He would simply go ahead on his own and file suit. As a result, the NAACP could no longer raise money from major cases like that of James Meredith—even though the public still thought the NAACP handled them.

Greenberg did not comment on these remarks. Wilkins went on to say that people did not appreciate the history of the NAACP—that it was the oldest organization and bore the most scars of battle. "People say we are only legalistic," Wilkins said, "but we have had picket lines." He berated all the other organizations, accusing Dr. King of trying to destroy the NAACP with his proposal that SCLC should become a membership organization. This would cut into the membership base of the

NAACP. Martin knew this, Wilkins said, and this was his basic reason for the proposal: He wanted to destroy the NAACP. While Wilkins made these remarks, he held his hands together out in front of him and slowly—continually—rubbed one against the other. I couldn't believe that I was actually hearing and seeing all this. There sat the mighty Roy Wilkins, caught up in a nervous gesture, absolutely convinced that people were out to "destroy" his entire organization.

Dr. King tried to reassure Wilkins that he was not out to destroy the NAACP. We all had the same destination, King said, and were just traveling down different roads. But we had to agree, as a minimum, that there could be different approaches.

Wilkins then lambasted CORE for not having a base and SNCC for not having any structure, for "raiding" the NAACP youth chapters in Georgia and for "making messes" that the NAACP had to clean up. The events in Albany were on the minds of all the participants and references to it constantly came up. Wilkins also went into a long diatribe on how SNCC was always "attacking" the NAACP, reminding us of the mild criticism that Jim Lawson had made of the NAACP when he was a guest speaker at the founding conference of SNCC.

Several things became clear at this meeting. It had been a mistake to ask the NAACP for legal assistance in the McComb cases. (Later we were to work out a legal arrangement with the NAACP Legal Defense Fund which lasted until we started working with the National Lawyers Guild during the summer of 1964.) It also became clear that we in SNCC had to do our work without worrying too much about relationships with other civil rights groups. We had a program of our own and to be overly concerned about the attitude of other groups would limit our effectiveness. Finally it became clear to me that aside from the extreme defensiveness and arrogant style of Roy Wilkins, there was also a problem of trust. During a coffee break at the meeting, he whispered to me that he would like to get together with us and try to develop some joint program. He felt that the NAACP could work with SNCC, he said, but not with CORE and Jim Farmer. They couldn't be trusted, he said. I made no reply, for I felt that Wilkins' remarks were insincere and that he could not be trusted.

In the early summer of 1963, before the March on Washington, we heard reports that there were large sums of money being raised for civil rights groups and that there had been meetings—called "civil rights breakfasts"—between these groups and donors. We called Jim Farmer of CORE to verify this. He said that there had been meetings and, in reply to our question as to why SNCC had not been invited, he said that he didn't know. CORE had been invited and had attended such meetings. Then we called Dr. King. SCLC had been invited and attended, he said. We objected to the ignoring of SNCC, and Dr. King agreed that we should certainly be invited to the meetings; he would raise this issue at the next meeting. He felt that SNCC should get some of the money which was being raised for civil rights organizations.

Some time after the March on Washington, we were invited to a meeting of the group. It took place at the plush Carlyle Hotel in New York. The meeting this time was not one of those much-heralded breakfasts, but a dinner. To me, it was a feast—whatever the name—and that was part of the whole style of the group. Looking around at the setting, the way people were dressed and talked, I knew I would have to stay on my toes not to be swallowed up by this slick band of competitors and circle of distrust. There I sat, representing an organization whose workers rarely had more than fifty cents in their pockets, hustled hamburgers to keep going, and wore overalls as a matter of course. The overalls had by that time become a symbol of SNCC. We wore them because they were adaptable to the way we lived, such as sleeping on floors as we did many nights; because most of the people with whom we worked also wore them; and, above all, to promote a proletarian viewpoint and life-style. For a few of our organizers who were from the middle class, the overalls represented an effort to transform themselves totally as they worked. But most of the work force at that time was poor Southern blacks, for whom wearing overalls came naturally. Those were the people I represented now in the Carlyle Hotel, and I felt the great gulf between the two worlds.

Representing the civil rights groups at the meeting were Roy Wilkins, Whitney Young, Jack Greenberg, Martin King, James Farmer, Dorothy Haight of the National Council of Negro Women, John Lewis, and myself. Representing the fund-raising force were Stephen Currier, president of the Taconic Foundation and married to one of the Mellons who owned the Gulf Oil Company (I could not help thinking of the boycott that the Gulf Oil Company had imposed on John McFerren in Fayette County, Tennessee, back in 1959); William Lloyd Garrison of the Taconic and Field foundations and later superintendent of schools in New York; Mel Dewitt, a tax lawyer who figured out the best tax arrangements for the donors; Jane Lee J. Eddy, executive director of the Taconic Foundation; and a young sister who was secretary to Mrs. Eddy.

We learned during the course of the discussion that meetings had taken place throughout the spring and that eight hundred thousand dollars had been pledged to the Council on United Civil Rights Leadership, the name given to the group. This new superorganization aimed to provide funds for the civil rights groups and a forum where they could meet and talk. But the primary thing which held the group together was the promise and the receipt of money.

During dinner there was a lot of chitchat about the need to have a forum for discussion and airing of grievances. After the eating was over, people got down to the subject of funds and their distribution—the real nitty-gritty. To the surprise of both Lewis and myself, a neat little formula by which a few crumbs would be thrown to SNCC had already been worked out in previous meetings. The first distribution of funds would be roughly 10 percent of each organization's annual budget for the previous year. Thus the NAACP and CORE would each get a hundred thousand dollars; the NAACP Legal Defense and Education Fund and the Urban League, one hundred twenty-five thousand dollars each; SCLC, fifty thousand dollars—the amount it had requested, since its fund raising around the Birmingham issue was going very well and SCLC felt it did not need more—and SNCC, fifteen thousand dollars. We objected to the formula, stating that distribution of funds should be made on the basis of need. We also argued that there should at least be an equal distribution of funds. All this was bargaining on our part, since we felt that we would come out ahead if either of those two formulas was adopted. Finally the group agreed that SNCC should present a list of its needs and expenditures for the past year. Additional grants could be made.

After that meeting, SNCC agreed that either John Lewis or I would represent the organization on the council. But it was usually I who attended the meetings. Young, inexperienced, from a small Southern town, John had fine qualities as a symbol of black resistance, but he was lost among these overpowering, tricky infighters. I was a good ten years older, had been through some infighting, and had become more or less responsible for SNCC's fund raising anyway.

But I relished neither the infighting nor the fund raising. Throughout my experiences with the Council on United Civil Rights Leadership, I felt we were in a jungle—a jungle of civil rights hyenas, each distrustful of the other, each with personal grievances against the other, each agreeing to curb some of his hostility so that he could get just a little more money for programs with which everyone else probably disagreed (although it was unpolitic to say so). I was never under any illusions that this so-called leadership coalition would have a long life. It would last only so long as there was money to split up. No one could seriously expect it to be a real forum for the airing of conflicts and grievances even if the meetings had been limited to black people, civil rights people. There was too much past distrust and too many experiences within the council to confirm that distrust. For example, the Council on United Civil Rights Leadership at one time planned to give a massive, private performance of artists with a television hookup as a method of raising funds for the council as a whole. Wiley Branton asked Wilkins to check the idea with the NAACP branches. Wilkins reported back to the council that he felt the plan was not feasible. But less than three months later, the NAACP announced it would hold a massive private television program by major artists . . . for the exclusive benefit of the NAACP.

Because he represented a source of funds, Stephen Currier probably did the most to hold the group together. He was originally elected co-chairman because of his fund-raising potential but later resigned because he felt sensitive to the fact that he was white and not a civil rights person. I felt that his resignation was in order.

It was Currier who first raised with me at length the question of SNCC's intention to use the services of the Lawyers Guild in the upcoming Mississippi Summer Project—a question that would bring the wrath of the mighty down on our heads. Currier had asked me to meet him alone one day at the Potomac Institute and there explained that he and others felt disturbed about our plan to use the Guild. I explained to him our position on civil liberties and Red-baiting, and that we were not going to change it.

On two later occasions Whitney Young tried to get the council to issue a statement saying there were no communists in the movement and that the civil rights groups did not want the help of communists. I fought against these resolutions as a violation of first amendment rights and freedom of association. The position we took on civil liberties only infuriated the other groups, except SCLC, which seldom attended. This was probably because Dr. King had an extremely crowded schedule; substitutes for the top officers of an organization were rarely allowed except in the case of SNCC; and SCLC probably did not feel at the time that the meetings were necessary for SCLC's fund raising. On one occasion when he did come, Dr. King supported my efforts to block a Red-baiting resolution.

As the 1964 Mississippi Summer Project approached, the groups became very nervous about SNCC's willingness to use the services of the National Lawyers Guild. A full meeting of the council took place where criticism of our position on civil liberties thundered through the room. Gloster Current, director of branches for the NAACP, was on this rare occasion standing in for Roy Wilkins and he objected violently. Jack Greenberg, who is white, turned whiter—as if he had just seen a ghost, the ghost of Lenin or something. I refused to relent on our position.

At a subsequent meeting, after the project had begun, Wilkins made other statements which indicate his operating style and personality. When Whitney Young and Dorothy Haight commented that the mass media were circulating the impression that the NAACP was part of the Summer Project, Wilkins blandly remarked, "We will ride this one out." We knew that he didn't enjoy the "ride," but that he wouldn't pull out officially because the NAACP was raising money on the basis of its participation—without having to make any expenditure. He later added that the NAACP was part of the project only because of Aaron Henry, a "problem" that the NAACP would have to deal with. "Aaron Henry isn't qualified to plan a project like that," he added, saying that Bob Moses was the brains behind it. I told Wilkins that I felt he should not discuss an NAACP officer in that manner before us.

Wilkins repeatedly criticized the Mississippi Summer Project on the basis that it was going to help Goldwater get elected—by encouraging a white "backlash." During the summer of 1964 a meeting was held at the home of Senator Jacob Javits which Bob Moses and I attended. There was at this time tremendous pressure on the federal government because of the three deaths—Chaney, Goodman, and Schwerner—and other incidents of brutality. Senator Javits was trying to find some ways to ease this pressure. At the meeting, Wilkins reiterated his position to Moses and me that the Mississippi Summer Project was a mistake for it could help elect Goldwater. He maintained that you should work on Mississippi from the outside and not from inside the state. This had been his position in 1961, when we first started our efforts in Mississippi, and it was his position when tremendous changes were occurring.

Fear of helping Goldwater get elected was Wilkins' professed motive again when he proposed a moratorium on demonstrations at a council meeting during the summer of 1964. With the aid of the Johnson administration, he had dreamed up the scheme of trying to get all civil rights organizations to call such a moratorium. Demonstrations might help propel Goldwater into the White House, he said again and again. All the groups were singing the praises of Lyndon Baines Johnson in those days and saying how the Texan would "fool 'em" when he got elected. (Not only did he fool 'em, but he sent five hundred thousand troops to Vietnam.) SNCC refused to agree to the moratorium and again Wilkins burst a blood vessel.

Aside from the pressures which it placed on SNCC to play games with the power structure, the council also tended to catch us up in ugly situations when member groups used the council for their internal fights. One example was the way in which Wilkins had denigrated Aaron Henry. Then, in the spring of 1964, the national office of CORE asked the council to pass a resolution condemning the stall-ins at the World's Fair in New York City which had been planned by some of CORE's dissident chapters. I was in London at the time of that meeting. Suddenly the statement of condemnation appeared with SNCC's name on it. I was angry and disturbed. Only after my return did I learn from John Lewis that he had not agreed to sign the statement, but SNCC had been listed with the others anyway. Our executive committee released a statement stating that the stall-in was a legitimate form of protest against long-standing grievances of black people in the United States. After that incident I tried to institute a rule with the council that the internal workings of organizations were not the legitimate business of the council.

That same spring the Red-baiting issue came up again. COFO sent out a memorandum proposing that a civil rights delegation visit the President to ask protection for the workers who would be coming to the Mississippi Summer Project that year. The memorandum went to heads of civil rights groups and various black organizers, including Jesse Gray, the Harlem rent strike leader who had been active on a grass-roots level. At a meeting of the council on May 13 James Farmer and Whitney Young vigorously protested any participation by Jesse Gray in such an action. They called it a "political problem," but I saw their opposition as disguised Red-baiting, although I had no direct knowledge of Jesse Gray's politics. They wanted the visit to be made in the name of the council. I pointed out that the decision rested with Bob Moses, director of the Summer Project, but I felt it would be unacceptable. Moses, COFO, and SNCC were trying to broaden the base of support for the Summer Project while these liberal-labor forces were trying to keep it in the straitjacket of the Establishment-oriented Red-baiters. The proposal was finally sent—with SNCC's backing—and the President ignored it.

By 1965 the Council on United Civil Rights Leadership was raising less and less money while trying to inflict more and more of its conservative positions on the movement. Meanwhile, SNCC did get some funds from the council after considerable wrangling, but never to equal those given to "the big five." The last meeting of the council that I attended concerned the war in Vietnam and again SNCC was under fire to modify its position.

The meeting took place in March, 1966, after the election of Floyd McKissick as national director of CORE. Following the regular gathering, there was an "after meeting" in Whitney Young's office with Dr. King, Whitney Young, and myself. He began by stating that he and many others were disturbed by SNCC's and SCLC's positions on the war in Vietnam. (SNCC had taken an official position against the war in January of that year, while SCLC as an organization had never opposed the war, but Dr. King did speak out against it as an individual—on the grounds of personal, moral principle.) Young contended that civil rights and the war in Vietnam were separate issues. "Johnson needs a consensus. If we are not with him on Vietnam, then he is not going to be with us on civil rights," said Whitney Young.

We tried to explain to Brother Whitney that our job was not to psychoanalyze Johnson but to adhere to certain principles. We understood that, given the corporations from which Whitney got support, his position on the war in Vietnam had to be different from ours. We pointed out that we were probably not going to change his mind and that he certainly was not going to change ours. I told Brother Whitney that it was indeed sad if civil rights organizations had to go around trying to please this person in the White House and then that one, hoping to win some concessions. None of our gains had been made in that fashion and we would get few in the future by that procedure. Brother Whitney admitted that the issue gave him personal distress, for he had a daughter at Bryn Mawr who was active in antiwar demonstrations and she could not understand her father's position on the war. The irony of all this is that some three years later, in 1969, Whitney Young would support the moratorium against the war. Better late than never. But of course by that time even forces in Wall Street were against the war.

Soon after the summer of 1966, the council was disbanded. By this time revolutionary blacks were no longer trying to maintain any facade of unity. The "civil rights" phase of our struggle had ended and the time had come when the Uncle Tom leaders had to be exposed for what they were, misleading thousands of people in the rank and file.

It is always an illusion to believe that groups with antithetical ideological positions can build a solid base of unity that will sustain itself. At best there can be efforts at cooperation on limited objectives for limited periods of time. The Council on United Civil Rights Leadership was a coalition for the purpose of acquiring more funds for the major civil rights groups. It was a fund-raising gimmick, based on the fact that civil rights had become a very popular issue in this country, and many forces sought ways to support (or use) the moral thrust of the movement. At the same time, the historical differences and approaches inherent in the various organizations made it impossible for a group of spokesmen at the top to work out patterns of lasting unity.

The insistence at first that SNCC be excluded from the council revealed a dislike that was never overcome. But the growing importance of SNCC in the field of human and civil rights made it impossible for those leaders to ignore its existence. Also it is reported that some potential donors objected to the exclusion of SNCC. Hence SNCC was brought into the council—not in an effort to achieve unity, but rather because it could not ignore the work we were doing. We in SNCC knew that we were entering into a temporary alliance with people who had strongly opposed us in the past. This alliance was necessary, we thought at the time, to increase the possibilities of getting financial assistance for the work we were doing. At no time did we think any real unity could come with those who were supporters of, and apologists for, the two-party system and the United States Government. Furthermore, we knew that the other organizations saw us as a threat—and correctly. The success of a SNCC meant to each that part of its base had been lost, especially the fund-raising base and influence on the masses.

But we also took the position then that it did no good to come out with public criticism of these organizations. It would have been too easy just to attack, without addressing ourselves to the question, What alternative do you, SNCC, offer? We had to concentrate on building an alternative for black people.

One of our biggest efforts to build that alternative was the Mississippi Summer Project of 1964. From Allard Lowenstein to Roy Wilkins, the liberal-labor syndrome and its black flunkies had for some time been making various moves to contain or undermine SNCC. But those moves turned out to be just an opening barrage. The Mississippi Summer Project brought out the big guns.

CHAPTER 48

Inside the Mississippi Summer Project

IN SNCC we had often wondered: How do you make more people in this country share our experiences, understand what it is to look in the face of death because you're black, feel hatred for the federal government that always makes excuses for the brutality of Southern cops and state troopers?

We often wondered: How do you make a fat, rich country like the United States understand that it has starving people within its own boundaries, people without land, people working on Senator Eastland's plantation for three dollars a day or less?

We often wondered: How can you make the people in the United States exercise their responsibility to rid themselves of racist politicians who fight every progressive measure introduced in the halls of Congress?

We often wondered: How can we find the strength to continue our work in the face of the poverty of the people, to do everything that shouts to be done in the absence of so many resources?

The Mississippi Summer Project was an attempt to answer those questions.

By the summer of 1964 the small guerrilla band that once fought for life in McComb, Mississippi, had expanded its influence throughout the state—not to mention the nooks and crannies of distant states. The Mississippi Summer Project of 1964, including the Democratic Convention challenge at the end of the summer, was a culmination and high point of all the work that SNCC had been doing since 1960. It represented a massing of forces and a consolidation of popular power perhaps unequaled in the history of American civil rights organizations. Its consequences were far-reaching within SNCC and within the larger society.

The story of the project as such has been told a number of times by other writers. It is a highly dramatic story of black people in Mississippi and how almost a thousand volunteers—mostly white students—came to the state to help work on voter registration, the building of the new Mississippi Freedom Democratic Party, the setting up of "freedom schools" as an alternative to the miserable black school system which taught black children little more than "their place," the establishment of community centers with classes in basic skills and libraries. The story opens with the gruesome murder of three volunteer workers by Klansmen in June of 1964, and continues with a relentless pattern of white violence through the summer.

But that story does not need to be repeated. My purpose here is to look at some of the larger implications of the Summer Project—its meaning within the history of SNCC as an organization fighting racism and economic exploitation on revolutionary terms in the United States. From this viewpoint we see two main effects of the project and the assault on the Democratic Convention which climaxed that summer's work. It gave SNCC a degree of power such as it had never attained before and thereby accentuated conflicts within SNCC that ultimately aided in our disintegration. That same power also led to an intensified campaign by the Establishment to destroy SNCC. Both processes took time to work themselves out, but their origins can be perceived in the events of that summer.

The project was theoretically a creation of COFO, the Council of Federated Organizations, but the force most active within COFO was SNCC, and leadership in the project came from SNCC. Bob Moses presented the idea at the December, 1963, meeting of SNCC's executive committee, the idea in large part based on the successful participation of Yale and Stanford students in the mock election of November, 1963. Many of us endorsed it. We felt that it was high time for the United States as a whole, a white-dominated country, to feel the consequences of its own racism. White people should know the meaning of the work we were doing— they should feel some of the suffering and terror and deprivation that black people endured. We could not bring all of white America to Mississippi. But by bringing in some of its children as volunteer workers, a new consciousness would feed back into the homes of thousands of white Americans as they worried about their sons and daughters confronting "the jungle of Mississippi," the bigoted sheriffs, the Klan, the vicious White Citizens' Councils. We recognized that the result might be great pain and sorrow, but we were not asking the whites to do any more than we had done. And our goal was not personal or simply vengeful: Any havoc that might be brought into the homes of white America would be acted out in the nation's political arena. As it was. Uppermost in the thoughts of some of us was the long-range implication for social change in the United States by exposing ever greater numbers to active struggle with poor people.

But there was intense resistance to the project by many staff members of SNCC and COFO. It centered around the consequences of having a huge number of white students in Mississippi. Great concern was expressed over the security problem that would be created: Whites in black neighborhoods would draw tremendous attention, intensify our visibility, make it harder for us to be absorbed in, and thus protected by, the black community. In addition to the security problem, staff members worried about the effects—especially psychological effects—of having many whites enter into work with black people that had up to then been primarily carried out by other black people. If it had not been for Bob Moses's strong stand in favor of the project—and his statement during one discussion that "I will not be part of a racist organization"—we might possibly never have gone ahead with it. I am sure that today Bob would not see opposition to bringing in so many whites as "racist," but that was his position at that time on that issue.

Plans for the summer rolled on, and the recruitment of volunteers began. CORE and SNCC had no money to support them, so every volunteer was told that he or she must have five hundred dollars. This meant that few black students from the South could participate, for they did not have access to money like that. Ruby Doris Robinson made a concerted drive to recruit some black people from the South, given the limitations of funds. In all the interviewing and recruiting of prospective volunteers, they were all asked if they would be willing to work under the leadership of blacks—often blacks without formal education. Their response to this question and other indications of their willingness to work with black leadership was crucial in deciding whether they should be accepted. It had been firmly decided that all community projects would be headed by black workers.

The original thinking behind the Mississippi Summer Project included the idea that the heated atmosphere caused by the presence of many volunteers, especially whites, would force the federal government to intervene—possibly with the use of troops. But this idea changed through discussion and analysis. It was realized that the federal government, the Johnson administration, was unlikely to send troops into Mississippi during the summer of 1964. And even if it did send troops, they would constitute no more than a housekeeping operation. At Oxford, Mississippi, Kennedy had sent in Federal troops during the James Meredith crisis and that had been only a housekeeping operation; it did not modify the overall pattern of violence in Mississippi.

Given this fact of life, we saw the local, long-range function of the summer volunteers as helping to break the pattern of white racism and helping to build viable institutions of, by, and for black people. This turned out to be a tricky proposition. The presence of so many white college students had a negative effect on SNCC workers and local people. One of our project directors, for example, began to feel ashamed of the fact that he had completed only the sixth grade in school and told people that he had graduated from college. In other areas, local black people who had been in the process of learning how to handle office work and administrative matters just got shunted aside as the whites came in with their already developed "skills." These problems were aggravated by the fact that the entire staff seldom came together during the summer for discussion and evaluation.

We had had a taste of these problems and tensions when the Yale and Stanford students came down for the Freedom Vote. But we did not worry about such problems too much in the summer of 1964 for one simple reason: It was never contemplated by anyone in SNCC that volunteers would remain after the summer. It was always assumed that they would leave. Here COFO and SNCC made a cardinal mistake, a disastrous miscalculation. We did not anticipate that the volunteers would either want to stay or that they would stay. We failed in our planning and we would pay dearly for this miscalculation.

The role of whites in the project was closely related to the issue of violence and, therefore, to the question of self-defense. A few days before the orientation sessions for volunteers were to begin at Oxford, Ohio, a meeting took place at which these interwoven problems assumed major proportions and were hotly debated—especially the question of self-defense. Up to that time, SNCC had never discouraged the use of arms for self-defense by the Southern blacks with whom we worked, but we did have a policy of not allowing staff members to carry weapons. At that meeting, the lines of debate were complex and intermingled, but generally speaking there was one contingent arguing that SNCC should publicly proclaim its belief in self-defense while others, including myself, argued that self-defense was something people should just do and not proclaim—for the announcement alerted the opposition. There were some actions that had to be carried out in a clandestine fashion and arming oneself stood high on that list.

In the spring of 1964 the concept of armed self-defense had been introduced in the Greenwood office but Bob Moses, with whom I agreed, sent Stokely Carmichael there to remove the guns and insist they not be kept in the office. My reasons were not that self-defense was wrong, but that having guns in an office so open to the public was a warm invitation for the police to crack down and raid that office. Moses was also not opposed to self-defense, but felt that too much repression would come down on SNCC people if it were widely known that we had a policy of arming ourselves. As things worked out, many SNCC people did arm themselves, and I placed a nightly armed guard around the Greenwood office which became SNCC's national headquarters for the summer.

At the meeting just before orientation began, it was finally agreed to take no public position on self-defense. In any case, we were minutes away from the beginning of the Summer Project and did not have enough arms for ourselves without even thinking of the volunteers. Certainly we could not have embarked on a mass arming of the summer workers— guns are not distributed in that manner unless one is unconcerned about whom the gun is pointed at.

But that debate was very significant, for it indicated a historical process at work, a process that had bypassed the use of nonviolence as a tactical weapon. It reflected developments not only within the organization but in the minds of black people all over the United States and eventually the world. For we were part of a worldwide process. I was once convinced by the words of Kwame Nkrumah that the use of positive nonviolent action could produce the necessary changes. But at the time he wrote that, Algeria was already engaged in a violent revolution, and Frantz Fanon would later argue that only violence could bring about decolonization. This seeming contradiction actually reflects a process of evolution—of ideas, institutions, and organizations. Astute leadership implies the ability to perceive in the maze of clashing tendencies the kernel of the historical process—for it is this which will grow to become a tree.

I did not realize it then, but the importance of leadership rests in its ability to plan. This means not only forecasting the direction in which history moves but also mobilizing energies to pursue that direction. Many black people and many black leaders—not just SNCC's leadership— failed in those early years to understand that beneath all popular struggles there must be built a firm foundation for armed struggle. By popular struggles, I mean struggles against the contradictions in the society— struggles for the redress of grievances, reform efforts. Today there are still people in the United States who do not yet understand that such struggles cannot win decisive victories if they are not coupled with armed revolutionary organization and struggle.

The Mississippi Summer Project was clearly a popular struggle. It confirmed the absolute necessity for armed self-defense—a necessity that existed before the project but which became overwhelmingly clear to SNCC people during and after it. One reason for our slowness to perceive this necessity was the lingering idea of the project as a means of putting extreme pressure on the federal government. As I mentioned, most of us ceased to think of this as one of the main purposes for bringing in white volunteers. But it probably continued to affect our thinking, because we had been playing for years on that fine line of contradiction. The result was that we failed to realize the need to protect ourselves and the people with whom we worked. More precisely, we failed to see that as part of the people, we had to protect ourselves.

In my own case, I was perhaps too much influenced then by a theory of history that says the masses will respond and act when they are ready. Carried to an extreme, this means that the organizer does not provide leadership at any stage. I have already mentioned perceiving this anti-leadership tendency, with its good and bad aspects, at my first SNCC meeting. Since that time, I would often ask myself if we were—in the name of developing poor people's leadership—actually misleading the people by advocating that demonstrations be nonviolent when many of us believed in nonviolence only as a tactic. We used other forms of struggle, but we thought that objective conditions in the South did not permit the articulation of other forms. When the masses were ready for violence, they would use it—I thought. But where is the individual's responsibility in history, I now wonder. Were we right to proceed on the assumption of a separation between ourselves and the masses? It seems to me that this kind of separation is typical of the old Left in the United States, of a middle-class attitude which unconsciously assumes a separation of oneself from the masses. The masses have to be organized, and I am personally convinced that the masses of black people could have been organized around self-defense and even aggressive forms of violence in the early sixties. Many facts confirm the truth of this.

One is a well-known incident that took place in the Mississippi Delta in May, 1963. In the hour before dawn, white men came and threw Molotov cocktails and fired guns at the home of Hartman Turnbow, a strong black man who had dared to register to vote. Turnbow fired back at them, sent them running, raced for buckets of water and saved his burning house. (The local sheriff, of course, arrested Turnbow and charged him with arson.) Self-defense—at least of one's home—was not a concept new to Southern blacks in 1963, and there was hardly a black home in the South without its shotgun or rifle. Robert Williams had organized around the idea of self-defense in Monroe in the late fifties. In 1961, in Nashville, students were fighting back. The creation of the Deacons for Defense also suggests the possibility of such organizing. So does the limited participation of young blacks in the student movement precisely because of its nonviolent character. And all this is to speak only of developments in the recent history of black resistance.

Perhaps we ourselves, in SNCC, were not completely ready for violence. We had not exhausted the legal means of protest and hence we were not emotionally prepared to articulate and teach other forms of struggle. In my own case, I knew our struggle would eventually take a violent form, and I was ready for the transition whenever it occurred. There was never any doubt that I was psychologically prepared to kill my oppressor by whatever means I had. But I didn't feel the time was ripe. Today I believe it was a great mistake not to organize, beneath our public efforts, a cadre to prepare for the inevitable period of armed struggle. I myself would not have been the person to initiate this, because my thinking had not yet reached the point it has now. If someone had articulated the idea and especially a plan for its implementation in the South, I probably would have been willing to execute it. I had worked with Robert Williams, an advocate of self-defense. But self-defense is an essentially static concept. One must mobilize the masses through popular struggles—and this Williams was unable to do—while simultaneously building for a clandestine, aggressive struggle.

For revolutionaries, how to combine political and military struggle is an important question. In the United States the extreme depths of frustration caused by racism and political and economic subjugation leads quite often to much rhetoric about violence. At the same time many people ignore the role of workers as decisive to revolutionary change and fail to attempt to disintegrate the military arm of the state. The use of violence and discussion of violence must be controlled political acts that lead to revolutionary change. Without the political mobilization of the masses it is impossible for acts of violence to accomplish their objectives.

All this thinking was yet to come, in the summer of 1964. At that time we had a thousand problems of all sorts on our hands, not the least of which was the old one of SNCC's relationship to COFO. The creation of COFO had always presented serious difficulties to SNCC and the Summer Project intensified them. Many people in SNCC, including myself, saw the continued existence of COFO as detrimental to SNCC's growth. Moses and the COFO staff argued for the independence of COFO, its right to make decisions for Mississippi. This position was honored by SNCC with great reservations, for it was full of dangers. It meant that we were working desperately to make COFO viable while the other organizations supposedly part of COFO did not assume their responsibilities. Acknowledging the independence of COFO meant submitting SNCC to the will of a body which could make decisions in conflict with important principles of ours. But the main reason for our reservations about COFO was that we did not like being in a working coalition with Toms and especially with the NAACP, given the history of Roy Wilkins's activity.

Relations with CORE were much less strained but problems existed in that area too. In the late winter or early spring of 1964, Bob Moses and I met with James Farmer, Marvin Rich, Norman Hill, and Gordon Carey of CORE's national office as well as Dave Dennis, who was in charge of CORE's operation in Mississippi. We were making every effort to involve the other civil rights groups, especially CORE, regardless of past friction. Farmer opened the meeting by stating that CORE was worried about its focus as an organization within COFO, it was important to their chapters and to their fund-raising efforts to have some identity specific to CORE. Therefore they wanted to carve out some territorial base in Mississippi for which they could be clearly responsible, and they proposed the Fourth Congressional District—which included Madison County, a stronghold of CORE activity. In essence this meant that SNCC had responsibility for the four other congressional districts in the state, because no one else was doing community organizing in the state except SNCC and CORE. We agreed to this arrangement.

The group then discussed plans for the project, including the challenge of the Mississippi Freedom Democratic Party—a new organization then in the making—to the "regulars" at the Democratic Convention scheduled for later that year. We were especially concerned that there be no public projection by this group—at this time—of the proposed challenge. Noth-ing should be done that would project a false image of the challenge, that would stand in the way of its being seen as the truly grass-roots effort which it had to become in order to succeed. This was understood, and the meeting ended with an agreement that there would be no further action for the time being. But the next week, on the front page of *The New York Times*, we read that CORE was planning to challenge the seating of the Mississippi Democrats at the convention.

No explanation was ever given by Farmer, and we were furious. It was not the first time we had had that kind of problem; during the Free-dom Walk, also a joint SNCC-CORE operation, CORE had issued press releases on its own. Many SNCC people now felt they could never trust the CORE leadership again. Throughout the Summer Project, there was intense hostility to CORE's national office—but not, however, to the brave and hard-working Dave Dennis and other CORE field workers who often had to suffer the consequences of actions by that office.

Ever since the fall of 1963 Moses had been pushing for the national office of SNCC to move from Atlanta to Mississippi for the summer as a way of putting maximum pressure on that state, of coordinating forces outside the state, and of insuring that national attention be given to the work of the project. Shortly before the project began, SNCC decided to make the move—to Greenwood, Mississippi—for the reasons men-tioned by Moses and also to assure that at the end of the summer there would still be a SNCC. Many of us saw within the Summer Project the possibility that SNCC itself might cease to be a force in the South, while having encouraged the existence of COFO with all its built-in conflicts involving the NAACP and CORE. SNCC's move to Mississippi was an important decision, for COFO folded after the summer of 1964, and many of the problems that were actually created by the independence of COFO became the problems of SNCC. The move to Greenwood had made SNCC stronger in Mississippi and, without that strength, we would not have been able to deal with many of those problems. As it was, they beset the organization for the next two years.

I was in charge of the national office in Greenwood that summer, although my original plans had been very different. Since mid-1963, I had intended to rest during the summer of 1964 and begin writing at long last. I was exhausted, having had no break in work and tension since I first started with SNCC. But the rest got postponed once again—the magnitude of the project, the shortage of trained people, the dangers faced by SNCC workers and the volunteers, made it impossible to take a break at that time. I did get a few days of relaxation, more or less by accident, during the spring. I had gone to a conference on economic sanctions against South Africa, held in London. There were representatives of many nations, including the People's Republic of China, with whom I would normally have jumped at the chance to talk. But I was sick throughout the conference, from a last-minute smallpox shot which had an unexpected effect. When the meeting ended, I decided to spend a week in Paris—it was so close, I was fairly fluent in French, and it seemed a chance to get some rest. I did, but it wasn't enough. My consciousness about colonialism was not as developed then as now but still I remember wondering, as I admired the beautiful gardens and buildings and wide streets of Paris, what price the people of Africa had paid to build that city. Then, while there, I learned of the statement supposedly signed by SNCC denouncing the stall-ins—which was very disturbing. I wanted to get back in a hurry.

In the Greenwood office, we had one of our four coordinators with SNCC offices and support groups in the North—Betty Garman. She was principally in charge of communications, via the nationwide WATS line we had installed in the office to communicate more efficiently with our friends. We used the WATS line to mobilize political support and to raise funds. Judy Richardson, my secretary, worked mostly on the statewide WATS line, taking down reports day after day of the various incidents occurring all over Mississippi. We developed a system whereby people could call either Greenwood or the Jackson office of COFO if there was any sign of trouble in their area. Our files became full with details on incident after incident of harassment and brutality. We relayed information quickly to Atlanta, where our efficient central staff went to work. They worked on a twenty-four-hour basis throughout the summer, as did the Greenwood and Jackson offices.

The internal pressures on SNCC and the Summer Project—the sheer logistics of handling that many newcomers to the state, the problem of so many whites, the delicate relations inside COFO—were heavy enough. External pressure in the form of white racist violence—killings, beatings, bombings, police harassment—never let up. But there was more. The liberal-labor syndrome and its black sellouts launched an intensified attack from many angles.

Allard Lowenstein did not come to Mississippi himself but he managed to make serious trouble, even at a distance. During the spring period of recruitment, we were told, he went to various college campuses telling people that they would be going to Mississippi under his direction. At Stanford University there was a reported split among the white students planning to go—some of them loyal to Lowenstein, some to the Summer Project as directed by SNCC and COFO. We know positively that Lowenstein set up his own recruiting office in the New England area, headed by Barney Frank. The jurisdictional question arose as to who was recruiting, the Boston Friends of SNCC, or Barney Frank. It was resolved with our Boston office left definitely in charge, and Lowenstein abandoned his efforts. But Lowenstein also pushed to have the Summer Project directed from New York, with a figure such as Bayard Rustin acting as central coordinator. In effect, he wanted power shifted away from Moses—away from SNCC—away from Mississippi.

But it was SNCC's decision to work with the Lawyers Guild that brought on the sharpest attack from the liberals. I have already mentioned instances of Red-baiting against SNCC and criticism of our accepting help from groups like SCEF and the Lawyers Guild. Now, with so much national attention focused on the Mississippi Summer Project, the Red-baiters threw a real fit.

We were not about to refuse the help of the Lawyers Guild—both because of our principles and because we were in a box legally. The suits being filed by the Justice Department were too few and usually inadequate. We also knew that many of the arrests of SNCC members were illegal and that there was a statute that provided for the transferring of these cases to federal court. On one occasion, Ben Smith of New Orleans—from the Lawyers Guild—filed a removal suit that saved us a lot of time and trouble. It was a simple procedure that any lawyer could have carried out if he had had the courage and willingness to openly fight the legal system of the United States.

In 1962, at our spring conference, Len Holt had tried to teach us how to file suits ourselves. His ideas were far ahead of the conservative legal profession and they earned him the enmity of many lawyers, who argued that you could not successfully transfer suits or engage in aggressive litigation with racists. Unfortunately, we ourselves did not take advantage of his advice. Arthur Kinoy, William Kunstler, Ben Smith, Howard Moore, Victor Rabinowitz, Michael Standard, Leonard Boudin, and Morty Stavis would prove the correctness of Len's position by their own work.

On many occasions we tried to get Jack Greenberg, successor to Thurgood Marshall as head of the NAACP Legal Defense and Education Fund, to transfer some of these cases to federal court. We also tried to get him to file aggressive suits which would tie up the state of Mississippi in legal work and would provide a forum for us to air some of our grievances. All these pleas were ignored. Greenberg was too much influenced by the policies and politics of the Justice Department. The fund's legal approach tended to be defensive.

So we were in a box, with almost no one then either willing or able to do the kind of aggressive legal work that we needed done—except members of the Lawyers Guild. During the spring of 1964, the COFO staff—including the CORE workers—agreed to use the services of any lawyers we needed and could get. Moses then wrote a letter to Jack Greenberg saying that this would be COFO's position. Greenberg sent a strong reply, stating that the decision was Bob's but that the Legal Defense and Education Fund would then pull out of Mississippi. Greenberg later modified his position to say that if we maintained our decision to work with the guild, he was going to come to the orientation sessions and ask each summer volunteer to choose in advance between being assigned a guild lawyer or a lawyer retained by the Legal Defense and Education Fund. He also said that in the future, the fund would not represent any SNCC person.

For Greenberg's sake, we were hoping he wouldn't have the nerve to come to orientation and raise that question. Our nonviolence was wearing thin. Greenberg stayed away.

The white liberal-labor syndrome and its black sellouts intensified their pressure on SNCC. By midsummer, it was coming from the heartland of the administration itself. Rumbling began one day when the brother of Congressman Bingham (New York) came to Mississippi to visit his son Steve, a volunteer in the project. Seeing the Lawyers Guild in operation there, he almost had a fit. Bingham later arranged a meeting in Washington with Burke Marshall of the Justice Department and asked several of us to come. The meeting was called ostensibly to discuss the situation in the Third Congressional District—the hill country of McComb and Natchez where the Klan rode strong. But when it finally took place, the Lawyers Guild seemed to be the main subject on the minds of our hosts.

Sitting around the paneled room in the Justice Department were Burke Marshall, John Doar, Arthur Schlesinger, Jr., Steve Bingham, and his father, with Bob Moses, Lawrence Guyot, and myself representing COFO. Burke Marshall pleaded with us to go slow on starting projects in the Third Congressional District; the Justice Department was trying to do some work in that area and it would take them time. We pointed out to him that all the United States Government had to do was throw one of the racist sheriffs in jail. This would prevent some of the brutality. We reminded him that the FBI had made one arrest in the Delta, indicating they had the power to make arrests if they wanted to. There was silence. We pressed the point and talked of the murders of James Chaney, Andrew Goodman, and Michael Schwerner.

Burke Marshall replied in that trembling voice of his that they were not going to fight a guerrilla war in Mississippi and if they arrested a sheriff, they would have to fight this type of war. We stated vigorously that he seemed more concerned about Mississippi's whites than the safety of black people. We did not agree with his position that the whites would start a war, and, if they were capable of that, then the issue needed to be forced.

Arthur Schlesinger, Jr., had said almost nothing up to then. Suddenly he spoke—and when he did, we knew he spoke with the consent of the government officials present and the elder Bingham.

"There are many of us who have spent years fighting the communists," he said, as if he had made this speech many times. "We worked hard during the thirties and the forties fighting forces such as the National Lawyers Guild. We find it unpardonable that you would work with them," he concluded.

Schlesinger's remarks came out of the blue. But, from that moment on, the subject of the Lawyers Guild dominated the meeting and I am convinced that the whole purpose of Schlesinger's presence was to raise this question. John Doar had already discussed with Moses the wish of the Justice Department that action be withheld in the Third Congressional District, so there was no real need for the meeting from that viewpoint. It would have been somewhat embarrassing for the Justice Department to raise the issue of the guild directly, and we had already heard Bingham's views on the subject. So it seems almost certain that Schlesinger had come to fire a new barrage against SNCC's position.

As the same old arguments against the guild were trotted out, we had to repeat once more our position on freedom of association. We also talked about the unwillingness of the Justice Department and the NAACP Legal Defense and Education Fund to take aggressive legal action in Mississippi. Bob Moses and Burke Marshall had a hot exchange on this point.

After the meeting, we walked outdoors. It was a Saturday and the streets of downtown Washington were quiet. I felt that the rupture with the government was complete and the issues absolutely clear. The words of Schlesinger echoed in my head, "We find it unpardonable . . . ." What blindness and arrogance, I thought. He knew nothing of the reality of our struggle in the South.

Not long after that trip to Washington, I was asked to make another trip North—this time to New York—by the family of Andrew Goodman. I did not know what to expect but I knew I felt badly about the murder of their son as well as of James Chaney and Mickey Schwerner. Our meeting centered around the efforts of the family to get the federal government to provide more protection for people in Mississippi. Marty Popper, a lawyer and a friend of the Goodmans', was also present and a phrase of his stuck in my mind. "The murder of the three boys was the first interracial lynching in the history of the United States," he said. These were people who had learned something about the reality of the South. But the Arthur Schlesingers of this country found it "unpardonable" that we should try to get help and protection from all possible sources.

By the end of the summer, it was firmly established in the minds of the sisters and brothers that SNCC was like an underdeveloped nation, struggling for its own self-determination. We would take help from anyone, always insisting that no one who gave us help had the right to dictate our policies. There could be no strings attached. That had been our policy in 1961 and it would not change. We knew only too well that there were people who wanted us to "fight communism," to engage in their factional skirmishes. Whitney Young was not the first nor would Arthur Schlesinger be the last. These forces would continue to attack us, claiming that by allowing the guild to participate in the Summer Project, SNCC was destroying years of hard work—years of Red-baiting, they should have said, and years of character assassination.

Once we had wondered: How do you make somebody understand that when people have dedicated their lives to moving history a few steps forward, and are willing to work not for money but for a cause, and are willing to die for it, then nobody from a comfortable setting in Greenwich Village or New York's upper West Side can tell us: "You're soft on communism" . . . "You don't have a statement in your constitution that bars people who believe in totalitarian government" . . . "If you would only do that, then we could get you as much money as you need. As it is we don't know anyone who would give you money."

We stopped wondering how to change those people.

We decided that the so-called fights of the thirties and forties were not really our fight, although some tried to impose them on us.

We decided that the House Un-American Activities Committee had better not subpoena any of us or we would create a total disruption of the hearing.

We decided that instead of engaging in the sterile memorandum politics of liberals and many of the Left, we had to work—to throw the dirt of the nation back in its face again and again, to gather a few more forces here and there, to build and then consolidate what we built.

We knew that the cold war, which provided the impetus for all the anticommunist pressures on us, was oppressive to human beings everywhere but also worked in our favor. For the United States did not want that dirt constantly made visible. It had to pretend to the people of Africa, Latin America, and Asia that the problem of the colonized Africans inside the United States was not really a problem. Black people just wanted to be good Americans—that was the line it had to sell the world. And so the government sometimes had to make concessions, open small doors through which we could hide—in order to expose still more of the dirty reality.

In effect, SNCC was breaking through the circle of fear that had been imposed on people by McCarthyism and which still lingered. It deserves infinite praise, I believe, for its attitude on freedom of association, because SNCC fought not only for its own freedom, but for the civil liberties of all.

In this spirit of refusal to compromise basic principles, we prepared for the challenge of the Mississippi Freedom Democratic Party (MFDP) to the lily-white regular delegation at the Democratic Convention in Atlantic City. I was both elated and yet disturbed about the challenge. I was elated because it seemed that at last we were building the type of organization that I had long hoped for. It had a broad base among black people and a clear structure that fed into counties and then into precincts. But I was concerned about the aftermath: the challenge had to be made, but we couldn't win at Atlantic City—how would the people accept their defeat? Would they see their attempt as a resistance effort in a long struggle or would they be discouraged and give up?

I discussed my concern with Moses and we agreed that I should make a tour of the state, trying to speak to as many people as possible. I wanted to alert people at the various county conventions and mass meetings of the MFDP to the fact that we might not win but that it was absolutely vital for the party to continue its grass-roots organizing effort. Francis Mitchell of SNCC and I traveled many hundreds of miles to Hattiesburg, Biloxi, Gulfport, Natchez, Vicksburg, Batesville, and other towns, keeping in close touch with Moses all the time.

Dr. King came to Mississippi at this time. The news of his imminent arrival led to a whole day's discussion among SNCC people. We wanted to make sure that when he came, he would give his support to the challenge. He agreed to do so. Knowing Dr. King's speaking style, his propensity for finding a memorable phrase and repeating it rythmically at intervals, I wondered to myself how he was going to handle this one— "Mississippi Freedom Democratic Party" is quite a mouthful. But Brother Martin did it again. "*Seat* the Freedom Democratic Party!" he cried, drawing out the first word, and it became, "Suh-*eet* the Freedom Democratic Party!" And he went on, "That's what we have to do at Atlantic City, ladies and gentlemen. . . . Suh-*eet* the Freedom Democratic Party! . . . Yes, my brothers and sisters in the struggle, with the Lord and justice on our side, I say to you that we will go there and we will do it—we will make them suh-*eet* the Freedom Democratic Party!"

The time for people to leave for Atlantic City drew near. Sixty-eight delegates from the MFDP, all but one of them black, were going there to demand that they be seated instead of the racist regulars from Mississippi. They were going armed with a detailed legal brief presenting their case. They were going backed by dozens of their brothers and sisters from the shacks and back roads of the poorest areas, many of whom had never been outside the state before. A sizeable number of the white volunteers also went.

I wanted to go with them but I had some major fund-raising events to attend in the North first, and would have to join the group later. Our fund raising had been going extremely well, although many of the old attitudes toward it still prevailed inside SNCC. At the height of the Summer Project, Harry Belafonte and Sidney Poitier had paid a visit to Greenwood—I had met them in New York and accompanied them south. Their visit stimulated them to help us further in our fund-raising efforts. They, together with many less famous people, had made it possible to finance the trip to Atlantic City.

The buses were drawn up on the street in Jackson and people got on board. I kissed Mrs. Hamer on the cheek as she stepped into the bus. She had been through many experiences since her first attempt to register to vote and she was moving the hearts of millions of people. She was SNCC itself. Despite the brutality, the murders, the hardship, a force was emerging on the national scene—the Student Nonviolent Coordinating Committee. It had started out in 1960 with the determination of four people in Raleigh, North Carolina, who were tired of segregation. From the April, 1960, meeting at Raleigh to Rock Hill, from the Freedom Rides to McComb, from Albany to Danville and Pine Bluff and Cambridge, from Greenwood to Selma, from New York to Boston to Chicago and San Francisco, a still small group of people had activated energies and wills to struggle for the creation of a new society.

No one dreamed of that new society more often and more thoughtfully than Bob Moses. I saw him now, slouched down by the window. He looked toward me and I felt the heavy load he carried. I knew many things about him, problems of his work and personal matters, and it was a tremendous burden. But he was going too, he would stand with the others on the boardwalk at Atlantic City. I felt very proud of him and Mrs. Hamer and the busloads of people, people, people, black people, and I knew they must be proud too.

We were a band of sisters and brothers, a circle of trust.

We were a circle of determined workers who had decided long ago that not to struggle against racism—this was a luxury we did not want nor could we afford.

We were young.

We had energy.

We had brains.

We had technical skills.

We had a belief in people and their power to change their lives.

We were willing to work with the most dispossessed—the sharecropper, the day laborer, the factory workers, and the mill hands.

We were not afraid of death.

We knew what we were doing was important not only for the South, but for our sisters and brothers in the North and throughout the world.

They needed models to raise their consciousness, to spur them on. And our work did this. Harlem, Watts, Detroit, Newark, the Black Panthers—all can be connected in the spiral of history with the determination of those who faced the Democratic Convention of 1964, culminating the work of five years, continuing the spiral of resistance set in motion by our ancestors on the shores of Africa when they resisted slavery.

I wanted very much to board that bus and ride with the people from Mississippi to Atlantic City, from inside the Summer Project to that bastion of racism—the Democratic National Convention. But I couldn't. The bus pulled off. I shouted "good-bye" to the people of Mississippi and I waved good-bye to Robert Parris Moses. They were on their way.

CHAPTER **49**

The 1964 Democratic Convention

AT THE 1964 Democratic National Convention in Atlantic City Hubert Humphrey, Walter Reuther, Senator Wayne Morse, Roy Wilkins, Bayard Rustin, Martin Luther King, Jr., Ralph Abernathy, Allard Lowenstein, and many other forces in the liberal-labor syndrome said that the Student Nonviolent Coordinating Committee did not understand politics.

We did not understand the political process, they said.

We did not know how to "compromise," they said.

We did not understand the Democratic Party, they said.

We in SNCC understood politics and the political process. We could compromise—but not sell out the people. And we knew a great deal about the Democratic Party. But the way that the liberal-labor syndrome looked at life was not the way we looked at it. We did not see the Democratic Party as the great savior of black people in this country. Therefore we did not have the habit of following blindly the ass, no matter how stupid he became . . . or how many times he kicked you . . . or did not move forward . . . or lost his way. We were not hooked on his smell. We understood, we understood all too well.

When I arrived at Atlantic City, two days after the others from Mississippi, Mrs. Fannie Lou Hamer had already testified before the Credentials Committee—the first step in the battle of the Mississippi Freedom Democratic Party delegation to be recognized as the rightful representatives at this convention. Mrs. Hamer has a way of describing her own life and the lives of other poor people in the Delta with such force that they become very real. Her testimony, carried over national television, stirred the hearts of many viewers. She brought to life the legal brief prepared by Joseph Rauh, general counsel for the UAW, whose true character we did not yet know, and by Eleanor Norton, a skilled black attorney. The brief argued that the regular delegates could not represent the Democrats of Mississippi because almost half of that state's population was excluded from the entire political process, including the election of delegates; that the regular delegation, aside from its racist basis, could not even be considered "loyal" to the national party because the state Democrats had several times bolted—most recently by coming out for Goldwater. These were solid arguments, but would they be heeded? We knew better, and went on pushing.

The atmosphere at the Gem Hotel, our base in Atlantic City, was exciting—and unusual. One of the first sights I saw was Ivanhoe Donaldson and Charlie Cobb, the blue jean twins of Mississippi, as we called the two veterans of the dirt roads and outhouses and grits, all dressed up now in Ivy League outfits. I couldn't believe it: suits, button-down collars, striped ties, the works. They had been lobbying with delegates from Northern states, and lobbying hard. Charlie Cobb was on his way to talk with Governor Peabody of Massachusetts, who would tell him that he felt the Freedom Democrats were right but . . . politically he couldn't support them, of course.

Everywhere in the lobby there were Mississippi farmers, all dressed up in their Sunday-go-to-meeting best. I greeted Mrs. Palmer; she was worried about what-them-white-folks-going-to-do. Upstairs in one of the rooms several of our delegates were stretched out on a bed. They had another meeting to attend, one-of-them-caucuses. Haven't been to so many meetings in all my life, one said. Back on the first floor, there was Francis Mitchell, handling public relations for the Freedom Democrats. He handed me a statement that they had issued upon their arrival.

Everything seemed well in hand, I thought. There wasn't even a floor for me to sweep.

Then a call came over the two-way radio: reinforcements needed on the boardwalk. Out there, in front of the convention hall, Stokely Carmichael was heading up a twenty-four-hour vigil. A group of us responded to the call immediately. Walking on the boardwalk, I wondered to myself what would happen to my brothers and sisters when the sellout came—as it had for me in 1956, as I knew it would again. We had worked an entire summer, done a tremendous amount of organizing, but we had not done enough to prepare people in Mississippi and in SNCC for the kind of political machinations, double crosses, and treachery that always went on at these conventions.

The vigil continued while high-level, closed meetings took place between the Mississippi people, regular delegates from various states, and others. I did not attend these meetings myself, because I was not asked; and, if I had been asked, I would have declined. This was the hour of the MFDP; I respected its integrity and the work that Moses had been doing. Mississippi was his bailiwick, in a sense, and I felt that he had things in hand. I knew enough about negotiating sessions to realize that only a limited number of people are necessary. But I did speak on behalf of the MFDP at a meeting of the Michigan caucus, and was ready to help in any way possible.

Moses was singled out by the powers at Atlantic City as the person who could make the Freedom Democrats accept any compromise that the Credentials Committee worked out. But he wouldn't—he couldn't, for it was not his decision to make. The situation became critical for the traditional brokers between black people and the Democratic Party. It seemed that Walter Reuther and Roy Wilkins, the long-time supersalesmen of human stocks and bonds, no longer had control of the ticker tape. This convention wasn't going right, from their viewpoint. Three days had passed since the Credentials Committee opened its hearings on the question. It was taking too long to settle this little matter. Wilkins had told Mrs. Hamer, after her testimony, that she and the other people from Mississippi had made their point—they should go back home now and leave politicking to those who knew how to do it. That was an insult that Mrs. Hamer never forgot, but she didn't go home and neither did the others. Too bad for the brokers.

For three full days, poor, working-class people and one middle-class white preacher—Ed King, who had run as lieutenant governor with Aaron Henry in the Freedom Vote—brought the great convention to a standstill.

Meanwhile, the word had flashed through the liberal-labor circle that Lyndon Baines Johnson, the man most likely to be nominated as presidential candidate, had said, If Hubert Humphrey doesn't settle this thing, he can forget about the vice-presidential nomination. And so the squeeze was now put on, full force. Congressman Charles C. Diggs, Jr., of Michigan obtained from Moses, by using heavy pressure and distorting his intentions, the names of people on the Credentials Committee who had said they would sign their names to a minority report if the full Credentials Committee did not vote to seat the Freedom Democrats. We do not know all the forms of the great squeeze, but we do know that a telephone call was made to one delegate from California by someone saying that her husband would lose his appointment as a federal judge if she voted for the minority position. She backed out, sorrowfully—she just couldn't go through with it. And we do know that Walter Reuther told Joseph Rauh that if there were a floor fight—another possible development, which we had real hope of seeing happen at one point—then he could forget about his job as general counsel of the UAW. We do know that Edith Green, congresswoman from Oregon, made a public statement later to the people from Mississippi that she never knew Johnson would stoop to some of the things he did.

Soon the squeeze began to be felt further down the line, closer to our own people. Bayard Rustin, considered a very good friend by Moses, Courtland Cox, and others at that time, had originally promised to help the Freedom Democrats. Now he began to work with "the greater coalition," as he saw it, and urged our people not to "wreck" the convention —we must allow Humphrey to become Vice President. Like the others, he thought that Humphrey's nomination would make it possible to bargain with the administration. The whole liberal-labor syndrome saw the possible election of Humphrey as their finest hour, the crowning glory to years of sellout, compromise, and so-called coalition. Humphrey was the shining knight of Americans for Democratic Action; he was the darling of some segments of the labor movement. No upstarts from Mississippi were going to destroy his chances. No "wild-eyed, idealistic bunch of kids" was going to say what's good for poor people in this country.

But the people of Mississippi had no faith in Humpty or Dumpty or any of those other smooth-talking jackals. They did have faith in us. They knew that none of those distinguished ladies and gentlemen had lain on the floor with them during the nights when the Klan rode by their houses firing guns. They knew that none of those fast-talking politicians had picked cotton with them to earn a meal, or lived on corn bread and grease and Kool Aid, or faced a sheriff like Jim Clark with murder in his eyes. They knew what party had sold them out before— the Democratic Party. And they knew the same party was trying to sell short their struggle again, sell short their years of waiting in lines trying to register to vote . . . their years of seeing neighbors shot at and many of them killed . . . their years of trying to make a living off the soil . . . their years of seeing children leave as soon as they were big enough, for the big city of Chicago, in hopes of eating a little better.

So they sat tight while the Credentials Committee and the other delegates squirmed—trying to find a bone to toss the people that would be accepted. On the boardwalk, our people sat and talked and walked— waiting for the word to charge the convention, if necessary. And the nation waited, too, and watched. At Atlantic City, in August of 1964, the whole Democratic Party was forced to deal with the black people of Mississippi.

It was Tuesday night, 8:30 P.M., and the convention was about to have its formal opening. As the chairman introduced George Lawrence, former governor of Pennsylvania, members of the Freedom Democratic Party entered the convention hall with passes obtained from sympathetic delegates. There they were, black Mississippians, led by Mrs. Fannie Lou Hamer, sitting in the seats of the Mississippi delegation. They had voted to reject the proposal adopted by the Credentials Committee—a proposal "giving" them a grand total of two seats as "delegates-at-large." This was not what they had come for, not by a long shot. So they came inside, all of them. This was their protest, their answer to Lyndon B. Johnson.

But Johnson's people had a trick bag for them. The word was passed in some delegations where we still had support that the Freedom Democrats had accepted the resolution of the Credentials Committee. I know this happened in the Michigan delegation, some members of which had been ready to fight Congressman Diggs and the administration. But when they got the false report that the MFDP had accepted the so-called compromise, they felt there was nothing they could do. The Credentials Committee report was adopted by the convention. Some people in SNCC and many in the MFDP were stunned—others were not.

I left the convention hall and gave my pass to someone else. The Democratic Party had imposed its will. It was the seat of government. With the Republican Party, it controlled the political process, merely alternating management of the national government, as they still do today. Both parties sought and seek to control the lives of all of us at any given time. Both parties made and make decisions that the people could not challenge. Both parties sought and still seek to physically destroy those forces that get in their way.

But the liberal-labor bigwigs were not satisfied. They wanted a meeting the next morning where they could try to convince the black people from Mississippi that they should formally accept the decision of the Credentials Committee which they had rejected the night before.

There was a telephone call for me at the hotel; it was Dona, the wife of Bob Moses. "They're going to hold a meeting this morning," she said. "They want to try to force the people from Mississippi to change their minds. They even got Senator Wayne Morse, who's going to urge them to accept the compromise. They got Farmer and King. All of 'em. Bob's the only one that's against it," she went on. "He's not sure he's going to speak. We want you to come down and speak for SNCC."

"But I haven't been to the meetings. I don't know anything about the inner workings of the decision," I said.

"That doesn't matter. The meeting's going to start at ten—you got fifteen minutes to get here. We'll try to hold it till you arrive."

I felt like a lawyer being rushed off to defend a client without knowing the facts of the case. As soon as I reached the church where the meeting was being held—the church where the MFDP had been eating and meeting, and where some SNCC people had been sleeping—I got a copy of the Credentials Committee resolution and read through it. I surveyed the room quickly. It was supposed to be a closed meeting with the MFDP delegates, SNCC staff, and those whom the delegates had invited to speak. No press. I kept my eye on Allard Lowenstein, sitting on the side. I also saw Congressman William Fitts Ryan's legislative assistant, who had been helpful at the convention.

The plan was to have presentations by all the speakers and then everyone except the delegates would leave the room. The delegates would then vote again on accepting or rejecting the "compromise."

Aaron Henry, chairman of the Freedom Democrat delegation, called out the list of speakers:

"Jack Pratt of the National Council of Churches.

"Bayard Rustin, the renowned organizer of the March on Washington.

"Martin Luther King, Jr., president of the Southern Christian Leadership Conference, whom we all know.

"Robert Spike, director of the Commission on Race and Religion of the National Council of Churches.

"Senator Wayne Morse, that great senator from the state of Oregon.

"Joseph Rauh, our legal counsel, who has stuck with us this far.

"Bob Moses, who needs no introduction.

"Art Thomas of the National Council of Churches.

"James Farmer of CORE.

"James Forman, whom we all know, from SNCC."

I listened to the list of names and said to myself, "They have really loaded this meeting." There we were, all of us amazed—dumbfounded —at the array of power that the administration had dished up, thinking that these distinguished gentlemen could deliver. They had to deliver, if they were going to continue their brokerage services at the same rates in the White House. So they began to speak.

Jack Pratt hailed the decision of the Credentials Committee as the greatest thing that has happened for the Negro since the Emancipation Proclamation . . . "I urge you to accept," he said.

I noted down a response to him. He would be easy to knock off in rebuttal. Dig this blond white man up there telling us that this is the greatest thing since Emancipation. He must have heard the chuckles in the audience. We were polite, although he seemed to get ruffled after making that profound statement.

Next came the master, Bayard Rustin, the man whom Bob Moses and Courtland Cox had invited to Atlantic City to try to convince Martin King that he should continue supporting the efforts of the MFDP despite the intense pressure put on Martin to discontinue that support. There was the master, a teacher of many who were in the audience, Stokely Carmichael, Courtland Cox, and others. There was the friend of Bob Moses, who had urged him to go South in the summer of 1960 and work for the Southern Christian Leadership Conference. To paraphrase Bayard:

"Yes . . . there is a difference between protest and politics. The former is based on morality and the latter is based on reality and compromise. If you are going to engage in politics then you must give up protest. . . .

"You must be willing to compromise, to win victories and go home and come back and win some more . . . .

"That is politics. And those of you, my friends, who are here from Mississippi and who have made such a valiant struggle, you are now engaged in politics. You must accept the compromise. If you don't, then you are still protesting.

"We must think of our friends in labor, Walter Reuther and the others, who have gone to bat for us. If we reject this compromise, we would be saying to them that we didn't want their help. In making our decision, we must remember our friends in labor for we will need their help in other matters."

Mendy Samstein of SNCC could sit still no longer, "You're a traitor, Bayard, a traitor! Sit down!" he shouted from the audience.

Aaron Henry urged the audience to let the speakers finish.

Stokely wanted to know if there would be a chance to refute and to ask questions.

The meeting was in an uproar. After Bayard sat down, Stokely, Courtland, and others hammered away at him, challenging his assumptions, defying the wisdom of the master. They had seen the light.

Then Martin Luther King, Jr., rose and stepped elegantly to the front. He said, very slowly, and I am paraphrasing, "Indeed there are many wrongs in our nation. . . . We have indeed paid a heavy price. Indeed we have a long road to travel. Indeed we cannot travel it alone. Indeed there is only one party that has helped the Negro in this country. Indeed there are segregationists in this party, but indeed the Democratic Party is the best we have and we must work to make it better. . . . I'm not going to counsel you to accept or to reject," King continued, "That is your decision. But I want you to know that I have talked to Hubert Humphrey. He promised me there would be a new day in Mississippi if you accept this proposal.

"He promised me he would get the Civil Rights Commission to hold a hearing in Mississippi, something we have been wanting for many years.

"He promised me they were going to make sure that segregation would leave the Democratic Party.

"He promised me there would be seats found on the convention floor for the entire delegation.

"And finally, my friends, I have been assured by Hubert Humphrey that the meeting you have been seeking with the President of the United States can be and will be obtained."

There was more applause for Martin than there had been for any of the other speakers. Yet there was not the general upsurge of emotion which usually accompanied his speeches.

A few questions were posed to Martin. As he spoke and answered them, I could not understand his naïveté. It seemed that he was telling the delegates to accept the compromise because Humphrey, whom he said was most likely going to be the next Vice President, had promised him that he would do this and that for the people of Mississippi. But what Humphrey had promised was not much.

After Martin spoke, Bob Spike said he objected mainly to the manner in which the delegates had made their decision. There did not seem to be enough time for deliberation. "Assumption is that with more time they would vote differently," I scribbled.

James Farmer spoke neither for nor against. He said it was true that there is a difference between protest and politics, but the MFDP was not one or the other. If you do this, then. . . . If you do that, then. . . . CORE is with you no matter what you decide. It was a decent statement.

Wayne Morse urged accepting the two seats. I couldn't understand why he was there. But later the reason would be revealed to me.

Joseph Rauh felt the two seats represented a victory, but "I am with you and I want you to know we're going to work to make the resolution work."

Bob Moses said we had to bring morality into politics. That's what was wrong with the country now. There is no morality in politics, otherwise we would not be here. He said he didn't want anyone telling him down in Mississippi about Walter Reuther needing help, Reuther hadn't come to Mississippi.

I recall that I started off my own remarks by saying, "I am not a part of the delegation. I was not a party to the decision made last night to reject the compromise, although I agree with it. I have been asked to speak for SNCC, but I cannot speak as though I am not one of you, for I am.

"I have worked in the state of Mississippi since 1961," I said, "although I was not actually there all the time. But I am part of an organization that has worked there. I have some other claims to being a Mississippian, as some of you know. I was raised in the northern section of that state, in Marshall County where Holly Springs is located. There my grandmother died without ever registering to vote because she couldn't. I shall not speak as if there is a division between us. Instead of saying "you," I shall say "we," for we are one.

"Let us remember that this resolution of the Credentials Committee has been adopted by the entire convention. In talking about 'reconsideration,' we are talking about a statement that will be released to the press by someone saying that the Freedom Democratic Party supports or doesn't support the resolution already adopted by the convention last night.

"That is a fact.

"Let us clearly understand it. The resolution of the Credentials Committee does not call for any action by the Freedom Democratic Party.

"It does not. You do not have to support it, or do anything.

"But let us read it and see what they are asking us to support. In paragraph two, they are asking us to agree that 'those members of the delegation of the regular Democratic Party of Mississippi are hereby declared to be the duly accredited delegates and alternates to this convention who have signed the following declaration.'"

I then referred to the brief submitted by the Mississippi Freedom Democratic Party to the Credentials Committee of the convention, in which the MFDP charged that Negroes had traditionally been excluded from participation in the state's Democratic Party. I reminded the delegates that most of them had been refused the right to attend precinct or county meetings of the Democratic Party. "And now they are asking you," I said, "to agree that in the face of all these injustices you still support this convention and still will agree that these people are entitled to seats no matter what they have done in Mississippi."

I also read out these words of Governor Johnson in a speech to the White Citizens' Council: "I am proud to have been part of the resistance last fall to Meredith's entrance at Ole Miss. Mississippi stirred the admiration of the world by her spirited stand against the federal invaders."

"And now, today," I went on, "we are being asked to say that the party which this man heads in the state of Mississippi should be the delegates to the National Democratic Convention.

"Paragraph eight of the Credentials Committee resolution welcomes you, the Freedom Democratic Party, as honored guests of the convention. But you came not to be received as guests. You came to take regular seats as delegates to the convention. To accept the status of guests is to deny the legitimacy, the rightness of your position. The regular or traditional Mississippi Democratic Party is clearly illegal and violates the rules of the convention. To accept the status of guests is to say they should have those seats.

"Paragraph nine adds insult to injury. The Credentials Committee has granted two delegate-at-large seats. But they have even gone so far as to name who the two delegates should be. Perhaps you, the delegation, might well have wanted two other people to represent you. Maybe you would want Mrs. Hamer or someone else. It is time we let people know that we are tired of having them name our representatives.

"Let us now consider some of the arguments as to why we should vote not to support the compromise," I began summing up. "Certainly this is not the greatest thing since Emancipation. That is very, very clear. Secondly, there may well be a difference between protest and politics, but as has been said, we must try to bring some morality into politics. Thirdly, there have been many arguments about what the federal government will do. Why is it that the Civil Rights Commission just can't do its job and come to Mississippi? And now they tell us we can get a meeting with President Johnson. Do we have to accept all their compromises to get that? How many meetings have we had with governmental officials and what good did they do? And where was President Johnson when we wanted to meet with him before the summer, before the death of Goodman, Chaney, and Schwerner? Aaron Henry, as president of COFO, sent him a letter long before the summer and he didn't even have the courtesy to send back a reply, even a reply saying that he had received the letter.

"And now they want us to be proud of the fact that somebody can arrange a meeting with President Johnson, if we accept his bribe.

"In making a decision to reconsider the vote of last night, we must always think of where we are from and whom we represent. Those of you who are here as delegates represent many people in the state of Mississippi. What effect will a decision to accept the honored guest status and the two seats-at-large, with the delegates named for you—what effect will this have upon your friends and your relatives and your fellow workers in the state of Mississippi?

"It seems you have no other choice but to reject support of this resolution.

"There is, however, something in the resolution which is only there because of the efforts to organize the Freedom Democratic Party and what has happened here at Atlantic City, namely the section dealing with the composition of the state parties and the call to be issued by the Democratic National Convention in 1968 to make sure that the delegation from Mississippi is democratically elected. In 1968 we must bring thousands of poor black folk such as ourselves and challenge once more the racism in the Democratic Party, the party of Lyndon B. Johnson."

After the speeches, everybody except the delegates left the room. I particularly noticed Senator Wayne Morse looking dejected, and I could not help but think that some high officials in the Democratic Party must want very much for the Mississippi Freedom Democratic Party to accept the compromise.

The delegates from Mississippi refused. They refused the crumbs offered them. They had come from Mississippi to challenge the seating of the regular Democratic Party and they felt they were entitled to the regular seats. "We didn't come all this way for no two seats!" Fannie Lou Hamer exclaimed.

Atlantic City was a powerful lesson, not only for the black people from Mississippi but for all of SNCC and many other people as well. No longer was there any hope, among those who still had it, that the federal govern-

ment would change the situation in the Deep South. The fine line of contradiction between the state governments and the federal government,
which we had used to build a movement, was played out. Now the kernel
of opposites—the people against both the federal and state governments
was apparent. Five years of struggle had radically changed the thought
processes of many people, changed them from idealistic reformers to full-
time revolutionaries. And the change had come through direct experience.

Not all of the participants in that early stage of the struggle would
make this change within themselves. Many were psychologically unpre-
pared for the lessons of those first five years, culminating in Atlantic City.
Many failed to analyze, to study, to advance their political education—
and it was one of the faults of SNCC that it did not provide a program
for this. Many people were, therefore, left to shift for themselves when
the forms of the struggle required change; when the need for making
sense out of a shifting situation stood high on the list of priorities. Some
crumbled as the spiral of history moved higher, for the transition was
painful. Others felt betrayed by the liberal-labor syndrome but could not
use that betrayal to push history forward.

So when the SNCC workers and the people with whom they worked
left Atlantic City heading back for the rural South, some were dejected
while others were angry, and still others were ready to move on. Everyone had learned something. The history of a people never repeats itself.
It is always in the process of change although often the forms of that
change are difficult to see. Atlantic City was a powerful lesson but we
still had more to learn—the lessons I call "profiles in treachery."

CHAPTER 50

Profiles in Treachery

AT THE Democratic Convention of August, 1964, SNCC had demonstrated not only that it sought political power in the national arena, but
also that it had power and the capacity to use it. The small group of
organizers who once cooperated with the Justice Department in obtaining information about voter discrimination had become a determined,
greatly enlarged, organized political force opposed both to the policies
of the Democratic Party and the liberal-labor Establishment.

We were alienated from the mainstream of American values and rejected those values, we sought power not for ourselves but for the very poor people with whom we had been working for four years. This drive for power for poor people signaled danger to the officials of the Democratic Party, especially President Lyndon Baines Johnson and vice-presidential hopeful Hubert Humphrey. Therefore, the destruction and neutralizing of SNCC's power became a must for the Democratic Party in 1964.

The power base operating for SNCC at Atlantic City had involved not only the Mississippi Freedom Democratic Party and its constituents. It also had the political and moral support of many students, churchmen, radicals, old and new—Americans moved to action by indignation about the blatant, brutal denial of the right to vote in the South. When SNCC forged a new coalition of these forces and brought it to bear at Atlantic City, it therefore not only disturbed Democratic officials but also disrupted the old arrangements between the officials of the Democratic Party and the white-dominated liberal-labor leadership circles. If this newly emerging political force led by SNCC were allowed to grow in strength, its influence in Mississippi and other parts of the country would further weaken the influence of the old-time brokers between the masses of black people and the Democratic Party. That possibility signaled danger—Red—to them for they could not control us and enlist our energies in their compromising, so-called coalition efforts, a great deal of which rested on the "struggle against communism."

But it was only after the convention that we began to understand all this fully, and to understand that some people we had thought to be friendly or at least neutral were in fact constantly operating against us and the people we worked with most closely. Their name for the game was "politics." Our name for it was treachery.

Two of these people were Senator Wayne Morse, who had walked out of that meeting of the Freedom Democrats looking so dejected, and Joe Rauh. Their true attitudes were revealed when I came into possession of excerpts from a letter Morse had allegedly written to a person whose name was not revealed to me. In it he said that he had had breakfast with Joe Rauh the previous morning, and they had analyzed the Mississippi delegation issue backwards and forwards. In essence, Rauh had stated that he thought the best hope would be to have both Mississippi delegations seated and had cited the precedent for such action in past Conventions.

Rauh had stated that he was satisfied that there was no longer any chance of having the so-called Regular Mississippi Delegation barred, but that he had hopes of having the Freedom Democratic Delegation seated, also. Morse had read all the briefs and memoranda that had been sent to him, including the excellent one prepared by Professor Robert E. Agger, Department of Political Science, University of Oregon.

Morse had come to the conclusion that he should not accept any role of leadership in the contest before the Credentials Committee or, subsequently, before the Convention, for the seating of the Freedom Democratic Party for the following reasons:

1. He was satisfied, and Joe Rauh shared his view, that the White House was unalterably opposed to any attempt to deny the seating of the so-called Regular Democratic Delegation from Mississippi. Further, he was satisfied that he could best serve the President in the campaign ahead on the civil rights issue, as well as other issues, by not involving himself in the Mississippi issue.

2. As Chairman of the Oregon Delegation of the Convention he was confronted by the fact that the overwhelming majority of the members of the delegation were opposed to involving the delegation in this controversy. Granted that what any individual member of the delegation did on this or any other issue was his own business, nevertheless, as Chairman of the Delegation, Morse had a responsibility of seeking to carry out the wishes of the majority.

He had favored putting the Mississippi delegation issue on the agenda of his Delegation meeting July 13 as recommended by a motion which had been presented at the meeting. However, the Delegation not only defeated the motion, which he had supported along with five others, but the Delegation decided by a vote of 17–6 that any further consideration of the matter should be postponed until the Delegation convened in Atlantic City.

Morse said that he had already sent notices announcing that the first meeting of the Delegation would be held at 5:30 P.M., Sunday, August 23, at the Pala Motel. At that meeting, he would place on the agenda the Mississippi Delegation issue.

However, he thought it would be most inappropriate for him, as Chairman of the Delegation, to sign any letters or accept any position of committee leadership or take part in any way whatsoever organizing a Convention contest on the Mississippi Delegation issue.

3. Next, Morse said that *the reelection of President Johnson, along with a vice-presidential candidate who he would eventually recommend, was Morse's major concern and interest* as far as both the Convention and the subsequent election were concerned. He did not think that the Mississippi Delegation issue should be allowed to supplant or endanger that objective. At least two of the liberal Democrats who were prominently mentioned as possible vice-presidential candidates, either one of whom he was sure he would be pleased to vote for at the Convention, could not be expected to involve themselves in the Mississippi Delegation controversy, especially in view of the White House opposition to it.

Morse said he wanted to be in a position to help either one of those men, if the President tapped either one of them for his running mate. He seriously doubted if the Mississippi Delegation issue would strengthen the chances of either one of them or of those who wanted to help them. He had decided to await the Oregon Delegation meeting on August 23 for a discussion of the entire matter at that time . . .

Morse said that Joe Rauh was the counsel for the Freedom Democratic Party, and had indicated the previous morning that he intended to see it through and give the group his best legal advice, as Morse was sure he would. However, Morse's own feeling was, expressed confidentially, that *Joe Rauh was very much concerned about the White House reaction to the issue, and he was also very much concerned about the effect of the controversy on one of the two potential vice-presidential nominees* referred to above. The other potential nominee, who was a Senator from the same state, would likewise be injured by a fight on the Mississippi Delegation issue.

Morse went on to make oblique references to conflicts within the Democratic Party. He referred to a memorandum which had apparently been circulated containing criticism of the policies followed by the Department of Justice in respect to Mississippi. And he concluded by saying: "I think it is clear that the recent pronouncements of President Johnson in respect to the Harlem and Rochester situations make clear that he has no intention of engaging in action in respect to any civil rights crisis that develops."

So much for what our supposed friends did at Atlantic City. Shortly after the convention, on September 18, a meeting was called by the National Council of Churches in New York which clearly revealed a campaign to undermine or neutralize SNCC by the liberal-labor Establishment and its brokers. Bob Moses and I, as well as others of SNCC happened to be out of the country at the time, and Courtland Cox had been left in charge of SNCC affairs. He and Mendy Samstein represented the organization at that meeting. Samstein took extensive notes, which will be reproduced here almost exactly as they were made.

First, let me introduce the other persons who attended the meeting as he noted their names:

1. Courtland Cox, then Program Director of SNCC.
2. Gloster Current, Director of Branches for the NAACP.
3. James Farmer, the Director of CORE.
4. Jack Greenberg, Director of the NAACP Legal Defense and Education Fund.
5. Bruce Hansen of the National Council of Churches. Helped with the orientation of students for the Summer Project at Oxford, Ohio, which had been financed by the National Council.
6. Anna Hedgeman of the National Council of Churches.
7. Allard Lowenstein.
8. John Morsell, Assistant Executive Secretary of the NAACP.
9. Jack Pratt, a lawyer who once worked for the National Council of Churches. Took leave during the summer or around the time of the 1964 convention to work for the National Democratic Party.

10. Joseph Rauh, general counsel for U.A.W.
11. Mendy Samstein of SNCC.
12. Robert Spike, Director of the Commission on Religion and Race of the National Council of Churches. [Was later mysteriously killed at the University of Ohio.]
13. Art Thomas of the National Council of Churches, a field worker in Mississippi.
14. Andy Young, Executive Director of SCLC.

Spike: Meeting has been called to discuss ways of cooperating in Mississippi in the future. If possible, let us try to avoid raking the coals of the past.

Current: I have questions about SNCC. Was attacked at a panel discussion in Cleveland, Ohio, last night by Ivanhoe Donaldson. Accused of not cooperating in Summer Project, of opposing direct action. I would like some evaluation of the Summer Project—for instance, the role of the Lawyers Guild. I object to Johnny-Come-Latelies. I also have questions about the MFDP and Moses. NAACP is nominally part of COFO, but its original purpose seems to have been subverted. If we are going to be partners, let's be partners. Let's determine the extent of cooperation. NAACP has a quarter of a million tied up in Mississippi.

Young: At last meeting, we expressed our frustrations with MFDP and generally. Meeting ended up with idea that whether we like it or not, we cannot escape our responsibility to make our work go as smoothly as possible. Must develop structure of cooperation—MFDP or COFO or some other ad hoc organization for funneling projects into Mississippi.

In evaluating the summer project, we must recognize that it ushered us into a new phase of civil rights struggle—from public accommodations to politics. . . . Now we must work to reestablish the coalition we had on Saturday and Sunday in Atlantic City. Our main concern must be to put this back together.

Spike: Mississippi is no longer a local problem. It exerts leverage on the national scene. Tension has been created between those who are moved by local considerations and those who must heed national considerations. The question now is, how to funnel resources into Mississippi without on the one hand manipulating local people, and on the other hand abdicating responsibility nationally. We must come to peace, eliminate the suspicion that exists among us.

Young: At the convention, we had a combination of moral power (Mrs. Hamer) and political power (King, Farmer and Wilkins). If this had been maintained, it could have been used to make the vote for Mississippi an issue in the election. We must re-establish national pressure for the right to vote in Mississippi.

Current: Has the way now been smoothed for winning the right to vote in Mississippi?

Rauh: The obstacles have not been cleared away.

Greenberg: We must assault the state, county by county. Have people go to the courthouse, follow that up with legal action. . . .

Rauh: What is needed is federal legislation that says: where less than one-third of the Negro population is registered, federal registrars will be sent in. But such legislation depends on the President and he is not likely to push it. So difficulties remain.

Current: We should concentrate on urban areas like Atlanta. The Freedom Democratic Party is a delusion. It causes confusion among local people. FDP units are developing in several places around the country and wherever they do, there are suspicious characters. . . .

In Jackson, Charles Evers has rapport with "downtown," so there will be little resistance to registration. Must develop campaigns, but cut out picketing and arrests because if people are jailed, others become frightened. Registration will be a slow, arduous effort. What kind of structure can we have? I expect not one with a director—I mean, Bob Moses—who dictates and we must take it or leave it. It must be democratic!

Farmer: Decision-making in COFO is the nub of the problem. Confusion exists on how decisions are made. We must agree on decision-making structure.

Morsell: It is a question of making the right decisions . . . problem is that Bob Moses and SNCC feel need for a single-line approach—perhaps because of their youth, frustration, indignation, bitterness. They must have understanding of strategic complexity. How are we to create this understanding? It's necessary to have that before we can have a structure.

Cox: Accusations are being made against Bob. Nobody has asked the people of COFO how decisions are made. People here must stop thinking in organization terms and stop dealing in recriminations. Must worry more about people of Mississippi than about an organization and its image.

The structure of MFDP and COFO is one in which decisions are made by the people of Mississippi and those who must face the consequences of any action taken. The attempt is made to have people in lowest economic situation be able to express their needs.

This whole meeting has been aimed against SNCC. It doesn't help to engage in a diatribe against Bob and SNCC.

Spike: We must try to get at the feelings of all participants here.

Young: Perhaps it would be helpful to review some of the history behind all this. COFO was originally formed as a structure to receive (VEP) Voter Education Project money. The participating organizations accepted it with varying degrees of interest—some only in name. After VEP, appeals for resources were made to the various organizations. SNCC gave the most, then CORE. NAACP gave to its branches and SCLC to its citizenship program. The idea in COFO has been that those who don't pay the piper don't call the tune. Whether or not it was a mistake to invest in the people of COFO rather than in the organizing of COFO, it is necessary to see present misunderstandings in that context.

Lowenstein: The past is done. Now the question is, how to maximize cooperation and not drive anyone out?

Rauh: But I would like to drive out the Lawyers Guild. I think it is immoral to take help from Communists. [Italics added.]

Lowenstein: I agree with you, but we must maximize cooperation. We need some understanding on how decisions are made. Right now, decision-making is metaphysical. We need a definite structure. We need a constitution. This new structure would be responsible for handling money and making other decisions.

It is true that SNCC was the main source of funds and resources, but this is no longer the case. Now students, labor, other groups are involved, so these must have a say. We must strike a balance with the people of Mississippi in decision-making. I would suggest that every group in the broadly based coalition that is committing people and money to Mississippi have a consulting role.

To sum it up, right now we need a commitment by the people here to the formation of a new, central body that will be regularized and democratized and broadened in its base. Questions like the Lawyers Guild would be submitted to this body and everybody would have to accept it. The problem now is that we have no appeal from decisions we disagree with. I was troubled at Atlantic City—but different points of view were not welcomed. We need structured democracy, not amorphous democracy.

Farmer: I agree with Al, but wouldn't you agree that not all who contribute should have a role in decision-making—only those who are part of the action?

Lowenstein: Yes, that's what I meant.

Spike: With Bob Moses and Jim Forman not here, we can't make any decision. We obviously can't decide for COFO or SNCC [he said, looking at Lowenstein].

Lowenstein: I deliberately didn't structure things . . . rather, I was trying to see if there is a consensus here on my proposal. If not, let's not take the time of Bob and others.

Morsell: We have a commitment to Mississippi, whether in COFO or not. The commitment is to our branches as an integral part of the NAACP structure. We must consider our national responsibilities—and this is the problem. In the event of decisions injurious to our national interests, no matter how democratic they might be, we must have a way out.

Lowenstein: In practice, we are bound by the decisions as they are now made. We can't leave Mississippi . . . though we might talk about it.

Morsell: Precisely the point. We're caught.

Lowenstein: Unless we write off Mississippi or engage in an open clash, then we must take this action which I proposed. There are now lots of committed people coming back from Mississippi—lawyers, doctors, students and others. It would be irresponsible if we were not to develop a structure. To avoid structure means to have decisions made which are not subject to the general will—authoritarian decisions made by small groups.

Thomas: The National Council of Churches (NCC) was invited to serve as a part of the COFO executive committee for the Summer Project. Does this willingness to include an NCC representative still exist?

Samstein: I couldn't say specifically . . . there was a general commitment to cooperation but there would have to be more discussion.

Hedgeman: We must get Bob and six or seven others, and have this over again. I understand the feelings of those on the firing line. I even have a good word for the Lawyers Guild.

Spike: We need clarification of what COFO is. Is COFO local groups plus local outlets of national organizations, or is COFO a confederation of national organizations? . . . We need to know exact relation of MFDP to COFO—are they separate? There should be two kinds of follow-up: 1) in Mississippi, need delineation of what COFO is; 2) we continue on a national level with this kind of meeting with Bob and Jim.

Morsell: There are positions taken by COFO which commit the contributing groups without their having any say.

Spike: There is no need for a new organization.

Lowenstein: I agree but there are pressing problems: resources are pouring in —over a thousand people this summer and probably close to a million dollars. There must be consensus on how this is to be utilized.

Thomas: There is an air of unreality about all this.

Lowenstein: We must have a consensus on the structure which we don't have.

Cox: We have begged and asked for help for COFO, as Andy explained earlier. People on the scene make the decisions. It so happens that most of the people on the scene are SNCC people, so SNCC plays a major role in decisions. But at Atlantic City it was the people, the MFDP, who rejected the compromise —Mrs. Hamer, Devine, and Miles. Jim and Bob spoke only after Pratt, Rustin, Thomas, King, etc. It is only democratic that we have the right to present our position. The actual decision was made at a closed meeting of the delegation.

Pratt: I would disagree with your reading of history. . . .

Cox: We asked for help but it was not given, as Andy indicated. I question whether groups are really prepared to come in now.

Lowenstein: There was no cooperation before because there lacked a structure to cooperate through.

Thomas: It is unreal, as far as Mississippi is concerned, for an ad hoc group to meet in New York and determine what should go on.

Current: I am not convinced by anything I've heard from those we have to do business with (meaning SNCC). . . .

Morsell: There have been over 1000 volunteers and NCC involvement in preparing them. Probably next summer there will be more. Something needs to be done immediately for guiding and directing the prospective invaders. This is a national question and so national interests are involved.

Thomas: Last summer we proposed to the NAACP a common training school for volunteers but there was no interest.

Morsell: Who did you talk to?

Thomas: I made the rounds last January and there were no takers but SNCC and CORE somewhat. SNCC is not naïve or inexperienced, as is often said.

Current: We didn't know about the Summer Project and the Oxford training program until we read about it in the newspaper and we saw that we were not involved. The NAACP is a disciplined army. No decision is made on lower levels without authorization from the top. Aaron Henry has got to get in line. If a decision is to be made, it has to go to Wilkins, Morsell or myself.

Morsell: In our organization, things take time to get done. We are bureaucratic. Many memos get to our desks, and have to await our decisions.

Spike: It's not just bureaucratic delay. I talked to Roy and he had grave doubts about the whole thing. . . .

Lowenstein: I have questions about decision-making. For instance, how was it determined that Henry should run for U.S. Senate? And how was it decided to substitute Victoria Gray for Dean Jones last spring? Seems that people are excluded who would like to partake in decisions and then they are stuck with those decisions. So who makes decisions?

Samstein: You should be careful to get correct information about what is happening. Henry was chosen by the MFDP meeting.

Lowenstein: But people are excluded or not notified of meetings, like Rev. Smith.

Samstein: Rev. Smith is not a member of the MFDP Executive Committee. The Executive Committee was chosen by the district caucuses about a week before the state convention. These caucuses were held in five different cities. Each elected three people to the Executive Committee. Records of meetings and names of Executive Committee members are on paper in Jackson. Every effort was made to get members to the Executive Committee meeting last Sunday. I was in McComb when they called several times from Jackson to make certain that Weathersby from Amite County got to the meeting, for example. . . .

Lowenstein: I was called by two Negroes in Mississippi and told that they couldn't understand what was going on. Rev. Smith considers himself a member of the Executive Committee. Feeling exists that local people are excluded.

Samstein: What you are saying amounts to a very insidious indictment. It is essential that you be in Mississippi and know what the facts are rather than make accusations without knowing what is really going on. . . .

Current: The whole program must be reviewed. We need a summit meeting of different groups to evaluate the whole situation. . . .

Cox: The need is for a low-level meeting. Get expression from people so we can help develop programs which speak to their needs. Henry and Evers cannot present the totality of the situation. Next meeting should be in Mississippi with people of Mississippi and based on interpretations from them.

Young: I suggest 5 people from each group working in Mississippi.

Spike: That might mean as many as 35 people.

Thomas: I disagree with the proposal. The National Council has no problem in communication. Have a program and open it to anyone who wants to add resources.

Current: The more I listen to Cox, the more I know we need a top-level meeting. *I have been listening to people from Mississippi cry for seventeen years.* [Italics added.] I don't want to listen to Steptoe. We need a high-level meeting so we can cut away the underbrush.

Spike: Both are essential. We see here represented some basic differences in ideological outlook. We need a high-level meeting but also must recognize the psychological importance of a low-level meeting.

Current: At Jackson, would have to meet with every Tom, Dick and Harry. And once we have them in, can't invite them out. We have to decide what to do in 1965. Budget considerations. These are top-level decisions, not to be made by the man in the field.

Morsell: We do have a national budget and constituents across the country. A knowledge of local situation is necessary but not alone sufficient. Can acquire vital knowledge without living in Mississippi. Some knowledge is to be gained by not being too close to forest. I would like another high-level meeting with Moses and Forman.

Lowenstein: At some point, we need to think of the volunteers, who are not being represented. . . .

Morsell: We don't have to caucus with Negroes in Mississippi. You want us to listen to people in Mississippi; we don't want to be attacked. We don't mind criticism but we don't like to be attacked.

Current: 1. Mississippi projection must be continued in 1965 under a coordinated agency. 2. We must think organizationally, that is, with budget considerations. These are realistic problems. Can't listen to grass roots. 3. We can go alone or be involved in broader commitment but we will have to decide at top-level meeting. We must consider many factors in allocating resources. We are planning now to move back to Alabama. It will have to get some priority and maybe it would be more important for us to work in Alabama than pour resources down the drain in Mississippi. We need a top-level meeting if we are going to commit resources.

Spike: I will try to get in touch with Bob and Jim and try to set up a meeting for as soon as they get back into the country.

Reading those minutes it is hard to know which is worse—the blatant "fuck-the-people" attitude expressed by the NAACP's Gloster Current, or the subtle, slick maneuvers of Allard Lowenstein. But it doesn't matter, both were out to get rid of SNCC. As might be guessed, the meeting with Bob and myself called for by that group never materialized. The group itself, with various personages added or subtracted, continued to meet between Christmas of 1964 and mid-January of 1965. SNCC was never invited again and just who called the meetings remains unclear. But at least one of them took place at the National Council of Churches headquarters in New York City. Discussion centered on the same themes: alleged resentment about decision making in COFO, based on SNCC's position at Atlantic City; criticism of SNCC and expression of the need to work around SNCC; the assumption that SNCC would reject changes in COFO decision making and, therefore, a new body had to be created.

At a meeting on December 29 younger people involved in the Summer Project, including representatives of the National Student Association and the U.S. Youth Council, were present; also Al Lowenstein and Michael Harrington. A national board was proposed which would include representatives of all the organizations putting resources into the state. Middle-class Negroes, who were considered to have been excluded up to now from COFO, would also be included. It, too, never came off.

All during this period when the liberal-labor syndrome was working to contain SNCC or remove it from the scene in Mississippi, we were forging ahead with new activities and programs. None of them were designed to make the "liberals" feel more secure. Immediately after the convention, SNCC began to plan a Black Belt Summer Project for 1965 that would extend from the Tidewater of Virginia to east Texas. Our goal was that by 1968 there would be a Freedom Democratic Party as well as independent political units throughout the Black Belt South. SNCC was also helping to plan a new challenge by the Mississippi Freedom Democrats—this time to the seating of the "regular" congressmen in the fall of 1965. No longer was Joseph Rauh SNCC's attorney; his place had been taken by Arthur Kinoy, William Kunstler, and Morty Stavis, with the help of many other attorneys.

While SNCC planned actions to stir further mass consciousness and exert more pressure on the domestic scene, it also made its first major move in the international arena. In October of 1964 ten members of SNCC including Chairman John Lewis paid their first visit to Africa together with Mrs. Fannie Lou Hamer. We went to the self-proclaimed socialist nation of Guinea and to other nations. Given all the efforts of the National Student Association to align African students with United States foreign policy and all the efforts of U.S. Government agencies to project in Africa an image of this country as democratic and progressive, our trip must have caused great alarm. Our trip to Africa almost coincided with one of Malcolm X's trips, and two of our staff talked with him by chance in the airport at Nairobi, Kenya. With this groundswell of radical blacks going to Africa, the government would decide it had better send James Farmer of CORE over there, in 1965.

Also in 1965 the USIA would put out its first issue of *Topic*, a magazine distributed exclusively in Africa. It showed pictures of Mrs. Hamer and Bob Moses supposedly winning representation for black Mississippians at the Democratic National Convention. This outright lie was intended to undercut the bad image SNCC had helped to generate in its four years of work, and the truth we told on our trip to Africa.

But no amount of tricks or treachery, from "liberal" or official sources, could stop the evolution of the black revolt. We went to Africa, we were broadening our struggle, we were going to become revolutionaries of the world.

CHAPTER 51

African Interlude

I STOOD alone on the verandah of the Villa Silla, looking out into the dark night. Around me grew the rich, tropical vegetation, and below the waves of the Atlantic Ocean lapped against the coast. The night was still.

I wondered if my ancestors had come from this land.

I wondered if they had been chained in the bowels of some slave ship docked on this coast.

I wondered if they had been taken from here to be stood on the selling block in some town of the Americas and auctioned off like animals.

I wondered how many of them had died in the long, brutal passage across that ocean out there.

I wondered what their names had been, how they looked, whether they had revolted against enslavement—or perhaps killed themselves rather than accept a life in chains.

The entire panorama of slavery swept before me as I stood on that balcony above the ocean. The long years of monstrous slavery, the hope of freedom, the Ku Klux Klan, the Mississippi Convention of 1890 which began the legal "reenslavement" of black people, the migration to Northern cities from the South, the Brown Decision of 1954 that ordered desegregation of the schools, Montgomery, Raleigh, the sit-in movement, the Freedom Rides, McComb, and Atlantic City—all filled my mind in the same moment. A thousand names and dates and images swirled through my head, blending together in a single horrendous truth. They were all part of a historical process, the life of a people separated from their homeland.

This was Mother Africa. We belonged here. This was our home. In the United States, we were strangers in a foreign land. We were separated from our people. We belonged here in Mother Africa, helping to build the continent of our brothers and sisters.

And then I thought of the millions of black people in the United States who could never get to Africa, whose lives were locked in the daily grind of racist poverty. We had to stay there and struggle inside the United States. We had to make a revolution to end the racism, the poverty, the crushing of our dignity.

But the choice came hard.

We were in Conakry, Guinea—ten of SNCC's officers and staff and Mrs. Fannie Lou Hamer. The trip had been proposed by Harry Belafonte when he came to Greenwood, Mississippi, and he also was in Guinea now with his family and members of a dance troupe that he had organized. His proposal had led to much discussion, for there were many people who wanted to join this first trip by SNCC to Africa. It had finally been decided that the following veteran workers would go: John Lewis, Bob Moses and his wife Dona, Julian Bond, Ruby Doris Robinson, Donald Harris, William Hansen, Prathia Hall, Matthew Jones (representing the "Freedom Singers"), and I. We had arrived at the beginning of September, 1964, planning to stay about three weeks.

As guests of the government, we were extended every courtesy. Comfortable living quarters and two cars were put at our disposal. But these physical conveniences did not explain the sense of well-being that filled all of us. The real reason was that we had come from several years of intense struggle to this place where there were no sheriffs to dread, no Klan breathing down your neck, no climate of constant repression. We had come from years of living as blacks in an enemy white world to this land of black people with black socialist rulers. We could relax at last. In the group we often talked about the tremendous pleasure of just being able to go to sleep at night without listening to every noise outside, worrying about bombings or armed attacks.

The pleasure of Mrs. Hamer in this trip was a pleasure for all the rest of us to see. She had traveled outside her home state very little and was exceptionally thrilled by everything in Guinea. President Sekou Toure sometimes came by the house where we stayed, and Mrs. Hamer always said, "Imagine the president coming to see us, when in the United States we couldn't even go to see the president." Today, Mrs. Hamer still talks about the psychological importance of black people from the United States visiting black countries where blacks run the government, industry, everything.

We felt particularly glad to be visiting Guinea, whose people and leaders deserve great respect. This small nation had ceased to be a French colony under the most difficult circumstances. In 1958 the government headed by President de Gaulle of France conducted a referendum asking each French colony (they are now called *départements* of France) if it wanted to remain under French rule—or not. This was no generous gesture by the so-called mother country, but an action forced on France by the Algerian War and the possibility of more Algerias. Only Guinea voted against remaining under France, and thus it became the second independent African nation. But when the French colonialists left, they took everything with them—even ripping out telephones in some cases. The Guineans had to start from scratch in every area of national life— and they survived.

Since that time, Guinea had declared itself a socialist country but non-aligned internationally. Our group saw these principles in action. We attended the opening of a new stadium on Guinea's Independence Day, October 2—a stadium built with the help of the Soviet Union. We visited the Patrice Lumumba printing plant, built with the help of the German Democratic Republic. And a match factory opened while we were there, built by the Chinese. We read Guinea's newspaper and were struck by the fact that African news, of a political nature, dominated its pages—not news about France or any other foreign country, and not accidents, scandals, murder. We learned about Guinea's one-party system and how it was organized, and did not regret the system of the United States with its fraudulent pretense of difference between the two parties. We saw a people working eighteen hours a day to build their nation and keep it afloat. Socialism made great sense for Africa, with its indigenous communal traditions and values that said, if one can eat, then none should starve.

In a hundred ways Guinea represented to us the antithesis of everything to which we had been exposed in the United States.

The trip was not as fruitful as it might have been in terms of political discussions, nor were we able to travel in the countryside as much as we would have liked. For one thing, our group was too large for good talks—I realized on this trip that three is the maximum number of people for a delegation that seeks to hold serious, intensive discussion. Also, as I recall, the General Council of Guinea was meeting then and many officials were tied up. But most importantly, a series of Cultural Competitions was in progress—nightly performances of Guinean dance, theater, music which kept many people in the capital busy. The fact that President Sekou Toure attended every performance himself from 8:30 P.M. to 1:00 A.M. indicated the political importance attached to these events. They represented a new society being built and the important role of youth in that process.

The cultural competitions formed a major step in the decolonization process. In a conversation with Diallo Alpha, director general of the Ministry of Information and Tourism, we learned just what the process meant for Guineans. Diallo told us that when he attended school, under French rule, students were taught that they were descendants of the Gauls—that their ancestors had blue eyes. When he later went off to school in Paris, he learned the names of all the rivers and towns of France —but knew very little about the geography of Guinea. The Guineans had to win back their identity. Diallo also told us about a day when President Toure came to Guinea's state-owned radio station. He called the staff together and said that music foreign to Africa could not go on Radio Guinea from that moment on. And it did not.

Our group spent its time resting, reading socialist literature (for the first time in most cases), talking among ourselves, attending the Cultural Competitions and occasionally meeting with officials. We had several talks with President Toure, a man with many important political ideas. He has given much attention to the internal development of Guinea's political party, the PDG (Democratic Party of Guinea), and in particular to how to develop political consciousness among the people.

I was impressed by his emphasis on leadership and organization, especially his statement that careful attention must be given to the selection of leaders because the people judge an organization by them. Later, in SNCC, I would push for open discussion of the strengths and weaknesses of various candidates for office—particularly the chairman. But this would be resisted strongly and SNCC would continue in several important cases to choose its officers more on the basis of personality than on careful examination of good and bad qualities.

The concept of criticism and self-criticism was not new to me as an idea. I had always believed in analysis of an organization's actions, including analysis of one's own mistakes. Only in this way are mistakes not repeated, conflicts resolved, and steady growth possible. But the trip to Guinea advanced my ideas about this process. Sekou Toure emphasized the need for people to examine the good and bad aspects of not only the party's section leaders but officials all the way to the top. The president, he maintained, must be criticized by the base and the base must have the strength to do it. I felt the truth of this very acutely, for I was aware of conflicts in SNCC which had been submerged for various reasons— and they included disagreement about my own role.

On one occasion we asked President Toure if he wished to say anything about our struggle in the United States. In that talk, he emphasized the need for political consciousness, good organization, and the correct analysis of our problems as black people in the United States. "It is fundamental that you see the problem as exploitation," he said. "While you should speak to black people first of all, it is the entire community that must be liberated." Later in SNCC, and throughout my experiences in the black struggle, I would recall these remarks of Sekou Toure. Ruby Doris Robinson and I would fight vigorously for an understanding of economic exploitation—not merely race—as part of the problems that black people faced. Unfortunately this concept would never be debated in an orderly fashion in the discussion about direction that would later come in SNCC.

I kept a long diary of our visit to Guinea, which formed the basis of a report I would later present to a SNCC staff meeting. The trip for me was a culmination of my life in several ways. Africa as a black continent, as our homeland, had always been on my mind. I had also dreamed for years of helping to build an organization to achieve popular power in the United States and then to relate it with one or more African countries for common revolutionary purposes. My African studies and the energy expended on learning French, which I did to be able to communicate better with Africans, were now being justified. All sorts of plans and activities whose purpose had once been abstract in a certain sense, were taking on concrete reality. My political and historical convictions about the importance of Africa to black people in the United States had become a living experience.

My mind was full of ideas and enthusiasm for formalizing and expanding this first link between SNCC, a base of black resistance in the United States, and the African struggle for total independence. It was imperative, I felt, that SNCC create an African bureau—something we should have done immediately after this trip but did not. Our trip was one of the first organized, group visits to Africa by members of a civil rights organization and, therefore, rather widely reported in the African press. We could extend our relations in Africa with more of such trips, I felt.

All these possibilities were buzzing in my mind, when suddenly we received a telephone call from Ivanhoe Donaldson and Betty Garman in Atlanta. They said that a meeting of the entire SNCC staff had been called by Courtland Cox, the person left in charge during our absence, and we must return immediately. The reason given was that some important decisions had to be made, including the question of what to do with the large number of volunteers from the Summer Project who had remained in Mississippi. But we were still baffled as to why Cox had called a staff meeting with the principal officers and project directors out of the country.

All of us except John Lewis and Donald Harris left Guinea after the October 2 Independence celebration. Lewis and Harris went on to Zambia and other parts of Africa. It was felt that they did not need to drop their plans simply to attend the staff meetings. But then, none of us understood what this meeting was about—and certainly nobody could have guessed how it would turn out.

CHAPTER **52**

Internal Disorder

THE STAFF meeting of October, 1964, to which we were so unexpectedly summoned turned out to be a historic event.

At the time of the meeting, SNCC was moving from one stage of its development into another. With the Mississippi Summer Project, we had acquired more power than ever possessed by a civil rights organization; we had also entered onto a very intricate, national political scene. We were prepared then to deal with neither our own power nor the powers against us. The fundamental question, although no one articulated it in this way at the time, was: Could SNCC grow from a cadre of organizers into a revolutionary organization seeking power?

Since its birth in 1960, the composition and orientation of SNCC had changed in several ways. The sixteen people who formed SNCC's first staff had been on the whole black, urban, and middle class in origin. Those in and around SNCC were primarily college students interested in change and in dealing with racism through nonviolent positive action. By 1964, with the shift of emphasis from public accommodations to the vote, SNCC had taken on a number of poor, rural blacks from the South and its focus was on that element as well as having more of an orientation toward adults like Fannie Lou Hamer.

By 1964, also, SNCC had proved that it could survive. When I first joined the organization, I had thought, if we can just survive as a group of agitators, we will someday be able to build a mass-based organization. I dreamed of the day when we would reach two hundred in number. Now it was happening.

All these developments encouraged my belief that SNCC could help build a lasting, mass organization of the poor that would seek power. This would, in my view, be a revolutionary organization. And I believed that SNCC itself could grow to become that organization. But others felt that SNCC should and would remain a small cadre group. Most, in fact, did not see themselves as creating an organization which would survive and seek power, but rather as working themselves out of business as a result of community organizing efforts that would spin off other organizations. Most did not see SNCC building a revolutionary organization. Some others and I were ready to shift gears in the fall of 1964; most were not.

This is not to negate the fact that the work SNCC had done was, in its time and place, revolutionary. We were not struggling for the vote as an end in itself, but to attain human dignity. And any struggle for dignity is revolutionary. SNCC was a pacesetter, a vanguard, in the early 1960s and would continue to be one. But it is possible to do revolutionary work in certain situations without being a revolutionary. This was what SNCC as a whole had done until then, and we had reached the point where it was necessary to become a revolutionary organization in every sense.

I thought SNCC would grow to see that need. But I failed to see clearly enough my own responsibility for sharing my dreams and infusing others with my spirit of organization. I also underestimated the danger of certain contradictions inherent in SNCC.

One of those initial contradictions had been the adoption of nonviolent positive action as a strategy. This contradiction we would be able to resolve. But there were others which would become intensified rather than minimized. A major one was the middle-class bias of SNCC's staff, stemming from the belief that college students had a very important role to play. I shared this belief, not because I was middle class myself but because I saw students as less shackled with the fear besetting older people in the South. The students—at least some of them—were the ones willing to work and to make great sacrifices. They had the technical skills which I thought should be put into service for the people of the rural South. As a result, the middle-class element continued to run strong even though a number of poor rural blacks joined the staff.

It was my mistake to think that this same cadre could go beyond being a catalyst of change and transform themselves into a mass organization with poor people. There had been warning signs—for example, a heated debate in 1961 as to whether one young black, who happened to be a high school dropout, should or should not be placed on SNCC staff—a staff of mostly college students. But no one, including myself, foresaw the crippling effect of certain habits and values common among middle-class students: a fear of one's own power, egoistic individualism, lack of discipline, generalized rebellion against authority, and self-indulgence. In more political terms, I think that the middle-class element saw SNCC basically from a reformist rather than a revolutionary point of view. One incident suggesting this occurred during a staff meeting in February, 1965, when Ella Baker was talking about certain actions SNCC had to carry out "if the organization is going to be revolutionary." At that point, one of the leaders of the middle-class element rose to declaim, "This is a liberal, democratic organization and it's not going to be pushed into violence."

Largely because of the Mississippi Summer Project, a Northern, middle-class, interracial element in SNCC had begun to predominate over the poor, rural, Southern black element. This shift greatly weakened the organization. For it created internal antagonisms just at the time when the dynamics of SNCC's work was forcing it to choose between reform or revolution, violence or nonviolence. And an organization that is seeking revolution, and willing to use violence, cannot afford the fear of power. It cannot afford weak or vacillating leadership; it cannot afford liberalistic forms of self-assertion. As a result of those internal conflicts, factionalism developed and split the circle of trust asunder.

We lacked the historic models which might have helped us to overcome that middle-class bias, those unrevolutionary habits of thought and action. Our need for internal political education was therefore great—for people do not grow automatically, they grow only with intensive political education and constant practice. And we had not adequately developed such a program. We also lacked a tradition of criticism and self-criticism, as I have already indicated. We had no mechanism for thorough, organized analysis of conflicts. Many people were simply too insecure to speak up.

Another factor that contributed to viewing SNCC as a reform organization was the constant turnover in staff. In 1961 I had felt that, if college students would take one year out of school, this would be a revolutionary step for it would signal a rejection of the virtues supposedly inherent in higher education. In 1961, it must be remembered, there were very few college students—black or white—who were willing to drop out of college and work for the movement. This trend, initiated by SNCC, would soon accelerate. But the constant turnover in staff, either as a result of people returning to college or just dropping out of the movement after they had worked for one, two, or three years, showed vividly that people were not committing themselves to the long-range struggle of building a revolutionary movement or making SNCC into a permanent organization. There were important exceptions to this, of course, including Ruby Doris Robinson. But the crippling effects of constant turnover became so acute that in 1965 I started talking about the need to recruit cadres for a five-year period.

The focal point of all these problems was SNCC's situation in Mississippi. We had acquired enormous power there, a power that called for expansion, a power that could have been greatly increased. As that New York meeting at the National Council of Churches made clear, our adversaries were just waiting and hoping for the chance to neutralize or destroy SNCC so that they could manipulate the movement in Mississippi as they wished. If we did not expand our power base there, all kinds of vultures would be waiting to descend on the vacuum thus created—from the NAACP through the unions up to the Democratic Party and the anti-poverty program vultures. And there were many signs that SNCC was going to let that base evaporate.

These, in broad outline, were the problems that surfaced at the October, 1964, staff meeting. Several major decisions were made there—and not made, which turned out to be equally important. First of all, SNCC failed to adopt the plan for the Black Belt Summer Project, which aimed to extend all over the South the popular power we had developed during the past four years. This broke the rhythm of our development and introduced a creeping paralysis into SNCC's program. Also, the meeting voted to put eighty-five new people on staff—almost all of them middle-class and Northern, and many of them white. Finally, SNCC grappled with the problem of its structure—the apparatus with which it would make decisions—and failed to resolve it.

All these issues were dealt with in a way that can only be called confused and chaotic. The style of SNCC meetings had never been orderly;

discussion always moved in a groping, circular way. But this time, the existence of problems seemed to become destructive. It would never have happened, I think, if SNCC had been a revolutionary organization seeking power.

The five-day meeting of October, 1964, is worth describing in some detail, for only in that way will the theories I have set forth take on real meaning. The goal is not to embarrass any individual or to justify my own actions, but to provide insight that might be of use to black revolutionaries today. It should also be said that I am giving a summary of events as I perceived them—and I recognize that my perception was not always the perception of others.

When I came back to the United States from Africa, I had no idea that the meeting ahead would be so momentous. I was primarily puzzled as to why it had been called. SNCC staff meetings were usually called by the Executive Committee with the consent of the state project directors. But much of the committee and all of the state project directors were away in Africa when Courtland Cox called the meeting. Technically he had the power to do so, for we had left him in total charge, but his action seemed an abuse of power. Courtland had become program director in the spring of 1963, a job I defined as helping me in working with the staff. I was desperate for assistance at the time, but choosing Courtland was an error in judgment. He had come straight from Howard University, had not then worked in the field, and some staff resented having such a person placed in a position of authority over them. They were right, and I should have been more sensitive to the dynamics of staff relations.

I arrived back in the United States five days before the meeting was to start, and immediately became sick with what was to become a recurrent ailment—inflamed sweat glands—and a deep abscess developed. It made me very feverish. Instead of going directly to Atlanta and preparing for the meeting, I decided to wait in New York until two days before it opened. When I reached Atlanta, I was too ill to do very much. The abscess had just been lanced and during the meeting I would find myself having to bathe the incision from a pot of water while listening to the debate and fighting off my general weakness. I was in bad shape for an important gathering.

Then the meeting itself got off to a bad start. It was supposed to begin on a Friday evening, at Gammon Theological Seminary in Atlanta, and many of the field staff arrived on time. But Courtland Cox was away on a speaking engagement and not due to return until Saturday noon. Since he had called the meeting, we waited for his arrival.

By Saturday morning, people were becoming impatient. The field staff had come a long way, they were busy with problems in their local areas and anxious to get back. I was concerned, because these gatherings of the entire staff took place only twice a year and everyone came to them with a tremendous amount of accumulated tension, anxiety, frustration. Collectively, this frustration could become very volatile and handling it called for great sensitivity.

To fill the time usefully until Cox arrived I began distributing to the staff for discussion a long report on our African trip which presented my ideas about how we could relate our struggle to theirs. The report generated tremendous interest.

Cox arrived at noon and wanted immediately to present his apologia to the staff for calling the meeting. I thought it would be better to go on with the discussion of Africa, not only for the sake of continuity, but also because that would delay the meeting until the arrival of Bob Moses —due that afternoon—whose presence was essential for discussion of the Black Belt Summer Project. But Cox insisted. Since he had been left in charge and since he did call the staff meeting, I reluctantly yielded.

Cox then made a few general, rather defensive statements about having called us all together because of certain urgent business including the question of what to do about the volunteers who had remained in Mississippi after the Summer Project. He then began reading the agenda he had prepared for the meeting. The question arose from the floor as to whether it was possible to change the agenda. Instead of replying that additions can always be made, Cox flatly answered, "No"—the agenda was set. This threw the meeting into an uproar. SNCC had always had an open agenda. And there was an additional grievance: At the preceding staff meeting we had postponed until this meeting a discussion of SNCC's organizational structure. It was an important question, scheduled for discussion now, and not on Cox's agenda.

I finally stepped in and tried to calm the waters by stating that we had always had an open agenda at SNCC meetings, that anyone could add anything to the agenda that he would like to see discussed, and that to resolve the immediate problem we had only to place on the agenda the question of our structure. This was done, but the hassle had lasted over an hour. It had set a bad tone for the meeting, generating an atmosphere of suspicion and distrust.

We proceeded to the subject of the Black Belt Summer Project. This was to be a massive undertaking in all the Black Belt counties from Virginia to Texas, with programs similar to those of the Mississippi Summer Project, but with the emphasis now on involving black college students. Moses and I were its chief proponents. The proposal had been thoroughly discussed by SNCC's Executive Committee before the trip to Africa. It required approval by the whole staff, but some preliminary work had begun. By the time of the October meeting, two staff members had prepared reports on the project stating that they had visited many counties in several states and people were ready to support the program. Campus travelers from SNCC had visited several colleges and many students seemed interested in working in the program. The Black Belt Summer Project had tremendous promise: it could serve to capitalize on the momentum of the Mississippi Project, but with our errors in Mississippi corrected, and to consolidate bases in a regional structure with national potential.

As we began to discuss the project, the meeting was again sidetracked. Frank Smith, a former SNCC staff member who had worked in Mississippi for two years, raised the question of who had decided on the Black Belt Summer Project. I was baffled then as to why he did this, and still am. Frank had been at the Executive Committee meeting where the project was thoroughly discussed, and knew that that body planned to seek the approval of the entire staff now—that the committee recognized such approval had to be given for the project to take place. I called attention to these facts, but it didn't help.

Lawrence Guyot, chairman of the Mississippi Freedom Democratic Party's Executive Committee and also a SNCC staff member, joined in the attack. The meeting then took a disastrous turn. A few people were raising the cry, "Who made that decision?" as if somebody had tried to sneak something over on them. These were not fundamentally the rural, Southern black staff members of the organization but Northern, middle-class elements—both black and white.

The meeting finally got off this track and moved on to discussion of the project itself. At this point Guyot walked out of the room, throwing his hands up in the air. Mendy Samstein, one of those who had done preliminary work on the project, was then asked to present his report. He said that it was difficult for him to do so if the staff really wanted to discuss decision making. This threw the meeting back into the morass we had just escaped. Mendy later told me that what had really bothered him was Guyot—for whom he had great respect—walking out of the room as he did. The situation had come to the point where the progress of this meeting seemed to depend on how one individual psychoanalyzed another's conduct.

The debate over decision making went on and on. Meanwhile, Bob Moses—one of the main people favoring the Black Belt Summer Project—never pushed for it. Never spoke in support of it. He was not one to talk often, but he usually had important things to say and people had great respect for him. Now he remained absolutely silent.

As a result of these developments, the Black Belt Summer Project of 1965 was tabled—never again to hit the floor of SNCC for discussion. The death of this proposal represented a crucial defeat. There are moments in history when an idea is ripe for implementation and can change the destiny of many people. But that moment must be seized for it may never come again. Failure to seize it will set back the clock of history. SNCC had reached a high point of power and influence, which had been slowly and painfully built since 1960. The Black Belt Summer Project would have extended the acquisition of power for poor people. But it was tabled, and the clock turned back.

The day after Guyot had taken his strong stand on decision making I saw him about to leave the meeting. I asked him why he was going, since he had pressed the issue so hard and the matter was then still under discussion. He told me that he was not really worried about decision making, he just didn't want the Black Belt Project to take SNCC resources from Mississsippi. I told him that was never the intention of the project. If Guyot had expressed his objections in a principled, clear statement from the floor, we could have dealt with them positively. Instead he told me his true feelings in a side meeting between the two of us. The irony was that he told me of his concern about resources while I was handing him a substantial check for the MFDP, part of SNCC's regular support for the party. In the spring of 1965 Guyot would state publicly in Mississippi that he had made a mistake in his stand at the SNCC staff meeting. But it was too late. The Black Belt Summer Project had died.

At one point during the hassle over decision making, I was sitting near Ivanhoe Donaldson and Stokely Carmichael, both of whom favored the project. Ivanhoe said some significant words to me in passing, "The leadership is not fighting for this proposal. Leadership has to fight for what it wants. Who is Frank Smith, to try and sabotage this program? He's already left the staff." To my deep regret, I did not heed his words about leadership—although they were not applicable to me alone.

The intervention of Frank Smith and our toleration of it reflected a liberalism that permitted people who had once been on staff to drift in and out of SNCC meetings. That liberalism allowed a Mendy Samstein to get so caught up with concern for the feelings of a Guyot—whose walking out was simply irritation with a political defeat—that he could not speak out for what he knew was right. That liberalism tried to give equal weight to all shades of opinion when there were two hundred people in the room. Since it was SNCC's practice to make decisions by consensus rather than by voting, that liberalism opened the door for meetings to be tyrannized by a minority. The vast majority of people present would, after hours of discussion, be ready to adopt a proposal; a very few would say they were not in agreement—and the meeting would bog down.

This kind of problem would have been unimaginable one or two years earlier. The sixteen people who formed SNCC's first staff had by 1963 become a tight group, moving on the assumption of great unity of purpose and good intentions as well as a willingness to compromise. We could make decisions by consensus rather than voting, and it was a good method. For the dangers that we all faced were too great to risk the possibility of someone not implementing a decision made by the group because he personally disagreed with it. We had to talk things out until we all agreed on all decisions.

This spirit prevailed from 1961 to 1964, and it was one reason that I called SNCC a band of brothers, a circle of trust. Ours was a decentralized operation. We imposed commands on no one. All this tended to reduce factionalism. Up to the fall of 1964 the careful planning and control of SNCC meetings was not seen as an absolute necessity. We could rely on a sense of common objectives and goodwill. The meeting now seemed to be lacking that sense. The great increase in SNCC's numbers partly explained the change, but there were other reasons.

The liberalism of which I have spoken tended to negate leadership as a valuable factor in an organization. This tendency was not something new. For a person to have stated publicly in SNCC at any time since 1961 that he or she represented part of the leadership would have been to invite scorn, derision, ostracism. There were good reasons for this, in a certain sense. SNCC's staff was young and idealistic. We rejected the "great leader" orientation of other civil rights organizations. We wanted no part of the corruption which attended that kind of attitude, the denial of the importance of people—especially poor people. We were fed up with hearing the words *leader* and *leadership*, especially from the press and so-called civil rights leaders. We believed in community organizing, in the power of the people to develop their own strength and direction.

But this attitude had become a kind of general neurosis in the organization, especially in the minds of the middle-class element and especially among those who had been strongly influenced by ideas about participatory democracy coming out of Students for a Democratic Society. What had been born as an affirmation became a simplistic negation. Instead of finding ways that people with natural leadership qualities could make their contribution and help to develop leadership qualities in others, this attitude simply said, Curb your leadership.

This attitude deeply affected Bob Moses, as his silence on the Black Belt Project indicated. Some staff members, including persons close to him, were always pointing out at meetings that he exerted too much influence over people. He shouldn't speak at all, they said, because his words carried too much weight as a result of the enormous respect people had for him and his work. He was made to feel guilty, I think, about his power—and lost sight of the fact that it was a power achieved not through manipulation and tyranny, not out of self-interest, but as a result of performance, good ideas, hard work, tremendous courage, self-sacrifice, and, above all, a spirit of humanity. Bob's attitude was crucial because people looked to him for leadership in Mississippi—and he was no longer providing it.

Bob and I had talked about this problem several times. "You got to do something," I said. "You cannot abdicate leadership or your administrative role unless there's somebody else there. If you abdicate, the thing will collapse. People don't know what to do." Bob once asked me, "At what point do you turn over leadership?" He was deeply disturbed by the amount of leadership that he had acquired and had to give. But it went even further than that; he was disturbed by an almost Jesus-like aura that he and his name had acquired. "Nobody would ever call me a mother fucker," he once said, or words to that effect, meaning that he was receiving a kind of respect which he considered false. He wanted to be just another worker. My position was that you just stand up and say, "Mother fucker, fuck you," and you'll be one of the guys then. But you don't abdicate leadership.

There must have been enormous pressures on Bob in addition to the burden of leadership. The brutality he had seen and continued to face, the constant administrative and organizational work, the treachery of the liberal-labor syndrome—all these factors weighed heavily. But I believe he might have been able to deal with them if it had not been for those staff members, primarily from the middle-class element, who constantly sniped at him about his supposedly excessive influence and strength.

It was not clear as yet, but a fundamental struggle had begun, to shift the power of decision making in SNCC from a rural, Southern, black base to a Northern, middle-class, interracial base. That shift received a momentous boost when the October, 1964, staff meeting voted to put an additional eighty-five persons on staff—most of them middle-class and Northern, many of them white.

This proposal was made at the meeting by a number of staff members for various reasons, including the need they felt for more personnel on their projects with certain kinds of "technical and linguistic skills." Most of the eighty-five people were from the group of over two hundred volunteers who had remained in Mississippi after the summer—completely contrary to our expectation. Before our trip to Africa, the Executive Committee had developed the concept of a "freedom force" to provide some structure for these volunteers as a separate group. Courtland Cox and Mendy Samstein were to work out the details for the freedom force while we were in Africa. But they did not do their homework. Now, at the October meeting, that concept got lost in the shuffle as pressure mounted to put the eighty-five directly on staff. A number of the volunteers had come to the meeting, lobbying for inclusion.

Ruby Doris Robinson and I led the fight against the proposal to put the eighty-five people on staff, for several reasons. First, it would change the racial and class composition of the organization. SNCC had begun with a staff that was all-black except for Bob Zellner, who came to work for us under a special arrangement made with SCEF. Bob was supposed to work in the white community; this proved impossible at the time and so he worked with us in the black community, but it is important to understand that original conception. It was over a year before another white person, Bill Hansen, joined the staff. Even when a few more whites were added, none of us doubted that SNCC always had been and should be black-led and black-dominated.

We argued further that people, whether black or white, should not be put on staff in one fell swoop—for security reasons. SNCC had built its staff very slowly, making sure that each new person was known and could be trusted. I had my own informal system of security checks, to guard against infiltrators and police informers. Unless a person was known to me or highly recommended by those I trusted, I usually hedged on an application to work with SNCC. I also had the habit of observing whether people were unwilling to do the unpopular jobs, such as mopping floors and emptying out wastebaskets. Most of the eighty-five people had worked with SNCC only for a summer—they were a largely unknown quantity.

Our third reason for opposition to the proposal was that we felt no one should be put on staff without a training session, without being educated in the history of SNCC and its objectives, and without being given a general political education. We had no setup for this, and it was a cardinal fault. For several years we had discussed the need to have training sessions for new workers, and on several occasions the Highlander Folk School conducted training sessions in voter registration. But SNCC itself had developed no formal process for orienting new workers. Our work on voter registration and public accommodations did not require that much skill, but there were things to be learned. Those already on staff needed some training sessions; I could not encourage the addition of a large number of people who would have no training and, therefore, aggravate an existing problem.

Finally, I saw no need to give staff status to the summer volunteers. We had the concept of the freedom force which could be implemented. I argued that Southern black people needed an organization where they could develop leadership and gain experience. Volunteers could find this through the freedom force.

The proposal was finally put to a vote, one of the very few times up to then that we employed this method of arriving at a decision. And we lost. That vote drastically accentuated SNCC's inherent problems, for it took power away from the Southern constituency and it added power to the middle-class element. While I didn't use such terms at the time, a different vote would have allowed SNCC the possibility of becoming a truly working-class organization, a mass-based organization.

One might get the impression that the reason for SNCC's difficulties at this stage was the presence of so many whites. But that would be to negate the importance of the class factor—a factor to which we did not give enough importance at the time. Much of the liberalism was being articulated by Northern, middle-class blacks.

SNCC already suffered from class tensions among the black staff workers. They ranged from young people with less than a high school education, and at least one person who could not read at all, up to college graduates and several people with master's degrees. We also had experienced racial tensions. Now the addition of so many whites increased racial tensions drastically, while also intensifying the class problem, since the whites were mostly middle class. We might have been able to resolve the class conflict if there had been only a minor racial problem. But the combination of problems was deadly.

The vote to include the eighty-five people also gave added strength to an egoistic individualism, rooted in the middle-class syndrome of values.

Some of us had seen that individualism takes an acute form in the state of Mississippi, where a phenomenon called "freedom high" was developing. The phrase was a humorous euphemism for workers and volunteers who, in late 1964 and early 1965, apparently felt that individual freedom was perhaps more important than organizational discipline. They felt no need to let any central office of SNCC or the MFDP know where they were, or what they were doing. They went about "doing their thing," often floating from project to project, responsible to no one but themselves. If workers were needed to help on a voter registration drive but they felt like writing poetry, they would write poetry. The freedom high people, most of them middle class, were often subject to an ailment known as "local people-itis"—the romanticization of poor Mississippians. This carried with it the idea that the local people could do no wrong; that no one, especially somebody from outside the community, should initiate any kind of action or assume any form of leadership. To some extent, this represented a reaction to the tendency of white volunteers to "take over" in black Mississippi, and in that sense it was a good thing to reassert the importance of local leadership. But too often "local people-itis" meant simply an excuse for inaction. It became almost a religion. People who had normally worked hard would go to Mississippi and become paralyzed. This whole set of attitudes drove Michael Thelwell, a very talented SNCC staff member, to write a paper called "Mississippi: A Metaphysic Wrapped in a Mystique." In this paper, Thelwell perceptively attributed "local people-itis" to what he called bourgeois sentimentalism.

It should be said immediately that SNCC and other elements bore much of the responsibility for the freedom high development. There was a structural vacuum in the state, as well as internal conflicts, which frustrated many people and left the remaining volunteers without clear direction. COFO had collapsed. SNCC workers were abandoning our hard-won bases in the state. They did this because of the lack of direction, the whole freedom high attitude, and, finally, because Bob Moses himself found it necessary to abdicate his leadership there. Bob had several reasons for doing so, a major one being his apparent feeling that he had become too dominating a figure. From my viewpoint, this feeling was in large part produced by the pressure on him of that liberalism which said, beware of your own leadership, your own power.

Another reason that SNCC workers left Mississippi was that relations between ourselves and the Freedom Democratic Party had become strained as a result of the internal chaos in SNCC and certain actions by the party. Many staff members found objectionable the manner in which Lawrence Guyot conducted his business. At the same time, the MFDP took the position of officially supporting Johnson and Humphrey in the 1964 presidential election. This dismayed and angered many people who had seen what happened at Atlantic City. Guyot had been in jail then and missed the convention, which was very unfortunate.

The MFDP needed to have its own character, to take its own positions. But it was a creature of SNCC's work. And SNCC made no significant effort to prevent the MFDP from becoming just another reform institution, to make it realize its fabulous revolutionary potential. This abdication of leadership, a leadership which many people in the MFDP wanted, contributed to the estrangement between the two organizations. It became characteristic of SNCC to spin off organizations and other vehicles of change in this loose way—which further aggravated our internal disorder.

At the October, 1964, staff meeting, we tried to cure some of that disorder as we grappled with the question of our organizational structure —the question which had been postponed from the previous staff meeting. In the discussion of this issue the effects of the shift in power from Southern black to middle-class, Northern and interracial elements were again a major factor.

From 1960 to 1961, SNCC had had only one staff member—Ed King —and decision making rested with student delegates from local protest groups who met every two months. In the fall of 1961 this structure was no longer viable and so the staff of sixteen people elected a temporary Executive Committee which functioned until the spring of 1962. At that time, a new constitution for SNCC was drafted. It provided that the full assembly of all student representatives would constitute the Coordinating Committee of SNCC's name, and that this would be the basic decision-making body. In that body, staff had a voice but no vote. The constitution also provided for an Executive Committee, on which the staff was represented by the executive secretary. Behind all these arrangements was our belief that the staff should be separated from the Coordinating Committee if SNCC was to be a Southern student organization. The staff simply worked for SNCC.

By December, 1963, SNCC's staff had grown to some seventy people and their representation on the Executive Committee became an issue. In practice, no decisions were made by that committee or the Coordinating Committee without staff approval. But some staff members were pushing for more formalized power. The problem was resolved temporarily by the addition of six staff members to the Executive Committee. In the spring of 1964 a move was made to have the entire staff become the Coordinating Committee. It was this question which had been tabled for discussion at the October, 1964, meeting, and we had to find a new decision-making structure because the old one was certainly obsolete.

Some people, including myself, argued for expansion of the Coordinating Committee to include not only more staff, but also representatives from student groups, community organizations and Friends of SNCC units. We felt that it was important to expand the base, that a decision to make just the staff into the Coordinating Committee would isolate student and other protest groups.

Our contention, and especially mine, was that many community organizations in the South wanted to be part of SNCC. Association with a national organization could give them more power, resources, ideas. But there was no formal way for them to do this. We were stimulating and organizing such groups, then leaving them isolated. I had in mind particularly our experience with the Albany Movement in 1963, when Slater King, Mrs. Jackson, and others had told me that they wanted to be part of SNCC—but how? We could offer no answer to their question, so they were going to affiliate with the SCLC. Thus we failed to offer people the means of doing what they wanted to do, with the result that the power of the people was being dissipated instead of consolidated and extended.

I also felt that the strong, growing network of Friends of SNCC groups in the North should have additional representation. In the case of black Southern student groups, our responsibility seemed clear. It was the recruitment of SNCC workers from Southern campuses which had given the organization its strength. The black campuses were an important, tangible base with great potential. A grant of eight thousand dollars to organize statewide student conferences would shortly become available to develop that base.

My position was based on my view of SNCC as the nucleus for what would eventually become a mass-based organization with a strong structure. I did not see SNCC as remaining a limited cadre of organizers who moved around instigating protest, and who might catalyze the emergence of such an organization—but never themselves grow to become it. We had to grow, I believed, and this meant expanding that base as well as creating a more centralized structure.

Other people opposed expanding the base—including Bob Moses, who spoke up strongly on this issue. Community groups should "hook up" with each other, student groups with each other, and so forth—but not with SNCC. SNCC should remain an organizing cadre. The staff and only the staff should be the Coordinating Committee. SNCC should close its rank with its present staff members.

Some people saw the debate as between a "Moses faction" and "a Forman faction." I think that such factions did develop, but I didn't view the conflict as merely a factional clash. To me, and others, the question was whether SNCC should be a strong, centralized organization expanding its power and moving toward becoming a mass organization, or a small elitist core of self-perpetuating organizers who provided no method for enlarging its ranks.

Bob's position had many supporters from the middle-class element of the staff. At one point, a staff member asked, "What is SNCC trying to become, the power on the throne?" This kind of remark exposed the germs of a negation of power which would infect SNCC mortally. The Atlantic City challenge had brought SNCC to a peak of power and influence—and some people were fundamentally afraid of power. "Power will corrupt us—we must maintain some kind of purity," was their attitude. Indeed, power can corrupt—but it depends on how power is used. In any case, the answer is not to run away from power, as this group sought to do.

One way to define this problem would be to say that many people in SNCC failed to distinguish between SNCC as an organization fighting for the creation of a better society, and SNCC as that better society itself. They could not distinguish between a revolutionary organization seeking power, and power as it had been corruptly wielded by the managers of capitalist America. There is no doubt in my mind that, to them, the slightest question related to the decision-making process or leadership was a very real issue. They were not basically insincere. But I think that they failed to resolve the relationship between their individual freedom within the organization and the liberation of people for which SNCC was supposedly fighting.

This element feared power for SNCC as an organization and also on an individual level. The overall negation of power created a fear of the power that I had in the organization. In retrospect, I think that the predominantly middle-class element was often not really arguing about the decision-making process but against me—because of some equation between the possession of power, which they found threatening, and myself.

The irony was that the fear of power coexisted with the desire to make SNCC a closed group—which amounted to a kind of elitism, in my eyes. While being so worried about SNCC dominating the people, this element was actually moving to isolate the people. One person at the meeting told me privately that she opposed the expansion of SNCC's base to include black student groups because "they haven't had our experience, they aren't up to our level of development." To work during the summer of 1964 in Mississippi was certainly an overwhelming experience for anyone, but many people let it justify a kind of mystique about SNCC and SNCC people—almost a snobbery, a feeling of belonging to an ingroup.

The debate on structure dragged on. By the fourth day of the staff meeting, a large number of the field staff—black Southerners—had left. Many of them later told me that they had come for a discussion of the Black Belt Summer Project and were frustrated as well as infuriated when this was aborted. They were tired of the vague hang-ups, the endless expressions of concerns that had no reality for them.

Their departure, together with the addition of the eighty-five new people, gave support to those who wanted to close the organization. Many of the new people felt no strong ties to the South or to the idea of Southern black people having a strong national organization at their command. My experiences in the South as a child and as an adult, and my theory that organization should begin where contradictions are the sharpest, certainly influenced my position. But I did not feel then, nor do I now, that this was any form of sectionalism or "tribalism." It seemed to me an assessment of realities. We had only begun to consolidate our bases in the Deep South, and there were many states where we did not yet have bases. The Black Belt Summer Project had been designed to carry forth that work. At the same time, we had started limited action in Northern cities, and the first major school boycott of the sixties occurred in Chicago under the direction of Chicago Friends of SNCC. There were many people from Northern cities on our staff, including myself, in a sense, and the North was not likely to be neglected. But we still had a big job to do in the South.

Those of us·who wanted to expand rather than contract SNCC's base failed to convince the majority of the people now at the meeting. And so, at one point, Bob Moses stood up and moved that the meeting adjourn and that the entire staff be called back for a new session, since so many had left and since the executive secretary had a minority position. Bob later explained that he had done this because SNCC had never asked people to implement programs or policies with which they did not agree.

I then rose to say that people should vote on the proposal and their decision would be binding on me. It didn't matter whether I personally had a minority position or not; it would not be the first time I had lived with decisions that seemed mistaken to me. I also offered my resignation as executive secretary as a sign of good faith and because it didn't make sense to disband that meeting and call in all the field staff again for this one decision. We had spent over five thousand dollars for the meeting. I was worried about this expense.

But my offer to resign threw the meeting into consternation. My motivation was probably misunderstood. I never discussed it with anyone, but people may have felt my offer was some kind of squeeze play to force adoption of my position or some aspect of a factional conflict people saw existing between me and Moses. I truly intended just to simplify the issue and bring about some resolution one way or another. Still my offer seemed to be a mistake and, after much discussion, I withdrew it. It was then decided that the meeting should be adjourned and another staff meeting called for November. In the meantime, some basic questions facing the organization were to be analyzed by an "Extension Committee" to provide guidance for the next meeting. Everyone was encouraged to write papers for discussion at the next meeting.

Much of the analysis of the staff meeting which I have given here— particularly the problem of the negation of power—was not clear to me at the time. But I did have the distinct feeling that the trust we had had for years was flawed and splintered. I saw hard-earned victories being tossed away. I saw Mississippi abandoned. I saw resources that we had finally obtained, after years of scraping by, about to be wasted. I saw our eight campus travelers with the four new cars we had at last managed to get for them, all set to go out and discuss the Black Belt Summer Project, now confused by the internal disorder. It was not simply a material problem. The time was ripe to move, we finally had the means —and, then, this paralysis.

One thing was clear, however: The trip to Guinea had been a serious mistake. It took away many people who should have helped to steer the organization in the period of transition from summer into fall. Instead of our small group going away, we should have had a long retreat for ourselves and others. People were tired. But we did not think three weeks would make such a difference, and we believed that all the important work was lined up for continuation. The trip to Africa seemed important and enormously appealing.

SNCC not only faced many problems of internal disorder; it also faced external threats on a complex, political level. SNCC was not prepared —structurally, ideologically, or psychologically—to deal with the kinds of enemies we encountered at the Democratic National Convention and afterward. Some of the staff still found it too painful to believe that we could be sold out by a Bayard Rustin or a Martin King. During the October meeting the staff had been given copies of the minutes which Mendy Samstein had made of the meeting at the National Council of Churches in New York. They could have been an important educational tool, to understand how the power structure operates. But the attitude of many staff members was, Oh, that's just some people in New York, and the minutes were never discussed.

In actual fact, a new period of history was upon us and called for a total reexamination of our role. The answer to "those people in New York" and others like them was to keep our power base in Mississippi. Instead, we were abandoning it. Allard Lowenstein and his cronies were on the outside waiting to descend, but we had among our own people those who—while not working for Lowenstein directly—represented his middle-class, liberal viewpoint. Our adversaries had only to wait, I thought, for SNCC to destroy its own power by failure to understand its historic role, by a fear of power among some of its members, and by a negation of leadership.

The problem of the class nature of the organization which I have discussed here is not just a problem facing us in the United States. It is the fundamental plague upon all the revolutionary movements in the colonial world, for most of these movements have been started by the Western educated elite who have failed to understand that any revolutionary movement cannot succeed if the power of that movement is not in the hands of the poor. The class composition of most of the independent African governments is middle class or petit bourgeois, as is that of the liberation movements among the colonized, including Latin Americans. Until this is changed one will not see much revolution in colonized areas. Therefore the problems I have raised with regard to SNCC are relevant the world around, I believe.

Between the October and November staff meetings, the Extension Committee met in Atlanta to consolidate and discuss some twenty to thirty topics with the overall title, "These Are the Questions." The questions had been broadly discussed at the staff meeting, and they were good ones: "What is SNCC?" "What is our role?" But the group that met, whom I dubbed "the postrevolutionary council," was convinced that the basic issue at the October meeting was decision making—the question first raised by Frank Smith. There were about fifteen or twenty people, and to me their attitude seemed condescending and patronizing. They never said, "I am concerned about decision making," but, "The staff is concerned about decision making." I was part of the staff and knew many others on the staff who did not feel that decision making had been the key issue. It had been forced on the field staff by some bourgeois sentimentalists who were mystifying and rationalizing their own desires in a very paternalistic way. The "postrevolutionary council" spent hours in what I can only call group therapy, a very personal and usually unpolitical examination of people's psyches.

I had a great deal of work to do in the office, and I was still ill, so I spent little time with the group. But I do remember one session vividly. Dona Moses was talking about "strong personalities" in the organization—two in particular, Bob and myself—and the need for them to be careful because of their great influence. Courtland Cox agreed and added that he had taken the job as program coordinator in order to curb some of my forcefulness—or words to that effect. This was a shocker. I had thought of Courtland as helping me in working with the staff, and his revelation suggested something like treachery. It did not help our relationship, which already contained important political differences, although we have remained friends.

The next day, October 16, I confronted some of "the postrevolutionary council" with the need to make a concrete, fast decision. The Executive Committee of SNCC had decided to purchase a large building in Atlanta to serve as SNCC's national office meeting place and as an educational institute. Five thousand dollars had to be paid for the option soon if we wanted to get the building. I asked the group what should be done. It was pointed out that no decision could be made until the November staff meeting, but Bob Moses felt that I could make the decision—as long as I would "take the consequences for it." I was very disturbed to see again the organization in a state of limbo at the height of its power, and decided to take those "consequences." I called around to the field staff, discussed the situation, and all agreed that we should pay the option. They would support me in case of any fight over the matter, they said. They were angry about the turn of events, their frustration, at the October staff meeting. With this support I went ahead with arrangements for the building.

The next day, Friday, I took a plane to Los Angeles to fulfill a speaking engagement. My arm was in bandages, and I had had little sleep. I planned to return and go to Mississippi the following Sunday to try to organize the field staff for a revival of the Black Belt Summer Project and against the negation of power. But these plans did not materialize. In Los Angeles, a few minutes before I was scheduled to speak, I became dizzy and then violently ill backstage in the auditorium. A doctor gave me some sort of injection and I managed to speak very briefly, but for the next two weeks I had to remain under constant medical care. My doctor, Brother Henry Paul, said that I might have a new, incipient ulcer. I must not go to Mississippi and I should rest for the next two months.

I was forced to follow his first piece of advice, but did not take the second, and began trying to put in writing some of my thoughts for the November meeting. This writing eventually became a long paper entitled, "What is SNCC?—A Band of Brothers, A Circle of Trust," which contained an analysis of SNCC's past history and some efforts to define our ideas, working methods, goals.

The very act of writing that paper represented an important break with my own pattern of work in SNCC, a pattern by which I gave little time to analysis, little time to sharing my experience with others in an organized way, little time to long-range planning. It is the function of leadership to do this—not to impose ideas, but to look at the total picture in perspective and come up with suggestions as to how an organization should move. It is also a function of leadership to develop strong people, by sharing its own experience and information, and by a constant process of education. I had many ideas in my head—ideas of how we could outmaneuver the racists, how we could hammer against the federal government, how we could consolidate our power and extend our influence. My great mistake was that I did not put my thoughts down on paper where others could read them, criticize and evaluate them. I had come to SNCC to write but I had written almost nothing since 1961.

There were several reasons for my failure to write, analyze, help plan— for the failure of all SNCC's leadership to do this. One was the simple fact that we were overworked. There were incessant demands upon our time. We were always tired. We had no time to plan, in effect, for we were too busy carrying out plans already made. In my own case, I was too busy with action, with organizing, with administration—and, above all, with the sheer survival of SNCC. This meant in a very nitty-gritty way, fund raising. By the end of 1964 the proper maintenance of SNCC called for raising forty thousand dollars a month. The ultimate responsibility for doing so had been laid on me alone. However, I do not want to leave the impression that there were not others involved in fund raising. There were many people who worked heroically to provide funds for SNCC, but the major portion of the staff saw the development of a fund raising machinery as my responsibility. I fought that kind of one-man responsibility constantly, knowing it was unhealthy in many ways, insisting that the whole staff face its collective responsibility, but without success.

A second reason was the oral tradition of our people, which discourages the habit of writing down one's ideas. This problem is exemplified by the so-called Reconstruction period in our history. Many black men became lawmakers, officials, sheriffs during that time—but there is little if anything written down by them. Many of them could write, but they left little for us to read about a very important experience. The oral tradition makes it very hard for us to pass on ideas and information to future generations. We must, I would come more and more to believe, get away from reliance on that tradition. We must write from our experience, and we must be the ones to do the writing, for only we can have full insight into what we mean.

A third reason, in my own case, was that I failed to realize the gap between my ideas of what SNCC should be and the ideas of most SNCC workers. This included the conflict between the idea of SNCC as a lasting, mass organization versus SNCC as a cadre, and with it the conflict between making a lifetime commitment to SNCC—as I had—and giving a few years to SNCC before going on to other things—as most of the SNCC staff saw themselves doing. I was in fact struggling against the internal dynamics of SNCC, but this wasn't apparent then; I thought we were out to build a mass-based organization. If I had been more aware of these conflicts, I would have tried to write more and communicate my ideas more forcefully and do more to solve the problem of internal political education in general.

There was also a personal, psychological reason for my failure to analyze, plan, and help educate others. I always felt that SNCC was fundamentally a youth organization and that it should remain that way. I knew the future belonged to young people and that I, as an older person, had to help create a forum and an organization where young blacks could struggle for their dignity and humanity. I saw myself from the time I went to work for SNCC as a tool of the organization with my main role, as executive secretary, that of helping to make the chairman able to perform more effectively. My sensitivity about my age and my feeling that SNCC had to be kept a youth organization reinforced the conception of my role as a more or less anonymous entity. I was not there to serve as an interpreter of or spokesman for SNCC.

I could not forget my experience with the Emergency Relief Committee in Chicago—the charges that I was trying to win personal power, when I knew this was a lie, and the crippling effect of the split which developed on the poor black people in Fayette County. I would never let anything like that happen again, if I could help it. So I sought to avoid publicity, although I got my share. I tried upon most occasions to avoid asserting myself forcefully with my fellow workers—except those in the Atlanta office and in some of the fund-raising offices under my direct jurisdiction. In those cases, I ran a tight ship, although I fought against being made into a father figure or big brother. With the field staff, the power of the project directors stood as supreme for me—inside whatever limits were placed on that power by the organization as a whole.

I think that from the beginning I probably exaggerated the conception of myself as merely an instrument of the organization. One example of this is the fact that, although I had been trained in African studies and felt passionately the need to link our struggle with that of Africa, I did almost nothing within the organization from 1961 to October, 1964, to promote that idea. This proved to be a major disservice. For, in later years, many brothers and sisters began to "discover" the African continent and failed to put certain matters in perspective. This kind of stumbling upon our African past and not comprehending the current realities of Africa could have been avoided with more discussion and proper planning.

At the same time, I was in fact giving leadership and direction to SNCC, to the movement as a whole. I would fight for the implementation of my ideas, if they seemed worthwhile, and fight very hard. Probably because I did often fight for my ideas, some people felt I was too forceful. Those with a taste for psychoanalysis might say that the young SNCC staff members opposed me as an authority symbol and were unconsciously fighting my leadership as they would fight the authority of a parent or teacher. Much of the opposition to various stands on program or structure which I—and others—took at meetings may have actually been based not on principles or politics but on a desire to break down my leadership. In other words, the opposition was not to an idea but to the person advocating it. I have mentioned earlier that I thought the fear of power, as part of a desire to make SNCC the ideal society rather than an instrument to attain that society, created hostility to me personally. This was one aspect of the problem; unconscious opposition to me as an authority symbol was perhaps another.

I sensed some of this. By the time of the October staff meeting, I had become so sensitive to criticism about being overly forceful that I was making constant efforts at self-negation. I was constantly holding myself back, negating my role. The reason why I had waited in New York instead of going straight to Atlanta after my return from Africa was not merely illness but also that I didn't want to seem compulsive about the direction of the meeting, always jumping in to run things. The result of that bit of liberalism in me was a meeting that fell apart because of faulty planning. The negation of power and leadership which had infected SNCC as an organization was getting to me personally as well.

Leadership, as I said, has the function of planning on a long-range basis. This means, among other things, training new workers to bring out their greatest potential and make them strong people. By the end of 1964 it was obvious that we desperately needed a program of internal education, including political education—not only for new workers, but for those already on the staff as well. We needed to discuss some basic issues of ideology. But we could hardly do that when some of the staff were unable even to read. The problem of internal education was a tremendous one and should have received the attention and resources given to our most important field projects.

My negation of leadership responsibilities—self-imposed and imposed by a tendency in the organization at that time—seems to me very unfortunate in retrospect. I feel today that I did a great disservice to my people and aided the enemy by not interjecting my ideas into our work through the writing of working papers, speeches, and other ideological efforts. I was in a better position than most people in the organization to see trends and directions, for I traveled widely and dealt with a wide variety of problems. I had also been with SNCC longer than all but a handful of people, and had a perspective.

Now, in California, I finally began to write down some of the fruits of all that experience. I was still far from understanding all the organization's problems. But a sharp light had been shed on our internal disorder and its potentially disastrous effects. As Bob Moses would write in a paper for the November staff meeting, SNCC was like a ship out on the ocean which needed to be repaired. How could we repair the ship and at the same time keep it afloat?

CHAPTER **53**

Power for Black People

THE STAFF meeting held that November, 1964, at Waveland, Mississippi, lasted seven days—and turned out to be a stalemate. The conflicts which had surfaced the month before were never resolved.

When I returned to Atlanta from Los Angeles, I found that talk about "the Forman faction" and "the Moses faction" had become rampant. There were rumors of "a coup against Forman"—which was made to sound like the deposition of Premier Khrushchev in the Soviet Union the week before—and even wilder rumors. The organization appeared to be split, and I quickly arranged for a meeting with Bob Moses. He came from Mississippi to Atlanta and, together with Ivanhoe Donaldson, we set about finding some way out of the mess.

They immediately raised the question of structure. I stated that I still felt it was a mistake to limit the Coordinating Committee to the staff, but for the sake of unity, I would not continue fighting the point. However, I thought it would be a political mistake for SNCC to declare that the staff alone constituted the decision-making body. Instead, we could make up a list of those who should be invited to the November meeting—staff and others. The people thus assembled would constitute the Coordinating Committee. Then, at the meeting, we could propose setting up a Call Committee which would invite people to future meetings and they would all have a right to vote. This would resolve the problem of structure temporarily; at the meeting itself we would have to work out our structure beyond the Coordinating Committee level. The formula was agreeable to the others, and adopted on the first day of the meeting.

On the first day I presented my paper "A Band of Brothers, A Circle of Trust" which contained a history of SNCC, answers to the questions, "How, Why, and Where We Organize," a discussion of our responsibilities to the Southern campuses, and a brief history of fund raising, together with an explanation of salary scales. I also urged that the staff evaluate my own role at this meeting. "I place my role up for examination and for criticism," I said, "but whatever is decided, I will have to take a few months' rest." In fact, I had wanted to step down as executive secretary— a job I had never wanted—since the end of the summer. I felt that I had completed the task of developing a strong administrative apparatus and that I could now get down to the job for which I had originally come to SNCC—writing and analysis. I wanted very much to write about our experiences.

One reason that I brought up the subject of my own role at that point was to encourage the process of self-criticism and criticism. Outside SNCC many people thought that it was an organization which practiced that habit. But the free-for-all collective style of our staff meetings had never reached the point of examining conflicts in an honest, thorough, collective way that would put problems in perspective and reduce frustration. Many times SNCC staff members would express criticisms of a meeting or an individual—outside the meeting, in private. I would urge them to speak out in the meeting itself, but there was great reluctance to do this. People remained unwilling to examine individual behavior and actions in an open, rational way, apparently out of fear that negative comments would inevitably threaten an entire relationship. Criticism of individuals had not moved beyond the level of personal grudges or personality conflicts.

People would also run to give me their ideas instead of speaking on their own. For a while this even included people like Ralph Featherstone and Cleve Sellers, who would later become outspoken critics within SNCC. I felt that everyone must acquire the strength to stand up, present their own ideas, fight for them if necessary, criticize the ideas of others, and recognize their own weaknesses. We all had to overcome the low level of political consciousness and insecurity—the lack of maturity— which caused these problems. But my attempt to do so, by initiating criticism of my own role, failed. So did other attempts to make the meeting a success.

Some thirty or forty, perhaps even fifty papers, of which mine was one, had been prepared by different staff members on "the questions" posed at the October staff meeting. The papers were distributed to everyone at Waveland. There was good material in them and they could have been the beginning of that much-needed mechanism for study and analysis, for internal education. But they called for a collective reading and discussion—the field staff obviously could not do much reading on their own. And no collective reading and discussion took place. People began talking as if the papers didn't exist, talking from their old standpoints, setting forth their same old attitudes, in a very individualistic way. The result was a staggering waste of time, thought, and effort by many people.

The irony was that many people who talked a great deal about the need for internal education didn't do anything about it. Mostly Northerners of middle-class background, they simply didn't understand the problem. When the Mississippi field staff talked about the need for education, they were talking about really fundamental problems—many of them couldn't read and write well and they wanted a remedial program to acquire those basic skills. But the middle-class element kept raising the question, "Why don't people talk in meetings?" as if it were some great mystery. The answer was obvious, Because they felt insecure—and the insistence on that question just made people feel more insecure. Finally one staff member from Mississippi got up and said, "Well, I don't talk 'cause I don't understand the words that you-all use!"

This conflict flowed in part from what I described as "local people-itis"—an ailment often contracted by middle-class elements when they went to Mississippi. Workers failed to accept their responsibility to teach and provide leadership. This problem reached a high point with the Work-Study Institute which was scheduled to follow the staff meeting, also at Waveland. Responsibility for the institute lay with a sister who had been made SNCC's education officer. Some of us had reservations about this, because of her Northern middle-class background and upper-class education at Vassar. Then, on the last day of the staff meeting, with the institute scheduled to start the following day, she suddenly announced, "I don't know anything, you people have to take over the institute." She, too, fell victim to that liberal, bourgeois abdication of responsibility.

We hit a dead end again in the discussion of structure and procedure. Many hours were spent arguing structure versus program—some people said, "What we need is program—then the structure will flow from that." I probably felt the need for structure most keenly, because I had too much responsibility for a single office, and because I felt that no two hundred people could function, no matter what the program was, unless they had a structure. We eventually broke down into three groups, each assigned to bring back a structure. But none of the proposals for a structure was ever adopted at this meeting.

Along with other people, I tried to introduce voting in the organization, because it had become too unwieldy to depend on consensus. The problem was that we had to reach agreement on this new way to reach agreement. In the same process I described before, the group would be about to decide on voting when one or two people would rise to say, "I disagree," or to insist on further examination of some fine points. From the middle-class element would come questions that I can only call intellectual masturbation. And so we again froze in inaction.

Once or twice during the meeting I went to Bob Moses and asked if he couldn't help to move things along. Bob simply said, "Things will start working out in a while." His reluctance to use his influence continued, and his alignment with the middle-class element and its attitudes seemed definite. I think that I understood the changes he was going through and felt sympathy for them, but the effects I saw were very disturbing. Shortly after the Waveland meeting, Bob would refuse to go to the first meeting of the Mississippi Project volunteers held since the summer. His reason: people were saying that if he went, discussion would be cut off and the ordinary workers wouldn't feel free to talk. I urged him at least to send a note or letter of explanation about his absence, but he did not.

The atmosphere of this Waveland meeting reached a new low in bad vibrations and secretive maneuvers. People were cutting each other up in small ways, but never openly criticizing a person. Instead of speaking out, a number of people could be seen circulating around the room, whispering. At one point, Stokely Carmichael came up to me and said, "Forman, don't you understand what's going on here? Those people are just angry 'cause you got so much power. And that's all they're trying to do, undercut that power."

I told him, "Man, if that's the thing, why don't they bring it out into the open instead of all this other nonsense about structure versus program and everything? Why don't you raise it in the meeting?"

So he did. "Why don't we stop all this?" Stokely jumped up and said. "You people are just afraid of the power of Forman." And he sat down. But nobody picked up on the point, at least partly because it had not been raised in a very political way. Open criticism and self-criticism were not the style of SNCC, and we needed more than Stokely's brief remarks to change that.

By the last days of the meeting most of the field staff had left in disgust—as they did in the October meeting—and it was mainly the Northern, middle-class element that remained. The Waveland gathering broke down finally on the question of firing people. We had specific proposals on the floor for disciplining staff members and firing them if necessary. Then came the argument: We can't fire anybody, we can only vote them out. If we voted them in, then we have to vote them out. It was absurd, but again confusion was created and decision became impossible. And I found myself forced to continue, virtually alone, dealing with personnel problems, although the administrative network that had been developed since 1961 was decisive in providing continuity and leadership in these troubled times.

The Waveland meeting revealed very clearly to me that we had a factional fight on our hands, and that it was necessary to organize in a way appropriate to such a fight. Only by pulling together the field staff would the fight be resolved. They had no basic problem with questions of leadership, structure, the distribution of power. I had not realized fully until Waveland how drastically the character of the organization had changed, that everyone was no longer moving on the desire to reach consensus, that we had become crippled by the will of a faction. Now I did, and the need to pull the field staff together was clear.

I had wanted to do that before the meeting but could not because of my health. It was so bad that I had to have a special diet and a room to myself during the Waveland meeting. And this was another lesson: It is a political mistake to abuse one's health. I had learned that before, in January, 1963, but it seemed to bear repeating. Everyone in the revolutionary struggle must try to maintain his health above all else. The body is an instrument of that struggle and must be preserved.

The Waveland meeting produced one other important realization. For the first time, I became aware of pot smoking as a serious problem in the organization. It had been introduced by the Northern middle-class elements, black and white, and was spreading to others. While I have no moral objections to pot smoking, I am convinced that anyone who is engaged in an intense struggle against the United States Government does not need to risk the luxury of smoking pot and the resultant penalties if caught. Even more critical than that problem is the fact that judgment can be impaired when vitally needed. The danger of this would show itself on a number of occasions.

Back in Atlanta, I returned to my usual work, but did not go to the office every day because I wanted to get as much rest as possible. I went to New York in December for more rest. I slept and slept and slept, something I had not done in a long time—certainly not at the staff meeting, when I would often get a total of only seven hours sleep in four straight nights.

As my health improved, I began to talk to many people from the field about what was happening in the organization, how we were losing a historic opportunity, our need for structure, the urgency of ending disorder. By February we had our goals mapped out—one of which was to make all decisions by voting and not consensus. We organized for the next meeting, scheduled to take place in Atlanta that month, very tightly and efficiently.

By the time the meeting started, I was back in good form and rested like a race horse. John Lewis opened it with a strong speech: "The organization must be black-led and black-dominated." Ivanhoe Donaldson: "There has to be strong discipline." I also spoke some opening words. But all that wasn't really necessary, because the field staff came to the meeting and said clearly, We want some structure, and we're tired of you all jamming up the organization. We ain't worried about no decision making. We want some officers in the organization.

And the same group of people who, back in October, were claiming that the staff was concerned about decision making now brought out a new argument, The meeting is too rigid, too controlled. You're intimidating us.

But the "field machine" held together. In terms of the class struggle taking place inside SNCC, the February meeting was a working-class victory.

Yet that victory took a heavy emotional toll. The meeting was stormy, even traumatic, and at times totally confusing—especially for the people with whom SNCC was supposed to be most concerned.

The battle over the Executive Committee contained some prime examples of that confusion. It had been decided by the Planning Committee for this meeting, some thirty persons who met beforehand, that we would begin the meeting with field reports and then move on quickly to structure, resolve that problem by the third day, and devote the rest of the meeting to a discussion of program. In the beginning this plan was basically followed, and by the second day we had agreed both to make all decisions by voting and to create a new and truly effective Executive Committee. This body, which was supposed to make decisions for SNCC in between meetings of the full Coordinating Committee, had not really functioned very well up to then and too many decisions were left to the Atlanta office—to me, in particular.

Jesse Morris offered a proposal for the composition of the Executive Committee: that all members be black, have no more than a twelfth-grade education, and be from the South. There were additional proposals, including one of my own for a geographic distribution of members that would give the field people control on the Executive Committee. Jesse's proposal was not discussed seriously, but its spirit had an important effect on discussion. We finally got around to nominations for the committee.

But, while the list of people nominated was being mimeographed for the purpose of voting, discussion was sidetracked in several directions— including the subject of program. A mood of uncertainty set in. Bob Moses then spoke for the first time, saying he wished to reintroduce Jesse's motion. Discussion resumed and then later Bob rose to pronounce, in a very quiet voice, a single statement to the effect of, "If you want to keep a slave, give a man the vote and tell him he's free." (His actual words may have been, "If you want to make a slave, you take a free man and give him the vote.") This remark, coming from a person so respected by the staff, left a baffled and disturbed expression on many faces.

Later Bob made his meaning clearer, "If you vote for that Executive Committee, and if you don't work out the programs, then don't tell me you're free. And I know you're not going to stay here and deal with programs. It will be left to the Executive Committee to do it, and I know how that committee works, so then it's going to be left to the administration. . . . So don't tell me you're free."

Mrs. Fannie Lou Hamer, a key nominee for the new Executive Committee said, "I just don't understand. You say you want people, local people who don't have twelfth grade education. I just don't understand this. Please withdraw my name, I just don't understand!" Others were also disturbed, "Bob, what do you mean we won't be free?" they asked.

I could feel the meeting disintegrate. Bob's concern was correct, basically, but I felt that he was expressing it at the wrong time and in the wrong way. It was unnecessary to reintroduce Jesse's motion, because all but two or three of the nominees in fact met the requirements of that motion.

I rose to make these points. I had decided early in the meeting that I was tired of people calling me names behind my back—"Grand Manipulator" or whatever—and this time I was going to fight back and also set the record straight. There had been too much distortion, too much twisting of the facts about my actions. Eventually it was moved that we vote on the nominations to the Executive Committee. The motion carried—we would proceed with the election—but it carried by 57 to 54. More people abstained than voted, mostly out of confusion or dislike for the general atmosphere. It carried, because the field people stuck together, but it was hard going.

We then elected officers. I had been opposed to the reelection of John Lewis and made my position clear in a long speech of criticism and self-criticism. It seemed to me that the position of chairman had been reduced to nothing more than spokesman for the organization; it was disfunctional. And John himself had not done a great deal personally to extend his role. But now, given our internal chaos and confusion, I reversed my position. We should not try to change the chairman at this time, I felt. Lewis was reelected chairman while I was reelected executive secretary and Cleve Sellers became program secretary.

The election of those officers was not a quick or easy matter, either, and emotionalism continued to ride high with many moments of bitter confrontation. For some people, the most difficult and confusing hour came late one night when Bob Moses announced that he was changing his name to Bob Parris—his middle name.

Although he did not explain at length his reasons for the change, it seemed clear enough that at least one of his reasons was the desire to unload the burden of charisma and influence which he had acquired as Bob Moses, and to assert a new direction for himself. I sensed also that Bob was under a terrific emotional strain. Whatever his reasons, they will be respected and he will hereafter be called Robert Parris in this story. There is no doubt that he was sincerely groping, as we all were, for direction and for some meaning in the process of building a revolution.

The February staff meeting made two decisions on future programs. It was too late to revive the Black Belt Project, but we did agree to hold a series of people's conferences throughout the South. And we decided to help organize a lobby of volunteers to go to Washington, D.C., that spring to support the MFDP in its challenge to the seating of the five racist congressmen from Mississippi.

After the staff meeting, the 'field machine" went to work to correct some of the disorder that had crept into the organization. Many people among those experiencing freedom high saw the decisions of the meeting as a threat to their "freedom" and began to resign or just drop out. Others were fired for not submitting to the discipline exerted by the program secretary or the Executive Committee—for example, not sending in at least a brief report on their whereabouts and activities. You could say that a purge was underway, but it was more than this. SNCC was an organization struggling against its internal contradictions, trying to shape itself into a truly revolutionary body, although this process was not clear to many at that time. The "field machine" had been caught off guard in October and November because it was operating under the assumption that we were still a circle of trust—when that circle had in fact been broken, essentially by certain middle-class elements who were afraid of power and freedom high. Now the "field machine" was functioning again. We were in the process of resolving the problem of negation of leadership and fear of power, which made it then necessary and possible to move ahead on basic issues in a political way. But the problem of individualism was still with us, as later events would show.

While the organization continued its struggle to overcome the internal chaos of late 1964 and early 1965, it also grew more militant. In addition to carrying on extensive action, particularly in Mississippi and Alabama, it began to develop self-defense networks in some areas. I announced SNCC's plan to help organize the Washington, D.C., lobby at a press conference in New York held shortly after the assassination of Brother Malcolm on February 21, 1965. Representatives of the Revolutionary Action Movement (RAM) had come to the conference and asked if they could make a statement after mine. They were under severe pressure, as the result of efforts to divide the black community on the issue of Malcolm's murder, and I agreed that they should speak. The association of SNCC with an organization advocating armed struggle created no problem for most of us in SNCC.

Shortly before his death, Malcolm had said it was the ballot or the bullet. The necessity of advancing from the ballot to the bullet had become clear to me by then; I knew that the ballot would never solve the basic problems of poor people—black people, Puerto Ricans, and Chicanos. For me, as for others, this period marked the approach of an end to any belief in—or willingness to engage in—large, nonviolent demonstrations. But I had one more experience of massive nonviolent action to undergo. This was the Selma-to-Montgomery March.

Selma, Alabama, had become a symbol of black resistance to flagrant denial of the right to vote. Events there in March, 1965, climaxed four years of agitation and finally forced the United States to end some of the abuses of the ballot. But this reform was not just a product of public opinion. The Democratic Party found that its own interests lay in that direction; more black voters meant more Democratic voters, it was believed. Thus the Selma-to-Montgomery March involved some backstage maneuvers by the Johnson administration, together with certain actions by the Southern Christian Leadership Conference of a type that SNCC had encountered before.

SNCC decided not to participate as an organization in the March, which was sponsored by SCLC. We felt that the possibility of violence against the people was too strong and we knew that self-defense would not be allowed on the March. But we did allow individual staff members to participate if they wished. Our fears of intense brutality proved correct on March 9, 1965, when many people were severely beaten and gassed at the Pettus Bridge—including our chairman John Lewis. That incident led us to send a large number of our two-way radio cars to Selma to help the people in whatever way possible, and many staff members also went there.

I arrived in Montgomery on March 11. A new attempt to start the March was scheduled for the next day, but then I discovered that Dr. Martin Luther King had privately acceded to the wish of the Justice Department that it be called off. He told the people at a mass meeting, however, that it would proceed and expectations ran high. I thought this a classic example of trickery against the people, and others also criticized Dr. King, including James Bevel and Hosea Williams of his own staff. Under this pressure, King called Attorney General Nicholas Katzenbach at about four o'clock in the morning to say that he had changed his mind. He could not call off the March, he said.

By nine o'clock that morning, the Justice Department had pressured Judge Johnson into issuing a temporary injunction to stop the March. But SNCC and other people went to work to create a climate of rebellion against the injunction. We had become convinced of the need for the March to proceed and we were certain that Gov. George Wallace would not permit violence by his state troopers this time. H. Rap Brown and other militants were at a private meeting in Washington, D.C., telling President Lyndon B. Johnson to go to hell. The climate across the nation was on our side.

But Dr. King and SCLC had more tricks yet to play. They worked out a deal with the Civil Rights Commission, headed by Leroy Collins, former governor of Florida, by which the thousands of people who had come to Selma from all over the country would march a few feet beyond the Pettus Bridge; Dr. King would kneel and pray, and then turn around to lead the people back into Selma where they would wait for a ruling on the injunction. A favorable ruling had been promised by the U.S. Government. The plan worked.

When the Selma-to-Montgomery March took place, at last, some SNCC people served as marshals but we had generally washed our hands of the affair. Aside from the problems with SCLC, it had become very clear to most of us that mass marches like the March on Washington and the Selma-to-Montgomery March had a cathartic effect. Their size created the impression that "the people" had made a show of power and changes would be forthcoming, but actually they served as a safety valve for the American system by taking the pressure off—pressure created by local activity.

By this time, students from nearby Tuskegee College had begun massive protests in Montgomery and asked for our help. It was there that I met Sammy Younge, Jr., a Tuskegee student who joined SNCC and who, in January of 1966, was murdered by a white gasoline station attendant when he tried to use the "white" toilet. I would later write a book, *Sammy Younge, Jr.: The First Black College Student to Die in the Black Liberation Struggle*, which tells the story of Sammy's life as well as the Montgomery demonstrations and the Selma-to-Montgomery March in detail.

The cycle of black resistance and white repression continued in full swing that summer. In Jackson, Mississippi, the state legislature was holding a special session to pass laws that would liberalize the state's voting requirements. This was a blatant attempt to take the edge off the arguments presented by the Mississippi Freedom Democratic Party in their legal challenge to the seating of the five racist congressmen and their demand for recognition of the MFDP. Demonstrations against the special session led to the arrest of over eight hundred people in June, 1965, and their imprisonment under conditions described by many observers as like a concentration camp. Many were brutally beaten and hospitalized. At the same time, black Mississippians were being arrested in Washington, D.C., for protesting the failure of the clerk of the House of Representatives to have printed the evidence submitted by the MFDP in support of its challenge.

SNCC was deeply involved in helping to mount and lead the Jackson demonstrations. I went there myself at one point, although I had become very leery of such demonstrations and of nonviolence even as a tactic. I had no intention of getting arrested. But at one point, I saw Mrs. Annie Devine, an MFDP leader, being arrested while she stood on the street speaking to a group of demonstrators. It was impossible for me not to take some action, so I walked over and asked the police, "What are you arresting her for? She hasn't done anything." I quickly found myself in the city jail, but that was the last time I got arrested in the Deep South.

SNCC was also active in the Delta again, where a strike of cotton choppers had started that spring and grown until, by early June, over a thousand workers were involved and the Mississippi Freedom Labor Union had been born. Its main demand was a minimum of $1.25 an hour instead of the average pay of $3.00 for work from sunup to sundown. Mechanization and suppression eventually defeated the strike but the fact that it happened at all showed how ready for action our people were—even the most intimidated and controlled elements.

Our project in Arkansas was also active, while over in Georgia SNCC staff member Julian Bond was elected to the state House of Representatives on June 16 as the Democratic candidate, but on an independent and radical platform determined by the black community. A number of SNCC workers campaigned for Julian. His election came about under the Supreme Court's "One Man, One Vote" reapportionment decision, which shifted power in the state legislatures from the rural counties to the metropolitan areas and created many new assembly districts where special elections had to be held—such as Julian's. In these new districts across the South, SNCC saw the possibility of creating bases of support for radical candidates who would use the elections as an opportunity for disruption and the raising of issues. The process of lifting consciousness, of revolutionary development, might thus be accelerated.

Julian's election proved that SNCC could rally mass support and that it had the potential for transforming itself into a political party. This potential was also being revealed in Alabama, under the sign of the black panther.

Near the end of the Selma-to-Montgomery March, a white supporter from Detroit named Mrs. Viola Liuzzo had been killed by Klansmen while she drove through Lowndes County. One night, at a meeting in Montgomery, we decided that SNCC's response to her murder would be to organize in Lowndes—a notoriously racist, terrorized area with an 86 percent black population that was acutely poor and with not one black person registered to vote. Stokely Carmichael became the project director for this county; Bob Mants, Courtland Cox, the Jackson brothers, and Ralph Featherstone were other SNCC staffers working there. I attended two of the early mass meetings in Lowndes but did not go there often. My nerves were in bad shape and, in any case, the other SNCC people had the situation well in hand.

Jack Minnis, head of SNCC's research department, discovered a little-known Alabama law that made it possible for independent political organizations to be formed and run candidates for office under conditions that were technically not difficult to meet. This legal loophole opened the door for the creation later that year of the Lowndes County Freedom Organization, with the black panther as its symbol. Minnis held a number of workshops to explain the whole process. The Alabama people in the Freedom Organization acquired a better understanding of what they were doing, and why, than any other political group that we had thus far developed. A tremendous excitement and new hope began to flow as the black men and women of Lowndes County moved to shake off a hundred years of white supremacy.

All this activity, and especially the birth of the Lowndes County movement, was giving SNCC the sense of a new lease on life when the November, 1965, staff meeting opened. We still faced internal problems, especially those created by individualism and a lack of self-discipline—no doubt about it. A previous staff meeting, in May of the same year, had made this clear enough. One incident centered around the fact that the person responsible for arrangements—room, board, transportation, and so forth—had set up a system of meal cards. It should be noted that the cost of our meetings ran into thousands of dollars; we paid for meals according to the number of people who ate; and there was often confusion caused by many unregistered hangers-on. With the meal cards, given to everyone legitimately attending the meeting for presentation in the dining hall before each meal, the conference coordinator hoped to solve this problem. But a few people raised the cry of "regimentation" and organized a meal card burning. Others, mostly Southern working-class blacks, were prepared to bar this small group from the dining hall, by armed struggle if necessary. A serious confrontation was finally avoided, but the incident revealed the lingering power of destructive individualism.

At the November, 1965, meeting, this problem was intensified by the resentment of some people against the disciplinary letters which they had been sent from the Atlanta office. But, by now, the staff had been sharply reduced in number, and most of the people at this meeting were ready to think in long-range revolutionary terms. We could talk and make plans in an atmosphere relatively free from personal trauma. It was high time—much had happened in the black community, including the Watts rebellion that summer, and if SNCC didn't get itself together, the revolution was going to leave it behind.

For me, the turning point became clear during a talk by Courtland Cox, who had been working in Lowndes County. He was talking about what the people there were trying to do and, at one point, he wrote some words on the blackboard. I think they said, "Get power for black people." And he continued, "The people want power, power to control the courthouse, power to control their lives." As he talked and I looked at the written words, something clicked in me. I felt then that we had emerged from the internal disorder, that we were in a new day, and that I personally could begin to work freely on the basis of my true beliefs—beliefs along the line I had indicated in my Greenwood speech about power.

I went up to the blackboard myself and wrote down, "Power. Education. Organization." "Fundamentally," I said, "the organizer has to see his role as instilling a tremendous political education toward forming basic organizations in order to achieve power." This was the first time that the discussion of power as such had come up in the organization. From that time on, SNCC began to talk more and more about power for black people, organization, and political education. We had attained a whole new level of objectives, we were once again moving in harmony with the needs of the masses of black people.

At the same meeting SNCC also began to discuss the war in Vietnam and to prepare a statement on it. Until that year, most of us—including myself—had considered the war not irrelevant, but simply remote. Its importance to black people had not come home to us. Bob Parris, however, had begun working that summer with some forces in the peace movement. He was concerned that students who had worked in the South—white students in particular—could remain relevant and also continue relating to the black movement in a healthy way after they left the South. His new activity also had roots in a general concern for peace, which had been manifested when he went on a Quaker mission to Japan in the late fifties. Bob worked that summer with the Committee of Unrepresented People, an ad hoc organization which aimed to bring together people from different movements and which held a large gathering in Washington, D.C., to confront the machinery of government with some of the people whose views—especially on the war—it was supposed to represent and did not. Bob also traveled around the country, meeting with various peace groups.

The creation of these and other links between the antiwar movement and what was still called the civil rights movement, together with the expanding consciousness of various SNCC workers, led us to the discussion of Vietnam. It was agreed at the November meeting that a statement should be drafted along certain lines; this work later took place and the statement itself came out in January, 1966—the first time a "civil rights organization" made a public stand against the war.

Release of that declaration was triggered by the murder of Sammy Younge, Jr., in Tuskegee, Alabama, on January 4. The killer was freed by an all-white jury. For myself, Sammy's murder marked the final end of any patience with nonviolence—even as a tactic.

SNCC's statement read:

The Student Nonviolent Coordinating Committee has a right and a responsibility to dissent with United States foreign policy on an issue when it sees fit. The Student Nonviolent Coordinating Committee now states its opposition to United States' involvement in Vietnam on these grounds:

We believe the United States government has been deceptive in its claims of concern for freedom of the Vietnamese people, just as the government has been deceptive in claiming concern for the freedom of colored people in such other countries as the Dominican Republic, the Congo, South Africa, Rhodesia and in the United States itself.

We, the Student Nonviolent Coordinating Committee, have been involved in the black people's struggle for liberation and self-determination in this country for the past five years. Our work, particularly in the South, has taught us that the United States government has never guaranteed the freedom of oppressed citizens, and is not yet truly determined to end the rule of terror and oppression within its own borders.

We ourselves have often been victims of violence and confinement executed by United States government officials. We recall the numerous persons who have been murdered in the South because of their efforts to secure their civil and human rights, and whose murderers have been allowed to escape penalty for their crimes.

The murder of Samuel Younge in Tuskegee, Ala., is no different than the murder of peasants in Vietnam, for both Younge and the Vietnamese sought, and are seeking, to secure the rights guaranteed them by law. In each case, the United States government bears a great part of the responsibility for these deaths.

Samuel Younge was murdered because United States law is not being enforced. Vietnamese are murdered because the United States is pursuing an aggressive policy in violation of international law. The United States is no respecter of persons or law when such persons or laws run counter to its needs and desires.

We recall the indifference, suspicion and outright hostility with which our reports of violence have been met in the past by government officials.

We know that for the most part, elections in this country, in the North as well as the South, are not free. We have seen that the 1965 Voting Rights Act and the 1964 Civil Rights Act have not yet been implemented with full federal power and sincerity.

We question, then, the ability and even the desire of the United States government to guarantee free elections abroad. We maintain that our country's cry of "preserve freedom in the world" is a hypocritical mask behind which it squashes liberation movements which are not bound, and refuse to be bound, by the expediencies of United States cold war policies.

We are in sympathy with, and support, the men in this country who are unwilling to respond to a military draft which would compel them to contribute their lives to United States aggression in Vietnam in the name of the "freedom" we find so false in this country.

We recoil with horror at the inconsistency of a supposedly "free" society where responsibility to lend oneself to military aggression. We take note of the fact that 60 percent of the draftees from this country are Negroes called on to stifle the liberation of Vietnam, to preserve a "democracy" which does not exist for them at home.

We ask, where is the draft for the freedom fight in the United States?

We therefore encourage those Americans who prefer to use their energy in building democratic forms within this country. We believe that work in the civil rights movement and with other human relations organizations is a valid alternative to the draft. We urge all Americans to seek this alternative, knowing full well that it may cost them lives—as painfully as in Vietnam.

Our statement caused the liberals and their black flunkies not to mention the racists, to raise a hue and cry against SNCC. These forces claimed that civil rights and the war were two separate issues, not related, and that SNCC as a civil rights organization had no business issuing a statement on the war. Our support among the liberals was sharply curtailed. Julian Bond would soon be denied his seat in the state legislature because he supported the statement. But we continued down the revolutionary path. SNCC began to engage in antidraft activity, and the Atlanta Project conducted demonstrations at the racist draft center in Atlanta, resulting in jail terms for ten people ranging from three years to six months. Later SNCC would create the National Black Anti-War Anti-Draft Union,

(NBAWADU). Courtland Cox would go to Europe to represent SNCC on the International War Crimes Tribunal called by Lord Bertrand Russell.

As 1966 began SNCC stood at the end of a period of internal crisis that had lasted less than a year and a half but had shaken the organization profoundly. We had resolved some of our internal contradictions, while others stayed with us. But in the process we had missed a historic opportunity. Too much power had been dissipated. Now we did seem to have entered a new day, and SNCC had clearly begun moving toward Black Power and the anti-imperialist position that it would later apply in all areas. We had also established ourselves in a new headquarters building, with great potential for many actvities, and acquired a forty thousand dollar grant for a printing operation that would enable us to proceed full-steam with the propaganda work that I knew we should be doing.

I, and also others, in SNCC felt battered and weakened—but hopeful. We knew that the dynamic of forging revolutionaries in the United States or anywhere is a long and complicated process. People must learn from their own experiences, although study can quicken the pace. We knew how great a handicap was the lack of historical models for our particular group. Radical youth organizations had always been attached in some way to an adult group; we were the first to move on our own and we had no predecessors for guidelines. People said it couldn't work. Our mistakes had to be momentous—and they had to be the mistakes of young people.

The revolutionary organization of our dreams might still emerge I thought.

CHAPTER **54**

Kingston Springs

AS SPRING came to Lowndes County, Alabama, the black panther was growling with increasing vigor. The weight of a century of fear seemed to be lifting—not for all the black people there, but for a number that grew larger every month. Our sisters and brothers in one of the nation's most oppressed and terrorized areas were showing the way. The people of Lowndes were going to make an organized try to take over county power. They were through with being intimidated and carried their guns to show it. They knew what they wanted, what they would do to get it, and where they stood in relation to the white world.

The same kind of clarity did not exist in SNCC. The basic question, "What is SNCC?" had not yet been answered. Our long-range goals had called for redefinition ever since Atlantic City, and especially since the 1964 and 1965 Civil Rights acts—which made obsolete many aspects of our early organizing work. Watts had exploded in August, 1965; could we still call ourselves "nonviolent" and remain in the vanguard of black militancy? If we were revolutionaries, what was it that we sought to overthrow? Was racism the only problem of black people, or was racism part of a larger system of oppression—a system that affected other peoples as well? Was our struggle simply one of black against white, or also a class struggle of the exploited against those who exploited them? What kind of society did we want to see replace the present one?

We had not dealt with these questions. The lack of ideology had become obvious, and that lack was crippling SNCC's growth. We were caught in the habit of thinking about short-term objectives only, and this was producing intense frustration. The brutality and racism that our workers constantly experienced, the denial of minimal rights, forced a psychological anguish upon us that could be overcome only if we had a long-range view of our historical role and objectives.

It will be remembered that SNCC's original statement of purpose drawn up in 1960 had been allowed to go unchanged long after that statement became completely obsolete. In May of 1962 someone tried to initiate debate on the statement with a view to changing it. We bogged down in ideological conflicts and dropped the matter, most of us feeling that the statement didn't matter anyway. Almost everyone felt that the emphasis on love and nonviolence was an anachronism which we could simply ignore.

That had been my own attitude. I, too, had resisted ideological discussions. I felt that our work against racism in the South, our campaigns against segregated public accommodations, our efforts at voter registration, our general struggle against repression, were sufficient to show where SNCC stood. I felt that long, ideological discussion was the habit of armchair revolutionaries who would rather analyze than work. In Chicago I had seen all sorts of groups on the left splintering themselves to death, this little group fighting that one, and all of them doing it only on paper. Memorandum politics was a trick bag and I didn't want SNCC to fall into it. Also, I had probably been influenced by a book which I had read some years earlier, in which the author—no doubt some social democrat—stated "the tighter the ideology, the greater the split." I saw no reason to risk wrenching SNCC apart for the sake of abstractions.

In addition, at that time there was still a legacy of fear imposed by the McCarthy period—a fear which made people reluctant to use words like *socialism* or *communism* or even *revolution,* a fear of appearing too militant. I had dealt with this problem in my novel, in a scene where the main character is telling another about the kind of society he wants to see built. "Be careful—that sounds like socialism," says the second character. "I don't care what you call it," the first replies, "it's what we need." But while unafraid of labels for myself, I had to recognize that many others in the organization remained influenced by the great American brainwash process. Their attitude could not simply be rejected; the problem called for a program of internal education. It was not enough for a few of us to feel that SNCC was a revolutionary organization, that racism was part of a larger system of exploitation, that we should prepare for an armed struggle against racism and capitalism and imperialism.

At the October, 1964, staff meeting, Michael Thelwell had presented a new statement of purpose and again the discussion led nowhere. It was a good, hard-hitting statement which led to sharp disagreement. At the November meeting of that year, I made some attempts to place racism within the context of the total American system. In my paper, "What is SNCC?" under the subject "Why do we organize?" I stated: "We have said that we want to change the system, the system of segregation, the system of discrimination. . . . Now, we did not carry the analysis of the system perhaps to other conclusions. We did not say, except in a few instances, that the system of segregation is wrapped up in the American system of political and economic exploitation. . . . When we spoke of changing the system of segregation, we did not completely speak of an overhaul in the economic and political institutions of this country."

A year later, when some of our internal problems had been solved, we began for the first time to discuss the relationship of race and class in the oppression of black people. I had begun talking about the need to understand international finance—imperialism—and to include class factors in our analysis. But it was a bare beginning.

Now the staff found itself gathered again, this time at Kingston Springs, Tennessee, in May of 1966. It was a very intense meeting at which the work we had been doing was thoroughly debated. We spent a day discussing the assumptions on which work had proceeded to date. All this was a prelude to changing the nature and direction of SNCC's work—a prelude to Black Power and to more intensive work in the black community. We were shedding the mantle of nonviolence as a tactic. We recognized the absolute need to gear all our energies toward the black community, including our fund raising and promotion.

The two burning issues at that meeting were the objectives of SNCC and the role of whites in the organization (there were about forty then). These were not mutually exclusive, but closely related. The definition of our goals depended on an understanding of our problems as black people, and this in turn put the role of whites into proper perspective.

I took the position at Kingston Springs that SNCC had to understand U.S. imperialism—international finance, as some of us called it—and certain Marxist concepts before it could resolve the question of what role whites should play in the revolutionary process. My ideas were violently opposed by many people who claimed that Marx was white and, therefore, had nothing to tell us. Ideological debate at Kingston Springs remained at this low level because it took place in a theoretical vacuum. Discussion of the role of whites took place in a framework that excluded an understanding of capitalism, imperialism, the class struggle, colonialism, and revolutionary nationalism. The organization had never engaged in systematic, collective study, and so our discussion simply reflected the personal opinions of various members on a variety of different subjects.

Confusion about the nature of our real enemy resulted. It was also very difficult to have any useful discussion of the question of nationalism—its roots, its meaning, its different forms, its weaknesses and strengths. I understood the gut reaction that many people had to the presence of whites in SNCC and realized that the struggle to create an all-black organization represented a revolutionary step if such action was accompanied by broader theoretical understanding.

The problems that people in SNCC faced in resolving the question of nationalism were not limited to our organization alone. Everywhere in the United States there are still many people who see the problem as exclusively one of race—an incorrect position. All colonized groups, all organizations fighting colonialism, experience painful moments when discussing the role of people who have the same skin color as the oppressor. Puerto Ricans, Chicanos, Indians, and Asian people in the United States have also debated or will be debating the same issue. In the absence of revolutionary theory—reading the works of Marx, Lenin, Mao Tsetung, Castro, Che Guevara, Ho Chi Minh, Fanon, Nkrumah, and others—the discussion usually focuses on the question of what should we do with whites, period.

In SNCC the roots of the debate lay in the entire history of the organization. SNCC had been founded on the thesis that nonviolence and redemptive suffering could change the course of history. Throughout its subsequent struggle, SNCC was evolving in opposition to that thesis—evolving into a revolutionary organization. But that process was painful and not clear to all participants. We were clearly victims of racism, and the most visible manifestation of that racism was white people. Lacking a clear understanding of the economic basis of racism and exploitation, black people will flail out against the most visible manifestation—white people. Unconscious or semiconscious racism in supposedly revolutionary whites adds to the distrust of all white people. (White liberals and out-right racists are something else.)

In an effort to lift the level of debate inside SNCC, I presented a paper at Kingston Springs in which I tried to trace the causes of the rise of nationalism among our members. The paper suffered from many weaknesses, especially the lack of a detailed definition of nationalism. I limited my definition to a feeling of racial solidarity and listed the following factors as general reasons for the rise of nationalism—ones that affected black people throughout the United States:

1. Emergence of the necessity for racial pride and for the feeling that we as a people can perform actions by ourselves.

2. A growing awareness of the importance of Africa to the black struggle in the United States.

3. The influence of the ideas of Malcolm X and Elijah Muhammed.

4. An understanding that the West, symbolized by white people, was responsible for the condition of black people.

5. Increased study of the works of Frantz Fanon.

In addition to these general reasons for the rising sense of nationalism, there were others peculiar to the SNCC experience:

1. The increased number of white workers in the South, resulting from the Mississippi Summer Project of 1964.

2. The unwillingness of whites to work in white communities.

3. The insensitivity of some whites to customs of the black community, which created hostility in black workers.

4. SNCC's reliance on a primarily white fund-raising base.

5. Our failure to recruit blacks to replace some of the black cadre members whom we lost.

6. The campaign waged by members of SNCC, especially in the Atlanta Project, to make SNCC an all-black organization.

The Atlanta Project was an example of how the failure to resolve the role of whites could do serious damage to a program aimed at winning power for black people. The project had originally been conceived in early 1966, when the Georgia legislature refused to let Julian Bond take the seat to which he had been duly elected because he refused to repudiate SNCC's statement on Vietnam. This struggle would go all the way up to the U.S. Supreme Court, which would finally seat Julian. Meanwhile, the Atlanta Project was meant to be an experiment in political organization of the community, but it became instead an attempt to organize SNCC around the issue of blackness, with emphasis on eliminating whites from the organization. Throughout the spring of 1966 I had often discussed the question of whites with members of the project, but nothing had been resolved.

After much debate at Kingston Springs on this question, I introduced a resolution that whites in SNCC should work in the white community and blacks in the black community. That motion actually represented a return to SNCC's original position on whites.

As mentioned earlier, Bob Zellner of Alabama had been the first white person to be put on SNCC staff, in 1961. He was originally recruited to work in the white community under the sponsorship of the Southern Conference Educational Fund. During 1962 it became clear that it was extremely difficult for him to function in the white community and we made a decision that he should work in the black community hoping that this would encourage other white Southerners to fight racism and economic exploitation. Dorothy Miller, later to marry Bob Zellner, had then come to work in the SNCC office as a communications secretary. Very soon a pattern of whites working both in the office and out in the black community was established which seemed almost impossible to break.

While racial antagonisms had always existed within SNCC, they were originally viewed as a manifestation of the system that we were fighting against. But, as the years passed, and the difficulties of working in the white community diminished, it was apparent to some of us that the whites in SNCC simply had to begin organizing white communities if we were serious about revolutionary change. By that time, however, a deep alienation from the white community was felt by the white field staff and they were very reluctant to tackle that job. Many of us felt that this alienation could be overcome, and the old pattern broken, only by the strenuous insistence of blacks that the role of whites was in the white community. There were others who felt that whites should be expelled from the organization. I never shared that position, maintaining that you do not expel people with whom you have worked, merely on the basis of their skin color. I felt that revolutionary whites could understand the rising nationalism in the black struggle and the necessity for whites to work in the white communities against racism and repression.

My proposal to this effect was adopted. But it did not end the arguments in SNCC over the role of whites.

New officers were scheduled to be elected at this meeting, and I had given much thought to this question. By the time of Kingston Springs, I had become exasperated with the difficult position in which I found myself: Supposedly, I was there to help the chairman but the chairman, in fact, did little inside the organization. Relations between John Lewis and me had become more difficult after the 1964 Waveland meeting where I had suggested that his was an essentially disfunctional position. More recently I had discussed all my thoughts on this subject with Lewis and suggested that we both resign at the Kingston Springs meeting. I felt that we were both growing conservative, due to our external dealings with other civil rights groups, fund-raising groups, pressure groups, and the White House. I suggested that we both needed to give up our titles, for these can act as brakes on a developing organization, and to give some of the younger staff members a chance to acquire the experience we had acquired.

The growing conservatism of John Lewis became apparent at an Executive Committee meeting where we discussed the proposed White House Conference on Civil Rights scheduled for late May, 1966. Lewis wanted to go, while the Executive Committee was against any participation by SNCC at this conference. Lewis took the position that he was going, whether the organization wanted him to or not. I did not criticize him at the meeting, for I felt I was there to serve the chairman, but later I talked with him in private about the absurdity of his position. He finally decided to follow the wishes of the organization, but he had not—when the Kingston Springs meeting started—decided whether to run for chairman again or not.

For my own part, I had firmly decided against serving any longer as executive secretary. I had wanted to resign since the fall of 1964 but had not because of SNCC's internal chaos and weakness; now I would do it. So that it would not come as an awkward surprise, I discussed my plan in the ranks of the organization before the meeting—and explained my reasons.

There were several. Fundamentally, I wanted to analyze and summarize the experiences of the early sixties—and the job of executive secretary left no time for thinking or writing. That urge to write stemmed from my belief that political figures have a responsibility to record their experiences if they want to help save others from making similar mistakes and thus help to speed up the struggle. Black people in particular needed to write about their lives and thought. I felt that from 1961 to 1966, I had made a historical mistake by not writing and analyzing for the benefit of my contemporaries and posterity. A personal aspect of this need was my feeling that I had not been growing politically. Always on the go, never reflecting, because there were too many immediate worries and problems to solve, I had fallen into a stagnant state.

Then, too, I wanted to spend more time working with the Southern field staff to help develop their strength and self-confidence, and to further develop their political consciousness. I have mentioned the lack of an internal education program before; our need for it now was greater than ever. If SNCC was going to become a revolutionary organization, it had to solve two problems: a low level of political consciousness and lack of maturity. Outside the position of executive secretary, I felt that I could fight more effectively to build that internal education and create the spirit of criticism together with self-criticism

Third, I felt it was unhealthy for me to remain executive secretary when others needed the experience. I also did not like the fact that, more and more, the press had begun to focus on me. I didn't see myself as a leader of black people and did not want that kind of projection—either within or outside SNCC. SNCC had to be about the business of building people, not leaders, I had always felt. No doubt my dislike for the growing publicity also contained an element of fear: By becoming more widely known, my chance of being killed by some racist increased.

That fear, or loss of nerve, was part of a general inability to be as responsive to the needs of SNCC as I had once been. I no longer had the stamina to run from project to project. And I often felt shaky in some of the rural situations in which we found ourselves—unarmed and subjected to much potential brutality.

Finally, there was certainly a large measure of personal frustration in my desire to resign. I was tired of the job, tired of the worries, tired of fund raising, and tired of dealing with certain kinds of internal attack. The fund raising is a clear example of this frustration. On the one hand, I saw a tremendous waste of resources—especally the abuse of cars—and I knew what effort it had taken to obtain them. On the other hand, I was subjected to increasing criticism because of the predominantly white fund-raising base that SNCC had acquired. I understood the criticism, but there were several factors to be considered.

One was the historical context in which that base had been developed. I had been in favor of a Southern (and black) fund-raising base, but this was vetoed by many staff people. Then our Northern fund-raising operation was supposed to have been mainly in the black communities, according to my plans and projections. But the fund raisers that we had found it easier to raise money in the white community. Meanwhile, the organization was always short of money and begging for resources; and I, with the responsibility of finding that money, soon reached the point of thinking, let's take it wherever we can get it. This compromise was counterbalanced by SNCC's position that no one who gave us money could thereby dictate our policies. SNCC, and only SNCC, would decide its programs and policies. This was a rule to which I certainly stuck, and there were no violations of it.

Still, the critics continued to complain about that white fund-raising base and, at the same time, they were not willing to work on fund raising—whether in the black or the white community. And, at the same time, they constantly demanded resources. It was a miserable situation, and I only hoped that my resignation would literally force others in the organization to go out and raise money.

This problem was part of my general weariness with a certain attitude toward me. I had often stated that I was not running in a personality contest, that I should be judged on the basis of my ideas and work. But still I felt unsure about how much leadership to demonstrate and I had wavered between self-negation and self-assertion. The charges that I was trying to maintain and increase my power had had their effect on me.

I often found myself in a minority position; later I would come to understand more thoroughly that leadership is always in the minority if it is planning correctly, but its job is to convince others of the correctness of its position. At the time of Kingston Springs, however, I had had my fill of problems about my own role.

At Kingston Springs I stuck to my position of refusing to be a candidate for executive secretary and Ruby Doris Robinson was finally elected to this position. Cleveland Sellers was reelected program secretary. John Lewis was defeated for the chairmanship by Stokely Carmichael, after a long night of discussion and a series of complicated events. I tried, during the nomination of candidates, to introduce the idea that we should thoroughly discuss their merits and weaknesses, because I knew that many people had ideas about the officers we might elect—ideas they never shared in an open forum but only in private conversations. Also, discussion of a candidate's weaknesses could help to correct them in future work. But, again, the proposal failed.

After the meeting, the Establishment press published a great deal of distortion about the election of Stokely Carmichael as chairman. There were reports that a "coup" had taken place in SNCC; that Lewis and Forman had been ousted by Carmichael and Robinson; that elements favoring violence and revolution had triumphed over the "moderates." All this was untrue, for I had supported both the candidacy of Carmichael and of Robinson. The greater militance and emphasis on blackness symbolized for many people by Carmichael, largely as a result of his work in Lowndes County, were in the natural order of SNCC's whole evolution. But in any case, the internal workings of SNCC were not for the consumption of the press. It was none of their business, and I decided not to comment publicly on the press's distortions.

John Lewis, however, could not remain silent and for years has kept a bitter memory about those events. In public interviews, he blamed me for his defeat. SNCC made every effort to conciliate him and to keep him within the ranks of the organization, as head of international affairs. But he finally resigned from that post and from SNCC, without ever giving any reason, and despite many pleas from the Central Committee (the new name given to the Executive Committee at the Kingston Springs meeting).

After Kingston Springs, I worked as the administrator of the national office in Atlanta—a position I accepted to make sure there was some orderly transition in our administration. But I would soon give it up, for it kept me involved in the same kind of responsibilities I had had before.

Looking back, I have often wondered if my resignation was a mistake. Had I myself been too liberal in yielding to the criticism of some that I had too much power (although this was only one factor in my resignation)? While there were disadvantages to my resignation, I think it was an important and correct decision, for I, too was in a period of transition and need for study. I had formulated a fairly good set of operating principles in the late fifties that helped to carry me through the early sixties, but these ideas centered around the creation of a mass consciousness among black people. It was time to move on and I needed time to reflect, to organize my studies, to write and to absorb some new ideas for the future of the struggle. It was a mistake for an organization such as SNCC not to provide time for its leadership to do this. On the other hand, leadership cannot take an elitist stand. It must be willing to do whatever needs to be done. It must combine its planning function with actual work, so that it can better plan to make the work more efficient.

These and other ideas were churning through my mind that summer. Meanwhile, the revolutionary struggle was propelling people and events forward. There are times when people help to shape events—but, more often, they are shaped by those events. And that is the best way that anyone can explain the cry that burst across the nation in the summer of 1966, the cry for Black Power!

CHAPTER 55

Black Power Strikes

"HEY JIM, I got an idea. I want to know what you think of it." It was Willie Ricks, the young SNCC field secretary who had acquired a reputation as a brilliant organizer of young people in Birmingham, Americus, and other hot spots in the South. He had stopped in the Atlanta office on his way to Mississippi. The Meredith March on June, 1966, was underway and Stokely Carmichael had asked Ricks to come over.

"Suppose when I get over there to Mississippi and I'm speaking, I start hollering for 'Black Power'? What do you think of that?" Ricks asked. "Would you back me up? You think it would scare people in SNCC?"

" 'Black Power'—sure, try it," I told him. "Why not? After all, you'd only be shortening the phrase we are always using—power for poor black people. 'Black power' is shorter and means the same thing. Go on, try it."

And that is how the cry for Black Power came to be voiced. Willie Ricks, whom the world at large has barely noticed so far, must rank as one of those unknown heroes who captured the mood of history. In calling for Black Power, he caught the essence of the spirit moving black people in the United States and around the world who were poor, black, and without power.

I did not go to Mississippi myself at the beginning of the Meredith March, for we were in the process of making a transition of leadership and I felt that I should stay away from those well-publicized demonstrations if the new team of Carmichael-Robinson-Sellers was to get proper projection. But on the last day of the March, I did go to Jackson for a brief visit. Ricks and others had been chanting "Black Power" and the words were becoming more and more popular, although some activists seemed frightened by them. John Lewis, for example, urged me to stop Ricks—he didn't like the phrase, it didn't make sense, he said.

Instead of stopping Ricks, Ruby Doris Robinson, a few others, and I placed ourselves in a strategic position directly behind a mass of people who were in front of the news cameras and joined in raising the cry of Black Power. Over and over, the chant resounded. We wanted black people in all parts of the United States to hear the slogan, to be stirred by it, to adopt it. It was a spontaneous move on our part, with nothing false about it. We felt, we knew, we could see that "Black Power" was a slogan of the masses.

Those two words electrified the nation and the world. Black people wanted power, the words said. Only power could change our condition. The type of Black Power we wanted still had to be defined, but this initial articulation meant that another stage of struggle had been reached It was a higher one than "One Man, One Vote" or "Freedom Now." We had moved to the level of verbalizing our drive for power—not merely for the vote, not for some vague kind of freedom, not for legal rights, but the basic force in any society—power. Power for black people, black power.

To achieve that power, poor black people had to take power from the racist, exploitative masters of the society, who are white. Revolutionary warfare is the ultimate weapon by which this is achieved. Therefore "Black Power" was more than a slogan to me. It was a concept pointing the way to a revolutionary ideology.

But, even on an immediate level, the slogan had tremendous force. It struck a responsive chord, because by 1966 the problems of black people across the United States had become similar in all their fundamentals.

Voting discrimination and segregation of public facilities had generally disappeared in the South after years of protest—that protest which produced the 1964 Civil Rights Act and the 1965 Voting Rights Act. At the same time, the newly established political rights of black people in the South were being undermined by whites in many ways: deliberate miscounting of votes, bribery, economic intimidation of voters. The South was becoming more and more like the North. The fundamentals of racism—inadequate housing, lack of jobs, insufficient medical attention, inferior education—remained basically unchanged throughout black communities, whether in New York or Mississippi.

Thus the call for Black Power drew substance from the realities of the lives of black people across the nation. With the equalizing of our problems in North and South, the concept evoked a national response. It had emerged from the Southern experience, but had meaning for black people everywhere.

A whole new rhetoric and a new set of attitudes as well as policies emerged at this time. The phrase "civil rights movement," long moribund, died forever with the birth of Black Power. At the same time, recognition of the need for black people to organize themselves and conduct their own struggle—together with the need for whites to fight racism in white communities—led to an increasing emphasis on all-blackness in SNCC as well as other militant groups.

Not surprisingly, accusations of "extremism" and "racism in reverse" filled the air. Those accusations reflected the fact that the slogan "Black Power" was frightening to white Americans in general and the U.S. Government in particular because of its revolutionary implications. That government knows that whites have power and blacks do not. The idea of poor black people united for power represented a major threat to white America. Black Power was very bad for the reformist image of the black movement which the U.S. Government tried so hard to project abroad, especially in Africa. Black Power especially threatened the Democratic Party, then the ruling party of the United States.

The Democrats had risen to power in 1932 and remained there by obtaining "the Negro vote" in many major cities. It was not surprising that this party, along with other ruling elements, now set out to discredit and destroy those supporting Black Power. The Democrats tried to accomplish this in various ways. First, Vice-President Hubert Humphrey flew to the 1966 national convention of the NAACP and made a major address in which he stated, "We must support the NAACP's goal of integration." To the best of my knowledge, this was the first time that a President or Vice-President of the United States had forthrightly enunciated that the United States Government favored integration.

Second, the administration and the mass media tried to discredit the concept by associating it with violence and by making the use of violence illegitimate and contrary to the "American way." The press attacks on SNCC became ferocious in this period, as reporters and columnists tried to make our spokesmen—particularly Carmichael—into monsters thirsting for the blood of whites. All of a sudden, the press conveniently forgot the lynchings, bombings, beatings, and jailings which met attempts to win the vote in the early sixties. By projecting Black Power as nothing more than "reverse racism," the press sought to divide black America, scare it away from supporting Black Power.

And then, seeing that they could not destroy the revolutionary thrust of Black Power, the powers of this nation adopted a new tactic—co-optation. It's the good old American way: Whom the gods cannot destroy, they try to buy off. We first saw this in the attempt to get Congressman Adam Clayton Powell to hold a Black Power conference in the auditorium of the United States Labor Department. This idea received some serious consideration in the ranks of militants, but SNCC took the position that to hold such a conference in such a place under such sponsorship would be to play directly into the hands of our enemies.

Several "Black Power conferences" did take place, and in all of them the revolutionary thrust was blunted either at the meetings or later. Some excellent resolutions were adopted at the Newark "Black Power conference," for example, but the direction for carrying out those resolutions rested in the hands of some very bourgeois elements who had no intentions of carrying them out. Nathan Wright, who held the reins over the Newark conference, felt compelled to announce when it was over that it had been financed primarily by white corporations.

The power structure used flunky and funky Negro politicians to say that Black Power meant Negroes must elect their representatives—to the power structure. Then President Nixon, succeeding Johnson, went all the way and said that Black Power meant "black capitalism." Through black capitalism, "we" can solve the problems of black people. That was the supreme act of co-optation and, in its way, a clever maneuver.

Black Power was not defined adequately at the time. If it had been, the government and its Negroes might not have been able to co-opt the term. Here, we in SNCC must assume some blame, for the term received no precise definition from us. We were stunned and overwhelmed by its immediate success. The most radical definition of Black Power that we could give at the time was "power for black people." Thus the door was left open for opportunists to define the term in any manner they chose. Of course we did not control the means of communication, so that any revolutionary definition that we might have given Black Power would not have outweighed the definitions by those Negroes with government backing. But that is not to excuse our own inability and unwillingness to define the objectives and program for achieving Black Power. We were caught by not having our own revolutionary ideology together.

Yet Black Power did represent a new form of resistance when the cry was first uttered. The Democratic Party correctly saw Black Power as a threat in large cities, where the welfare system has failed to pacify the people of the ghettos. In most metropolitan areas black people form between 20 and 45 percent of the so-called inner city population. In Newark, New Jersey, and Washington, D.C., black people are more than half the population. In all these areas the trend is for blacks to become more numerous while whites move out to the suburbs. The result, potential bases of black political power. These population changes have become a serious problem for the Democratic Party, upsetting old systems of control, including graft and patronage. For example, after the rebellions in Cleveland in 1966, that city moved to become a "metropolitan area"—bringing people from the suburbs inside its boundaries in order to offset the growing black population. Party leaders in such cities must give up graft from the counties and carve out new domains when this happens.

The city of Philadelphia typifies the population shift. Its black population is 35 percent. With a normal growth and no "regerrymandering," black people will be 50 percent of the city within a few years. When Black Power was brought to Philadelphia by SNCC in 1966, the reaction of the city's power structure was exactly what you might expect: Move to destroy. But we didn't expect them to use dynamite.

CHAPTER 56

Dynamite in Philadelphia

ON AUGUST 13, 1966, newspapers in Philadelphia carried screaming headlines that four SNCC offices had been raided and four SNCC members had been arrested for possession of dynamite.

But only one SNCC office had actually been raided. The other places belonged to various human rights groups working in the city.

And only one of those arrested was actually a SNCC member. The other people belonged to a local group named the Young Militants.

And the only dynamite found was in an apartment not belonging to or used by SNCC people.

It was a frame-up.

The frame-up took place because Philadelphia had become the first major metropolitan area in which SNCC was developing the concept of a national freedom organization with the panther as its symbol. SNCC's work there was going well. Response in the ghettos had been good and relations with other organizations had been built. Philadelphia had all the classic characteristics of an "inner city" in which Black Power represented both a real possibility and a scary threat to whites.

Philadelphia was the city in which the Black Power movement had to be crushed—immediately.

At about five o'clock in the morning on Saturday, August 13, Fred Meely — director of Philadelphia SNCC — called the Atlanta office where I happened to be at the time and said that his office had been raided. He didn't know where his people were; the police had raided an apartment too; he didn't know exactly what was going on.

Later that morning, about nine o'clock, we found out that four people had been arrested for supposed possession of dynamite: Barry Dawson, George Brower, Eugene Dawkins, and Caroline West. Of the four, only Dawson was associated with SNCC. In court that morning they were arraigned and bound over on fifty thousand dollars bond each for a preliminary hearing. (There are three steps between arrest and trial on a felony case: arraignment, preliminary hearing, and then an indictment or "no true bill" by the grand jury.) Cecil Moore of the NAACP was representing them, but he did not show up at the arraignment. The preliminary hearing was set for August 22, which was the last possible day according to Pennsylvania law.

All that morning we met in Atlanta—Stokely, Cleve, Ruby Doris, other members of the Central Committee and the office staff—and discussed the information that Fred was telephoning to us throughout the morning and into the afternoon. It was decided that I should go to Philadelphia as soon as possible. Len Holt was in town, and I asked him to go with me. Fred was extremely concerned about the role being played by Cecil Moore, a local lawyer who was president of the Philadelphia NAACP chapter and who had represented four people arrested and jailed in the Girard College demonstrations during the summer of '65. Fred wanted very much to try to get a lawyer other than Cecil Moore for Barry Dawson, the defendant who had been working with SNCC, because he felt that Moore would try to kill politically what SNCC was trying to do in Philadelphia.

We got word about seven or eight o'clock Saturday night that Barry Dawson had signed some sort of confession or statement about having brought dynamite into the SNCC office. The police then put out a fourteen-state warrant for three other SNCC workers—Fred Meely, Morris Ruffin, and George Anderson—who, until about five or six that evening, had been in the Philadelphia SNCC office. But we did not jump to conclusions about this so-called statement or confession of Barry Dawson's. We were skeptical about its validity and suspected that it had been beaten out of him or that he had in some way been tricked into making it.

Later we learned that Barry Dawson had, in fact, been beaten on August 10, three days before being arrested. He had been given a lift to

Thirty-third Street and Poplar. As he got out of the car, someone called him by name. He was beaten on the street by some whites, then dragged into a park, cut in his fingers with a knife, and kicked into unconsciousness. When he came to, several hours later, he was taken to St. Joseph's Hospital. It was then about one o'clock in the morning, but he did not get treatment for three or four hours. The only whites whom Barry knew were police, and his attackers called him by name: The facts speak for themselves. A statement by Barry about the beating had been released by the SNCC office and was read to us now in Atlanta. It clearly revealed that he was in a state of exhaustion and anxiety.

About eleven or twelve o'clock that Saturday night we learned that there was only a group of mostly young sisters in the SNCC office in Philadelphia. We were wondering where all the men were—not Fred Meely, Ruffin, and Anderson, who had by then disappeared, but the men in the community. We then called Ivanhoe Donaldson and Matthew Jones of SNCC in New York, and also Marion Barry and Lester McKinney of our Washington office. They should get over to the Philadelphia office immediately. Both groups arrived in Philadelphia about four o'clock Sunday morning.

Before they got there, however, the police paid another visit to the office. Over the telephone, the sisters told us what was happening as it happened. Six police arrived, claiming they had a search and seizure warrant. The sisters asked to see it and the police refused to show it. The sisters refused to let them search. After an argument, the police finally left. It was then about two or two-thirty in the morning.

Meanwhile, Len Holt had been trying to make contact with several lawyers and finally got a Philadelphia attorney named Bill Akers to go down to the office and see if he could be of help. Earlier we had told Fred that the key thing was to try to get Barry Dawson's mother to give a written statement authorizing Fred to get a lawyer for Barry. The mother didn't give him a written statement, but what she said was fine; she didn't want Cecil Moore handling the case and Fred should try to get a lawyer. Fred then called Clarence Harris and asked him to try to call a lawyer. The person called was Bernard Seigel, a white lawyer in Philadelphia. Seigel told Barry's mother that he would represent her son but that he would have to talk to her first. She was on her way out of town because her sister was very ill, and told Seigel to go ahead and do whatever was necessary. Saturday evening, when the story came out in the press about Barry's confession, Seigel apparently felt that it would jeopardize his possible representation of the other people if he went to talk with Barry—a position that we disagreed with very vehemently. The key thing from our viewpoint was to try to get to Barry and tell him not to say anything more for the time being. Instead of talking with Barry, Seigel was in effect pressuring Clarence Harris and us to try to get Meely, Ruffin, and Anderson to turn themselves in, on the assumption that we knew where they were.

Len and I finally got off to Philadelphia Sunday evening. We arrived in New York about one o'clock Monday morning and picked up a rented car which Ruby Doris had reserved for us by telephone. We were extremely careful about what we said in the car while driving to Philadelphia—a mild degree of paranoia might have set in by that time, but there was also the fact that Len Holt had been involved in other cases where microphones had been planted in cars and the tapes thus made used as testimony. This was done in the Statue of Liberty case, 'where people had supposedly been involved in planning to blow up several national monuments.

About thirty miles outside of Philadelphia, we called Ivanhoe. He told us to come straight to the Sheraton Motor Inn, room 520. When we got to Philadelphia, we found no Sheraton Motor Inn, but we did see a Sheraton Hotel with a motor inn across the street. We assumed he had meant the Sheraton Hotel, took our bags out of the car and walked into the lobby.

As we walked straight back to the elevator, the elevator operator ran over and woke up a black man asleep on a couch who was obviously a detective. He hustled and bustled and put on his coat and snapped his brim and came into the elevator with us. When the elevator operator asked us what floor, I turned to this other fellow and said, "What floor are you going to?"

"Five," he answered.

When we got to five, which was of course the floor we were going to, the elevator stopped and the detective stepped out. Then he extended his arm out to us and said, "Aren't you all getting out here too?"

Len and I were so taken aback at this audacity, or stupidity, that we had to look at each other and smile. Our paranoia was working, and correctly—that is to say, it wasn't really paranoia but just caution. "Yes," I said. (There were only eight floors in the hotel and there was no point in riding up and down, as would have happened if we had not gotten off.)

We saw that 520 was to our right and started in that direction as did the detective. He then told us his name and I said mine was Brown. As we got to room 521, which was next to room 520, he stopped and said, "I'd like for you-all to stop here a minute."

"For what?" I asked.

"Just want to ask you a couple of questions."

"Questions about what?"

By that time he had knocked on the door of 521, the door opened, and some white pig with his shoes off and his belly lapping over, half-dressed, ran out of sight back in the room. Apparently he was putting on his pants.

Another black cop, well-pressed, came out into the hall. "What's going on?" we asked.

They said they were detectives and they began to show their badges. "What do you want with us?" we persisted, talking very loudly now to let the people in 520 know that these police were right next door.

One of the black detectives said that they had been stopping everybody that came up to the fifth floor. "Are we under arrest?" we asked.

"No, you're not under arrest."

"Well, let's go," I said, "we don't have to give you any information."

We walked down the hall past 520, and then walked back because there was no exit that way. As we were walking past 521, still trying to decide exactly what to do, we heard the white detective say, "They didn't give you their names?"

Then came the answer, "No."

"Well, they should have given you their names."

We kept on going, to the elevator. Downstairs, we called on a pay phone to room 520 and explained to Ivanhoe, who answered the telephone, what had happened. To our chagrin, he said, "Well, yeah, we knew they were next door. They've been there for about three or four hours." We were a little upset that he and the others had let us walk into this kind of a situation, knowing full well that the police were there, but I presumed that there was nothing else that they could do.

We went across the street and waited for them to join us. Then we went to a friend's house where we all met with the SNCC office staff of Philadelphia. Len and I decided we had to stay in the city. The people from Washington then went back to Washington and the people from New York to New York.

In the next few days we began trying to do some investigative work. On Tuesday afternoon, I think, we went into the office for the first time —I opened it up. Community people started coming in about 5:30, talking about the importance of keeping the office open. From them and others, we learned that the police had kicked the door of the office open and broken a window when they came that Saturday morning. Apparently no one was there. We talked to a lot of people that day and night . . . talked to more people Wednesday . . . followed up many leads. It became very obvious to us that a frame-up had occurred, but the key question was, How could we prove it?

We got a break in the case Wednesday night in the form of information about the "confession" that Barry Dawson had made, which was entirely contrary to the press reports. But the break had to remain secret, and we faced the problem of how to use what we now knew. We planned to hold a press conference on Wednesday and then on Thursday, but on both days things happened which made it impossible to do so. The press of Philadelphia had practically tried and convicted SNCC for having dynamite. We did not feel that our first concern was to win the battle of the press, but we did want to let the black community know there was another side to the story. The police had pulled various tricks to prejudice people against SNCC. An Inspector Meers, for example, called in some so-called Negro leaders and showed them photographs allegedly of men taking dynamite out of the SNCC office.

On Friday, August 19, 1966, we held a press conference on the street directly in front of the SNCC office. Many community people attended and shouted their approval as we attacked Acting Police Chief Frank Rizzo and other officials.

We charged that Rizzo knew there was only one SNCC office and that there was no dynamite in it.

We charged him and Inspector Meers with violating the constitutional rights of people by imposing exorbitantly high bonds.

We further charged that Mayor Tate was acting in complicity with the police by issuing statements that Stokely Carmichael, that monster advocate of Black Power, should be barred from all Northern cities in the United States.

We made it clear to the terrorized black community that we intended to keep the office open and that I would serve as temporary director and Fred Meely as director-in-exile.

We stated that we intended to intensify the work started by Meely, Ruffin, and Anderson to develop a freedom organization in Philadelphia with the black panther as a symbol.

We said that we intended to wage an aggressive campaign for quality education, decent housing, adequate jobs, payment of welfare funds, and against police brutality.

We announced plans to hold a Black Power conference in Philadelphia.

In our statements, we asserted as positively as we could that Rizzo would be fought, that he was the real mayor of Philadelphia. We centered our attack on Rizzo because of his reputation for terrorizing black communities. He had been known as the "Cisco Kid" ever since his earlier days when he wore two pearl-handled pistols.

Frame-up! Frame-up! was the general tenor of our remarks at the press conference. We had fairly good evidence that the dynamite found in the apartment had been planted, and we knew that SNCC was being framed generally in the public consciousness. We started pushing this line in the community. It was an uphill battle because of the press. All along, they had been running headlines like "Dynamite Found in Four SNCC Headquarters" and constant references to "four SNCC Headquarters." Even after the press conference, they were coming back with such headlines as "SNCC Suspects Still Being Held."

But we kept pushing and things began to roll in the black community. We started mimeographing forty-five thousand copies of a leaflet charging a frame-up and asking people to come to the preliminary hearing on Monday morning. That Friday night, we found a printer who ran off some thirty thousand copies of the leaflet in large type while we kept two or three mimeograph machines going. It was about four o'clock on Saturday morning when we stopped. By Sunday afternoon all the leaflets had been distributed. The mobilization was somewhat haphazard, but still effective. We bought two megaphones and began talking to people on street corners. There were street corner rallies all day Saturday and Saturday night, telling people to come down to the preliminary hearing. This was a very important part of our whole campaign.

A lot—too much—was happening at once. On Friday night I was over in North Philadelphia passing out leaflets and talking to George Brower, head of the Young Militants, who had been bailed out of jail, and some other people. It was about two o'clock in the morning. The police picked up George Brower, primarily because of those leaflets. We had gathered some people around, in a street corner rally, in case anything happened and now there was a group of us there charging harassment by the police. A police car drove up slowly behind us, and hit Len Holt—not hard, but very deliberately. We held another "sidewalk press conference" on Saturday about these events.

But the lead story in the Sunday papers was that Rizzo planned to subpoena me to testify Monday morning on the frame-up evidence. Sure enough, about noon on Sunday, a plainclothes cop arrived at the SNCC office with the subpoena. "Where's Forman?" he asked.

"What's this about?" I asked him, not identifying myself.

"It's a subpoena for Forman."

"He's not here," I answered. "He might be in the back." I was standing by a desk at that point, and started getting ready to leave the office.

The cop walked over to another person in the office, and spoke to him. "Oh, Forman's over there by the desk," the person said.

They were going to give me the subpoena one way or another, so that bit of bungling didn't really matter—but it indicates the kind of security problems we have had. I marked an X on the subpoena instead of signing my name, as a small act of protest.

We issued a press release saying that I had been subpoenaed, to arouse people in the community further. Meanwhile, Barry Dawson's mother had returned to town and she asked Len Holt to represent her son. Barry himself had also sent a letter asking that Len represent him at the hearing on Monday morning. These procedures sound petty, but they can be important, especially in political cases—since a lawyer is not supposed to enter a case unless very specifically requested by the client or his representative. Things were looking up. A lot of the evidence that we had turned up could be exposed at the preliminary hearing only if we had a lawyer who was for real. Otherwise, it would have had to wait until Fred

Meely and the other brothers had either given themselves up or had been caught. And we were afraid that Cecil Moore, representing the other defendants, was just going to breeze through the hearing and that it would be over in a matter of minutes—unless we had a lawyer like Len Holt.

As we drove down to City Hall, we saw some of our brothers and sisters on their way there in African dress. We felt that it was going to be a very exciting morning, but we never expected to see such a crowd at the hearing: more than seven hundred people. All the mobilization efforts had not been in vain.

During the hearing, the following story emerged:

The police had raided four places with so-called search and seizure warrants. One was the SNCC office at 521 South Sixteenth Street. The next was a house on North Seventeenth Street where Fred Meely, Morris Ruffin, and some others slept. They had intended to use it eventually for a freedom school. The third place was the Freedom Library run by the Northern Student Movement (NSM). The fourth was the home of George Brower, at 909 North Sixteenth Street, where the Young Militants sometimes met. The Young Militants was a local group which had grown out of the Girard College demonstrations and which was at that time very closely aligned with Cecil Moore.

Only in one place did the police claim that they found dynamite, and that was in the apartment of George Brower. It is not a place where SNCC had held any meetings, although the press initially reported that this was a meeting place used by SNCC, CORE, and the Young Militants.

The search and seizure warrant used for the raids was signed by an FBI agent named Dean. It stated that Dean had been told by an informant, who had given him information two hundred times in the past which had led to two hundred arrests, that there was dynamite in the SNCC office and that he had heard people talk about how they could use it to destroy life, liberty, and property. (According to the Pennsylvania statute, for the possession of dynamite to be a crime, one must have intent to use it so as to inflict bodily harm, destroy property, etc.)

The confession of Barry Dawson was introduced at the trial. It stated that he had received some sticks of dynamite from a man named Ealy, who said that he had got it from a construction worker named Jenkins. (Ealy and Jenkins had subsequently been arrested and were before the judge at this preliminary hearing along with the four persons originally arrested.) Dawson had brought the dynamite to the SNCC office while Fred Meely was out of town, the statement said. When Fred came back he was very upset and told Barry that the dynamite had to be removed from the office. Fred, Barry, and Morris Ruffin wrapped it up in three packages. Each of them was going to take a package and throw it in the river.

When Barry left the office he felt that he was being followed by a police car. He stopped at 909 North Sixteenth Street and the car was still pursuing him. He saw some white men getting out of the car who looked like the same people who had beaten him the night before. He threw his package over the fence.

There is no question that dynamite was involved in the case against SNCC and that Barry Dawson had made a mistake in bringing the dynamite to the SNCC office, a serious error in judgment. But for the police to try to build a huge case on the basis of Barry's action and indict Fred and Morris Ruffin, who were simply trying to extricate themselves from a bad situation, was not only preposterous, it was clearly a matter of political persecution.

Fortunately we had Len Holt representing Barry Dawson at the hearing. Judge Weinrott, who presided, is known as the "hatchet man" for the city. He was a bastard, from my point of view, and at the very least a patronizing old white man who kept telling Len to "hurry up. These things don't usually take so long—we're not usually here very long; I don't understand why you keep dragging this thing out." Holt was masterful, bringing out as many details as he possibly could to prove the frame-up and to discredit the city and the newspapers which had slandered SNCC. It was apparent from the testimony of Inspector Meers, the first witness, and the police photographer, that the Philadelphia police had the SNCC office under intense surveillance long before the dynamite incident. Meers, by the way, later left Philadelphia to work in the New York City Police Department.

At the end of the hearing Barry Dawson was bound over for the grand jury with bail set at seventy-five hundred dollars. Ealy and Jenkins were also bound over, with bonds of one thousand dollars apiece. The case against the three other defendants was dismissed. The case of Barry Dawson never came to trial, nor those of Ealy and Jenkins. However, Dawson—who had other cases pending—eventually spent some time in a mental institution and also served a two-year parole term.

In November of that year Fred Meely, Morris Ruffin, and George Anderson turned themselves in after successfully evading the police network. In April, 1967, the case against them was dismissed for lack of evidence.

"The Great Dynamite Case," as some people sarcastically referred to the attempted frame-up, kept me in Philadelphia for a month and for periods of time after that. In an attempt to draw from the experience some lessons for general use, I wrote a "Philadelphia Black Paper." Among other points made in it were these:

REPORT AND RECOMMENDATIONS TO SNCC

1. Don't talk unnecessarily over the telephone . . . WRITE!! There's no point in always taking the attitude that they know anyway.
2. Anything you want kept secret, DO NOT DISCUSS in our offices.
3. REGULAR searches of our offices should be made for planted dynamite and SHIT.
4. Scramblers for our phones should be bought.
5. DO NOT TALK TOO MUCH in certain cars; you must ASSUME that certain devices can be planted there.
6. References of people who CLAIM to be friendly SHOULD BE CHECKED OUT.
7. Anyone who is vulnerable to the man, by virtue of his current activities such as the numbers racket, use of narcotics, etc., should NOT BE ALLOWED to become associated with the organization. In several cases, informers have had pressure put on them by the man, i.e. "Help us or we convict you of narcotics, etc., violations."
8. I think that all of SNCC has to begin talking more about mass mobilization, especially if you're talking about the cities. Standard operating equipment has to be 2 or 3 sound trucks and megaphones . . . where you really get out into the black community with sound, music, rhythm and constant leaflets . . . that's the kind of pressure that helps build a political base in a city. City administrations are afraid of this type of pressure. It's far better to have seven people talking on corners at rallies in the black community than to picket a single store downtown. No substitute for a group of people out in the community on Friday and Saturday nights and sometimes in the morning getting to those natural gathering places. We're convinced that the whole change in attitude from the DA is really a political thing. It's not a question of his having a change of heart. There's been a lot of pressure put on him by the black community and people are questioning him, talking about a frame-up.

What had happened in Philadelphia was that SNCC turned a defensive situation in which it found itself into an offensive attack on the city and the police. By building up pressure in the black community and hitting hard with our charges of a frame-up, we had put the district attorney in an awkward position. He was stuck with a bad case launched originally by the city and the police. Furthermore, the district attorney was a Republican while the mayor was a Democrat, and I suspect that the DA felt he could make some political hay in the black community by avoiding vigorous prosecution of a phony case. Whatever were all the factors involved, he did not press hard and the "Great Dynamite Case" against SNCC boiled down to nothing in the end.

But the police had won a larger battle. The momentum generated by our activities in the black community declined and SNCC lost its base in Philadelphia. The police effectively stopped SNCC from organizing around the symbol of the black panther in a major metropolitan area by putting our organizers in jail or driving them underground for months. The following year in Chicago a SNCC organizer and head of the project there, Monroe Sharpe, would leave the country for Tanzania because of intense harassment by the police. He, too, had been organizing around the symbol of the black panther. Thus in two attempts to organize political units in Northern cities, SNCC found itself stymied by the police and the repressive apparatus of government.

These defeats were also SNCC's fault to a large degree. We failed to sustain the momentum which had been injected into Philadelphia's black community because we lacked sufficient trained workers to deal with the complexities of organizing in an urban, Northern situation. Our forces were too dispersed. SNCC had extended itself from Arkansas to Alabama, Texas to Virginia, and was working in the North as well. When the attacks came in Chicago and Philadelphia, driving people into hiding or out of the country, SNCC had insufficient personnel to maintain operations. We lacked a systematized recruiting and training program.

But Philadelphia proved to me that the total power structure of the United States—with the press as a willing tool—was out to destroy SNCC. It provided a foretaste of the kind of openly fascist tactics that police departments would use increasingly in the years that followed. At that time, the growth of Birchites in the New York Police Department was just being revealed, and black militants had only begun to be aware of how the police operated to suppress people in the inner city—meaning mostly black people. Philadelphia showed that we needed to analyze all the elements of control in the corporate state.

If the nation was out to destroy SNCC, then it was also clear that we needed support from many black people—all those who responded to the call of Black Power. SNCC faced the absolute necessity of transforming itself into a centralized political party embracing the many aspects of black people's struggles and with a tight ideological framework. It could no longer exist as a cadre of organizers going into situations and helping people to "do their thing." At this time I proposed the idea of a Black Power conference to take place on February 1, 1967, the seventh anniversary of the sit-in movement. I thought it important to link these two movements—the sit-ins and Black Power—in a very public way. The 1960 movement had helped to produce the historical forces that ushered in Black Power. But I did not push the idea of such a conference in SNCC, because I felt that SNCC did not have its own ideological position together. It would be a tremendous mistake for us to call a conference on Black Power and fail to give it ideological direction.

The Philadelphia dynamite frame-up was one of the first acts of massive repression in the urban North against the current black movement. But for SNCC, it was only the latest in a series of acts to weaken or destroy us. The power structure had pulled out a quintuple-barreled shotgun with which to blast SNCC away, as we became more and more threatening. There it went:

SNCC opposes the war in Vietnam—
Lowndes County—year of the Black Panther.
Coup in SNCC—Lewis and Forman "ousted."
Black Power—
Dynamite in Philadelphia.
Boom! Boom! Boom! And away we go!

While the big blasts were resounding, the government was also moving to undermine SNCC in quiet little ways behind the scenes. In the same period as the Philadelphia frame-up, we learned for the first time how one of the lesser-known federal agencies operates to undercut revolutionary organizations. The Bureau of Internal Revenue plays its cards more quietly than the Philadelphia police, but it can be almost as repressive.

CHAPTER 57

The Bureau of Internal Revenue Attacks

THAT THE United States Government had declared SNCC an enemy was beyond question in the year 1966. Militant opposition to the whole American system had more and more become the style and content of SNCC. Our stand against the war in Vietnam and U.S. foreign policy in general, our articulation of Black Power, the hard-hitting speeches of such spokesmen as Carmichael and Brown—all this, combined with the mood of aggressive violence developing in the larger black community, made SNCC an anathema to the nation's power structure.

The American Government has many ways to fight those opposed to its policies, and one of the most powerful is the Bureau of Internal Revenue. The bureau zeroed in on SNCC in September, 1966—shortly after we began calling for Black Power—and plagued us steadily for two years. Its excuse was that SNCC had not filed an income tax return as an organization, although it had always paid personal income tax on the subsistence pay of staff members. The bureau also demanded that SNCC produce its complete financial records—including the names of people who had made donations to the organization.

SNCC's battle against the Bureau of Internal Revenue became time-consuming, expensive, and harassing—which was clearly the intention of the bureau, or powers behind it. As Ruby Doris indicated in many letters, SNCC was willing to pay any taxes it might legitimately owe. It could not, however, figure out which form it should use to file a return, since none of the standard forms applied to SNCC. We were an unincorporated association, for which no apparent precedent existed. The process of determining which form to file led to a confrontation discussed in the following exchange of letters between SNCC and the Bureau of Internal Revenue:

November 7, 1966
Mr. Austin
District Director
Bureau of Internal Revenue
Atlanta, Ga.

Dear Sir:
This afternoon, on instructions of Mrs. R. D. S. Robinson I went to the offices of the Internal Revenue Service to pick up forms for the filing of income tax returns by SNCC. I asked the girl on the information desk for the forms for a nonprofit association. She could not find such forms.

The girl referred me to a Mrs. Phelps. Mrs. Phelps did not know what form applied. She got in touch with Mr. Orr and he came to Mrs. Phelps' office to discuss the matter.

Mr. Orr told me that there was no way of knowing what form would be appropriate for SNCC's filing until it was determined into which organizational category SNCC fits. He said that at this time he did not have sufficient information about the organization to make such a determination.

Mr. Orr provided me with what he said were all possible forms (990—exempt organizations; 1120—corporations; and 1065—partnerships). Mr. Orr and I examined all the three forms and agreed that, since SNCC is neither exempt, a corporation, or a partnership, none of them were appropriate. However, since these were the only forms available, according to Mr. Orr, I told him I would take all three and turn them over to our accountants and lawyers in an attempt to determine which, if any, would be appropriate.

During the course of my visit to the IRS offices an incident occurred of which I think you should be aware. While I was seated at Mrs. Phelps' desk, she took occasion to ask the name of the organization with which I was concerned. I identified it as SNCC. She then inquired what I was doing in the organization, in obvious reference to my white skin. Again, she asked me if I was not afraid of "Black Power." Then, a short time later, during a telephone conversation, she referred to me as a "white man" representing SNCC.

At no time during my visit to the IRS offices was anyone, including Mrs. Phelps, discourteous to me in what I took to be their concept of courtesy. Nevertheless I wonder if Mrs. Phelps' enquiry, and her reference to me as a "white man" constitute approved modes of conduct for employees in your office.

Very truly yours
Jack Minnis

cc:
Mr. Orr
Mrs. Phelps

U.S. TREASURY DEPARTMENT
INTERNAL REVENUE SERVICE
District Director
275 Peachtree St., N.E.
Atlanta, Georgia 30303

November 10, 1966

Mr. Jack Minnis
Student Nonviolent Coordinating Committee
360 Nelson Street, S.W.
Atlanta, Georgia 30313

Dear Sir:
Your letter of November 7, 1966, has just come to my attention. If you will recall, Mr. Orr and I talked with you Monday concerning the tax forms your Organization would need to file their returns.

The remarks made by Mrs. Phelps relating to "Black Power" are, indeed, unfortunate and should not have been made. Mrs. Phelps assures me that no reflection on you or your Organization was intended and certainly she did not mean to offend you when she referred to you as a "white man" representing SNCC in her telephone conversation with another person.

I can understand your feeling in this matter, and I want to thank you for calling our attention to it. We, in Internal Revenue Service, are charged with the responsibility to treat everyone with courtesty, dignity and respect. We strive to have all our people attain perfection in this relationship, and we sincerely want to improve in any area we fall short.

Very truly yours,

J. L. Austin
Group Supervisor
Field Audit Group 2

The Bureau of Internal Revenue backed down on that exposure of its real attitude toward SNCC, but our troubles were far from over. We continued to be pressured for that list of donors. I was with Ruby Doris Robinson on several occasions when she had confrontations with the bureau and, together, we argued that we would give them our records of receipts and disbursements—we were willing to cooperate to that extent, although we knew that the whole investigation was part of a harassment campaign—but we would not turn over any information concerning our donors.

Ruby Doris never relented in her absolute refusal to reveal those names. Many of us were prepared to go to jail on this point. We would do anything necessary to protect the right of a person to make a contribution to SNCC without his or her name winding up in the files of the FBI, the Senate Internal Security Committee, the House Un-American Activities Committee, or any other repressive agency of the U.S. Government. Still, the government persisted.

We finally won a ruling from the Washington office of the bureau that we did not have to reveal the names of our donors. In 1967 we decided to file a return as a nonprofit corporation—which we were not, but we hoped it would get the bureau off our backs. The harassment abated for a while, but then the bureau renewed its pursuit of SNCC.

A battle over income tax may seem like a small thing, but it is important for people to know how the Internal Revenue Service can play the role of political investigator and agent of harassment. Any radical organization handling a substantial amount of money should never forget the tax collector. He is Uncle Sam's boy, as much as the FBI agent. People are sometimes surprised when the United States Government or some of its local pigs tap telephones or frame activists on trumped-up charges as they have done with the Black Panthers, Rap Brown, Reies Lopez Tijerina, and many others. But these forms of persecution, intimidation, and harassment are to be expected. The United States Government today, as in the past, will kill its enemies inside the country and abroad, in Chicago or in Vietnam. For it is a government founded on the extermination of the American Indian, the bloody enslavement of African people, and the colonization of the Chicanos and Puerto Ricans. Under such a government, anything goes—as long as it helps to maintain the domestic and world control of the capitalist power structure.

The person in SNCC responsible for dealing with the tax mess was Ruby Doris Robinson, who served as executive secretary until she became too sick with what proved to be a fatal illness. Ruby had been affiliated with SNCC longer than any other person in the organization at that time. Active in the Atlanta student movement of 1960, she was one of four SNCC people arrested at Rock Hill in February, 1961, and spent thirty days in jail there. That was considered a very long term in those days, and it left Ruby with a stomach ailment from which she suffered the rest of her life. After Rock Hill, Ruby joined on a Freedom Ride with Lucretia Collins and others, and spent forty-five days in Parchman Penitentiary. She had begun coming to the Atlanta office to do volunteer work while still in school and came to work with us full time in the early part of 1963.

Ruby and I worked very closely and she was enormously efficient, hardworking, committed. But Ruby was far more, both to me and to the organization, than just a vital prop in the administrative structure. She had brilliant ideas—ideas always more advanced than those of many others in SNCC. Her political perceptions and understanding of people were amazingly sharp. She acted as a mentor of mine in many ways. SNCC staff members became angered by Ruby's actions sometimes; she often had to make unpopular decisions about paychecks, cars, and other resources, and stick to them. Whether they wanted to admit it or not, Ruby Doris was one of the few genuine revolutionaries in the black liberation movement.

If SNCC had had twenty workers like Ruby, our internal problems would never have grown as overwhelming as they did at the end of 1966. Nothing that the city of Philadelphia, the Bureau of Internal Revenue, or any other enemy did to destroy us equaled what we were doing to ourselves. It was the point I have called "rock bottom."

CHAPTER 58

Rock Bottom

BY JANUARY, 1967, I had started reading the words of Mao Tse-tung; I studied in detail his essay "On Contradiction," trying to fit my experiences into some theoretical framework. I was coming to realize how much the lack of revolutionary reading on my part had handicapped me. I had a great deal of practical experience, but it lacked synthesis; it was just a disorganized mass at that point. I was also coming to realize more than ever before that oral argument was not enough in political discussion. No longer would I be content just to talk, to try to win political points verbally.

The necessity for me to analyze and write was one reason I had resigned as executive secretary, but new pressures and crises had prevented that plan from materializing. Now I knew it was no mere necessity, but a must. The truth of this struck me especially after a staff meeting which SNCC held in December, 1966, at a resort owned by Peg Leg Bates, a popular black entertainer of the thirties and forties, in upstate New York.

At Peg Leg Bates's, debate over the role of whites in SNCC reached a new pitch of intensity. After many hours and days of discussion, it was decided that whites could not be members of the Coordinating Committee, SNCC's policy-making body, although they could work for SNCC. There were only seven nonblacks left in the entire organization at that time, and they all worked in a fund-raising capacity except one person in the Atlanta office and one who planned to work in the white community. Nevertheless, their presence had led to some highly emotional debate. But I was more concerned with the underlying causes of those emotions.

The cause sprang from SNCC's unresolved disagreement about the nature of the problems that black people faced: Did our oppression spring from exclusively racial causes or from a combination of racial and class factors? This issue hit the floor with great intensity, again and again. There was still deep resistance in some people to dealing with the question of capitalism. And the debate still did not rise above the level seen at our Kingston Springs meeting. The message now was the same as before: Any organization, group or individual that lacks a systematic education in revolutionary thought, that fails to read, cannot help but become immersed in sterile arguments about the cause of our oppression and about white people.

The meeting revealed to me that we were at rock bottom on other levels, too, especially in our leadership. Here again, SNCC suffered from its own history. Leadership had been negated, although there was always in fact a leadership. But, by this time, the leadership of the organization had become corrupt in several damaging ways.

A great deal of marijuana smoking and pill dropping had been introduced into the organization by then. The problem had become so grave that a resolution had to be passed against it—which many people in leadership quickly overlooked. At Peg Leg Bates's, we received news that police had raided our Chicago office on charges of possession of marijuana. When we called a meeting to plan action on this situation, some of the leadership were so high from smoking pot that they could not participate in any meaningful discussion. I wanted to knock "the shit" physically out of one leading personality, for I felt that he encouraged this corruption of the organization.

Unwillingness to study, believing that one has the right answers all the time, pot smoking, pill dropping, and other forms of individualism—all these were manifestations of the middle-class attitudes which still plagued SNCC. (However, it should be noted that excessive pot smoking and pill dropping are also problems in black organizations that do not consider themselves middle class.) By the time of the meeting at Peg Leg Bates's, the class conflict among blacks had sharpened acutely. Some people with college educations showed their disdain toward people who were slow readers or could not read at all. A few black staffers were making such comments as "Mrs. Hamer is no longer relevant" or "Mrs. Hamer isn't at our level of development." This conflict was related to the debate over whites, for the same middle-class blacks who spoke this way of working-class people like Mrs. Hamer also refused to look at "the white question" in anything more than a racial context. The trend toward middle-class elitism was fundamentally responsible for the fact that SNCC had thus far been unable to develop a mass political party. For that would have involved close work with the unemployed, with working-class people, and there weren't many of those in the SNCC leadership then.

Negative individualism and elitism prevailed despite the fact that the "field machine" had pulled together in February, 1965, to overcome the freedom high tendency. That had proved to be only a temporary victory, for several reasons. First, workers with a middle-class orientation continued coming into the organization. Secondly, some of the key leaders in SNCC who had been thought of as belonging to the "field machine" turned out to be very individualistic and unrevolutionary. The "field machine" developed its own problems of individualism by a process of contagion and corruption which could not be stopped. Southern blacks who had come to SNCC as disciplined, dedicated workers became dysfunctional and disgusted within a year or two. The freedom high element left SNCC, but then so did many in the "field machine." SNCC's long, confused, very charged debates over whites and its lack of direction certainly made them feel confused and aimless, helping to drive them away. In this situation, the middle-class element—now all-black—once again came to dominate.

So many contradictions faced SNCC at Peg Leg Bates's that I put on the floor a motion to dissolve the organization and send any surplus funds to Guinea for liberation movements in Africa. I was dead serious about this motion, although I had failed to organize around it and, therefore, did not expect it to pass. But I wanted to force a discussion of the contradictions that beset us. Only serious, prolonged discussion could resolve our conflicts, I believed.

The motion was defeated. The meeting went on to vote a new program, to create freedom Organizations, political parties that would not simply make election promises but truly serve the day-to-day needs of the people. This was, I felt, a step in the right direction—of creating a mass political party, with the black panther as its symbol. The groundwork for this decision had been laid with our work in connection with Julian Bond's election and then with the Lowndes County Freedom Organization, which made the black panther a symbol of resistance for black people. In the summer of 1966 I had pushed vigorously inside SNCC for people to understand the importance of creating a mass political party with the black panther as its symbol. In Philadelphia Fred Meely had tried to implement this concept. By the time of the Peg Leg Bates meeting, a general agreement existed in SNCC on the panther party goal.

After the staff meeting I went to work on a paper that I hoped would lay the basis for a political education program and help to settle SNCC's contradictions. It was entitled "Rock Bottom," and it posed a series of questions in four areas of critical importance: leadership, the group as a political unit, ideology, program and work. Many people have found this paper useful, and I think it is worth quoting parts of its introduction —an introduction in which I was deliberately hard on myself because I still hoped this would help develop the organizational habit of criticism and self-criticism that we needed to move ahead on the revolutionary road.

INTRODUCTION

Throughout my history with the Student Nonviolent Coordinating Committee, there have been various discussions about the importance of an education program for the members of the organization. At some time or another, this person or that one has assumed the responsibility for working on this program or aspects of it. It goes without saying that each day we work, we engage in various forms of political education. However, there still has not been a systematic attempt to educate ourselves; to train new members; to instill a sense of the history of the organization, its objectives, success and failures; to discuss and analyze many events occurring in the world.

I assume some responsibility for the failure to implement this internal education program. It was a mistake always to give in to the demands of the moment and not insist in a more active manner that we create and implement a program for the intellectual and political development of our staff. My present evaluation stems from observing and participating in the effects of the failure to do this, from my own development, and from accepting the criticism of many who have been crippled by the lack of an internal education program. Without question, every time we allowed a new member to join our staff without undergoing some indoctrination program, we were contributing to misunderstanding, suspicion, ill-will, wasted effort and time lost. . . .

Today, 1967, six years after the student movement started in February, 1960, we are at Rock Bottom. There is nowhere to go but up or under. We have finally emerged, from my point of view, from many obstacles and can realistically assess what in fact has been true for more than two years: namely, that the massive attack on public accommodations and voter registration has been successful and we have played no small part in that success. With the passage of the 1965 Civil Rights Bill, the entire character of this organization changed. Some of us saw this, but we were unable to convince the organization of this shift and of the absolute need to revamp our programs. One of the reasons for this failure stemmed from the lack of an internal education program. As has been true throughout our history, we have been backed up against many walls, and changes have been forced upon us.

Today, we must face the reality that we have been successful, no matter what may have been all the shortcomings, and we must quickly revamp our entire style of operation—or there is no other way for us to go but out, nothing to do but destroy our effectiveness through lack of direction, lack of confidence in the future, a sense of failure, fatigue, despair, frustration and bad health. These conditions in turn lead to internal bickering, feuding, factional fighting, inertia, inability to work, loss of morale, hanging-on, resignation, walking-out, Fuck-it, it ain't worth it. . . .

By facing our success and evaluating that, I am saying that the framework within which the organization worked is no longer valid.

The question is no longer the right to vote, but the nature of the politics in which we should engage. The question is no longer segregation in public accommodations, but addressing ourselves to certain rock-bottom problems in the society. For instance, should we as an organization actively work to do something about inadequate housing, inferior education, the inequities of welfare, unemployment, insufficient medical attention, the malignment nature of America's racist foreign policy (stemming, of course, from a racist country and the exploitative wars in which we are asked to fight and to support).

At our December, 1966 meeting at Peg Leg Bates's, we decided many things, but we also recognized that the nature of our struggle had changed. We did this in voting to create Freedom Organizations in the country. We voted that these Freedom Organizations would be all-inclusive political parties; namely, that these political parties would have within their structure a housing, a welfare, an educational, a cultural, an economic and a youth division. We did this in full realization that politics in this country is usually election day campaigning. We wanted to help create political units that would speak in the name of the unit about day-to-day needs of the people we hope to organize.

We voted to do this, given our entire history of protest, voter registration efforts, and organizing people into political units. However, within our own organization we face the problem of who is going to do this work. We not only face that problem but we face many others given the nature of our history and again the nature of ourselves, the people in the organization. Therefore, it becomes crystal clear that the need for a political education program within the STUDENT NONVIOLENT COORDINATING COMMITTEE is a must. There are some basic questions in any internal education program that must be raised and answered and agreed upon by the members of a political unit. If there can be no agreement on certain fundamentals, or at least continuous discussion while one works, then SNCC as a political unit cannot survive.

We are in fact a political unit although we do not call ourselves that. We still cling to the rhetoric that we are a group of organizers. If we are successful in the development of the Freedom Organizations, we will inevitably become a political cadre within a political party. Whether we can assume our responsibilities and help move forward the struggle of black people—and thereby all people as we have done in the past, this is another question. It is quite possible that we cannot. It is also possible that we may not be able to overcome the inertia, the stagnant state in which we find ourselves.

During the spring of 1967 I continued to devote much time to reading revolutionary thought and putting past experiences into some political perspective. I was encouraged as I saw the revolutionary process unfold inside the United States. A change in consciousness had taken place and the rebellions in black communities all over the country were accelerating that pace. But I was still troubled about the transition that SNCC had to make in order to meet the challenge ahead. It began to occur to me that perhaps we might never become the ones to carry forth the struggle at the level where it needed to be sustained, to develop a mass political party with the black panther as its symbol. We still lacked clear-cut objectives, an understanding of world economics, an international outlook. Yet time and study could help us to articulate our goals in a revolutionary way and to reach an organizational position against racism, capitalism, and imperialism—the three enemies of black people, as I was coming to see.

While I searched for and explored ways that might still push forward the pace of SNCC's development, Ruby Doris Robinson—then our executive secretary—had fallen very ill and was confined to a hospital in New York. Living in that city, and always having been close to Ruby, I became the person who attended to her the most. This experience had a deep effect on the revolutionary process in me.

At the time, I had started a study of the works of Frantz Fanon and realized that she was dying from the same illness—leukemia—that had killed another revolutionary. It was a terrible, painful feeling to see her sinking into death over the months—to see a quirk of fate taking from this earth a brilliant sister who had the ideas and spirit to change many things. Ruby had suffered under the weight of administrative responsibility, like others, and seen much effort demolished through carelessness and immaturity, yet her commitment had never diminished.

Ruby's illness and eventual death gave me a new sense of urgency. For years I had said that the fact of death was inconsequential for revolutionaries. But now I felt that we must speed up time, we could not let the years slip by, because you never know how much time you really have. I felt that caution on my part, and an attitude of waiting for changes to come about in SNCC, were no longer valid. No longer could I muffle my voice and my thoughts in the slightest degree, or fear consequences. I had to wage the ideological struggle with intensity, push hard in the effort to develop new forms of struggle.

I was also influenced by the fact that Ruby had endured vicious attacks from some of those people in SNCC—particularly in the leadership— who embodied the middle-class, egoistic individualism that I have described. They also embodied male chauvinism in fighting her attempts as executive secretary to impose a sense of organizational responsibility and self-discipline, trying to justify themselves by the fact that their critic was a woman. Ruby had often seen the dangers represented by those individuals before I did.

After her death, I tried to steel myself with revolutionary thought that would sustain me for the rest of my life. I read *Malcolm X Speaks* carefully. His criticism of the term *civil rights*, and his advocacy of *human rights* in its place, led me to formulate a resolution that was adopted at the June, 1967, staff meeting of SNCC.

This resolution declared that SNCC considered itself to be a human rights organization working for the liberation not only of black people in the United States but of all oppressed peoples, especially those in Africa, Asia, and Latin America.

At the same meeting H. Rap Brown was elected chairman of SNCC. It was our hope that he would carry out the program adopted at the

December, 1966, staff meeting to develop freedom organizations with the black panther as a symbol, which the previous leadership had not done. But this would not come about. It was SNCC as a whole that failed to carry out the program, primarily because of a lack of organizational discipline. People failed to work consistently on programs assigned to them and engaged more in helter-skelter random activity—some of which was positive, of course. Thus another program would fail to materialize and it would be left to others to popularize the black panther.

Stanley Wise was elected executive secretary at the meeting and Ralph Featherstone was elected program secretary. I myself became director of the newly created International Affairs Commission, based in New York, a position that I held until the summer of 1969. Working on international affairs, I felt that I could help inject an anti-imperialist position not only into SNCC but into the black movement as a whole. For all the people and nations with whom we would want to have international associations were against racism, capitalism, and imperialism. In addition, they were striving in the main to build socialist societies. I was never able to get SNCC to declare itself for socialism, but I did not worry about that too much at the time. To have achieved a realization that our fight was against racism, capitalism, and imperialism represented a major victory in itself. It represented a way up, a progression from the rock bottom position in which we had found ourselves.

CHAPTER 59

The Indivisible Struggle

JULY 14, 1967—On board a plane to Dar Es Salaam. As I travel to East Africa, a 15-year-old conflict is reopening in my mind. Should blacks who have technical skills stay in the United States or should they go to Africa, live and work? When I first began debating this seriously, there were only two independent black countries south of the Sahara: Ghana and Guinea. The options were not as great then, but today there is a demand for skilled black personnel. Should we as a colonized people remain in a sick decaying country that is doomed for total collapse? The question is a serious one. Frankly, I say no, we should leave! We should return to Africa. We should use our skills where they are wanted.

That is my firm conviction and then comes the halter—what about those blacks who can't? Shouldn't some of us stay and encourage them to live to fight America from within? My work with SNCC has been predicated on many assumptions, but one of them has been the necessity for some of us to stay in the United States and struggle from within. I elected to do this after serious self-examination covering a period of more than four years, during which time I tried to prepare myself for the day when I would help to join the African and the Afro-American struggle. The indivisible link has always been there, but at this time in my life I have the opportunity to forge stronger links.

I am concerned about the dedication of those who would go to Africa and come back, about our willingness to subordinate self for the cause. We have been raised in a highly individualistic society where profit and social-climbing are paramount. These have had their effects upon all of us. The caliber and dedication of those who go to Africa and return will determine how many more of us our brothers in Africa will want!

July 15. In less than two hours we shall arrive in Dar Es Salaam. This has been a very long journey, the longest I've taken by plane and I'm worn out. A little while ago, we landed at Djibouti, on the eastern coast, near Ethiopia. It is controlled by the French and many Freedom Fighters from the area are in jail. One could feel an intense heat rising from the ground, pressing down from the sky, squeezing from all directions of the sandy wind that shot through one's body. A sauna bath is the closest parallel I can describe. The airport seemed deserted, but it wasn't. There was a freight plane from Pacific Western there and some old training planes. I saw a rack for Air Ethiopia.

Inside the restaurant the idle sense of just waiting for the plane was very evident. Air France, with its colonial history and present neo-colonialism, dominated the room. There were the new French stewardesses who were taking the place of those that left Paris some *millions* of years ago. The so-called fresh stewardesses seem pale, haggard and worn out from the heat. They just sat there waiting and hoping the time would come for them to board the plane; then they would be out of the heat (refrigeration and air conditioning are trades we must learn). I walked around the restaurant and they had cameras and radios for sale. I saw a few strings of beads, probably made locally. Colonialism is tricky and efficient sometimes. Here France digs out oil and sells back cameras.

I got into an understanding type discussion with a brother who was waiting tables. I ordered an orange juice. They didn't have change for an American dollar, so the brother told me to drink it with sign language and a few encouraging words in French. I later asked him about the independence movement and he walked away. Then he returned and showed me his hands clasped, which meant people were in jail. There had been considerable agitation in and around here for independence.

On the plane we have talked to only one person, the Secretary of the Mauritian Friendly Society in London. Mauritius is an island below Malagasy (or Madagascar). There are approximately 1,000,000 people there under the colonial rule of Britain. The poor man is a political activist and he has not slept since we left Paris.

I wrote those lines and more as Howard Moore, Jr., SNCC's legal officer, and I traveled together to an International Seminar on Apartheid, Racism, and Colonialism in Southern Africa, scheduled for July 24 to August 10, 1967, and sponsored by the United Nations. It was my first trip to Africa since 1964 and I was enormously excited to be returning.

Howard and I both felt that our attending the seminar would be a milestone for black people in the United States. We had been officially invited by the United Nations to present our views at an international forum. We had no illusions that the United Nations could bring about our liberation, or the liberation of Africans on the continent; we knew it was controlled by Western imperialism. But, like the late Malcolm X, we believed that pressure upon the United Nations could be useful nevertheless in shaping public opinion. To make the most of our opportunity at the seminar, Howard and I had carefully prepared a SNCC position paper entitled "The Indivisible Struggle Against Racism, Colonialism and Apartheid." Dr. St. Clair Drake, a longtime activist in African affairs and my teacher at Roosevelt, had helped us. We strove to make our paper as political as possible, including in it many facts to show the direct connection between American oppression of blacks in Africa and of blacks in the United States.

We also hoped to make contacts for the development of the Afro-American Skills Bank Program—a project we had designed to get black people from the United States to work in select African countries for periods of two to three years. The program had grown out of my thinking about ways in which we could relate to the emerging African nations, and it was a sort of compromise between my feeling that all Afro-Americans should go to Africa and my feeling that we should stay to participate in the struggle here. There were many black people in the United States with technical skills, including farmers, who could be helpful in the building of an African continent. The Skills Bank aimed to tap this resource. The program could not be co-opted by the United States Government, for its orientation was against the Peace Corps and other official agencies—it was pro-African in an anti-American way.

As Howard Moore and I arrived in Dar Es Salaam, Tanzania, on our way to the seminar, then scheduled to take place in Lusaka, Zambia, we knew that we were not just two Americans visiting East Africa. We were representatives of Africans living in the United States, and would be seen as such. Africa is full of "Negroes" who serve as agents for the CIA and other agencies of the United States Government. The last black "dignitary" who visited Tanzania had been James Farmer, then director of CORE, in 1965. The Tanzanian Government had arranged for a private helicopter to take him to Zanzibar. Upon arrival there, the United States Embassy had a car waiting and he got in it—a gross insult to the Tanzanians but no real surprise, since Farmer's whole trip had State Department blessings.

The story of Farmer's behavior would be told to us by many people in Tanzania, and we would try desperately to offset negative feelings about American "Negroes." We repeatedly took the position that Africans should not assume every black American was a friend. We wanted to be judged by our actions alone; they would determine if we were true brothers. We felt very strongly about this, for at the time we arrived in

Tanzania, Newark was in flames and the torch would soon be lighted in Detroit too.

Our first four days in Dar Es Salaam lifted our spirits high, and we wanted to remain in Africa for the rest of our lives. Dar Es Salaam struck me as the most beautiful city I had ever seen and the island off its shore where Kivikoni College is located—a school for the training of government cadres—the closest thing to paradise on earth. Everywhere people were working to build Tanzania, and we wanted to help. Earlier that year Tanzania had issued the Arushua Declaration, calling Tanzania a country trying to build socialism. This declaration was under intense discussion in political circles. The freedom with which people talked of socialism, armed struggle, the liberation of Africa, was a liberation in itself for Howard and me, coming as we did from the repressive atmosphere of the United States.

We had long discussions with representatives of liberation movements and many talks with Brother Babu, a government official from Zanzibar who had come to the United States and spoken in Harlem at a rally sponsored by Malcolm X. As we listened and exchanged ideas I could feel a growing passion for revolutionary ideas. Surrounded by a pleasant atmosphere, visiting in a country where I felt one did not have to worry about police spies, I wished that all black people from the United States could be there too.

Howard and I visited the Chinese book store in Dar Es Salaam and bought books for our friends in the United States. For myself, I bought several works of Lenin's. I was acquainted with the life of Lenin and I had read some of his thoughts, but in Tanzania I began to make a systematic study of his ideas—looking for ways to apply his thoughts usefully to our struggle. I became more aware than ever before of the crippling effect of miseducation in the United States. The need for constant political reeducation and the study of all revolutionary writers nagged at me as I thought of how much time we in the black movement had wasted by having been denied the opportunity to learn from those revolutionaries who preceded us.

One of our most successful experiences was our talks with President Julius Nyerere and other high government officials about the Afro-American Skills Bank. Everyone was enthusiastic in principle about the program. We all agreed that some of the technical skills that black people had acquired from living in industrialized America would be helpful in Africa. Politically we all saw this program as a counter to the Peace Corps. It would demonstrate concretely the rising interest in Africa on the part of blacks in the United States, with a program whose goal was not control and co-optation but revolutionary unity. Later, when we went to Zambia, we would have additional discussions about the Skills Bank with government officials there and they, too, would express enthusiasm.

Allard Lowenstein popped up while we were in Dar Es Salaam, like a sudden nightmare. We assumed that he was there on behalf of the State Department or the Central Intelligence Agency. We knew that he did not have the Tanzanian Government's interest at heart, and saw his presence in the framework of the liberal-labor syndrome's efforts to maintain control even in faraway Africa. The influence of that treacherous element in Africa has been great, especially in some of the trade unions. Lowenstein turned up again on the plane with us as we headed for Zambia and the Seminar on Apartheid, Racism, and Colonialism in Southern Africa.

July 19. We are now flying on East African Airways. This company is owned, I'm told, by the governments of Tanzania, Uganda and Kenya. A curious condition exists on this plane. The stewardess and stewards are all black and the passengers are white, except for a few Indians and two Overseas Africans, Howard and me. We are beginning a campaign among Afro-Americans to declare themselves Overseas Africans, a people ruptured from their culture, colonialized, who only live in the United States. We have been pushing this position hard with all the Africans with whom we have talked. It is important that the brothers and sisters in SNCC begin pushing this position, for there is a gulf in culture between us, the Overseas Africans, and those on the continent, but our political situation is the same for the most part. Colonialism and Western imperialism have shackled us, and all of us must wrench ourselves free by any means possible. Our brothers on the continent are able to do this with greater ease, for some of them have become independent of certain forms of political domination and are struggling to free themselves from neo-colonialism.

July 23. Just a note on a confused Sunday morning far away on the other side of the world where the West and East struggle for Africa. The conference opens Tuesday in Kitwe, not Lusaka. So now we go back to Kitwe. We met with the Foreign minister and the General Secretary of the UNIP (United Nationalist Independence Party). I am convinced we are a lost tribe and our main responsibility is to struggle against the U.S., although I am also convinced that wherever one struggles today he is fighting the U.S. and its Western allies.

July 24. Howard and I are having our last meal at the Ridgeway Hotel before leaving for Kitwe. This hotel is a relic of colonialism. We are sitting next to a large pool which is in the center of the hotel. The sprinklers, the goldfish, the tadpoles, the water lilies, are all in muddy green water. Around the pool, having lunch, are white people, God only knows from where, but not the U.S. It has been cold here, requiring two blankets at night. I'm told by John Lang, a South African white, that the Ridgeway is the center of social life. There is truth in that since all the liberation representatives and lower echelon civil servants and all foreigners, including us, are here from time to time. This place is designed to make a person from the States hate the colonialists. Here are all these Europeans dining well while we saw some Africans having a roll and pop for lunch. That is not to say that the economy of the Africans is not better here than in some other countries.

July 26. Today is the second day of the conference. We are meeting in a community center. Speaking now is the representative of the OAU. He speaks of the death of Chief A. Lithuli (a South African liberation leader who had supposedly been killed by an accident when a train hit him while he was out walking). We called for an investigation, for we fear murder. The OAU representative now supports that position of his being murdered. Says we must revise thinking about the question of nonviolence. Appeals to seminar to consider whether nonviolence is relevant. All liberation groups are opposed to it in Southern Africa. We too!

The first two days and the next will be devoted to opening statements and then we go to the agenda. Good thing about this conference is that Liberation Movements and nongovernmental organizations have been invited. Personally I do not believe much will come from the UN but the forum is good for us and other liberation struggles to air points of view. This speaker hitting hard again on nonviolence. This morning, the brother from the Congo was great! Mercenaries assume great importance at this meeting, for we are not far from the Congo and all independent nations fear invasion by mercenaries to create disorder in their territories.

There are moments in history when you realize you yourself are making it. Howard Moore and I felt that way as we stepped before the microphone to address the assembled delegates of the United Nations and the liberation fighters. We had no illusions about the United Nations but, at the same time, there were delegates and liberation fighters around the very large rectangular table who were going to hear and to transmit to their sisters and brothers some of the ideas we would present. Moreover, we were going to raise in this body some of the issues that had confronted us for many years and we had a good chance of drawing more support to our cause.

The chairman of the seminar, Mr. Malechela, ambassador from Tanzania to the United Nations, introduced us. It was decided that I should speak. Although we had a written paper, the recent rebellions in the United States compelled me to begin by talking about those events and putting them in perspective. I pointed out that, notwithstanding the efforts of the United States Government to label them "riots," they were in fact rebellions against the forced enslavement of a people who had been wrenched from the African continent. I particularly called attention to the case of Chairman H. Rap Brown, who had become a symbol of resistance in the summer of 1967, emphasizing that the United States Government had decided he must become a scapegoat for the rebellions that black people were mounting. As I said this, I thought the United States representative at the seminar would surely interrupt me and object to my remarks, but he just sat there turning red as I spoke.

There was more in store for him, as I began to give the position paper we had prepared. It is worthwhile, I think, for readers to know at least parts of what we said, since the American press carried no report at all of our remarks:

Afro-Americans have watched with sympathy and concern the struggle against apartheid and white-settler domination in eastern and southern Africa over the past twenty years. We rejoiced with all freedom-loving people when the victory was won in Kenya. Today, we express our solidarity with the Freedom Fighters who languish in prisons and detention camps of southern Africa awaiting the day when the heroic efforts of those who are still free to fight will wipe out these inhumanities of man to man once and for all, and place the destiny and welfare of the people in their own hands.

It is only natural that we in SNCC should be deeply concerned over the course and outcome of this struggle, for our own members have been engaged for seven years in struggle against a particularly vicious form of apartheid that has existed for centuries in the United States. We can understand South Africa because we have seen the inside of the jails of Mississippi and Alabama and have been herded behind barbed wire enclosures, attacked by police dogs, and set upon with electric prods—the American equivalent of the *sjambok*. There is no difference between the sting of being called a "kaffir" in South Africa and a "nigger" in the U.S.A. The cells of Robin Island and Birmingham jail look the same on the inside. As the vanguard of the struggle against racism in America, SNCC is not unfamiliar with the problems of southern Africa.

SNCC has never visualized the struggle for human rights in America in isolation from the worldwide struggle for human rights. It was inevitable that a time would come when it would formally declare itself, as it did this year, a "Human Rights Organization interested not only in Human Rights in the United States but throughout the world," and would apply to the United Nations for status as an affiliated non-governmental organization. SNCC has made it clear by recorded vote at its May, 1967 conference that: "It encourages and supports the liberation struggles against colonialism, racism and economic exploitation wherever these conditions exist, and that those nations that assume a position of positive non-alignment express a point of view most consistent with its own views. Therefore, although our name indicates the original form of our struggle, we do not foreclose other forms of struggle. . . ." The organization's participation in this conference is evidence of its desire to render intensified support to the fight against racism, apartheid, and white-settler domination on the continent of Africa.

As an organization technically composed of American citizens, SNCC's first obligation to the worldwide struggle for human rights is to take a firm stand against violations of these rights by the American government.

It is our firm conviction that American intervention in Vietnam militates against any possible constructive action by the U.S.A. in other areas of Latin America, Asia, and Africa. It distorts any clear analysis of the problem, since policy makers tend to interpret all such struggles in terms of Cold War rivalries. (The shameful intervention in the Congo between 1960 and 1965 was justified on the grounds that it was "necessary" to curb Soviet and Chinese influence in Africa.) Policy makers of the U.S. government divert resources and energy that should be applied to financial and technical assistance—without strings —for developing areas, including the ghettoes of the United States. It destroys the confidence of Africans, Asians, and Latin Americans in the good intentions of *any* American nationals, laying the pall of suspicion that there may be CIA among them. SNCC took a formal position against the Vietnam War in January, 1966. . . .

The problem of Vietnam is organically related to the position of the United States with regard to southern Africa. The United States is formally committed to a half-hearted participation in economic sanctions against Rhodesia, but it has vigorously resisted all attempts to commit itself to such a policy with regard to the Republic of South Africa. Although it repeatedly deplores the existence of apartheid there, the United States views the Republic of South Africa as an integral part of a worldwide military system—a site for tracking stations and a haven for sailors going to and from the Far East.

World opinion has moved to the point where it is prepared to support the imposition of sanctions on South Africa in the hope of averting a violent conflict in the future. The U.S. opposes such sanctions—and not only because of its involvement in an East-West conflict. The volume of its investments and its desire not to "rock the boat" are matters that have been well documented by the United Nations and other non-governmental organizations. . . .

Since its inception in 1960, SNCC has always been interested in the African phase of the struggle against racism. In 1965, on the anniversary of the Sharpeville massacre, SNCC became active in attempts to mobilize pressure against the system of apartheid in South Africa by conducting a week of demonstrations in the offices of the South African Consulate and the South African Mission to the UN, both in New York. It has also participated with other organizations in the attempt to get Americans to withdraw their accounts from banks doing a large volume of business in the Republic of South Africa.

Increasing numbers of Afro-Americans—and their allies—are beginning to recognize the indivisible nature of racism. The Chase-Manhattan Bank, for instance, has large-scale investments in South Africa and profits greatly from apartheid. SNCC has recently been lending its support to black employees of Chase-Manhattan who are victims of racist personnel practices. A total of 12 Negro employees have filed charges against the bank with the New York City Commission on Human Rights, charging the "baas" mentality among supervisors, denial of promotions and job training opportunities, and intimidation, harassment and constant surveillance after they had dared to challenge these practices. Finally, nine employees were dismissed for seeking redress of grievances. This struggle continues.

The parallels between the African Liberation movement and the struggle of Afro-Americans are striking. As both movements have matured and the lessons of previous struggles have been drawn, they have increasingly emphasized the extent to which their fate has been linked—without their consent—to Great Power struggles. They have also seen the need for increasing their effectiveness by stressing the right to make their own decisions, uninfluenced by pressures from other racial and ethnic communities even though they may sustain close working relations with them as allies. In the United States, this has taken the form of the "Black Power" movement with SNCC in the lead. Within the United States, conservative organizations—some of them represented at this conference—as well as all levels of government have tried to undermine, contain, or simply destroy the organization.

Numerous incidents might be cited, but a very recent one will illustrate the point. This month, five SNCC-affiliated students from Texas Southern University will go on trial in Houston, Texas. Their trial is the outgrowth of events on May 16, 1967, when 500 Texas police armed with rifles, machine guns, shotguns and dogs, fired upon and then invaded two dormitories at the University. In the wild shooting, one policeman shot another and a patrolman was killed. Despite the fact that the patrolman was shot on the side of a building where there were no doors or windows, and despite the fact that at least two of the five accused students can prove their absence from the scene, these five have been charged with murder. The brutal conduct of the police inside the dormitories, where they destroyed property indiscriminately, kicked a dormitory house mother, and arrested 487 students (some of whom they also beat)—with these crimes, the state of Texas is unconcerned. This is the same state which the President and the Attorney General of the United States call home. This is only one of many recent incidents of massive police brutality. Such occurrences led the New York office of SNCC to issue an appeal to the African and Asian missions to the United Nations on June 13, 1967.

This, then, is a brief summary of some aspects of SNCC's recent activity and experience which have relevance for those gathered here. What conclusions and recommendations may be drawn for the consideration of this conference?

We see the worldwide fight against racism as indivisible. Southern Africa as a stronghold of the Herrenvolk mentality has high priority in the struggle. To win the battle there is to hasten the victory in the U.S.A. SNCC is dedicated to a joint struggle of all who fight for Human Rights in Africa and in the U.S.A., each backing up the other, each rendering what support it can to the other. Therefore, SNCC has come to this conference not only to express its condemnation of apartheid and colonialism, already affirmed in previous statements, and to offer its moral support to all Africans engaged in liberation struggles. We also come to assert that we consider ourselves and other black people in the United States a colonized people; a colony within the United States in many ways similar to colonies outside the boundaries of the United States and other European nations.

The fight against racism is a responsibility of all who believe in Human Rights, but it is the victims who bear primary responsibility for waging struggle. We have accepted our responsibility for the attack on the American front. We salute those who are waging the battle in southern Africa. We welcome their assistance in our struggle and pledge ourselves to theirs. But we also affirm that strategy and tactics must be decided by those who bear responsibility for waging the struggle, on both fronts.

Among African leaders, a remarkable degree of consensus has developed during the past five years on the acceptance of the strategy of a multi-pronged attack upon apartheid, racism, white-settler domination, and the remnants of colonialism in southern Africa. As part of that strategy, they have enlisted the support of the United Nations in arraigning South Africa before the bar of world opinion; in condemning oppressive policies in Portuguese territories; in voting to assume administration over Southwest Africa; and in declaring economic sanctions against Rhodesia. These leaders have also tried to bring the UN to the point of voting sanctions against South Africa. We support that effort to obtain action in the United Nations and, as our recent appeal to the Afro-Asian nations indicates, we shall attempt to do the same for our own struggle.

SNCC has *never* accepted the position that racism in the U.S.A. is a domestic issue that should not be aired before the United Nations. We call attention to the case of Julian Bond, a SNCC staff member who was duly elected to the Georgia State Legislature and then denied his seat because he refused to repudiate the SNCC statement condemning the U.S. war in Vietnam. For almost a year, Brother Bond was denied his seat and the people of his electoral district were thus denied representation. The legislature's action was clearly motivated by the fact that he was a black militant, an affront to the white supremacist legislature. During this period, Brother Bond was invited to lunch by a number of African delegations to the United Nations. Extensive pressure was brought to bear on delegations not to attend the luncheon, on the grounds that his case was a matter of domestic concern—an internal affair of the United

States. Most of the delegations resisted this pressure, recognizing that racism in the United States is a matter of international concern. . . .

As African liberation movements intensify their armed struggle, what will be the response of the nations in the UN and its associated organizations? Will certain powers decide to intervene to protect "missionaries" and "white civilization," raising the cry of "Communism" to strangle liberation efforts, as happens within the United States whenever blacks vigorously oppose the *status quo*? Will organizations concerned with human rights provide humanitarian assistance to the casualties of this struggle, as they do in the cases of international warfare, or will they define Africans as "savages" (rather than Freedom Fighters) and deny such assistance? Will those who sing praise of the heroes of the French, Russian and American Revolutions define the black heroes as "Satanic creatures of darkness?" Is it possible, even now, before the climax of the struggle comes, to define positions, if and when such situations arise? We believe that to do less is not only unrealistic but also a betrayal of the values which all opponents of apartheid say they support.

We concluded our position paper with ten specific recommendations to the seminar. After our presentation, Mr. Malechela, chairman of the conference and a man of tremendous energy and organizational ability, indicated ways that we could help to make the conference more successful. The seminar had four agenda items and we spoke on each of them. We made a number of recommendations including these two: that the Afro-Asian delegations to the United Nations find ways to curtail the domination of the UN by the colonial powers (the United States, Great Britain, and France); and that the United States withdraw its investments and civilians from South Africa before the revolutionary armed struggle reaches the point of killing those citizens and blowing up those investments.

Every time we spoke, we raised the issue of the oppression of black people in the United States and compared it in some specific way with racism in Southern Africa. It was impossible for the delegate from the United States to object since we were sticking to the agenda. For years the United States blocked any presentation of the problems of black Americans at the United Nations on the technical grounds that this was a domestic—not international—concern. This was their excuse for putting heavy pressure on the delegates not to attend that luncheon for Julian Bond. Now, at Kitwe, we overcame that obstacle. Later in the fall of 1967, when I spoke before the Fourth Committee of the UN dealing with conditions in colonial territories, I would again evade the technicality and describe some aspects of the colonized condition of black people in the United States.

Given our hard-hitting indictment of the United States and the West in general, it was no surprise that the American press failed to carry any news of SNCC's presentations at the seminar—though our remarks were widely disseminated in Africa. For years, black people had tried to take their case to the United Nations. In the 1940s, William Patterson drew up an extraordinary document entitled "We Charge Genocide" in an attempt to push the UN into discussing American racism. At Kitwe we had, in a sense, finally managed to bring our case before that organization. From the viewpoint of the United States, the less that people heard about it, the better.

We also learned that, at the seminar itself, the United States delegation spread a lie to discredit SNCC. We were informed by one delegate that the American representative had told him SNCC was the only civil rights organization invited, and that there were other groups which did not share our opinions. This was not the true story of the invitations. SCLC and CORE had also been invited originally. Then the United States, through its ambassador to the United Nations, Arthur J. Goldberg, objected furiously to the exclusion of the NAACP and the Urban League. He claimed that the African delegations, especially Tanzania and Guinea, had no right to split the so-called civil rights movement (as if it was united, or even could be). The NAACP was later invited but the Africans would not, as I recall, yield on the Urban League. At the seminar, only we of SNCC appeared and presented a position paper. Representatives from SCLC and the NAACP were not in attendance, an insult to the Afro-Asian delegations. CORE did send a delegation which arrived at the very end of the conference, stating they were unable to make it earlier because of the armed rebellion in the United States.

In our final address before the seminar, we struck out once more against the United States and the West. We called on all the delegations to notify their governments that Afro-Americans say they are victims of the same colonialism that established apartheid, that the struggle against racism is indivisible. We affirmed that our efforts inside the United States would hasten victory for the liberation struggle in Southern Africa, and that the struggle in Africa would hasten a better life for Africans living in the United States. We recognized that it was from the sweat and the riches of Africans, among other peoples, that those who live high and mighty in Western capitals have derived their positions.

We also expressed our full support of the resolutions introduced by the liberation organizations and others, and reiterated the recommendations we had made ourselves during the seminar. We also acknowledged that SNCC and other Afro-Americans had not done as much as they could to mobilize public opposition to American policies in Southern Africa, and promised to correct this. Then we concluded:

Our brothers and sisters are dying in the streets of the United States as we utter these words. They are engaged in rebellions and revolts against white people who have denied them their liberty and exploited our labor for centuries. Yet the United States representatives sit at this conference and talk about freedom blowing in the wind. There is indeed something blowing in the wind, Mr. Chairman. It is blowing all over the world and it is a determination by the oppressed black, brown and colored people who form a world majority that the day of the white man exploiting all of us is over.

The summer of 1967 became the hour when liberation fighters all around the world took full notice of and were inspired by the black struggle in the United States. The fierce rebellions in Newark, Detroit, and fifty-five other cities served warning that black people in the United States had escalated their resistance. They would fight with any means available to them. Meanwhile, Stokely Carmichael and other members of SNCC were in Havana, Cuba, at the Organization of Latin American States (OLAS) to strengthen bonds between our struggle and that of liberation fighters all over the Americas. Still other SNCC representatives had gone or would be going to the Far East. We were building solidarity with the freedom struggle in Africa, Latin America, and Asia at the same time that the struggle inside the United States reached a new peak. The cry of Black Power had for SNCC become an international one.

During this period, SNCC also took a position on the Arab-Israeli dispute. We saw that dispute as part of the fight against racism, capitalism, and imperialism. The indivisible struggle intensified.

CHAPTER 60

The Arab-Israeli Dispute

WHILE THE United States rocked with the rebellions of 1967, the Arab-Israeli War in the Middle East was making the summer even hotter. I had just become SNCC's director of international affairs when the issue of the war confronted us. I felt that SNCC might eventually take a position on it, and that we should begin some intensive discussion inside the organization. Before leaving for Tanzania and Zambia I, therefore, set down my own thoughts about the war in two letters to Stanley Wise, then executive secretary:

June 7, 1967

Dear Brother:

I assume you have been following the debates over the current Middle East crisis in the newspapers and over television. I assure you that it is most important that we all do this, for I am convinced this will not be a short war. It already has been a long protracted struggle (the conflict between Israel and the Arab nations) and it will continue to be one. There are certain events which must be of major concern to those of us in SNCC.

1. Within the United States there is a large public opinion which is very favorable to the Israelis. There are many Jewish organizations that operated and do operate within the framework of the liberal-labor leadership circle. Rabbi Prinz spoke at the March on Washington. He is now a chief spokesman for organizations urging more United States action in support of Israel.

Within this circle of leadership, there are many Negroes who have sought the support of these Jewish organizations and who . . . usually support United States foreign policy. For instance, A. Philip Randolph spoke at Manhattan Center Tuesday night and said that 30 million Negroes were behind Israel. Martin Luther King has come out in full support of Israel. I am told there was a rally in Paris and Sammy Davis Jr. led the parade.

Any black person of national stature who speaks against Israel must expect a certain isolation from the press—all white-controlled and so forth. Again, I am trying to make an analysis and I am not saying that we should be worried about these matters, but we do need to analyze them.

2. The class struggle in the black community will become sharper if the war continues. Obviously the "gut" reaction in many people is against Israel and for the Arabs, reflecting the black-white tension, the hardening of racism, and the particular circumstances in which we find ourselves in this country.

However, it becomes very necessary for those of us in the organization, especially those of us in leadership positions, to study the historical development and the contemporary economic policies of Israel. Actually Israel represents an extension of United States foreign policy as well as an attempt by the Zionists to create a homeland for the Jews. The latter merges with the former in many countries, especially the United States, Great Britain and France in some respects.

The implications of the last paragraph for us, it seems, is not to fall party to a reactionary position that even the Syrians and the Egyptians do not articulate: namely, a hatred for the people of Israel. Rather they detest what Israel represents—an extension of imperialism and a violation of territory of the Arabs, to put it mildly.

3. We must, and we must, and we must, stop putting it off—*we must get busy and get financial support bases in the black community*. If by chance or by design we were to take a position on the Arab-Israeli war such as we took on the war in Vietnam, the reaction would be fantastic against us. What are some of the possible reactions?

A. Why was it necessary for SNCC to issue a statement? What does this statement do for the people we are organizing? Why did we do this when the issue was and remains touchy in the country?

B. SNCC is wrong. Did not the Jews help SNCC in Civil Rights? Is this not a minority issue and SNCC should support minorities in this country? How could SNCC dare be so inhumane as to not recognize the rights of the people of Israel?

C. This is not any of our business, Period.

D. SNCC must be isolated further and it must be destroyed and never forget that it came out in favor of the Arabs (assuming we do that).

Now I am just giving some thoughts as to possible reactions and I am not personally sure we can take a position at this moment. This assumes that we would take a pro-Arab position. Sitting here in New York and watching that television and reading these newspapers daily, I am horrified at this country and the prospect for blacks in this country. I am sure I am developing a war psychosis or war neurosis. This man will roll over or attempt to steamroll any standing in the way of his foreign policy desires—namely the saving of this capitalistic system with its international tentacles all around the world. . . . I am also absolutely convinced that we can go nowhere in the future in terms of programming if we do not accentuate a class analysis of the national and international scene. We cannot, for instance, just explain glibly the events in the Middle East as a struggle of blacks against whites when the actors themselves have a different viewpoint. That is not to say we must not speak of racism, for racism is involved in the Middle East crisis. But it is a serious error to even think one can eliminate racism without dealing with the fundamental cause of exploitation, the unequal distribution of wealth throughout the world, and the desire of those who have control of the wealth to keep it.

I stress this point very seriously. It is interesting to note that the countries supporting the Arab nations are fundamentally socialist nations or those striving for socialism. At some point in our struggle, and that day is not too long off, we ourselves must begin to declare that this too is one of our objectives in the building of a new society.

Why am I stressing this point? For those of us in SNCC who are called upon to speak and whose words do get international projection, clarity about the nature of our problem is called for if we are to have meaningful relations with forces in Africa, Asia and Latin America.

We must understand what is meant by imperialism, neocolonialism, socialism . . . we must ask ourselves why is it that the Chinese and the North Vietnamese—why is it that all these forces constantly say we are not against the people of the United States; we are against the rulers of the country, the power elite, who wage these unjust wars?

If we are aware of these factors, then what is our responsibility? Is it not our responsibility to educate, to persuade, to inform ourselves, those with whom we work and those with whom we are in contact? Is it not sheer opportunism to keep silent for the sake of trying to please the crowd? Is the role of leadership always to think that it is enough to know what people are thinking, and only to say those things we know will be acceptable? How are we going to lead people within the United States and relate them to international forces, when we ourselves are afraid to say those things which we know are true?

What I am arguing, Brother Stanley, is that in mid-1967—when obviously we are linked in a world-wide struggle and know it—then the leadership and the members of SNCC must struggle for clarity of ideas and clarity of expression about the causes of our oppression, and seek to give direction to those with whom we are in touch.

We must continue to act!
We must organize!
We must mobilize!
We must study!

We must read!
We must educate ourselves!

Dear Brother Stanley,
This letter is a continuation of the one I wrote the other day and also deals primarily with the international affairs program especially the Middle East crisis.

. . . Today I had an appointment with Ambassador Maroff of Guinea for one o'clock. It just happened that McKissick and Lincoln Lynch (of CORE) also requested an appointment at the same time. He saw us as a group and then I talked to him privately about some other matters.

McKissick and Lynch were very concerned that certain African nations, especially Guinea and Tanzania, understand why CORE had not come out with a position on the Middle East. They obviously support the position of the Arabs in their fight against imperialism. But, they stated, they felt their organization could not survive in the country if they took a public, anti-Israel position.

Maroff said that any reasonable man could understand this position, but that he was glad we had not made statements in support of Israel as Whitney Young and some others had done. He stated that it was good we were there and he would convey their position to the Chairman of The Arab Delegations so that they would know there are people in the United States, black people, who support their position.

As I write this, I am reminded of something I just read of Julius Nyerere, stating there is a difference between an African state encircled as is Zambia, trying to free itself of the colonial legacy, which therefore has to take a moderate position on certain matters, and the action of Tshombe, which is anti-African unity. I thought of that as I listened to Lynch and McKissick. And I fully understand their position. It is even more complicated because they feel that a pro-Arab stand would split their organization. Since they have been struggling to maintain their anti-war stand and support of Black Power, they obviously have had tremendous internal problems, given the nature of CORE prior to McKissick's arrival. They have struggled and this I know for a fact.

However, I stated to them in front of the Ambassador that I felt the dynamics of the Middle Eastern situation were going to force both CORE and SNCC to take a position. I said that our Central Committee had not met since the crisis but the item was up for discussion. Regardless of whether we take a position, there is an understanding among the progressive nations at the UN through their ambassadors about our concern. Also, we have written from the office a letter to all the Arab countries asking to be put on their mailing lists, asking for information on the formation of Israel, the Palestinian refugee question and the involvement of the United States in the Middle East. We also asked for copies of their speeches. Considering this and the visit we had today, I am sure all the delegates will understand where SNCC and CORE stand privately.

I assure you Martin King has cooked his goose with the African countries by his consistent support of Israel. He would have been much better off if he had not said anything. But given his limitations in perspective and his involvement with the liberal-labor leadership circle, his actions are expected. . . .

Frankly I have not changed my position on the Middle East crisis since I last wrote. A public stand ought not to come before there is a special meeting and education of the staff. I would hate for someone in Alabama to read about the position of the Central Committee and no education on the question. Secondly, I am worried about SNCC's ability to withstand the external pressures. I know we would almost be united internally, but the external pressures would be fantastic, especially in New York. Thirdly, the situation is very muddy in the Middle East and I think we should give some time to see what is going to happen. *One has to be concerned about the wording of any position, for that is a very delicate question given the nature of the governments of some countries.*

When I returned from Africa to the United States in August, I found SNCC under violent attack by many Jews and Zionists. During my absence, SNCC had published a newsletter revealing a pro-Arab position. It was not an official statement of SNCC's stand on the conflict, but a series of questions and some cartoons which indicated support for the Palestinian guerrillas. The material had been hastily edited and the questions were not framed to make the kind of educational presentation desirable—especially for the black movement.

At the same time, the newsletter was not in my opinion anti-Semitic. Furthermore, Ralph Featherstone, program secretary of SNCC, had held a press conference at which he clarified SNCC's position on the Arab-Israeli dispute. But none of this really mattered to some. SNCC had come out in support of the Arabs, as far as the Zionists were concerned, and that was enough.

No formulation of our position would have satisfied the Zionists and many Jews. Leading Jewish organizations had joined others in the liberal-labor syndrome to attack us as too radical back in the days when the subject was not the Middle East but Mississippi. We were too radical then, for not supporting domestic policies of the administration, and we were too radical now—for opposing American foreign policy, for seeing Israel as an imperialist power in the service of, and serving, that policy.

While I supported SNCC publicly for its general position on the Arab-Israeli War, I had my disagreements internally, for I felt that the newsletter was in fact a position and this meant that my counsel to Stanley had been ignored. Furthermore, I felt that as international affairs director I should have been involved in any decision dealing with the Arab-Israeli War. The confusion in lines of responsibility characterized by this action would plague us further in later months. But as I had done in many other situations and decisions, I continued to function, for I knew that we had to support the people of the Arab world in their fight to restore justice to the Palestinian people—regardless of how raggedy the formulation of our position. Our position against Israel, as I saw it, took us one step further along the road to revolution. For SNCC to see the struggle against racism, capitalism, and imperialism as being indivisible made it inevitable for SNCC to take a position against the greatest imperialist power in the Middle East, and in favor of liberation and dignity for the Arab people.

At that time, preparations were being made for one of the largest assemblages of white leftists, black militants, and liberals in the history of the sixties. This was the meeting of the National Conference for New Politics, held in Chicago. Both racism and the Arab-Israeli dispute were likely to be hot items on its agenda. I knew that many elements from the liberal-labor syndrome would be there and that the old question of how that syndrome tries to control or undercut the black revolutionary thrust would probably arise again. It was time to speak out—and sharply—about our own experience. It was time to force a confrontation on some explosive issues.

CHAPTER 61

Blacks Assume Leadership

AT THE huge gathering held by the National Conference for a New Politics on Labor Day weekend of 1967, the issues of self-determination, imperialism, and the role of whites erupted and became traumatic for many. The Arab-Israeli War has already created its conflicts. The increasing insistence of black people that our struggle was against the United States Government, and linked to the worldwide struggle against imperialism in general, upset many of the old arrangements between whites and blacks. The growing awareness that black people must assume leadership in the revolutionary struggle in the United States had also displaced the former power and social relationships. But in any social upheaval there is always a hardening of the lines at first. Later, events move to a new stage. Often circumstances that seem confused, disturbing, and bewildering at one level then blend to produce new forms of struggle on a healthier basis and at a higher level.

The National Conference for a New Politics, originally established as an ad hoc organization, helped to finance the political campaigns of many reformists. In the summer of 1967, it had decided to hold a very large gathering, a convention of diverse people, to find a so-called new direction in politics. There was talk of running Dr. Martin Luther King for president, or Dr. Benjamin Spock for president with Dr. King as his running mate. Whatever the combination, there were many who felt that reform politics had a tremendous value in the political spectrum of the United States. The convention called by the National Conference was supposed to explore these and other possibilities.

After returning from the United Nations Seminar on Racism, Apartheid, and Colonialism, I was invited to speak at a plenary session of the NCNP convention. I thought about it, consulted with my brothers and sisters in SNCC, and finally decided to go. It meant breaking a long silence—I had not spoken in public in the United States since the Philadelphia dynamite case. That silence had given me time in which to analyze my experience, clarify my ideas, study, and grow. Now I felt ready to speak, and I also felt a responsibility to do so. Over four thousand people from all over the United States were expected at the convention and I had some important things to say about the liberation movements in Africa. I owed it to them to spread the word about their struggle and try to get support for it. I also had an analysis of the liberal-labor syndrome that I wanted to present. And, finally, I felt that black leadership of the struggle in the United States must be firmly asserted at the convention—but that this leadership must be revolutionary and not reactionary.

Many people contacted me before the convention, asking what could be done to insure that it produce some meaningful result. One of these persons was Lincoln Lynch of CORE. I suggested that a black caucus be formed both at the planning sessions and the convention itself, in order to separate the black militants from the white liberals who were coming in full force. Discussion of our program could evolve from the caucus. This came to be the strategy adopted.

When I reached Chicago on Friday, September 1, the first day of the convention, I found that the black caucus had split. On the one hand, there was the Black Peoples' Convention that did not want any part of the convention called by the NCNP. Most of the black delegates, however, decided to remain inside the convention structure as a caucus but they were pushing strongly for 50 percent of the voting power and a condemnation of Israel as an aggressive, imperialist power. There were other demands, but these two caused the greatest consternation among the whites present. The convention ushered in a new set of dynamics in relationships between blacks and whites; after it, black caucuses sprang up all over the country demanding 50 percent of all power in relationships with whites. The importance of this demand is that it puts leadership in the hands of the dispossessed, where it belongs.

That Friday night I spoke at the Black Peoples' Convention and the next day before the black caucus. By this time, I had put aside my old habit of speaking from a few notes or none at all, and had begun writing down what I had to say in advance. I called my speech before the black caucus "Profiles in Treachery," although it was not limited to the subject alone.

I began with some remarks about the trip to Africa which I had just made with Howard Moore and then went on to say:

The Liberation groups, especially the African National Congress, indicated to the entire Seminar that they were going to take up arms and fight the illegal regime in South Africa. They said they were not going to fight like our fore-fathers, who threw spears against the white man's rifles. They are going to exchange automatic weapon fire for automatic weapon fire. They have stated that the struggle there will be long and bitter but they will win.

They will win and those of us in this room who are black and talking about New Politics must have one major objective: we must help them win, even if this means that we must take up arms and die in the Southern African Liberation struggle. We cannot any longer be quiet and not show active concern in the face of the death of our brothers at the hands of the brutal white suprema-cists who rule South Africa and other territories comprising Southern Africa, namely Mozambique, Angola, Rhodesia, South West Africa.

The Liberation Movements consider the entire Southern tier of Africa as one, even though different colonial powers occupy and control various coun-tries—the Portuguese in Angola and Mozambique, the white minority called Unilateral Declaration of Independence (UDI) in Rhodesia, the Afrikaners in South Africa. Naturally there is an alliance between all the white Western Powers supporting these dictatorial white regimes. . . .

There are wars of Liberation going on in all these areas and, in the last two weeks, the African National Congress (ANC) and Zimbabwe African Peoples' Union (ZAPU) have decided on a massive direct armed revolutionary struggle against the governments of Rhodesia and South Africa. There is the imminent possibility of the United States sending troops to Southern Africa and espe-cially to South Africa to fight on the side of the Vorster, the Afrikaners, the white Nazis of South Africa. There are more than 15,000 American white Nationals in South Africa and millions of U.S. dollars invested in plants there. Walter Reuther is supposed to have said that the goose gets fatter no matter how much they cut off. The weakness in his analysis is that he fails to realize that General Motors and most other monopoly concerns in the United States are getting fat on the lives of black people in Africa and all over the world. For him and other so-called union leaders to attack the problem of more wages for some but not all American workers, and to participate in the slaughter and murder of our people in South Africa, is in fact for them to make themselves enemies of the people. . . . these unions are not taking the necessary action to halt the investment of United States capital, machinery and buildings in Southern Africa. They are in no sense of the word internationalist, but in fact reactionaries trying to make every American worker, except many of our black brothers, into emerging and satisfied capitalists. They must be considered an enemy of the people.

. . . . There can be no new form of politics unless the people engaged in it are willing to actively support the armed liberation of Southern Africa. There must not only be resolutions demanding the withdrawal of American invest-ments from South Africa and its nationals, but there must be a concerted effort to force this withdrawal. We cannot wait until the cargo planes go with soldiers to protect the White American Nationals and their dollars. We must begin mobilizing now, to neutralize the possibility of the United States intervening as it did in the Congo, in Vietnam, in Santo Domingo, in Cuba! We must make it very difficult for those companies that invest in South Africa. In fact we must punish our enemies by whatever means necessary, including the use of force if they continue to help in the murder of our people.

I also assure you that the white power structure is planning in a deliberate manner to punish the voices that speak out against its imperialism. But it cannot silence all of us and those who live must solemnly swear they will carry on. Remember: from the blood of martyrs flow the seeds of revolution. . . .

Chairman Rap Brown has said that violence is necessary and is as American as cherry pie. That is true. So are revolutions. Remember, this country led the way in breaking away from colonialism by armed revolutionary struggle . . . but no country can really be free if it keeps a large segment of its population in slavery and allows the wealth to be concentrated in a few hands. White America was unable to realize the potential discord of stating on the one hand that all men are free and then forcing those of us who are black to a slave position on the other hand. The discord created by this dichotomy will exist so long as the United States remains an imperialist country sucking the life blood and the profits from people and countries all over the world in order to enjoy the highest standard of living of all mankind. We speak of standard of living in the mechanical sense, the industrial and technological sense; certainly not in the sense of human values, for here the United States is the low man on the totem pole.

I went on in that speech to give an analysis of how the liberal-labor syndrome operates against black militants. Much of that material has already been presented in this book but I also said:

It is absurd to talk of a new form of politics, if in fact history is going to be repeated—the collaboration of young black militants with the liberal-labor white alliance and its Negro counterparts. Also, if there is to be any new brand of politics, it cannot just be based on a peace movement designed to stop wars when they are full-blown. . . .

When we returned from Africa we heard of this convention and some of the trouble the staff was having with some of the white liberals on its board. It became apparent to us that the young black militants who were coming from all over the country were being put unknowingly in a trick, if certain facts about the liberal-labor leadership circle in this country were not made known.

We in SNCC and those in CORE have had our experience with the liberals and the moderate labor wing that believes in coalition politics as a dogma, to the extent that the main exponents in the liberal-labor leadership circle will try to tell black militants there is no organic connection between the war in Vietnam and the so-called Civil Rights Movement in the United States. . . . Even as we talk today, Whitney Young is in Vietnam, protected by the United States government and its soldiers, in order to witness the mockery of so-called free elections in Vietnam. That this Negro consents to allow himself be used by the government is a disgrace to all black people but understandable when one realizes that the Urban League is backed by, among others, the Rockefellers, the strongest capitalists in the world whose interest in the Chase Manhattan Bank and oil is well known.

We in SNCC have been the victims of the liberal-labor circle's lies, their false propaganda, their attempts to destroy our organization, their misleading of the masses of people in this country, and we say *NO*. No longer can we allow young black militants to assemble in the presence of these double-crossing, liberal-labor coalition exponents, both Negro and white, without raising our voice in protest and without telling those who have not experienced what we have experienced the truth about some of the activities of this syndrome, the liberal-labor leadership circle.

Failing to speak out and to inform our black brothers and our white allies, who are also ignorant of the inner workings of this nefarious, undermining, Democratic-party-oriented circle, is in fact to retard the liberation of all black people around the world and especially here in the United States. Make no mistake about it: while they have kept our attention on the internal problems resulting from race in this country, they have been busy exporting the line that the United States is good and that all Negroes in the United States simply want a fair shake at the cream of American society. That is a lie; there are those of us who are black who are bitterly opposed to the policies of the United States government, both internally and internationally. We have a responsibility to inform our brothers and sisters of what has gone down. If we don't then we in fact become a reactionary force.

. . . . It is now necessary to talk about the nature of the leadership of oppressed people. Black people in the United States have undergone the worst form of oppression for the longest time known to mankind, so far as I am concerned. We are a people who have been wrenched from our native continent and dispersed throughout Latin America, the Caribbean and the United States. It is we who have built the great foundations of modern, western society. This is a fact and cannot be refuted. Paris, which is indeed a beautiful city, has been able to survive because of the exploitation of our brothers' labor in Africa. England would certainly not enjoy the position of wealth that it has if it had not been for the colonies she directly controlled and still controls through neo-colonialism. West Germany today is building a new empire through the export of capital and machinery through the world, but let us not forget that Germany had control for a long time of Tangyanika.

I hardly need talk about the exploited labor of all of us who are black and who tilled the fields without pay while the white man reinvested the capital from our labor.

Therefore, even today, here in the United States, we are the lowest class on the economic ladder. We suffer the most from racism. What does this mean? This means that we and we alone have the responsibility to wage our own war of liberation as we see fit to do that, and no one who has not suffered as we have has the right to dictate to us the forms of our struggle. Those of us who will pay with our lives for our liberation must insist upon the right to determine the manner in which we will fight. This is our right. This is our responsibility *and anyone who does not like it can go to hell*.

. . . . The so-called white progressive and radical is still white, and cannot understand fully the impact of racism upon us. He may understand the nature of the class struggle and he may well want to change the system that produces racism. We welcome his help. But he has not experienced the racism we have. For the black militant to abdicate his leadership is to betray a historical role he has to perform. That does not mean the black militant does not look for allies. The mere fact that we are here at this conference gives the lie to the fact that we black militants believe that we can change the system by ourselves, but we must give leadership to our struggle.

There are trade unions and other organizations all over the country supposedly working for the betterment of mankind, yet the leadership of all these unions and many other organizations is primarily white and even in some trade unions there is blatant discrimination. So far as I am concerned, there is only one way to break the stranglehold of conservative union leadership and that is for black men and women who are workers to form black caucuses and demand that they have positions of leadership. . . .

There can be no new concept of politics, no new coalitions, unless those of us who are the most dispossessed assume leadership and give direction to that new form of politics. If this does not happen, we are going to see the same old liberal-labor treachery of very rich white folks and Democratic-party-oriented whites and Negroes trying to determine what they can do for us. The best thing that anyone white can do for us is merely to support that for which we call. If he cannot do this, then we should not despair but tell him to go on his merry way and not get in our path, for we shall liberate him whether he wants it or not.

We must say to all our black brothers: assume leadership. But there are two types of leadership: reactionary and revolutionary. We are talking about revolutionary leadership and that only comes when people are committed to changing the system of economics and the resulting political structures that have kept us in bondage these many years. This is fact, brothers and sisters, and we must not forget it. We must assume leadership in a revolutionary fashion. We must not have black leadership that is striving to make black men capitalists like our exploiters.

Any leadership that does not recognize the legitimacy of revolutionary armed struggle inside and outside the United States is a reactionary leadership and must be replaced.

. . . . If SNCC has contributed nothing else to the cause of the black man's struggle, it certainly has forged a consciousness in all black people that we as a people can do something about our condition and if we don't, no one else will. There is only one thing the man can do to us in SNCC: kill us. We have accepted the possibility of death, for being killed is inherent in taking revolutionary positions. The technical destruction of SNCC is irrelevant, for too many brothers have taken up the cry: Freedom or Death! If all the current activists in SNCC are killed, we will die knowing that we have moved history ahead a few steps. We do not despair or fear the future.

The impact of the speech was tremendous on the already charged black delegates. Meanwhile, inside the main auditorium, whites were debating the demands of black delegates and many could not agree with the demand for 50 percent of the voting power.

All that Saturday, Saturday night, and Sunday morning there were caucuses and meetings. I did not know if I would speak to the plenary session, as I was originally invited to do, or not. That was a decision for the black caucus to make. Chairman H. Rap Brown of SNCC arrived on Saturday night and delivered a dynamic speech to the black caucus. He spoke forcefully about the dispossessed in the United States—the people of African descent, the Puerto Ricans, the Mexican-Americans or Chicanos, Indians, and many poor whites. The development of SNCC's relations with these other groups was advanced at the convention by our first meeting with Reies Lopez Tijerina, president of the Alianza Federal de los Pueblos Libres in New Mexico, a leader of the Chicano struggle for land and justice who would become a political prisoner in June, 1969. A short time after the NCNP meeting, Ralph Featherstone of SNCC would attend an Alianza convention in Albuquerque and confirm a pact between the two organizations.

On Sunday morning it was decided that I should speak at the plenary session, with black people sitting up front, after which the sisters and brothers would leave to let the whites hassle over our demands for 50 percent of the votes and the condemnation of Israel as an imperialist power.

My speech on Sunday morning before the four thousand delegates was widely reported and televised. It was essentially the same as what I had said to the black caucus, but I took the opportunity to read to the entire audience a statement that we had made at the International Seminar on Racism, Colonialism, and Apartheid in support of the ANC and ZAPU guerrillas. The convention then approved it.

Many whites saw me as the symbol of the black defiance at the convention, if not the actual instigator of the 50 percent demand. But this was an absurdity. There were many other people at the convention who had the same ideas and had long been active politically. However, it is true that I was trying hard to assert black leadership. I saw the debate in Chicago that weekend as a justification of the position that SNCC had taken on whites at its Kingston Springs meeting. The role of whites had never before been discussed by whites on such a broad scale and so thoroughly. The intense work that many white people would later do in white communities and on the Vietnam War issue stemmed in part from that NCNP discussion.

The ideas in my speeches before the Black Peoples' Convention, the black caucus, and the entire convention were the forerunners of ideas that I would develop and articulate with more precision in later years. I had struggled for years to find ways in which black people in the United States could deal with racism, class conflicts, and the question of leadership. At the NCNP conference, the need for blacks to assert leadership seemed of special importance. There was also the possible trap of thinking in the year 1968 that electoral politics—the original focus of the NCNP convention—offered a solution to people.

But I was also disturbed by the ideas of many black people who called themselves leaders. Putting a simple label of racism on all our problems and attacking individual whites had led many people astray. I had to use whatever power, experience, and strength I had acquired to help wage the ideological fight against racism, capitalism, and imperialism. Passionate arguments that our problem was purely racism had to be fought in the arena of ideas. But I did not want to confine my fight against these incorrect concepts to SNCC. The whole black liberation movement had to hear some new ideas. This feeling was strongly confirmed by another trip to Africa which I made shortly after the NCNP convention.

CHAPTER 62

The Organization of African Unity

DURING THE summer of 1967, the repression of SNCC chairman H. Rap Brown had begun its steady climb toward the point at which Brown had to go underground to survive. The long and vicious story started in Cambridge, Maryland, on July 24, 1967, when Rap came to speak at the invitation of the local sisters and brothers. Four hours after he had left town, an elementary school which had been condemned twelve years earlier as unfit for human habitation—a school that had been set on fire twice before—was burned for a third time.

Rap had left quickly for Washington, D.C., because he had been shot in the face by a Cambridge deputy sheriff and it seemed safer for him to be elsewhere. A fugitive warrant for his arrest was immediately issued. The charge said "counseling to arson," supposedly because he had commented while in Cambridge, "That school should have been burned down a long time ago," referring to the previous fires. This was made into a federal warrant because he had crossed state lines. It was then arranged by Rap through his attorney, William Kunstler, that he would turn himself in at the FBI headquarters the next morning in New York. This agreement was broken when the FBI arrested him as he arrived by plane in New York.

The FBI took him to Alexandria, Virginia, and jailed him there. The federal government dropped its case a few hours later and Rap walked out of the courthouse—only to find the Alexandria police waiting for him with the original fugitive warrant. After that, he found himself in some fourteen courts in fourteen different parts of the United States, facing every kind of charge and legal harassment. At the same time, he was becoming increasingly popular with our people. His way of speaking, his whole style, has a grass-roots quality that gave him mass appeal. When I heard his famous statement, "Violence is as American as cherry pie.

If America don't come around, we'll burn her down," I knew that a new stage of struggle had been reached in the United States.

It had become clear that the government would go all the way to eliminate Rap Brown from the scene, and SNCC was working hard to combat the repression for which he had been singled out. I myself spent considerable time on this effort. Then, in September of 1967, I saw what seemed to be a new opportunity to build support for Rap. The Organization of African Unity was meeting in Congo Kinshasa that month and I felt it would be of tremendous value if Rap, following in the footsteps of Brother Malcolm several years earlier, could attend this meeting where the heads of state of many African nations would be present.

His name was already widely known in Africa; the newspapers there had carried major stories about the persecution of Rap by the U.S. Government. His personal presence at the OAU meeting could increase international support for him. It would, furthermore, help to cement ties between Africans in the United States—ourselves—and those on the continent. I also felt that attending the meeting would broaden Rap's knowledge of African and world affairs. As our new chairman, he could greatly profit by such an experience.

I was not, of course, happy about the fact that the OAU meeting was being held in Congo Kinshasa. Its history and present situation weighed heavily on the minds of all black revolutionaries. The existence of Congo Kinshasa, we might recall, emerged from the Berlin Conference of 1886 which divided the Congo into two parts—Congo Kinshasa becoming the "property" of Belgium and Congo Brazzaville the "property" of France. In 1960 the Belgian sector had become officially independent. Then the French Congo also became independent of France and began moving far to the left of Congo Kinshasa. Belgium continued to reassert its authority in the Congo by fomenting a civil war in which Moise Tshombe led the reactionary forces. The United Nations was called in to suppress that war and its intervention proved disastrous for the government of Patrice Lumumba, who was killed. By 1967 General Mobutu had for all practical purposes suppressed the progressive forces engaged in armed struggle. But white mercenaries in the pay of right-wing Belgian and Portuguese forces continued to harass the Mobutu government.

Shortly before the OAU conference was scheduled to begin, the mercenaries were still fighting in the Congo and many people feared that the conference might be disrupted by this turmoil. But eventually they were driven out of Congo Kinshasa and the 1967 OAU meeting would be held without that problem.

I was generally aware of this history, and acutely aware of the murder of Lumumba. Although I realized that neither the Congo Kinshasa nor the OAU could be considered revolutionary and although I had no illusions about the unity of opinion among African states or their freedom from Western political influence, I still thought it would be worth an effort to get H. Rap Brown to the conference. The tremendous impact of the 1967 black rebellions and the widespread attention given to Rap's actions and words might, I thought, have created a climate in which the OAU could give him some diplomatic recognition. I believed that there would be delegates at the conference favorable to the black struggle in the United States. Then, too, I knew that we Africans in the U.S. had to make every effort to link our struggle with the African continent. No stone should remain unturned in our effort to win support for Rap Brown, the victim of brutal repression by the American Government.

Although I had no official invitation to the OAU meeting, I knew that Bob and Dona Moses had attended a similar one in Accra, Ghana, in 1965 as representatives of SNCC and there was also Malcolm's attendance at an OAU meeting. It seemed possible to make some kind of arrangement for Rap to be invited, once I got to Africa. The desperate need to win international support for him made me think it was worthwhile at least to try this. So it was decided that I would go ahead, while Rap obtained his passport. Several different people promised to make the trip with me, but at the last minute I had to leave alone.

When my plane landed in Kinshasa, there was a protocol officer at the airport to meet some arriving delegates. I introduced myself and explained my situation, and he agreed to take me to a downtown hotel where the delegates were staying. He doubted, however, that I would be able to get a room since all available rooms had been assigned to the OAU. He was right.

I immediately went to the large white building where the OAU was meeting. It was heavily guarded and no one without a pass could enter. I stood outside the entrance gate, explaining my situation in French to people who entered. Finally one brother brought a press registration blank back to me at the gate. I explained that I was not a member of the press, but by this time another brother who had heard of my predicament came and took me inside with him so that I could go to the protocol office of the conference.

Once inside the building, I saw many people I had met in Kitwe, Zambia, especially representatives of liberation movements in Angola, Zimbabwe, Mozambique, and others. They explained that they were having difficulties with the OAU themselves, for even they were not allowed to attend sessions. They had only the "privilege" of standing in the halls and talking to delegates as they entered and left the meetings or stood around in the halls. They could not even attend those sessions at which the liberation movements in Southern Africa were discussed. The best they could do was to present papers that would be read to the meeting by someone else. I thought this absurd.

The Organization of African Unity was a mockery. This became even more apparent as I talked to some of the delegates later. Many complained about the tight grip that the conservative nations had on the OAU.

Several protocol officers with whom I spoke told me that my presence at the conference was a political problem. One, from the Congo, wanted to make sure that my organization was not illegal in the United States. "We have good relations with the United States," he said frankly, "and we receive a lot of aid from them. We have to be careful about political people from the United States." He further explained that there was a company of United States troops, including blacks and whites, stationed near the Kinshasa airport to help the Congo Government if they were needed.

His remarks explained why, when still standing out at the gate, I had seen a car marked "United States" and flying an American flag drive through the gate and the two people in it then enter the building where the Organization of African Unity was meeting. The United States was not a member of the OAU in any capacity, but still its officials were allowed the privilege of entering the meeting at will. Apparently officials of the United States could enter where liberation movement spokesmen of Africa could not. But this was Congo Kinshasa and the United States has a great hold on its economy.

I finally met with Diallo Telli of Guinea, the secretary-general of the OAU. He indicated that I could not get any kind of official status at the meeting but that no one would remove me from the halls of the building. I then requested time for Rap Brown to speak, knowing full well by now that it was hopeless. Diallo Telli explained that only issues raised at the meeting of ministers of foreign affairs from OAU member nations, which met two weeks before every OAU meeting, could be presented. He added that, at meetings of the OAU, the host country had the right to invite special guests to attend the sessions. That explained to me the presence of the United States officials. Clearly, we would not get any kind of help from the Congo Kinshasa Government at this time.

The Congo protocol officer who had explained the realities of the Congo's relationship to the United States did find me a place to stay. At first he had indicated he would take me to a hotel downtown, but decided against that since I would be exposed to the press and the Congo Government didn't want any press to know that I was at the meeting. I was then taken to a hotel on the outskirts of town, far from the meeting.

After the first day, I cabled Rap suggesting it best not to come. It would have been a security problem for us, for if they were nervous about me, then I imagined they would have had real jitters about H. Rap Brown. As it turned out, Rap could not have come in any case because the United States Government would not give him a passport.

During the next four days I availed myself of the opportunity to talk—

508 THE MAKING OF BLACK REVOLUTIONARIES

privately—with many people from various countries. I gave them SNCC's position paper on the recent guerrilla actions in Zimbabwe and copies of material we had presented at the United Nations Seminar in Kitwe, Zambia. They were very interested. I circulated among the delegates a SNCC petition in support of the guerrillas fighting in Zimbabwe (Southern Rhodesia) and another calling for the release of Ambassador Achmar Maroff from Guinea, who was at that time detained in the Ivory Coast (Guinea had wanted to send troops through the Ivory Coast to Ghana after the coup against Nkrumah).

I also discussed with various delegates the idea of the Afro-American Skills Bank which Howard Moore and I had first raised on our trip to East Africa. There were some specific, positive responses from them. But in the months after my return to the United States from the OAU, none of these responses materialized into concrete action. For reasons which will probably remain a diplomatic mystery, the program was held in abeyance by the African countries involved. Some African officials have indicated that we did not follow up with enough vigor. This might be true, but the idea is a sound one and is being carried out in 1970 in various forms, especially through the Pan African Skills Bank sponsored by the National Committee of Black Churchmen. Both President Kaunda of Zambia and President Nyerere of Tanzania have consistently voiced their approval of having Africans from the United States work for a period of time in those countries.

After five days, I left the OAU meeting because it seemed unwise for me to spend too much time in the country where Lumumba had been killed—and which was now under the control of many of his killers. As I returned to the United States, the full impact of my hasty trip struck me very forcefully. I had not, before going to Congo Kinshasa, realized fully the impotence of the OAU and the degree to which it was controlled by conservative African states—themselves, in turn, controlled by the imperialist powers. The degree to which the United States has extended its power throughout the world could still surprise me. Reading about imperialism and neocolonialism is never, I realized once again, the same as watching those forces operate firsthand.

The complexities of nation building, the reality of changing a former colony into a truly independent country, is often a bewildering process. If one does not have a clear ideological position, the African reality will often produce a distorted perception. Bourgeois nationalism is the trap waiting for everyone who lacks that position, especially those of us in the United States who are of African descent. The need to fight against the bourgeois nationalists, who bury the issue of exploitation under the rallying cry of nationalism, was becoming ever more apparent to me. My studies of Frantz Fanon were of particular help in this.

Although I had thought and talked about reactionary nationalism before, especially in my speech to the black caucus of the NCNP, it was when I got back from my trip to the OAU meeting that I started a full-fledged campaign against it. Ideas about class and race that I had been developing over the years received full treatment in a speech that I gave in Los Angeles on Thanksgiving weekend. It was entitled "Liberation Will Come from a Black Thing."

CHAPTER 63

Liberation Will Come from a Black Thing

AFTER MY return to the United States from the OAU, I was asked to deliver the keynote address at the Western Regional Youth Conference in Los Angeles, California, during the so-called "Thanksgiving" weekend of 1967. Over eight hundred black youths attended that conference as delegates from schools in the western part of the United States. The impetus for it stemmed from the Black Power conference held in Newark the preceding summer, and the Western Regional Youth Conference was perhaps one of the most meaningful results of the Newark conference. Plans for black athletes to boycott the 1968 Olympics in Mexico City were also formalized that Thanksgiving weekend.

When I was told the theme of the conference—Liberation Will Come from a Black Thing—I pondered how to give depth to its meaning and a formulation that could stand the test of time. By now I was deeply involved in a serious study of the works of Fanon—not just a one time reading but a reading and a rereading. In his essay "Concerning Violence" in the *Wretched of the Earth*, I found a passage that shaped the poem I wrote to introduce my speech: "Decolonization is the veritable creation of new men. But this creation owes nothing of its legitimacy to any supernatural power; the 'thing' which has been colonized becomes man during the same process by which it frees itself."

In preparing my speech, I also decided to take this opportunity to present some views not usually heard from speakers in the black movement—views that had to become popular if we were going to move toward liberation. I knew my ideas on class and race were not shared by all and I felt that my speech in Los Angeles should open a campaign to wage an ideological struggle in the public arena concerning the fundamental nature and causes of our oppression in the United States. In addition, I wanted to indicate certain directions that would help to sustain us in the future. Here are parts of the speech, delivered on November 23:

Brothers and Sisters:

On behalf of the Student Nonviolent Coordinating Committee I should like to thank the coordinators for inviting me to this conference. I think we should give Brother Jahid, Brother Crook, Sister Blake, and all the rest a resounding Thank You for their work. H. Rap Brown is not here because he is a political prisoner on the island of Manhattan, and that is part of a plan to isolate voices of black people that are opposed to the Government of the United States. Brother Snelling has said that one way the man destroys a people is to kill off its leaders. That is true, but in a movement well grounded in the masses, there must always be others to rise when one falls. Rap Brown sends you his greetings.

I have prepared a poem for this conference, based on its theme. I should like to dedicate it to Ruby Doris Robinson, the former Executive Secretary of SNCC, who died of a rare blood disease at the age of 25, and who had been involved with SNCC since she was seventeen years old. She was my ace boon coon. I should also like to dedicate it to Huey Newton and all the unsung heroes of the rebellions since Watts, 1964.

LIBERATION WILL COME FROM A BLACK THING

They are outright racists.
They are too militant.
They will push us to counteract violence.
They do not understand.
They seem to be anti-Semitic.
They used to be wonderful.
They used to talk to us.
They look at us with funny eyes today.
They have just gone too far.
They want to tear up the country.
They do not understand it takes time.
They are hurting their cause.
They are communists.
They are violent.
They.
They.
They.
Rap Brown.
Stokely Carmichael.
Huey Newton.
Ron Karenga.
LeRoi Jones.
The Student Nonviolent Coordinating Committee.
Non-Student Violent Committee.
Black Power.
Black Panthers.
SNCC.
RAM.

Self Defense.
Newark.
Watts.
Detroit
Black Power Convention.
No whites allowed.
National Conference on New Politics.
They.
They.
They.
They have gone mad.
Insane.
And down in Los Angeles they talking 'bout liberation will come from
    a black thing.
What thing?
What kind of thing is this?
It's us.
We, them there things.
Remember.
Your shoe shine boy, all stooped over rubbing your feet and shuffling
    mine.
It's us.
Remember.
Standing in your kitchen, all pretty and fine while I don't have no
    time to stay in mine.
It's us.
Remember.
Down in Alabama, across in Mississippi, all through Texas, even out
    here in California,
U.S.A., can't make a dime, just hanging around loving and fighting
    my women all the time.
It's us.
Remember.
We your soldiers.
Fought in all dem wars.
Brother Crispus Attucks the one to fall first.
And now you got me fighting against my own kind—Santo Domingo,
    Vietnam, Congo.
Dontcha hear me.
Hell No.
Not this time!
It's us.
And don't you forget it.
The youngbloods.
We ain't got nothing to lose. All these books ain't right. You been
    teaching me wrong. Now I'm trying to keep my mind on taking
    care of business, not go into business.
My folks are out there, been there, but you fooled me; you kept tell-
    ing me I was an individual, I had democratic rights, personal
    freedom, esthetic sensibilities, a sense of perspective, rationality,
    a profound primitive instinctual capacity, to remain the thing,
    praying to your god, making money for you, fighting your wars,
    killing my people.

It's us.
All of us.
We, the things.
Transformed.
Dig it.
Standing tall.
The Man.
The Woman.
All uptight.
Together.
Now, what you gonna do with your thing?

LIBERATION WILL COME FROM A BLACK THING
The only correct way to discuss those words is in a historical context. Too often we look at an event, a situation, a slogan, a life history, a rebellion, a revolution and assume that its present characteristics have always been its past. For instance, in Vietnam we see a heroic struggle occurring in which the Vietnamese people are using revolutionary armed force to repel their aggressors. Sometimes we fail to understand that the South Vietnamese had a policy of self-defense for at least four years—from 1955 to 1960—before they engaged in offensive armed struggle to liberate their country from the repression of the Diem regime and its United States backers.

When the student movement started in February, 1960, many of the activists thought they had begun the black revolution. Many of us failed to understand the historical conditions which produced us and the actions we were taking against segregation in this country, especially, the Deep South.

While it is beyond the limits of my time to go into a long discussion of the history of our people, it is absolutely essential to see our history as one of resistance. Our ancestors began to resist enforced slavery long before they left the shores of Africa. Those of our brothers who sold their kin into slavery found that there was resistance in the interior of Africa. The captured African did not voluntarily go to the shores of Africa and willingly board the slave ships that brought our forefathers to this alien land. They resisted in Africa.

They resisted the moment they were wrenched from the shores of Africa.
They resisted on the high seas.
They resisted in Virginia, Texas, Mississippi, South Carolina, whenever they were forced to work as slaves building the so-called great white civilization of the United States and the Western World.

We must resist today!
We must continue, at every step of the ladder of our liberation, to view those previous rungs as battles which we fought, as battles for which we paid dearly in our blood, sacrifice and toil, as battles which we could not win unless those below were willing to resist, dead though they may be, unknown, unsung, many of them names no one knew. But they resisted and they died in the liberation struggle.

Those of us who live are obligated to keep the unknown martyrs before our consciousness and to dedicate ourselves to more resistance until there are no more rungs of resistance, no more ladders of resistance, but only the ravines, the fields, the mountains, the inner cities and streets of revolution.

The opposite of resistance is accommodation. It is certainly true today that many of our people are accommodating themselves to the system of capitalism in which we live. Personally, I do not view much of the history of our people as accommodation. There may have been a few who accommodated themselves to slavery, a few informers. But our basic history is one of resistance. After the Emancipation Proclamation, a neo-slavery was created and again there were some who accommodated themselves. But the period of Reconstruction, the Niagara movement, the Garvey movement and most of the civil rights movement must be seen in my opinion as the history of a people who were and are resisting neo-slavery.

It is true that much of the visible leadership in the past has often been characterized as accommodating leadership, but I am not discussing just the visible leadership. I am talking about the masses of our people and they have never accommodated themselves to the United States.

And it is among the masses that our youth must work.

Only from the masses of Black people will there come revolutionary leadership, a leadership that will not accommodate itself, that will continue to resist as our ancestors resisted, a leadership that will not mind dying for the independence and freedom not only of blacks but of all the oppressed.

For those of us who consider ourselves freedom fighters, it is imperative that we view our history in this manner, a history of resistance, not of accommodation. It is imperative that we realize that our culture and our people have been able to resist in order to survive and to make it possible for us to deal more death blows to our oppressors.

Why have I devoted so much time to interpreting our history as one of resistance? There are several reasons. First, I assume all of us have certain factual knowledge of our history and those of us who do not will soon acquire that. But I am convinced that many of us have not interpreted those facts correctly. Certainly my interpretation is open to debate, a debate in which I am prepared to engage. Secondly, I am convinced that a faulty interpretation of our history is often damaging to our cause.

For instance, Johnny Wilson, a member of SNCC, recently attended a conference in Czechoslovakia where there were many representatives of the National Liberation Front and the government of the Democratic Republic of North Vietnam. The Vietnamese there assembled, people who are fighting and dying daily by the hundreds for their freedom, asked the American representatives to sing the song, "We Shall Overcome." They stated that they had sung the song often, for it gave them inspiration and hope. One of the brothers from Newark attending the conference, who may or may not have participated actively in the rebellion, jumped up and said: "No. We don't sing that song. The people who sang that song were crazy. They were nonviolent and we ain't."

The Vietnamese were stunned. They are not crazy for singing it and I do not think all of us who sang it were crazy. People do not sing it today for many reasons. But the brother from Newark was only in Prague because there was a historical relationship between his presence there and the manner in which he got there. I am well aware that my presence here is due to many factors but if it had not been for the people who sang "We Shall Overcome," there is no question in my mind that I would not be here today.

To view our history as one of resistance is to recognize more clearly the colonial relationship that we have with the United States. Traditionally, when one thinks of colonialism, images of foreign powers occupying another land and subjecting its people are the kinds of mental pictures we frame. But our own colonial status is unique in that we are the descendants of people enslaved and transplanted into a colonial status. The rhetoric, the false claims, the meaningless phrases, all these try to tell us that we are citizens. We are Americans. I will not dwell on the absurdity of that, for we all know too well that the internal rebellions in this country, led by Watts, would not occur if in fact that was the case.

The serious conditions in which we find ourselves as a people demand that we begin talking more of the colonized and the colonizer. If we begin to use those terms more, and to describe their inner workings, especially the economic base on which colonialism is founded and the industrial military complex of Western countries which sustain it, we shall definitely advance the cause of our liberation.

Any colonized people are exploited people. But all exploited people are not colonized. That is to say, we can have in certain situations, as we do in many countries around the world, people exploited because of their class positions in society. Within the United States there are many exploited whites, but they are not colonized. In most instances, they form a part of the colonizing group. . . . When Fanon says we must stretch the Marxist analysis when we look at colonial situations, he is referring to this condition, even though he didn't explain it.

Unless my historical understanding is incorrect, the colonial relationships since the fifteenth century have all involved white Europeans and their American white descendants colonializing the darker people of the world. Therefore race is intimately involved in the colonizing experience.

My own experience in various situations with my brothers and sisters has led me to conclude that it is necessary to view ourselves in these terms, the colonized and the colonizer, if we are not to fall into the trap of seeing the cause of our problems as merely skin causes, black skin versus white skin. A purely skin analysis of the cause and continuing responsibility for our condition is not only theoretically incorrect but, because it is theoretically incorrect, it will lead to some serious mistakes in programming.

When we view our colonial situation in the United States, it is easy, it is emotionally satisfying at times, and it may be the first step in nationalism—which we must promote—to view the cause as solely one of skin. But if our analysis remains there and if we do not work to broaden our understanding, we are headed for a trick, a frustrating pit of despair.

A purely skin analysis, for instance, makes it very difficult to guard against reactionary nationalism. For instance, Dr. Hasting Banda of Malawi would undoubtedly and without question tell you that he is an African nationalist. A man with black skin, yet he visits Taiwan, tells us the United States is right in Vietnam, and is willing to open diplomatic relations with South Africa.

There is an aspect of our colonial experience which we often fail to examine, to look at, to determine its meaning for today and tomorrow, and which may help to shed light on the skin analysis. Hence, too often we overlook that our enslavement involved a duality—an alliance by some of our African ancestors with white slavers. The ruling class of many African territories and nations, the African victors in many skirmishes and wars with other Africans, cooperated with the white ruling classes and their merchants to get us to this country. This examination should in no way imply that I do not place the greatest burden upon Western Civilization for our enslavement, but I do not think it does much good to overlook that many Africans were willing to make a profit off of our bodies.

Today in many instances we see similar situations—exploitation of blacks by blacks, especially in parts of Africa, and I could call a list of those countries, and here in the United States. This exploitation has its own historical roots, and any effective programming which we will do in the future must take it into account. A more profound analysis of this problem, the cooperation of the ruling-class Africans with the white slave merchants, has been made by a young historian, Walter Rodney, whom we met in Tanzania.

Brothers and Sisters, bold analysis of the last six or seven paragraphs of this paper places into sharp focus three ways of looking at the fundamental causes of our problems: One, we can take the position that says we are exploited solely because of our skin color. This I call the exclusive skin analysis. Two, we can take a second position that says our exploitation is solely due to our class position in this society. This I call the exclusive class analysis. We can take a third position that says that our exploitation results both from class positions as well as from our race. Given all that I said, it is obvious that I hold to the third position.

The absolute necessity for me to raise this as a discussion item arises from my own experience within the movement. Once during a discussion with one of my brothers, I used the word *Marxian*. He jumped up and pounded on the table and yelled: "But Mother fucker, Marx was not a black. He was not black, do you hear! He was a white writer."

Just recently we have come through some painful discussions in the New York area and we have seen some very deep tensions in the black community resulting from conflicts on this issue. For instance, the march on the Pentagon was advertised in the *Inner City Voice*, a revolutionary journal that started in Detroit after the rebellion. This journal called upon blacks to join the confrontation at the Pentagon. In the meantime, there had been all sorts of discussion among some black militants on the East Coast as to what should be the relationship of black militants to the March. The brothers and sisters from Detroit did not know about these conflicts and therefore came to Washington to participate in the demonstration. They wanted the National Liberation Front, so they said, to know that there were blacks opposed to the war. However, at the march they were torn asunder because there were brothers and sisters who began to say: "Black people are not relating to that thing. That's a white thing." And one so-called spokesman for a Black Power Committee said: black people are interested in their communities. The whites started this war so let them end it. We're tired of marching. We're headed for a black thing and that thing don't include marching on the Pentagon. We're concerned, this Black Power spokesman said, about the cutbacks in the Poverty program. We want jobs and better communities.

Within SNCC today, we are discussing revolutionary Black Power as opposed to reactionary Black Power, for we have seen instances where conservative forces have tried to explain away or excuse the revolutionary aspect of Black Power. But an understanding of what is meant by revolutionary Black Power hinges on how one sees the fundamental causes of our condition today. From this analysis will flow many things and many decisions and many ways of solving our problem.

Within the concept of the colonized we must begin to speak more of the dispossessed. It must be clearly understood that the nature of the colonial experience is that racism is inherent in all its manifestations. Even though the dispossessed unite with the dispossessed, or even if the exploiters who are responsible for the colonizing are kicked out, the legacy of racism and remnants of the colonial experience remain and must be uprooted. The Chinese are saying, in part through their cultural revolution, that even though one eliminates the structural forms of capitalism, there are capitalistic ideas and thoughts that still remain and must be combatted. . . .

It is our job to go forth from this conference using whatever means necessary to liberate ourselves and other oppressed people, not only in the United States but throughout the world. In order to do this, we must wage an unrelenting struggle against racism and the exploitation of Man. We must work, not for ourselves, but for the unborn generations that will carry humanity and our people to new heights, to a world without racism, to a world of no more resistance but only a community of concern. For this world we must be prepared to fight and to die. And we must believe that we will win. We must believe that our fight and our deaths are not in vain.

How do we organize and what do we organize? One year ago, within SNCC, we called for the formation of all-inclusive political units, independent of the Democratic and Republican parties. We have called for the formation of the Freedom Organizations. You can choose any name, so long as it is an independent political organization that will service the needs, the total needs of the people. . . . It is up to us, those of us with the commitment to total change, with energy and time, to go to the masses and organize them to do this work. One may well speak of revolution, but unless there is day-to-day, block-to-block, city-to-city and nationwide organizing, there can be no fundamental changes in our lives. Those of us who consider ourselves politically hep, those of us who feel we have a consciousness, those of us who are prepared to take care of business—must recognize that unless there is mass participation by black people in efforts to bring about revolution, then that revolution will not occur. No matter how long we talk about it, rhetoric is not a substitute for work.

And as we work in the inner cities and in the rural areas we must be prepared to guard against the sabotaging of our work, the infiltration of our cadres, by the FBI and the CIA and local police agents. We must not allow the McClellan Committee, the Eastland Committee, the House Un-American Activities Committee, to isolate SNCC, to destroy the Panthers, to arrest and imprison other militants. . . . We have to build visible defense committees and link all the militants in some confederation so that it will be more difficult to isolate and destroy any of us. Inner city newspapers must be established to provide alternative methods of communication, for all of us know that the man is not going to print anything but negative news of our movement.

Finally, we must protect our brothers and sisters, and even as I say this there are some brothers in jail about whom there is not much active concern because we have allowed our own internal contradictions to divide us. This brother may not have done something the way some brothers would have done it. Therefore, he is left isolated. And to the degree that this occurs, all of us stand to be destroyed. Granted that the forward thrust of the movement cannot be stopped, it can be halted and set back. Time and energy, the two most important assets we have, can be uselessly spent if we are not immediately responsive to a crisis or even to take legal action in behalf of brothers that are arrested. This last point cannot be overstressed, for the man is picking up brothers all over the country and sometimes there is no response to their arrest. This is not the case with respect to visible symbols of leadership. Stokely Carmichael, Rap Brown, and so forth and so on and maybe even myself. But it must also be true for the man behind the mimeograph sheet or the one who is taking care of business. In other words, we have to work to eliminate the class bias that is often apparent in many of our organizations and efforts. . . .

Now I want to discuss several things that we must do to counteract possible attempts to destroy us by the man. The first thing we must do is to stop all this loose talk, to keep our mouths shut. Because cats are sitting around doing loose talk and the man is gathering information and intelligence. The man is piecing together all this loose talk and making up conspiracy charges and what have you. . . . I know this is what happened with the Statue of Liberty case, because Policeman Woods was the man who conceived of the idea, pushed the brothers into it by making them feel guilty because they weren't militant enough, arranged for the dynamite, took a brother to pick it up and then testified against them in court. The result was they served three and one-half years and Woods is still free. That is a fact and you'd better read about the Statue of Liberty case before you go out every night talking about the revolution with any and everyone.

The second thing deals with these research programs. I have been gathering some intelligence on them and I have discovered that in one city, Detroit, three researchers with some money talked to over 250 brothers who discussed details of the rebellion, plans and stages for future activity. The researchers have taken the material back to the foundation. What do you think that it has done with it? Obviously the man has it. This has happened all over this country. Immediately during and after the rebellion, you saw brothers talking to television cameras saying what they're going to do soon as the National Guard pulls out. They are just selling wolf tickets and giving out information on themselves. The man has an intelligence file on everybody. And he has gotten that information in part because we have been running off at the mouth cooperating with some research project about a rebellion. You don't describe a rebellion until after it's all over.

The third question deals with rumor mongering. For the last two or three weeks I've gotten telephone calls from people saying that this person or that person is "the man" and when I check it out, there doesn't seem to be much basis in fact for the kinds of rumors that are spreading. Such evidence as "this chick looks funny or she talks funny." I am not saying that there are no informers. There are enough FBI and CIA agents, even in this room, that we don't know about. We do not need to make the situation worse by spreading rumors that have no foundation based on facts and reality. One must check out these things before fingering a person.

What is the danger of rumor spreading? The danger is that the man uses this as a divisive technique. He wants to create suspicion, he wants to divide and conquer, he wants to put the finger on cats by spreading ill-founded rumors. This has happened all over Africa. Liberation fighters have had to combat suspicions placed on them by the fingers of the man. And if we give in to this type of rumor mongering, we are contributing to that type of activity.

The fourth thing which is extremely important deals with splitting activities. As Brother Snelling said, "Everybody's black." Blackness is granted; it may not be sufficient, but certainly it is granted. But the reality is that the man is wearing Afros today, he is wearing dashikis. You dig it? He's wearing them. I've seen them in the crowds. When we were in Philadelphia on the so-called dynamite frame-up case, a cop, of whom we were suspicious and had not seen for weeks, came around in a dashiki and a turban identifying with the masses. The brothers easily identify with me because I'm wearing a buba, the other brother is over there clean and taking care of business. See, we're in a trick. We have to watch out for this kind of activity because it is happening all over. That is why the man has so much intelligence in Harlem, because he has gone in there on that kind of basis and he's doing it everywhere else and we have to watch out. . . .

Remember, this government will use any means to control the upsurge of insurrectional activity coming from the inner city and we must not help him. We just do not have the time to fight among ourselves. The masses get bewildered and they are not willing to go out on the streets if they feel they have to fight with brothers. . . . We must understand, brothers and sisters, that this is going to happen time and time again—situations where we will be unnecessarily provoked will occur.

Brothers and sisters, I am going to close. But I want to emphasize that we have brought a lot of information in papers to this conference and we urge you to go back to your campuses and get this material distributed. Get your student activities office to stencil this material and you can pass it out. Do you realize that most books don't sell over 10,000 copies? When we mimeograph 15,000 copies of something we are beating Random House. What difference does it matter if it is not printed by one of the New York publishing houses?

We have got to work. I am old and I know that, but I also know that most cats are shucking and jiving. They simply do not want to do any work. They want to sit down and talk about how black I am and how bad the man is, but they will not even get up and raise a quarter for a black organization.

Now I ain't going into no cultural historical analysis of that. It ain't nothing but out-and-out laziness.

Finally, we must be concerned about the future. It is a trap to think in terms of our lives. Do you think that if those North Vietnamese soldiers were worried about their lives, they would put up the fight that they do at Dak To hill? And if you are too worried, you are again expressing individualism. You are not concerned with the future. When you are not worried about your life and you are concerned about the future, concerned about all the unborn Huey Newtons, all the unborn Emmett Tills and Charles Mack Parkers and Sammy Younges and Ruby Doris Robinsons, and when you are concerned about your own children, then you are ready to take care of business. And you ain't got no business having any children if you ain't gonna fight for their freedom.

Thank you.

The reaction to this speech was tremendously positive. Many people printed and widely distributed it. I felt that the ideological points raised in it were not only correct but had to be further refined and propagated. Within SNCC, most people had arrived at the position I articulated in this speech but debate continued over what we were fighting for. There was an emerging agreement that we were fighting against racism, capitalism, and imperialism, but a consensus on the type of world that we wanted to see built after the destruction of the United States as an imperialist power had not crystallized.

This conflict was reflected in the problems that SNCC had with Stokely Carmichael, and Carmichael was certainly one of those to whom key parts of that speech were addressed. This situation must be explained in some detail, not as an indulgence in personality problems but for its historical and political lessons.

I had first met Stokely in Nashville in 1961 at the Southern Student Leadership Conference sponsored by the National Student Association when I was still a teacher in Chicago. Stokely had just been released from Parchman Penitentiary in Mississippi for participation in a Freedom

Ride. As mentioned earlier, my students and I had sent a letter of support to James Farmer, also behind the bars of Parchman then. Stokely told me in Nashville that the letter had been the only one received by the jailed group, and that Farmer had read it aloud. I felt very good about this news, and Stokely and I began to develop a warm friendship that grew in the years that followed.

While I was serving as executive secretary of SNCC and involved in its field work from 1961 to 1964, Stokely was a student at Howard University and participating in the Nonviolent Action Group, an affiliate of SNCC's. When plans for the Mississippi Summer Project were being drawn up, Moses encouraged Stokely to bring some students down from Howard University as volunteers on the project. He did so, and that summer he himself held the important post of district director of the Second Congressional District, with headquarters in Greenwood. We saw each other from time to time but had no extensive contact.

That fall, when SNCC's problems of internal disorder began rising to a crisis level, I had many talks with Stokely and often urged him to take more leadership in the discussion. The failure of SNCC people to do this, a weakness that I have mentioned before, was puzzling in the case of Stokely because he had experience and was very articulate. We did have many debates in private at that time, particularly on the subject of pot smoking, which was becoming a major problem in SNCC.

Some time before the Kingston Springs meeting, where I planned to announce my intention not to serve any longer as executive secretary, Carmichael stated that he would run for chairman with the goals of working to strengthen SNCC internally and to lift some of the weight off my shoulders. His statements to me about his willingness to work inside the organization—a quality lacking in John Lewis—were very appealing. He also sided with me at that time on the black-white issues that beset the organization. I thought he would make a good chairman—he had field experience, many good ideas, and the ability to express them well—so I voted for him. There were others who had worked with Carmichael on a day-to-day basis and who were opposed to his election but failed to express their feeling and the reason for it in the open meeting. Only later did I learn of their objections.

During Stokely's year as chairman, SNCC had no ideology to provide him with guidelines in the many public statements he made. We were still struggling for direction. As a result, Stokely was left free to say whatever he liked. He made public statements in what was almost a vacuum—statements that often did not reflect positions adopted by the organization. At one point, Ruby Doris Robinson introduced a motion to silence him for six months; she felt that his statements favoring armed struggle and other violent acts brought down too much heat on the field organizers and general repression on black people. Ruby Doris believed we should organize quietly for armed struggle rather than preach it constantly and openly. But this motion was tabled after much discussion.

At first I did not pay much attention to Stokely's public statements—which was an error—but then I began to listen to him in the spring of 1967 when the term *honky* became common in his speeches. I felt that this was creating a polarization of the struggle around the single issue of race rather than class and race. At that time, I had been appointed by him to serve as one of three organizational secretaries assisting the chairman, and I spoke to him about my concern privately during the May, 1967, staff meeting. His response was that "the blood on the street will kill you if you talk about class."

I talked with him at length about the function of leadership and its obligation to raise consciousness. I disagreed with his belief that "the blood on the street" would not respond to a discussion of capitalism as an oppressive force. I felt Stokely could at least talk about the honky banker, the honky landlord, the honky capitalist. This discussion formed part of the long debate we had been having in SNCC over race and class, but now resolution of the conflict was particularly important for we needed to build a platform from which Carmichael could speak without creating confusion and internal antagonism.

That conversation with Carmichael, together with many other conflicts at the May, 1967, staff meeting, exposed the sharp differences in ideology and leadership concepts that had developed between Carmichael and myself. This development was an important factor in my decision to begin speaking for SNCC and to introduce—as at the Los Angeles youth conference—some new ideas in the black movement that would advance us from the exclusively racial analysis dominating the speeches of Stokely and other black leaders. My decision was strengthened by Stokely's speech at the OLAS (Organization of Latin American States) conference in Havana in July, 1967.

In that speech, he did speak of imperialism and its effects, and I was glad for that. I hoped that his travels abroad were giving his thought a new direction; I also hoped he was not just being opportunistic and making the kind of speech he thought the Cubans wanted to hear. But other parts of the speech disturbed me in a very concrete way, in particular when he stated that until the cry for Black Power, our people in the United States had "coexisted" with capitalism. I, as well as others in SNCC, felt that this was an entire negation of the slave revolts, of the long history of black resistance.

When Carmichael returned to the United States, after visiting not only Cuba but also Algeria, Guinea, Tanzania, Syria, and North Vietnam, the criticism of his OLAS speech and other public statements made on that trip was fully aired. Many staff members of SNCC, including its officers, wanted to expel him in the fall of 1967. For there were not only the problems with his statements but the basic fact that his entire trip had not been authorized by SNCC's overseas trip committee, consisting of H. Rap Brown, Ralph Featherstone, and myself. Carmichael made arrangements to go to OLAS entirely on his own, while away on an approved trip to London. He did so despite the fact that the overseas trip committee had appointed two others to represent SNCC at the OLAS meeting and we had prepared a position paper for that meeting. And he went on from Cuba to the other countries I have mentioned despite the fact that Executive Secretary Stanley Wise and others told him by telephone to Havana to return to the United States immediately.

That sequence of actions by Stokely was a serious violation of organizational discipline. In addition, Carmichael had placed SNCC's director of international affairs—myself—in a very awkward position. He had gone traveling around the world and involving himself in international affairs while the director of that department had no idea where he was going next or what he would say.

Nevertheless, I argued against expulsion on the grounds that the masses of black people would see it as similar to the Malcolm X-Elijah Muhammed dispute and once again be confused by conflicts on the leadership level. We simply had to suffer the consequences of Stokely's actions, I argued. The final decision was against expulsion.

But the problem of Stokely stayed with us. People also began to notice that Stokely's line while speaking abroad was not the same as inside the United States. Several revolutionary governments would be turned off by SNCC, at least temporarily, when Stokely spoke at a rally for Huey Newton in 1968 and said that socialism and communism were irrelevant for black people. He was creating more and more confusion and distrust in the movement.

Much of what Stokely said while abroad was good, but his general attitude represented the zenith of an individualism that has hurt the black struggle in many quarters. His actions indicated that he was more interested in building a cult of personality rather than a strong organization. I felt that he had betrayed his own promise to help strengthen SNCC internally. At the same time, there is also no doubt that SNCC must bear the final responsibility for the lack of discipline and collectivism represented by Stokely. His admirers must bear a major part of the blame for this, and I, too, must accept my own responsibility.

In August, 1969, Stokely would be finally expelled from SNCC at a meeting which I did not attend. If I had been there, I might well have again argued against expulsion for the same reasons as before. Nevertheless, Carmichael would tell many people that I was responsible for his expulsion. This, like his other actions, suggests that law of history which says that revolution unfolds in stages and many people are unable to climb the next rung on the ladder of mounting resistance. They jump off, go backward, or are crushed beneath the pressure of those willing to escalate the tempo. It is a law that often works tragically, with great potential and energy lost in the shuffle.

SNCC's failure with Stokely was more than a matter of discipline and ideology. We also failed to organize the tremendous upsurge of energy in the black community created by the cry for Black Power and Carmichael. By the fall of 1967, I was becoming increasingly doubtful as to whether SNCC could transform itself into the builder of a mass black political party. It had to be done. It was theoretically and practically necessary at this juncture of black history. But could SNCC make it?

In California there were people already at work organizing a party around the symbol of the black panther. I soon found myself back in Los Angeles, in January of 1968, on a trip that led to SNCC's deep involvement with the Black Panther Party for Self-Defense, which later became simply the Black Panther Party.

CHAPTER 64

The Black Panther Party

SNCC IN DECLINE AFTER 8 YEARS IN LEAD
PACE-SETTER IN CIVIL RIGHTS DISPLACED BY PANTHERS
By C. Gerald Fraser
The Student Nonviolent Coordinating Committee, which emerged from the rural South eight years ago to become a pace-setter in the national Civil Rights movement, is in serious decline.
It has lost much of its power and influence to the northern slum-born Black Panthers as the rights movement has grown into the "black liberation struggle." And it has also lost to the Panthers its leading apostle, Stokely Carmichael. These losses, and this transition, have not come about without anxiety and pain.
PISTOL INCIDENT RECALLED
Members of the Black Panthers walked into James Forman's office at the committee on Fifth Avenue in late July, according to Federal authorities. One of them produced a pistol and put it into Mr. Forman's mouth. He squeezed the trigger three times.
The gun went click, click, click. It was unloaded.

from *The New York Times*, Monday, October 7, 1968.
When I read that vicious lie, stating that a gun had been placed down my throat, I immediately called Eldridge Cleaver in San Francisco. Kath-

leen Cleaver, whom I know very well and who had once worked for SNCC, answered the phone. After we exchanged warm greetings, she handed the telephone to Eldridge. It was early in California, about nine o'clock in the morning, and near noon in New York. I asked him to get a copy of the newspaper and read the story.

It was obvious, I told Cleaver, that the federal government had decided to escalate the conflict between SNCC and the Panthers, if federal authorities were saying that a gun had been placed down my throat. Cleaver, Bobby Seale, David Hilliard, and many other Panthers knew that this was a lie and I knew it. That there had been serious differences between the Panthers and myself, and between the Panthers and SNCC, some nearly involving gunplay, was a fact. But the *Times* story was a lie. I told Cleaver that I believed the article was written to create a fratricidal situation between our two organizations. I felt that some public denial was necessary, in order to eliminate the confusion that it would cause. Notwithstanding any differences between SNCC and the Panthers, it was necessary—in the face of that article—to articulate a position that we would not be led into organizational fratricide by incorrect and vicious staten ents in *The New York Times*, I said. He agreed that we should keep "it" on that level. I suggested that he contact Bobby Seale and call me later that afternoon to decide on a joint statement.

Cleaver never called me back, and that became the last time I spoke to him.

Relations between SNCC and the Black Panther Party went back almost to the time of the party's founding in October, 1966. Aside from the link in the symbol of the black panther, used first in Lowndes County and then in California, we also felt a clear political need for relations with and support of such organizations as the Black Panther Party. SNCC was under such severe repression that we doubted how long we could survive; we had to support every emerging Black Power group in the country so that if we did go under, others could carry on the work we had started. It was in this spirit that Stokely Carmichael, George Ware, and Rap Brown of SNCC talked with the group on various occasions in 1966 and early 1967. We also worked to rally support for the Panthers when they went to the state legislature in Sacramento, guns in hand, to oppose changes in the California gun laws.

Then came the 1967 confrontation of the party's minister of defense, Huey P. Newton, in which one cop was killed and another wounded. Huey became the most important black political prisoner in the United States, at about the same time that H. Rap Brown became confined as a political prisoner to the island of Manhattan, waiting for the many courtroom trials that the government had set for him. Repression was also running high against Stokely Carmichael, although he did not have heavy charges hanging over his head. I considered these three—Newton, Brown, and Carmichael—extremely important symbols of resistance in the black liberation struggle. People had to speak out and organize in their defense, for all political prisoners are innocent and the U.S. Government is always wrong. That is the political truth, regardless of so-called "legal" technicalities.

In January, 1968, there were three different groups of people organizing around the symbol of the black panther: the Black Panther Party for Self-Defense, the Black Panther Party of Southern California, and the Black Panther Party of Northern California. I went to Los Angeles that month to speak at the invitation of the southern California group and the black caucus of the NCNP. There were many groups then hassling in Los Angeles—the Black Congress, a collection of black organizations in the area; US, the organization headed by Ron Karenga; and the two Panther parties active in that area. Each had intense differences with the other.

Stokely Carmichael was scheduled to speak in Los Angeles on February 18, at a rally co-sponsored by the Black Panther Party for Self-Defense and SNCC. I set about to resolve some of the differences between the various groups, to insure that the rally would be a success. I also felt a responsibility to try to help because of my belief that such conflicts are of service only to the enemy. Furthermore, I knew that all of these groups were trying to build self-defense units in California and in tense situations it can become easy to point the gun at one another rather than at the oppressor. After hours of discussion, with some of the individuals involved separately and then getting some of them to sit down "face to face," I succeeded in ironing out many of the difficulties.

The month before, the U.S. Government had handed down indictments against Dr. Benjamin Spock and the Boston Five for antidraft activities. I knew this signaled more intense repression inside the United States and against black militants in particular. If the government was prepared to move against a man of Dr. Spock's popularity and reputation, it would not hesitate to open guns on black people. For this reason, I agreed to speak at mass rallies for Dr. Spock in New York City and California. It was at one of these rallies, in Berkeley, California, on February 4, 1968, that I first met some of the leadership of the Black Panther Party for Self-Defense. Chairman Bobby Seale, Eldridge Cleaver, Kathleen Cleaver, and several other Panthers attended the rally that night. Eldridge told me afterward that the speech was tremendously liberating, for it articulated many points he had been thinking about but not yet raised in a public forum.

I opened by commenting, "This is the third rally in a week in support of the Boston Five at which I have spoken. I've agreed to do this primarily because I think it is absolutely essential to show solidarity, first of all with Dr. Spock, who at the National Conference on New Politics convention made a crisis decision. Many of his liberal white friends in SANE (Committee for a Sane Nuclear Policy) were urging him to leave the NCNP. The blacks had taken over. We were racists. We were anti-Semitic. We were against Israel. He shouldn't be in any kind of coalition with the demagogues and the dictators."

But Dr. Spock did not leave. "And we feel," I continued, "that it is absolutely important to support him as an individual because of his decision."

Those opening remarks were mild, but they cut into the sensitivities of some in the audience who were there to hear the baby doctor. The words that followed posed the fundamental questions facing many who would call themselves white radicals or revolutionaries:

We, as black people in this country, understand we are the revolutionary force which is going to be the vanguard in the final destruction of this system of government under which we live. We understand that. And we are not going to abdicate our leadership to anybody. As that vanguard force, for which we will pay with our lives and blood as we have been doing, we are not going to give up our leadership to anybody. We are not going to share the leadership, and that should be crystal clear. We are not going to give up the leadership and then have our struggle aborted as we have seen it aborted in the labor struggle movement in this country, as we have seen it aborted many other times. . . .

Will white people be willing to kill for black people when they seal off the ghettoes of this country? Will you be willing to take up a gun and shoot a cop who's shooting in Oakland? That's the fundamental question. Because you say you're against the war in Vietnam. You're for the Viet Cong. You're for the NLF. But are you for the black liberation fighters in this country and will you support them and give them sanctuary and will you kill for them?

I went on with some comments that hit home even more specifically. Some of these concerned the Peace and Freedom Party of Northern California, which had refused to accept the formula of the NCNP convention that blacks should have 50 percent of all voting power in any relation with whites. They had skirted this issue by entering into a coalition with the Black Panther Party for Self-Defense. This is what I said:

The indictment of Dr. Spock was a calculated attempt to test the reaction. It was a calculated attempt, we contend, also to show that if you indict five prominent white men, one of whom is the pseudo-father of many people, that it becomes open season on black people. Remember that he was not arrested. None of the five were arrested. No bail was originally set on them. Look at the situation in terms of black people. How much bail is on Rap Brown? How much bail is on Cleveland Sellers, who faces five years on the draft? Take the situation of Eddie Oquendo, a black man in Brooklyn facing five years, confined to the borough of Brooklyn, who cannot leave in order to go around the country to mobilize support. Rap Brown is confined to the island of Manhattan. And the racist judges say that he cannot leave; he cannot go around the country to hold mass rallies because they are afraid of what he has to say.

I think that we must definitely understand the connection between the black liberation struggle and these indictments. Why? Because the draft is only one prop to the system. If in fact there is no draft, there can be nobody to defend Goldwater, Rockefeller, Lyndon B. Johnson, General Dynamics, Dow Chemical, and what have you. The draft is a prop which must be knocked out, because without the draft you cannot fight the war.

But there's another prop. And that's us, the colonial subjects, black people, our labor. And we are beginning to knock out that particular prop, and that's why all the confusion. That's one of the reasons why it becomes imperative that NCNP's concept of absolute equality in terms of positions on committees is accepted. And that may go against the grain of some people, particularly in the Peace and Freedom Party. But your day is coming and it has to be rectified if in fact there is to be a true Peace and Freedom Party in California. That's a fact. It doesn't matter about numbers. We're not talking about numbers. We're talking about a colonial condition and who is the revolutionary force in the country. We've suffered from the racism in this country. You have not.

That position did not endear me to the Peace and Freedom Party, but I would continue to take it throughout the history of my relations with the Black Panther Party. Eldridge would tell me that whenever I spoke, the telephones began to jump; members of the Peace and Freedom Party complained that I was not talking about coalition but about black dictatorship.

But the ideas about retribution which I set forth at this Berkeley meeting were even more disturbing to some people:

We will not stand by and allow black leadership to be assassinated, as Brother Malcolm was assassinated, without full retaliation. And I say this, and I'm going to tell you what my price is, and you pick out which one you want to contribute to. My personal price for assassination is:

ten war factories destroyed
fifteen blown-up police stations
thirty power plants destroyed, demolished
no flowers
one Southern Governor
two mayors
five hundred racist cops dead.

Now this is no theatrics. The price on Stokely and on Rap is triple my price because all of them have been receiving assassination threats. We intend to put an end to that. They may be assassinated. Nobody can stop assassination. But we say to the CIA people who are in the audience, to the local police agents, to the FBI, and to everyone else that their deaths will not go unseen. . . .

And I tell you this: the sky is the limit if you kill Huey Newton. The sky is the limit if Huey Newton dies.

That was the first time that the slogan of "the sky is the limit" for Huey was articulated. To my mind, raising the issue of retribution and trying to organize to implement it seemed the best defense that one could make to help protect the lives of black militants. That included my own defense, for the work that I was doing in international affairs had led me to realize that I was becoming a more and more serious embarrassment to the United States Government, one that they would have liked to eliminate.

After the meeting that night, I experienced a refreshing treat. I heard Bobby Seale speak for the first time. We were gathered in the house of a sister in Berkeley and many sisters and brothers had come to this meeting. His analysis of the social system in the United States and the dynamics of our struggle revealed an understanding of some of the thought of Mao Tse-tung and Frantz Fanon. His emphasis upon class factors as well as racial factors as fundamental to understanding the black experience struck a responsive chord in me. I knew then that I would try to help the Panthers in whatever way that I could, for there was a maturity and intellectual level of development in Bobby Seale that seemed lacking in many other black spokesmen.

My attraction to the Black Panther Party was based on deep beliefs about how the revolutionary struggle had to be waged in the United States. The creation of the party by Huey P. Newton and Bobby Seale was the extension of work that many of us in SNCC had been doing over the past seven years and a natural outgrowth of the intense struggle that had been waged since 1960. One of the reasons that I had come to SNCC was to help create a mass consciousness that we as a people could fight with our own resources and strength inside the United States against the injustices that confronted us. Once that consciousness had been developed, some of us knew that the next step was to form a broadly based party with the panther as a symbol. But we were too trapped in our own contradictions to build that party ourselves.

The Black Panther Party for Self-Defense was able to grow where we did not for many reasons. Central to its development was its formulation of a clearly defined set of goals in its ten-point program and statement of beliefs. The courage and tenacity of its founders and early members were also a key factor, for they sustained the party in periods of intense repression. The emphasis on recruiting street brothers, young people from the "ghettos," rather than college students, gave it a large base and eliminated some of the class tensions which we had experienced. Finally, the Black Panther Party had begun to articulate the need for armed self-defense and revolution just at the time of growing militancy in the black liberation struggle. The symbolic effect of Huey P. Newton in prison—and later on trial—for the murder of a policeman was tremendous. And the ability of the party to mount a powerful, national defense campaign in support of Huey P. Newton contributed greatly to its growth. So would the Panthers' working alliance with SNCC and the drafting of three from SNCC's leadership into the party.

The day after I spoke in Berkeley and attended the meeting with Bobby Seale, I went to visit Huey P. Newton in jail. He told me that he had read my speech "Liberation Will Come from a Black Thing" and liked it very much. Later that day, I accompanied a Panther delegation headed by Bobby and Eldridge to Los Angeles in an effort to resolve some of those interorganizational problems which I mentioned before and which had not been permanently resolved. We were met at the airport by a contingent of US members, headed by Ron Karenga. Both Karenga and Seale exchanged cordial greetings and talked for several minutes at the airport. LeRoi Jones was arriving at the same time and this was perhaps the last meeting between all these forces at one time. In my mind I was hoping that a joint list of articles of retribution could be drawn up by all the black forces that had gathered on that bright Monday, February 5, 1968. I also thought a public statement of unity would reveal to the masses of black people that solidarity within the black struggle was emerging.

A series of meetings followed and on Wednesday, February 7, 1968, there was a large gathering at the Black Congress of the diverse elements. A working unity was established that lasted through the rally in Los Angeles on February 18, although it was filled with tension and minor breaks.

During the time we spent in Los Angeles, I was asked to hold a political education class for members of the Black Panther Party for Self-Defense. The Black Panther Party of southern California had dissolved itself in January, 1968, and become the SNCC chapter in Los Angeles. The one in northern California had basically disintegrated. This left only the Black Panther Party for Self-Defense operating in California.

At the political education class, I came to know young Bobby Hutton, the party's treasurer, who was later assassinated by police in Oakland after a 1968 shoot-out, and David Hilliard, the party's chief of staff. There I presented the concept of the ten-ten-and-ten method of organizing a city. This was a refinement of the method I had outlined in my novel for the organization of a mass movement of black people in the United States. It is based on a very simple theoretical principle which involves dividing a city into ten sections, establishing ten subsections in each of these, and ten sub-subsections in each of these. The principle can be extended to any length depending upon the number of recruits one finds. The only magic is in its implementation. It takes hard work, but it is the basis upon which any urban political party should be organized. My trip to Guinea and study of the Democratic Party of Guinea also led me to formulate this plan.

Bobby Seale told me that he had been searching for a method to broaden the base of the party and, when he went back to Oakland, he began implementing the ten-ten-and-ten idea. It worked for the Black

Panther Party. He also accepted the high command principle, an adaptation of the concept of democratic centralism, designed especially to help the Panthers keep their paramilitary orientation and centralized leadership but at the same time allow the base to participate in decision making. In making a major policy decision, for example, the party would circulate a proposal through the rank and file and call for discussion of it at various levels. To my knowledge this procedure was never implemented.

Armed with these two concepts—the ten-ten-and-ten plan and the high command principle—the party had the structural machinery for broadening its base throughout the United States. At that time, it was mainly confined to northern California, although it was spreading in Los Angeles. The birthday rally for Huey Newton, scheduled for February 17, 1968— the day before the Los Angeles rally at which Stokely was to speak— loomed in the minds of many as the occasion to kick off a campaign that would build a massive national and international reputation for the Black Panther Party.

While in Los Angeles, I met with Eldridge Cleaver one day at the teen center where Alprentice Bunchy Carter was working (Bunchy was later killed by members of the US organization headed by Ron Karenga). Cleaver asked what I thought of a decision that the Panthers had made to draft Stokely Carmichael as "prime minister of the Afro-American nation." I said that I thought the decision was premature and ill-advised for several reasons. First, the Panthers were not yet a national organization and it would seem presumptuous for them to speak in the name of all black people. It would be wiser to build the party up to a national level and then discuss that possibility. Second, I felt that many people throughout black America might question the choice of Stokely. Naming him could cause unnecessary problems and ill will toward the party. Third, I indicated to Eldridge that there were serious conflicts within SNCC concerning the role of Stokely, and a split between him and H. Rap Brown. The selection of Stokely over Rap for prime minister would intensify those conflicts. I suggested that if any status was to be conferred on Stokely, then Rap should receive the same—they could both become deputy chairmen of the party, for instance.

Cleaver answered that it would be difficult to follow my suggestions, for, during a trip to Washington, he and Bobby Seale had already indicated to Stokely that they were going to inaugurate him as prime minister of the Afro-American nation. I was sorry to hear this, but considered the matter settled and prepared myself to live with the Panthers' decision. However, my comments seemed to have had some effect because the Panthers later changed the title bestowed on Stokely to prime minister of the Black Panther Party only, and they also decided to draft H. Rap Brown as minister of justice.

During that same conversation, Cleaver said they wanted to draft me into the party too. I explained that I would accept such a draft, but only in the areas of foreign affairs and political education. Cleaver said that I would be drafted as minister of foreign affairs and director of political education. I indicated that titles were not that important, but I did want to work in those fields.

All this was to be announced at the birthday rally. For the first time, two leading organizations in the black liberation struggle would announce that they planned to create a working alliance to strengthen the revolutionary forces and to combat repression—a repression expected to mount sharply. At the rally in Los Angeles on February 18, Reies Lopez Tijerina of New Mexico would also speak—thus broadening the base of resistance even further. Building this kind of united front seemed to me absolutely vital and our alliance with the Panthers in particular had top priority. Of all the people in SNCC, I was probably the one who wanted most to see this alliance develop. I saw working with the Black Panthers as not only a way of fighting our mutual repression and a way of implementing decisions SNCC had reached but could not carry out, but also of benefit to the Panthers specifically. Members of SNCC had acquired a great deal of expertise in organizing that could be of help; we also had many friends and contacts which could be used to help strengthen both organizations.

Contrary to some public reports and newspaper articles, there was nothing wrong or unprecedented about members of SNCC accepting positions in the Black Panther Party. SNCC had not developed as a tightly sectarian group—a factor which gave it strength. Relations between the Panthers and SNCC had been very good, and other SNCC people had worked on an ad hoc basis for the Panthers. To establish a working alliance—the term I used in our discussions, to which all seemed agreed—was no violation of organizational discipline. If the officers of one organization accepted positions in another, that clearly meant there was a working alliance.

When I went back to California for the birthday rally on February 17, the hall in Oakland was packed and beautiful sisters and brothers were dancing. Eldridge Cleaver told me that the prime minister of the party—meaning Stokely—had objected to my being drafted as director of political education because he had serious political differences with me. The Panthers had sided with Stokely and I was not to be drafted as director of political education. Cleaver said he hoped that at some later time, the conflicts could be ironed out. Meanwhile, I would be drafted as minister of foreign affairs.

This meant that the Panthers' political education department and program would not get off the ground at that time. I, therefore, reacted rather strongly to this news, for I felt that the party needed a department of political education more than anything else. I had learned much in SNCC about the serious mistakes that can flow from the lack of a revolutionary political education program. But, I told Cleaver, I was willing to work with the Panthers in any capacity and did not really need any titles. I felt deeply committed to doing whatever I could to forge more unity in the black struggle. But at the same time I would not relinquish or compromise my basic political ideas.

As the rally began, Eldridge asked me to speak first. Introducing me, he said that I would explain the "merger" between SNCC and the Black Panthers. I was very surprised; this was the first time that term had been used, although we had not decided definitely on another. But the clear spirit of our discussions had been to create a working alliance. And I certainly would not have involved SNCC in a "merger" without discussion throughout the organization. So I explained to the audience that it was not exactly a merger but an attempt to create a working alliance in order to deal with repression and bring further unity within the black struggle. However, across the country the news flashed that SNCC and the Panthers had "merged." I was severely criticized by many people for leading SNCC into a "merger," when in fact there had been no merger or any discussion of one.

After the meeting, I suggested to Eldridge—in front of Ethel Minor, SNCC communications secretary, who was traveling with Stokely—that the word *merger* was inappropriate. Unfortunately, in the Panther newspaper itself the relationship was always described with that term. But I could live with these historical inaccuracies. They did not seem that important; the crucial point was that a joint attempt was being made by SNCC and the Panthers to strengthen the liberation struggle.

The international affairs office of SNCC had been working in Brooklyn and, when we entered into our working alliance with the Black Panthers, we encouraged the development of a Panther chapter in the New York area. In fact, the first chapter in Brooklyn was organized with some of the leading members of the cadre of SNCC's Brooklyn project. Until July 23, 1968, the international affairs office served as the principal headquarters for the Panthers in the New York area.

After the murder of Bobby Hutton in Oakland and my attendance at his funeral, I made an international trip representing both SNCC and the Panthers. I went in April to a conference in Sweden where people from the United States, from North Vietnam, and from the National Liberation Front of South Vietnam discussed mutual problems. From there I went to Paris and spoke at a huge rally in solidarity with the Panthers and SNCC. This was the first representation of the Panthers abroad. By this time, I had decided to write a book on the life and thought of Frantz Fanon and preparations for this project took me to Algeria, where I also wrote a series of articles. One of them, entitled "In Defense of Huey P. Newton and the Black Panthers," was published in *El Moujahid* on May 6,

1968. (Frantz Fanon had been an editor of *El Moujahid* during the Algerian revolution, and it was his wife, Josie—a journalist—who had arranged for me to do the series of articles.)

These were only a few of various ways in which I, and others in SNCC, worked to build support for, and solidarity with, the Panthers. Unfortunately there were other forces at work behind our backs. Many rumors had been spread, some by forces unknown to me, that SNCC was trying to take over the Panthers or that SNCC needed the Panthers for fundraising purposes. Many white commentators on the black movement helped to fan these rumors, this I know for certain. I also suspect that confusion was created and distrust sowed by my enemies, together with enemies of SNCC in the Peace and Freedom Party and other groupings of whites that saw themselves winning a new lease on life through the Black Panther Party.

At the annual SNCC staff meeting in June, 1968, I introduced a resolution stating that SNCC would work to help build the Black Panther Party, of which Huey Newton is the minister of defense and Bobby Seale the chairman, as a national organization. The honest intent of this resolution, which passed, was to commit SNCC formally to make available whatever resources and skills that it had to help build the Black Panther Party. The references to Huey P. Newton and Bobby Seale were included to eliminate any confusion if another Black Panther Party arose (there had been many in the past). The language of that resolution was clear and it meant precisely what it said. It was not ambiguous in the least. But two newspaper articles that appeared after the meeting did create confusion in an already difficult situation.

First, Robert Allen, a staff reporter for the *Guardian*, published what he called "findings" of the SNCC staff meeting, in which he said that SNCC had rejected the ten-point program of the Black Panther Party. The source of his information has remained a mystery to me. For his report was inaccurate and misleading, and did not carry any mention of our actual resolution, one that we wanted submitted to the public. As a result, suspicion began to increase about the intentions of SNCC.

Actually, I had encouraged a discussion of the ten-point program of the Panthers during the SNCC meeting as a class in political education and as a background to the resolution to help build the Panther Party as a national organization. There was some disagreement with sections of the ten-point-program. I myself had and have objections to the section calling for a plebiscite by the United Nations. The United Nations is clearly a tool of the imperialist camp which has excluded China, North Vietnam, and North Korea from membership because of U.S. pressure. To make the demand for a UN plebiscite one of the ten points seemed to me to give the UN undeserved validity—especially when that demand was not projected as a way of using the UN for propaganda purposes (which can be effective) but as sacred dogma.

But that did not mean I couldn't work to help build the Panther Party as a national organization. I had lived for seven years with a religious statement of purpose issued by SNCC in 1960 and I do not consider myself religious. It is a mistake to split hairs or to think that one can seek perfect agreement on all points before one begins to work. In the final analysis, I am convinced that all theoretical positions that exist in the world today among all revolutionaries will evolve and modify themselves. As Brother Mao points out, the contradictions that exist—the differences in opinion between members of the Central Committee of China—stem from the differences in life-style, history, and class background of its members. If this is true for China, then certainly in the United States, the heart of imperialism, we must expect many differences. People grow, learn new ideas, and the struggle forces changes. In the very beginning, the Black Panther Party was not articulating socialism as one of its goals. In the beginning, no one in SNCC was talking of armed struggle, but rather of nonviolent positive action.

Hence I have always felt that, even if there was disagreement in SNCC with some of the ten-point program, Robert Allen and the *Guardian*—while claiming to be revolutionary—did both SNCC and the Panthers a disservice by printing incorrect reports.

The second incorrect report was an interview given by Phil Hutchins, who had just been elected program secretary of SNCC. (At the staff meeting, we abolished the offices of chairman and executive secretary and set up, instead, a system of several deputy chairmen plus a program secretary. This was to prevent the U.S. Government from focusing its oppression on a single leader and thus hampering the struggle, and also to streamline a decision-making structure that had long been awkward.) Phil Hutchins stated in a *New York Times* story that SNCC had decided to build a nationwide black political party. This was not the motion we had voted and it further caused suspicion and distrust, by implying that we intended to build something other than the Black Panther Party.

On July 13, 1968, I was scheduled to go to Oakland to speak at a rally and participate in demonstrations to free Huey. His trial was to begin in two days and efforts were being made to mobilize as much support for him as possible. I had just left the hospital, where I had undergone minor surgery, but I planned to go to California anyway because Huey's defense seemed much more important than any consideration of health. While in the hospital, I had called Eldridge Cleaver and explained what we had really voted at our staff meeting. Hutchins was coming to California, I said, to discuss ways to implement the resolution. Unfortunately, this did not happen, which meant that I would again have to be the one articulating SNCC's intentions—on that July 13 trip to Oakland.

I took with me to California copies of the new statement of purpose that SNCC had voted at the June, 1968, staff meeting, indicating that its fight was against racism, capitalism, and imperialism, and also copies of an interorganizational memorandum I had written interpreting the decisions we had reached at that meeting. In that memo I explained how SNCC had come to its decision to assist in the building of the Black Panther Party as a national political party—the history of our plans to develop freedom organizations, the class problems that had caused those plans to fail, and the establishment of a working alliance between our two organizations as made concrete by the drafting of three SNCC people into the Panthers. The memorandum concluded that there was only one legitimate role for SNCC to perform in this period of history, "to assist in the development of the Black Panther Party. This means that we must use our resources, our contacts, our experiences, our minds, our revolutionary zeal to further expand the Black Panther Party."

On July 17, 1968, a rough meeting took place between four members of SNCC—Willie Ricks, John Wilson, Brother Crook (deputy chairman for the Western region), and myself—and members of the Black Panther Party including Bobby Seale, Eldridge Cleaver, David Hilliard, Field Marshal Donald Cox, and Emory Douglas. Because I felt so keenly the need for SNCC and the Panthers to make their working alliance effective, and because I expected to hear serious questions raised about SNCC's resolution, I got up early in the morning on the day of the meeting and prepared an outline of remarks that I planned to make there. I showed them to David Hilliard, at whose house I was staying, and asked for his comments and suggestions. After he indicated approval of what I had drafted, I asked him to take me to Bobby Seale's house so that I could get the chairman's opinion too. Bobby also expressed approval. I, therefore, had high hopes for a successful meeting.

But, when we all sat down together, I was stunned to hear Eldridge insist that our relationship was that of a merger. Cleaver also asked if SNCC was trying to co-opt the Black Panther Party. At one point he asked, alluding to the black leather jacket—a Panther uniform item—worn by one of our group, if we from SNCC were in fact Panthers or SNCC. In my mind, it was not an either-or question; we were involved in joint activity. But Cleaver's insistence on such matters continued, in a clearly hostile fashion.

After the meeting I felt that not only the integrity of SNCC but also my own political integrity had been challenged. At the same time, I felt strongly that the alliance between SNCC and the Black Panther Party had to survive. I knew that no two organizations could enter into a working alliance without experiencing difficulties and the job of sincere militants is to work out these difficulties. Therefore I would resign as minister of foreign affairs, to help ease tensions, and continue to work for the party without a title.

We met again the next day with Panthers Cleaver, Seale, Hilliard, and Carter to discuss ways of rallying support for Huey Newton. His trial was just beginning and we wanted to create favorable public opinion before the jury was picked. The group agreed that SNCC and the Black Panthers would organize mass rallies in New York City and a press conference at the United Nations, both in support of Huey Newton with the leadership of the Panthers and of SNCC on hand. We would also enter the UN building itself, using the pass SNCC had acquired as a nongovernmental organization, and lobby for Huey among delegates in the lounge there.

I was placed in charge of making arrangements for all these events in New York, scheduled to begin in less than four days. As we were preparing to leave California for New York, I handed my letter of resignation to Bobby Seale, stating that I wanted him to read it although I would not submit it at that time in light of our decision to hold the joint press conference at the United Nations. That original letter, which was later stolen from my desk in the New York office, reviewed in detail the history of my involvement with the Panthers and stated that, although I was resigning, I would still work with the party. I told Bobby that it was his decision to accept or reject my resignation, but I felt that I had to offer it in order to make sure that the working alliance between SNCC and the Panthers continued. He rejected it, stating that he found my services useful and very important to the party.

Two Panthers, David Hilliard and Bill Brent, and I caught a late plane from San Francisco to New York, arriving Friday morning, July 19, after some complications in the flights. By this time I had become extremely exhausted for I had worked intensely while in Oakland. I was in no physical condition to continue working without rest, but I felt that I could exert myself a few more days to complete the assignment. Working for the political defense of Huey was a principle I held dear. And I thought that the press conference at the United Nations, together with rallies in New York, would mount tremendous pressure on the United States Government. But I was stretching my own capacity far beyond the limits of the human body. In the midst of this extraordinary output of energy, there were the tensions between SNCC and the Panthers, between myself and members of the Panthers, created by continuing distrust and suspicion of intentions. The relationship between SNCC and the Panthers was a delicate one that called for great diplomacy. A slight spark could split it asunder.

The task of organizing three rallies and a press conference between a hot Friday morning in July and the following Monday morning is not an easy one. But the people in the SNCC office and the New York Panthers went to work and, on Saturday, July 20, we began to distribute the following leaflet, which indicates the kind of job we were trying to do:

FREE HUEY   FREE HUEY   FREE HUEY   FREE HUEY   FREE HUEY   FREE HUEY
From: James Forman

Chairman of the International Affairs Commission, SNCC
Minister of Foreign Affairs, Black Panther Party
July 20, 1968
CRISIS: THE NECESSITY FOR ORGANIZING A MASS MEETING IN TWO AND THREE DAYS
Rallies to be held: Monday July 22, 1968 6:00 P.M. *Brooklyn.* Fulton Park
                    (Fulton Street and Schenectady Avenue)
                    Tuesday July 23, 1968 6:00 P.M. *Harlem.* 125th Street and
                    7th Avenue
                    Tuesday July 23, 1968 8:00 P.M. *Newark.* Community
                    Center, 9-11 Holland Street.
Speakers: Bobby Seale, Chairman of the Black Panther Party.
                    Eldridge Cleaver, Minister of Information for the Black Panther
                    Party
                    David Hilliard, National Captain of the Party.
                    Phil Hutchins, Program Secretary of SNCC.
                    James Forman, Chairman of the International Affairs Commission
                    for SNCC and Minister of Foreign Affairs for the Party.

ALL MEMBERS OF THE BLACK PANTHER PARTY IN THE METROPOLITAN NEW YORK AREA ARE EXPECTED TO WORK HARD AND TO DO THE FOLLOWING THINGS UNDER THE INSTRUCTION OF THEIR CAPTAIN, LIEUTENANT, SECTION LEADERS. IT IS EXTREMELY IMPORTANT THAT WE MOBILIZE THOUSANDS OF PEOPLE IN THIS AREA TO SUPPORT AND SHOW SOLIDARITY WITH BROTHER HUEY P. NEWTON, MINISTER OF DEFENSE AND FOUNDER OF THE BLACK PANTHER PARTY. IN ORDER TO MAKE THIS EMERGENCY MOBILIZATION SUCCESSFUL, IT WILL BE NECESSARY FOR EVERY MEMBER OF THE BLACK PANTHER PARTY TO CARRY OUT THE FOLLOWING:

1. EACH PERSON IS TO CALL 10 PEOPLE AND ASK EVERY PERSON TO CALL 10 OTHER PEOPLE. Members are requested to study, use, and adapt to their audience the following message incorporating the information given above concerning place of rally and speakers.

> THE MESSAGE: Prominent members of the Black Panther Party will be at_____. This is going to be a very important event because the rally is a show of support to mount political pressure to free Huey. Huey Newton is currently being tried by the illegal jury of the Oakland Police Department. We want you to come out because the more people who turn out at the rally, the more pressure there will be to free Huey. Your help is urgently needed. How about it? Will you be there?

Each person who calls is to stress time and time again and exact a promise from the people that they will call 10 others. Each Party member is to list the names of people he called. The names are to be brought to the next meeting for they form a basis of membership solicitation in the Party. Each person who calls is to use tact, persuasion, patience and a convincing attitude that this is indeed a very important event. If people say they can't come, ask them why. Record their reasons for evaluation to be made by staff. This is important. If they can't come, at least exact a promise that they will make the 10 calls. At the next membership meeting there will be a review of the activities of the Party members during this crisis time.

2. MOBILIZATION OF YOUNG PEOPLE. A HAND BILL WILL BE PREPARED FOR THE CHILDREN TO HAND OUT.

3. ORGANIZE CADRES TO GET CHURCH MEMBERS TO ANNOUNCE THE RALLY. USE BULLETIN BOARDS AND POSTERS.

4. DISTRIBUTE HANDBILLS AT THE END OF CHURCH SERVICE.

5. STEADY BLASTING IN COMMUNITIES WITH SOUND TRUCKS TALKING ABOUT THE RALLY, explaining the necessity for people to be there to show support to free Huey. The person speaking over the microphone should say, "This is the voice of the Black Panther Party. We're asking the members of the black community to come to a rally to free Huey Newton."

6. MAKE RADIO ANNOUNCEMENTS. All Captains should call the radio stations and ask to make a public announcement about the rally.

7. CALL THE HEADS OF ALL ORGANIZATIONS AND ASK THEM TO CONTACT THEIR MEMBERSHIP ABOUT THE RALLY.

8. AFTER MAKING THEIR TELEPHONE CALLS, ALL PANTHERS ARE TO BEGIN TO WORK IN THEIR SECTIONS explaining the need for people to come to the rally, talking about the principles and ideology of the Black Panther Party, urging people to sign temporary membership forms and to give a donation. The last point is extremely important because the Party is in desperate need of funds. A dollar given is a political act. It must be clearly understood that this is not begging but asking the black community for support in this situation. Another dollar given helps in the campaign and efforts to free Huey. Panthers must explain to those people to whom they talk that it costs money to run a political organization; it costs money to get the national officers to the rally. They must stop bullshitting. The people must support the Black Panther Party. SNCC must not be destroyed. We must resist.

FREE HUEY   FREE HUEY
FREE HUEY   FREE HUEY
FREE HUEY   FREE HUEY
FREE HUEY   FREE HUEY
FREE HUEY   FREE HUEY

YOU HAVE HEARD THE VOICE OF THE BLACK PANTHER PARTY.

After all that work and intense preparation for the rallies, the press conference, and our lobbying at the United Nations, the working alliance between SNCC and the Panthers split asunder. Petty personality differences, suspicion, distrust, excessive drinking, deep-seated political conflicts, and deep-seated, neurotic, egotistical power drives on the part of many people surged to the front. The press conference had to be cancelled, as did plans to enter the United Nations.

The press conference was scheduled to take place at the Methodist Church Center Auditorium, near the United Nations, at 10:00 A.M. Monday morning. I arrived there shortly before the hour and sat at the front table awaiting the Panthers. Several of them, with Stokely Carmichael, entered the room and stayed a short time, then left. I tried to find them in the building, but could not, and assumed they were in caucus. The press arrived, and the Panthers did not appear. I urged the press representatives to stay, but by 1:00 P.M. I realized that the Panthers were not coming and had to cancel the press conference. Our plan to have a joint delegation of SNCC officers and Black Panthers go into the United Nations on my pass could not materialize at that point. Later, some Panthers spread the lie that I had simply refused to go into the UN, and also that I had called off the press conference all on my own, not because of their actions.

The mass rallies were held, but under the most strained circumstances, with intense hostility between members of the two organizations. The public had been informed of the meetings and they had to be held. By midnight of July 22 I was in a state of near collapse and subsequently forced to take several months of rest. I had assumed too much responsibility for this working alliance and allowed myself to work too hard and too long without adequate sleep. I resigned from the party as minister of foreign affairs that midnight.

My resignation from the party was based on significant political and organizational differences. First, I did not like the lack of internal security within the Black Panther Party. I felt that the party opened itself to infiltration and frame-ups by the loose method of recruiting that it employed and other practices. Always apprehensive of frame-ups with myself involved, I often urged Bobby Seale to tighten internal security while there was still some chance and hope to do it. To assume that the United States Government would not try to infiltrate and set people up for arrests and killings was a mistake of the highest order, for this country is not going to allow any group of black people to talk about the gun publicly. It will try to frame members of that group.

Since July, 1968, as I have heard and read about the large number of internal purges within the Black Panther Party, the police infiltration and frame-ups, I have often thought of those days when I talked to Bobby Seale about the need for security in the party. Constant purges are an indication that initial recruitment leaves a lot to be desired and the frame-ups reveal clearly the most direct method the United States Government uses today to stifle militant organizations—infiltration. This was an issue to which I made public reference in my speech, "Liberation Will Come from a Black Thing."

A second reason for my resignation was the fact that I could not function properly with the party unless its administrative apparatus was drastically restructured—and it seemed clear that this was not about to happen.

All during my last trip to California, we had talked about setting up a more efficient administrative network and I had drawn up many plans, but efforts to discuss these in more detail were constantly frustrated by changing events and plans. I felt that the lack of proper administration caused many personality differences and confusion over lines of authority. As an officer in the organization, I needed to know the limits of my powers, the scope and function of my duties in relation to other officers and parts of the organization.

Third, the failure of the Panthers to appear at the press conference without discussion with the person who had been placed in charge of it

—myself—was a violation of organization discipline that I could not tolerate. It reflected a serious violation of that collectivism and democratic centralism necessary in any revolutionary organization or relationship of organizations. I had invested too much energy in that weekend and in my entire relationship with the Black Panther Party to be treated in that fashion. And I did not feel that this was just a personal reaction, for there were other things that indicated breaches of lines of authority and collectivism.

Authoritarian behavior is a very dangerous tendency in a movement and must be combatted at all times. An authoritarian process or person will cancel out a good and revolutionary content. The destruction of many plans, programs, and organizations can be laid to authoritarian people or an authoritarian process. Authoritarianism in men often takes the form of male chauvinism and complete disregard for the rights of others, especially women.

Within the Black Panther Party I was not about to become the patsy of anyone or negate my years of trying to build collective leadership. I had too much strength and commitment to my people to allow any authoritarian person or process to crush my rights or destroy my work.

Fourth, too much had happened in California and New York for me to trust certain forces in the Black Panther Party at that time. I had never worked in an organization where I felt my personal security and safety were threatened by internal elements and I did not intend to start doing so then.

Following my resignation, and notwithstanding all the conflicts, SNCC made several overtures to the Panthers to discuss future relations. It even sent a written letter urging a meeting to discuss our relationship. As far as I was concerned personally, I did not allow what had happened to stand permanently in the way of some type of future relationship with the Panthers in the name of black unity. It was in this spirit that I made that telephone call to Eldridge Cleaver after reading the *Times* article on October 7, 1968, three months after the abortive press conference incident. When I talked to Eldridge that day, I urged him to call Bobby Seale and in fact tried to call Bobby myself. I still had hopes that, in a thorough discussion session, with all parties being honest and frank about their problems and misgivings, some form of unified front could still be exhibited for the sake of black America.

In June, 1969, a Panther official asked me, upon the instructions of a higher official, if I would be willing to conduct political education classes for them. I told him that I would, but I wanted a written request from the Panthers to do this. I did not want to be put in another trick, but at the same time I would not refuse giving political education to those who requested it. The letter never arrived and I didn't pursue the matter.

My experiences with the Black Panther Party taught me several important political lessons. First of all, the nature, scope, and limits of any type of alliance that two organizations form must be absolutely clear to both parties. Without this understanding, the seeds of distrust will be planted immediately. The facts of this understanding must be known not only to the leadership of the organizations but throughout their ranks also.

Here I would make some serious criticism of myself. I failed to inform all the leadership of SNCC and its rank and file of why I thought that a draft of three people from SNCC into the Panther Party would be a good way to fight the mounting repression against black people. After the widespread press coverage stating that SNCC and the Panthers had "merged," I had to submit to much criticism from SNCC people for "leading them into" that situation. Some of these attacks on me were justifiable. At the same time, H. Rap Brown was also involved in decisions made with the Panthers and he was still chairman of SNCC at that time, thus bearing responsibility too.

But the fact remains, both organizations needed a more precise definition of what was intended by the draft of three SNCC people into the Panthers. Certainly the question of whether this was a merger or a working alliance called for absolute clarification, for there is a tremendous political difference between a merger and a working alliance. To merge means to give up your identity and become something new. If one organization merges with another, then the two become one, but if two organizations simply have a working alliance, then they keep their own identities, but work for a common purpose or on a common program. More and more we are going to hear one organization stating that it needs an alliance with another. My experiences with the Panther-SNCC alliance teaches me there must be precise answers to such questions as:

What is the purpose of this alliance?

What is its ideological basis?

Are the two organizations similar in ideological approaches?

Are there written ideologies which can be evaluated? Or are there ever-changing ideologies which depend upon the whim or the latest enthusiasm of some of the participants? This is not to say that an organization must have developed an airtight ideology before another group can make an alliance with it because, as I have said before, the working out of an ideology is a constant process of resolving contradictions. But it is important to have some idea of an organization's basic principles.

Is the alliance opportunistic—to get publicity, money or prestige—or is it based on political principles?

How will the alliance be financed if finances are needed?

Will the common objective for which there is an alliance further the revolutionary struggle? Will it retard it?

What is the background of the leadership of the organizations making alliances? What are their strengths and weaknesses? What have they written and said?

In my eagerness to deal with repression in the United States, I urged a working alliance between two organizations that were in the process of evolving their ideologies and few of the questions I have listed here were raised or answered in my mind. This was a political mistake. I have come to the conclusion that the SNCC-Panther alliance was made in too much haste and one could even say that there was no alliance between SNCC and the Panthers, but rather that three leading personalities from SNCC and the black struggle had been drafted into the Panthers—Carmichael, Brown, and Forman. In addition, for some of us, it was an alliance of principle but for others it was an alliance of opportunism.

The final lesson was one which I had learned before, on at least two occasions. A person can do only so much in any situation, and I had driven myself beyond all limits. History is not shaped by the actions of one person only, and nobody should abuse his or her health—for this only shortens the time he has to do revolutionary work.

There is an African proverb that says, When two elephants fight, only the grass gets hurt. Expressed in another way, When forces on the left are unable to resolve differences and to form working alliances, only the right benefits. Another formulation, When there are splits inside the black liberation struggle, they tend to weaken the participants and strengthen our white oppressors and the repressive forces. Hence it is always in the interest of the United States Government and local pig agencies to witness, foster, and encourage division between those who are opposed to the United States.

During internal and interorganizational fights, emotions run high, issues become confused, and minor points are transformed into overriding matters of principle. When cooler days come, it is often too late for reconciliation, for the cards have been played wrongly and the players always remember the stacked deck. By this time, organizational and individual egos have been hurt. The inability to criticize and self-criticize, to minimize and submerge past differences, makes it impossible to create a common bond, a working alliance, a united brotherhood that would give more strength to the revolutionary forces.

The ability to engage in self-criticism and analysis of past mistakes is one of the hallmarks of truly great revolutionaries. Not many people understand the political importance of thorough discussion to see where the pitfalls existed, why they occurred, who was responsible, and what steps should be taken to correct these mistakes. Usually errors in judgment, bad tactics, distrust, and suspicion of motives get rationalized into abstract and profound ideological differences that split asunder the elephants. The masses are confused, divided, and unwilling to trust any of them, for who knows what new turn of events might not revive the old hostilities, the uncertainties, the public fights, the confused news stories and grapevine reports?

In the midst of all of this, the people and the most direct victims of repression suffer. Fred Hampton, Huey P. Newton, Morton Sostre, Bobby Seale, David Hilliard, Eldridge Cleaver, are well-known names of black people victimized by the repression of the United States. In the case of H. Rap Brown, we can see the government at work with its full arsenal of tools for repression. Rap was kept under house arrest, not allowed to leave New York City, from 1967 to 1970. Then, in March of 1970, Rap was supposed to stand trial in Belair, Maryland, for his alleged crimes in Cambridge. Ralph Featherstone and "Che" Payne Robinson, a staff member of the Black Economic Development Conference, went to Belair to make arrangements for Rap's arrival. They were both killed in their car by an explosion of dynamite, almost surely planted by some government agency. H. Rap Brown was nowhere to be found.

There are also many other lesser-known people, such as the five brothers murdered in Augusta and two more in Jackson, Mississippi; Carl Hampton killed in Houston; the De Soto brothers in Chicago; Brother Melvin X in California. There is Lee Otis Johnson, a SNCC political activist in Texas now serving thirty years on trumped-up charges of possession of marijuana; Donald P. Stone and ten other SNCC people serving three years for allegedly destroying government property during an antiwar demonstration in Atlanta. There are many other victims of repression from the Black Panther Party such as the New Haven group and the Panther 21 in New York. The so-called RAM Seventeen still suffer under the New York indictments of 1967. The list could go on and on, for there are thousands of still lesser known people and many victims who have not been too active politically. They were just black and their skin color was an invitation to murder or indefinite imprisonment.

The trial of the Chicago "Conspiracy Eight" and the persecution of the Weathermen clearly show that the current repression in the United States crosses any color line. And we should not forget how the American Indians were almost exterminated; how the white majority went on to colonize the Mexican people and the Puerto Ricans and how it helped kill such revolutionaries as Che Guevara and continues today to massacre innocent Vietnamese, how everywhere men and women and children are dying under the fist of American imperialism.

Notwithstanding the above, the elephants fight . . . and the grass gets hurt.

The attacks on the Black Panther Party are only symptomatic of the attacks that this government has been directing at black people for over four hundred years. Thousands of black men and women have suffered at the hands of the pigs, murdered day after day, night after night, with-

out any organized resistance. The call for resistance issued consistently by
the Black Panther Party is a heroic effort. Its attempt to win the minds of
many young black people toward political and military struggle stands
as a hallmark in the resistance struggle of black people.

CHAPTER 65

The Black Manifesto

ENSLAVED

Oh when I think of my long-suffering race,
For weary centuries, despised, oppressed
Enslaved and lynched, denied a human place
In the great life line of the Christian West;
And in the Black Land disinherited,
Robbed in the ancient country of its birth,
My heart grows sick with hate, becomes as lead,
For this my race that has no home on earth.
Then from the dark depth of my soul I cry
To the avenging angel to consume
The white man's world of wonders utterly:
Let it be swallowed up in earth's vast womb,
Or upward roll as sacrificial smoke
To liberate my people from its yoke!*

Claude McKay

AFTER MY experiences with the Black Panther Party, and a decrease
in my activity with SNCC, I felt that I should travel in the United States
and observe what other groups of black people were doing. In early 1968
Mike Hamlin—one of the founders of the League of Revolutionary Black
Workers—telephoned me and invited me to visit Detroit so that I could
observe the league in action. Mike had read some of my writings and
discussed my political position in our telephone talks. It sounded as
though the trip would be very worthwhile, and I agreed to come in April.

There was a second reason for my going to Detroit at that time. A
conference on National Black Economic Development had been sched-

*From *Selected Poems of Claude McKay*, New York: Harvest Books, Harcourt,
Brace & World, Inc. Copyright 1953 by Bookman Associates, Inc.

uled to take place in that city by IFCO, the Interreligious Foundation for Community Organization, a creature of the major Protestant denominations whose function was to award funds to groups for community organizing. Lucius Walker served as its executive director. This conference had been called to discuss ways to develop the black community economically. I was asked to speak by Dorothy Dewberry, a member of SNCC working with the conference planning committee.

I told Dorothy by telephone that I did not feel the conference would be of much use or importance, since I believed there could be no solution to the economic problems of black people within the framework of capitalism. She urged me to accept anyway, saying that I should speak on whatever topic I chose and present my viewpoint as I wished. I finally accepted the invitation, mainly as a way of financing my trip to Detroit so that I could meet with the league. The National Black Economic Development Conference was low on my list of priorities. But events would soon change this.

In Detroit, Mike Hamlin and I had many conversations which deepened our respect for each other and led to a solid friendship. We discussed the league, the revolutionary struggle of black people, the importance of black workers, SNCC, the Black Panthers and other organizations. Mike introduced me to many of the brothers and sisters active with the league, and I learned much about its history as well as current programs.

The league was organized in 1968 by black auto workers after the rebellions in Detroit. Mike Hamlin, John Watson, and others soon began publishing the *Inner City Voice*, a newspaper articulating the importance of class factors in the black struggle and the need to build a strong organization of black workers. Members of the league began to develop independent caucuses of such workers, the best known being DRUM—the Dodge Revolutionary Union Movement. These caucuses constitute the league, and the *Inner City Voice* is their revolutionary journal.

Since its formation, the league has been involved in many strikes protesting racist practices, inadequate safety conditions, speed-up, and other hazards facing those who worked under the grueling conditions of Detroit's auto plants. In the summer of 1971 Mike Hamlin, John Watson and most of the progressive forces in the League left the organization and began working with the Black Workers Congress, an organization that is seeking to unite black, Chicano, Puerto Rican, native American and Asian workers as a fighting force against imperialism and to give class leadership and direction to the revolutionary struggle in the United States.

I also talked with members of the league about the National Black Economic Development Conference, which was about to begin. We knew that such conferences usually involve great expenditure of money and produce little concrete result. We agreed that a conference with the declared purpose of helping black economic development should not take place in a city like Detroit without producing some definite programs beneficial to the black community. And we decided that the only way to make this conference relevant was to take it over completely and then make sure that an organizational framework was created to carry out the programs formulated by the meeting.

Since the conference was being staged by "Christians," we felt it was the right occasion to demand reparations from the Christian churches for the centuries of exploitation and oppression which they had inflicted on black people around the world. (We later decided to make the Jewish synagogues an additional target for our demands.) Reparations did not represent any kind of long-range goal in our minds, but an intermediate step on the path to liberation. We saw it as a politically correct step, for the concept of reparation reflected the need to adjust past wrongs—to compensate for the enslavement of black people by Christians and their subsequent exploitation by Christians and Jews in the United States. Our demands—to be called the Black Manifesto—would not merely involve money but would be a call for revolutionary action, a Manifesto that spoke of the human misery of black people under capitalism and imperialism, and pointed the way to ending those conditions.

On April 26, 1969, at 7 P.M., the hour arrived for me to address the conference with the Manifesto. We had completed all the arrangements for taking it over. The National Black Economic Development Conference would become a permanent organization with that same name (later we would drop the word "national," for our plans included the creation of chapters outside the United States). Lucius Walker had agreed to serve as its chairman. We felt that we needed his participation to carry out our coup more smoothly. These are important facts, for in some circles the legend exists that James Forman simply walked into the conference and took it over.

Two weeks after the conference took place, U.S. Attorney General John Mitchell and J. Edgar Hoover ordered the FBI to interview all the participants and the Justice Department convened two special grand juries to investigate the National Black Economic Development Conference. Some people cooperated with the government, but many didn't. The federal government obviously considered the Black Manifesto a dangerous document. Perhaps it considers me dangerous, too, since the Manifesto was issued over my name and it was I who entered Riverside Church in New York City on May 4, 1969, to interrupt a church service and proclaim the Manifesto.

Religion and so-called Christianity fucked up my young life in terrible ways, instilling in me a deep fear wrapped in images of a fiery hell. The preachers in rural Mississippi tried to convince me that I was sinful at the age of twelve and only the mourners' bench could cleanse my soul of all the crimes I had committed against a blond, blue-eyed Jesus and his father, the white God who sat on the throne of judgment granting to white people the right to persecute and enslave black people. At school in Chicago, the Catholic nuns worked a con game on all the innocent black children, telling us that heaven was like a city, with suburbs for the rich and slums for the poor, and you were rich or poor according to how much good you did on earth. I fell for the con game until I peeped the hole card of the lying sisters, whose lives were supposedly devoted to Jesus who was the supposed lover of my soul. But only in my mid-twenties did I finally see the lie in believing that there was some super-natural power that made the world the way it is.

All those wasted years, my whole life, the lives of all poor black people, swelled up in me as I stood looking at the granite of Riverside Church on the morning of May 4, 1969—the date set by the Black Manifesto to begin the disruption of the racist churches. I thought of the millions of people throughout the world who have been hooked on the religion habit. I thought of the slave ships sailing across the Atlantic Ocean full of my people, whipped and starved by the "Christian" sailors and sea captains. And when the ships landed on the shores of the United States, more "Christians" came to put my mothers and fathers, my brothers and sisters, on the auction block where they were sold to the highest white "Christian" bidder. Bid 'em up in the name of Jesus and his father and the holy ghost!

As my ancestors built the foundations of the "Christian" West, the good white "Christian" lived in luxury and prayed through his priest to a "Christian" God who loved all men—meaning all white men, the men who shackled blacks and stole their land in Africa and raped their women in the Americas. And when those good "Christians" wrote the Declaration of Independence saying that all men were created equal under God, with life, liberty, and justice for all, they were talking about a white God and white justice and white men. Black people were only three-fifths human —this they wrote into their Constitution. Black people were slaves, chattels, hewers of wood, pickers of cotton, studs and breeders of dignified people sold for the profit of the sons and daughters of the fairest lord Jesus—rock of the ages, but cleft for me.

All this and more swelled up in me as I mounted the steps of Riverside Church and walked into the monument to "Christianity" that John D. Rockefeller had built with the millions he stole from poor people, the millions he made with oil stolen from the earth—the people's earth. All the lies that "Christianity" had used to enslave the poor stared me in the face. There stood the temple of the liars—quick-talking, double-dealing

John F. Kennedy, Lyndon Bloodbath Johnson, Richard Tricky Dicky Milhous Nixon, and Funky Spiro Agnew—all these Americans who prayed to their white gods, their white popes, their white Billy Grahams, their white sweet lord Jesus, while they sent napalm to burn our sisters and brothers in Vietnam. And crooked Harry Truman, who asked the lord of white lords for "wisdom," for "guidance," as he bombed Hiroshima and Nagasaki. And all the other rulers of the West, white "Christians," despots, sadists, greedy pigs.

I was more than angry as I walked up into the nave of Riverside Church and stood behind the pastor, waiting to announce that the Black Manifesto demanded five hundred million dollars in reparations from the racist white "Christian" churches and the Jewish synagogues. I felt my action as one more rebellion against the vast system of controls over black people and their minds, of which the church and religion stood as a prime example. For years I had been fighting many of these control mechanisms —the educational system, the segregated lunch counters, denial of the right to vote, the court system, the racist Democratic Party and its conventions. My learning about international finance and how imperialism supported racism had deepened my awareness of these controls.

Prime among the mechanisms was the concept of citizenship—the way that the United States Government and all its institutions try to trick us into believing that we are citizens so that it can control us and make us submit to its tyranny. And then the way that the educational system teaches us to believe in the U.S.A. and salute the flag and go off to Santo Domingo, the Congo, or Vietnam fighting for this white "Christian" nation. And the way that the mass media controls our people with flashes of "Julia," doses of "Kit Carson" and "I Spy." On down the list—the police, the profit system, the love of life and fear of death taught by Western culture, the fear of ideologies that call for revolution . . . control, control, control.

Colonized people must be controlled. Poor people must be controlled. We must never think of revolution. The "Christian" church and the Jewish synagogue must teach us that love and patience are good. But if this doesn't work—then assassination, the ultimate control.

The program outlined in the Black Manifesto was a specific answer to some of the controls. We demanded five hundred million dollars to be spent in various ways, including the establishment of a Southern land bank for the use of poor people; four major publishing and printing enterprises for black people; four TV networks to provide an alternative to racist and capitalistic propaganda; a training center for the teaching of skills used in communications; a Black Labor Strike and Defense Fund; a black university. These were not gimmicks or Band-Aids but part of a whole campaign against the controls. Colonized people must be controlled. An analysis of the control factors operating on any colonized or oppressed people is essential to any liberation struggle.

And almost anywhere, the church can be listed among these.

Ernest Campbell, pastor of Riverside Church, trembles now at the sight of a black revolutionary standing in his church. He tries to speak, I try to speak. He calls off the service and walks out of the church. I stand quietly, hatred of the West and its "Christianity" and its controls giving me strength and determination. Hated of injustice carries the seed of love for humanity and the dialectic sustains the revolutionary.

I am filled with visions of a new day, a world without racism, a Chicago without slums. Sharecroppers like Georgia Mae Turner are no longer the wretched of the earth. All the pigs have been killed or fled. The lying white politicians are gone. Africa stands proud and truly free. Around the world, the large white rat lies motionless—forever.

The organist at Riverside Church plays loudly, trying to drown out my voice. But I am silent. I can wait a thousand years, for the white boy's time is up. His wars of aggression, his murders at home, his polluted cities and dying fish, his choked air and totally brutal life—all are going to pass. The world is in an uproar. H. Rap Brown. Ralph Featherstone. Brothers Che Robinson and Guevara. The Weathermen. Tupamaros. Ho Chi Minh. Lumumba. Malcolm X. Sammy Younge. Ruby Doris Robinson. From the blood of the martyrs flows the seed of revolution. We can wait and while we wait, we prepare. For the day is fast approaching—a bloody day, a clash of Left and Right, rich against poor, blacks against white racists. Chicanos and Puerto Ricans and Indians and Orientals, all in an uproar, patient no longer with the bloody Anglo.

The organ is quiet. The oppressors have conceded. I speak, "We have come from all over the country, burning with anger and despair. . . ."

The Black Manifesto is the product of centuries of struggle by black people in an alien land. We will not relinquish our stake, the stake of our labor. With the Black Manifesto, we serve notice on white America and its "Christian" churches. The Black Manifesto is a timeless document, like the precious rights of the people, the right to work, to peace, to dignity, to liberty, to justice—to be free of racism and exploitation.

Reparation is one more step toward these goals.

Unfortunately, the Black Economic Development Conference had actually received less than $300,000 in reparations by the summer of 1970. Most of the money voted was carefully turned over to organizations *other than* BEDC.

Of the funds received by BEDC, the great part was invested in a revolutionary publishing house called Black Star Publications, located in Detroit with Mike Hamlin as the director. Most of the people involved in preparing the Black Manifesto were all agreed that starting a black publishing house must be our prime objective. Black writers and revolutionary thinkers often find it difficult to get their ideas printed by the big commercial publishers. Then, too, these houses are part of the capitalist system and engage in exploitation. Their values must ultimately be in conflict with the ideals of the revolutionary. Our writers find themselves in a squeeze, for the commercial publishers have distribution systems that make it attractive to publish with them and we certainly cannot now foresee the day when Black Star will compete with Third Avenue. But it is not designed for that purpose; instead, it is an outlet for radical ideas.

The original plans of the Black Economic Development Conference also called for a massive organization, but our work since April 26, 1969, has had to be conducted on a limited budget with constant struggle against many other problems as well. Throughout the summer of 1969, we concentrated on distributing and publicizing the Black Manifesto. That fall, we settled down to intensive community organizing and established bases of support throughout the United States but particularly in Philadelphia, New York, Detroit, Chicago, and Los Angeles. At the 1969 national convention of the Presbyterian church, we extended our demands to include those of the Chicano movement for the return of lands in the Southwest held by the Presbyterians.

Many forms of support that we thought would be forthcoming failed to materialize. Key to this was the retreat of IFCO from support of the Black Manifesto. In Detroit, Lucius Walker had given his unqualified support to the Manifesto and pledged that IFCO would donate an operating budget of $290,000 for a staff of fifty people for one year. But when he returned to New York and came under pressure from the IFCO board, he resigned as chairman of the BEDC. IFCO issued a ruling that it would not turn over any money to BEDC that had not been specifically earmarked for us. The latter point was critical, for I had gone around the country speaking before the national church bodies and urging them to send money for reparations to IFCO. In effect, our publicizing IFCO caused it to receive much money, especially a grant from the Methodist church, which refused to give money directly to BEDC. But then IFCO became greedy itself and saw the Black Manifesto as a way to increase its own power and funds, so we never received the fruits of our work.

We also expected to get support from the black caucuses in the white denominations. At first they did help us, and fought the white racists, but most of them later began to pimp off our efforts and to take money for their own programs in very opportunistic ways. Some of them rewrote parts of the programs in the Manifesto and presented them for funding from their own denominations. This betrayal by greedy black churchmen was a serious disappointment.

But the fight for reparations has been a positive struggle and many black churchmen have supported us without reservation. There is a growing alliance between black churchmen and revolutionaries, an important development that helps to radicalize other church people and offers bases of material and moral support for revolutionaries.

Meanwhile, my work with the Student Nonviolent Coordinating Committee diminished. At a June, 1969, staff meeting of SNCC I proposed that the organization officially adopt the BEDC as a major program. This was rejected. There were conflicts, essentially factional rather than substantive, which caused the organization to disintegrate and become inactive for a time. Later, one faction reconstituted itself as the Student National Coordinating Committee. Within the new structure, I was removed as director of international affairs.

As I reflect on the many people I have known through my experiences with SNCC, I have strong, warm feelings. If we all had our lives to live again, naturally we would do many things differently, but that is idealism and we must accept our lives as we have lived them, always examining our actions and trying to improve on our past experiences. There is a bond of unity between some sisters and brothers, forged in struggle during the sixties, that still carries on in the seventies. Many of us have changed the organizational form of our struggle, but the content of fighting injustice wherever we are remains the same.

In the winter of 1969–70, I made a trip to Martinique to gather material for my book on Frantz Fanon. One evening I interviewed his mother, who was then seventy-eight years old and still very strong although her memory was fading. It was a moment that I had lived before, when interviewing the mother of Sammy Younge to prepare the book on his life. It was the same moment, for I was talking to the mother of another dead black hero, another man of Africa who had given his life to humanity. It was also a different moment, for the lives of the two women and their sons had been very unlike. But in essence it was the same. There was no real division between the sugar cane fields of Martinique and the cotton fields of the American South, between the French racists and the American ones, between the mental colonization that Fanon fought and the psychological oppression of young black Sammy Younge.

We are all colonized. Je suis français, the Queen of England rules over me, Belgium *gave* us independence after Livingston discovered us, I am clean like my Dutch friends, I am an American. The day will come when we will no longer cry that we are French, English, Belgian, Dutch, or American, but assert our African allegiance, our black togetherness. We will fight for an end to racism, colonialism, capitalism, and imperialism.

Before we reach this point, we will have to fight a repression whose full force has yet to be felt. To do this, we will have to develop new forms of struggle, not the least of which will be a conspiratorial method of fighting the United States. All black people are already a conspiracy against the United States. Since our arrival here, we have been treated as if we were permanent conspirators.

We will have to pursue the ideological struggle. We must see clearly what we are for, as well as against. Some time ago I came to the conclusion that only under socialism can the problems of black people and of all humanity be solved. This does not mean that a socialist revolution can end racism overnight. But racism can never be eliminated unless the people control the means of production—the fields and the factories, the land and the cities. Nor will I engage in polemics about the various forms that socialism might take. I am simply talking about a socialism in which all the wealth of the United States is used to the benefit of all mankind; a form of socialism in which the workers, the poor farmers, and all the other wretched of the American earth have control and in which the vanguard force of revolutionary change will be black people, Indians, Chicanos, Puerto Ricans, Orientals.

The dynamics of racism in the United States make it difficult for some black people to decide what to do about whites, or to believe that there will ever be whites willing to fight imperialism all the way—to the point of killing white racists if necessary. But recent events stand as an argument for this possibility. I know there are and there will be some whites who clearly understand the kind of struggle that must be waged and the need for the black and other Third World forces to lead the revolutionary struggle in the United States, a struggle that will help build world socialism. An ideological struggle will certainly take place on this question, but that is part of the revolutionary process.

The ideological position of black revolutionaries must state clearly that it is the poor, the working class, who are to achieve power. During the sixties, we concentrated too much on the middle class. Most of our short-range victories resulted in the black middle class entrenching itself further. SNCC's failure to organize actively with black workers and put them at the center of decision making is a serious indictment, as is our failure to hold the power we had acquired in the rural South.

My own activity in this decade, the seventies, will be concentrated upon waging the ideological struggle and creating bases in urban black communities centered near the means of production. We must organize and learn from black workers, constantly summarize our total experiences, discover laws of revolution in the United States, unite with sincere anti-imperialist forces and always give class leadership, resting ourselves in the particular historical forces that have shaped our people.

Above all, I will wage the ideological struggle—the drive for political education. I will continue this work that I have tried to do most of my life with vigor. For it is my duty to help make black revolutionaries.

Armed with a correct ideology, pursuing all efforts to make sure that the black working class has power and gives direction to the revolutionary struggle, working to develop all forms of popular struggle as well as a network of unknown revolutionaries, preparing for the long-range armed struggle inside the United States, uniting all into a disciplined, central-ized, mass party or organization—thus we will surely advance our struggle in the seventies. We will be carrying on the work of all the black sons and daughters who have died in every corner of Africa and the Americas under the whiplash of racism, colonialism, capitalism, and im-perialism. And we shall win without a doubt.

> In brotherhood.
> Remember Lumumba.
> Fanon pointed the way!

Postscript

Attica. Attica. Black men, brown men, white men—shot down at Attica by the command of Nelson Rockefeller and supported by the Nixon Administration. Black women, brown women, white women, families, friends, lovers, wives, millions of people mourning the loss of those slaughtered at Attica, killed on American soil by weapons developed in the Vietnam War. Many people are talking about Attica, the increasing repression against the prisons and the general population. But Attica is only the latest of a long process of attempted extermination and brutality that rich white people have used against the poor of all colors who have threatened their control and drives for profits.

George Jackson, lying in his grave, shot "while trying to escape" from San Quentin. Prisons are turning into revolutionary schools, and George Jackson will live forever.

Angela Davis and Ruchell MaGee, fighting for their lives in San Rafael. Walter Collins, Donald Stone, thousands of other brave sisters and brothers doing time as political prisoners. In the new society there will be no need for prisons and people will come to understand that all prisoners were trapped by the cruel workings of a capitalistic society.

Unemployment, high rents, rats and roaches, bad housing, chemical warfare in the form of heroin and other drugs, mounting assaults by the pigs and constant repression by the Federal government. Pollution, ir-relevant movies, trash on television, thought control in the schools, sterilization and the Vietnam War expands into Indochina and becomes fully automated.

All these problems. But I have little despair. I am full of hope and confidence. The future of revolutionaries is bright, especially in the United States. Around the world the U.S. government is under attack for its cruelty to humanity. The capitalistic economy is in serious trouble—the dollar crisis, the balance of payments, inflation. And the workers of the United States are forced to pay for these ills.

People are organizing, talking about the need for total change, studying revolutionary theory and grappling with the role of the working class as the decisive force in the making of history.

Naturally the massacre at Attica outrages me. The murder of George Jackson intensifies my anger. But revolutionaries must not submit to repression and terror but use them to further organize resistance and propel the revolutionary struggle forward.

You have not died in vain, Comrade George.

Your lives will be long remembered, victims of Attica.

You shall be free, political prisoners.

Organize and struggle, the only road to revolution.

October 4, 1971

INDEX

INDEX